The Jews in the Modern World: A History since 1750

Hilary L. Rubinstein
Dan Cohn-Sherbok
Abraham J. Edelheit
William D. Rubinstein

A ARNOLD

A member of the Hodder Headline Group
LONDON
Co-published in the United States of America by
Oxford University Press Inc., New York

First published in Great Britain in 2002 by
Arnold, a member of the Hodder Headline Group,
338 Euston Road, London NW1 3BH

http://www.arnoldpublishers.com

Co-published in the United States of America by
Oxford University Press Inc.,
198 Madison Avenue, New York, NY10016

British Library Cataloguing in Publication Data
A catalogue record for this book is available from the British Library

Library of Congress Cataloging-in-Publication Data
A catalog record for this book is available from the Library of Congress

ISBN 0 340 69162 X (hb)
ISBN 0 340 69163 8 (pb)

Production Editor: Jasmine Brown
Production Controller: Iain McWilliams
Cover Design: Terry Griffiths

Typeset in 10/12 Sabon by Phoenix Photosetting, Chatham, Kent
Printed and bound in Great Britain by MPG Books Ltd, Bodmin, Cornwall

What do you think about this book? Or any other Arnold title?
Please send your comments to feedback.arnold@hodder.co.uk

Contents

List of maps

The source of all maps is Dan Cohn-Sherbok, *Atlas of Jewish History* (Routledge, 1994)

Preface

During the past thirty years, the study of modern Jewish history has moved from the periphery to the centre of academic historiography. Hardly taught at the university level a generation ago, and all but ignored in mainstream history textbooks, modern Jewish history has become a widely-recognised subject attracting considerable interest and a vast, ever-growing volume of monographs, journals, conferences, and dissertations. In part this has occurred because of the centrality of the Holocaust to contemporary consciousness, of a general awareness of the Jews as the archetypal persecuted minority, and of the popularity of ethnicity as a mode of social analysis. In part it has occurred because of the breakdown, regretted by many, of the familiar 'kings, dates, and battles' history oriented around the nation-state, and its supercession, in part, by categories derived from social history. In part it has occurred because of the sheer volume of writing on this subject, generally by Jewish scholars, but often and increasingly by non-Jews.

While this explosion of interest has resulted in a vast profusion of monographs and specialist studies, rather curiously there has not been an equivalent increase in general textbook studies of the topic, and *Jews in the Modern World* is designed to fill a real gap. So far as we are aware, the major textbook in this field remains Howard M. Sachar's invaluable *The Course of Modern Jewish History*, now more than forty years old. Our work reflects somewhat different emphases, as well as the great increase in scholarship in this field during the past generation; it is, we hope, just as comprehensive as Sachar's work, and perhaps more so. We have, for example, included more on women, on Sephardim, and on socio-economic and demographic trends.

Given the controversial nature of much of modern Jewish history and the different viewpoints which exist within the Jewish matrix, we have tried very hard to be neutral while reflecting a consensual viewpoint where one exists within this matrix and, in addition, to be fair and even-handed to all elements within Jewry, especially in the religious sphere. There is also the question of the transliteration or spelling, in English, of Yiddish and Hebrew terms. Here, we have tried to reflect the most reasonable transliteration where no consensus exists.

Margaret Broadway and Gill Parry skilfully typed the manuscript, and Vanessa Mitchell was a helpful copy-editor, for which we express our gratitude.

Acknowledgement

The publishers would like to thank Taylor & Francis for permission to reproduce the maps that appear in this book, all of which are taken from Dan Cohn-Sherbok: *Atlas of Jewish History* (Routledge, 1994).

Chronology of Jewish history from 1750

1750	Moses Mendelssohn attempts to launch first periodical of the Haskalah, *Kohelet Musar*.
1753	(May) – The 'Jew Bill' (Jewish Naturalisation Bill) passed by Britain's Parliament but repealed in December.
1754	G.E. Lessing's play *Die Juden* (written 1749) published.
1756	Excommunication of Jacob Frank, scandalous 'pseudo-Messiah' and founder of the Frankists, by Podolian rabbis.
1760	Death of the *Baal Shem Tov* (Israel ben-Eliezer, founder of Hasidism).
1760	Foundation of the Board of Deputies of British Jews.
1772	Death of Dov Ber, *Maggid* of Mezhirich.
1772–95	Partitions of Poland; hundreds of thousands of Jews become subjects of Prussia, Austria, and, especially, Russia.
1781	C.W. von Dohm issues essay 'On the Civil Improvement of the Jews'.
1782	*Toleranzpatent* issued by Austria's Emperor Joseph II.
1783	Publication of Moses Mendelssohn's *Jerusalem*, a plea for religious tolerance.
1783	Moses Mendelssohn and the Friends of Hebrew launch *Ha-Meassef*.
1786–91	Beginnings of the Pale of Settlement by decrees of Empress Catherine II.
1789	Abbé Grégoire's *Essai sur la régénération physique, morale, et politique des Juifs* published at Metz.
1789–91	Jews given equal rights in France following the French Revolution of 1789.
1790	Enactment of the American Bill of Rights, which guarantees freedom of religion and forbids the establishment of any religion.
1792–1810	Removal of many Jewish disabilities throughout Europe by Napoleon's conquering armies.

1803	Establishment of the famous *yeshivah* in Volozhin, Lithuania.
1804	Shneur Zalman (1747–1813), founder of the Chabad movement, settles in Lyady.
1804	Tsar Alexander I issues Statute concerning the Jews.
1805	Frankfurt-born Nathan Mayer Rothschild (1777–1836) moves from Manchester to London and establishes the English branch of the celebrated bank.
1806–07	'Assembly of Jewish Notables' deliberate in Paris.
1807	Convocation of the 'Grand Sanhedrin' of Jewish leaders by Napoleon.
1809	Death in battle of Berek Joselowicz, Poland's Jewish military hero.
1810	Earliest Reform Temple (at Seesen) completed (closed 1815).
1814–15	The Congress of Vienna instructs the German states to grant citizenship rights to Jews.
1815	Reform services begin in Berlin.
1827	Imposition of the brutal Cantonist Decrees in Russia.
1831	Recognition of Judaism as a state-supported religion in France.
1832	Abraham Geiger (1810–74), pioneer of Reform Judaism, becomes rabbi at Wiesbaden and institutes religious reforms.
1833–69	Gradual emancipation of the Jews in the German states.
1835	Tsar Nicholas I defines Pales of Settlement.
1838	Sir Moses Montefiore becomes president of the Board of Deputies of British Jews.
1840	The Damascus Affair.
1843	Establishment of B'nai B'rith in New York.
1848–49	Revolutions throughout continental Europe advance Jewish rights, but their failure causes thousands of Jews to flee to America, especially from Germany.
1851	Samson Raphael Hirsch (1808–88), most influential German neo-Orthodox leader, becomes rabbi of Frankfurt-on-Main.
1856	Modification of the Cantonist Decrees in Russia.
1858	Admission of a practising Jew, Baron Lionel de Rothschild, as a member of the British House of Commons.
1858–59	The Mortara Affair.
1860	Establishment of the Alliance Israélite Universelle in Paris.
1862	Judah P. Benjamin (1811–84) becomes secretary of state of the Confederacy.
1862	Moses Hess publishes *Rom und Jerusalem*, the first Zionist classic.
1868	Benjamin Disraeli becomes Britain's prime minister.
1870	Abolition of the Rome ghetto, the last in Europe.
1873	Economic depression in Germany heightens antisemitism.
1877	Saratoga Springs Hotel bars a prominent Jewish banker from staying there, one of the first instances of social antisemitism in the United States.

1878	Foundation of the antisemitic Christian Workers Party in Germany by Adolf Stöcker.
1879	Wilhelm Marr coins the term 'antisemitism', with the introduction in Germany of the Antisemiten-Liga (League of Antisemites), the first organisation anywhere to carry such a title.
1881	Violent pogroms in Russia lead to the mass emigration of Jews to the West, especially to America.
1881	Eliezer ben-Yehuda, pioneer of modern spoken Hebrew, settles in Jerusalem.
1882	(May) – Promulgation of the notorious May Laws in Russia (repealed 1917).
1882	Publication of Leon Pinsker's *Auto-Emancipation*, a pioneering work of Zionism.
1882–1903	The 'First Aliyah' to Palestine; *Chibbat Zion* movement founded in Russia.
1885	Nathaniel Rothschild (1840–1915) takes his seat in the British House of Lords as Lord Rothschild, the first practising Jew there.
1891–92	Expulsions of Jews from Moscow and St Petersburg.
1894–1906	The Dreyfus Affair in France; Captain Alfred Dreyfus is arrested, tried for treason, convicted, and sent to Devil's Island (1894); retried (1899); pardoned (1906).
1896	Theodor Herzl publishes *Der Judenstaat*, central work of modern Zionism.
1897	First Zionist Congress held in Basle, with Herzl as President.
1897	Establishment of the Bund (General Federation of Jewish Workers) in Vilna.
1902	Publication in Russia of *The Protocols of the [Learned] Elders of Zion*.
1903	Joseph Chamberlain, British colonial secretary, offers East African territory to the Zionist movement as a possible Jewish homeland.
1903	Kishinev pogrom, and publication of H.N. Bialik's famous poem 'In the City of Slaughter'.
1904	Herzl unexpectedly dies, aged only 44.
1904–05	Further murderous pogroms in Russia.
1904–14	The 'Second Aliyah' to Palestine.
1906	Oscar Straus becomes the first Jewish member of an American Cabinet.
1906	Zenith of Jewish immigration to the United States: 154,000 Jewish immigrants arrive.
1909	Herbert Samuel enters the British Cabinet as the first practising Jew.
1912	Foundation of Agudas Israel, Strictly Orthodox political party.

1913	Trial of Mendel Beilis (1874–1934) in Kiev on a charge of ritual murder.
1913	Foundation of the Anti-Defamation League of B'nai B'rith.
1914–18	The First World War has a profound effect on European Jewish life.
1915	Extension of the Pale of Settlement by the czarist government, effectively abolishing restrictions on Jewish settlement.
1917	Russian liberal (February) and Bolshevik (October) revolutions; the latter greatly heightens antisemitism in the West and leads to the repression of Jewish life in Russia. Trotsky emerges as Bolshevik Russia's war leader.
1917	(November) – Promulgation of the Balfour Declaration: Britain promises Palestine to the Jewish people as a 'national home'.
1919–23	The 'Third Aliyah' to Palestine.
c.1919–22	Heightened antisemitism in the West with widespread distribution of the *Protocols of the [Learned] Elders of Zion*.
1921	Albert Einstein awarded the Nobel Prize in Physics.
1921	Arab riots in Palestine.
1921; 1924	Quota restrictions placed on most European immigrants to the United States.
1922	The League of Nations formally awards Palestine to Britain as a mandate and constitutes a Jewish Agency to head the Jewish community there; Transjordan separated from Palestine.
1922	Ahad Ha-am (1856–1927), philosopher of 'Cultural Zionism', settles in Tel Aviv.
1924–29	The 'Fourth Aliyah' to Palestine.
1924	Adolf Hitler publishes *Mein Kampf.*
1926	Foundation of the Hebrew University of Jerusalem.
1928	Henry Ford repudiates the antisemitism in his *Dearborn Independent* newspaper.
1929	'Wailing Wall Incident' in Jerusalem begins clashes between Jews and Arabs.
1932–40	The 'Fifth Aliyah' to Palestine.
1933	(January) – Adolf Hitler comes to power in Germany as chancellor, becoming *Führer* (leader) in August 1934.
1933	(April) – Most Jews removed from government and university positions in Germany.
1935	The 'Nuremberg Laws' exclude Jews from German citizenship, etc.
1936	World Jewish Congress founded.
1938	(March) – The *Anschluss*: Germany annexes Austria, resulting in extreme persecution of Jews there.
1938	(November) – *Kristallnacht*. Destruction of most Jewish institutions and synagogues throughout Germany. In 1938–39 hundreds of thousands of Jews flee the German Reich.

1939	(May) – MacDonald White Paper limits Jewish immigration into Palestine.
1939	(September) – Beginning of the Second World War. Germany invades Poland, which is divided (1939–41) between Germany and the Soviet Union. Jews forced by Nazis to move into ghettos throughout Poland and, later, throughout eastern Europe, prior to mass murder.
1941	(June) – Nazi Germany invades the Soviet Union, beginning the mass murder of Jews in the conquered territory and the Holocaust.
1941–47	The 'Sixth Aliyah' to Palestine, amid great difficulty.
1942	(January) – Wannsee Conference co-ordinates policy of mass extermination of European Jewry.
1942–45	Mass murders of European Jews, chiefly in extermination camps such as Auschwitz, Treblinka, and Sobibor.
1942	(May) – 'Biltmore Program', calling for an independent Jewish state in Palestine, adopted by the Zionist movement.
1943	(April–May) – Warsaw Ghetto uprising.
1945	(January) – Auschwitz liberated by Soviet army; (February–May) – Liberation of concentration camps by Allied Armies.
1945–46	Defeat of Nazi Germany; Hitler, Himmler, and other top Nazis commit suicide; others (e.g. Göring, Frank) hanged after the Nuremberg Trials.
1946–48	Anti-British guerrilla war in Palestine.
1947	(November) – United Nations divides the Palestine Mandate into Jewish and Arab states.
1948	(May) – Declaration of Independence of the State of Israel.
1948–49	Israeli War of Independence.
1949	(May) – Israel admitted to the United Nations.
c.1948–53	'Black Years' of Soviet Jewry under Stalin. 1952: 'Doctor's Plot' and the Slansky Trial in Czechoslovakia.
1956	Sinai War.
1960	Adolf Eichmann captured by Israeli agents in Argentina; brought to Israel, tried (1961–62) and hanged (1962).
1963	David Ben-Gurion retires as Israel's prime minister.
1967	(June) – Six Day War.
c.1968	Beginning of wave of Arab terrorism and hijacking.
1972	Ordination of the first American woman rabbi by the Reform movement.
1972–73	Several hundred thousand Jews emigrate from the Soviet Union.
1973	(October) – Yom Kippur War.
1973	Henry Kissinger becomes US secretary of state.
1975	The UN General Assembly adopts a resolution declaring Zionism to be a form of racism (repealed 1991).

1977	Menahem Begin becomes Israeli prime minister.
1978	Camp David Accords between Israel and Egypt; Begin and Sadat, the Egyptian president, awarded Nobel Peace Prize.
1982	Israel invades Lebanon to root out the PLO.
1984–91	*Glasnost* followed by the collapse of the Soviet Union and Communism in Europe. Hundreds of thousands of Jews emigrate from the mid-1980s onwards.
1987	'Intifada' on the West Bank.
1991	Gulf War; Iraq launches 'Scud' missiles at Tel Aviv.
1993	Opening of US Holocaust Museum in Washington DC.
1993	Oslo Accords between Israel and the PLO.
1993	John Demjanjuk, alleged Nazi war criminal, acquitted by Israeli Supreme Court.
1994	Peace treaty signed between Israel and Jordan. Death of Menahem Schneersohn (1902–94), the Lubavitcher *rebbe*, attracts world-wide publicity.
1995	Israel's prime minister, Yitzhak Rabin, assassinated by a right-wing extremist.
1996	Binyamin Netanyahu elected Israeli prime minister.
1996	Madeleine Albright, of Czech Jewish descent, becomes America's first woman secretary of state.
1999	Ehud Barak elected Israeli prime minister.
2000	Senator Joseph Liberman, an Orthodox Jew, selected as the US Democratic party's vice-presidential candidate.
2000	Renewed violence on the West Bank despite near-agreement between Israel and the PLO on a final peace treaty.
2001	Ariel Sharon decisively defeats Ehud Barak in a nation-wide election for prime minister.
2001–2	Relations between Israel and the Palestinian Authority deteriorate after suicide bombings by Palestinian extremists leave over 100 Israelis dead; Sharon retaliates by invading Palestinian towns.

The authors

Dr Hilary L. Rubinstein is a former Research Fellow in History at the University of Melbourne. She has taught modern Jewish history at Monash University, Australia, and at the University of Wales, Lampeter. She is the author of several books and numerous articles on philosemitism and Australian Jewish history, and for a number of years contributed the Australian section of the *American Jewish Year Book*. She delivered the 1998 Lady Magnus Lecture of the Jewish Historical Society of England, and is a Fellow of the Royal Historical Society.

Rabbi Professor Dan Cohn-Sherbok is Professor of Judaism at the University of Wales, Lampeter. He received his doctorate at Cambridge University and has been a Visiting Professor at the Universities of Essex, Middlesex, St Andrews, and Vilnius. He has written or edited over forty books on Judaism, Jewish affairs, and comparative religion, including *An Atlas of Jewish History, Understanding the Holocaust, The Jewish Faith, Modern Judaism*, and *Issues in Contemporary Judaism*.

Dr Abraham J. Edelheit is an Assistant Professor of History at the Kingsborough Community College of the City University of New York. He also serves as Historian in Residence at the Conference on Jewish Material Claims Against Germany and as Director of the Moreshet Zvi Institute for Jewish Communal Studies. He has authored or co-authored ten books on Jewish and European history, including *History of the Holocaust: A Handbook and Dictionary* (1994) and *History of Zionism: A Handbook and Dictionary* (2000), both of which were written with his late father, Hershel Edelheit.

Professor William D. Rubinstein is Professor of Modern History at the University of Wales, Aberystwyth. He has written numerous books and articles on modern British history and on Jewish history and affairs, including *A History of the Jews in the English-Speaking World: Great Britain* (1996) and *The Myth of Rescue: Why the Democracies Could Not Have Saved More Jews From the Nazis* (1997). Before coming to Aberystwyth in 1995, he was Professor of History at Deakin University in Australia and is a Fellow of the Australian Academy of the Humanities, the Australian Academy of the Social Sciences, and of the Royal Historical Society.

1

The Jews from their origins to modern times

Jews in the ancient world

As in so much of their history, the early experience of the Jewish people is both similar to that of their neighbours and yet categorically different. From the first, the history of the Jews (or Hebrews, as they were more commonly known) was bound up with the history of one place, Palestine, the land which contained the ancient kingdoms of Israel and Judah, and now contains the State of Israel. It revolved, as well, around two men of fundamental importance to the Jews over the subsequent millennia – Abraham and Moses, whose lives and achievements put their stamp forever on their people. Abraham, who lived probably around 1800 BCE, is regarded as the Patriarch of both the Jewish and Arab peoples. Born in Ur of the Chaldees, a Babylonian city which had reached a high level of civilisation by that time, Abraham migrated to Palestine, living among the Canaanite and Philistine inhabitants, travelled to Egypt, and settled in Hebron (today on the Palestinian West Bank). God – the one God of the monotheistic religions – appeared to Abraham in a vision and promised that his progeny would inherit land 'from the river of Egypt to the Euphrates'. God entered with Abraham into a covenant (*brit* in Hebrew), a formal agreement denoting God's special relationship with Abraham and his progeny, symbolised by the rite of the circumcision of male babies – practised ever since by Jews and Muslims. (Christians believe that God entered into a 'new covenant' with the followers of Jesus Christ, which made the rite of circumcision unnecessary.) In addition, God tested Abraham's loyalty by ordering him to sacrifice his eldest son Isaac, a killing stayed by God only at the last minute. Traditionally, Abraham is regarded as a wise and gentle man, the original wise old man. What Abraham brought to the development of the central concepts of the Jewish people cannot be overstated: monotheism, the concept of God's covenant with the Jews, the most basic of Jewish rites, such as circumcision. While Jews traditionally believe that they are descended from

Abraham through his sons Isaac and Jacob (the second and third of the Patriarchs), Arabs also believe that they are descended from Abraham through his son Ishmael.

More important still to the origins of the Jewish people was the role of Moses, the Lawgiver and founder of the Jewish religion, who lived probably around 1225 BCE (although some historians place his life two centuries earlier, around 1445 BCE). The life and achievements of Moses are almost too familiar to mention. Moses the Lawgiver was, according to the Biblical account, born in Egypt, hidden among the bullrushes when the Egyptians decided to slaughter newborn Hebrew males, was adopted by an Egyptian princess, and grew up with a deep desire to right the wrongs inflicted on the Hebrews, in bondage in Israel. On Mount Horeb, from out of a bush which burned but which miraculously was not consumed by the flames, Moses received a Command from God to lead his people out of Egypt. The pharaoh agreed to release the Israelites only after Ten Plagues had been inflicted on his country. Moses and the Hebrews miraculously crossed the Red Sea, received the Ten Commandments at Mount Sinai from the immediate hand of God, and enacted the Hebrew legal code. Moses's brother Aaron became high priest, and Joshua, Moses's chosen successor, led the Israelites into the promised land after the death of the Lawgiver. Moses, who spoke to God 'face to face', was, at least by the Biblical account, effectively the founder of the Jewish religion and of Jewish history as we know it.

At this point, Palestine was controlled by the Canaanites, Philistines, and other local tribes. Over the next few centuries, the Hebrews gradually conquered Palestine, under the Israelites' three supreme leaders, Saul (proclaimed king around 1013 BCE), David (proclaimed king around 1006 BCE), and Solomon (reigned approximately 973–933 BCE). Saul laid the groundwork for an independent Israelite monarchy. This process was completed by King David, who married Saul's daughter. David is renowned for slaying the Philistine giant Goliath, for conquering most of Palestine, and, above all, for establishing Jerusalem, in the hills of central Palestine, as the capital of the Jewish state. There he moved the Ark of the Covenant, the wooden chest in which the original tablets of the Ten Commandments were kept. David's son and successor, Solomon, renowned for his wisdom, built the Temple in Jerusalem, and is traditionally regarded as the author of the 'Song of Songs' and Ecclesiastes in the Bible. Under Solomon, the ancient kingdom of Israel reached its greatest extent, wealth and glory, its realm extending from Egypt to the Euphrates. At the heart of the Temple of Solomon was the 'Holy of Holies', wherein was kept the Ark of the Covenant. Only the high priest of Israel could enter the Holy of Holies, and only on *Yom Kippur*, the holiest day of the Jewish calendar. While the Temple existed, Judaism was much more of a priestly religion, with the high priest being in some sense an intermediary between God and ordinary believers, than was the case after the fall of the Temple. Today only the

Western Wall of the Temple of Solomon – the most sacred holy place for Orthodox Jews – exists to recall Solomon's ancient glory.

After these great reigns, ancient Israel went into a long period of decline and internal conflict, strongly reminiscent of many other smaller kingdoms in the Middle East and elsewhere. In particular, the unified state of David and Solomon split into two separate kingdoms, Israel and Judah. Israel was the more northerly of the two, and the wealthier. Its history, roughly from 933 till 721 BCE, was one of constant violence and intrigue, with its leaders frequently meeting sudden death, as in many unstable states then and since. Judah, the smaller, poorer and more isolated of the two, was more peaceful in its internal history and more religious. In the ninth and eighth centuries BCE, Assyria, a powerful kingdom in what is now northern Iraq, launched a series of attacks against the Jewish states which weakened and debilitated them. Babylon (now probably central Iraq) in turn conquered Assyria and, in the period around 597–586 BCE, also conquered Palestine, deporting much of its Jewish population and destroying the Temple. The 'Babylonian Exile' of the Jews lasted approximately seventy years, until about 538 BCE, when Cyrus of Persia permitted the Babylonian Jews, who had maintained their distinctive customs, to return to Palestine (where a nucleus of Jews had remained).

A second Temple was erected by the returning exiles and, in religious terms, this was a period of great advance for Judaism. It would seem that the first synagogues were built and used during the period of exile, while Ezra the Scribe, who worked around 450 BCE, helped to codify, and write down in its currently accepted form, the Pentateuch (the first five books of the Bible, traditionally ascribed to Moses). Sabbath-keeping was rigorously enforced. The Prophets, from Isaiah and Ezekiel in the sixth century BCE, had introduced the notion that the travails suffered by the Jews were ordained as divine punishment, but that the redemption of Israel would be vouchsafed by God in order to enhance Israel's role as a moral exemplar and covenant people.

The Hellenistic and Roman periods were just as tumultuous as anything which had occurred to the Jews previously. Palestine came successively under Greek and Roman rule. Many Jews left Palestine, spreading out through Egypt and Asia Minor. Greek probably became the vernacular language of most Jews in this period, and the intermixture of Greek and Hebrew philosophies had a profound influence, especially on early Christianity. Side by side with this went a contrary trend, the revival and assertion of Jewish nationalism and a drive for Jewish national independence, exemplified for instance by Judah the Maccabee (died *c.* 160 BCE), who led a briefly successful revolt against the Hellenic ruler Antiochus Epiphanes, occupied Jerusalem, and purified the Temple. In 64 BCE the Roman general Pompey conquered Jerusalem, a rule which would continue for centuries, with profound consequences for the world. The kingdom of Judea received a kind of semi-self-governing colonial status under Antipater and his son Herod the Great (73–4 BCE). Judea was seething with ferment of every kind, and the expectation of a 'Messiah' – in the Jewish context, a human priest-king who would lead the Jews out of bondage – was strong. New, extremist sects like the Essenes emerged. At the crossroads of the Roman Near East, Judea absorbed many previously alien doctrines and philosophical schools; the message offered by these religious and philosophical schools could be widely dispersed throughout the Roman world very quickly. It was in this milieu and this atmosphere that Jesus of Nazareth (whose dates are generally given as 4 BCE–29 CE) taught and died in Judea. Everything about the life of Jesus, and the relationship of his teachings to the Jewish world from which he emerged, remains a matter of both the keenest interest and the greatest controversy. There are, it should be noted, no indisputable contemporary or near-contemporary and independent Jewish sources which record anything about the life of Jesus, with the possible exception of some contested passages in the *Jewish Wars* of the great historian Josephus (38–107 CE), which was probably written about 95 CE. Jesus lived just before the catastrophe which produced the revolt in Judea (66–70 CE) and the Fall of Jerusalem to a successful Roman army led by the future Roman emperor Titus. Jerusalem fell in September 70 CE after a five-month siege. The famous mountain fortress of Masada, the site of one of Herod's palaces, held out as a bastion of Zealots (one of the Jewish sects) until 73 CE when the 960 remaining committed suicide to avoid being captured by the Romans. The Temple was destroyed and the Sanhedrin (the assembly of seventy-one scholars which probably acted as the governing council of the Jews as well as a kind of Supreme Court for interpreting Jewish law) abolished, as was the institution of high priest. In the next century, led by the priest Eleazar and the nationalist Simeon Bar Kokhba (d.135 CE), another major revolt was launched against the Romans. The Romans routed the Jews, seizing their last stronghold, Betar, near Jerusalem, around 135 CE. Thousands of Jews perished or went into exile, and Judea was virtually despoiled of Jews.

Judaism accommodated itself to these unprecedented crises as best it could. In particular, rabbinical Judaism, no longer directly associated with the Temple in Jerusalem, began to flourish, under such notable scholars as Hillel (who lived in the first century CE) and Johanan Ben Zakkai, his pupil, who established an academy at Jabneh (or Yavneh) near Jaffa. This academy, and others like it, were the progenitors of the *yeshivot* and Talmudic academies of many centuries later. Additionally, the record of academic and judicial discussion of Jewish law began to be codified in the Mishnah and the Talmud after 200 CE.

The Judaism which survived the destruction of the Temple had thus evolved from a priestly to a rabbinic religion, that is, from one centred exclusively at the Temple in Jerusalem to one which could be transplanted to any place that a Jewish community existed. As important was the change which occurred in the lands of the Diaspora, where most Jews lived. From the time of Constantine (Roman emperor 312–337 CE), the Roman world became increasingly, and then officially, Christian in religion. While Christianity was wholly an offshoot of Judaism (adding some Hellenic philosophical concepts and pagan symbols and customs), and while Jesus and his disciples were all Jews, Christianity became virulently anti-Jewish, doing everything possible to denigrate and ostracise Jews and Judaism. Antisemitism (hostility to Jews) had already existed in the ancient world, but was greatly strengthened by the official position which Christianity enjoyed in the Western world after the middle of the fourth century CE. Attempts to distance Christianity from Judaism in every conceivable way became an obsession with many Christians. For example, the Council of Nicaea of 325 CE adjusted the calendar so that Easter never fell on the same day as Passover (*Pesach*), despite the fact that the Last Supper of Jesus and his disciples was a Passover celebration. At the end of the Roman period, the Jewish people thus found itself without a nation-state, bereft of its holy city, driven into seemingly perpetual exile, dispersed throughout the Roman world, and increasingly victimised as 'Christ-killers' by the newly-dominant Christian religion.

At the dawn of the Middle Ages, the Jewish people emerged from their already lengthy history with a number of characteristics and attributes which would continue to mark them until the present time. At the core of Jewish identity was stringent religious monotheism, perhaps unique in the ancient world. A priestly religion for many generations while the Temple of Solomon existed, Judaism was in the process of successful evolution to a rabbinic religion, which no longer required the existence of a single temple or shrine to survive. Judaism emphasised the unique covenant entered into between God and the people of Israel, wherein Jews were seen as God's 'chosen people'. Nevertheless, implicit in the moral code of Judaism was at least the basis of a universalistic ethical and religious code, and the creation stories in the Hebrew Bible tried to explain the origins and early history of the world and of all humanity. The universalistic moral code implicit in Judaism was increasingly emphasised by the Hebrew prophets and became the basis of Christianity and (later) of Islam. Judaism, however, categorically remained the religion of one small people; indeed, its scriptures are the history of one people. It never sought mass proselytising (although converts to Judaism always existed) and remained endogamous and largely hereditary. The dichotomy between the unquestioned particularism of Judaism and the implicit universalism of its central message remains one of the central points of tension, and also of creativity, in Judaism.

In the Hellenistic and Roman periods, Jewry spread out from its promised land in Palestine to the whole Roman world (and even beyond), but never lost the centrality of the Land of Israel as one of its core tenets. Most Jews spoke the language of the countries in which they found themselves, or a specifically Jewish tongue based in the vernacular, rather than Hebrew, although the latter remained the language of Judaism and religious worship. Jewry thus also developed another perhaps unique dichotomy, between a lost, but geographically specific and still desired homeland, and their current place of residence and culture. It is often said that the Torah became the Jews' 'portable homeland' during their centuries of wandering. Because Jewry was endogamous and largely hereditary, Jewish identity was also nationalistic and ethnic, as well as religious, in a sense which has remained the case ever since. Judaism's sacred texts were the history of a single people, of common descent.

The fierce monotheism of the Jews and, after Christianity became the general religion of the West, their failure to worship Jesus as the Messiah, aroused tremendous hostility to them, turning them, in the centuries which followed, into a pariah people in Europe. In the Hellenistic and Roman periods some creative interaction with other peoples was possible, but was largely lost during the centuries which followed. The Jews became 'a people who dwell apart'. The flexibility of Jewish forms, side by side with the rigorous insistence on a core of a particular unique religious identity, gave the Jewish people surprising and tremendous strength which enabled them to survive the centuries of persecution which followed.

There were also some respects in which the Jews of ancient times displayed very different traits from those with which the Jews came to be associated later. Most Jews in ancient Palestine were farmers, peasants, and agriculturalists (like the great majority of non-Jews). They were not urban-dwellers, and had no particular reputation in the ancient world as merchants or financiers. Nor were they renowned for their contribution to the Western world's philosophy, science, or culture apart from the dimensions set by Jewish religious frames of reference. Other peoples gained a reputation for these areas of endeavour, but not the Jews.

Jews in the medieval and early modern world

What happened to the Jews in the centuries following the fall of the Temple and their dispersion from Palestine is unclear and open to dispute. As elsewhere, the ensuing period was a 'dark age', although for the Jews not so dark as for the people among whom they lived. A small Jewish population remained in Palestine, but Jews were now spread out everywhere in the Roman world and in Babylonia. In Babylonia, a flowering of Jewish culture occurred, leading to the creation and editing of the Babylonian Talmud between about 200 and 750 CE. Jews everywhere now began to acquire strikingly different socio-economic characteristics from those which they demonstrated in the past, or of the peoples among whom they lived. They abandoned the land, becoming, even then, a people of cities, and became known as money-lenders and merchants. Their role as money-lenders, which continued for centuries, was brought about by the fact that both Christianity and Islam banned usury (lending money at interest). This brought Jews popular opprobrium but also an assured role as court financiers, which continued into the eighteenth century. Jews were also prominent as mercantile traders, especially over long overland or sea routes, and as artisans and craftsmen. In the early part of the seventh century CE whatever remained of the unity of the former Roman world was ended forever by the career of the Prophet Mohammed (570–632 CE) and the rise of Islam, the religion he preached. Within a century of Mohammed's death, the world between India and France (including Spain and Portugal but excluding what is today Turkey) had been converted to Islam. In many respects Islam was much more akin to Judaism than was the form of Christianity which emerged triumphant in the later Roman Empire. Islam, like Judaism, was unequivocally monotheistic, and many of its customs (like circumcision) and dietary code were virtually identical to those of Judaism. Arabs also claimed descent from Abraham. Jews (and Christians) as 'People of the Book' were treated as *dhimmis* ('the protected ones') and were allowed to practise their religion and live freely in Muslim lands, provided that they paid a special tax and acknowledged the sovereignty of Islamic rulers. They were forbidden to carry weapons or ride horses, and were subject to a variety of minor humiliations. As a rule, Sunni Muslims were more tolerant of Jews than were Shi'ites. Some Shi'ite Islamic rulers, like Al-Hakim B'Amr Allah, the eleventh-century caliph of Egypt, were particularly intolerant of Jews. The yellow badge of shame, so notorious a feature of medieval Europe, was a Muslim innovation, introduced by a caliph of Baghdad during the seventh century CE. Nevertheless, by and large, Islamic rule was one of toleration for the Jews, and most Jews lived at this time in Islamic lands, ranging from Spain to Persia. This point should be emphasised: from the early Middle Ages until perhaps as late as the mid-eighteenth century, most of the world's Jews lived in the Islamic, Afro-Asian world, not in Europe. Their language, customs and lifestyles increasingly resembled those of their neighbours, albeit always in a distinctively Jewish way. For instance, many Jews in the Arab world began to speak, as their vernacular language, such tongues as Ladino (Judeo-Spanish), which they evidently first spoke when resident in Spain and Portugal prior to their expulsion in 1492.

During this period, or even earlier, Jews spread far, to form communities in extremely unlikely places. Several groups of Jews established themselves in India, notably the so-called Cochin Jews, who existed in the Cranganore area on the south-west coast from around the sixth century CE, and the Bene Israel ('Sons of Israel'), an ethnically Indian Jewish community around Bombay. A Jewish community existed in the Far East, around Kaifeng in central China, from about the year 1000 CE, apparently founded by merchants from Persia. By the time Westerners learned of its existence in the eighteenth century, this isolated community, owing to intermarriage, was wholly Chinese in appearance and custom. The well-known Jewish community of Ethiopia (a mixed Hamitic and black Christian kingdom in northeast Africa), widely known as 'Falashas' ('exiles'), but more officially and acceptably as Beta Israel ('House of Israel'), by repute descend from King Solomon and the Queen of Sheba, but in actuality probably from converts to Judaism from the late pre-Christian era. They speak a number of Ethiopian dialects and are, in appearance, dark-skinned Hamites. A sect of Jews who accepted the Bible but not the later Oral Law – the Karaites (a term usually taken to mean 'People of the Scripture') – emerged in Persia about the seventh century and survive to this day in Russia and Israel. Perhaps the most remarkable addition to Jewry in this period were the Khazars, a Turkic tribe of the lower Volga area of Russia, north of the Black Sea, whose king and nobility converted to Judaism in the late eighth century CE. Khazaria was a powerful kingdom from the eighth to the tenth century, and was, strangely enough, the largest territory in terms of area ever ruled over by Jews. Much about Khazaria is subject to dispute and even legend. It is generally believed that only a minority of Khazars were Jews, not the entire nation. In the twentieth century, extravagant claims were made that the Khazars were, in fact, the ancestors of most European Jews. This seems highly improbable, since the Khazars certainly spoke a Ural/Altaic language, akin to Hungarian or Turkish, while eastern European Jewry spoke Yiddish, a dialect of German (written in Hebrew letters) consistent with their migration from the Rhineland. The Khazars gradually disappeared after the Tartar invasion of 1237, although remnants continued to exist for several more centuries.

Jews in the Muslim world produced a flourishing and remarkable culture. The most notable among them included such luminaries as Judah Ha-Levi (*c.*1075–1141 CE), a Spanish-born poet and philosopher who was a proto-Zionist and died in Egypt on his way to Palestine. The most famous and remarkable of Jewish intellectuals from this milieu was Moses Ben Maimon, known as Moses Maimonides (1135–1204), or the *Rambam* (from the Hebrew initials of his name). Also born in Spain, he lived for most of his life in Egypt, where he was a prominent physician. Maimonides set out the famous Thirteen Articles of Faith of Judaism, and an influential Code of the Talmud, *Mishneh Torah*. An even more famous work, *Dalalat al-Ha'irin* ('Guide of the Perplexed'), also attempted a clear exposition of Jewish belief, and was heavily influenced by Aristotelian philosophy.

This golden age of medieval Jewish thought in the Muslim world gradually waned, especially after the expulsion of the Jews from Spain in 1492, but such later philosophers as the codifier Joseph Caro (1485–1575), continued to produce important works. Caro, born in Spain but spending most of his life at Safed in Palestine (which re-emerged as a centre of Jewish learning), wrote the famous *Shulkhan Arukh* ('The Prepared Table'), a brief codification of previous commentary on the Law which remains central to Orthodox thought. Besides the mainstream of Orthodox Jewish philosophy and commentary, there also emerged during this period another mystical Jewish strand, the *Kabbalah* ('tradition' in Hebrew), which was codified around the twelfth century CE. Kabbalah, which has links with the ancient

philosophical schools of Gnosticism and Neoplatonism, postulated the existence of semi-secret ways of gaining insight into the nature of the Divine
which could become known to acolytes through rigorous training. It also
had a more mystical appeal as well. Probably the best-known work of the
Kabbalists was the *Zohar* ('brightness' in Hebrew), a commentary on the
Bible apparently written in Spain in the twelfth or thirteenth century.
Kabbalism influenced many strands in the development of Judaism: the
pseudo-Messiah Shabbetai Zevi (or Zvi, 1626–76) and, later, the Hasidic
strand in Orthodox Judaism both owed much to Kabbalism.

The Jews who lived in the Christian world, especially in Europe, for
many centuries did not fare so well. The attitude of Christianity towards the
Jews generally became one of stark simplicity: the Jews were, originally,
God's chosen people, but forfeited this role with the mission, crucifixion
and resurrection of Jesus Christ. Indeed, by being held chiefly responsible
for the crucifixion of Jesus, the Jews became an accursed people, to be
universally condemned and ostracised unless and until they accepted the
divinity of Jesus. Increasingly, Christians read the Old Testament to find evidence of the foreshadowing of Jesus, especially in the books of the Prophets.
By the early Middle Ages, Jews were everywhere subject to many restrictions on their behaviour, with more and more occupations closed to them,
and greater and greater levels of insult and condemnation hurled against
them. By the high Middle Ages, Jews in Europe generally had no rights
except those which were specifically conferred on them by local kings and
princes. They were, however, subject to their own internal governance and
law codes, and were often under the direct protection of the local ruler. Jews
in Europe gradually came to monopolise the position of money-lender and,
often, tax collector, such that Jews became synonymous with the role of
money-lender. This obviously produced enormous hostility to them almost
everywhere, although it often made them absolutely necessary to the
running of the medieval state.

Hostility to Jews in medieval Europe grew, and manifested itself in a
variety of ways. The crusades, the attempts by Christian rulers and their
armies to recapture the Holy Land from the Muslims, were accompanied by
ferocious and violent attacks on Jewish communities, especially by
crusaders preparing to set out for Palestine. In Europe, violent antisemitism
probably increased significantly, especially with the promulgations of the
'blood libel', the allegation that Jews murder Christians, especially Christian
children, to obtain blood for *matzah* at Passover. This notorious allegation
apparently originated with the case of William of Norwich, in England in
1144; other infamous medieval examples include that of Hugh of Lincoln
(1255 in England) and Simon of Trent (1475 in Italy). Violence against Jews
increased for other reasons. For instance, over a hundred Jews were killed at
York in England in 1190, at the hands of a mob probably stirred up by local
aristocrats to whom they had lent money. The Black Death of 1348–49 led
to murderous attacks on Jews, especially throughout Germany; Jews were

alleged to have begun the plague by 'poisoning wells'. From the twelfth century CE Jews who refused to convert were often expelled *en masse* from European countries – from England in 1290, France in 1306, and, most significantly, perhaps, from Spain and the Spanish dominions in 1492, ending the great period of Jewish intellectual endeavour there. In some countries, the expulsion of the Jews occurred at the same time as the rise of a Christian financial sector (or, as in England, the immigration of Lombard bankers from Italy) in a more sophisticated economy.

Although the first legally-defined ghetto dates only from that established in Vienna in 1517, from the eleventh century the Church tried to forbid contact between Jews and Christians. During the Middle Ages, indeed, Jews frequently segregated themselves from Christians, often in walled enclosures, in large part for self-protection from mobs, but as well to maintain their individual cultures. From the early sixteenth century, however, ghettos were legally established in parts of Europe, especially in Italy and Germany, as districts in which Jews were compelled to live. Ghettos were, typically, walled enclaves from which Jews could not leave after dark. Despite being overcrowded, squalid and impoverished, a vigorous Jewish culture often flourished. Jews were also often forced to wear distinctive badges and were subject to conversionist sermons. Ghettos, it should be noted, never existed in some parts of Europe, nor in the English-speaking world. The Jewish district (*mellah*) of Islamic societies was an eastern version of the ghetto. The earliest had been established at Fez, Morocco, in the fifteenth century, not to humiliate its inhabitants but to make them less vulnerable to physical attack during outbreaks of popular hostility. *Mellahs* were subsequently set up in other towns with the intention of penalising Jews rather than protecting them; they were uniformly wretched in appearance and their inhabitants subject to night-time curfews.

Within Europe, the chief regions of Jewish residence also gradually shifted, away from the Mediterranean area to eastern Europe, especially to Poland, then a powerful, independent kingdom. Jews first arrived in Poland as early as the ninth century CE, but were encouraged by the country's monarch to migrate there as merchants after the Tartar invasions of 1240. Although they won a charter of protection in 1264, gradually, owing to antisemitic pressures, by the mid-fifteenth century their rights had been whittled away. Nevertheless, as the backbone of the small mercantile class, they remained more or less secure as businessmen. As was the case much later in the tsarist empire, the fortunes of the Jews ebbed and flowed, depending on the whims of each king or local nobleman. In general, the sixteenth century saw an upturn of their fortune, which then waned again in the seventeenth century. In Poland, Jews spoke Yiddish and formed *kehillot* (organised, self-governing local communities). A central organisation of Polish Jewry, the Council of the Four Lands (*Vaad Arba Aratzot* in Hebrew), was formed in the mid-sixteenth century, a remarkable proto-parliament which met twice yearly. It assessed the taxes to be paid by the

Jewish community and regulated a range of Jewish activities, including schools and charities. The Council declined in the eighteenth century and was, in effect, abolished in 1764. The Yiddish-speaking Jews of Poland comprised most of the Ashkenazi Jews,[1] the majority of Jews in the modern world, especially in Europe and America.

The religious conflict which divided Europe for nearly two hundred years from the early sixteenth century could not fail to affect the status of the Jews. Medieval western and central Europe was exclusively Catholic. While Jews were persecuted and marginalised, in a sense their status was secure. They were the only non-Catholic religious minority whose existence was permitted, and, occupationally, they often formed the backbone of the proto-middle class of financiers and merchants. *De facto*, they were often left alone to evolve their own communities and their own religious culture. The Reformation begun by Martin Luther (1483–1546) in 1517 divided western and central Europe into warring Catholic and Protestant religious groups. Protestantism, with its doctrine of individual salvation and its rejection of the authority of the pope, contained at least the seeds of greater toleration for the Jews. It should, however, be noted that Martin Luther was himself a ferocious antisemite whose teachings have sometimes been seen as laying the foundations for later Germanic hostility to Jews. Nevertheless, more radical forms of Protestantism, especially the sects associated with the French-born Swiss religious reformer John Calvin (1509–64), were often more philosemitic than were most strands of Christianity for many centuries, placing great emphasis on reading the Bible, and even encouraging contact with Jews. In addition, the nations won over to the more radical forms of Protestantism, especially the Netherlands, Britain, and its North American colonies, often encouraged religious toleration, freedom of expression, and the removal of caste-like barriers to social mobility, for the whole population. These countries were also bastions of capitalism, which did not view Jewish economic activities in an unfriendly light. Moreover, the division of western and central Europe into warring Catholic and Protestant camps itself made Jews less vulnerable to persecution as religious deviants and unbelievers in Catholic countries. Protestants (for example, the Huguenots in France) now filled this role, while Protestant nations often witnessed the development of fierce anti-Catholicism.

The seventeenth century saw a deep divide in the fortune of Europe's Jews. In western Europe Jews tentatively but often successfully began to engage in the wider European politics and culture, for the first time in centuries. Benedict, or Baruch, Spinoza (1632–77), a Sephardi Jew in the Netherlands, became internationally renowned as a philosopher and metaphysician, although his highly unorthodox views on religion and the Bible shocked Jews

---

1 The word *Ashkenaz*, originally used of a people mentioned in Genesis and Jeremiah, became linked in the Middle Ages to German Jewry, and thus Jews of central and eastern European background are known as *Ashkenazim*.

and Christians alike. Jewish merchants and financiers became respectable as 'court bankers' to royalty on the European continent and as successful entrepreneurs in Britain, the Netherlands, and overseas. In eastern Europe, however, catastrophe struck the Jews in the form of the massacres launched by the Cossack leader Bogdan Chmielnicki (1593–1657) in 1648. In an episode strongly presaging the Holocaust three hundred years later, hundreds of thousands of Jews were massacred; unlike Hitler, however, Chmielnicki generally spared Jews who accepted baptism to Christianity. The Chmielnicki massacres helped to lend support to the colourful Shabbetai Zevi, who proclaimed himself the Messiah, and actually led many of his followers to Palestine. Given the choice by the Turkish Sultan of converting to Islam or being put to death, Zevi converted to Islam, although his many disciples continued to believe that he did so in order to accomplish his messianic purpose. Nearly half of the world's Jews, the Sephardim,[2] lived in the Afro-Asian world, especially in the Turkish empire. It has been estimated that one million of the world's 2.5 million Jews in *c*.1780 lived in the Afro-Asian world, almost all living the traditional lifestyle of many centuries.

The bulk of Jews in eastern Europe who survived the Chmielnicki massacres continued to practise traditional Orthodox Judaism as they had for centuries. An elite of *yeshivah*-educated Talmudic scholars emerged, with many 'ordinary' Jews feeling increasingly cut off from full participation in Jewish life. Most Jews in eastern Europe continued to live in a *shtetl* (Yiddish for 'small town'), speaking Yiddish and remaining obviously distinct from their Christian neighbours. Most were small traders or merchants, with only a small minority employed in agriculture, unlike the great majority of their Christian neighbours. They enjoyed few civil rights, and were subject to widespread ostracism and persecution. Jews had no nation-state of their own, although many hoped in due course by divine means to be restored to Palestine, which they had been forced to abandon seventeen centuries earlier. Very quickly over the next few generations, all of these realities were to be challenged and gradually changed, by forces within the Jewish community and outside it.

Further reading

Shmuel Almog, ed., *Antisemitism through the Ages* (Jerusalem, 1988)
Richard D. Barnett, *The Sephardi Heritage* (New York, 1971)
Salo W. Baron, *A Social and Religious History of the Jews*, 18 vols (New York, 1952–83)

2 From the word *Sepharad*, used in Obadiah 1:20, denoting a region north of Palestine to which Jews from Jerusalem were exiled following the sacking of the First Temple, and then given in the Middle Ages to Spain. Thus the Jews of the Iberian peninsula and their descendants, as well as those of the Near and Middle East, became known as *Sephardim*, in contrast to the so-called *Ashkenazim* of central and eastern Europe.

Judith R. Baskin, *Jewish Women in Historical Perspective* (Detroit, 1991)

H.H. Ben-Sasson, *A History of the Jewish People* (London, 1976)

Robert Chazan, *Church, State and Jews in the Middle Ages* (New York, 1980)

Anna Foa, *The Jews of Europe after the Black Death* (Berkeley, Cal., 2000)

Jonathan Israel, *European Jewry in the Age of Mercantilism, 1550–1750* (Oxford, 1985)

David S. Katz, *The Jews in the History of England, 1485–1850* (Oxford, 1994)

Jacob Katz, *Tradition and Crisis: Jewish Society at the End of the Middle Ages* (New York, 1971)

H.J. Leon, *The Jews of Ancient Rome* (Philadelphia, 1960)

Ivan G. Marcus, *Rituals of Childhood: Jewish Acculturation in Medieval Europe* (New Haven, 1996)

G.F. Moore, *Judaism in the First Centuries of the Christian Era*, 3 vols (Cambridge, Mass., 1971)

Heiko Oberman, *The Roots of Antisemitism in the Age of Renaissance and Reformation* (Philadelphia, 1984)

Leon Poliakov, *The History of Anti-Semitism*, 4 vols (London, 1974)

Cecil Roth, *A Short History of the Jewish People* (London, 1969)

Gershom Scholem, *Sabbati Sevi, the Mystical Messiah, 1626–1676* (Princeton, 1957)

Robert M. Seltzer, Jewish People, Jewish Thought: *The Jewish Experience in History* (New York, 1980)

Bernard D. Weinryb, *The Jews of Poland* (Philadelphia, 1973)

|2|

Enlightenment and emancipation in continental Europe, 1750–1880

After the Renaissance, both European Jewry and the majority populations among whom they lived underwent a process of what many social scientists term 'modernisation' which transformed both Jewish and European life. This process did not occur evenly throughout Europe. Western Europe experienced it first; eastern Europe later and more fitfully or, indeed, in some countries to the most limited extent before the First World War. For the nations of Europe, the process of modernisation entailed such changes as the institution of parliamentary government and a universally applicable legal system in place of monarchical absolutism and medieval 'estates' (nobles, merchants, peasants, etc.), urbanisation and economic development, and religious freedom. Inhabitants of European nations were increasingly perceived as equal citizens of their respective countries, their status defined by their place of birth or naturalisation rather than their hereditary class background or by their religion. Although these changes affected all Europeans whose countries experienced 'modernisation', they affected the Jews more than virtually any other people. Throughout Europe, Jews remained, until the modern period, a pariah people who were virtually outside of and apart from the majority of people among whom they lived. As a rule, Jews were tolerated aliens, who were liable to expulsions. Almost everywhere, they paid special taxes and were subject to a range of legal disabilities. In some places they continued to be confined to compulsory ghettos. Most Jews were traditionally Orthodox, living in an almost wholly Jewish milieu where rabbis and other Jewish leaders – not kings, noblemen or (obviously) bishops – were regarded as leaders of the community. Throughout eastern Europe, most Jews spoke Yiddish, a language spoken by no one else. Few Jews lived in large cities (as opposed to small towns or villages) and virtually none had attended a university or made much of an impact on the wider European culture.

The roots of modernity

By the late nineteenth century, the nature of both European and Jewish society had changed enormously. Most of western and central Europe had constitutional government, often elected by universal manhood suffrage. Citizenship rights were accorded equally to everyone who was born or naturalised in a particular country, and all male citizens were seen as having equal rights and responsibilities (for instance, in many countries all young men had to perform military service for some years). The status of Jews had also altered categorically. Ghettos and legal disabilities had been swept away, and in law Jews were almost everywhere the equals of gentiles, Russia being the most important exception. Many Jews had moved to cities; most Jews in the West had abandoned traditional Strict Orthodoxy and spoke the language of the majority population wherever they lived. Jews were often at the forefront of 'modern' culture and scientific advance, as well as capitalist enterprise and socialist ideologies. Indeed, the prominence of Jews in these areas was a potent cause of the 'new antisemitism'.

Certainly, 'modernisation' is a useful concept only up to a point. All societies had their own pathways to 'modernity' and almost nowhere were 'pre-modern' elements in society entirely eliminated until 1918 or long afterwards. It is often argued, for instance, that Germany took a 'special path' to modernisation, in which pre-modern forms of militarism and autocracy continued to dominate German society perhaps until 1945, and that Germany never really experienced a 'liberal' phase. Many social scientists have questioned the usefulness of the concept of 'modernity' as such, and it may well be that the concept is in part confused and confusing. In today's Israel, for instance, Strictly Orthodox Jews, whose lives revolve around the most stringent observation of their millennium-old religion, often work as computer programmers in the most modern part of 'hi-tech' industry. Nevertheless, the concept of 'modernisation' is at least partially valuable in viewing the evolution of both European and Jewish societies since the seventeenth century, however superficial it may be.

Most historians view the crucial intellectual transformation of modern Europe as having occurred in the eighteenth century, during the period known as the 'Enlightenment' or 'the Age of Reason'. The spirit of the European Enlightenment gave rise to emphasis on the Rights of Man (although not, despite the efforts of early feminists like Mary Wollstonecraft, the Rights of Woman), a trend summarised in the Swiss-born philosopher Jean-Jacques Rousseau's famous indictment of the *ancien régime*: 'Man is born free, but everywhere he is in chains'. The European Enlightenment gave rise to a specifically Jewish Enlightenment, known as the *Haskalah*, among westernised sections of the European Jewish intelligentsia, as will be discussed below.

The Enlightenment found its roots in the liberal, secular premise that man is not inherently evil, as the Christian Church, with its doctrine of

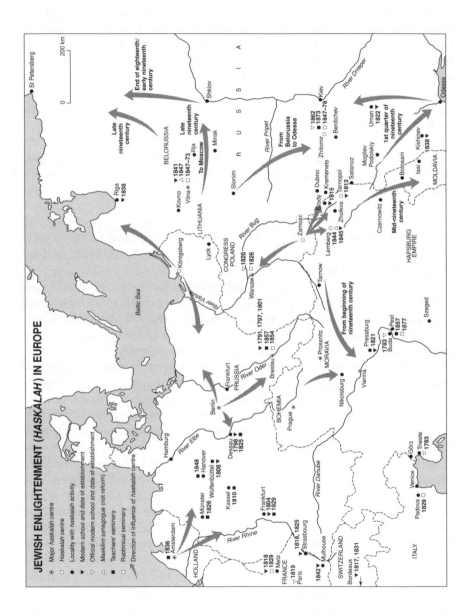

JEWISH ENLIGHTENMENT (*HASKALAH*) IN EUROPE

◉ Major *haskalah* centre
○ *Haskalah* centre
● Locality with *haskalah* activity
▶ Modern school and date of establishment
▷ Official modern school and date of establishment
◀ *Maskilim* synagogue (not reform)
■ Teachers' seminary
□ Rabbinical seminary
→ Direction of influence of *haskalah* centre

0 ____ 200 km

original sin, insists. Rather, man is capable through the power of reason of rightful conduct, and this has the potential to perfect the good life on earth through his own conscious efforts rather than the promise of 'reward or punishment' in the next world. As a preliminary to the perfection of society, man's mind must be liberated from the shackles of ignorance and superstitious authority, whether in the form of the Church (especially the Roman Catholic Church) or of feudalism. Many have argued that the ideas of the Enlightenment led to the French Revolution of 1789. Moreover, a rather different strand of liberalism and constitutional government emerged in the English-speaking world, emphasising constitutional liberties and representative government, through Britain's 'Glorious Revolution' of 1688 and the American Revolution of 1775–83. Both strands emphasised the equality of all citizens before the law, and (perhaps reluctantly in the British case) came to view religious freedom and equality as one of the bedrocks of free government. The American Constitution of 1787–90 forbade the state establishment of any religion, setting all religions on equal footing. The obvious implication of this view of the role of citizenship and of religion is that Jews would be treated as equal citizens of the countries in which they lived. All offices of the state would be open to them, as would all state schools and all occupations. The religion practised by the Jews, in common with all other religions, would become a purely private matter.

Today, these ideas seem so commonplace as hardly to be worth mentioning. It must be appreciated, however, that in the eighteenth century they were literally revolutionary. There was hardly a place in Europe where Jews did not suffer from a variety of legal disabilities and there was no place where Jews were free to hold political office. It took nearly 200 years for all the disabilities of the Jews in western society to be removed. Many historians have identified three periods in the history of what is known as Jewish Emancipation: a preliminary period covering the decades of the Enlightenment (roughly 1730–89) preceding the French Revolution; secondly, the nine decades (roughly 1789–1878) between the French Revolution and the Congress of Berlin when Jewish equality was achieved in western Europe and America and then in central Europe; and thirdly, the six decades (roughly 1878–1933) between the Congress of Berlin and Hitler's rise to power when Jewish emancipation was achieved everywhere, but side-by-side, paradoxically, with the rise of the 'new antisemitism' and other extremist ideologies which were eventually to bring catastrophe to European Jewry. The first two periods are surveyed in this chapter.

Traditional Jewish society

It should also be realised that a redefinition of Jewish identity as consisting of full equality in every sense with their non-Jewish neighbours, with religion sidelined as a purely private matter, was not necessarily welcomed by all Jews and also required a difficult reinterpretation of the nature of Jewish identity. For many centuries, Jews had voluntarily seen themselves as 'a people apart', God's chosen people, waiting patiently to be restored by Him to the promised land. All Jews were required to observe a large number of religious rituals which determined their lives from cradle to grave. They were supposed to marry among themselves, and to deal with their Christian neighbours at a distance. Thus, for example, not all Austrian Jews wished to be regarded as Austrians, or Italian Jews as Italians. Since the Enlightenment, many Strictly Orthodox Jews have continued to live in the observant manner of their ancestors, deliberately separating themselves, in so far as possible, from their non-Jewish (and Jewish non-observant) neighbours. The nature of Jewish identity itself was (and remains) highly ambiguous. The Zionist movement, for instance, regarded the Jews as a separate ethnic group or nationality who deserved a state of their own. Until the foundation of the State of Israel in 1948, many Jews rejected and contested this view of the nature of Jewish identity.

By the second half of the eighteenth century about 1.5 million of the world's 2.5 million Jews are believed to have lived in Europe. The great majority of those lived in eastern Europe, with perhaps 900,000 in the kingdom of Poland and 170,000 in the Hapsburg lands. Another 175,000 lived in the German-speaking realms of central Europe apart from Austria. Much smaller numbers lived in western Europe: for instance, about 50,000 Jews lived in Holland, 40,000 in France, and 20,000 in Britain. Sephardi Jewry were more prominent in western and south-eastern Europe than subsequently, and were regarded as more highly assimilated and in some senses more socially acceptable than the mass of Yiddish-speaking Ashkenazi Jews.

By and large, the Jews of Europe followed much the same lifestyle as their forebears had done for centuries. Education for Jewish males was exclusively religious and almost wholly judeocentric, involving study of the Torah and Talmud at a *heder* (private elementary school, usually in one room; plural *hadarim*), or at a *Talmud Torah* (a communally-maintained elementary school, often for the poor). Secondary education occurred, if at all, at a *yeshivah*, where Torah and Talmud were analysed day and night by close intense study and debate known as *pilpul* (literally 'pepper'), typically in a hairsplitting way. Jewish men were expected to make time throughout their lives for daily Torah study. They were expected to marry young, preferably at 18, in the hope that they would 'be fruitful and multiply'. From the time they became *Bar Mitzvah* (literally, 'Son of the Commandment') at the age of 13, all 613 commandments inherent in Judaism were binding upon them, affecting their lives every hour of every day. Jewish women had only a few commandments binding upon them, but were expected to marry young, bear children and keep house in the traditional way. Rates of literacy for both Jewish men and women were among the highest in Europe.

Jews were still more or less cocooned from the ideological influences of the outside world, with the possible exception of a small minority of assimilated Jews in the West. Even when ghettos were abolished they tended to live in the same neighbourhoods, within walking distance of a synagogue, since Jewish law forbids Jews to use any form of transport on the Sabbath. Overwhelmingly, they spoke languages which were distinctive to themselves: Yiddish (a dialect of German written in Hebrew letters) throughout eastern and central Europe; or languages such as Ladino (Judeo-Spanish, with Portuguese elements) in the Sephardi world, which also were written in the Hebrew alphabet. Hebrew was the language of prayer, liturgy, and sacred texts; it was also used in many Jewish documents, although it was not the vernacular language of the Jews. Throughout eastern Europe, Jews often wore distinctive clothing, such as the long black robes (the 'caftan' of stereotype) and large fur-trimmed hats for men; high-necked, long-sleeved gowns for women, their hair hidden under close-fitting caps or shaven and replaced by wigs.

Jews had developed an extensive system of elected local self-government, the *kehillot* (singular *kehillah*), with elected leaders (*parnassim*). In time the *kahal* – a term meaning the executive leadership of the *kehillah* – had become an oligarchy based on wealth and family influence. It imposed taxes on the local Jewish community to pay for a communal infrastructure of synagogue, schools, and charitable institutions. It appointed the *Beth Din*, the Jewish court which judged criminal and civil cases coming before it in accordance with *Halakhah* (Jewish law). One dreaded weapon inflicted upon miscreants was the *herem* (rabbinic decree of excommunication), whereby the wrongdoer was stigmatised, curses were invoked on him, and he was shunned by all members of the *kehillah*. The celebrated Dutch freethinker Benedict (Baruch) Spinoza was probably the most famous victim of a *herem*, although as he lived in western Europe, largely outside the Jewish community, this sentence was not as serious as it might have been elsewhere. At this time, rabbis did not routinely lead synagogue services or perform many of the functions of clergy, as they would normally do today in the Western world; their chief function was to use their expertise in Jewish law to advise on religious matters and settle civil disputes within their community, and also to attend the *Bet Hamidrash* ('house of study') to teach Torah, perhaps delivering a Talmudic discourse at the beginning of each term. Synagogue services were led by an official known as a *baal tefillah* ('master of prayer'), although the rabbi might preach on certain occasions. Jewish communal autonomy reached its most developed form in Poland before that country's partition in the late eighteenth century. There a multi-layered system of local, municipal, and provincial government existed for the Jewish community. At the provincial level there existed the Council of the Four Lands (*Vaad Arba Aratzot* in Hebrew), composed of representatives from local *kahals*. It collected the special taxes which the Jewish community was required to pay, and had a host of other communal functions. The Council was abolished by the Polish government in 1764 since, after a major recession, it proved unable to collect the requisite taxes. Government officials assumed that task.

Jewish legal disabilities

Throughout Europe before the French Revolution, Jews suffered from innumerable forms of legal discrimination. Almost everywhere (Britain was a notable and striking exception) Jews or the Jewish community were required to pay a special tax to the local ruler in order to live in his country, a tax not paid by Christians. In many cities, especially in German-speaking lands and Italy, Jews were required to live in ghettos, tiny, horrifyingly insalubrious neighbourhoods consisting of only a few blocks, which Jews were prevented from leaving between sundown and sunrise. They were forced to wear distinguishing headgear and/or badges (usually yellow), and were also subject to many other irksome restrictions. Notable ghettos existed in such cities as Prague (the *Judenstadt*, or Jews' town), with its famous medieval synagogue, the Altneushul, Frankfurt-on-Main, famous as the ancestral home of the Rothschild family, and Rome, whose ghetto became notorious not merely as one of the worst in Europe but the last to survive, being abolished as late as 1870. Jews were often required to take part in insulting ceremonies – in Rome, for instance, each Saturday and every Good Friday, 150 of them were marched from the ghetto to a nearby church where they were forced to sit through a fiery conversionist sermon. Many European countries, from Spain to Switzerland to Sweden, refused to allow Jews to settle in their territories, and these bans continued to exist in some cases until the mid-nineteenth century. In most countries, Jews could not own land or be admitted to many trades and professions. This was one of the major reasons why Jews became so heavily involved in finance, commerce and petty trading, as well as in such areas as money-lending, pawnbroking and itinerant peddling. In some countries with substantial Jewish populations, Jews were forbidden to settle in the capital city or other large centres. For instance, Vienna was off-limits to most Jews, as were Moscow and St Petersburg. In most German states and elsewhere, Jews entering the country were obliged to pay the *Leibzoll* (body or head tax), levied on them as if they were livestock. This tax was imposed each time a Jew crossed the boundaries of the numerous petty states. Only in a few places in Europe, such as Britain (after 1656) and some (but not all) of the Dutch provinces, could Jews enter and settle freely. During the eighteenth century, too, Europe's absolutist rulers decided the fate of their Jewish populations in a virtually whimsical manner. In 1744, for example, Austria's Empress Maria Theresa (who reputedly could literally not stand the sight of Jews) issued a decree expelling all Jews from Bohemia and Moravia. Owing to adverse international pressure, driven by Britain and Holland, she was forced to suspend the decree indefinitely; Jews returning to Prague, however, were forced to pay higher taxes.

In Germany and the Italian states, and in certain other parts of Europe also, Jews testifying before public officials were required to swear a special oath (*more judaico*) with demeaning wording. In some localities, Jews had to take the oath while struggling to keep their balance standing on a wobbly stool, or standing on the skin of a pig. From 1466 until 1668, the Jews of Rome were compelled by papal injunction to participate in a bizarre ceremony for the amusement of revellers at a winter carnival: representatives of the community, originally teenage boys but later unfit old men, had to race on foot through the streets of Rome clad only in loincloths. Later the Jews were replaced by horses, with Jews being made to pay for the race. A representative of the Jewish community had to appear at the start of each carnival dressed in ludicrous attire; he was forced to pay public homage to Rome's civic dignitaries and request permission for Jews to remain in Rome for another year. This was given with a haughty warning that if the community gave cause for complaint permission would be withdrawn. He was then literally kicked aside.

Myths about Jews continued to be commonplace. Many still believed that Jews could be detected by a characteristic fetid odour they exuded, which miraculously disappeared whenever a Jew converted to Christianity. Many supposed that Jews had tiny horns on their heads, denoting their supposed kinship with the Devil. The 'blood libel' – the notion that Jews kidnapped Christian children at Passover, ritually murdered them, and used their blood to make *matzah* (unleavened bread eaten by Jews at Passover) – persisted, and induced a serious spate of violence against Jews in Poland in the mid-eighteenth century which caused them to ask the Vatican to intervene. The special investigator, Cardinal Ganganelli (later Pope Clement XIV, reigned 1769–75) condemned the ritual murder charge as nonsense. As pope, he pursued a relatively moderate policy towards the Jews of the Papal States, ending some of the worst abuses against them. This policy was reversed by his successor Pius VI (reigned 1775–1800), who reinstated all the old ordinances against them, and added some new ones. In 1777 Venice (an independent republic ruled by an oligarchy of noble families) issued a particularly oppressive set of regulations affecting its Jews which forbade them to participate in many professions and trades. On the eve of the French Revolution relics of medievalism underlay the treatment of Jews in most parts of Europe.

Jews and European rulers – enlightened despots

Admittedly, during the late seventeenth and early eighteenth centuries there were many positive developments for the status of Jews in Europe. Following the Thirty Years' War (1618–48), the rulers of the fragmented European states required financial support and reliable providers of goods and services. Often, they used Jewish entrepreneurs to provide these requirements. Jews were outside the feudal power structure, maintained international contacts at a time when this was rare, and were regarded as competent and reliable. These Court Jews (*Hofjuden*), as they are often known, acted as moneylenders, contractors, brokers, and commercial advisers to many German rulers. They provided credit, acted as army provisioners, and even undertook diplomatic missions. They tended to dress in the fashion of the day, rather than in distinctly Jewish garb, and were often exempted from the special taxes on Jews. They were frequently permitted to reside in places forbidden to Jews. They tended to marry among themselves, and interrelated dynasties of Court Jews emerged. Nevertheless, they were also precariously placed. Probably the best-known Court Jew was Joseph Süss Oppenheimer (*c.*1698–1738), known in literature and films as 'Jew Süss'. He was a relative of two other famous Court Jews, Samuel Oppenheimer (1630–1703) and Samson Westheimer (1658–1724), both based in Vienna. Joseph Oppenheimer, Court Jew to the Duke of Württemberg, set about centralising the state administrative system and modernising the economy, with the aim of freeing the duke from dependence upon grants from the local 'estates'. Oppenheimer's policies made him many implacable enemies, and when the duke died suddenly in 1737 he was arrested the same day, tried and found guilty on trumped up charges of embezzlement and offences against the state, and publicly hanged in Stuttgart. His corpse was exhibited in a suspended iron cage.

Europe's rulers occasionally tried to lure Jews to their kingdoms because their presence was seen as conducive to economic prosperity. Although continuing to discriminate vigorously against Jews in trades he despised, King Frederick William I of Prussia (reigned 1701–40) offered subsidies and inducements to Jews willing to move to Prussia to build up the local silk and satin industries and other desirable enterprises. Jews sometimes came to occupy important roles as manufacturers in fields which local rulers wished to encourage. In the 1780s a Jew was appointed head of the state tobacco monopoly in the Hapsburg Austrian realms – the first to hold a public administrative post under that dynasty. In Prussia and Austria there gradually grew up, during the eighteenth century, a class of Jewish factory owners producing such items as luxury textiles and fine linens, jewellery, chinaware and glassware, all deemed desirable by local rulers.

Together, these groups of affluent, westernised Jews represented one of the earliest milestones on the long road to the emancipation of European Jewry. Most retained their ties with Judaism, and Court Jews often acted as emissaries or go-betweens (*shtadlan*) between Jewish communities and their local rulers, using their influence on behalf of Jewry. During the attempts in 1744 to expel Jews from Bohemia and Moravia, Wolf Wertheimer (d.1763), the son of Samson Wertheimer and Court Jew to the King of Bavaria, prevailed on his influential contacts in European ruling circles to intercede on behalf of the Jews of Bohemia and Moravia. Other affluent Jews obtained permission for the building of synagogues and other benefits for Jews in their home towns, secured as favours from grateful rulers. Neither the privileged Jews nor the European rulers had any intention of granting general emancipation for the Jews, and the privileged Jews confined their activities to trying to remove the worst features of oppression or in granting further privileges to themselves and their kinsmen as special favours. The achievements and limitations of this situation might be seen in the case of Austrian Empress Maria Theresa, who disliked Jews so much that she reputedly agreed to an audience with a wealthy Jewish entrepreneur only while seated behind a screen so that she would not have to look at him. Nevertheless, she prohibited the baptism of Jewish children against the will of their parents (a common practice in some Catholic countries) and forbade the voicing of the 'blood libel'.

The eighteenth century in Europe before the French Revolution is often said to be the era of 'enlightened despots', kings who saw themselves as promoting the interests of their states in innovative ways, often against the wishes of the feudal aristocracy and the churches. Among the more famous of 'enlightened despots' were King Frederick William II of Prussia ('Frederick the Great', reigned 1740–86) and Maria Theresa's son Emperor Joseph II, who ruled jointly with his mother from 1765 until her death in 1780 and then singly until his own death in 1790. These rulers saw themselves as paternalistic guardians of the interests of the state, and they believed that the promotion of those interests was conducive to the public welfare of Jews. This often meant the enshrinement in legislation of the concept that some Jews, in beneficial occupations or occupying positions of status, were useful to the realm, and were to be given more privileges than the mass of Jews. While all Jews remained second-class citizens, some were deemed less second-class than others. In many European countries, this represented the earliest instance in modern times of Jews being officially tolerated, even encouraged, to become part of the societies in which they lived. Nevertheless, these privileges were often extremely limited in their range and did not constitute real emancipation in any sense.

The official code regarding the role and status of Jews in Prussia, issued in 1750 by Frederick the Great, divided Jews into those who were given 'regular protection' and those given 'special protection'. For those in the former category, they and one (but not more) of their children could remain in Prussia; in turn, only one child of that child could remain in Prussia. Those given 'special protection' could not transmit the right to remain in Prussia to any of their children. This code also spelled out those trades in which Jews were permitted to deal on an equal basis with Christians (which included dealing in tea, coffee, chocolate, horses, used clothing, and money-lending) but closed most other trades to them. The number of Jews with transmissible 'regular protection' remained extremely small, being fixed at 203 for Berlin and 63 for other parts of Prussia. Nevertheless, it was in Prussia, and especially in Berlin, among the wealthy and protected Jews of this class, that the *Haskalah* or 'Jewish Enlightenment' took root.

The best-known enactment by an 'enlightened despot' which affected

Jews was the Edict of Toleration (*Toleranzpatent*) of 1782, issued by Austrian Emperor Joseph II. It was drafted with the help of Joseph von Sonnenfels (1732–1817), court interpreter to the emperor and professor at the University of Vienna, a Catholic of Jewish parentage. The goal of the Edict was 'to make the Jewish nation useful and serviceable to the State, mainly through better education and enlightenment of its youth as well as by directing them to the sciences, the arts, and the crafts.' It arose in part from the fact that the Jewish population of the Hapsburg realms had grown enormously as a result of the First Partition of Poland of 1772, which brought Galicia and other parts of Poland under Austrian control. The Edict abolished all discriminatory taxes affecting Austrian Jewry, the yellow badge, and prohibitions on Jews leaving their homes on Sundays and Christian holidays. It permitted the Jews of Vienna to trade freely, and opened the state schools to Jews. There were also many limitations. Jews could not become peddlers, and no foreign Jews were allowed to reside in Vienna without special permission and had to pay a special sum (the *Toleranz*), intended to keep poor Jews out while allowing some successful Jews to settle there. As in Prussia, the goods in which Jews were permitted to deal were restricted. Since Joseph II expected all 'estates' and pre-modern corporations to yield power to the state, he curtailed the power of the *kehillah* by recognising the status of individual families, rather than the Jewish community, in relation to the state. Jews were not allowed to hold public religious services or open new synagogues. In the mid-1780s Joseph abolished the jurisdiction of the rabbinic courts. Despite these restrictions, the aim of the *Toleranzpatent* was expressly to 'almost place the Jewish nation on an equal level with other religions in trade and employment'. In 1787 came what would be a momentous ruling, the requirement that all Jews take fixed surnames. From this date they began to acquire the 'typical' Jewish surnames, often German-sounding, which distinguish them in the western Diaspora, in place of patronymics (for instance, Aharon ben Shlomo – Aaron son of Solomon – whose son might be Moishe ben Aharon – Moses son of Aaron) by which they were previously known. The *Toleranzpatent* also initiated a mood of Jewish goodwill towards the Hapsburg monarchy which lasted until its overthrow in 1918. While the rising Jewish merchant class of central Europe generally welcomed these changes, many rabbis, especially in traditional communities, rightly feared it as an encroachment on their way of life and authority. They thus did not necessarily welcome emancipation, especially if this was likely to take Jews away from their religious obligations under *Halakhah*.

Dohm, Lessing and Mendelssohn; the Haskalah

By this time, the latter half of the eighteenth century, a number of European writers and philosophers were advocating the extension of all citizenship rights to Jews. Among them was the Prussian constitutional lawyer Christian Wilhelm von Dohm (1751–1820), who in his essay of 1781, 'On the Civil Improvement of the Jews', advocated the removal of all legal discrimination against Jews and their full admission to civil society. This would have the effect, he argued, of making Jews 'useful members' of society while diminishing their 'clannish' tendencies and other undesirable features. Discrimination against Jews was 'a remnant of the barbarism of past centuries, a consequence of a fanatical religious hatred' which was 'unworthy of our enlightened times.' 'In a few generations the Jews will be just like all other citizens,' Dohm concluded. Another influential German intellectual who favoured Jewish emancipation was the distinguished critic and dramatist Gotthold Ephraim Lessing (1729–81), one of the leaders of the Enlightenment. His one-act play *Die Juden* (*The Jews*), written in 1749 and published five years later, is believed to have been the earliest literary work by a continental European gentile to portray a Jew in a sympathetic light. Lessing's dramatic poem *Nathan der Weise* (*Nathan the Wise*), written in 1779, depicts Judaism, Christianity, and Islam as three brothers, each possessing an identical gift from their father, and each claiming that his alone is of value. It is Nathan, the Jewish character, who preaches an enlightened approach based on common humanity.

Both Dohm and Lessing were Freemasons, members of the semi-secret fraternal order whose imagery derives in part from ancient Hebrew roots. Freemasonry, which became popular in western and central Europe from the seventeenth century, was often joined by liberals and free thinkers, and was one of the earliest secular organisations which generally accepted Jews as members. In such bodies as the Freemasons, Jews and gentiles often mixed relatively freely, for the first time in modern history.

Dohm and Lessing were also influenced in their attitude towards the Jews by admiration for their Jewish friend Moses Mendelssohn (1729–86). The character of Nathan was based on him. Moses Mendelssohn was a major – perhaps the major – transitional figure in the *Haskalah* or Jewish Enlightenment, the parallel to the European-wide Enlightenment of the eighteenth century. Born Moses ben Mendel (Menahem) in a north German town, the son of a Torah scribe, he received a traditional Jewish education. At the age of 14 he moved to Berlin, where he mixed with the secularised families of that city's small Jewish economic elite, learning German, other languages, and a range of secular subjects. He became known as a rationalist philosopher of note. In 1763 he was awarded first prize by the Prussian Royal Academy of Sciences for a treatise on metaphysics; Immanuel Kant, the most famous of all German philosophers, was the runner-up! There were, however, limits to Mendelssohn's ascent, for he was nominated for membership in the Academy, but denied admittance as a Jew. Nevertheless, he became known as the 'German Socrates' in the intellectual salons of Berlin, which substituted for a modern university in the cultural life of the city. Frederick the Great awarded him the status of a 'protected Jew', thus ensuring his residency in Berlin.

Mendelssohn found himself, in part against his better judgement, defending Judaism in debates with Christian theologians. His views on Judaism were centrally expressed in his book *Jerusalem*, published in 1783. He argued that Judaism was the most rational of religions. Its core tenets, such as the existence and unity of God and the immortality of the soul, were the products of human reason, not of divine revelation. He did believe, however, that God had revealed His laws and commandments at Sinai, and it was accordingly incumbent upon Jews to keep them. In keeping with Enlightenment thought, he believed in the separation of church and state, and held that religion was a matter of private conscience. He therefore argued that the government and the church must never attempt to coerce an individual to accept a particular religious viewpoint. Mendelssohn greatly admired Judaism because (in contrast to Christianity) it did not attempt to make converts, but he equally opposed the judicial powers of rabbis and Jewish communal leaders to impose a decree of excommunication upon those of whom they disapproved. While he believed in mutual toleration for all religions, he also believed deeply that the Mosaic code was God's revealed will for the Jews, and remained an observant Jew throughout his life. Nor was he in any sense a precursor to Reform Judaism, arguing that even if Jewish law conflicted with the demands of modern life, Jewish law must prevail, and that Jews must forsake emancipation rather than abandon Judaism. Mendelssohn was rather lukewarm towards the *Toleranzpatent*, suspecting the Austrian Emperor of wanting to convert Jews to Christianity.

Moses Mendelssohn was probably the most illustrious Jew of his time, welcomed, and comfortable in, gentile Enlightenment circles – yet remaining a practising Jew who became a leader of Berlin Jewry. Mendelssohn believed that the emancipation of European Jewry would come, since as he put it, 'the betterment of the situation of the Jew is identical with the progress of mankind'. Yet there was much that Jews, too, had to do to advance themselves. They must, he argued, abandon their exclusive preoccupation with Talmudic education that kept them ignorant of the modern world. They must cease to use Yiddish, which he considered a debased jargon, and turn to languages which held the key to secular knowledge. For this reason, he translated the Pentateuch into German, using Hebrew letters. It was published, along with a commentary in Hebrew which reflected modern influences, in 1780–83. In this task he was assisted in writing the commentary by several like-minded scholars, including Naphtali Herz Wessely (1725–1805) and Naphtali Herz Homberg (1749–1841). This commentary provoked the ire of traditional rabbis, but Mendelssohn was unfazed. Indeed, he and his collaborators hoped by such works to enable Jews to revive Biblical Hebrew as a living language. In the long run, this proved to be a formative influence on the revival of Hebrew advocated over a century later by the Zionist movement. Mendelssohn's disciple David Friedländer (1750–1834) founded a school for Jews in Berlin which was guided by principles he enunciated, together with other acculturated Jews of the day:

besides German, French, arithmetic, science, and other secular subjects, it taught Hebrew and Biblical studies. It thus provided both a comprehensive general education and a specifically Jewish one, although in a way very different from that taught in traditional, pre-modern Jewish communities.

From these roots, the *Haskalah*, or Jewish Enlightenment, developed and made its lasting impact upon German and then European Jewry. Beginning with a group of acculturated Jews in Berlin, of whom Mendelssohn was the most prominent, it aimed at a synthesis between German Jewry and German culture that in later decades became so marked a feature of the German–Jewish community until the Nazi period. The term *Haskalah* (Hebrew for 'Enlightenment') was not employed until 1832, when the movement had spread beyond its German home. Its adherents were known as *maskilim*, a term rooted in the Hebrew for 'to have understanding'.

The *Haskalah* posed a series of very difficult questions of self-identity to European Jewry, questions which are not fully resolved in the Jewish world today. Of what does Jewish identity consist in the modern world? How far should Jews go towards compromising with secular influences? To what extent are Western notions of progress compatible with Judaism? Traditionally, Jews had been particularist and inward-looking, relatively untouched by the surrounding gentile culture except in some milieus, such as medieval Spain. In contrast, the *maskilim* regarded the involvement of Jews in wider society as both desirable and feasible, a goal which might be termed integration. They wanted Jews to adapt themselves to modern conditions in order to end their age-old status as outsiders, but certainly did not advocate the disappearance of Jewry altogether. They stressed the common humanity which united Jews and gentiles, regarding the differences dividing them as secondary. Jews, they argued, should meet the growing possibility of emancipation half way, modernising their educational system, dress, language, and attitude towards their gentile neighbours. Jews would thus be deemed worthy of citizenship by the governments of the countries in which they lived, and would exercise the same rights and be bound by the same obligations as any other citizens. They would no longer be either a people apart or a people despised and persecuted.

The ideas of the *Haskalah* were aired in *Ha-Meassef* ('The Gatherer'), the pioneering secular Hebrew-language periodical launched by a group of Prussian *maskilim* in 1783 known as 'The Friends of the Hebrew Language'. Leading thinkers, including Mendelssohn, were contributors; the movement specialised in producing books in Hebrew on Jewish history and other topics, and in opening Jewish schools with a mixed curriculum of modern and Jewish studies. During the 1780s over 200 such schools were established in Austria, over 100 of them in Galicia. From its German centre the *Haskalah* spread by the 1830s to other parts of Europe, especially to Poland and Russia. Increasingly, the *Haskalah* and its tenets were strongly opposed by Orthodox rabbis and leaders, especially in eastern Europe. Increasingly, too, *maskilim* attacked traditional Judaism in satirical terms.

By the mid-nineteenth century, however, the *Haskalah* movement was entrenched in the eastern European heartland of traditional Judaism, particularly in Vilna in Lithuania. A sharp, perhaps unbridgeable gap thus opened up in Jewish ranks between traditionalists and modernisers. Interestingly, there was much less evidence of the *Haskalah* in western Europe and the English-speaking world (where the Jewish population was, of course, very small), where there was no pre-existing mass of traditional Jews and much less extreme hostility towards Jews than in eastern Europe.

Impact of the French Revolution

In the decades leading up to the French Revolution of 1789, many notable French thinkers turned their attention to the possible future role of Jewry in an enlightened and reformed society. The great French thinkers of the Enlightenment were liberals and radicals who viewed the feudal aristocracy and, in particular, the Catholic church, as enemies of progress that would be reformed or swept away in a reformed society. One might, therefore, expect their attitude to a persecuted minority like the Jews to be highly sympathetic. Yet, with individual exceptions, the attitude of the great French Enlightenment thinkers towards the Jews, and especially towards Judaism as a religion, was often surprisingly negative and hostile. The two-edged attitude of European radicals towards the Jews was to become something of a feature of gentile attitudes towards Jews over the next two centuries, influencing radical movements like Marxism and also radical nationalistic movements, including the roots of Nazism. To many eighteenth-century French radicals, Jews were steeped in superstition and backwardness. This was the attitude of Denis Diderot, editor of the famous *Encyclopédie*, who believed that Jews bore 'all defects peculiar to an ignorant and superstitious nation'. He believed that since they had nothing beneficial to offer the world they should disappear from history, laying aside their unacceptable beliefs and practices and blending as individuals into the rest of the population. Voltaire, the great satirist and philosopher who was central to the French Enlightenment, was even savager. He hated the Catholic Church, which he regarded as the pillar of backwardness, and was equally venomous in his criticism of Judaism; indeed, his writings on Jewry are seen by many as overtly antisemitic. He saw Judaism and its practitioners as relics from ancient times, steeped in rituals and laws which were barbaric and bigoted. In an article strongly presaging later European antisemitism, Voltaire labelled Jews the 'most contemptible of all' of the world's peoples and denied that they had made any impact upon civilisation. 'A great people cannot have received their laws and their knowledge from a small, obscure, and enslaved people.' Jews were adept 'in no act save that of usury' and 'an ignorant and barbarous people, who have long united the most sordid avarice with the most detestable superstition and invincible hatred for every people by whom they are tolerated and enriched.' The French materialistic philosopher Paul d'Holbach, a younger contemporary of Voltaire, was yet more extreme, describing Jews as 'cruel, inhuman, intolerant', 'the enemies of the human race', 'a nation of robbers' who 'have become notorious for deception and unfairness in trade' and 'have always displayed contempt for the clearest dictates of morality and the law of nations'. To be sure, other celebrated figures of the French Enlightenment were friendly to the Jews, understood their sufferings, and deplored all manifestations of persecution aimed at them. Montesquieu, Bolin, Rousseau, and Mirabeau, for example, were notable philosemites and enemies of antisemitism. Rousseau saw the survival of the Jews as one of the wonders of the world and even considered the possibility of a Jewish state. Mirabeau was particularly impressed by Moses Mendelssohn, wrote a book about him in 1787, and used arguments similar to Dohm's in favour of Jewish emancipation.

As the French Revolution neared, the question of the fate of the Jews in modern societies was gradually becoming of considerable interest to many of the intelligentsia and to the governing classes. In 1785 Pierre Louis Roederer, a liberal intellectual in Metz, organised an essay competition under the auspices of the local Royal Society of Arts and Sciences on the subject 'Are there possibilities of making the Jews more useful and happier in France?' The joint winners, announced in 1788, were a Catholic priest, a Protestant lawyer, and a Jewish linguist from Paris. All agreed that the Jews must lose their visible distinctiveness and become integrated into French life, but differed in details. The winning essay by Abbé Henri Grégoire (shortly to become prominent, during the French Revolution, in campaigning for equal rights for the Jews) was particularly interesting in rejecting the notion, widely held among Catholics, that Jews must suffer for the Crucifixion. He believed, however, that Jews were led astray by rabbinic authority, that they would eventually convert to Christianity and would, indeed, be restored to Jerusalem, heralding the 1000-year reign of Jesus on earth. The Jewish essayist, Polish-born Zalkind Hourwitz (*c*.1740–1812), a disciple of Mendelssohn, also argued that Jews should break free of Talmudic influences and rabbinic control and that enlightened society could help them to do so by granting them equality. During the Revolution he became a Jacobin, joined the National Guard, and actively lobbied for Jewish emancipation.

On the eve of the French Revolution, there were signs that the civic status of French Jewry might be heading for improvement. In 1787 an act was promulgated which gave civic rights to 'non-Catholics'. It was aimed at restoring to Protestants the toleration they enjoyed before the revocation of the Edict of Nantes in 1685. French Jewry thought that their hour had come, and pressed for their own rights, but found that the term 'non-Catholics' was narrowly interpreted to exclude them. Nevertheless, a breakthrough had been achieved, since French citizenship was no longer confined to Catholics. In 1788 a French minister, Chrétien de Malesherbes, established an informal committee, including many leading Jews, to advise him on the future status of Jewry. Unfortunately it failed, in part because Ashkenazim and Sephardim (the older, better-integrated component of the community) failed to achieve consensus.

The events of the French Revolution, which broke out in 1789, had the most profound effect on the status of French Jews. In August 1789, one of the first acts of the newly-established National Assembly was to pass the Declaration of the Rights of Man, a bill of rights drawing on British and American precedents and also many of the ideas associated with the *philosophes*. Among other things, it guaranteed freedom of conscience for all, 'provided that their opinions do not disturb the public order as established by law'. This paved the way for the full emancipation of Protestants in December, but there was considerable resistance to giving parity to French Jews. Abbé Grégoire introduced a motion giving Jews full citizenship. 'Fifty thousand Frenchmen arose this morning as slaves; it depends on you whether they shall go to bed as free men,' he declared. But there was considerable resistance. Some deputies were apathetic to the Jewish question; some were blatantly hostile, siding with the representatives of Alsace and Lorraine, who vilified Jews as usurers and exploiters of the peasantry and undeserving of citizenship. Some believed that as non-Christians the Jews should not be enfranchised. Other argued that the Jews were not a religious sect, like the Protestants, but a nation, subject to its own laws, and which (as one deputy put it) 'constantly turns its eyes towards another homeland', who were, in effect, resident aliens unable to exercise the rights of full citizens. In a well-known speech to the Assembly, Count Stanislas de Clermont-Tonnerre, a radical deputy, encapsulated both the arguments of emancipists and the qualms about Jews. He favoured granting full citizenship to the Jews, hoping to make them into useful citizens. 'Men who have only money can be only as good as money is; there lies the evil. If they had land and a fatherland they would not lend money any more; there is the remedy.' But he also declared, in a celebrated phrase, that 'Jews should be denied everything as a nation, but granted everything as individuals.' By this he meant that Jews had to become full and loyal Frenchmen, giving up any 'dual loyalties' as a separate nation within a nation. (He was not implying that Jews should change their religion.) However much he might well be misunderstood, Clermont-Tonnerre pointed to a significant ambiguity in the nature of Jewish identity which resurfaced many times, often at the hands of antisemites.

The principles which animated the French Revolution could not, however, permanently deny citizenship to French Jews. The French Sephardim, located mainly in Bordeaux and south-western France, were granted full citizenship in January 1790, following a petition stating that they were indeed French, since their Portuguese ancestors had been naturalised in 1550, a status reconfirmed by all successive monarchs. The Sephardim were keen to dissociate themselves from the Ashkenazim of the north-east, newer arrivals who were less integrated and more unpopular. A campaign led by the middle-class Ashkenazim of Paris led to the granting of full French citizenship to all Jews in September 1791, providing that their separate corporate status was ended and they became fully French. During the Reign of Terror (1793–94) synagogues were burned and destroyed by revolutionary mobs, while Jews also remained deeply unpopular with extreme conservatives and local antisemites. Nevertheless, by the early 1790s French Jewry had gained full, or virtually full, legal equality with other Frenchmen, the first time in the history of continental Europe that an entire national Jewish community achieved full legal equality. This occurred virtually contemporaneously with the adoption in 1790 of the Bill of Rights in the newly-established United States, which separated church and state and placed all religions on an equal basis in law.

Napoleon and the Jews

The period after the Revolution and the Reign of Terror in France saw the government of the republican Directory (1795–99), and the irresistible rise to power of the Corsican Napoleon Bonaparte (1769–1821), who achieved eternal renown as one of the most successful military leaders in history. From his *coup d'état* in November 1799 until 1804 Napoleon was first consul (together with two other inferior consuls appointed by him), in effect the dictator of France. In May 1804 Bonaparte proclaimed himself Emperor Napoleon I, ruling until 1814. A military genius of the highest order, he virtually conquered Europe, placing his relatives and supporters on the thrones of the countries he had overrun. For much of this period only Britain maintained continuing hostilities against Napoleon and France, gaining control of the seas with a celebrated naval victory against France at Trafalgar in 1805, and finally defeating Napoleon at Waterloo in 1815 when he attempted a brief comeback.

Napoleon possessed a keen knowledge of history, and in 1798–99 had conquered Egypt and parts of Palestine, briefly taking Jaffa (today's Tel Aviv), the first European to have ruled over any part of Palestine since the Crusades. Napoleon had a continuing but somewhat desultory fascination with the Jews. As a product and in many respects a representative of the French Revolution, he opposed the overt persecution of them. Like many Frenchmen of his day, however, he was puzzled as to what role Jews were to play in the new order – in this case, the new regime instituted and headed by Napoleon – and sought to make them into loyal, patriotic Frenchmen. Napoleon also agreed with many Frenchmen that Jews were not integrated into France and were, from his viewpoint, a 'nation within a nation' whose group characteristics included (as he saw it) the practice of usury and the exploitation of debtors. Napoleon was particularly aware of the depths of antisemitism in places like Alsace, where Jews were, it was claimed by their enemies, heavily involved in usurious money-lending to peasants. After Napoleon became emperor he attempted to gain legitimacy for his regime by restoring the Catholic Church, the aristocracy, and other pre-revolutionary elements of French society to their former place. Ultra-conservatives – who often detested Jews and regretted their emancipation – were given positions of influence under Napoleon. Among these was Vicomte Louis de Bouald, who had emigrated from France during the Revolution but returned in 1808 and became minister of instruction under Napoleon. Bouald jointly edited an ultra-conservative newspaper with another royalist erstwhile emigré, Vicomte René François Chateaubriand, in which he argued that sympathy towards the Jews entailed the undermining of Christianity and accused Jews of aiming to control the world. In this and his other published works Bouald set the scene for the anti-liberal, anti-semitic, ultramontane strand in French Catholicism which would remain extremely influential until 1945. He was also one of the first modern writers to view the Jews as part of an international conspiracy of evil, a theme which became central to modern antisemitism.

In Alsace and Lorraine relations between peasants and the local Jewish population deteriorated further. Napoleon came under considerable pressure to expel the Jews from these provinces. Instead, in 1806 he issued an edict which accused Jews of practising usury, declared his intention of protecting their debtors, and announced that Jewish defects of character would have to be reformed in order to instil in them 'sentiments of civil morality which, unfortunately, have been stifled in many of them by the abject state in which they have long languished'. In May 1806, therefore, Napoleon took the extraordinary step of summoning an assembly of Jewish 'notables', to be appointed by the Jewish communities of France and northern Italy, who would meet together in Paris. The ensuing Assembly of Jewish Notables, consisting of 111 members (they seldom met together all at once) was held in Paris between July 1806 and April 1807. It was probably the first officially-constituted national Jewish assembly in modern times which was summoned by a national leader to consider the Jewish viewpoint on questions of national concern. Count Louis Mathieu Molé, Napoleon's adviser on Jewish affairs (and no friend of the Jews), drew up a list of 12 questions which the Jewish notables were to answer, in order to convince Napoleon that he could 'reckon' them as 'faithful servants, determined to conform in everything to the laws of France'. These included such curious queries as whether Jewish men could marry more than one wife, whether divorce was valid among Jews, or marriage to a Christian; more seriously, the Assembly was asked to declare whether 'in the eyes of Jews are Frenchmen considered as brethren or as strangers,' whether Jews born in France 'consider France as their country' and if they were 'bound to defend it', the nature of the powers of the rabbis among Jews, and whether Jewish law permitted usury.

Since the Jews of the Assembly feared that Napoleon might have been considering the revocation of Jewish emancipation, they had to consider their answers carefully. The questions were framed so as to evince fairly predictable responses. According to witnesses, when Molé asked the Assembly whether Jews were bound to defend France, 'the whole Assembly unanimously exclaimed - Even to death'. After deliberating, the Assembly came to such conclusions as that 'In the eyes of Jews Frenchmen are their brethren, and not as strangers' and that they considered themselves to be Frenchmen and bound to fight for France. By the laws of Moses, Jews were 'generally forbidden ... to lend upon interest to our fellow-citizens of different persuasions, as well as to our fellow-Jews', and that if some Jews were indeed usurers, the whole community should not be blamed for their excesses. The Assembly concluded that it would declare 15 August, Napoleon's birthday, a day which Jews would celebrate with 'prayers, thanksgiving, and all the demonstrations of a pure and lively joy'.

Molé informed the Assembly that (not surprisingly) Napoleon was 'satisfied with your answers', and then announced that, most remarkably, the emperor had decided to summon a Grand Sanhedrin to transform them into binding precepts. Full citizenship would be guaranteed to the Jews, but Napoleon required a 'religious pledge for the strict adherence to the principles contained in your answers'. The Sanhedrin was to be similar to the Great Sanhedrin of Palestine which existed before and after the destruction of the Temple (finally being abolished in 425 CE), the supreme religious and judicial body of ancient Jewry. The Sanhedrin of Paris would similarly consist of 71 members, two-thirds of whom were to be rabbis. This Sanhedrin actually met in Paris early in 1807, endorsing the answers the Assembly had given about the behaviour of Jews, their complete loyalty to the French state, and determination to act ethically towards non-Jews.

In many respects, the Paris Sanhedrin was a seminal event in modern Jewish history, turning French Jewry at a stroke into loyal 'Frenchmen of the Mosaic persuasion', integrated into the framework of civil society. This new identity was reinforced in 1808, when an edict extended the consistorial system governing Catholics and Protestants to Jews. Under this edict, a central *Consistoire* was established in Paris, together with other regional ones. Their purpose was to organise French Jewish life, with Judaism recognised as a religious denomination like any other. (Although it was not until 1831 that rabbinical salaries were paid out of the public purse, like the salaries of Catholic priests and Protestant pastors.) Nevertheless, outside France many Jews were very dubious about these developments. In particular, many traditional Jews of eastern Europe viewed Napoleon as an agent of secularism, especially as his troops conquered much of Europe. In 1808, shortly after Napoleon convened the Sanhedrin, he appeared to reverse many of his liberalising measures through what became known as the 'Infamous Decrees'. These attempted to restrict the economic role of the Jews in France, limited further Jewish settlement in Alsace and Lorraine, and removed the right of Jewish conscripts (unlike others) to find substitutes to replace them. French *départements* were given the right whether or not to implement these decrees; at the time of Napoleon's fall, 44 of 68 *départements* continued to do so. After 1808, however, Napoleon took little or no further direct interest in Jewish affairs, being almost wholly concerned with military activities. Had Napoleon's rule lasted, one can only speculate as to what the future might have held for the Jews under French rule.

Influence of French policy

Perhaps even more revolutionary than the impact of the French Revolution and Napoleon upon the Jews of France was their effect in other parts of Europe which came under French rule. Between 1792 and 1815 France spread its rule throughout much of continental Europe, always sweeping away ancient constitutions and regimes and proclaiming the spirit of 'Liberty, Equality, Fraternity'. Everywhere, ghettos were abolished and the Jews placed on a legal equality with other inhabitants. This occurred when French armies conquered Belgium in 1793, the Netherlands in 1796, Switzerland (more insecurely) in 1797, and much of Italy in 1796–7: the Jews greatly benefited and age-old restrictions were abolished. Between 1792 and 1794 much of the Rhineland came under French rule, and, as a result, Prussia (in 1787) and Bavaria (in 1799) abolished the 'body tax' on Jews. The kingdom of Westphalia (including much of central Germany) under Napoleon's brother Jerome gave Jews equal rights in 1808, while the Frankfurt ghetto was abolished in 1811.

Most semi-independent countries remaining in Europe were forced to concede rights to Jews. Prussia (which remained independent) gave citizenship for the first time to a Jew in 1791, to Prussian Court Jew Daniel Itzig. Liberal reforms followed in 1808–12, with Jews gaining municipal rights in 1808. In 1812 King Frederick William III (reigned 1797–1840) issued the 'Edict Concerning the Civic Condition of Jews' which granted citizenship to Jews and removed virtually all previous restrictions on them, although they could not hold public office above the local level.

As in France, the previous judicial powers of Jewish communal leaders were revoked, and Jews were required to use German in their commercial transactions and in official documents. They became eligible for military service, and were required to take hereditary surnames. Many also germanised their forenames, with Moses changed to Moritz, Solomon to Siegfried, Isaac to Isidor. Marianne, Henriette and Fanny were favourites among women. Many of these names, for instance Isidor, were little used by Christians and became hallmarks of Jewish identification, while names like Moritz, Siegfried, Charlotte, and Henriette became so closely identified with Jews that Christian parents shied from using them for their own children. Many Jewish surnames, such as Cohn, Moses and Levy, immediately signified the ethnicity of their bearer. In adopting names intended to make them seem more 'German', Jews often found that they had exchanged one pejorative label for another. Nevertheless, as in France, many German Jews began to describe themselves (famously) as 'Germans of the Mosaic persuasion', Hebrews, Israelites, or some other euphemism. Germany's ever more assimilated and acculturated Jewish community increasingly saw itself as fully accepted and acceptable. Historians have often argued whether this was a generally accurate impression which was negated only by the wholly unexpected rise to power of Adolf Hitler in 1933, or whether the perception of full acceptance was illusory from the start.

Reaction and rights lost

Napoleon foolishly invaded Russia in 1812, began to lose decisively to the allies (Britain, Prussia, and French royalists) in 1813–14, and abdicated in April 1814, when he was banished to Elba. Louis XVII (reigned 1814–24), half-forgotten younger brother of Louis XVI, guillotined in 1793, was placed on the French throne, and a major gathering of European statesmen was assembled to decide the future of Europe at the Congress of Vienna from September 1814 to June 1815. In March 1815 Napoleon returned to the mainland, entering Paris, and again took up the post of emperor. In June, he was decisively defeated by Wellington and Blücher at Waterloo, and the emperor found himself banished to the remote island of St Helena. The defeat of Napoleon meant the restoration of reactionary, pre-revolutionary regimes throughout Europe, with the principle of 'legitimacy' (pre-existing dynastic rule) becoming the watchword of most of Europe's rulers, especially the leaders of the 'Holy Alliance' (initially Italy, Austria, Prussia, and Russia). Only Britain, previously Napoleon's arch-enemy, remained to champion constitutional liberalism. The decades after 1815 also saw a general drift to the ideological right in many spheres, with Romanticism's revival of medievalism in art and culture, and a renaissance of Catholicism among its hallmarks. This period also saw liberalism driven underground, but becoming more radical than ever, with the memory of the French Revolution central.

The effects of these changes upon the Jews of Europe were, as might be expected, deleterious, although not to the extent that many Jews might have feared. The 'Jewish question' was specifically considered at the Congress of Vienna – the first time an international conference had discussed the Jews – with Jewish representatives present to lobby on Jewish issues. Somewhat surprisingly, the major Germanic delegates, Prince Metternich of Austria and Karl von Hardenberg of Prussia, favoured the maintenance of Jewish emancipation, while the smaller German states like Bavaria were opposed. Initially, the Congress drafted a constitution for a proposed German Confederation which gave Jews 'all rights heretofore accorded them in the several states'. Fierce opposition, however, forced the alteration of 'in' to 'by', meaning by the states themselves, not as a result of French conquest, enabling any German state to rescind Jewish rights if it wished. The Congress was also notable for its brilliant Jewish salons, led by Jewish women, including associates of Moses Mendelssohn's daughter Dorothea, where much discussion took place. In France, too, Napoleon's 'Infamous Decrees' of 1808 were not renewed by Louis XVIII when they lapsed in 1818, and as a rule the gains made by Jews during the revolutionary period were made permanent.

Elsewhere, however, much of the pre-revolutionary oppression returned. The ghetto of Rome was re-established in 1814, with Jewish representatives forced to pay annual ceremonial homage to the civic authorities. In 1826 the ultra-conservative Pope Leo XII (reigned 1823–29) reimposed the oppressive papal edict of 1775 concerning Jews, and, throughout Italy, age-old persecution of the Jews grew. In Tuscany, for example, university undergraduates were permitted to revive a bizarre custom which was officially ended by the conquering French, that of marking the beginning of winter by weighing the fattest Jew they could find and exacting his weight in confetti from the local Jewish community. During this period, the papacy became firmly identified with judeophobia of the most backward, medieval kind.

Since the mid-eighteenth century, Jewish advancement had gone as far in the German states, especially in Berlin. Jews enjoyed equality on the Berlin Stock Exchange and a Jewish banker had been elected as municipal councillor in 1809. Several factors, however, came together to prompt a significant antisemitic backlash after 1815. German nationalism had been fanned by the efforts to rid the country of the French conquerors, whose universalistic ideology of forced libertarianism was looked upon by German nationalists as un-German and perverse. Adherents of the growing Romantic movement increasingly promoted the concept of an 'organic Christian state'. As a result, from 1815 there was an upsurge of overtly antisemitic publications and propaganda in Germany, especially in Berlin. Jews were depicted as a 'state within a state', and accused of a range of anti-social characteristics. Much of the language employed was extreme, presaging twentieth-century antisemitism. One antisemitic pamphlet termed Jews a 'united gang of criminals' and facetiously suggested that Jewish men should be castrated, sold into slavery in America, forcibly repatriated to Palestine, or even put to death, the pamphleteer stating 'I do not regard the killing of a Jew as a sin or a crime.'

As a result, antisemitic activities increased markedly. Students' associations at German universities declined to accept Jews as members. In 1819 and 1820, anti-Jewish rioting broke out across many German states, and spread throughout northern Europe from Alsace to Riga. Jewish financiers were blamed for post-war economic misfortunes, while peasants resented Jewish moneylenders and livestock dealers. There were many injuries and much damage to property. For reasons which remain unclear, the rioters' rallying cry was 'Hep! Hep!' It was the cry used by goatherds in southern Germany, where the earliest outbreaks occurred. It might have been adopted because it was an abbreviation of the Latin phrase *Hierosolyma est perdita* ('Jerusalem is lost') reputedly used by the crusaders. The 'Hep! Hep!' riots remained notorious for many years. When George Eliot, the famous novelist and philosemite, wrote an article several decades later on the rise of modern antisemitism on the Continent, she entitled it 'The Modern Hep! Hep!'

Despite the social and economic advances made by European Jews at this time, many – probably more than in any previous period – underwent conversion to Christianity. There is no definitive way of knowing how many or when conversions peaked, but the zenith was probably reached between about 1790 and 1850. At the end of the nineteenth century, it was estimated that 45,000 Jews in Austria-Hungary and 23,000 in Germany had converted to Christianity. Most probably they had converted because of the attitude summarised in the famous phrase of the convert Heinrich Heine (1797–1856), the famous German poet, that his baptismal certificate was 'an admission ticket to European culture'. Heine adopted Lutheranism in 1825, expecting to reach high places in German academic life or the civil service, but found that doors were still closed; many German Christians still regarded him as a Jew, and an opportunist to boot. Typical of this milieu, Heine maintained a very ambiguous attitude towards his Jewish origins, although in his final years he claimed that he had not returned to Judaism 'because I never left it'. In some highly acculturated German Jewish circles, conversions to Christianity took on epidemic proportions. The children of Moses Mendelssohn, who had striven so hard to show that a person could be both a Jew and an active participant in society, nevertheless became Christians. One of Mendelssohn's Christian grandsons was the celebrated composer Felix Mendelssohn-Bartholdy (1809–47). Likewise, the father of Karl Marx, the founder of Communism, converted to Lutheranism in 1824 when his son was six, to enable the boy eventually to practise law. Karl Marx (1818–83) became not merely the most famous of radical theorists, but a particularly bitter foe of Judaism, a trait which permeated Communism for much of its history. Moses Mendelssohn's son Abraham and his wife converted to Christianity in 1822 'because it is the religious form acceptable to the majority of civilised human beings'. This, too, was an important motive for converting at that time, a sense that Judaism was a fossilised relic, particular to one small group, whereas Christianity was a universalistic religion embodying principles which ought to govern the behaviour of all peoples. There was much less of a sense then than subsequently of the miraculous nature of Jewish survival over the centuries, and of the universalistic message within Prophetic Judaism.

Liberalism and the quest for Jewish rights

Revolutions broke out in France in 1830, where the liberal 'citizen-king' Louis-Philippe (reigned 1830–48) replaced the Bourbons, and then throughout much

of Europe in 1848, the 'year of revolutions'. The aims of the 1848 revolutionaries were, broadly, to establish constitutional democracies throughout
Europe; for the first time, too, a revolutionary socialist movement emerged
(the *Communist Manifesto*, by Karl Marx and Friedrich Engels, appeared in
1848). Parallel to this was a strong nationalistic movement throughout
Europe, which aimed at achieving national independence in countries like
Greece and Poland, and national unification in Italy and Germany, which
remained as disunited petty states with generally reactionary rulers and
regimes. All these trends appeared to be favourable to the goal of full Jewish
emancipation. Jews participated in the Polish uprisings against the tsars in
1830–31 and 1863–64, in the Italian *Risorgimento* (drive for national unification), and in liberal uprisings in Germany and Austria in 1848, although as
a small component of broad movements. Nevertheless, the nationalistic component of these movements was not necessarily favourable to Jews. Many
extreme nationalists increasingly viewed Jews as an alien body in their respective societies, potential members of an international conspiracy adverse to
their host countries. This attitude provided the foundations of the 'new antisemitism'.

The years between about 1830 and 1880 nevertheless marked the high
tide of the liberal movement in Europe, and the period when Jews received
full, or virtually full, emancipation almost everywhere, tsarist Russia (see
Chapter 4) being the clearest exception. Emancipation was achieved in part
because of the campaigning of Jews, for example the works of the German
Jew Gabriel Riesser (1806–63), whose 1831 pamphlet *On the Position of
the Adherents of the Mosaic Faith in Germany* demanded the full emancipation of the Jews and called upon them to lobby for its achievement. In
1848 Riesser was elected a vice-president of the liberal Frankfurt parliament, which was briefly constituted during the revolution of that year, and
later (1859) became the first Jewish judge in Germany.

Nevertheless, it is probably fair to say that full Jewish emancipation was
achieved in the mid-nineteenth century simply because most of the Christian
majority had become convinced that it was both impossible and undesirable
for Jews to remain as legally-proscribed second-class citizens. Regarding
German-speaking states, all remaining restrictions on the Jews' right of
residence, acquisition of real estate, and choice of occupation were
abolished in 1861 in Bavaria, in Württemberg in 1862, Baden in 1864, and
the North German Confederation, comprising Prussia and 26 other states,
in 1867. In 1869 the parliament of the North German Confederation
abolished all remaining Jewish disabilities on the grounds of religion and
affirmed the eligibility of members of all religions for public office. When
the German Empire was established in 1871, this sweeping law was applied
to all Germany. Although these reforms clearly benefited Jews most directly,
it should also be kept in mind that Protestants and Catholics in areas of
Germany dominated by the other religion were also the victims of discrimination, and Protestant–Catholic hostility (especially Protestant fear of

Catholicism) was probably more important in German life at this time than was the position of the Jews. By 1871, it appeared that the Jews of Germany had been fully emancipated.

Elsewhere in western and central Europe, there was the same bumpy road to full emancipation. In Austria in 1849, under Emperor Francis Ferdinand (reigned 1848–1916), parliament forbade discrimination against Jews. But in 1851 the relatively liberal post-1848 constitution was revoked and some discrimination against Jews, for instance in the purchase of real estate, was reintroduced. From 1860 there was again an improvement, with full emancipation coming in 1867. In the Papal States, Pope Pius IX (reigned 1846–78) removed the worst of the humiliating restrictions on the Jews. During the 1848–49 revolution in Italy, full freedom was granted in most Italian states, but was revoked in the counter-revolution that followed. Indeed, Jews were targeted with particular vigour, being seen as having been prominent supporters of the liberal revolution. Ghettos were reimposed in four cities, and conversionist efforts against the Jews were redoubled. In 1858 there occurred the notorious case of Edgardo Mortara, a seven-year-old Jewish boy who was kidnapped from his home in Bologna after his Catholic housemaid admitted to baptising him during his infancy when he was close to death. Despite an international outcry, he was never released and, indeed, became a Catholic priest. Full emancipation for Italy's Jews came only in 1866–70. In 1866 King Victor Emanuel invaded and unified most of Italy; in 1870 he sent a substantial army into Rome, ending the temporal powers of the pope and unifying the whole country. Thenceforth (except during the Nazi period) Italy's Jews were legally equal to other Italians. Other parts of Europe which discriminated against Jews, such as Switzerland and the Scandinavian countries, gradually gave full equality to Jews in the period between the late 1830s and the mid-1870s, although often not without surprising difficulty. By the mid-1870s (probably the high-water mark of nineteenth-century liberalism) the Jews had achieved more or less full equality almost everywhere in central and eastern Europe. Before the growth of the 'new antisemitism' based only on racial definitions of Jewishness, it appeared as if the future of Europe's Jews, outside the eastern region, was bright, and that full emancipation had been achieved as if by an inevitable force.

Eastern Europe

In eastern Europe, where the great mass of European Jews lived, the *Haskalah* gained ground, although until the late nineteenth century the majority of Jews were traditionally Orthodox. In Galicia (in Austria), a centre of *maskilim* emerged, led by such thinkers as Nahman Krochmal (1785–1840) and Joseph Perl (1773–1839). Here, however, the *Haskalah* was more moderate than in Germany, less keen to challenge traditional religious practice and also more conscious of Jewish group cohesion. Outside Austria, however, both enlightenment and emancipation were long deferred; indeed, emancipation did not come to Russian Jewry until after the First World War.

Poland at the time of its Partitions in the late eighteenth century was a monarchy organised on semi-feudal lines. The relatively numerous nobles elected Poland's kings, and the population was divided into separate estates of nobles, townsmen, Catholic clergy, and peasants. The Jews were a community apart, belonging to no estate, ruled for internal matters by the officially-recognised *kahals*. Many Polish towns were closed to Jews, and many Jews lived in private towns owned by the nobility. In eastern Poland, Jews helped the nobility to administer their estates and functioned as a major component of the capitalist class, running distilleries, breweries, sawmills, and bleaching works; they functioned as middlemen and merchants for the sale of produce from nobles' estates and were especially prominent in the production and sale of alcohol. Jews also played a conspicuous part in rural transport, conveying travellers and freight by wagon and ferry. There grew up a network of small towns, largely if not wholly inhabited by Jews. A small town of this type was known in Yiddish as a *shtetl* (plural *shtetlekh*) Most were small, consisting of only a few thousand inhabitants. It was not a ghetto: Jews were not required to live in a *shtetl*. They had no walls and Jews often lived adjacent to gentiles. The *shtetl* became a distinctive feature of eastern European Jewish life until the Holocaust, and is often viewed today with considerable nostalgia, as in such works as *Fiddler on the Roof*. Yet in reality life was often grim, marked by extreme poverty, overcrowding, and disease.

Relations between Jews and their gentile neighbours varied enormously. Many Catholic nobles and intellectuals were reasonably friendly to Jews, whereas Catholic peasants and townsmen often viewed them with suspicion and fear. In eastern Poland, predominantly inhabited by Ukrainians and other non-Poles, hostility against the Jews was probably much more visible, hallmarked by a tradition of often violent antisemitism going back to the mid-seventeenth century. From the mid-nineteenth century, there was a considerable Jewish inflow into the larger Polish towns, especially Warsaw and Lodz, where Jews comprised one-third or more of the total population. Jews form one of the main components of both the urban business middle classes and the industrial working classes. A distinctive ideological division emerged among Polish Jewry. By the eve of the First World War, Polish Jewry was divided into Zionists, socialists of the Bund and other groupings, and Strictly Orthodox adherents of *Agudas Israel*. As elsewhere in eastern Europe, there was an enormous volume of emigration abroad, especially to the United States.

Just before the Partitions of Poland, serious calls were made there to remove restrictions on the Jews and integrate them into Polish society. There was, however, much opposition to such proposals, especially by the

conservative nobles and Catholic townsmen, who feared the Jews as potential rivals. After the Partitions, however, many Jews retained a continuing
attachment to Poland and fought for Polish independence. Most notable
among them, perhaps, during the Napoleonic period was the Lithuanian-
born Berek Joselowicz (*c*.1765–1809) of Warsaw, who made common
cause with Poland's liberal nationalist leader Tadeusz Kosciuszko and
organised a Jewish cavalry unit to fight for Polish independence against
Russia and Prussia. Composed of 500 young men, it was enthusiastic but
inexperienced, and was virtually annihilated by the Russian army.
Joselowicz went on to become a distinguished military commander, dying in
battle against Austria in 1809. Significantly, he became both a Polish and
Jewish national hero, something which would have been far more difficult
in a later generation.

The kingdom of Poland (the central part of the Polish realm, often
known as 'Congress Poland') became a semi-autonomous part of the
Russian Empire before and after a brief semi-independent existence under
Napoleon. While Polish Jewry were promised civic rights, in reality they
remained subject to many of the discriminatory measures affecting other
Jews in the tsarist empire. As Polish nationalism grew and revolts against
Russian rule occurred, the situation of Polish Jews deteriorated further.
During the Polish uprising of 1830–31 against Russian rule Joseph
Berkowitz (1789–1846), son of Berek Joselowicz, organised a Jewish militia
unit of 850 to fight alongside the Polish rebels. Originally lampooned, they
earned the respect of Polish nationalists, one of whom said that their efforts
'should convince everyone how much we have sinned against the Jews'.
Jews and Poles continued to fight for Polish independence, and the support
of Polish Jews continued to be sought by Polish gentiles. In 1848, for
instance, the famous Polish poet Adam Mickiewicz (who, incidentally, was
of Frankist ancestry) issued a manifesto in the name of anti-Russian Polish
patriots which pledged 'To our elder brother, Israel, respect, fraternity, and
help on his way to eternal and earthly welfare; equal rights in every matter.'
This spirit continued in the 1863 Polish revolution, when many Jews again
actively supported the Polish cause.

From the mid-nineteenth century, however, Polish–Jewish relations
began to deteriorate. There was a pogrom in Warsaw in 1881, and an
openly antisemitic Polish journal *Rola* ('The Soil') began publication in
1883. Many Polish nationalists increasingly regarded Jews as an alien force
in Polish society. They feared Jewish economic influence, especially the visibility of Jewish bankers and textile magnates, and also feared Jewish participation in the socialist movement. They regarded Jews as an urban,
cosmopolitan people inherently distinctive from the rural Catholic Polish
masses. Indeed, the socio-economic and demographic differences between
Catholic and Jewish Poles were very great, and unquestionably a source of
much of the friction which tragically developed between the two groups. In
1912 the National Democratic Party, a Polish nationalist party founded in

1912, called for an economic boycott of the Jews. These tensions continued in an even more extreme form after the re-establishment of the Polish state in 1918, down to the Holocaust.

Romania had been a Turkish possession. The two principalities of 'Old Romania', Moldavia and Wallachia, achieved virtual independence in 1856 following the Crimean War, and full independence at the Congress of Berlin in 1878. In 1856 the Treaty of Paris gave full religious freedom and civil rights to everyone in the Romanian principalities. Nevertheless, the Romanian authorities refused to end discrimination against the Jews. Indeed, Prince (later King) Carol I (reigned as prince 1866–81 and as king 1881–1914; he is sometimes known as King Charles I) implemented a series of anti-Jewish measures which were rivalled only by the Russian tsar in their intensity. For instance, Romania evaded its obligations to give equality to its 250,000 Jewish inhabitants by declaring them to be aliens, not Romanian subjects. They could not enter the professions, hold positions in the civil service, purchase land, or vote in national elections. This situation, paralleled in Europe only in Russia, continued until the First World War, despite continuing protests by Jewish groups in the democracies.

Further reading

General

Alexander Altmann, *Moses Mendelssohn* (London, 1973)

Allan Arkush, *Moses Mendelssohn and the Enlightenment* (Albany, N.Y., 1994)

Pierre Birnbaum and Ira Katznelsohn, eds, *Paths of Emancipation: Jews, States, and Citizenship* (Princeton, N.J., 1995)

Ronald Detterer *et al.*, eds, *Jewish Settlement and Community in the Modern Western World* (Selinsgrove, Pa., 1991)

Todd M. Endelman, ed., *Jewish Apostasy in the Modern World* (New York, 1987)

Jonathan Frankel and Steven J. Zipperstein, eds, *Assimilation and Community: The Jews in Nineteenth-Century Europe* (Cambridge, 1992)

Jacob Katz, *Jews and Freemasons in Europe, 1723–1939* (Cambridge, Mass., 1970)

Jacob Katz, *Out of the Ghetto: The Social Background of Jewish Emancipation, 1770–1870* (New York, 1973)

Jacob Katz, ed., *Toward Modernity: The European Jewish Model* (New Brunswick, N.J., 1987)

Rainer Liedtke and Stephan Wendehorst, eds, *The Emancipation of Catholics, Jews and Protestants: Minorities and the Nation State in Nineteenth-Century Europe* (Manchester, 1999)

Frances Malino and David Sorkin, eds, *From East and West: Jews in a Changing Europe, 1780–1870* (Oxford, 1989)

Paul Mendes-Flohr and Jehuda Reinharz, comps and eds, *The Jew in the Modern World: A Documentary History*, 2nd edn (Oxford, 1995), Parts I, II, III, VI, VII.
David Sorkin, *Moses Mendelssohn and the Religious Enlightenment* (London, 1996)
Selma Stern, *The Court Jews: A Contribution to the History of the Period of Absolutism in Central Europe* (Philadelphia, 1950)

Austria-Hungary
William O. McCagg, *A History of Habsburg Jews* (Bloomington, Ind., 1992)

France
Phyllis Cohen Albert, *The Modernisation of French Jewry: Consistory and Community in Nineteenth Century France* (Hanover, N.H., 1977)
Frances Malino and Bernard Wasserstein, eds, *The Jews in Modern France* (Hanover, N.H., 1985)
Frances Malino, *The Sephardic Jews of Bordeaux: Assimilation and Emancipation in Revolutionary and Napoleonic France* (Tuscaloosa, Ala., 1978)
Michael Graetz, *The Jews in Nineteenth-Century France: From the French Revolution to the Alliance Israélite Universelle* (Stanford, Ca., 1996)
Arthur Hertzberg, *The French Revolution and the Jews* (New York, 1968)
Paula E. Hyman, *The Emancipation of the Jews of Alsace* (New Haven, Conn., 1991)
Simon Schwarzfuchs, *Napoleon, The Jews and the Sanhedrin* (London, 1979)

Germany
H.G. Adler, *The Jews in Germany From the Enlightenment to National Socialism* (Notre Dame, Ind., 1969)
H.I. Bach, *The German Jew: A Synthesis of Judaism and Western Civilisation, 1730–1930* (Oxford, 1984)
Dietz Bering, *The Stigma of Names: Antisemitism in German Daily Life, 1812–1933* (Ann Arbor, Mich., 1992)
Michael A. Meyer, *The Origins of the Modern Jew: Jewish Identity and European Culture in Germany, 1749–1824* (Detroit, 1967)
Jehuda Reinharz and Walter Schatzberg, eds, *The Jewish Response to German Culture: From the Enlightenment to the Second World War* (Hanover, N.H., 1985)
David Sorkin, *The Transformation of German Jewry, 1780–1840* (Oxford, 1987)

Italy
Cecil Roth, *The History of the Jews of Italy* (Philadephia, 1946)

Poland

W.T. Bartoszewski and Antony Polonsky, eds, *The Jews of Warsaw* (Oxford, 1991)

Raphael Mahler, *Hasidism and the Jewish Enlightenment: Their Confrontation in Galicia and Poland in the First Half of the Nineteenth Century* (Philadelphia, 1985)

Magdalena Opalski and Israel Bartal, *Poles and Jews: A Failed Brotherhood* (Hanover, N.H., 1992)

Antony Polonsky, ed., *From Shtetl to Socialism: Studies from Polin* (London, 1993)

Antony Polonsky *et al.*, eds, *The Jews in Old Poland 1000–1795* (London, 1993)

Moshe J. Rosman, *The Lord's Jews: Magnate–Jewish Relations in the Polish–Lithuanian Commonwealth during the 18th Century* (Cambridge, Mass., 1990)

3

Modern developments in Judaism

The era of the Enlightenment and emancipation confronted European Jews with problems as to their religious identity, just as it did in other areas of life. For many Jews, the old certainties of Jewish identity were fast disappearing. Before modernity, Jewishness was inextricably bound up with keeping all of the commandments ordained by God and of living within the community of Israel (*Klal Yisrael*), a people covenanted to God as 'a kingdom of priests and a holy nation'. Alternative, secular notions of Jewish identity did not yet exist.

During the eighteenth and nineteenth centuries, however, Jews were no longer cocooned and shielded in self-governing, isolated communities, but came increasingly in contact with the lifestyles, social customs, cultural values, and religious beliefs (or lack of them) of their fellow citizens. As Jews acquired civic equality they often became indifferent to Judaism; they flouted the dietary laws and avoided the synagogues except on the High Holy Days. Increasingly, they opened their businesses on the Sabbath, and many intermarried with Christians. Many Jews, at least as many as among other groups, became rationalists who declined to accept the literal truth of the Bible.

These changes compelled many Jews to alter their religious practices and to forge new forms of Judaism which were, in their view, more consistent with modern knowledge and contemporary realities. Some wished for a type of Jewish religious practice which was broadly similar to that of their Christian neighbours and allegedly more acceptable to them. From the early nineteenth century, some Jews denied the everlasting, binding nature of *Halakhah* and made changes to the time-honoured liturgy and ritual. They were known as Reform Jews, while by the beginning of the nineteenth century the term 'Orthodox', coined by Reform Jews, had come into general use to describe those who upheld Judaism's traditional tenets and practices.

Accommodating modernity: moderate Orthodoxy

As Jews found themselves in societies which were increasingly willing to tolerate them as equal citizens, many wished for a compromise in religious position which would enable them to maintain their traditional religious tenets in modern form. Many religious leaders declined to meddle with *Halakhah*, but nevertheless believed that the forms and practices of the ghetto were obsolete. For Jews of this viewpoint, the solution lay in a modernised form of Orthodoxy which, while insisting upon the unalterable nature of God's Torah, would prove flexible enough to accommodate modernity. The proponents and practitioners of moderate Orthodoxy viewed Reform (discussed below) as an inauthentic form of Judaism which went too far in altering the laws of *Halakhah* to suit the mere convenience of modern life, whimsically changing hallowed liturgy and ritual. Nevertheless, proponents of moderate Orthodoxy were not immune to the example of change set by the more extreme proponents of Reform, and were themselves viewed with alarm by traditional Orthodox Jews.

Prominent among the pioneers of moderate Orthodoxy was Rabbi Samson Raphael Hirsch (1808–88), whose position is usually termed that of 'neo-Orthodoxy'. Born in Hamburg to an observant family but one influenced by the *Haskalah*, Hirsch received both a traditional Jewish religious education and broader secular schooling. He briefly studied such subjects as classical languages, history, and philosophy at university. In 1830 he became a rabbi in Oldenberg, and later held the position of chief rabbi of Moravia (1846–51) and rabbi of the Orthodox community of Frankfurt-on-Main (from 1851), whence his influence spread throughout Germany. Hirsch was centrally concerned with the fact that Jews were no longer organised in Germany as a *kehillah* (a separate community with its own laws) for that had now been replaced, legally and in actual fact, by a *Gemeinde*, a 'community of faith', bound together by religious practice but subject to the laws of the state. Membership in the *Gemeinde* was voluntary, with increasing numbers of persons born as Jews now indifferent to religion or likely to convert to Christianity. How should Orthodox Jews react to this new and disturbing phenomenon? Hirsch's most famous work, *Nineteen Letters to a Friend* (1836; also known as *Nineteen Letters of Ben Uzziel*), offered an answer. The essence of Hirsch's response lay in a phrase which he adapted from the Talmud but made famous: *Yafeh Talmud Torah im Derekh Eretz*, 'the Torah is good together with the way of the world'. (This phrase is often cited as *Torah im Derekh Eretz*, roughly 'the Torah in the wider world'.) By this Hirsch meant that while *Halakhah* was eternally binding on all Jews, it should be observed side-by-side with taking one's place in the wider world in every sense and fully participating in the opportunities now offered to Jews as equal citizens. Hirsch and those who argued with him thus rejected both the position of traditionally Orthodox Jews, who remained voluntarily in ghettos, cut off from their gentile neighbours, and also the position of Reform Jews, who were willing to alter *Halakhah* whenever it suited them.

While Hirsch believed that the Torah was literally of divine origin and that no alteration, however small, in Torah observance was to be permitted, he was willing to make changes in the traditional Jewish liturgy. He sanctioned such innovations as sermons in German and the use of choral music, in order to appeal more widely to the modern sensibilities of his day. Neo-Orthodoxy became a typical stance adopted by many (certainly not all) of Germany's Jews before the Holocaust. It hoped to achieve a comfortable, practical balance between its adherents' dual identities as professing traditional Jews and German citizens. It encouraged its followers to downplay their distinctiveness from their non-Jewish countrymen in everything but religion, and to participate in national life while remaining observant Jews. Because of Hitler, it is easy to view those who believed themselves to be 'Germans of the Mosaic persuasion' as hopelessly naive and over-optimistic, but no one could have foreseen the rise of Nazism. Neo-Orthodoxy also spread to the English-speaking world, placing its stamp on Ashkenazi congregations in Britain during the period as chief rabbi of the German-born Nathan Marcus Adler, beginning in 1845 (see Chapter 10).

Reform Judaism

The Reform movement went much further than neo-Orthodoxy. Its central aim was (and remains) to keep Jews within the Jewish fold who are unable, in the conditions and belief-systems of the modern world, to accept either the dogmas or the strict practices of Orthodox Judaism. In the nineteenth century, Reform Jews maintained that modern Biblical scholarship rendered untenable the view that the entire Torah was written by Moses (as Orthodox Jews hold). Rather, they argued, the Torah was compiled by different authors over several generations. While divinely inspired it was not the final Word of God, whose Will was revealed not once and forever at Sinai, but gradually over the centuries. The Torah reflected the social mores and presumptions of ancient Israel; therefore, insisted the Reformers, *Halakhah* could and should be altered to reflect changing socio-economic circumstances and modern ideas of progress. Aspects of Jewish law which had become obsolete or which offended contemporary sensibilities could be discarded or altered. The spirit of Judaism was more important than the letter. Jews could, for example, ride to synagogue on Sabbath, although this contravenes Jewish law. (Reform Jews have often pointed out that many Orthodox Jews actually drive to synagogue on Sabbath, hypocritically violating their supposed religious beliefs.) During the nineteenth century, most Reform Jews rejected the use of prayers calling for a return to Zion and the restoration of the ancient Temple, maintaining that Zion was to be found in any land where Jews lived as equal citizens. In the twentieth century, with the rise of Nazism and, later, the re-establishment of the State of Israel, Reform Jews have reversed this stance, becoming strong Zionists. In the twentieth century, too, Reform Jews have insisted on the equality of men and women in all Jewish matters and have in recent years ordained many women rabbis. (Orthodox Jews cannot ordain women as rabbis.)

Reform also altered many prayers and introduced several other innovations and changes into synagogue practices. Like neo-Orthodoxy, it introduced sermons and prayers in the vernacular language of the congregants, although it never entirely discarded Hebrew. The ambience of Reform services (like neo-Orthodox ones) emphasised decorum and prohibited the din and secular conversations found in many Orthodox congregations. It also introduced organ and choral music. To the dismay of the Orthodox, the early Reform movement broke the traditional dietary regulations, and allowed male congregants to pray bare-headed.

Reform Judaism originated in the German Duchy of Brunswick in the early nineteenth century, and Reform congregations sprang up elsewhere in central and western Europe. It spread in particular to the United States, and to other parts of the 'New Diaspora'. A Hungarian, Aaron Chorin (1766–1844), was apparently the first traditional rabbi overtly to espouse the cause of Reform. The earliest Reform congregation was established in the small Brunswick town of Seesen by Israel Jacobson (1768–1828), a wealthy mercantile contractor strongly influenced by the *Haskalah*. Jacobson's Reform Temple, completed in 1818, followed his establishment in Seesen in 1801 of a trade and agriculture school for Jewish boys which, extraordinarily, also admitted Christian boys seeking vocational training. Jacobson's congregation was known as the Reform Temple, and the term 'temple' (as opposed to 'synagogue' or 'congregation') would be widely used by the Reform movement, in conscious imitation of the Temple in Jerusalem. (Most Orthodox Jews would regard the use of this term for a synagogue, before the Divine Restoration of the Jews to Jerusalem, as provocative if not sacrilegious.) The dedication ceremony was attended, most remarkably, by Christian clerics and public dignitaries, something briefly possible during the period of Napoleonic reforms but not easily imaginable a few years later. At the dedication Jacobson declared that Jews must omit from their rituals whatever was 'offensive to reason and to our Christian friends' and implored Christians to consign anti-Jewish prejudice to the past. Except for the ladies' gallery the Temple did not closely resemble a traditional synagogue, and its use of German and its choir and organ music were departures from tradition.

In 1815, after Napoleon, the Prussian authorities closed the Seesen Temple; Jacobson (who had moved to Berlin) began to hold services in his home. These soon attracted hundreds of German Jews, necessitating its transfer to the spacious residence of Jacob Herz Beer (1769–1825), a wealthy banker. Beer's son, Jacob, known to us as Giacomo Meyerbeer (1791–1864), the famous composer of operas, wrote musical scores for the new congregation. Among Reform's innovations was the use of Sephardi pronunciation of Hebrew rather than the Ashkenazi pronunciation normal among eastern European Jews, perhaps to differentiate German Jews from the 'uncivilised' eastern Europeans. In any case, Reform Jews believed the Sephardi pronunciation to be closer to that of ancient times, and its adoption became a defining characteristic of their movement. In 1817, Reform introduced a confirmation ceremony for girls, loosely similar to the *bar mitzvah* ceremony for boys, another remarkable innovation for its time, and Reform has always been at the forefront of gender equality within Judaism. It also welcomed the application of secular knowledge to Jewish affairs. In 1819 some Berlin Reform Jews (including Heinrich Heine, later an apostate) founded an organisation whose translated title is the Society for the Culture and Scientific Study of the Jews. It sought to investigate Jewish history, literature, and religion by modern research methods, under the assumption that Jewish society evolved in much the same way as other societies. One of the most important members of this organisation was Leopold Zunz (1794–1886), later a Reform rabbi, who is generally viewed as the founder of what is known as the *Wissenschaft des Judentums* ('Science of Judaism'), which grew into a broad movement of the sociological and historical investigation of all aspects of Jewish life – what is known today as 'Jewish studies'.

Reform in Germany was gradually allowed to take root, and became a major force in German Jewish life under such leaders as Rabbis Samuel Holdheim (1808–60) and Abraham Geiger (1810–74). It increasingly took a universalistic stance, with a prayer book written by Geiger in 1854 omitting any nationalistic Jewish content. Holdheim went even further, allowing men and women to sit together (as in a church) in the Berlin Temple he headed; exhorting men to remove their hats during services; completely expunging Hebrew from his services; and even substituting Sunday for Saturday as the Sabbath. These innovations were literally revolutionary for their time, and would still be regarded as far too extreme by many Jews. In fact, over the decades Reform gradually withdrew from some of its more advanced stands, for example over observing the Sabbath on Sunday rather than Saturday, although it has continued to hold progressive views on many other subjects.

From 1840 Reform spread to the English-speaking world. In that year 24 prominent (mainly Sephardi) London Jews, concerned at flagging synagogue attendance, called for 'a revised service ... at hours more suitable to our habits' and in the fashionable West End of London rather than the East End, where the existing Sephardi synagogue was located. As a result, a very moderate Reform congregation, the West London Synagogue of British Jews, was established in 1842, intended for both Ashkenazim and Sephardim. By 1900, Reform synagogues had been established in Manchester and Bradford, where many German Jews had settled. However, British Reform lacked popular appeal until the arrival of refugees from the

Nazis in the 1930s. Reform also spread, but only sporadically, to other parts of continental Europe. It became especially strong in Hungary, where the *Neolog* (Reform) stream challenged the primacy of Orthodoxy. In eastern Europe, however, Reform remained a minor element compared with Orthodoxy. In today's Israel, Reform is largely restricted to immigrants from English-speaking countries and faces heavy restrictions to its growth from the Orthodox rabbinate.

British Reform introduced only piecemeal innovations, which for many did not go far enough. Nothing was done, however, to establish a more radical form of Jewish practice in Britain until the twentieth century. In 1902, a small group of acculturated Jews established the Jewish Religious Union, which became the spearhead of Liberal (later known as Progressive) Judaism in Britain. Among its founders was Lily Montagu (1873–1963), whose father, Samuel Montagu, Lord Swaythling (1832–1911), was, ironically, staunchly Orthodox and the founder of the Federation of Synagogues, representing a group of uncompromisingly Orthodox synagogues located mainly in the East End of London. Another prominent British Reform Jew was Claude G. Montefiore (1858–1938), a grand-nephew of the celebrated Sir Moses Montefiore. As the movement's chief theorist, he expounded an uncompromisingly modernistic, ultra-universalist, yet deeply spiritual version of Judaism. This approach was reflected in the liturgy and ritual of the Liberal Jewish Synagogue, opened in London in 1911, and headed for 40 years by a radical Reform rabbi from the United States, Israel Mattuck (1883–1954). While Reform and Liberal Judaism have become established in Britain, numbering about 20 per cent of all British Jews who belong to a synagogue at the present time, it never became the religious stream of the British majority and never challenged the popularity or hegemony of the neo-Orthodox United Synagogue movement, headed by the British chief rabbi. The British situation thus differs from that in the United States, where members of Orthodox synagogues have been in a minority for most of the twentieth century.

In the United States, about 25 per cent of professing Jews belong to Reform congregations at the start of the twenty-first century, with a larger number belonging to the Conservative strand in American Jewry. In America, demands for moderate alterations to Orthodox ritual were made as early as 1824 by members of the acculturated, largely Sephardi Beth Elohim congregation in Charleston, South Carolina. Regarding certain parts of the existing ritual as 'inconsistent with the present enlightened state of society', they requested such innovations as shorter services and the inclusion of English. When their request was denied they seceded, and in the mid-1830s rejoined their old congregation, transforming it into a Reform synagogue.

Reform Jews soon found the United States to be a country where their beliefs could flourish. There was virtually nothing in the way of a pre-existing Orthodox Jewish community in that country, especially of an

Ashkenazi rather than Sephardi background: until the 1840s there was not a single ordained traditional rabbi there. The nation's entire underlying ethos emphasised such values as progress, rationality, individualism, and democracy, and drew a sharp distinction between America 'the promised land' and the backwardness of Europe. It was almost impossible in America at that time for Orthodox Jews to lead a full Jewish lifestyle. Until the 1880s Jewish immigrants to the United States had been chiefly either Sephardim or (after the 1840s) German Ashkenazim, groups from which, in other countries, Reform had originated. America had (and has) no national Jewish religious hierarchy and nothing to compare with the British Chief Rabbi. Since, by law, religion was purely a private matter, there could by definition be no *kahal* or Jewish consistories in America as there are in Europe. For all of these reasons, a flexible, modern, progressive variant of Judaism such as Reform was certain to attract a wide clientele in the United States.

In 1842 a Reform congregation was founded in Baltimore by Jews of German background whose model was the Hamburg Temple. Three years later a similar group founded what became the celebrated Temple Emanu-El in New York; this congregation immediately engaged a rabbi, who preached exclusively in German yet composed a prayer book in which Hebrew prayers were supplemented by translations into English. In 1855 Baltimore's Reform congregation engaged David Einhorn (1809–79), a Hungarian rabbi, who was to play a major part in the development of American Reform.

Einhorn was a radical innovator in terms of religious usages but was highly particularistic in terms of his vision of the Jewish people. He saw that people as a collective version of the personal Messiah whom he (and Reformers in general) rejected. He abhorred any suggestion of proselytism and argued that conversions to Judaism should be made more difficult. On the other hand, in ethical matters he was a radical, in particular over the issue of slavery which was then tearing America apart. Einhorn was an abolitionist who clashed with such pro-slavery rabbis as Dr Morris Raphall (1798–1868), each man citing scripture in support of his case. Einhorn, who later served in Philadelphia and New York, refused requests to remain silent on this controversial issue. From that time, American Reform has almost always been known for its willingness to become vocally involved in controversial political questions, generally from a left-liberal perspective. This was particularly evident in the struggle for black civil rights after the Second World War, in which Reform Jews were prominently involved.

There was, as well, a more moderate wing of American Reform, headed by Isaac Mayer Wise (1814–1900). Born in Bohemia, he moved from Prague to Albany, New York in 1847; he was soon dismissed by his synagogue board for heresy. Undeterred, he turned up to conduct services on *Yom Kippur* confident that he enjoyed the support of the majority of congregants: a fist fight ensued between him and the synagogue president, with the local sheriff forced to intervene. Wise formed a congregation of his own, later moving to Cincinnati, where he made his home. He campaigned for the use of English in services, hoping thereby to win over American Jews who knew little Hebrew. In 1857 he produced *Minhag America* ('The American Rite'), a home-grown version of the traditional ritual which he hoped would appeal to both Orthodox and Reform Jews. It was rejected by the Orthodox but adopted by moderate (but not radical) Reform. He even hoped to attract non-Jewish converts to the Reform movement. His central importance lay in his seminal role in the organisational development of American Reform. In 1873 he played a prominent part in the formation of the Central Conference of American Rabbis, the rabbinic wing of the American Reform movement and its central policy-making body. He also founded the Hebrew Union College, the Reform movement's rabbinic seminary in Cincinnati, and served as president from its inception in 1875 until his death.

Although Wise remained a relative moderate, American Reform was captured by religious radicals. At the dinner held in 1883 at the Hebrew Union College to celebrate the ordinations of its initial graduates, oysters and shellfish, forbidden by dietary laws, were on the menu. For years this notorious dinner, widely known as the '*trefa* [non-kosher] banquet' was invoked by traditionalists to highlight the excesses of Reform. In 1885 the American Reform movement set out its basic tenets in the so-called 'Pittsburgh Platform', inspired chiefly by the German-born Rabbi Kaufman Kohler (1843–1926), who succeeded Wise as president of Hebrew Union College. The Platform accepted 'only such ceremonies as elevate and sanctify our lives' and rejected 'all such as are not adapted to the views and habits of modern civilization'. Among those spurned items were the traditional dietary laws. It regarded Jews as 'no longer a nation but a religious community', ruling out a restoration to Palestine. It also asserted the duty of Reform Jews to 'solve on the basis of justice and righteousness' the problems of modern society.

Although the Pittsburgh Platform specifically disavowed Jewish hopes of 'a return to Palestine' and 'the restoration of any laws concerning the Jewish state', the rise of a significant Zionist movement and, above all, the advent of Hitler, caused it to revise its traditional hostility to Zionism. This change is associated with, among others, Hungarian-born Rabbi Stephen S. Wise (1874–1949), who became the best-known clerical Jewish leader in the United States and was particularly close to President Franklin D. Roosevelt. Wise was significant as a Zionist activist from the First World War. In 1937 the American Reform movement adopted the 'Columbus Platform', which modified its 1885 Platform significantly. It welcomed 'the rehabilitation of Palestine . . . [where] we behold the promise of renewed life for many of our brethren', and asserted that it was 'the obligation of all Jewry' to rebuild Palestine as 'a Jewish homeland'. In other respects, too, American Reform asserted a collectivist, neo-traditional view of Jewish 'peoplehood' greatly at variance with its former universalism. Although Reform retained many enemies of the establishment of a Jewish state until 1948 or even later, during the recent past it has become as pro-Zionist as any other strand in the Jewish matrix. While American Reform has in many respects become more traditional in its attitude towards Jewish usages and communal life, its stance on controversial social issues has emphatically not done so, especially in the sphere of gender and sexual matters. It took the lead, in the 1970s, in ordaining women rabbis and, much more controversially, in granting legitimacy to homosexuality. It has also loosened the notion of matrilineal Jewish descent as a defining criterion of Jewish identity to include those whose fathers were Jewish (but not their mothers) as Jews. Such changes as these have unquestionably widened the gap between Reform and Orthodox Judaism, a gap which has probably grown in recent decades.

Conservative Judaism

The vacuum within nineteenth-century German Jewry between Reform and Orthodoxy left room for yet another movement which attempted to include the best features of both. In 1845 Zecharias Frankel (1801–73), a Dresden-based rabbi, quit the Reform rabbinical conference in Frankfurt in protest at its radical agenda. 'Maintaining the integrity of Judaism simultaneously with progress, this is the essential problem of the present', he warned participants. Frankel became a leading figure in the *Jüdische Wissenschaft* movement which, unlike the neo-Orthodox school of Samson Raphael Hirsch, accepted that the Torah was not beyond modern scholarly investigation, and that some aspects of law and practice might be discarded. Unlike Reform, however, he championed adherence to law and tradition as a vital link between the Jewish past and future. He thus sought to steer a midway course between the unchanging stance of Orthodoxy and the readiness of Reform to abandon Jewish tradition. He was, moreover, conscious of the distinct peoplehood of the Jews, and objected to the early Reform movement's opposition to liturgy relating to Zion.

Accordingly, he founded what he described as 'Positive–Historical Judaism': 'positive' because it recognised an evolutionary dynamic within Judaism. Until 1854 he headed the Jewish Theological Seminary in Breslau, which under his influence turned out graduates imbued with 'Positive–Historical Judaism', a viewpoint which became increasingly prevalent among German Jews. Conservative Jewry – as this trend increasingly became known – also took root and flourished in the United States where, indeed, it became the largest single strand in American Jewry. The founder of Conservative Jewry in America is generally regarded as Isaac Leeser (1806–68), another German-born rabbi who went to Philadelphia in 1829, and was an early pioneer of English-language sermons. The driving force behind American Conservatism is, however, widely seen as Solomon Schechter (1847–1915), a Romanian-born rabbi who taught at Cambridge and London universities before becoming president, in 1902, of the Jewish

Theological Seminary in New York. The Seminary had been established in 1876 to counter the Reform movement's Hebrew Union College. While the Seminary had been founded on the pre-existing strand of popularity for the Conservative position in America, under Schechter's leadership it became a bastion of the Conservative movement. Like Frankel, Schechter and his colleagues rejected both the readiness of Reform (particularly American Reform) to discard Judaism's age-old forms and the unwillingness of Orthodoxy to make any changes whatever in traditional Jewish practice. Firmly underlying Conservative Judaism was the idea that the consensus of the Jewish people as a whole must be the ultimate source of the practices and doctrines of Judaism. It never discarded the concept of Jewish people-hood, and it has always cherished the centrality of *Halakhah*, as is apparent in the writings of one of its most distinguished scholars, Louis Ginzberg (1873–1953), who put his stamp on the movement as professor of Talmud at the Seminary for half a century. Conservatism affirms the divine origins of *Halakhah*, and regards it as permanently valid. But in any conflict between *Halakhah* and what is referred to in rabbinic literature as 'great principles' – basic statements of ethical values – it believes the latter should prevail. In recent decades American Conservatism has, like Reform, removed barriers to women's participation in services and has ordained women rabbis. About 50 per cent of American Jews currently belong to Conservative synagogues, by far the largest slice of American Judaism. Conservative Jewry never spread, however, to other Jewish communities to the extent one might have expected in advance for this moderate, sensible middle way. In Britain, for instance, Conservatism was virtually unknown until the so-called 'Jacobs Affair' of 1962–64, which became celebrated in modern Anglo-Jewish history. Louis Jacobs (b.1920), an eminent rabbi belonging to the (Orthodox) United Synagogue organisation headed by the Chief Rabbi, had expressed views mildly critical of Orthodox literalist views on the origins of the Torah. Consequently, Britain's chief rabbi blocked his bid to become, first, principal of Jews' College (the United Synagogue's rabbinical seminary) and, subsequently, rabbi of a prominent London syna-gogue. The 'Jacobs Affair' became nationally-reported news, and Jacobs and a group of his followers broke away from the United Synagogue to found, in 1964, the New London Synagogue, which became the first of several British congregations affiliated to the Masorti ('traditional') move-ment, affiliated with the world-wide Conservative movement. Although the Masorti movement continues to exist, unlike its American equivalent it has never become widely popular.

Reconstructionism

The Reconstructionist movement is an American strand in Judaism which was launched by Rabbi Mordecai M. Kaplan (1881–1983).

Reconstructionism maintains that Judaism is not a revealed religion but the inspiration of the Jewish people, a religion created out of their needs, and constantly evolving. Judaism is the core of an entire dynamic civilisation that comprises art, literature, music, folklore, and custom, all of which nurture the Jewish spirit. Israel is the centre of Jewish civilisation, but the Diaspora has an important supporting role. God, in Kaplan's view, is not a Being transcending the universe but the force present in the human mind which makes for righteousness and ensures that righteousness will ultimately prevail. Kaplan, a Lithuanian-born rabbi ordained at the Jewish Theological Seminary in New York, published his controversial ideas in his important 1934 work, *Judaism as a Civilization*. From the 1920s Reconstructionism developed as a separate strand in American Jewry, with separate synagogues and institutions. Its liturgy is somewhat similar to that employed by Conservative Judaism, although the Reconstructionist concept of God has, obviously, been widely condemned as virtually atheistic. Reconstructionism continues to be a small (perhaps 3 per cent of synagogue members) but important component of American Judaism, although it has made little impact elsewhere.

Orthodox Judaism: the Musar Movement

Orthodox Jewry also had to respond to the pressures of modernity. The Vilna Gaon (see below), the outstanding Lithuanian rabbinic scholar of the second half of the eighteenth century, was by no means adverse to secular learning; he wrote authoritatively on topics ranging from astronomy to philosophy. Nevertheless, he adamantly opposed the *Haskalah* because for him secular knowledge was only a means to better understanding the Talmud. Others in the world of the *yeshivot*, for instance the well-known Soloveitchik rabbinic family, also welcomed a push to studying the Talmud which avoided hair-splitting casuistry (*pilpul*). Additionally, starting in medieval times, there had developed alongside the Talmud and other sacred texts a body of Jewish literature aimed specifically at imbuing its readers with a sense of upright conduct. It became known as *musar* ('instruction') literature. During the mid-nineteenth century Rabbi Israel Salanter (1810–83), a learned Talmudist in Lithuania who was disturbed at the inroads which the *Haskalah* was making, founded a new movement which encouraged its followers to read such instructive works. Salanter believed that a knowledge of Jewish law did not necessarily lead to ethical conduct. But he went beyond mere sermonising to internalise ethical conduct among his followers. In order to penetrate the subconscious minds of readers he encouraged the repetitive reading of a limited number of *musar* texts amid dim lighting and gloomy music. He expected his followers to dwell introspectively on their character faults and how these might be rectified, suppressing their evil impulses through willpower.

The Musar Movement began in Vilna in 1842 with a single-roomed study centre in which Jewish men of various occupations gathered as dusk fell in order to study the relevant texts. Initially, the movement met with severe criticism both from *maskilim,* who opposed its introspection and narrow-mindedness, and from traditional rabbis who considered studying *musar* writings unnecessary. Nevertheless, despite strong rabbinical resistance, the movement spread, especially among students at the great *yeshivot* in Lithuania. Eventually, it became widespread, producing scholars whose personal conduct would be guided by (in Hebrew) 'the fear of Heaven'. It continues to be taught at Lithuanian-style *yeshivot* in Israel, the United States, and elsewhere. Its austerity has often been contrasted with Hasidism (see below), known for its joy, although the use of Hasidic material in discourses on *musar* at *yeshivot* is by no means unknown.

The rise of Hasidism

'Hasidism' (which derives from 'piety' in Hebrew) was a religious revivalist movement which developed among the Jews of eastern Europe during the eighteenth century. Challenging received notions of religious practice, it aroused fierce controversy among the rabbinic authorities but, nonetheless, gained a mass following. By 1830, when its dynamic growth stabilised, perhaps nearly half of the Jewish communities of the region were under its sway. Originating in the Ukrainian provinces of Podolia and Volhynia, it made great headway among rural and *shtetl* Jews, becoming particularly influential in the eastern parts of the Pale of Settlement (see p. 65), Hungary and northern Romania. In contrast, Lithuania was largely resistant, as were Jews in western and central Europe and elsewhere. Today, flourishing and very visible groups of *Hasidim* ('the pious ones') exist in many countries. Because of their high birth-rate, resistance to assimilation, and (among some groups) outreach programme to other Jews, they have grown significantly since the destruction of their major bases of support in the Holocaust. They dress much as their predecessors did in early modern times, men distinguished by their long black coats, black or fur hats, bushy beards, sidelocks, and, especially on the Sabbath, white hose worn as a symbol of purity. Hasidic women always wear modest clothes, and after marriage cover their heads with berets, scarves, or wigs.

Hasidism derived in large measure from kabbalism, or medieval Jewish mysticism. Borrowing from such non-Jewish concepts as numerology, kabbalism envisioned the sweep of human history as unfolding inexorably towards the coming of the Messiah, and interpreted every act as contributing to that end. Kabbalists attributed divine powers to every Hebrew letter, and minutely searched the Hebrew text of the Bible for concealed codes and hidden meanings. Just as the name of God is never directly mentioned in Orthodox Judaism (with euphemisms such as *Ha Shem*, 'The Name', being employed), the designation *Baal Shem* ('Master of the Name') was given to practitioners of wonder-working powers in eastern Europe. Such men were often credited with miraculous powers to cure diseases and drive out demons. One of the most popular of the wonder-working mystic healers was Isaac ben Eliezer (*c.*1700–60), founder of Hasidism. Born into poverty in a *shtetl* in Podolia and orphaned as a child, he played truant from school and worked at a variety of humble occupations. In his spare time, however, he became well-versed in the Torah, Kabbalah, and other aspects of Jewish learning. Reflecting on the glories of nature as a lime carter in the Carpathian foothills, he turned to a pantheistic belief in the presence of God in all created matter, as taught in the Kabbalah. From his mid-thirties he wandered the countryside as a faith-healer and dispenser of wisdom, gradually acquiring an enormous following. His admirers gave him the title *Baal Shem Tov* ('Master of the Good Name') often abbreviated to the acronym of Besht. He left no writings, and some later scholars have doubted his existence. However, research into Polish archives has proved that he indeed existed.

The Besht combined a charismatic personality with vivid homespun imagery that made him comprehensible to the masses of eastern European Jews unversed in the complexities of the Talmud. His grandson recalled that his philosophy was based on three kinds of love – love of God, love of Torah, and love of man. The Besht emphasised God's love for the lowly and unlearned. His career is associated with the town of Medzibozh, a town in Podolia, Ukraine, where he settled permanently.

The tradition of studying at the feet of an acknowledged master was well-entrenched in Judaism, and those anxious to learn from the Besht travelled to Medzibozh. Apart from the unlearned masses, a number of scholarly rabbis also became his followers, such as Rabbi Jacob Joseph of Polonnoye (d.1782), whose book *Toledot Yaakov Yoseph* ('Jacob Joseph's History') is our primary source for the teachings of the Besht. By the end of his life the latter had an estimated 10,000 devotees.

Developing from the Besht's teachings, Hasidism maintains that God dwells literally in all things, and therefore the human heart cannot help but be joyous. Human beings are obligated to liberate the 'holy sparks' within all matter from the demonic forces entrapping them: every evil deed ensures that those sparks remain imprisoned, whereas every good deed helps to release them and will ultimately restore the cosmic harmony which was shattered by Adam's disobedience in the Garden of Eden. Consequently, as a result the Messiah will come. Each Jew, learned or unlearned, can thus help to achieve a state of redemption by loyalty to the *mitzvot* (commandments), releasing the 'holy sparks' within themselves. Sadness leads to despair and sinfulness, but joy helps to overcome the evil impulse and thus to release the 'holy sparks'. An abstemious lifestyle is to be avoided, since it is necessary to enjoy the good things of life. When going about their daily affairs, Jews should perform every task, no matter how trivial, with God fully in mind, a doctrine known as *devekut* ('attachment to God'). This attachment must come from the innermost soul, and natural impulses should be enlisted in God's service.

Following the Besht's death, leadership of the movement passed to Dov Ber of Mezhirich (*c.*1710–72), known as the *Maggid* ('preacher') of Mezhirich. He was chiefly responsible for the spread of Hasidism to other parts of eastern Europe, sending preachers far and wide to spread Hasidic doctrines. He was particularly successful in attracting young men who were disillusioned with the arid, hair-splitting nature of Torah study at the traditional *yeshivot*. Dov Ber was an awe-inspiring figure, perhaps as charismatic as the Besht. Hasidism spread quickly in those areas of eastern Europe which had experienced the antisemitic massacres of the 1600s, and where Shabbetai Zevi and Jacob Frank (1726–91) had raised messianic hopes. Large sections of the Jewish 'masses' remained uninspired by Talmudic learning in the *yeshivot*. They often felt excluded by the scholarly *yeshivot* elite, by the wealthy oligarchy controlling the *kehillot*, and felt continuously persecuted by the Christian authorities of wider society. Low-paid religious functionaries such as cantors and teachers in *hadarim* were attracted to the Hasidic movement, as were small shopkeepers, innkeepers, peddlers and other financially struggling or impoverished elements within eastern European Jewry. Hasidism gave them a message of hope and a sense of spiritual empowerment. Hasidism has been compared by some historians to Methodism in England, which arose at about the same time, and which also attempted to give a living, deeply-felt spiritual dimension to the stagnant Anglican religiosity of its time. Like Hasidism, it was founded by a charismatic leader, John Wesley. It emphasised such aspects of sincere religious belief as the experience of personal conversion, and appealed to some of the same socio-economic strata among the English population. Yet there were also differences – such as Wesleyism's emphasis on hellfire and damnation, very different from Hasidism's message of religious joy.

Some aspects of Hasidism were highly controversial to many Jews of the day, and attracted growing criticism and hostility. The movement placed importance on deeds performed in a spirit of *devekut*, including acts of the flesh such as eating and sexual relations. *Hasidim* often formed prayer groups in small houses of worship known as *shtieblekh* (singular: *shtiebel*, meaning 'conventicle'). They used the Sephardi pronunciation of Hebrew for prayers, and, during prayer swayed vigorously in order to arouse their entire body into a mood of wholehearted devotion; some rolled their heads around as well. Onlookers reported *Hasidim* praying with 'weird motions', 'whirling about in circles', 'swaying, clapping hands', in continuously 'noisy' prayer. Some early *Hasidim* performed somersaults during prayer, praying 'upside down and bottom up', according to one enraged contemporary. At festive gatherings, wine flowed freely and *Hasidim* often danced arm-in-arm in a circle, in near-ecstasy over their awareness of God. The Kabbalah was raised to the status of a key Jewish text, complementing the

Torah. Many Orthodox Jews in eastern Europe, and acculturated Jews in the West, were scandalised by such behaviour.

Among Dov Ber's disciples were charismatic individuals who became 'Hasidic masters' in their own right. Each became known as a *zaddik* ('righteous man'), reviving an earlier tradition in Judaism, but altering its meaning to denote mystics of great power. Each *zaddik* attracted devoted bands of followers, who came to study at the feet of the master. By the 1780s the tradition of *zaddikim* had become well-established in Hasidism. Each *zaddik* was regarded as a virtual king, with his own court, whose followers treasured his every utterance. Some, but not all, *zaddikim* began to enjoy princely lifestyles, becoming a kind of Jewish aristocracy in eastern Europe. The next step was the creation of hereditary courts among the *zaddikim*, based on the concept that the *zaddik* was capable of fathering sons in whom his powers were inherent, owing to the holy thoughts that he, in the spirit of *devekut*, entertained during sexual intercourse with his wife. As a result, the eldest son came to be considered the 'crown prince' of the dynasty, to succeed upon his father's death. In the absence of a competent eldest son, succession went to a younger son, a nephew, or a talented son-in-law. Thus rival Hasidic dynasties came into existence, each of their *zaddikim* being known as *rebbe* ('my teacher'), a familiar Yiddish variant of the word rabbi. Dynasties were named for the towns of their *zaddikim*, where each offered a slightly different slant on Hasidic doctrine. Occasionally dynasties fragmented, or came together through a marriage alliance among the offspring of their leaders. By the First World War, probably 30 major Hasidic dynasties existed, each with thousands of followers. Although the events of the twentieth century, especially, of course, the decimation caused by the Holocaust, greatly reduced their numbers, many Hasidic leaders managed to flee to America or Palestine, where (see below) they often re-established their dynasties and today are believed to have as many followers as before 1939.

One of Dov Ber's most notable followers was Shneur Zalman of Lyady (1745–1813), a brilliant Talmudist from Belorussia. Eventually, he succeeded to the leadership of the Belorussian *Hasidim* on the death of his colleague Menahem Mendel of Vitebsk (1730–88), and proceeded to publish his sayings as the *Tanya* (Aramaic for 'It was taught') in 1796. In this and in other writings, such as his revision of Joseph Caro's *Shulkhan Arukh*, he enunciated a philosophy of Hasidism which had a wide impact. He held that the *zaddik* was, essentially, less a miracle-worker than a spiritual guide, who, through his ability to withstand the evil impulse must be deemed a saint. Unlike the bulk of the Hasidic movement he placed reason above emotion. Reason, he argued, consisted of *hokhmah* ('wisdom'), *binah* ('understanding') and *da'at* ('knowledge'). The abbreviation of these words is *Habad*, and this acronym has been used ever since of the stream of Hasidism which he founded. Shneur Zalman placed great emphasis on the study of the Torah, especially the 'secrets of the Torah' contained in the

Kabbalah, and also required his followers to study the Talmud. Habad was thus more intellectual than other strands in Hasidism, and acted as something of a bridge to the *mitnaggedim* (see below). Habad gave rise to the Lubavitcher dynasty, which took its name from the Belorussian town in which Shneur Zalman's son and successor, Dov Ber Schneerson (1773–1827) settled.

Opposition to Hasidism

From the outset, Hasidism encountered fierce opposition from traditional rabbinical scholars (and, later, from *maskilim* as well). Known as *mitnaggedim* ('opponents'), the traditionalists denounced the new movement for its apparent reversal of old values. They condemned the Hasidic view that God is present in all things as heretical and deplored the contention that it was possible to worship Him through bodily acts. Certain imagery in Hasidic writings was regarded by the *mitnaggedim* as obscene. The veneration of *zaddikim* was denounced as bordering on idolatry, and the attribution of supernatural powers to them was regarded as ludicrous. Seeing clear resemblances to such previous movements as Shabbatai Zevi's, they feared the emergence of a new false messiah movement among the *Hasidim*, and were alarmed by their assault on traditional established authority.

Hasidism proved to be relatively weak in Lithuania, which was outside the area where the antisemitic massacres of the 1600s had occurred. Lithuanian Jews possessed a far higher level of Jewish learning than Jews in areas receptive to Hasidism, and were not as likely to be won over by the movement's elevation of prayer over scholarship. Nevertheless, Hasidism gained a foothold in Lithuania in the 1770s, leading to a furious internecine war between the two camps. The main opponent of Hasidism was the Vilna Gaon (Elijah ben Solomon Zalman, 1720–97), the most illustrious Talmudist of his day, renowned for his scholarship and learning. He regarded Hasidism as heretical, and aimed to extirpate it from Lithuania. In 1772 and again in 1781 he proclaimed excommunications on the adherents of the movement. *Hasidim* and their families were ordered out of Jewish communities, their texts were burned, and numerous other measures were directed at removing them from the Jewish community. *Hasidim* responded with retaliatory counter-measures, and allegedly verbally and physically abused traditional rabbis and scholars. In 1797 the Vilna Gaon called on Jews everywhere 'to wipe them off the earth'. At his funeral in 1797 *Hasidim* openly rejoiced. A lengthy campaign between the two groups continued, with denunciations by *mitnageddim* against Shneur Zalman leading to his arrest on two occasions by the Tsarist authorities.

Eventually, the conflict between the two sides cooled. The *mitnageddim* realised that they and the *Hasidim* faced a common enemy in the *maskilim*, the opponents of Orthodoxy. As the *Hasidim* grew in numbers, they became a source of revenue for the local Jewish communities, through paying taxes on kosher slaughtering, and became an economic force which could not be ignored. The tsarist statute of 1804, which allowed all Jewish sects within the *kahal* to open their own synagogues and forbade measures of excommunication, made their persecution impractical. By the mid-nineteenth century, too, Hasidism had placed an emphasis on Torah study which resulted in the opening of several Hasidic *yeshivot*. In the twentieth century, while the differences between the two groups have narrowed, there are still discernible distinctions between 'Lithuanian' Strict Orthodoxy (representing the latter-day descendants of the *mitnaggedim*) and *Hasidim*, with 'Lithuanian' *yeshivot* in Israel and elsewhere still more oriented towards study and scholarship than are most *Hasidim*.

Today, there are sizeable concentrations of *Hasidim* in Jerusalem, New York, London, and a variety of other places around the world from Melbourne, Australia, to Antwerp, Belgium. Many *zaddikim* once again have thousands of followers, who regard their *rebbe* as their spiritual and denominational leader. Among the most prominent dynasties in the contemporary world are those founded at Belz in Poland, Ger in Poland, and Satmar in Hungary/Romania. They form an important political block in Israel, frequently using their political strength to influence legislation. A large 'Lithuanian' Strictly Orthodox community also exists in Israel.

The Hasidic dynasty with the highest profile (although several others may be larger in size) is unquestionably the Lubavitcher, whose followers, if men, wear black trilbies rather than fur hats, and never don white hose. Until 1994 leadership of the dynasty was vested in successive generations of the Schneerson family. Greatly suffering under both the Communists and Nazis, after the 1940s the Lubavitchers achieved wide international fame under the leadership of Menahem Mendel Schneerson (1902–94), the seventh Lubavitcher rebbe. Schneerson came to America in 1940 and, from his famous headquarters in Brooklyn, New York, embarked on an 'outreach' programme to non-observant Jews which saw an army of *habadniks* (as they are often known) travel the globe and spread their message to universities and prisons, urging Jews to observe the *mitzvot*. 'Habad houses' were established by his followers around the world. Tens of thousands of Jews were brought back to Torah observance in this way. From his Brooklyn headquarters, Rabbi Schneerson held regular public addresses for his followers known as *farbrengen*, attended by thousands. By the end of his life Schneerson was regarded by some of his followers as the Messiah. His death in June 1994 became headline news around the world. He was childless: for this reason, and because of the widespread conviction among his followers that he was the long-awaited Messiah, no successor as the eighth Lubavitcher *rebbe* has been named by the movement.

The re-emergence of a growing Strict Orthodoxy in the post-1945 Jewish world, after generations of secularisation, the Holocaust, and 75 years of Communist persecution, has been one of the religious wonders of the modern age, a phenomenon which few would have predicted 60 years ago. Some sociologists have seen in the re-emergence of Strict Orthodoxy a parallel to the rise of fundamentalism in most other religions in recent decades, although specifically Jewish factors are probably more significant. At the present time, Judaism is arguably as fractured as at any stage in its modern history. The growth of an absolutely observant Strict Orthodoxy at the same time as non-Orthodox forms of Judaism have become even less traditional on issues like the ordination of women rabbis, homosexuality, and abortion, make it most unlikely that there will be any narrowing of the differences between the various sects within Judaism in the near future, if ever.

Further reading

Jacob B. Agus, *Modern Philosophies of Judaism* (New York, 1971)

Alexander Altmann, ed., *Studies in Nineteenth-Century Jewish Intellectual History* (Cambridge, 1964)

Moshe Davis, *The Emergence of Conservative Judaism* (Philadelphia, 1965)

Todd M. Endelman, ed., *Jewish Apostasy in the Modern World* (New York, 1987)

Avraham Yaakov Finkel, *Contemporary Sages: The Great Chasidic Masters of the Twentieth Century* (Northvale, N.J., 1994)

Roman A. Foxbrunner, *Habad: The Hasidism of R. Shneur Zalman of Lyady* (Tuscaloosa, Ala., 1992)

Neil Gillman, *Conservative Judaism* (West Orange, N.J., 1993)

Hillel Goldberg, *Israel Salanter* (New York, 1982)

Arthur Green, ed., *Jewish Spirituality: From the Sixteenth-Century Revival to the Present* (New York, 1988)

Louis Jacobs, *The Jewish Religion: A Companion* (Oxford, 1995)

Mordecai M. Kaplan and Arthur A. Cohen, *If Not Now, When? Toward a Reconstruction of the Jewish People* (New York, 1973)

Jacob Katz, ed., *The Role of Religion in Modern Jewish History* (Cambridge, Mass., 1975)

Steven T. Katz, ed., *Frontiers of Jewish Thought* (Washington, D.C. 1992)

Anne J. Kershen, ed., *RSGB, ULPS: 150 Years of Progressive Judaism in Britain* (London, 1990)

Raphael Mahler, *Hasidism and the Jewish Enlightenment: Their Confrontation in Galicia and Poland in the First Half of the Nineteenth Century* (Philadelphia, 1985)

Frances Malino and Phyllis Cohen Albert, eds, *Essays in Modern Jewish History* (Rutherford, N.J., 1982)

Jacob R. Marcus, *Israel Jacobson: The Founder of the Reform Movement in Judaism* (Cincinnati, 1972)

Dow Marmur, ed., *Reform Judaism: Essays on Reform Judaism in Britain* (Oxford, 1973)

Paul Mendes-Flohr and Jehuda Reinharz, comps and eds, *The Jews in the Modern World: A Documentary History*, 2nd edn (Oxford, 1995), especially Part IV

Michael A. Meyer, *Response to Modernity: A History of the Reform Movement in Judaism* (Oxford, 1988)

Jacob Neusner, *American Judaism: Adventure in Modernity* (Englewood Cliffs, N.J., 1972)

Aubrey Newman, *The United Synagogue, 1870–1970* (London, 1976)

Ada Rapoport-Albert, ed., *Hasidism Reappraised* (London, 1996)

Kopul Rosen, *Rabbi Isaac Salanter and the Musar Movement* (London, 1945)

Noah H. Rosenbloom, *Tradition in an Age of Reform: The Religious Philosophy of Samson Raphael Hirsch* (Philadelphia, 1976)

Lou H. Silberman, *American Impact: Judaism in the United States in the Early Nineteenth Century* (Syracuse, N.Y., 1964)

Leo Trepp, *Judaism: Development and Life* (Belmont, Ca., 1982)

Bela Vago, ed., *Jewish Assimilation in Modern Times* (Boulder, Col. 1981)

L. Wallach, *Liberty and Letters: The Thought of Leopold Zunz* (London, 1959)

Jack Wertheimer, ed., *The Uses of Tradition: Jewish Continuity in the Modern Era* (New York, 1992)

Nisson Wolpin, ed., *The Torah World: A Treasury of Biographical Sketches* (Brooklyn, N.Y., 1982)

4

The Jews of the Russian Empire, 1772–1917

Between the late eighteenth century and the end of the First World War, more Jews lived in tsarist Russia than in any other country. Russia remained an absolute monarchy until 1905, ruled over by the tsar from the House of Romanov. By the early twentieth century Russia was the last remaining absolutist state in Europe, lacking a parliament and synonymous with political repression and arbitrary rule. While many of the key developments of modern Jewish history occurred elsewhere, it was in Russia that the bulk of Jews lived and where many of the important movements in modern Jewish thought – Zionism, socialism, Strict Orthodoxy – began or had their greatest impact. Tsarist oppression meant that millions of Jews fled from Russia to seek new lives for themselves or their children elsewhere. The ancestors of millions of Jews who today live in the United States and other parts of the Diaspora, or in the State of Israel, had lived in tsarist Russia, emigrating, in particular, after the pogroms of 1881. In 1795, it is estimated, at least 800,000 of the world's total of 2.5 million Jews (at least 32 per cent) lived in Russia (including Russian Poland). Because the birth rate of Russian, especially Polish, Jewry, was so high, by the year 1900 about 5.1 million of the world's total 10.5 million Jews lived in Russia (about 49 per cent). In the twentieth century, independence for Poland, followed by the Holocaust, the creation of the State of Israel, and, after the late 1980s, by the emigration of many of the Jews of the former Soviet Union, meant that Russian Jewry, while not insignificant, has dwindled to become a relatively much smaller component of world Jewry than in previous times. Tsarist Russia was itself a vast multinational empire, numbering perhaps 120 million inhabitants at the start of the First World War, dominated by Russians, but also comprising millions of Ukrainians, Poles, Belorussians, Balts, Finns, Armenians, central Asian nationalities, and many other groups, most of whom groaned under tsarist repression. Widely known as the 'prison of nations', tsarist Russia was an autocratic, quasi-medieval regime ripe for revolution. While Jews were probably treated worse than any other group, many other minorities also saw themselves as being persecuted and oppressed by the tsarist regime. To be fair, it should also be noted that nineteenth-century Russia was a place of remarkable intellectual ferment and originality, producing a host of remarkable figures in every field, from Tolstoy and Dostoyevsky to Tchaikovsky, Mendeleyev and Pavlov.

The Pale of Settlement and legal restrictions

For the most part, by 'Russian Jewry' we actually mean the Jews of the Pale of Settlement. The 'Pale of Settlement' was an area in tsarist Russia consisting of twenty-five provinces in Poland, Lithuania, Belorussia, the Ukraine, Bessarabia, and Crimea, where Jews were permitted permanent residences. Except in limited circumstances, Jews were not permitted to live elsewhere in the Russian Empire. This residential restriction persisted until just before the overthrow of tsardom in 1917. Areas where Jews were generally not permitted to live included Moscow and St Petersburg, as well as in the interior areas of the country. Exceptions were made for certain types of Jews, such as those in the liberal professions, wealthy businessmen, and ex-Cantonists (former conscripts in the Russian army), who could live elsewhere in Russia. There were, as well, old-established communities of Jews in the Caucasian areas and central Asia, who continued to live there, while Jews could gain exemption from these residential restrictions by converting to Christianity. For the bulk of Jews of the Pale, however, permanent emigration to areas of Russia outside the Pale depended on the arbitrary whims of the local governor of each province, and, even when granted, could be (and often were) revoked at a moment's notice. For instance, Jews were tacitly allowed to live in Moscow, but, in 1891, some 20,000 were arbitrarily expelled to the Pale of Settlement. The tsarist government never explained or justified this policy, which was probably designed in large measure to keep Jews from 'taking over' the Russian economy and 'dominating' its large cities. Most of the Pale of Settlement was situated in Poland, and Poland was *par excellence* the centre of Jewish life. This meant that Polish Jews also experienced a very mixed relationship with Polish Christians (and, indeed, with most other non-Russian minority groups in tsarist Russia), being at times their allies in the face of common oppression by tsardom but also, tragically, the victims of much indigenous antisemitic hostility.

Apart from the residential restrictions imposed by the tsarist regime upon its Jews, Russian Jewry also suffered from a labyrinth of legal restrictions on virtually every aspect of their lives. Shortly before the 1917 Russian revolution, laws and enactments concerning the Jews were collected in book form: it totalled nearly 1000 pages, and touched a gamut of activities, ranging from Jewish participation in the government and civil service to the military. As a general rule, in tsarist Russia Jews were forbidden to do almost anything which was not explicitly granted by laws or ordinances. The phrase

THE JEWS IN THE RUSSIAN EMPIRE
IN THE LATE NINETEENTH
CENTURY

St Petersburg

LIVONIA

Baltic Sea

KURLAND   Riga

PSKOV

KOVNO
212,700   Dvinsk

LITHUANIA   VITEBSK
                        175,600

Kovno   Polotsk
                     Vitebsk   SMOLENSK

GERMANY   Vilna   Smolensk   Moscow

SUWALKI
59,300

Suwalki   VILNA
                 204,700   Kaluga

PLOCK 51,500 Lomza   Minsk   Mogilev   Tula

Plock   Grodno   BELORUSSIA
        LOMZA   Bialystok   MOGILEV
KALISZ 91,400   203,900
71,700 POLAND   Warsaw GRODNO   Slutsk   Orël
Kalisz 351,900 WARSAW 280,000   ORËL
        Lodz   Siedlce Brest-   Bobruysk Gomel
222,600 SIEDLCE Litovsk
PIOTRKOW RADOM 121,100   MINSK
        Radom 112,300   Pinsk   345,000
Czestochowa   CHERNIGOV
                Lublin   114,500   Kursk
Bedzin Kielce LUBLIN   KURSK
                156,200 VOLHYNIA Chernigov
        KIELCE   395,800   U K R A I N E
        83,200

                Zhitomir   POLTAVA
AUSTRIA-HUNGARY   110,900   Kharkov
                         Berdichev   KHARKOV
                PODOLIA KIEV   Poltava
                370,600 433,700 Cherkassy Kremenchug
                Kamenetz-
                Podolskiy   Uman   Yekaterinoslav
                Mohilev-   Yelisabetgrad YEKATERINOSLAV
                Podolskiy   NEW RUSSIA   101,100
        Beltsy   Balta
                         Bendery   KERSON   Rostov
        ROMANIA   339,900
                Kishinev   Nikolaev
                         Odessa   Kherson
                Bendery   TAURIDA
                                            60,800

⊙ Large city with at least 40,000 Jews
● Community of 30,000– 40,000 Jews
⊗ Community of 20,000– 30,000 Jews
• Community of 10,000– 20,000 Jews   CRIMEA
○ City barred to Jewish residence (by order   Black Sea
   of Nicholas I)
── Pale of Settlement   Sevastopol
---- Regional boundary   0   100 km   Yalta
.... Provincial boundary

58,000 Jewish population of province

'excepting the Jews' became a commonplace feature of Russian legislation until virtually the end of the regime.

Hostility to the Jews of Russia was of long standing. In the late fifteenth century, there occurred the so-called 'Judaising heresy', in which some clergymen in Novgorod were converted to Judaism by Jewish traders, leading to a spate of similar conversions. In panic, a wave of antisemitism occurred, with 300 Jews drowned at Polotsk and Vitebsk in 1563 for refusing to accept baptism. The ruling Orthodox Russian Church and the tsarist regime became fiercely antisemitic, with Jews expelled from Russia in 1727, 1738, and 1742. In 1753, 35,000 Jews were expelled from Russia. Hostility to Jews was based squarely on religion: when Catherine the Great's minister was asked by Prussia's King Frederick the Great why Jews were no longer welcome to settle in St Petersburg, Russia's capital, he replied 'Because they crucified our Lord'. Additionally, Jews were seen as wily, shrewd financiers, always likely to take advantage of the naive Russian peasantry, and also likely to introduce subversive ideas into the Russian autocracy. Jews were, moreover, widely associated with magic and the supernatural, perhaps owing to the spread of the Kabbalah, and were often feared by the illiterate, superstitious Russian peasantry for this reason. As elsewhere throughout Europe, Jews came to be seen as an alien people, with a different and separate history, language and system of beliefs from Russians, who were mainly Orthodox Christians.

In the late eighteenth and early nineteenth centuries, the number of Jews living in the realm of the tsars increased dramatically with the three Partitions of Poland. By stages in 1772, 1793, and 1795, the independent kingdom of Poland disappeared from the map, not to reappear until 1918. Three great continental powers, Russia, Prussia and Austria, conquered and annexed all of Poland. By the first Partition (1772), Prussia took Prussian Poland, and Austria took Galicia and other areas of southern Poland. At the same time Russia took the easternmost portion of the former kingdom of Poland. These three powers annexed still more in 1793 and 1795, with Russia grabbing the most, a vast area including Lithuania and the Ukraine. In 1795, Prussia took the Warsaw area of central Poland, while Cracow went to Austria. In 1815, as a result of the Congress of Vienna, Russia gained central Poland, which technically became the kingdom of Poland, with the Russian tsar as sovereign. Originally given a relatively liberal constitution, the kingdom of Poland came more and more directly under Russian rule, with Poland's constitution abrogated after an ill-fated Polish revolution in 1830–31. The majority of the Jews of eastern Europe thus found themselves living under the rule of the tsars, with a minority of Yiddish-speaking Jews under Austrian rule (in Galicia and other parts of southern Poland) and a much smaller minority under Prussian rule. This situation persisted until the end of the First World War.

The tsarist government thus found hundreds of thousands, and eventually millions, of unwanted Jews on its hands. For the entire period between the Partitions of Poland and the 1917 Russian revolutions, government policy towards the Jews pursued a course almost always centred in their repression and exclusion from the main arenas of Russian life, with the exception of a small minority of highly assimilated, wealthy, or well-educated Jews, numbering no more than perhaps 5 per cent of the Jewish population of Russia, and of Jewish converts to Christianity. This was not a straight course. Some tsars proved more liberal than others, while the stick was, from time to time, replaced by the carrot. Nevertheless, for every step forwards there was always one step (often two) backwards, and never during the history of the tsarist regime was there a general liberation of Russia's Jews and an end to their repression.

Catherine the Great: confronting the Jewish question

The first Russian ruler obliged to deal with a vastly enlarged Jewish population was Catherine the Great (Catherine II) who ruled from 1772 to 1796.[1] German-born Catherine did not begin by hating Jews. She prided herself on being guided by the principles of the Enlightenment, and initially viewed the settlement of additional Jewish merchants in Russia as helpful to the country's development. After the First Partition of Poland, Catherine took a number of positive steps towards the Jews. She declared herself in favour of 'the free exercise of religion . . . for one and all'. Jews 'will be left in employment of all those liberties which they possess at present' so long as they lived 'as faithful subjects' and pursued 'genuine trade and commerce'. In 1776–83 Jews were declared to be a legitimate part of the 'estates' of merchants and townsmen, midway between the estates of the nobility and of the serfs. Jews would still be subject to a special tax (as they were throughout much of Europe).

From the mid-1780s, however, this liberal policy was gradually eroded and reversed. Pressure to suppress the rights of the Jews came from a variety of sources. Much of the nobility and the office-holding classes detested Jews, while Christian Russian merchants viewed them as rivals. The French Revolution of 1789 abruptly ended the tradition of 'enlightened despotism' which had existed among many central and eastern European rulers of the mid-eighteenth century. Nervous hereditary rulers were now keen to crack down on any show of liberalism that might lead to a repetition of the fate which overtook the French king and queen, and much of the French aristocracy. The Second and Third Partitions of Poland added vast numbers of Jews to Russian rule, which made the rulers of Russia particularly fearful of any perceived growth in Jewish power or wealth.

The tenor of laws, *ukases* (ordinances), and decisions concerning Jews

---

1 Catherine II was not a Russian, but was born Princess Sophia Augusta of Anhalt-Zerbst. She married Tsar Peter III and converted to the Orthodox faith. Her husband, a weak and incompetent ruler, was deposed by elements of the aristocracy and killed, and Catherine was allowed to rule as tsarina. The son of Peter III and Catherine II, Paul, succeeded her.

thus turned against emancipation. In the latter decades of the eighteenth century, the rights of Jewish merchants were severely curtailed. For instance, an imperial *ukase* of 1791 refused Jews permission to enrol in merchant corporations or enjoy the rights of townsmen outside Belorussia and some recently annexed areas in or near Crimea (where Jews often continued to be granted permission to settle, in the interests of economic development). By an edict of 1794, Jews who wished to become merchants throughout much of the Pale had to pay double taxation. Jews were also increasingly expelled arbitrarily from villages on the pretext that they could be 'enrolled' only among townsmen.[2]

After Catherine's death, the position of tsar came briefly to her tyrannical and mentally unbalanced son Paul (reigned 1796–1801), who was assassinated. Several developments at this time marked the beginnings of a new and darker period of Jewish life in Russia. At the behest of the nobility, heavy restrictions were placed on Jewish participation in alcohol production and the liquor trade, an area of the economy with a large Jewish input. Proposals were made by the governor of Vilna, Ivan Friesel, and the future minister of justice, Gavriil Derzhavin, for far-reaching restrictions on the Jewish community in Russia with the aim of 'russifying' them and replacing 'Jewish ... superstitions' with 'the education' of the Jewish people. Under Friesel's proposals, Jews were to be required to send their children to state schools, to dress like other Russians, and to be forbidden to marry before the age of twenty, in order to lower the Jewish birth-rate. Derzhavin, who described the Jews as a 'dangerous people' who must be made 'useful to themselves and to the society in whose midst they lived' advocated a central institution to regulate Jewish religious affairs throughout Russia, and oversee all Jewish schools. He sought an end to rabbinical intrusion into secular affairs and the abolition of the *kahals* (Jewish community councils). He wanted Jews driven out of such occupations as liquor-selling into 'productive' trades, and a mass settlement of Jews in newly-developed agricultural regions. These themes, especially that Jews should become 'useful' members of society, recurred again and again during the history of the tsarist empire. While some Jews might well have welcomed some of these proposals, they were not accompanied by any parallel initiatives to relax the discriminatory legislation from which Jews suffered. This blatant contradiction in aims continued to hallmark the tsarist regime's policy towards the Jews to the end. It wished Jews to become 'useful' members of society and leave their 'superstitions' (i.e. religious and traditional practices) behind, and pointedly refused to allow Jews to become free and equal citizens, which alone might have brought about an impressive Jewish contribution to the Russian state and their loyalty to the regime.

2 A small sect of Jews known as the Karaites were specifically excluded from discriminatory legislation. The Karaites, who lived in southern Russia, found favour with the tsarist authorities because they allegedly had left Palestine before the crucifixion of Jesus and also rejected the Talmud, a work which the tsarist regime deemed particularly dangerous and offensive.

Alexander I: making Jewry 'useful'

The murder of Paul brought his son Alexander I (reigned 1801–25) to the throne. Alexander's reign was momentous for seeing Napoleon's ill-fated invasion of Russia, followed by the Congress of Vienna of 1814–15 and the formation of a 'Holy Alliance' among the conservative European powers: Russia, Prussia, and Austria. Alexander I's policy towards the Jews has been described by the great historian Simon Dubnow as 'a mixed tendency of "benevolent paternalism" and severe restrictions'. It clearly built on the ideas about what to do with the Jews which had gained currency during Paul's reign. In 1802 Alexander appointed a Committee for the Amelioration of the Jews, which reported the following year; its recommendations formed the basis for the Statute concerning the Jews of 1804, aptly described as 'a mixture of liberties and disabilities'. Although liberal and emancipatory voices were heard in this committee, the 1804 Statute enacted many of the proposals of Friesel and Derzhavin, restricting the authority of the *kahals* and the rabbis. Jews were to be allowed to speak Yiddish and Hebrew among themselves (and to practise Judaism) but all official documents were to be written in Russian, Polish, or German, the three acceptable languages of the tsarist empire, and Jewish schools were to be established to teach in those tongues. From 1812 only Jews literate in one of those languages could hold office in the *kahals* or as a rabbi. Worse, from 1807 Jews were no longer to be allowed to lease agricultural land, manage inns or other liquor-selling outlets, or reside permanently in villages or hamlets. On the other hand, Jews registered in approved categories were to be allowed to purchase land in new regions of development and be relieved of their double taxation burden. The Statute also allowed Jews to enter the Russian state educational system. As a result of the Statute, Jews were, in fact, driven in substantial numbers from the countryside, while few settled in newly acquired areas of Russia. In 1812 the tsarist regime was obliged to backtrack on some of these harsher proposals.

Alexander I and his ministers feared that Jews would prove disloyal to the regime in the wake of Napoleon's invasion, as the Poles had been. These fears proved groundless; in fact, many Strictly Orthodox Jews actually feared the secularising tendencies which Napoleon and the legacy of the French Revolution would bring. As a result of the Jews' loyalty, Alexander I promised in 1814 to 'ameliorate their condition', but the remainder of his reign, driven by the extreme conservative ideology present on the continent in the post-Napoleonic period, proved a disappointment to Jewish hopes. Alexander increasingly favoured the conversion of the Jews as a solution to their ills. Material inducements were offered to Jews to adopt Christianity, and in 1802 a large tract of land was set aside in New Russia for 'Israelitish Christians'. There were few takers. A renewal of the policy of expelling Jews from the countryside began, with 20,000 expelled from rural parts of Belorussia in 1823, and a further expulsion from the rural border zone of Russia's western frontier two years later.

Nicholas I: worsening oppression

Alexander I died in December 1825. There was considerable doubt about the succession, which eventually came to his youngest brother Nicholas rather than the second brother Constantine. In the confusion, there occurred the liberal Decembrist uprising, which was quickly suppressed. Nicholas I (reigned 1825–55) proved to be a determined enemy of liberalism and a firm believer in autocracy and absolutism. In 1830–31 he was faced with a determined revolution in Poland, which was suppressed; as a result the Poles lost most of the liberties they retained from before the Partitions. Under Nicholas the bureaucracy grew, while a new law code, enacted in 1832, resulted in a drastic repression of all liberal tendencies in the Empire. A powerful, sinister secret police (the 'Third Section' of 'His Majesty's Own Chancery') came into existence; its legacy was to be a central feature of Russian life under many regimes until the 1990s. Strict censorship of all deviant ideas and official championing of orthodoxy and autocracy became the rule. Russian intellectuals became broadly divided into two schools, the 'westerners', who wished Russia to follow the social and political models of western Europe, and the 'slavophiles', who rejected western models of development, especially liberalism, arguing that Russia's historical pathways of evolution ought to be independent of western trends. In 1853–56 Russia became involved in the ill-fated Crimean War, and was defeated on Russian soil by France and Britain.

For the Jews of Russia, the period of Nicholas I's rule was one of the worst they experienced anywhere in the nineteenth century. He required them to adopt surnames, to facilitate bringing them under bureaucratic control. His guiding principles were much the same as those of his predecessors, moving Jews into 'useful' activities and professions without granting them any increase in their fundamental rights, but he took the negative aspects of this policy much further than anyone else. Most notorious and painful were the Cantonist Decrees of 1827. ('Cantonist' battalions were the term adopted for a similar scheme in eighteenth-century Prussia, denoting a military recruiting district.) From 1805, all Russian male youths were subject to military conscription for enormously long periods of time. In 1827 Nicholas applied these requirements to Jews for the first time. He did this with the implicit aim of converting many such recruits to Christianity. Under the terms of the Cantonist Decrees, each Jewish community was required to supply, annually, a certain number of recruits between the ages of 12 and 25, who were obliged to serve in the Russian army for the incredible period of 25 years! The quota figures assigned to the Jews were double those required by non-Jews; conscription could begin at 12 rather than the normal minimal age of 18; *kahal* officials were obliged to provide the annual quota figure of recruits or be fined. Moreover, Jewish recruits were also often obliged to serve a six-year preliminary training period in the

Cantonist battalions *before* they began the 25-year period of conscription, meaning that they had to serve in the army for 31 years![3]

Jewish youths caught up in this diabolical scheme faced a bleak future. They were usually taken to the eastern provinces of Russia, including Siberia, billeted only in Christian homes, and were forbidden to observe Jewish religious customs or converse in Yiddish. Typically, they were given the Russian staple diet of cabbage soup flavoured with hog's lard, and were compelled to listen to sermons by Russian Orthodox priests. They were allowed to recite Jewish prayers as long as this did not interfere with the duty roster, but could expect no time off for Jewish holidays or the Sabbath. Only Christians could be promoted to the rank of non-commissioned officer or above. Jews were promised eligibility for the civil service on the completion of their service, but few were ever admitted.

Cantonism fell most heavily on the Jewish poor. Rabbis, merchants, and graduates of state educational institutions were exempted, while anyone with money could purchase exemption or provide a 'volunteer' to take his place, provided he too was Jewish. *Kahals* were obliged to recruit Jews who fell behind in paying taxes, or were guilty of vagrancy or 'other misdemeanours'. Leaders of the *kahals* sometimes resorted to press gang tactics to find recruits, by appointing *khappers* (literally 'catchers'), who descended on Jewish neighbourhoods, typically at nightfall, to kidnap boys and young men. These would be snatched from *yeshivot* or even dragged from their mothers' arms. Owing to the commonness of early marriages, many were already husbands, whose families were simply abandoned. This entailed economic hardship for the families and also the risk of leaving wives as *agunot* (Hebrew for 'chained women'), unable to remarry so long as their husbands' deaths remained unconfirmed.

So many potential Jewish conscripts evaded induction that in 1850 Nicholas ordered that for each one missing the *kahal* in question was compelled to provide three others in their twenties. The following year he announced that a relative, even if the family's sole breadwinner, would be conscripted in place of every draft evader. Kidnapping by *khappers* reached a peak during the Crimean War, when a Jewish quota of 30 out of every 1000 conscripts was required. In all, until 1859 when the system ended, some 40,000 Jews were taken into Cantonist battalions. After 1843, efforts to convert Jewish conscripts to Christianity increased significantly, in part because the tsar became convinced that Jews did engage in ritual murder. Jewish recruits were often flogged or tortured until they agreed to conversion. Many committed suicide, sometimes when being immersed in a river to undergo baptism.

In 1835 Nicholas issued another *ukase* defining the boundaries of the Pale of Settlement, which from that date until 1917 officially consisted of

---

3 The Cantonist *ukase* did not apply to Karaites, nor to Jews in the former kingdom of Poland until 1843, and then in a less rigorous form.

fifteen provinces in western Russia plus ten others in the former kingdom of Poland.[4] A number of places where Jews could formerly live (such as the province, but not the city, of Kiev) were made off-limits to Jews. With rare exceptions, no practising Jew could live anywhere else in Russia, an area many times the size of the Pale.

At this time, too, Nicholas applied the rigorous censorship which existed in all of Russian society to the Jews. In 1836, books in Hebrew, chiefly religious works, were confiscated by the state censors and, the following year, many thousands were taken to St Petersburg and destroyed. On the other hand, in 1840 Nicholas had, rather surprisingly, visited a Jewish school established by *maskilim* in Odessa and had been favourably impressed by its teaching of secular learning and a knowledge of wider culture, which he saw as combating the obscurantism of Orthodox Jewish education. In 1849 the Minister of Public Instruction, Count Sergei Uvarov, proposed that a network of such schools should be established throughout the Pale as instruments for Jewish integration. Instruction would be in Russian, but owing to the shortage of teachers fluent in that language German would be accepted as a short-term substitute. As a result the Bavarian-born educator Dr Max Lilienthal (1815–82), a clean-shaven German educator of reformist views who was the principal of a modern Jewish school at Riga, was brought in to advise the government. Despite fierce opposition from many Orthodox Jews, the committee headed by Lilienthal recommended the establishment of a modern system of Jewish schools alongside the traditional Orthodox educational network. Parts of this plan were proclaimed by a *ukase* of 1844, which promised to inaugurate a largely secular system of Jewish schools, to be paid for by a special tax on Jews. In addition, modern Jewish seminaries for training rabbis and teachers were to be established at Vilna and Zhitomir. The worst feature of the 1844 *ukase* proclaimed that once these new schools had been established in sufficient numbers, traditional Jewish schools would be closed. Furthermore, only Christians could be headmasters of the new schools, and after 20 years, teachers would have to be graduates of the two modern seminaries. Owing to fierce opposition, little came of this *ukase*, and Lilienthal emigrated to the United States.

The 1844 *ukase* was only one of a wide range of measures by the tsarist regime during the time of Nicholas I targeting traditional Jewry and attempting to make Jews 'useful' to the state. In 1845–50, traditional Jewish dress was prohibited throughout the Pale, and in 1851 Orthodox Jewish women were prohibited from shaving their heads upon marriage, an ordinance which proved impossible to enforce. At the time of Nicholas' death in 1855, the government had far-advanced plans to transport tens of thousands of Jews in 'useless' occupations to the newly-established areas of central Russia. As early as 1843, as a precaution against smuggling, the Russian government forbade Jews to live within 50 versts (33 miles) of the

4 The ten Polish provinces did not officially become a part of the Pale until 1864.

border with Austria and Prussia. This and other anti-Jewish measures attracted widespread condemnation in the West, especially from leaders of Jewish communities in the democracies such as Sir Moses Montefiore.

One of the most ironic aspects of the repressive measures introduced by Nicholas I and his ministers was that the Jews of Russia were evolving naturally into the very directions which the tsarist regime apparently wished to bring about: towards modernity and economic 'usefulness'. While the majority certainly continued to live in *shtetl* communities as traditional, Orthodox believers pursuing the traditional Jewish occupations, a more 'modern' community was emerging in the largest cities of the Pale and, occasionally, elsewhere. Large-scale bankers and industrialists, especially in the sugar industry, as well as in textiles and woollens, began to appear. The *Haskalah*, previously centred in Germany, moved eastwards, especially to Jewish centres, such as Vilna, which previously were dominated by Strict Orthodoxy. Pioneering Russian *maskilim*, such as the prose writer Mordecai Aaron Gunzburg (1796–1846) and the poet Abraham Dov Lebensohn (1794–1878), turned Vilna into a centre of Hebrew literary renaissance. Odessa, Kishinev, and Riga also became known for the modernising Jewish intelligentsia who appeared there. Jewish merchants travelling from Galicia to commercial centres within the Pale helped to spread the *Haskalah*.

The major obstacle to full and loyal Jewish participation in the development of Russia was that provided by the tsarist regime itself, which regarded its Jewish population with fear, hostility, and contempt. The drive to turn Jews into 'useful' citizens was thwarted by the failure to grant them any significant measure of rights, or to make them feel an accepted component of the Russian population. Tsarist treatment of Jews was only a component of repressive handling of all Russia's inhabitants, especially its ethnic and religious minorities.

Alexander II: the limits of liberalism

Jewish hopes rose with the death of Nicholas I and the accession to the throne of his son Alexander II (reigned 1855–81), who became known as the 'Tsar Liberator'. His reign was marked by a number of important reforms and moderate liberalism which gave hope to the Jews. In particular, he is associated with his Emancipation Edict of March 1861, freeing the serfs, the vast number of rural peasants who were virtual slaves. In 1864 he established a system of local self-governing councils (*zemstvos*) and reformed the judiciary system; in 1870 he reformed the urban government system of Russia. These far-reaching reforms appeared to replace the old, quasi-feudal legal system of Russia, with its legally-designated separate 'estates' among the population (nobles, town-dwellers, peasants, etc.) with a post-French Revolution concept of universal citizenship in which all inhabitants of a country enjoyed equal rights. Russia's Jews naturally expected that a shift in governmental attitude in the direction of equality would benefit them. The weaknesses in Russian society revealed by the country's defeat in the Crimean War also enhanced the feeling that far-reaching reforms were in the air.

Initially, Alexander II took some steps to benefit Jews and to reverse the oppression of his father's reign. In 1856 the worst of the Cantonist system was abolished, with conscription among Jews henceforth to be 'primarily from among those unsettled and not engaged in productive labour'. In 1858 the western border area from which Jews had been expelled by the *ukase* of 1843 was reopened to them. Influential voices from the Russian elite increasingly argued that discriminatory legislation against the Jews was counterproductive to Russian interests. Some far-sighted commentators saw that it was the legalised discrimination against Jews which caused their allegedly debased condition. As Count A.G. Stroganov, the governor-general of New Russia and Bessarabia, put it: 'By offering them a place among us, let us utilise their energy, readiness of wit, and skill as a new means for satisfying the ever-growing needs of our people.'

Some further, albeit limited, reforms followed. In 1859 Jewish merchants of the first guild – the very wealthiest – were given the right to reside and trade throughout Russia. In 1861 this privilege was extended to Jews with university degrees, including physicians. In 1879, all Jewish graduates of higher state educational institutions were permitted to live outside the Pale, including pharmacists, dentists, and midwives. In 1865, Jewish artisans, mechanics, brewers, and distillers were also allowed to live in the Russian interior, albeit with severe restrictions as 'temporary residents'. In 1867 former Cantonists obtained this right. Other limited but visible liberal reforms of this kind occurred throughout the first part of Alexander II's reign. Not all of the reforms of this period benefited Russian Jews, however. The end of serfdom brought ruin to thousands of Jewish middlemen and traders, while in 1861 the Russian government took over the sale and distribution of liquor, impoverishing the many Jews involved in that trade.

Alexander II increasingly showed that he was no liberal in the Western sense, and the latter part of his reign proved that he was little better, if at all, than his predecessors. Russia at this time remained an autocracy, with Alexander refusing to concede the most basic step of all, the establishment of a national parliament. Russia's central government remained in the hands of the tsar and his closest ministers.

Alexander turned specifically against the Jews. It is not entirely clear why this occurred. It is said that in 1870 he had been repulsed by the sight of hordes of *Hasidim* with their old-fashioned black garments and sidelocks, and became concerned, as his predecessors had been, to destroy the 'exclusiveness' of Jews or any hint of a 'state within a state' by russification and repression. In addition, the 'new antisemitism' which was beginning to emerge throughout much of Europe found its Russian proponents. One of the earliest and most extreme was a Jew who had converted to Christianity,

Jacob Brafman (*c*.1825–79), who harboured a long-standing grudge against the leaders of the Hevra Kadisha (Jewish burial society) of his home town. In 1868–69 he published two books attacking the *kahals* as a 'state within a state', alleging that Russian Jewry was engaged in a European-wide plot to subjugate Christians to Jewish power, aided by French and British Jews and Russian liberals. In 1879–80 a former Catholic priest of Polish extraction, Ippolit Lutostansky, produced a work in Russian, *The Talmud and the Jews*, alleging that an international conspiracy by Jews and Freemasons existed to take over the world, one of the first times this common fantasy of the extreme right wing was explicitly enunciated. Following the high-water mark of semi-liberalism in the late 1860s, events turned darker for Russia's Jews. Violent outbreaks against Jews occurred in Odessa in 1871, the precursor to the murderous pogroms which began a decade later. In order to diminish the 'excessive influence' of Jews in the urban areas of the Pale, a law of 1870 decreed that two-thirds of town councillors must be Christians and that no Jew could be appointed mayor. A law of 1876 declared that 'Jews are aliens, whose social rights are regulated by special ordinances'. By the end of Alexander II's reign in 1881, hopes for an era of true liberalism had been dashed.

Many of the Jews of Russia continued along a path of voluntary russification during this period, especially during the tsar's liberal phase. In 1863 a group of leading Jewish merchants and intellectuals of St Petersburg founded the Society for the Promotion of Culture among the Jews. With the motto 'education for the sake of emancipation', it set out to promote a knowledge of Russian among Jews, and furthered secular education. A number of Russian-language newspapers for Jews appeared in this period, and some Jewish intellectuals favoured the replacement of Yiddish by Russian as the Jewish vernacular. Some argued that all public signs of Jewish distinctiveness should cease, with Jews merging into the Russian people and religion shrinking to be a private matter. 'Be a Jew in your tent, and a man in the street' was the advice given by Judah Leib Gordon (1830–92), a leading Russian *maskil*, who also attacked the legalistic obscurantism of traditional rabbinic Judaism. Some Russian *maskilim* were instrumental in advocating the revival of Hebrew as the resurgent creative language of the Jewish people (a stance associated a few decades later with the Zionist movement). From the mid-1850s Hebrew-language newspapers, carrying the message of the *Haskalah*, began to appear.

Increasingly, significant numbers of secularised Jewish youth abandoned the traditional Jewish lifestyle, a trend which had begun earlier but now accelerated. In the 1860s, at the height of Alexander II's period of semi-liberalism, Jewish students at secular institutions expected antisemitic discrimination to end, as it apparently did throughout much of Europe. 'We felt as though we belonged to a new society, wherein there were neither Judeans nor Hellenes,' a Jewish student at the University of Moscow later recalled. Some (as elsewhere in Europe) rejected Judaism entirely, accepting baptism as Orthodox Christians in order to rise in Russian society. It was the famous orientalist Daniel Khvolson (1819–1911), baptised in 1855 in order to obtain a professorship at St Petersburg University, who, when asked if he sincerely believed in Christianity, made the celebrated reply that he sincerely believed that it was better to be a university professor in St Petersburg than a *melamed* (Jewish elementary school teacher) in Volozhin. Baptised Jews now often rose to eminent positions in Russian society, for instance the brothers Anton (1829–94) and Nikolai Rubinstein (1835–81), founders of, respectively, the St Petersburg and Moscow Conservatories of Music; Tchaikovsky, a close friend of both, dedicated his First Piano Concerto to Anton.

As the short-lived mood of liberalism faded, however, small but very visible groups of Jews joined Russia's growing revolutionary movements. By 1880, Jews were estimated to comprise 4 per cent of the revolutionary movement, which aimed at overthrowing the tsarist autocracy and bringing democracy to Russia. Some radical Jewish youth now embraced socialism. Revolutionary cells in both St Petersburg and Moscow were headed by Jews, and Vilna became a hotbed of revolutionary activity. Occasionally, but probably more frequently than among the general population, these revolutionaries were women, who felt doubly oppressed as Jews and as females. While the majority of Russian Jews continued to live a traditional or semi-traditional lifestyle, the minority of revolutionary Jews were obviously especially despised by the tsarist authorities as both revolutionaries and Jews. A number of Jews certainly participated in plots to murder the tsar, and one of them assassinated the governor-general of Kharkov, an interior province just outside the Pale. On 1 March 1881 Tsar Alexander II was assassinated by a bomb in St Petersburg. Among the six terrorists convicted for the crime was a Jewish woman, Hesia Helfman (1855–82; her name is sometimes given as Gesia Gelfman), who had arranged 'safe houses' for revolutionaries sought by the police. Although not directly responsible for the assassination, she was sentenced to death. As she was then pregnant, her execution was delayed, but she died in prison a few days after giving birth.

Alexander III: pogroms and May Laws

The new tsar was Alexander III (reigned 1881–94), eldest son of his predecessor. He was determined to suppress the revolutionary movement and all signs of Western liberalism. His chief adviser, Konstantine Pobedonostsev (1827–1907), who was made procurator of the Holy Synod, the governing body of the Orthodox Church, was an arch-reactionary and unbending advocate of autocracy in all spheres of Russian life. A drastic and general repression of all revolutionary activity and the silencing of even mainstream, reformist liberalism, occurred. Religious minorities and advocates of minority nationality rights were, in particular, targeted by the new government, with Jews at the very head of the queue.

For Russian Jewry, the next few years are remembered in particular for the first of the great wave of pogroms, the May Laws of 1882, and the beginning of truly mass migrations, on an unprecedented scale, to the 'New Diaspora', especially the United States. For millions of Jews in the Diaspora, the coming to power of Alexander III proved momentous in the history of their families, causing them to seek a new life in the democratic world. For the majority of Jews who remained behind in Russia, life now became worse than ever. In April 1881, during the turmoil following the tsar's assassination, pogroms against the Jews broke out in southern Russia, beginning at Yelisavetgrad and spreading to Kiev, Odessa, and elsewhere. A 'pogrom' ('devastation' in Russian) is an organised massacre of any group, but more specifically of Jews and Jewish communities, usually entailing mass murder, rapes, and the damage and looting of property. There had been pogroms in Russia before – in Odessa in 1821, 1849, and 1859 – usually organised by Greeks (who were economic rivals of the Jews) around Easter time. These were comparatively mild; a more serious one occurred, also at Odessa, in 1871, organised by Greeks and Russians. The pogroms of 1881 continued sporadically until June 1884. Centred (as noted) in southern Russia, mob violence also spread to Warsaw at Christmas 1881. Hundreds of Jews were killed, often in the most barbaric and brutal way possible; there were innumerable rapes, and the mass pillaging and destruction of Jewish property. Nothing like this had been seen in the 'civilised' world for centuries: while Jewish life in tsarist Russia was hallmarked by oppression, murderous attacks had previously been unknown or very rare. Outside Russia, persons of good-will were appalled by this seemingly inexplicable outburst of barbaric medieval antisemitism, and rallies supporting the Jews were held throughout the Western world. The pogroms unquestionably acted to increase hostility towards the tsarist regime outside Russia.

The causes of the pogroms of the 1880s have been widely debated by historians. There has been much speculation, but no conclusive evidence, that the tsarist authorities deliberately engineered the attacks on the Jews to divert attention from the failings of the regime. While this is plausible, the scale of the violence clearly took the regime by surprise. It was arguably not in the interests of the government to organise mob violence on such a scale, lest it get out of hand. Although historians do not agree on a single explanation, it has been noted that most of those who took part in the attacks on Jews were young men from the northern provinces who poured into the Ukraine, the centre of the anti-Jewish outbreaks, seeking work. Cast loose from their traditional milieus and often experiencing unemployment, they turned on the Jews, who played a conspicuous and visible part in the trade of the region. These young men were often joined by tradesmen and craftsmen, economic rivals of the Jews. There was also a strong pre-existing tradition of antisemitism which was fanned by newly-produced antisemitic works and growing Russian ultra-nationalism.

The new tsar and his ministers blamed the Jews for their own plight, rejecting requests from leading Jewish spokesmen that a *ukase* be issued against the pogroms. Instead, Alexander III's minister of the interior, Nikolai Ignatiev, blamed the disturbances on the Jews' disproportionate role in commerce and industry, their acquisition of land, their 'clannishness' and their 'exploitation' of 'the original inhabitants [Russians], primarily the poorest classes'. Instead of condemning the rioting, he promised 'to shield the Russian population' from the 'harmful' activities of the Jews. As a result, the government issued the infamous 'May Laws' of 1882 (named for the month in which they were promulgated). They prohibited Jews from living outside the Pale or acquiring property there, from moving into the countryside within the Pale, and from trading on Sundays and Christian holidays. The May Laws were designated 'Temporary Rules', so that they could be speedily enacted, but they remained legally in force until 1915. They created bitterness among Russia's Jews and resulted in a loss of earnings among Orthodox Jews, who could not trade on Saturday (their Sabbath), nor, now, on Sunday, or Christian holidays.

Although commissions appointed by successive tsarist regimes to investigate the Jewish question recommended that discriminatory legislation against the Jews be repealed in order to make them into loyal Russians, the influence of Pobedonostsev and other influential arch-reactionaries in the administration ensured that precisely the opposite occurred, and that restrictions on Jewish activities were tightened still further. This particularly affected education, where strict quotas on the maximum number of Jews permitted to enter schools and universities throughout Russia were imposed. In 1886 the Jewish quota for admissions to schools and universities were set at 10 per cent within the Pale and 5 per cent outside it, except in St Petersburg and Moscow, where it was only 3 per cent. With their traditional emphasis on education in the context of a largely illiterate Russian majority, Jews obviously suffered from a sharp diminution in the numbers allowed to receive an education compared with what those numbers would have been had all schools been open to Jews without discrimination. The authorities were well aware of this, and feared that vast numbers of well-educated Jews would present a direct threat to the hegemony of the conservative Russian ruling elite. In 1893 *hadarim* (with over 300,000 pupils) were forbidden to teach Russian; this was done to impede the chances of Jews acquiring state secondary education. Measures such as these – and there were many others – compelled Jews to seek higher education outside Russia, especially in Germany, France, and Switzerland. When they returned, however, Russian Jewish students of such institutions found their way in the professions barred by rigorous antisemitic quotas applied to many occupations. These barriers accentuated the drift of young Jews to the extreme left.

Moreover, from the mid-1880s the government again applied the May

Laws in all their rigour, especially in attempting to reduce the Jewish presence outside the Pale to the greatest possible extent. As a result, there was a marked decline in the number of Jews owning or leasing land. In 1891, the tsar's brother Grand Duke Sergei became governor-general of Moscow, where about 30,000 Jews lived. Sergei ordered the expulsion of almost all the Jews from Moscow. About 28,000 were uprooted, often under brutal conditions, and removed to the Pale, where they were often pauperised. At this time Jewish numbers in the Pale grew significantly, reaching over 5 million by the beginning of the twentieth century. The Pale was crowded and economically backward; its inhabitants had little or no chance of moving to the growing areas of the Russian Empire; dire poverty was rampant, along with endemic illnesses like tuberculosis, previously little-known among the Jews. As some industrialisation began in the Pale, Jews often moved to cities and towns there, becoming factory workers in Warsaw, Lodz, Cracow, and other urban centres.

For many Jews this situation of continuing oppression was untenable; the only realistic solution was emigration overseas. Even this was not straightforward for, legally, passes were required to leave Russia, and Jews of conscription age were especially in danger of seizure by tsarist border guards, so migrants tried to get out undetected, waiting for nightfall. The destination of the majority was, of course, the United States, the land of liberty where official religious discrimination was outlawed and where the 'rags to riches' story was the central national myth. Over 2.5 million Jews emigrated to the United States between 1881 and 1924, mainly from the Pale, transforming America into the largest Jewish community in the world and the *goldene medina* ('golden country') of Jewish hopes. America was, to quote the words of a writer in a Hebrew-language periodical serving the Pale, 'a new motherland' to which Jews 'go out to freedom from laws of iniquity and oppression to live as citizens in a free country'.

Many other countries also saw their Jewish population rise enormously at this time, from Argentina and Brazil to Germany, France, and Britain. Most Jewish newcomers inevitably settled in recognisable eastern European Jewish ghetto-like areas, most famously in the Lower East Side of Manhattan and the Whitechapel area of east London. Often the presence of so many obviously different and alien Yiddish-speaking newcomers caused a rise in antisemitic hostility from the majority population; many well-assimilated Jews also regarded the presence of a vast number of Jewish immigrants as potentially dangerous and threatening to their status. The Zionist movement looked to Palestine as a centre of Jewish settlement and, eventually, nationhood, but the number of Russian Jews who settled there remained small, almost insignificant compared with the number who crossed the Atlantic to New York.

But most Russian Jews did not emigrate, and after Poland won independence in 1918, that country (containing most of the former Pale) still contained 2.5 million Jews, the second largest community in the world. Since immigration to America and other countries was virtually unrestricted before the First World War, it seems strange to us that any Jews at all stayed in the tsarist dungeon. Many Strictly Orthodox Jews remained because they viewed the secular, hedonistic societies of the West as inevitably corrupting to Orthodox practice. 'Who is the man who wants to be free of the commandments of God? – Let him go to America, a land which collects all those who forget God and abandon religion,' one Polish rabbi warned. Despite the barriers erected by tsardom, some Russian Jews managed to become reasonably successful, or, at least, managed to get by, and the prospects of travelling thousands of miles to an alien country where no Yiddish was spoken except by newly-arrived immigrants was too daunting to undertake. Many, too, imagined that sooner or later the worst features of tsarist oppression would be mitigated or vanish entirely, for instance via a liberal or socialist revolution. For whatever reasons, more Jews remained in Russia than left. The attitude of the tsarist authorities towards the Jews of Russia was summarised in Pobedonostsev's reputed remark that 'one-third of the Jews will convert, one-third will die, and one-third will flee the country'.

Nicholas II: the last of the tsars

In 1894 Alexander III died, and his eldest son Nicholas II (reigned 1894–1917) became tsar. Nicholas proved to be the last of the tsars, in a reign racked by turmoil and revolution. He was an intelligent but weak-willed man, indecisive on most subjects. On that of the Jews, however, he was firm and resolute, unwavering in his hostility to them and maintaining the pattern set by his predecessors. Nicholas's reign saw Russia's catastrophic military and naval loss to Japan in the Russo-Japanese war of 1904–05, leading to the 1905 revolution. He was forced to concede the creation of a Duma (parliament), the first in the nation's history. Russia also emerged emphatically as the champion of the Slavs of south-eastern Europe, and allied with France and Britain against Germany and Austria-Hungary. The assassination of Austrian Archduke Francis Ferdinand in Sarajevo in June 1914 led to the outbreak of the First World War, a conflict which proved disastrous to Russia and fatal to the Romanov dynasty. In March 1917 (February under the old calendar used in Russia) a revolution ended the tsarist regime and a liberal government headed by Alexander Kerensky took power, the only Western liberal government in the history of Russia until the 1980s. In November 1917 (October in the Russian calendar) the Kerensky regime was in turn overthrown by the Bolsheviks headed by V.I. Lenin, ushering in the first Communist government in history, and establishing a dictatorship which lasted until 1991.

The reign of Nicholas II also saw great economic expansion in Russia, which was rapidly industrialising and becoming one of the world's economic powerhouses. The rapid capitalist expansion of Russia is associated with Sergei Witte (1849–1915), minister of finance, and later with the prime minister Peter Stolypin (1862–1911). Despite all the obstacles placed in their way, many Jews benefited from these policies and became important entrepreneurs, although the majority lived in grinding poverty. Additionally, Russia saw the continuing emergence of a nationalist, pan-Slavic extreme right which was virulently antisemitic and anti-liberal, and welcomed violence against the Jews. Russian Jewry responded to the new situation in a variety of ways, especially in becoming more politically sophisticated. By the outbreak of the First World War at least three political tendencies had a wide following among Russian Jewry. The Zionist movement, given its modern form by Theodor Herzl, rapidly gained a following. Agudas Israel, the Strictly Orthodox party representing traditional religious Jews, was founded in 1912. In 1897 the Bund (the abbreviation of *Allgemeiner Yiddisher Arbeterbund in Litte, Polin un Russland*, 'The General Federation of Jewish Workers in Lithuania, Poland, and Russia') was formed in Vilna. Soon spreading all over the Pale and beyond, the Bund was a socialist party of the Jewish working classes in Russia, closely associated with the trade unions. It had close links to non-Jewish socialist and Marxist parties, and, like them, was outlawed by the tsarist regime. The various Jewish political groupings also fought with each other. Both the Bund and Agudas Israel fiercely opposed Zionism. At the left-wing extreme of Jewish politics were revolutionaries, some associated with the Bund, some more extreme. Some of the thorough-going socialists within the Bund joined the Menshevik opponents of Lenin, such as Leon Trotsky (born Lev Davidovich Bronstein, 1878–1940) and Julius Martov (born Iulii Zederbaum, 1873–1923), who became leading figures in the Communist regime after 1917. Smaller numbers joined Lenin's more rigorously Marxist Bolshevik party.

As with the preceding reign, the regime of Nicholas II saw its full share of anti-Jewish violence. The most notorious pogrom to occur under Nicholas was that at Kishinev, the capital of Bessarabia (now Moldavia), in April 1903. A peasant boy was found stabbed to death and Kishinev's crudely antisemitic newspaper claimed the Jews were responsible and that revenge was necessary. Two days of mayhem and murder followed, leaving 47 Jews dead and 424 wounded. Graphic accounts of the barbaric atrocities committed at Kishinev shocked the entire western world, and even Russian liberals. The famous Hebrew poet and Zionist Haim Nahman Bialik (1873–1934) wrote his best-known poem *Be Irha-Haregah* ('In the City of Slaughter') about alleged Jewish inaction during the Kishinev pogrom. The precise causes of the Kishinev pogrom remain unclear. There is no compelling evidence that it was directly instigated by the tsarist authorities (who were, however, very slow to protect the Jews) and most of the participants in the pogrom appear to have been Moldavians, Macedonians and Albanians, not ethnic Russians. Before Auschwitz and Treblinka, the name 'Kishinev' was probably the most infamous and potent eponym for murderous antisemitism in the modern world. As a result of that event, Jewish self-defence units were formed, who were ready for the next outbreak of violence. This occurred a few months later, in the summer of 1903, at Gomel in Mogilev, where rioting developed between Jews and Russians. Here, although ten Jews were killed, Jewish self-defence units protected their people from the worst excesses of the mobs, and, in contrast to Kishinev, the tsarist authorities quickly restored order.

The unpopular and disastrous Russo-Japanese war of 1904–5 sparked another round of pogroms, with 40 perpetrated in 1904 alone, more than half attributable to the war. The revolutionary movement of 1905 sparked yet another wave of pogroms in response to perceptions of Jewish involvement in the radical movement, with no fewer than 650 separate occurrences in the year following October 1905. More than 3100 Jews were killed and at least 17,000 injured. Many attackers were incited by the newly-emergent extreme right-wing, ultra-nationalist, anti-liberal movement, the Union of Russian People, whose local branches were commonly known as the 'Black Hundreds', a term which has become notorious for perpetrators of anti-Jewish violence in late tsarist Russia. Most of the pogroms of this period took place in south-western Russia, especially in the Ukraine. At the worst of these, at Odessa in 1905, no fewer than 800 Jews were killed by rioters and 5000 injured. Economic factors, especially the increasing visibility of Jews in the commercial life of the region, were in part to blame for these outbreaks of violence, although they were instigated by right-wing anti-semites. The pogroms of 1905-06 led to the highest-ever levels of emigration to the United States and elsewhere, with over 100,000 Jews migrating to America annually at this time, mainly from the Pale.

As if this was not enough, there were other highly significant instances of antisemitism in late tsarist Russia. The infamous forgery known as *The Protocols of the [Learned] Elders of Zion* was published in Russia in December 1905, after previously circulating at the imperial court in manuscript form. Purporting to be the transcript of a secret meeting of world Jewish leaders and rabbis to take over the world by manipulating revolutions, wars, and the economy, the *Protocols* have been termed a 'warrant for genocide' and influenced Hitler. They first appeared in the third edition of a book by Sergei Nilius, a mystical writer popular with the tsar, but research in 1999 revealed that they were actually written by Mathieu Golovinski, a Russian nationalist with links to the Secret Police, living in Paris. The *Protocols* remain in circulation among extreme right-wing propagandists and anti-Israel Arab groups around the world to this day.

In 1911, a few years before the outbreak of the First World War, there occurred one of the most famous of all cases of Russian antisemitism, the trial of Mendel Beilis (1874–1934). Beilis, a Jewish clerk in a brickworks in Kiev, was charged with ritually murdering a 12-year-old Christian boy whose body, bearing multiple stab wounds, had been discovered on the city's outskirts. The police believed the crime to be the work of a local criminal gang, but agitation by the Black Hundreds led to a fabricated charge against Beilis, who was put on trial. The Beilis case split Russia. Most Russian liberals and intellectuals knew the charge was preposterous, and many, including Maxim Gorky and members of the Tolstoy family, actively campaigned to have Beilis released. A petition in favour of Beilis was signed by 159 eminent non-Jewish Russians. The strength of support for him is indicative of the fact that Russian economic growth and contact with the West had produced a significant liberal middle class in late tsarist Russia, who viewed the regime's antisemitism as one of the worst relics of medieval barbarism and tsarist autocracy. The growth of a relatively liberal Russian middle class also showed itself in other ways, especially in the elections to the Russian Duma (parliament) established in 1906. As well as liberal and moderate Russians and others, 12 Jews were elected to the first Duma. An international agitation on behalf of Beilis also grew throughout Europe, reminiscent of that on behalf of Dreyfus 15 years earlier. In 1913, after a lengthy postponement of his trial, Beilis was acquitted, striking evidence that Russia was arguably evolving in a Westernised direction. (He moved to the United States; the Beilis Affair formed the basis of Bernard Malamud's famous novel *The Fixer*.)

Nevertheless, one should also not exaggerate the growth of Russian liberalism in this period. In 1911 the Duma debated a bill for the abolition of the Pale; the measure was shelved in committee, and many reactionary members of the Duma made luridly antisemitic speeches in opposition. The tsar still remained virtually absolute in practice, and was as antisemitic as ever. Jews were arbitrarily expelled from many Russian cities by local governors, and a rigorous quota system on Jews continued to be enforced, with arguably even greater rigour than before, until the end of tsarist rule.

In the summer of 1914 the assassination of Austrian Archduke Francis Ferdinand led to a chain-reaction of belligerent activities among Europe's great powers; within a few months virtually all of Europe was at war. Tsarist Russia found itself the ally of liberal Britain and France (and, after May 1915, of Italy) against Germany, Austria-Hungary, and Turkey. The tsarist army was, potentially, a fearsome instrument, and the threat of millions of Russian soldiers – the so-called 'Russian steamroller' – irresistibly pouring their way into central Europe genuinely frightened Germany and its allies. In the initial phases of the war, the Russian army actually penetrated into East Prussia and Galicia in Austria-Hungary. In August and September 1914, however, the Russian army was routed at the Battles of Tannenberg and the Masurian Lakes. The Germans, under Field-Marshal Paul von Hindenburg and General Erich von Ludendorff, completed the defeat of the Russians later in the year. Thereafter, the First World War turned into a catastrophe for Russia and the tsarist regime, although they (literally) soldiered on until 1917 as allies of Britain and France. By mid-1917 Germany was in control of one-third of European Russia, and was in the process of establishing puppet kingdoms from the Baltic to the Black Sea area. The military and political infrastructure of the tsars crumbled during the First World War, its backward bureaucracy and elite structure proving no match for Germany's ruthless efficiency. By mid-1917 it appeared probable that Germany would win the war, turning the whole area of the Pale into a German satellite state. While Germany had its own traditions of anti-semitism, one should not confuse the German imperial regime with that of the Nazis. Many, perhaps most, Jews of the Pale would have preferred the relatively modern and liberal rule of Wilhelmine Germany to that of the tsars, as would millions of Poles, Balts, Ukrainians, and others.

Initially, in a manner reminiscent of virtually the entire population of the belligerent nations, most Russian Jews supported the Russian war effort, as strange as this may seem. No fewer than 400,000 Jews served in the Russian military during the First World War, many of them volunteers returning from abroad. Nevertheless, the tsarist regime continued to the end to denigrate the Jews. Heavily-censored newspapers refused to mention Jewish heroism, but scapegoated the Jews as Russian armies became mired in defeat. In the belief that they would be disloyal to the tsarist regime, thousands of Jews were expelled from the war zone, with others leaving of their own accord. It is estimated that no less than 600,000 Jews left the war zone in the Pale during this period, many thousands dying of starvation and exposure. In 1915, as Jews began to crowd into Russia's interior, the tsarist regime grudgingly extended areas where Jews were permitted to live to include three additional provinces (but not St Petersburg or Moscow). To the very end of the tsarist regime, full participation in Russian life was denied to the Jews. On 22 March 1917, immediately following the liberal revolution and the seizure of power by Alexander Kerensky and other reformers, full civil equality was at last granted to the Jews, and the oppressive legacy of tsarism was at last swept away. Although most Russian Jews thought that the long dark night was over, it proved to be a false dawn.

Further reading

I.M. Aronson, *Troubled Waters: The Origins of the 1881 Anti-Jewish Pogroms in Russia* (Pittsburgh, 1990)

Norman Cohn, *Warrant for Genocide: The Myth of the Jewish World Conspiracy and the Protocols of the Elders of Zion* (London, 1967)

Simon M. Dubnow, *History of the Jews in Russia and Poland*, 3 vols (Philadelphia, 1916-20)

Jonathan Frankel, *Prophecy and Politics: Socialism, Nationalism, and the Russian Jews, 1862–1917* (Cambridge, 1981)

Jacob Frumkin *et al.*, eds, *Russian Jewry (1860–1917)* (New York, 1966)

Christoph Gassenschmidt, *Jewish Liberal Politics in Tsarist Russia, 1900–14: The Modernization of Russian-Jewry* (London, 1995)

Louis Greenberg, *The Jews in Russia: The Struggle for Emancipation*, 2 vols in one (New Haven, 1965)

Erich E. Haberer, *Jews and Revolution in Nineteenth Century Russia* (Cambridge, 1995)

Zvi Halevy, *Jewish Schools under Tsarism and Communism: A Struggle for Cultural Identity* (New York, 1976)

Gershon D. Hundert and Gershon C. Bacon, *The Jews in Poland and Russia: Bibliographical Essays* (Bloomington, Ind., 1984)

John Doyle Klier, *Imperial Russia's Jewish Question 1855–1881* (Cambridge, 1995)

John D. Klier, *Russia Gathers Her Jews: The Origins of the Jewish Question in Russia, 1772–1825* (De Kalb, Ill., 1985)

John D. Klier and Shlomo Lambroza, eds, *Pogroms: Anti-Jewish Violence in Modern Russian History* (Cambridge, 1992)

Eli Lederhendler, *The Road to Modern Jewish Politics: Political Tradition and Political Reconstruction in the Jewish Community of Tsarist Russia* (New York, 1989)

Ezekiel Leikin, *The Beilis Transcripts: The Anti-Semitic Trial that Shook the World* (Northvale, N.J., 1993)

Heinz-Dietrich Löwe, *The Tsars and the Jews: Reform, Reaction and Anti-Semitism in Imperial Russia, 1772–1917* (Chur, Switzerland, 1993)

Paul Mendes-Flohr and Jehuda Reinharz, comps and eds, *The Jew in the Modern World: A Documentary History*, 2nd edn (Oxford, 1995), especially Part VIII

Hans Rogger, *Jewish Policies and Right-Wing Politics in Imperial Russia* (Berkeley, Ca., 1986)

Michael Stanislawski, *Tsar Nicholas I and the Jews: The Transformation of Jewish Society in Russia, 1825–1855* (Philadelphia, 1983)

|5|

Sephardi and oriental Jewry since 1750

Following their expulsion from Spain and from the Spanish-owned island of Sicily in 1492 and their flight from the Portuguese Inquisition during the sixteenth century Sephardim had settled in great numbers along the Mediterranean seaboard. They were especially prevalent in the Italian peninsula, in North Africa, and the Turkish Empire (which included the Balkans and Greece), joining Jews whose ancestors had settled in those regions many centuries earlier, typically in antiquity. Some made their way to Palestine. Sephardim also settled in France, Holland, England, and the New World. In those lands they regarded themselves, and were widely regarded by others, as the 'aristocracy' of Jewry in contrast to the Ashkenazi settlers who arrived later. Gradually the term 'Sephardim' has come to embrace not only the refugees from Spain and Portugal and their descendants but, loosely, Jews of non-Ashkenazi background in eastern countries.

The prominence of Ashkenazim on the stage of Jewish history in modern times must not obscure the fact that at one time most of what was creatively and culturally significant in the Jewish world lay with the Jews of the Iberian peninsula and the Islamic lands: hence the pride of Sephardim and so-called Sephardim in their ancestry. During the Middle Ages Ashkenazi Jewry was the smaller component of world Jewry, an appendage to the more numerous Jews of Spain, Portugal, North Africa and the Middle East, with whom the Ashkenazim were in contact and from whom they received guidance and inspiration.

But by the early modern period Ashkenazi Jews had overtaken them in numbers and relative significance. In 1700 there were perhaps 716,000 Jews living in Europe (most of them Ashkenazim) and 370,000 Sephardim and so-called Sephardim in North Africa and the Middle East. By 1825 the figures were about 2,730,000 and 540,000 respectively, although there were thousands of Sephardim in the New World. The Ashkenazi component of world Jewry steadily outstripped that of the Sephardim thereafter. Sephardim described Ashkenazi Jews as *Tudescos* ('Germans'), while the

Sephardim were known in Yiddish as *Franks*. In the Levant and along the so-called Barbary Coast of North Africa the term 'Frank' was given by local Muslims to Europeans, both Jewish and Christian, who settled in the region in modern times. (This was the origin of the surname taken by the Polish mystic and notorious pseudo-Messiah Jacob Frank who sojourned for at least a decade in the Ottoman Empire.)

Sephardim in Christian Europe

There were communities of Sephardim along the Mediterranean seaboard as well as inland on the European continent. One of the most successful and prominent communities was that of Amsterdam, which developed important trading connections with east and west and whose contribution to the Dutch economy was appreciated. By the second half of the seventeenth century the Sephardim of Amsterdam were especially visible in the diamond industry, which they went on virtually to monopolise, as well as in book printing. They also played a noteworthy part in silk manufacturing and sugar refining. They were active in the stock market and were among the most important shareholders of the powerful Dutch East India Company. Some ventured across the Atlantic to fill trading niches in the New World opened up by the Dutch West India Company. Court Jews arose from their ranks. But during the eighteenth century Holland experienced a slump in trade, and reckless speculation and a series of economic crises ruined many Sephardi families there. The French conquest of the Netherlands in 1794 heralded a further decline in prosperity. By the close of the eighteenth century two-thirds of Amsterdam's 3000 Sephardim had been pauperised, while few rich families had escaped serious financial loss. However, the situation improved in the second half of the nineteenth century, largely owing to the robust development of the diamond industry.

The commercial life of the great Hanseatic port of Hamburg had also benefited from a Sephardi influx as had several Italian towns, particularly Livorno (Leghorn) in Tuscany. In the sixteenth century the Medici ruler of Tuscany, keen to develop Livorno, persuaded Jews of Spanish and Portuguese background to settle there with an assurance of freedom of religion. He and subsequent rulers had honoured that pledge. The Jews of Livorno were especially active in the coral trade. They worked, cut and polished the coral, much of it imported from Tunisia, sending it on for export or crafting it into fine beads. Sir Moses Montefiore, the illustrious British Jew and centenarian who laboured ceaselessly on behalf of oppressed Jewries, was born in Livorno in 1784 into a family of straw hat manufacturers. The grandfather of another great nineteenth-century Briton, the prime minister and novelist Benjamin Disraeli, father of modern Toryism, was a merchant of Turkish background who emigrated to England from Ferrara in the Papal States.

Although the expulsion edict of 1492 remained unrepealed in Spain, the revolutionary regime which in 1868 temporarily toppled the monarchy there introduced a constitution guaranteeing freedom of worship. Strenuously contested by the Catholic clergy, the principle of religious toleration nevertheless survived the restoration of the monarchy in 1870. This encouraged a number of Jews to emigrate to Spain, but organised communal life was slow to establish. Legislation of 1924 gave the Sephardim of Alexandria in Egypt, as well as of Salonika (Thessaloniki) in Greece, but formerly part of the Ottoman Empire, the right to claim Spanish nationality and settle in Spain if they so desired. This provided the basis for the government of General Franco – who is believed to have been of Jewish extraction, and well aware of it – to extend Spanish consulate protection to certain groups of Jews in Nazi-occupied countries during the Holocaust period. A renaissance in Jewish and Hebrew studies blossomed in the 1960s, and there was a degree of rapprochement with the Catholic authorities in Spain. A statute of 1966, giving non-Catholics the right to conduct public worship, instruct their children in their religion, and maintain organised institutions, implicitly included Jews. In 1968 the edict of 1492 was formally abolished. At that time there were about 8000 Jews in Spain, mostly in Barcelona (3000) and Madrid (2500). At the close of the twentieth century the total number was about 12,000. Barcelona's Jewish population held steady at the 1968 figure, but Madrid's had climbed to 3500.

As for Portugal, although the powers of the clerical authorities there were undermined by secular legislation during the second half of the eighteenth century, burning of heretics took place as late as 1791. Marranos continued to flee the country during that period. The Inquisition there was not abolished until 1821. During the opening years of the nineteenth century a number of Jews from Gibraltar and from Morocco settled in Lisbon. An organised community gradually developed there, but had to wait for formal recognition until 1892, when the Portuguese government officially granted it permission to hold religious services, maintain a burial ground, provide charitable relief for its poor, and keep records of its members. In 1912 the republican regime which had come to power in 1910 confirmed the Jewish community's rights. The distinctive presence of Marranos in Portugal had been long assumed to have ceased when, in 1917, a remnant was discovered by chance in a remote mountainous region by a Jewish mining engineer from Poland whose work had taken him there. Regarded as Jews by their Catholic neighbours, they retained folk memories of Judaism, looked forward to a messianic coming, and married among themselves. Their discovery aroused considerable interest among Sephardim abroad, especially in Britain and Holland, who wasted little time in fostering links and making efforts to reacquaint the Marranos with their spiritual heritage. During the inter-war period several hundred refugees from Nazism found refuge in Portugal, which meant that Ashkenazim joined the established Sephardim. At the close of the twentieth century there were 500 Jews in the country, centring on Lisbon.

The Alliance Israélite Universelle

One of the most distinguished members of France's Sephardi community was Adolphe Crémieux (1796–1881), who came from a family long settled in the old papal state of Comtat-Venaisson. He was a lawyer and politician who held ministerial office. Like – and on occasion with – Sir Moses Montefiore he campaigned tirelessly on behalf of downtrodden and persecuted Jewries. In 1862 he became president of the Alliance Israélite Universelle, an important Jewish self-help organisation founded in Paris in 1860 in the wake of the Mortara Affair (see Chapter 2). With the Hebrew motto *Ehud* ('Unity') the Alliance came to the aid of oppressed Jewish communities by defending their rights and working towards their civil emancipation and an improvement in their socio-economic status. Energetic and assertive, it was the first Jewish organisation of its kind, and in 1871 the more restrained Anglo-Jewish Association was set up in London in pale imitation of it. The existence of the Alliance was seized upon by Jew-haters, especially after the rise of political antisemitic movements from 1870, to promote the charge that Jews were involved in a sinister international conspiracy against gentiles; this was, of course, the stuff of which Nazi propaganda was also partly fashioned.

Between 1862, when it set up its first school in Morocco, and 1945 the Alliance established schools for Jews of both sexes in various localities around the Mediterranean, including the Balkans, North Africa and the Middle East. A network of primary schools grew up in those areas, based on the positivist and secular French system of education. They were staffed by graduates of the Alliance's teachers' training college in Paris. Supplementary kindergartens and vocational schools equipping both boys and girls for trades regarded as suitable to their respective genders were set up in some countries. The aim was to prepare young Jews in 'backward' societies for citizenship and help them attain secure, respectable employment. Tens of thousands of children benefited. But in the Arab world the introduction of such schools compounded antisemitism which accompanied the Arab nationalism that gained momentum in the twentieth century, for graduates of Alliance schools were identified with western interests. Following the Second World War Alliance schools were closed in most Arab lands.

Sephardim in the Americas

'New Christians' of Jewish background helped to finance Columbus's voyage of discovery in 1492; Marranos were among his crew, and there has been speculation that he may have been of Jewish origin himself. At least one Marrano landed with the Portuguese in 1500 in Brazil which, with Argentina, is the most important of the Latin American countries with a

Jewish presence. A flourishing community of Sephardim, with familial and trading links to Sephardi merchants in Dutch Curaçao and other Caribbean islands, was established in the South American colony of Surinam during the seventeenth century.

People unable to prove their 'pure' Christian ancestry were forbidden to settle in the colonies of the two Iberian nations, ruling out those descended from Jews and Moors. This meant that overt Jewish migration could not proceed until the Latin American colonies won their independence in the nineteenth century. Nevertheless, from the beginning of the colonial era numerous Marranos surreptitiously entered, and their apparent legacy can be seen among certain judaised Indian sects that remain. The Portuguese were especially lax in enforcing the immigration regulation, for New Christians were at the forefront of cultivation of the dyewood which was sent to Portugal for colouring cloth, and they played a dominant role in Brazil's sugar industry. The Inquisition, however, spread its tentacles to the New World. It was formally set up in Spanish colonies, while inquisitors from Portugal travelled to Brazil at intervals and sent suspected judaisers and heretics for trial to Lisbon. When each colony achieved independence the Inquisition was abolished.

Freedom from Spanish and Portuguese rule was also eventually followed by liberal enactments protecting the rights of religious minorities and of constitutions guaranteeing freedom of worship and thus allowing the foundations of Jewish communal life in Latin America. For example, Argentina gained independence from Spain in 1810, established the principle of freedom of immigration in 1812, and the following year that of liberty of worship on private premises. The principle of religious equality was enshrined in the constitution of 1853. Jewish immigrants, mainly from western Europe, began to arrive in the 1840s, and by the end of the nineteenth century had been joined by Sephardim from Morocco and Syria. During the eighteenth century there were persecutions of Brazilian Marranos by Portuguese inquisitors, resulting in a number of executions and the disruption of the sugar industry and of trade with Portugal. But the situation improved following the king of Portugal's decree of 1773 abolishing all discriminatory legislation towards New Christians in his domains. Meanwhile folk memories of Jewish liturgy and custom grew increasingly dimmer as more and more Marranos married Catholics and completely assimilated into the majority population. A constitution which was adopted following Brazil's independence from Portugal in 1822 gave non-Catholics the right to worship in private; in 1891 a constitution adopted by the newly proclaimed Brazilian republic put adherents of all religions on an equal footing. Jewish immigration into Brazil had been pioneered in the 1820s by Moroccans attracted by the burgeoning rubber industry, and over a century later during the 1950s there was a further influx from Morocco as well as from Egypt.

In 1630 the Dutch, bent on acquiring Portugal's overseas possessions, had occupied north-eastern Brazil. Under their benign rule many Marranos there had become openly professing Jews and were joined by large numbers of Jews from Holland, including members of that country's fledgling Ashkenazi community. But in 1654 the Portuguese had seized back the territory and the Jews, like the Dutch, had been forced to leave. Amsterdam proved the most popular destination. Some Jews, however, opted for Caribbean islands, where they introduced sugar cane, while (as noted in Chapter 10 below) 23 sailed to Manhattan Island and the Dutch town known as New Amsterdam, later named New York, where two Ashkenazim were living already. This group of newcomers was not exclusively Sephardi, but it pioneered Jewish communal life in North America with the establishment in New Amsterdam of a synagogue that followed the Sephardi rite. With further Sephardi immigration more 'Spanish and Portuguese' synagogues ensued along the Atlantic coast. Sephardi merchants played a significant part in the early commercial development of the United States. Sephardim migrated there from Holland and France, as well as from Dutch and British possessions in the Caribbean; until the large-scale migration from Germany in the mid-nineteenth century theirs was the dominant influence in American Jewry. During the twentieth century Sephardi and oriental Jews migrated to the United States from Cuba, the Balkans, North Africa, and the Middle East.

Jews in Muslim lands

Most Sephardim lived in the Afro-Asian world, especially in the area which comprised Turkey's Ottoman Empire which lasted from the fifteenth century to the end of the First World War. Most of the Jews in Muslim countries lived in the Turkish lands, for the Ottomans had established their rule in Algeria, Tunisia, Libya, Egypt, Syria, Iraq and Yemen during the sixteenth century. They also held parts of the Balkans, which had become Muslim, and Greece, which had not. Bordering, but standing outside the Ottoman domains were Morocco and Persia (as Iran was known until 1935). Jews had lived in all these lands since antiquity. During the sixteenth century and subsequently, large numbers of Sephardim had flocked into the Turkish Empire. Salonika, the great commercial port in Turkish-held Greece, was a particularly noteworthy Sephardi population centre. There had been Jews in Greece since Hellenic times, and in the sixteenth and seventeenth centuries there was an important influx of Iberian Jewish refugees into Salonika, from where some moved on to the island of Rhodes. In Salonika they were especially prominent as merchants, brokers and manufacturers, and dominated activities connected with the running of the port to such an extent that those activities came to a standstill on Jewish Sabbaths and festivals.

In the modern period Sephardim came in particular from Livorno in Italy, settling in significant numbers in North Africa, to which they were attracted by expanding commercial opportunities. The old-established Arabic-speaking communities and the newer, Ladino-speaking Sephardi ones traditionally had little to do with one another. They differed not only linguistically but culturally. By and large, the Sephardim of the Ottoman lands were of a higher socio-economic status than their 'indigenous' co-religionists, for whereas the latter were mainly small dealers, pedlars and craftsmen, Sephardim were heavily involved in large scale trade and commerce, and some families and individuals served the Ottoman regime and its local representatives in important capacities of a financial and diplomatic nature.

In order to understand the treatment of Jews in Muslim lands we have to appreciate the attitude of Islam towards them. Contempt for Jews was learned from the Koran, which described them in such terms as 'transgressors,' 'enemies of God,' cheats and traitors, so cursed that some of them were turned into 'apes and swine'. Their 'abasement and poverty' was decreed everlasting. Anti-Jewish invective in the Islamic oral tradition (*hadith*) also contributed to their degradation, which in modern times was practised markedly in Yemen, Persia and Morocco. Folkloric sayings such as 'No two Jews meet except to plot the death of Muslims' and insults such as 'apes', 'dogs', and 'sons of carrion' circulated into modern times. The Jews' offence in Muslim eyes was their failure to foresake their Mosaic tradition for the one revealed to Mohammed. While Muslims recognised the affinity between their own religion and that of the Jews they regarded Islam as a purer form of monotheism than Judaism, and saw Mohammed's revelation as the ultimate one, supplanting both Judaism and Christianity. The patriarch Abraham (preferred in Islam to Moses) and Jesus were regarded as prophets by Mohammed, but their followers were viewed as having corrupted their message – hence the need for Islam and hence the epithets of scorn in Koran and *hadith*. But Islamic prejudice towards Judaism stopped short of the hatred so easily engendered by Christian dogma: Islam condemned Jews for allegedly killing Jesus, one of the bearers of God's word, but unlike Christianity, which saw Jesus as part of the godhead, it did not equate Jews with deicide, the lethal change that made Jewish life so precarious in the pre-modern Christian world and continued to bedevil Jewish–Christian relations into the twentieth century. Jews, for their part, tended to regard Christianity, with its idea of the Trinity, as ambiguously monotheistic. Consequently, when faced with a choice between forcible conversion or death, Jews in Christendom generally chose the latter. This contrasted with their behaviour in the same circumstances in Muslim lands, where apostasy was typically chosen over martyrdom since Islam was seen as uncompromisingly monotheistic as Judaism itself.

Being designated in Islamic thought *Ahl al-Kitab* ('People of the Book'), Jews and Christians (as well as Zoroastrians, monotheists with their own sacred text) enjoyed in Muslim societies the status of *Ahl ad-Dhimma* ('Protected People'), and were known individually as *dhimmis* ('the protected ones'). The tolerance extended to these three non-Muslim groups in Islamic lands was begrudging, and *dhimmi* status came at a price. Despite their protected position *dhimmis* were regarded as infidels who must eventually appreciate the error of their ways and adopt Islam. Until they did so it was necessary constantly to remind them of their flaws, their inferiority, and how despised they were: it was this that basically determined the status of Jews (and Christians) in Muslim lands. In return for protection Jews had to acknowledge the superiority of Islam. They were obliged to pay a special annual poll tax (*jizya*) and there were rituals when paying it to the relevant official that symbolised their debased status. For instance, they had to walk, not ride, to the place of payment; they had to stand while the tax official sat; he could manhandle them at will; their hand had to be below his when the money was exchanged. Within Muslim society positions of authority were denied to them. They were obliged to wear distinguishing clothes, usually consisting of blue, violet or dark-coloured turbans and robes: the yellow badge of shame, so notorious a feature of medieval Europe, had been a Muslim innovation, introduced by a caliph of Baghdad during the seventh century CE. They were forbidden to bear arms – this in societies where to do so was usual – or to ride horses, having to make do with donkeys instead, and no saddles. The horse, as one eighteenth-century European traveller learned, was 'too noble an animal to be employed in the service of such infidels'. Synagogues were not to be taller than mosques; existing ones could be restored but no new ones built. Jews had to remove their shoes when passing a mosque. In some localities they had to go barefoot altogether when outside the *mellah*. When walking in the streets after dark Muslims and Christians carried lanterns, whereas Jews were allowed only a bare candle, readily blown out by the wind. Presumably this regulation was based on the Koranic saying that 'As often as they [Jews] light a fire, God will extinguish it.' They had to acknowledge their inferiority by walking on the left side of Muslims. Names such as Joseph and David, which they shared with Muslims, had to be spelled by them in a distinctive way so that they might not be mistaken for followers of the true faith.

Although some of the regulations – but not the all-important *jizya* – were in certain periods and places allowed to lapse or were enforced only half-heartedly, enough of them existed at various locations in modern times to merit the attention of Christian travellers. While it is true that travellers are liable to obtain an erroneous impression of the societies which they visit, especially where a language barrier exists, sufficient European visitors recorded similar observations regarding the status of Jews in Islamic countries for us to heed them.

The *mellah* (the Jewish quarter), in which so many European visitors found themselves, was an eastern version of the ghetto in Europe, modelled, indeed, on the old *juderias* of Spain. The residents were subject to night-time curfews. The earliest *mellah* was established in the first half of the fifteenth century by the authorities at Fez in Morocco, not to humiliate its inhabitants but to make them less vulnerable to physical attack during outbreaks of popular hostility. This did not prevent the Jews of Fez being nearly exterminated during a revolt nearly 30 years later. *Mellahs* were subsequently set up in other towns with the intention of penalising Jews rather than protecting them. The *mellah* at Tarudant, Morocco, was described in 1789 as 'a miserable place' whose inhabitants 'are in the most abject state of poverty and subjection'. Tetuan, another Moroccan town, was in 1839 branded 'filthy, uncivilised, barbarous, and beastly', its Jewish quarter being 'the most wretched of all'. That very quarter, another account explained, 'was divided from the Moorish by gates which are closed at a certain hour at night'; its streets were covered in 'filth'. A visitor noted around the same time that Jews inhabited 'the most wretched quarter' of Cairo. The situation was similar throughout the Middle East.

Appearances, however, could occasionally mislead. Although poverty and degradation were the prescribed lot of Jews under Islam, and despite the almost uniformly dilapidated appearance of their dwellings in the *mellah*, there were (as described below) wealthy and important individuals among them. A British writer and traveller, who visited Turkey at the beginning of the eighteenth century, discovered that 'There are many of them vastly rich, but take care to make little public show of it, though they live in their houses in the utmost luxury and magnificence.' Since impoverishment denoted their deemed degraded status as infidels, most affluent Jews in Muslim lands prudently concealed the extent of their prosperity from the Islamic masses. Before going outside they would usually exchange the finery they wore at home for plain, unostentatious garments. The outward shabbiness of their houses was often deceptive, ill-preparing the visitor for the brightness, in some cases opulence, of what lay inside.

In addition to assuming roles which brought them into contact with Christians, such as interpreting, commerce and diplomacy, all avoided by Muslims, Jews in North Africa and the Middle East were clustered in other occupations which Muslims did not pursue. These included gold- and silversmithing, for working and dealing in metals was believed by Muslims to pollute those involved and jeopardise their immortal souls, as well as the trades of tanner, dyer, and butcher, despised as being demeaning and dirty. For the same reason Jews across much of the Islamic world were employed as public executioners and as removers of refuse. (In the Yemenite town of Sana'a the Jewish community was forcibly made responsible from 1846 to 1950 for cleaning the municipal sewers.) Jews also dealt in wine and other alcoholic beverages, a trade eschewed by Muslims, whose religion forbids the consumption of alcohol. The occupational structure of Jews in Muslim countries thus paralleled, to a certain extent, that of Jews in Christian Europe.

Jews were generally better treated in the Ottoman Empire – with the exception of Yemen – than in Persia and Morocco. The Yemenites and

Persians belonged to the strict, minority Shi'ite strand within Islam, which was inclined to show less forbearance towards Jews and other 'infidels' than was the Sunni Muslim mainstream. Although not Shi'ites, Moroccans were very strict Muslims, and the Jews of Morocco, as the country's only non-Islamic minority, were as reviled as their co-religionists in Yemen and Persia were. In all three countries physical assaults on Jews were common – apparently much commoner than in Turkey, for example. But the Jewish victims were unable to defend themselves, since if they hit back they would have a hand chopped off in retribution for striking a 'true believer'. They thus had no choice but to exercise almost superhuman restraint when goaded and ill-treated. Even children manhandled and insulted them, regarding them 'as fair game, much in the same light as a dog', to quote one appalled European eyewitness. Jewish women were not spared intimidation and violence when walking in public, as travellers' reports make clear. In Yemen and Persia Jews were regarded not only as infidels but as ritually unclean people whose very touch brought defilement. Thus every Yemenite or Persian who accidentally came into physical contact with a Jew rushed to cleanse themselves thoroughly. Jews buying merchandise from Muslims were required to stand well away from the goods and point to what they wanted, taking care not to brush against the stock. Jews were forbidden to go outside in wet weather lest the rainwater running off their bodies should pollute Muslims.

Ottoman Jewry

The Jews of the Ottoman Empire had over the centuries enjoyed a tolerance denied to their co-religionists in Christian Europe, and for the most part they were reasonably treated. The Ottoman sultans were content to leave them and other non-Muslims alone so long as they caused no trouble and paid the special taxes imposed on them. There was no attempt to convert them. The Ottomans placed considerable reliance upon the commercial skills of Jews, who accordingly reached positions of trust and importance. The regime preferred them to Christians, regarding them as less likely to collude with elements in Europe hostile to Turkish interests. The Jews' financial expertise made them invaluable as bankers, money-changers, and customs agents. They also functioned as physicians and druggists. During the seventeenth century they had been plunged into an economic crisis which proved to be an fertile breeding ground for messianic expectations crystallising around the 'pseudo-Messiah' from Smyrna (Izmir), Shabbetai Zevi. Following the collapse of his pretensions and the consequent disillusionment incurred, the rabbis established a conservative stranglehold over Turkey's Jewish masses. At the same time, their shared difficulties encouraged the unity of the several groups which comprised Turkish Jewry, culminating in the rise to cultural and religious supremacy of the Sephardi tradition, and to the use of Ladino among Turkish Jews regardless of background.

Men of Sephardi origin played important roles not only in places such as Constantinople (as Istanbul was known until 1930) and Salonika but in Turkey's possessions in the Arab world. Jews largely of Livornese background were an economic elite in North Africa, generally favoured by local rulers (known according to rank as beys or deys). In Tunisia, for example, they collected customs duties and worked in the mint, and were granted monopolistic control of the coral and tunny fisheries as well as the trade in tobacco, ostrich feathers and wool: over 50 per cent of woollen and silk goods manufactured in Tunisia by Jews were prayer shawls exported to Eastern Europe via Livorno and Trieste. In 1784 the local ruler, the bey of Tunis, declared war on the Venetian Republic for failing to compensate Jewish merchants for the loss of cargo carried in its vessels. In the nineteenth century a number of high government positions were filled by Jews. During the long period of Ottoman hegemony Algerian corsairs scouring the Mediterranean for potential 'Frankish' galley slaves made the Barbary Coast notorious for piracy, and leading Jews of Livornese background proved invaluable to European governments in helping to ransom their citizens who had been captured there. In 1830 the bey of Algiers, trying to assist two interconnected Sephardi families of grain exporters to recover large debts owed to them by France, irately struck the French Consul, giving the French government an excuse to invade.

Owing to economic opportunites created by the powerful, Western-oriented reformist regime of Albanian-born Mehemet Ali, Governor of Egypt from 1805 to 1848, and by the opening of the Suez Canal in 1869, which transformed communication between Europe and the East, Sephardi entrepreneurs from Italy, the Balkans and the Levant flocked into Egypt. In Iraq Jewish merchants of 'native' origin traded with neighbouring lands such as Syria and Persia as well as with destinations further afield such as Bombay, Calcutta, Singapore, London and Vienna. Among the commodities in which they dealt were silks and other fabrics, pearls, gemstones, ironware, glassware and porcelain, as well as medicaments, foodstuffs and liquors. Among the most successful of Iraqi Jewish emigré families were the Sassoons, who have been called 'the Rothschilds of the East'. They descended from Sassoon ben Salah (1750–1830), who was financial adviser and agent to the Ottoman pashas (governors) of Baghdad. His son, David ben Sassoon (1792–1864) moved to Bombay in 1834. There he set up as a textile merchant and with the help of his sons expanded his company into a formidable business empire with links throughout the East. He was a devout Jew and a noted philanthropist. A few years before his death he posed for a much-reproduced photograph with three of his sons. It shows him wearing the turban and robes characteristic of Baghdadi Jews and only one of his sons in western attire. But the family's adaptation to modern influences was rapid. His son Abdalla, who wore eastern garb in that photograph, later moved to Britain, became a freeman of the City of London, and was knighted as Sir Albert Sassoon (1818–96). Sir Albert's son, Sir Edward Sassoon (1856–1912) sat as a Tory in the House of Commons.

The situation of the Jewish economic elite in Islamic countries was not, however, without its hazards. Occasionally the rulers they served proved capricious and spiteful. In eighteenth-century Egypt certain wealthy Jews who served as financial agents to successive governors and administrators were executed for giving offence, real or imagined, to their overlords. Numerous cases are recorded of Ottoman rulers and governors milking the local Jewish communities of their wealth, or of capriciously having Jews murdered.

From the eighteenth century Ottoman Jews found lucrative callings as agents to 'Frankish' merchants who regularly brought European manufactures to the Empire and purchased Ottoman products to sell at home. Such merchants became increasingly willing to contract this work to Jews, whose ability to deal with clients of various backgrounds as well as with frequently tricky officialdom was well proven. Historically, European consuls concerned themselves with the status of Christians under Ottoman rule, ignoring that of Jews. In the nineteenth century the situation changed. Britain was particularly protective of Jews' interests. In 1838 Lord Palmerston, the British foreign secretary, instructed British consular officials throughout the Ottoman realms to investigate 'oppression or injustice' against the Jews and protest against it. One of the most famous examples of this occurred during the so-called Damascus Affair of 1840, a 'blood libel' (ritual murder accusation) involving the alleged disappearance and murder of a Catholic priest and his servant in the Jewish quarter of Damascus, leading to incitement against local Jews and the torture of leaders of the community aimed at securing 'confessions'. A wide outcry in the west, headed by Sir Moses Montefiore and Adolphe Crémieux, and backed by Britain, led to an official condemnation by the Ottoman sultan of the ritual murder charge.

Britain also protected the interest of Jews in that area in other unexpected ways. In 1850 there occurred the renowned 'Don Pacifico' affair. David Pacifico (1784–1854), a Sephardi merchant residing in Greece, had been born in Gibraltar and was therefore a British subject. He had substantial monetary claims against the Greek government which he doggedly pursued. In 1847 an antisemitic mob burned his house in Athens. This led Lord Palmerston to order a blockade of Piraeus (Athens's seaport) by the Royal Navy in 1850 in support of his claims. Palmerston, celebrated for his vigorous use of British military power around the world, defended his actions in a speech in the House of Commons – which became one of the most famous orations of the nineteenth century – declaring citizenship of Britain to be like that of ancient Rome, when any Roman citizen could invoke the protection of the law with the phrase *Civis romanus sum* ('I am a Roman citizen'). 'A British subject shall feel the strong arm of England will protect him,' Palmerston declared, attacking the proposition that 'because a man is of the Jewish persuasion he is fair game'.

In the first half of the nineteenth century the Ottoman authorities, realising how weak Turkey – soon to be dubbed 'The Sick Man of Europe' – was compared to Christian powers, embarked on a programme of reform and modernisation. As early as 1839 the sultanate vowed its intention of giving full equality to all Ottoman subjects regardless of religion. This meant that Jews and other non-Muslims became eligible for public office, and during the middle of the century Jews in Turkey began to secure important state, judicial and professional positions, which made their situation compare very favourably with that of their Jewish contemporaries in Christian Europe. In 1855 the traditional tax that Jews and other non-Muslims paid in return for exemption from military service was abolished, since they had become eligible for such duty along with Muslims. If they preferred not to serve, as many Jews (and Christians) did, they could pay a new military substitution tax levied on members of all religions alike. However, in 1910 this tax was abrogated, owing partly to pressure from the Istanbul-based chief rabbi, a powerful figure whose official communal functions, restored in 1835, went far beyond spiritual leadership. He was keen to demonstrate that Jews were eager to serve their country. From then onwards non-Muslims were routinely conscripted.

Another innovation that the sultan's regime made in the mid-nineteenth century was the establishment of state schools with sciences and languages on their curricula, which would prepare Ottoman youth of all religions for life in a modern society. But, heeding the fierce opposition of the rabbis, whose conservative stranglehold had not yet loosened, most Jews continued to send their children to traditional, inward-looking Jewish schools. Secular education for Jews in Turkey did not really get underway until 1874, when the Alliance Israélite Universelle established a school in Istanbul based, like schools it set up elsewhere in the Ottoman Empire, on the French educational system.

The modernisation of Turkish Jewry

The sultan who ruled from 1876–1909 was well disposed towards Jews. Under him they recovered their former position as the 'most favoured minority community' in the Empire, to quote one historian. The sultan resisted the plan for an autonomous Jewish state in Palestine under his suzerainty, as outlined to him in 1901 by Herzl, partly owing to the negative attitude of most prominent European Jews and partly to his own wariness of the Ashkenazim who had come to outnumber the Sephardim there. But he was sympathetic to the plight of persecuted Jews. During his reign refugees from the Ottoman's former possessions – Greece, Serbia and Bulgaria – as well as from Romania and Russia, settled in Turkey.

This accommodating ruler was deposed in the Young Turk revolution of 1908. Despite his goodwill towards them Jews gave considerable tacit support to the Young Turks' constitutional movement, and some were close to its leadership. But there was a price to pay. In the immediate prelude to the First World War the new regime's secularising zeal brought the decisions of judges in Jewish religious courts and the curricula of Jewish communal schools under review by state authorities. A law of 1917 which transformed marriage and divorce into secular contracts undermined the role of rabbis.

The Jews' robust support for the Ottoman war effort, characterised by enthusiastic enlistment, contrasted sharply with the stance taken by Christian minorities. As the First World War progressed many Christians were deported, resulting in a lack of serious economic competition for Jews. However, the victorious Western Allies who occupied Istanbul turned the property of Jews (and Muslims) over to returning Christian claimants. Several prominent Jewish supporters of the Young Turk movement were arrested. Thousands of Jews (and Muslims) were killed by Greek troops who occupied south-eastern Anatolia in 1919, and until the region was recaptured by the Turks in 1922 several antisemitic incidents occurred there.

President Mustafa Kemal Ataturk's modernising government, which came to power following the First World War and the crumbling of the Ottoman Empire, aimed at curtailing the pervasive influence of Islam in Turkish public life and was thus welcomed by Jews. But it did entail a sacrifice on their part. Shortly after the signing of the Treaty of Lausanne (1923), in which Turkey's post-war boundaries were settled, the chief rabbi renounced his community's special legal status and rights guaranteed in that document, his example being reluctantly emulated by Christian minorities. Their communal autonomy and right to levy taxes thus ceasing, Jews had to rely on voluntary contributions in order to maintain their separate institutions; they were now subject to the same laws and regulations as everybody else; their personal status was now under the jurisdiction of civil courts; religious marriages were prohibited; the chief rabbi was no longer a state-recognised functionary. Turkish became the obligatory language of instruction in schools, and lessons in religion were banned.

There was a movement among some Jews, especially in Salonika, to turkify themselves including their names, in order to demonstrate their acceptance of Turkish nationalism, which they feared might otherwise turn against them. But they had little reason to fear. During the 1930s the Turkish government generously admitted many refugees from Nazism, most anti-Jewish activity during that period coming from Greeks and Armenians. Although Turkey managed to remain neutral during the Second World War its sympathies were with the Allies against the Axis powers, and it refused to deport its Jews to death camps as the Nazis demanded. In 1942 a tax aimed at raising the enormous sum needed to finance the huge army defending western frontier regions against possible German invasion struck hardest at urban merchants, most of whom were Jews and Christians. Consequently they incurred severe financial losses, even ruin, and faced a term of hard labour if unable to pay. Although not aimed at Jews as such, this episode left a bitter legacy, and, along with Zionist influences, resulted in a large-scale emigration of Turkish Jews to Israel soon after the war. This was despite the fact that the government had relaxed its uncompromising stance towards religious education, and despite demands by some Turks that emigration of Jews should be halted since it would harm the national economy. During the 1960s and 1970s there was another significant, although much smaller exodus, and at the close of the twentieth century the community which on the eve of the Second World War had numbered well over 80,000 stood at about 25,000 people.

Modernisation and persecution in other Muslim lands

The French who invaded Algeria in 1830 soon began tampering with the self-governing Jewish communal apparatus there. The judicial power of rabbinical courts was transferred to state tribunals, and a new leadership structure put in place. Consistories on the French model were established at Algiers and other large towns. During this period of upheaval many Jews with familial links to Livorno returned there, and numbers of middle-class Jews crossed into Morocco and Tunisia. On the other hand, there was a flow of Moroccan and Tunisian Jews into Algeria, attracted by French rule. An Alliance school was opened in 1894. Meanwhile a Jewish intelligentsia sprang up, composed mainly of men of Livornese origin, and from its ranks the first Algerian Jews to enter the liberal professions emerged.

In 1870 Adolphe Crémieux, France's minister of justice, signed a decree giving French citizenship to Algerian Jewry. This move antagonised many French colonists, and inflamed antisemitic sentiments among them. In a sporadic series of riots that continued until the end of the century Jews and their property were attacked; synagogues were looted. The unrest, exemplified by mob violence at Algiers in 1882 and Oran in 1883, intensified during the Dreyfus Affair (1894–99). It was fuelled by the right-wing antisemitic propagandist Edouard Drumont, who was elected deputy for Algiers in the French National Assembly, and the equally judeophobic mayor of Algiers, Max Regis. There were serious pogrom-like incidents at Algiers in 1897 and 1898. The ugly mood affecting colonists was reflected in the outrageous and unlawful decision of the municipal authorities at Constantine to bar Jewish patients from the town's hospitals. But an antisemitic party that was launched failed to win mass support, with Muslims remaining aloof, and it soon collapsed. Although the colonists' attitude towards Jews improved as a result of the bravery of France's Jewish soldiers during the First World War, hostility did not subside altogether, and was encouraged by Hitler's rise to power in Germany. There was a massacre of Jews at Constantine in

1934, and following the fall of France in 1940 the Crémieux Decree in Algeria was abrogated and the Vichy government's racial laws were rigidly applied. Jewish children could no longer attend state schools, and quota systems operated in the higher educational sector. Ultimately the Vichyite administration in Algeria forbade Jews to receive higher education at all.

During this time the local resistance movement was organised by Jews. An Algerian Jewish doctor sat among the distinguished French emigrés, including two Jewish future prime ministers of France, who comprised General de Gaulle's anti-Vichy French Committee of National Liberation, which based itself at Algiers from 1942. Following pressure from President Roosevelt on the French administration in Algeria the Crémieux Decree was restored in 1943. After the war the struggle within Algeria between the French colonists and Muslim activists bent on national independence largely shaped the fortunes of Algerian Jewry. During the 1950s and early 1960s the nationalists used intimidatory tactics, including murder, to convince Algerian Jews to join their cause. Highly gallicised in culture and allegiance, yet not fitting comfortably into the milieu of the French colonists, Algerian Jews found themselves caught in a war of terror and counter-terror waged between paramilitary pro- and anti-independence groups. With the coming of the country's independence in 1962 the majority of Jews emigrated. Several thousand opted for Israel but most went to France. From the middle of the decade those who remained in Algeria found themselves burdened with heavy taxes, subjected to severe discrimination, and attacked by a hostile press angry at Israel's victory in the Six Day War of 1967. All synagogues but one were turned into mosques. Heavy emigration ensued, so that by the end of the twentieth century fewer than 150 Jews were left in Algeria.

The situation was similar throughout North Africa. In 1912, the year marred by the massacre of Jews in Fez, Morocco became a French protectorate. Under French rule the situation of Moroccan Jewry eased and they were no longer obliged to live in designated neighbourhoods. But during the early 1940s, when the Vichy government's legislation was enforced, they were herded back into *mellahs*, where the consequent severe overcrowding caused epidemics to break out; they were allotted only half the food ration given to others; they were subjected to a quota system in schools. Following the creation of the State of Israel in 1948 there was recurrent pogrom-like violence against Jews in Morocco. Alliance schools were set ablaze. Over the next few years mass emigration took place. With independence from France in 1956 the Moroccan monarch granted Jews full equality, and several gained senior public and judicial positions. But this optimistic period was shortlived, since official opposition to Zionist activity was soon stepped up and some Jewish organisations were forced to close. Consequently, despite an official ban, further mass emigration ensued. The ruler who ascended the throne in 1961 demonstrated his goodwill by legalising emigration and appointing several Jews to important state posts. However, anti-Jewish propaganda, vigorously promoted by the Minister of Islamic

Affairs and the party to which he belonged, infected the press and sections of the public. There were cases of young Jewish girls being kidnapped and compelled to accept Islam. The situation deteriorated as a result of the Six Day War, and the consequently renewed mass emigration included many affluent Jews who had been encouraged by the monarch's tolerance but were now convinced that there was no future for them in Morocco. Many of the affluent went to France or Canada rather than to Israel. By the close of the twentieth century Moroccan Jewry had very substantially diminished, although it still comprised about 10,000 people.

In 1857 a French squadron was sent to Tunisia after a Jew alleged to have insulted Islam was put to death despite the pleas of the French consul. Accordingly, the bey of Tunis, evidently deciding that discretion was the better part of valour, formally declared the equality of all his subjects irrespective of religion. Discriminatory legislation against Jews was repealed and a new constitution was framed. But an angry backlash from Muslims incensed at equal rights for 'infidels' ensued. Anti-Jewish riots broke out, and the egalitarian constitution was revoked.

An Alliance school opened in Tunisia in 1878. The country became a French protectorate in 1881, and from 1910 Tunisian Jews became entitled to apply for French citizenship. Following the First World War, during which many Tunisian Jews fought in the French army and unruly Tunisian troops ransacked the Jewish quarter at Tunis and elsewhere, increasing numbers did so. During the inter-war period relations between Jews and other Tunisians was relatively calm. But after the fall of France Vichyite discrimination was enforced, and the situation deteriorated under the German occupation of the country from 1942–43, with mass round-ups of Jews resulting in deportations to death camps in Europe, and the detention of thousands of young Jewish men in local labour camps.

Jewish communal life was renewed in all its vigour after the war, along with increasing gallicisation and a tendency of middle-class parents to send their children not to schools run by the Alliance, since they offered only primary and commercial education, but to French-style state institutions. Jews entered the liberal professions in large numbers. But when Tunisia became independent of France in 1956 a programme of Arabisation began which had a deleterious impact on the Jewish population. The rabbinical court was abolished, the communal leadership structure tampered with, and the Jewish quarter in Tunis demolished. Jews were accused of unpatriotic activity. This charge heightened with the Six Day War between Israel and the Arab states, and there were acts of anti-Jewish arson. Emigration to Israel, which commenced in 1948, intensified, and a large-scale exodus to France (and to a lesser extent Canada) depleted Tunisia's Jewish population.

In 1911 Libya passed from Ottoman to Italian rule, and during the next 25 years the country's Jews lived in security and prosperity. Rather than send their children to the Alliance school, established in 1895, many Jewish parents in the capital, Tripoli, chose the Italian-type educational system instead. But from 1936 Mussolini's discriminatory legislation was imported from Italy. Jews carried compulsory documents displaying proof of their 'race,' and those who refused to open their shops on their Sabbath were punished. During the 1940s Jewish shops were systematically pillaged. There were inhumane deportations of Jews into the desert region, as well as forced labour under atrocious conditions, and many died of starvation and disease. In 1945 there were anti-Jewish riots by Muslims in Tripoli and elsewhere, and further mob violence broke out in 1948 with the establishment of Israel. As a result, most Libyan Jews emigrated, with Israel the usual destination. The constitution of 1952 proclaimed equal rights for the few thousand still living in Libya, but arrests and violence following the Six Day War ensured that the Gaddafi regime which came to power in 1969 inherited only a small remnant. They were forbidden to leave the country, and their property was nationalised.

Owing to the great influx of Jews who entered Egypt during the nineteenth century Alexandria, having recovered its former status as an important commercial metropolis, rivalled Cairo as a centre of Jewish life. In the immediate aftermath of the First World War Sephardim from Salonika and elsewhere in Turkey settled in Egypt. A vibrant communal life thrived, and several leading Jewish financiers achieved high political office. But following the seizure of power by Colonel Nasser in 1954 many arrests of Jews took place and the Jewish community was forced to donate money for military purposes – effectively against the State of Israel. Those arrested were charged mainly with Zionist or communist activity, and a number of Jews faced a show trial that year on charges of spying for Israel, two receiving the death penalty. In 1956 thousands of Jews were expelled from the country, having been forced to sign over their property to the government and to undertake never to return. Before long Jews whose livelihoods had been snatched away joined the exodus. The Six Day War caused Jews still holding public positions to be dismissed, and hundreds of Jews were arrested, beaten and tortured. Intervention by foreign countries, notably Franco's Spain, resulted in some being released and allowed to emigrate. During the 1970s further departures occurred, which robbed Egypt of all but a few hundred Jews. The history of the Jews in the former French colony of Syria followed a similar course, with a particularly extreme series of nationalist regimes after 1945 forcing the destruction of virtually the entire Jewish community, accompanied by especially brutal repression. By 1969, most Syrian Jews had fled to neighbouring Israel. This familiar pattern occurred in Iraq. Following that country's semi-independence in 1932, its once very influential Jewish community came under increasing threat from Iraqi nationalists. After 1948 most Iraqi Jews, perhaps as many as 125,000, fled to Israel. At the end of the twentieth century only about 150 remained in Saddam Hussein's Iraq.

The situation of Jews in Yemen is worth noting because of the extreme backwardness of both the Jewish community and of Yemenite society. Most

Jews in Yemen were craftsmen and pedlars living in the principal town, Sana'a, situated in the centre of the country, although in the seaports Jewish import–export merchants were to be found, dealing particularly in coffee. Since they were regarded as serfs without rights, Yemenite Jews found it necessary generation after generation to place themselves under the protection of Muslim patrons, who for a fee would avenge violence done to Jews and their families and recover property stolen from them by Muslims. Owing to their forlorn condition messianic expectations were high, and during the nineteenth century several pseudo-Messiahs appeared.

Ottoman rule in Yemen ended in 1911. Under the strict Muslim regime which lasted there from 1904 until 1948 Jews were heavily oppressed, and all orphaned Jewish children had to be converted to Islam. Since the Jews of Sana'a were, compulsorily, the town's hereditary sewer cleaners they had to pay ransom money to be allowed to emigrate. Large-scale emigration to Palestine had commenced in 1882 and in the years preceding the establishment of the State of Israel it exceeded the percentage of Jews moving there from any other country. From 1949 to 1950 no less than 43,000 Yemenite Jews moved to Israel in an airlift dubbed 'Operation Magic Carpet'. Most of the remainder emigrated to Israel during the 1950s, and within a few decades the Jewish presence in Yemen came to an end. 'Operation Magic Carpet' became celebrated – in part because many of those flown to Israel had never previously been on a wheeled vehicle of any kind.

An improvement in Persian Jewry's lot seemed to be heralded with the accession in 1736 of a Sunnite shah. But he was assassinated in 1747, when Shi'ite intolerance resumed its grip. The liberal-minded Shah who reigned from 1896 to 1907 abolished the discriminatory regulations facing his Jewish subjects, but under his traditionally-minded successor the Jews' high hopes of emancipation stalled. The founder of the Pahlevi dynasty, who became Shah in 1925, was a Western-oriented moderniser whose reforms curtailed the omnipotence of Islamic law in state affairs. Consequently the notion that Jews were ritually unclean gradually weakened, although it persisted in rural areas. Jews won the right to elect a representative to the parliament of Iran, as the country had become known. But only Muslims could become judges or government ministers. Although eligible, few Jews entered the public service. Their general status under the Pahlevis was generally good and their relations with the rest of the Iranian population mainly cordial. Nevertheless, in the decade immediately following the foundation of Israel many thousands of Iranian Jews settled there, and in Iran episodes of populist antisemitism, occasionally turning violent, broke out during times of turmoil and uncertainty. In 1960 the Shah courageously announced Iran's recognition of Israel. Opposition to his pro-western outlook and his progressive domestic policy gathered pace, leading to full-scale revolt, and in 1979, an ailing man, he fled Iran. The Ayatollah Ruholla Khomeini, a fundamentalist religious leader who was the symbol of the anti-Pahlevi revolutionary movement, returned from exile abroad and established a

strict Shi'ite regime. Khomeini's fierce animosity towards Israel was
reflected in the execution of several Jewish communal leaders with Zionist
sympathies. Anxieties regarding his rule led to renewed emigration, with
50,000 Iranian Jews settling in the United States. About 25,000 Jews
remained in Iran. Following Khomeini's death in 1989 Iran's Islamic revolution appeared to lose its ferocious edge. But the arrest ten years later of 13
Jews, including a teenager, on charges of spying for Israel, provided a
reminder that hardline elements had not been eclipsed.

Remote communities

Jews, generally described as part of the Sephardim, lived in remote places
throughout Asia and Africa, including India, China, and Ethiopia. The
presence at Cochin on the Malabar coast of south-west India of Jews who
physically resembled the native population had been known dimly in the
West since the Middle Ages. Of obscure origin, these so-called 'Black Jews'
of Cochin were subsequently joined by mainly Sephardi arrivals from the
Ottoman Empire and elsewhere, who were dubbed the 'White Jews'.
Influenced by the Indian caste system the two groups did not intermarry,
and also kept separate from a subsidiary group of Jews at Cochin, the converted descendants of native slaves, known as 'Freedmen,' who had to wait
until 1932 to be fully accepted by the other two. Further north along the
Indian coast, in the Konkan region south of Bombay, lived a community of
village-based agriculturalists who observed the Sabbath and other fundamentals of Judaism. Of Hindu appearance and speaking an indigenous language, they called themselves Bene Israel ('Children of Israel') and claimed
descent from shipwrecked Jews who had fled persecution in ancient
Palestine.

From 1663 to 1795 the Dutch ruled the Malabar coast, displacing the
Portuguese and ensuring freedom of religion for Cochin Jewry. Many Jews
became merchants and bankers, and others served the Dutch East India
Company as negotiators and interpreters. Their long isolation from their co-
religionists was ended, for the Jews of Amsterdam maintained continuous
links and supplied them with Hebrew books, and emissaries from Palestine
made visits. In the eighteenth century the Bene Israel emerged from their isolation, making initial contact with the Jews of Cochin, whom they greatly
outnumbered. Political instability in the Konkan region and a search for
new economic opportunities prompted some Bene Israel to move to
Bombay, and as a result their existence became generally known.
Subsequently, they were guided towards traditional Judaism by Baghdadi
Jews who settled in Bombay. A number of Bene Israel enlisted in the British
army in India as members of locally recruited regiments. They secured a
reputation as excellent soldiers, and some attained officer rank.

The Jews of India also proved to be capable civil administrators. They were demonstrably loyal to British interests. In Bombay and Calcutta many were employed in cotton, jute and tobacco processing works owned by co-religionists including the Sassoons. During the Nazi era many European Jewish refugees, mainly professionals, found a haven in India. But when India gained independence from Britain in 1948 the Jews there tended to feel uncomfortable. Although not discriminated against by the new regime, they were identified with the old one, and the mercantile enterprises in which many were engaged were largely undermined by government economic policies such as restrictions on the export of capital and on the importation of non-essential goods, and an impetus towards industrialisation. At the same time, strong Zionist feelings were spontaneously aroused by the establishment of the State of Israel, especially among the Jews of Cochin. Consequently, most of them settled in Israel. Many of the Bene Israel did too. In 1882 the Black Jews of Cochin had been declared to be true members of the Jewish people by the Chief Rabbi of Jerusalem, and the Bene Israel were declared such in 1954. Many others settled in Britain. But while the Cochin community had all but ceased to exist there was still, at the end of the twentieth century, a sizeable number of Bene Israel remaining in India, mostly in Bombay.

During the Dark Ages Jews reached China via accepted overland and overseas trade routes. In the tenth century, at the invitation of the Chinese emperor, who was keen to develop cotton fabric production in his country, a community was established at Kaifeng. It gradually assimilated, intermarried, and lost all traces of its Jewishness, its synagogue succumbing to decay in the nineteenth century. From the 1840s Jews from Iraq and India began to arrive in British Hong Kong. The most prominent of these settlers were the Kadoories, whose large mercantile interests in Hong Kong and Shanghai were laid by Sir Ellis Kadoorie (1865–1922), a British subject who had been born in Baghdad and educated at the Alliance school there. Several thousand Russian Jews settled in Harbin after the 1917 Soviet Revolution, and up to 20,000 refugees from Nazism found refuge in Shanghai. Following the Second World War most Jews in China relocated to Israel, the United States, and other countries. The Hong Kong community, founded in the 1850s, continues to exist.

The Jews of Ethiopia, physically indistinguishable from their fellow-countrymen, called themselves Beta Israel ('House of Israel') but were known as Falashas, an Amharic word meaning 'wanderers' or 'exiles'. Their origins were shrouded in legend. Living in a mountainous inland area where they worked at various crafts, they suffered much hardship for their religion, a form of Judaism based essentially on the Bible. They had been known to the West since the eighteenth century, but it was not until 1868, when the Alliance Israélite Universelle despatched a Paris-based Jewish orientalist to Ethiopia to investigate reports of Christian missionary activity among them, that European Jews made contact. Sustained attention was not paid to them until another Paris-based Jewish orientalist, who subsequently settled in Tel Aviv, made a series of visits beginning in 1904 and took up their cause. Determined to save them from extinction and bring them within the Jewish fold, he interested European and American Jews in them, and between the wars monetary donations from such wellwishers enabled schools for the Beta Israel to be set up in Ethiopia. Efforts to teach them Hebrew and introduce them to mainstream Judaism were resumed following the Second World War with the help of Israeli emissaries. The birth of the Jewish state excited the Beta Israel, who had long harboured expectations of settlement in Palestine. In 1975 the government of Israel acknowledged their right to immigrate under the 'Law of Return'. In 1984 and 1991 they were taken to Israel in dramatic rescue operations, and few remained in Ethiopia. By the last quarter of the twentieth century the process of *aliyah* to Israel had all but ended the existence of these ancient, remote Jewish communities, but a new life in the Jewish state had begun.

Further reading

Esther Benbassa and Aron Rodrigue, *Sephardi Jewry: A History of the Judeo-Spanish Community, 14th–20th Centuries* (Berkeley, Ca., 1995)

Arnold Blumberg, *Zion before Zionism 1838–1880* (New York, 1985)

Benjamin Braude and Bernard Lewis, eds, *Christians and Jews in the Ottoman Empire*, 2 vols (New York, 1982)

Shlomo Deshen and Walter P. Zenner, eds, *Jews among Muslims: Communities in the Precolonial Middle East* (London, 1996)

André N. Chouraqui, *Between East and West: A History of the Jews of North Africa* (New York, 1973)

Eli Faber, *A Time for Planting: The First Migration 1654–1820* (Baltimore, 1992; 'The Jewish People in America' series)

Jonathan Frankel, *The Damascus Affair: 'Ritual Murder' Politics, and the Jews in 1840* (Cambridge, 1997)

Harriet Pass Friedenreich, *The Jews of Yugoslavia* (Philadelphia, 1979)

Albert M. Hyamson, *The Sephardim of England: A History of the Spanish and Portuguese Community 1492–1951* (London, 1951; repr. 1991)

Albert M. Hyamson, ed., *The British Consulate in Relation to the Jews of Palestine* (London, 1939)

David Kessler, *The Falashas: The Forgotten Jews of Ethiopia* (London, 1996)

Bernard Lewis, *The Jews of Islam* (Princeton, 1984)

Sonia and V.D. Lipman, eds, *The Century of Moses Montefiore* (Oxford, 1985)

Aron Rodrigue, *Images of Sephardi and Eastern Jewries in Transition: The Teachers of the Alliance Israélite Universelle, 1860–1939* (Seattle, 1993)

Chaim Raphael, *The Sephardi Story: A Celebration of Jewish History* (London, 1991)

Stanford J. Shaw, *The Jews of the Ottoman Empire and the Turkish Republic* (London, 1991)

Nir Shohet, *The Story of an Exile: A Short History of the Jews of Iraq* (Tel Aviv, 1982)

Norman A. Stillman, *The Jews of Arab Lands: A History and Source Book* (Philadelphia, 1979)

Shifra Strizower, *The Children of Israel: The Benei Israel of Bombay* (Oxford, 1971)

Vicki Tamir, *Bulgaria and her Jews* (New York, 1979)

|6|

Antisemitism and philosemitism

Down the ages, Jews have probably experienced more hostility and hatred than any other single human group. Hostility to Jews forms a most important thread in the history of the Jewish people – so important that it must be discussed separately in this account of modern Jewish history. Jews were forced to live in ghettos; they were murdered in pogroms and massacres; during the Nazi era they were the victims of a genocide as terrible as any in history. However, down the ages there were also friends and admirers of the Jews who attempted to support them in times of persecution. It seems likely that their number has increased significantly in recent times.

Hostility to Jews, sometimes known as judeophobia, is usually termed 'antisemitism', a word coined by the German Wilhelm Marr, who is discussed below. Such hostility can take, and has taken, many different forms down the ages. Nevertheless, it has become common to distinguish two basic forms of antisemitism: religious and ethnic or racial. During the Middle Ages, and in some milieus since, antisemitism was fundamentally religious in nature, with Jews typically the objects of Christian hostility for 'crucifying Christ' and stubbornly refusing, ever since, to accept Jesus as the Saviour. Since the eighteenth century, particularly in reaction to the perceived prominence Jews gained in the economic and cultural life of Europe as a result of emancipation, most Western antisemitism has been ethnic or racial in nature, with Jews being attacked as a separate race or ethnic group which allegedly worked against the interests of the host population in which Jews found themselves. In modern times, Jews have also been defended by individuals sympathetic to their plight and opposed to antisemitism. Philosemitism – support and admiration for Jews by non-Jews – has also been a major theme of Jewish–Gentile relations in the Western world, especially in the English-speaking world, and must also be considered by historians.

The medieval legacy

In medieval Europe most hostility to Jews came from the Catholic Church (which was, until the Reformation, the only Christian Church in western and central Europe). Clerical hostility to Jews centred in the claim, mentioned above, that the Jews crucified Jesus and, ever since, have stubbornly refused to accept his messianic status. References in the Catholic Mass to 'perfidious Jews' (removed officially in the 1960s) kept hostility to the Jews alive throughout Catholic Europe, while Catholic usage emphasised the Passion (suffering) of Jesus at Easter, the anniversary of his crucifixion at the hands of the Jews. Easter often saw an upsurge of violent antisemitism and antisemitic acts. Medieval Christianity asserted that Jesus's crucifixion had negated the covenant between God and Abraham, and that the Jews were no longer God's chosen people, having been superseded by Christians.

Throughout Europe from the later Middle Ages, Jews were often confined, chiefly owing to Church teaching, to 'ghettos', that is, to Jewish quarters of towns which they could not leave at night. As shown in Chapter 2, the term 'ghetto' derives from the Jewish quarter of Venice, when Jews were first segregated in 1517, although the idea of confining Jews to separate residential areas was first mooted in the Lateran Councils of 1179 and 1215. Ghettoisation occurred throughout Europe, although it was not the invariable rule, and was particularly common in the areas of Italy which were most strongly dominated by the pope, and in what are now German and Czech cities like Frankfurt and Prague. Jews in ghettos enjoyed internal autonomy, but were also often compelled to wear a distinguishing badge wherever they went. Ghettos never existed in areas settled by Jews after the sixteenth century, such as Britain and parts of France. They were abolished from the late eighteenth century onwards, although, amazingly, the last European ghetto, in Rome, was not abolished until 1870. In 1939 the Nazis reintroduced the 'ghettoisation' of Jews in eastern Europe, in a vastly more brutal form, preparatory to the 'Final Solution'. (Nazi 'ghettos' were derived from Hitler's racist ideology and were not a direct continuation of the ghettos of medieval Europe.)

The medieval Church was also responsible for a number of other key components of clerical antisemitism. The crusades, the wars waged by Christian Europe between 1096 and about 1291 to reconquer the Holy Land from the Muslims, were often accompanied by the massacre of Jews in Europe by soldiers on the way to Palestine. Massacres of Jews occurred, especially, in the Rhineland in 1096–99, while zeal by English crusaders about to depart was also responsible in part for the infamous York massacre in 1190.

Two of the most notorious antisemitic accusations aimed by Christians against Jews also had their origins in medieval Europe, the so-called 'blood libel' and 'host desecration'. The 'blood libel' is the allegation that, at Passover, Jews murder Christian children in order to use their blood to bake *matzah*. A version of this grotesque and absurd claim was apparently first made in ancient times, but was first recorded in the Common Era in 1144 when a Christian child named William was found murdered at Norwich, England. It was claimed that William of Norwich, as he became known, was ritually murdered by Jews. The 'blood libel' accusation spread to the Continent in 1171. Apart from that of Simon of Trent in 1474, probably the best-known such accusation in medieval times concerns another English case, Hugh of Lincoln, in 1255. As a result of the discovery of the body of this boy, nearly one hundred Jews were executed and Hugh was popularly considered a saint. (Geoffrey Chaucer used this story as the basis for his 'Prioress's Tale' in *The Canterbury Tales*.) Although most intelligent Christians knew the 'blood libel' claim to be preposterous, it continued to surface even in relatively recent times. Probably the three most widely known 'blood libel' accusations in modern times were those made at Tisza-Eszlar in Hungary in 1882, Polna in Bohemia in 1899, and Kiev in Russia in 1911 (leading to the Beilis Affair of 1911–13). In the latter, the discovery of the body of a murdered boy in Kiev in 1911 led to the arrest of Mendel Beilis on a charge of ritual murder. In 1913 Beilis was tried and (remarkably in tsarist Russia) acquitted by a Russian court. The Beilis case led to world-wide protests on his behalf. Petitions by leading intellectuals appeared in America, Britain and Germany. Charges of 'ritual murder' continued in Eastern Europe during the inter-war era.

The second such charge made against Jews was that of 'host desecration', that is, the accusation that they defiled or poisoned the blood and bread employed by Catholic priests in the Mass. The first 'host desecration' charge occurred in Belitz, Germany, in 1243, and then spread throughout medieval Europe, leading to the persecution and massacre of local Jews. Besides these two well-known antisemitic charges made against Jews in medieval Europe, Jews were subjected to many other kinds of verbal, pictorial, and physical abuse. Engravings and other visual depictions of Jews frequently portrayed them with cloven hooves, with the disgusting *Judensau* (Jews' saw), and as the murderers of Christians.

The Reformation and the Enlightenment

The effects of the Reformation on the perception of Jews by others was mixed. In societies that were heavily influenced by Calvinist Protestantism, like the Netherlands and Puritan England, the situation for Jews became relatively better than it had been in pre-Reformation Europe. Protestantism largely dis-carded the Catholic emphasis on the Crucifixion and the sufferings of Jesus allegedly at the hands of the Jews, and was also more associated with con-stitutional guarantees of equal rights and with capitalism than was medieval Catholicism. On the other hand, the founding figure of the Reformation, Martin Luther (1483–1546), was notorious for his antisemitism. A German priest who broke with the Catholic Church in 1517, Luther originally spoke favourably of Jews and, in the hope of winning them to Protestantism, condemned Catholic antisemitism. When the Jews did not convert he became a ferocious Jew-hater. In 1543 he published *Concerning the Jews and their Lies*, which advocated, among other things, burning synagogues to the ground 'for the honour of God', destroying Jewish homes, forbidding rabbis to teach Jewish law, and expelling Jews from Germany. Luther's ferocity and virulent hatred of the Jews began a long tradition of German Protestant antisemitism (although it was seldom as extreme as that of its founder), and in some respects was a precursor of the fearsome language and imagery of the Nazis. About the only consolation is that Luther used equally extreme language about the pope and the Catholic Church, and about 'Turks' (Muslims).

As discussed in Chapter 2, the eighteenth century saw the Enlightenment and the Age of Reason. At first glance, the underlying principles of the reason and rationality embodied in the Enlightenment should have benefited the status and perception of Jews, especially by attacking the medieval superstition at the heart of so much clerical antisemitism, yet the major figures of the Enlightenment proved to be surprisingly mixed in their attitudes towards the Jews, and were often hostile. This strange paradox is probably best explained by the fact that many leading Enlightenment figures regarded the Jewish religion and the culture it produced as being just as much the products of primitive superstition and barbarism as the Catholic Church (which they especially detested). They rejected any claims made by the Jews that their religion was entitled to a special place because it was the ancestral faith of Christianity, and often accepted the stereotype of Jews as avaricious and miserly usurers. They insisted that in an enlightened society, one from which superstition was banished, all Jewish persons would enjoy the same rights as anyone else, but anticipated that Judaism would disappear as an organised religion. Many of these arguments are especially noticeable in the writings on the Jews by Voltaire (1694–1778), probably the foremost intellectual figure of the French Enlightenment.

This paradoxical mixture of views continued long afterwards, and was indicative of the difficulties which many on the Continental left, and among the European radicals, have had with Jewish corporate identity. Many on the European left wished to give to Jews the rights of all citizens, but were extremely uneasy with Jewish claims to a separate group identity with its own distinctive traditions. Jews were fully acceptable as Frenchmen (or Germans, or Austrians) but were unacceptable as Jews, if that meant that they had loyalties or ties above and beyond that of their fellow-citizens. The most famous exposition of this viewpoint is the often-quoted remark made in 1790 by the Count de Clermont-Tonnerre, a delegate to the French National Assembly, that Jews, as a nation, deserved nothing, but Jews, as a people, deserved everything. Indeed, over the next 200 years the European left often demonstrated surprising hostility to Jewish demands for recognition as 'a nation', especially to the Zionist attempt to create a Jewish homeland or state. This hostility persisted among some left-wing groups, especially Trotskyite parties, into the 1980s or later.

On the other hand, the figures of the Enlightenment, despite their views, never sought to persecute Jews as such, and regarded the persecution suffered by the Jews at the hands of the Catholic Church as barbaric. In France, those who viewed themselves as heirs of the Enlightenment, and who fully accepted the French Revolution's legacy of 'Liberty, Equality, and Fraternity', were almost always opposed to antisemitism and to the persecution of Jews when this became an issue, as during the Dreyfus Affair of the 1890s. Furthermore, the nature of Jewish identity has always been ambiguous. The increasing equality found by Jews in most European nations after the mid-eighteenth century also meant that they had to address and answer the question of what it meant to be a Jew in a modern nation-state, and for instance, how, if at all, Jewish Frenchmen differed in their loyalties and outlooks from non-Jewish Frenchmen. Were Jews only a religious entity, or were they also something more, with other forms of transnational group identity? There was never a consensus among Jews on this question, and perhaps only in the English-speaking democracies has it been successfully resolved, while for generations charges of 'dual loyalties' were hurled at Jews (and other minorities).

Nationalism and racism

Such ambiguities emerged chiefly because of the rise of the modern nation-state, where nationality was normally a matter of a distinctive national identity and of shared historical and cultural characteristics, including a common language. The status of the Jews in a world of nation-states was genuinely problematical. Until 1948 Jews had no state of their own, but regarded other Jews wherever they lived as, in some sense, their kinsmen. Religious Jews prayed every Passover that the coming year would see them in Jerusalem. In eastern Europe and elsewhere, Jews spoke a different language from their non-Jewish neighbours, often had different customs, and almost everywhere a distinctive socio-economic structure. *Could* Jews also be Poles, Romanians, Germans or Frenchmen? Could they be good, loyal and equal citizens of a country and still be Jews? What, indeed, was a Jew – an adherent of a religion, of a national/ethnic group, or of a distinctive culture demarcated by, for instance, a common language? If France fought Germany, would (or should) French Jews fight German Jews? Should Jews strive for a country of their own, such as every other European people was trying to achieve at that time, and where should it be? These questions have no straightforward responses, or were answered, if at all, by wider historical events often outside the control of the Jewish people. Certainly, until the second half of the twentieth century, there was absolutely no consensus among the world's Jews on any of these questions; indeed, the breadth of the responses offered by Jewish thinkers and ideologies to these questions was arguably wider than among any other people, who seldom had to decide the most basic questions of their national identity.

The rise of European nationalism was also responsible to a considerable degree for the rise of the 'new antisemitism'. The 'new' antisemitism differed from the old, described in Chapters 1 and 2, in defining Jews as primarily a racial or ethnic group (rather than a religion) and in centring its hostility to them in terms of the alleged ethnic differences between Jews and their host populations. To a certain extent the 'old' and 'new' antisemitism had a good deal in common. In both, Jews were depicted not merely as different (from Christians and from their host ethnic populations) but as evil, often as the embodiment of evil characteristics and as engaged in a great conspiracy of wickedness. Neither 'old' nor 'new' antisemites made much effort to understand the Jews and their history or to sympathise with their plight, and both, of course, regarded them as permanent outsiders to their own cultures. Nevertheless, there were, equally, differences between the two. Jews could escape from the opprobrium of antisemites of former times by converting to Christianity, but, in most formulations of the 'new' antisemitism, Jews could never escape from their Jewishness by conversion, assimilation, or other means. In the words of the notorious French antisemite Edouard Drumont (of whom more below): 'When a Jew converts, there is one more Christian, but there is not one less Jew.' (Nevertheless, apart from the German Nazis, most antisemitic theorists in late nineteenth- and early twentieth-century Europe agreed to tolerate a small, highly integrated and acculturated 'patriotic' Jewish minority in their country.) This left mass emigration as the solution to what became known as the Jewish 'problem', and many antisemites favoured the Zionist project for this reason. Hitler, of course, took the 'solution' to the Jewish 'problem' to its logical conclusion.

Closely allied to the nationalistic element in the 'new' antisemitism was racism, which insisted that the Jews' alleged bad traits were genetically innate. A 'racist' view of human society predated the nineteenth century but was apparently given scientific credence by the theories of Charles Darwin (1809–82), whose work *On the Origin of Species* (1859) was probably the most influential book of the nineteenth century. Darwin appeared to show that human beings are descended from animals (and were not divine creations as postulated in the Bible) which 'evolved' by a continuous struggle entailing (in the phrase of the philosopher Herbert Spencer, not of Darwin) 'the survival of the fittest'. Darwin himself was an English radical freethinker and naturalist (and most certainly no antisemite), who never at any time drew any conclusions of a political nature from his theories. Yet almost immediately his theories were used to give seemingly scientific underpinning to an amazing variety of ideological perspectives. For instance, *laissez-faire* liberals in Britain and the United States (such as Herbert Spencer) used Darwinism to justify unrestricted capitalistic competition and to oppose state benefits for the disadvantaged. At the other end of the spectrum, Karl Marx saw parallels between Darwinism and his own historical theories of 'dialectical materialism' and often compared himself to Darwin as a theorist. Most commonly, perhaps, Darwinism was used to justify racism and ultra-nationalism, with one particular race or nationality being seen as superior to others. Most commonly it was used to justify the theory of the 'Aryan' (northern European) race or races. Jews were usually seen by such theorists as constituting a different, inferior race, or a race that was different from and intellectually equal to the 'Aryans' but engaged in a permanent struggle for domination with them. Social Darwinism (the application of Darwin's work to theories of how society should be organised, especially by ultra-nationalists) came to underpin much political and social thought in late nineteenth-century Europe. It was often directed not merely against Jews but against anyone deemed different and 'primitive', especially Asians, Africans, American Indians, and even southern Europeans and the Irish. Social Darwinism came, in particular, to be a predominant element in European right-wing thought from about 1870 until 1945, usually with an explicitly or implicitly antisemitic edge to it.

It is somewhat difficult, however, to differentiate the nationalistic from the racialist elements in the 'new' antisemitism. Further, it was also the case that nationalism was often a liberating (and liberal) force, and that Zionism – Jewish nationalism – was also a product of these same forces. The nationalistic element in the new antisemitism long preceded the racist element. For instance, in 1793 Johann Gottlieb Fichte (1792–1814), the German philosopher, described 'the Jewish Nation' as 'a state within a state' which 'is infiltrating almost every country in Europe', was 'in a state of perpetual war with all these countries', and was 'founded on the hatred of mankind'. Fichte also stated that 'I can see absolutely no way of giving them civic rights' and 'no other way to protect ourselves from the Jews, except if we conquer their promised land for them and send all of them there'. (Fichte, however, also stated somewhat confusingly in the same work that Jews 'must have human rights . . . for they *are* human and their malevolence does not justify our becoming like them'.)

During the nineteenth century there emerged a number of key figures in the evolution of the 'new antisemitism' whose names are well known to students of this subject. Additionally, there also were a number of persisting themes which came to be found again and again among European antisemites. Joseph Arthur, Comte de Gobineau (1816–82), a French diplomat, produced, in 1853–55 (shortly before the publication of Darwin's *Origin of Species*) his *Essai sur l' inégalité des races humaines*, one of the revered texts of modern racism. Gobineau argued that the white race, especially the Nordics, were superior to other races. Gobineau was not an antisemite, but his work was widely used to justify racist theories depicting Jews as inferior to Aryans. So was that of the celebrated German philosopher Friedrich Nietzsche (1844–1900), with his glorification of blond, blue-eyed northern

Europeans, from whom he expected a race of supermen to develop. Nietzsche was not explicitly anti-Jewish but his views nourished the pan-Germanism which arose in the nineteenth century, and greatly influenced the Nazis.

The pan-German movement was founded on the idea and idealisation of the *Volk* – all people of Teutonic stock. It aimed at the unification of all German-speaking states including Austria. It regarded Jews as outsiders, for they were not part of the *Volk*. It viewed contemporary history as a struggle between Jewry (*Judentum*) and Germanism (*Deutschtum*). This image of inexorable conflict was reinforced by the writings of such men as Paul de Lagarde, Julius Langbehn, and Heinrich von Treitschke. Lagarde (1827–91), was a well-known Bible scholar and orientalist who wrote that Christianity 'is doomed to extinction because of the Jewish elements which it absorbed'. Like many antisemites of his type he saw Jews as the agents of modernism, liberalism, and cultural decadence. He described them as 'at least in Europe the masters of the non-Jews ... a terrible misfortune for every European people'. Jews, he wrote, were 'the carriers of decay and pollute every national culture, they exploit the human and material resources of their hosts, they destroy all faith and spread materialism and liberalism'. He saw their numerical preponderance in the higher professions and the universities as evidence of their determination to subjugate Germans, who were ill-advised to allow Jews to live amongst them: 'Every Jew is proof of the enfeeblement of our national life and of the worthlessness of what we call the Christian religion.' Jews, he wrote in one place, were 'usurious vermin'; in another he described them as 'trichinae and bacilli [worms and bacteria] who must be exterminated as quickly and thoroughly as possible'. Despite this biological imagery and intemperate language, reminiscent of Hitler's in *Mein Kampf*, he denied that he was a racist since he knew Jews who had succeeded in 'purifying' themselves of their undesirable characteristics. In 1885 Lagarde, who felt that Germany should colonise eastern Europe, advocated deportation to Madagascar for the Jews of that region.

Langbehn (1851–1907) was an antisemite of similar anti-modern, anti-liberal ilk. In a tract published in 1890, full of *völkisch* ideas, he conceded that Jews of the old-fashioned, pious type were tolerable. But in an enlarged edition published two years later he inveighed venomously against Jews of non-Orthodox inclination and modernistic outlook. 'The aspiration of present-day Jews for spiritual and material domination evokes a simple phrase: Germany for the Germans,' he declared. 'A Jew can no more become a German than a plum can turn into an apple.' Emancipation was a mistake; even Lessing, its arch-champion, would regard it as such if he could observe its consequences. Jews were 'a poison', 'a pest and a cholera', which would have to be eradicated. Langbehn was a relatively obscure figure, but his nasty little work proved a bestseller, and appealed especially to members of the neo-Romantic German Youth Movement, who hankered after an agrarian, non-urban national idyll.

Heinrich von Treitschke (1834–96) was a professor of history at Berlin University and the Prussian state historian. Originally a liberal, he became more and more intensely nationalistic. To him, Germany, as a 'young' nation – it had achieved unification in 1871 – needed protection from destructive foreign influences, of which the Jews were a serious example (he also condemned many other foreign influences in the country, and was an anti-Catholic). Owing to his towering academic reputation Treitschke became one of the most heeded antisemitic voices. Especially influential was a series of articles he wrote in 1879–80 in a journal which he edited. Warning, *inter alia*, that the children and grandchildren of the seemingly inexhaustible hordes of *Ostjuden* who were pouring into Germany from Poland would eventually dominate key institutions such as the press and stock exchange, he used the phrase 'the Jews are our misfortune'. It became a well-known and much-repeated rallying cry in antisemitic circles, and was taken up by the Nazis. Although he was a comparative moderate who condemned antisemitic excesses, Treitschke lent German antisemitism much respectability.

Another confirmed antisemite and German nationalist was Richard Wagner (1813–83), the celebrated composer, who may well have been the son of a Jew named Geyer. In 1850 Wagner published, under a pseudonym, a work entitled *Das Judentum in Die Musik* (*Jewry in Music*) which contrasted the nationally-rooted musical creativity of most European nations with the rootless, popular but (to him) worthless music produced by such Jewish composers as Meyerbeer and Offenbach. According to Wagner, Jews represented a threat to the national musical cultures of Europe. Although he never again carried his antisemitism into the public sphere, he detested Jews and always wore a glove when having to shake hands with Jewish performers. His operas, such as *Siegfried* and *Gotterdämerung*, celebrated the ancient Nordic gods and decried the power of money and gold. Long after his death, he became Hitler's favourite composer (for which, of course, Wagner was not responsible) and orchestras in Israel boycotted his works until the year 2000, when one of them performed the *Siegfried Idyll*. In 1908 his daughter married Houston Stewart Chamberlain (1855–1927), another notable antisemite. Born in Southsea, England, the son of a British admiral and a German mother (and incidentally no relation to the famous Chamberlain family of politicians), Chamberlain lived for most of his life in Germany, which he idealised. In 1899 he wrote *The Foundations of the Nineteenth Century*, in which he took Gobineau's racial view of human development, and explicitly advanced the theory that Aryans and Jews were in more or less permanent conflict. He maintained that the fact that Jews married only among themselves gave them enormous 'racial' strength. He deplored their increasing influence in modern Europe. Although not a vicious Jew-hater, he lived long enough to befriend Hitler and – rather amazingly, given the Nazis' obscurity at the time – hail him as the coming man of German nationalism. Alfred Rosenberg termed the antisemitic book he wrote *The Myth of the Twentieth Century* in honour of Chamberlain's work.

The economic recession of the mid-1870s to early 1890s, precipitated by the stock market crash of 1873 and accompanied by an increase in urban unemployment, saw the rise of antisemitism as a political movement in Germany. There were demands for repeal of the emancipation law. Perhaps the first party to engage in demagogic antisemitism was the Christian Social Workers' Party, founded in 1878 by Adolf Stöcker (1835–1909), a Lutheran minister who would later take his seat in the Reichstag, Germany's parliament. Stöcker attacked 'Jewish capital' which, he alleged, ran the banking system and exploited Jewish labour, and the Jewish destruction of traditional values. He advocated limiting the number of Jews in public life. His main appeal was to the lower middle class of artisans and tradesmen who had suffered as a result of the 1873 crash. Much of his rhetoric and attraction surfaced repeatedly among other German antisemitic movements, including the Nazi party. Another antisemitic political theorist was Eugen Dühring (1833–1921), a philosopher and economist who taught at Berlin University and was influential in the Social Democratic Party. In 1881 he published a book called *The Jewish Question* (*Die Judenfrage*), which explored the themes of race, morals and culture, and made the expulsion of the 'incomparably inferior [Jewish] race' from public office and economic life a matter of German 'racial honour'.

By this time the word 'antisemitic' had been introduced into the vocabulary, with the foundation in 1879 by Wilhelm Marr (1819–1904) of the League of Antisemites (Antisemiten-Liga). Marr was a journalist who had already written two anti-Jewish works, one of them entitled *The Victory of Judaism over Germandom Considered from a Non-Religious Point of View*, which had reached its twelfth edition by 1879. Despite apparently denoting all 'semites' (the actual or supposed descendants of Shem, one of Noah's sons), Marr's term does not refer to Arabs or any other 'semitic' people apart from Jews. He coined it to cover the 'new' hostility which defined the Jewish people as a race rather than a religious group; it has come to describe all forms of antipathy to Jews. His League aimed to save Germany 'from complete judaisation and to make life tolerable there for the descendants of the original inhabitants'. It marked the earliest attempt to create a popular mass political movement based on hatred for Jews, linking people from various parties and backgrounds.

In 1880 an Antisemites' Petition, as it was known, was circulated by disgruntled young political activists in Berlin. Claiming that an 'alien tribe' had rapidly gained the upper hand in Germany since unification, it demanded a curb on the immigration of *Ostjuden*, the exclusion of Jews from senior administrative and political posts as well as from state primary school teaching, and the introduction of a special census to monitor Jewish demographics. This petition gathered over 250,000 signatures, 10,000 of them in Berlin. In 1881 it was presented to Germany's chancellor, Bismarck, but had no effect. Since antisemitism was the only issue holding the activists together, their alliance soon disintegrated. It should be noted that these end-of-century antisemitic parties never received more than a tiny per cent of the vote in national elections, and that none of the antisemitic bills introduced into the Reichstag between 1880 and 1914 was passed or had the slightest chance of being enacted.

In neighbouring Austria, which had over twice as many Jews as Germany, hostility to Jews also increased during the nineteenth century, especially in Vienna. That city saw an enormous increase in its Jewish population between 1860 (6000 Jews) and 1910 (175,000) mainly as a result of an influx of newcomers following emancipation in 1867. Many Viennese felt that their city was being invaded by Jewish paupers (*Betteljuden*), peddlers and petty dealers from Galicia. By and large, Galician Jews were poor, economically backward, religiously traditional and secularly uneducated – a very visible, seemingly unabsorbable and most unwelcome presence in the cultured and sophisticated Austrian capital. (Watching developments from Germany, Treitschke described Austria as being 'unspeakably corrupted by semitism', and so it appeared to many Austrians.) As in Germany, resentment against Jews was exacerbated by the positions of influence and access to the higher professions many had attained since emancipation. The high number of Jews in law and medicine was greatly disproportionate to their percentage of the Austrian population. Most newspaper proprietors were Jews, and like Jews in general they were associated with political liberalism, which antagonised conservatives. The majority of banks in the capital, indeed in the entire country, were in Jewish hands, and Jews were prominently involved in entrepreneurial finance. When Austria was hit – and hit particularly hard – by the economic depression of 1873, culpability for the ruin of numerous small investors was ascribed to Jews.

Such developments concerned a radical populist politician from a recently ennobled family, Georg Ritter von Schönerer (1842–1921). At first his antisemitism confined itself to attacking what he saw as the deleterious impact of 'Jewish' capitalism on the livelihoods of artisans and peasants, decrying the 'judaised' press and Liberal Party. But during the 1880s, with his increasing commitment to pan-Germanism, his anti-Jewish rhetoric acquired an unmistakably racist edge. He campaigned for the 'removal of Jewish influence from all sections of public life' and founded an explicitly antisemitic party. There are indications that his political credo, with its blend of nationalism, quasi-socialism, and Jew-hatred, influenced Hitler. It certainly appealed to sections of the economically disadvantaged lower classes, and of the intelligentsia disgruntled by Jewish competition in the job market, as well as to other elements in the population seeking scapegoats for perceived societal ills or personal setbacks. But he never acquired a mass following, and his political star dimmed after 1888, when he and several associates broke into the premises of a Jewish-owned newspaper and beat its staff with sticks. For this crime he served a short term of imprisonment and was stripped of his aristocratic rank.

Schönerer has been described as a 'sincere' antisemite, in contrast to the prominent Jew-baiter of *fin-de-siècle* Vienna, Karl Lueger (1844–1910), whose influence waxed as Schönerer's waned. As mayor of Vienna from 1897 until 1910 Lueger dismissed Jewish officials, harassed Jewish peddlers, and tried to create schools for gentiles only. His mayoralty legitimated antisemitic debate. Adolf Hitler's youthful sojourn in Vienna, where he derived his antisemitic world-view, began during Lueger's regime. Rather astonishingly, Lueger had numerous Jewish associates; indeed, a rumour, apparently without foundation, circulated during his period of office alleging that he had a Jewish grandparent. He became famous for asserting, 'I decide who is a Jew.' He was a political opportunist who used the Jewish question to gain power in the municipal politics of the city that was perhaps the classical battleground in Europe between a progressive, modernist Jewry and Jewry's antisemitic, anti-modernist foes.

Even in France, the nation of the great 1789 Revolution and of the slogan 'Liberty, Equality, Fraternity', Jews were – as we have seen – by no means invariably regarded sympathetically, even by the political left. The Revolution rent the French nation politically and ideologically, divided between those who accepted its legacy and those who did not. The French right wing, which generally did not, originally preferred France to be ruled by an absolutist monarchy closely linked to the Catholic Church and the aristocracy. As the nineteenth century wore on, the right increasingly favoured the idea of an authoritarian dictator, a 'man on horseback' – such as General Boulanger, whose National Party and bid for power attracted considerable support in the late 1880s – who would lead the nation and save it from its enemies. These enemies were, as far as the right was concerned, so-called Protestants (a very small component of the French population), Freemasons, and Jews. Antisemitism became a significant component of the French right surprisingly early (perhaps as early as in Germany), and remained integral to its thinking until the overthrow of the Vichy regime. One reason for this was the great prominence in France of the Rothschild family, who in the 1840s were certainly the richest and most economically powerful family in the country. Moreover, in the wake of emancipation many Jews from the north-eastern border areas had flocked to Paris and become successful, affluent businessmen.

Throughout the nineteenth century there was an underground antisemitic feeling in France, which began to surface from about 1870. It had been fed by the pens of several propagandists. For instance, in 1845 Alphonse de Toussenel (1803–85), a popular writer on natural history, brought out a book in which he portrayed Jewish industrialists and entrepreneurs as avaricious parasites, ruining hardworking peasants and craftsmen and wantonly destroying the geographical environment with their factories and railways. Tellingly, it was titled *Les Juifs, rois de l'époque*. Toussenel drew his ideas from those of the well-known social reformer François Fourier (1772–1837), who in a book published in 1808 had denounced Jews on economic grounds, calling them the most 'despicable' people in history and decrying their emancipation. (Fourier, however, had gone on to become, in effect, a Zionist, expediently advocating the return of Jews to Palestine, where they would form a nation run on socialistic principles.) A book by Henri Gougenot des Mousseaux (1805–76), published in 1869, entitled *Le Juif, le judaïsme et la judaïsation des peuples chrétiens*, presented the existence of the Alliance Israélite Universelle as evidence of a sinister plot by Jews, aided by liberals and Freemasons, to dominate the Christian world. A similar theme was taken by a reactionary Catholic cleric, Abbé Chabauty, in a book which appeared in 1882. An acclaimed poet and novelist, the Boulangist Maurice Barrès (1862–1923), who as a leading right-wing politician and theorist regularly denounced what he regarded as Jewry's overpowerful presence in France's economic life, described antisemitism in 1889 as a 'national union' in which Frenchmen of various social backgrounds felt driven to make common cause. As in Germany, cartoons appeared in antisemitic publications, caricaturing 'typical' Jewish physiognomic features to the point of presenting Jews as hideously ugly and repellent, and depicting Jews – in a variety of symbolic poses – in control of the destinies of the world through their cunning and 'money power'. Unflattering stereotypes of Jews, stressing their alleged alienness, rapaciousness, social climbing, and stranglehold over the nation, appeared in works by such well-known nineteenth- and twentieth-century literary figures as Alphonse Daudet, Guy de Maupassant and André Gide.

The most significant antisemitic theorist in nineteenth-century France was Edouard Drumont (1844–1917), who was dubbed 'the pope of antisemitism'. His two-volume work *La France Juive*, published in 1886, had a phenomenal sale down to the First World War. Drumont blamed the Jews, and their allies – a familiar assortment of Freemasons, Protestants, cosmopolitans, foreigners, liberals and atheistic freethinkers – for the misfortunes which had befallen France. Clericalist-authoritarian (ultramontane) forces linked with sections of the Catholic Church proved especially receptive. So did small shopkeepers and workers in traditional handicrafts, the type of people who supported Boulanger. Resentful of economic competition from new department stores and mass production and nostalgia for the old Paris that had been transformed by modern buildings and boulevards, they found through Drumont's pen a scapegoat in Jews. France's defeat in the Franco-Prussian War of 1870–71 and the consequent cessation of most of Alsace and Lorraine to the victor exacerbated suspicions that the Jews of those provinces were pro-German; this, together with Drumont's explicit aspersions in his antisemitic newspaper *La Libre Parole* on the fidelity of Jewish officers in the French army provided the background to the Dreyfus Affair (considered below). During the 1890s *La Libre Parole* enjoyed a healthy circulation of 200,000.

Russian antisemitism tended to remain more heavily based in the 'old' Christian antisemitism than that of western and central Europe, something to be expected in view of the pre-modern nature of Russian society under the tsars. Tsarist Russia was notorious both for the extent of its anti-semitism and for the anti-Jewish violence of the pogroms which began in 1881. By the late nineteenth century, however, many of the familiar themes of modern antisemitism had entered Russian life, with the Jews depicted as an evil international conspiracy, a world-wide economic elite, agents of revolutionary movements, and the like. Indeed, as shown in Chapter 4, probably the most infamous of all the texts of modern antisemitism emerged from tsarist Russia at this time, the so-called *Protocols of the [Learned] Elders of Zion*. This was a forgery, apparently instigated by the regime (see Chapter 4), and appears to date from the turn of the century (although it seems to have been based on older, similar works) and was first published in Russian in 1905. Its purports to be the transcript of a speech made by the head of the 'Elders of Zion' to other senior Jewish leaders putting forth a plan for Jewish world domination, in league with Freemasons, liberals, and socialists. According to the *Protocols*, every means – the economy, the press, the educational system, and so on – would be employed throughout Europe to achieve Jewish international domination. It is difficult to see how any sane person could take this farrago seriously, yet, especially in the troubled period immediately following the First World War, the *Protocols* enjoyed enormous international popularity, even, at least initially, in countries such as Britain. Some saw it as the means to link and explain all the recent horrors of European society, together with the perceived prominence of the Jews in the Russian Revolution and other revolutionary movements. The *Protocols* influenced the Nazis and, although shown to be a forgery as early as 1921, it continues to be disseminated, even today, by far right-wing and Arab extremist sources.

Few of the most important theorists of antisemitism emerged from the English-speaking world. Indeed, most antisemites in modern Britain and the United States appear to have been strongly derivative of modes of hostility to Jews clearly deriving from Europe, which may in part account for the rel-ative lack of success these have enjoyed. In Britain and still more the United States, to talk, for instance, of Jews 'controlling' the national economy was much less plausible than in many continental countries, since they plainly did not control the economy of either country and, indeed, were virtually unrepresented among the multi-millionaires and 'robber baron' tycoons of America's post-Civil War 'gilded age' capitalism. Perhaps the only anti-semitic work which is generally discussed in histories of antisemitism to emerge from the great English-speaking democracies is 'The International Jew', a series of articles published in *The Dearborn Independent*, a Michigan newspaper owned by Henry Ford, the motor car manufacturing multi-millionaire. These articles subsequently appeared in book form (4 vols, 1920–22; single vol., 1924), and sold 500,000 copies. As with so many antisemitic tracts, *The International Jew* blamed the Jews for virtually all the ills of the modern world, especially the Russian Revolution and the alleged undermining of moral values in the post-war world. It is difficult to know just how much of the text was actually written by Ford, since the author demonstrates very sophisticated knowledge (such as a discussion of the philosophy of Spinoza), which the poorly-educated tycoon was unlikely to have possessed. It is difficult, too, to understand why his aversion to Jews arose. Ironically, the mass marketing of the Model T Ford probably contributed as much to the undermining of traditional moral values in America as anything else, and Ford's blaming of the Jews may be an interesting example of what psychologists term 'projection'. In 1921, in response to Ford's outburst, 121 eminent Americans signed a keynote petition against the emergence of antisemitism in the United States. 'We believe it should not be left to men and women of the Jewish faith to fight this evil, but that it is in a very special sense the duty of citizens who are not Jews by ancestry or faith,' they explained. Signatories included President William H. Taft, ex-President Woodrow Wilson, other political luminaries, distinguished educators, editors, lawyers, businessmen, and clergymen of all denominations. Many signatories were no strangers to the Jewish cause, having been prominently involved in protests over tsarist persecution; many were to crusade against Nazi antisemitism. In 1927 Ford publicly recanted his antisemitic views and apologised to America's Jewish leaders. But *The International Jew* had already caused an increase in antisemitism among many Americans of the isolationist 1920s.

Apart from these major landmarks in the evolution of the 'new' antisemitism, there were also a number of key incidents or antisemitic crises which became well known and which often had a seminal effect upon the responses mounted by the Jewish people to antisemitism and upon relations between Jews and non-Jews as well, on occasion, as upon much wider events. Some of these should certainly be noted in any account of modern antisemitism. They included the so-called 'Hep! Hep!' riots which occurred in Germany in the summer of 1819 and then spread to Denmark (see Chapter 2, p.36). The German authorities used these riots to argue that the emancipation of Jews in Germany would generate a popular anti-Jewish backlash, and would be unwise. The blood libel in Syria in 1840 known as the Damascus Affair (see Chapter 5, p.98) was chiefly important because of the outrage it aroused in Western Jewish and liberal circles. In particular two of the main Jewish leaders of the West, Sir Moses Montefiore and Adolphe Crémieux, personally intervened on behalf of their beleaguered brethren in Damascus. Moreover, the Damascus Affair was one of the very first occasions in which emancipated and politically powerful Western Jews used their influence to combat antisemitism in a country where Jews were oppressed, and constituted an important precedent for the notion that Western Jews had an obligation to defend their persecuted co-religionists. It also witnessed the coming to the limelight of the powerful Western Jewish leader, often a man of wealth and influence in his own country, to speak and act on behalf of less fortunate Jews, a tradition which continues to this day. As well, it formed a landmark in the development of a modern international consciousness among Western Jews of antisemitism and power politics.

Less than twenty years later there occurred the Mortara Affair. In 1858, a seven-year-old Jewish boy named Edgardo Mortara was kidnapped by papal gendarmes in Bologna and brought up as a Christian. This was, of course, not normal, and the pretext for kidnapping was the claim that six years earlier his Catholic nurse had informally baptised him when she believed him to be dying. As we saw in Chapter 2, an eighteenth-century pope had ruled that baptisms by lay people were valid. The Mortara Affair aroused world-wide indignation in Jewish and liberal circles. The Catholic Church was widely condemned for employing medieval, barbaric tactics. Montefiore and the leaders of French Jewry attempted unsuccessfully to secure the boy's release. Ironically, Mortara not merely remained a Catholic, but became a priest. One lasting outcome of the Mortara Affair was the foundation in Paris of the Alliance Israélite Universelle, a body founded in 1860 to defend Jewish rights internationally and to provide assistance to Jewish communities in developing countries.

The most horrifying wave of anti-Jewish violence in nineteenth-century Europe comprised the pogroms which occurred in Russia (especially southern Russia) between 1881 and 1906. (Further violent outbreaks against the Jews also occurred in Russia in 1917–21.) 'Pogrom', which means 'devastation' in Russian, denoted mass outbreaks of anti-Jewish violence, in which many thousands of Jews were killed. Historians have debated their causes and, in particular, whether they were spontaneous or organised by extreme right-wing groups, probably with the co-operation of the tsarist government. The pogroms of 1881–2 led directly to the mass emigration of millions of Russian Jews to America and elsewhere. Probably the most infamous pogrom occurred at Kishinev (in what is today the Republic of Moldavia) in June 1903 following a 'ritual murder' rumour. The Kishinev massacre was also notorious for the fact that the police not merely refused to stop the rioters (who numbered only between 100 and 300) but, according to eye-witnesses, pointed out Jewish houses and businesses to them. This atrocity gave strength to the emerging Zionist movement as well as leading to a further wave of migration by Russian Jews to the 'New Diaspora'. Mass rallies condemning the violence were held in America and elsewhere. The topic of the pogroms is covered in more detail in Chapter 4.

One of the most infamous antisemitic events of the nineteenth century was the Dreyfus Affair. Alfred Dreyfus (1859–1935), a Jewish captain on the French general staff, was accused in 1894 of having sold secret documents to the German military, tried, and condemned to life imprisonment on Devil's Island off French Guiana. Dreyfus protested his innocence, and there seems little doubt that his Jewish background played a major part in his conviction, which was based wholly on forged evidence. A national campaign by French radicals and liberals to clear his name, spearheaded by the celebrated (non-Jewish) writer Emile Zola, with his famous essay *J'accuse* (which appeared in Georges Clemenceau's journal *L'Aurore* in January 1898), divided France. Dreyfus was eventually pardoned by the French president, and restored to his former rank. Most of the French right wing, including much of the Catholic Church and the military, remained convinced that Dreyfus was guilty, in part because he was a Jew (and in addition because he was born in German-speaking Alsace). Even more than before, antisemitism became a major component of right-wing French politics. Nevertheless, in the end the pro-Dreyfusards (as they were known) triumphed, and in 1905 secured the separation of church and state in France. Dreyfus also enjoyed widespread support throughout the world. For the Jewish people, the most momentous outcome of the Dreyfus Affair was that it led directly to Theodor Herzl's conversion to Zionism and his publication of *Der Judenstaat*.

While the amount of antisemitism in Britain and the Empire (later Commonwealth) at that or any other time must not be exaggerated there were certain manifestations of it. In 1881 the eminent left-liberal political economist Goldwin Smith published a series of disturbingly antisemitic articles in a leading periodical. Radical antisemitism, with wealthy Jews and their 'finance capital' in its sights, became evident during the Boer War (1899–1901) with, for example, the Trades Union Congress passing a resolution condemning that conflict as an attempt to 'secure the gold fields of South Africa for cosmopolitan Jews most of whom had no patriotism and no country'. This view echoed that of another famous leftist economist, J.A. Hobson. This kind of thing was also evident in labour circles in Australia and elsewhere. During the Edwardian period unpleasant Jewish characters, especially grasping moneylenders, crept into the pages of popular British fiction, especially detective fiction. Two of the most notable British writers of the first half of the twentieth century, Hilaire Belloc and G.K. Chesterton, were well-known for their anti-Jewish remarks, although Chesterton, like several other prominent Britons who had indulged in mild antisemitism, would repent of his prejudice when confronted with the excesses of Nazism.

The First World War

Historians generally believe that the First World War was a great misfortune for the Jews. Although tsarism disappeared and, on paper, Jews secured legal equality in all of the successor states to the former continental European regimes, in practice the situation of Jews generally and increasingly deteriorated while the amount of antisemitism grew. The war itself, together with the Bolshevik Revolution of 1917, greatly enhanced the virulence of the antisemitic extreme right throughout Europe, who saw the Jews as heading a vast international conspiracy of evil and as being responsible for the Russian Revolution. The perception of Jews as Marxists was kindled by the prominent part played by such socialistic Jews as Leon Trotsky in Russia, Rosa Luxemburg in Germany, and Béla Kun in Hungary, as well as by the many prominent revolutionaries and Communists who were not Jews yet were assumed to be. In Germany and elsewhere it was believed in right-wing circles that all this activity was part of a Jewish–Marxist plot eventually to rule the world. As a Munich newspaper put it in 1919: 'These are dreadful times in which Christian-hating, circumcised Asiatics everywhere are raising their bloodstained hands to strangle us in droves.' Hitler wrote: 'If with the help of his Marxist creed the Jew is victorious over the peoples of the world, his crown will be the funeral wreath of humanity.' He tersely pronounced the remedy to be 'Annihilation and extermination of the Marxist world-view'.

In 1907 Charles Maurras (1868–1952), who like Maurice Barrès was a leading intellectual exponent of antisemitism, founded (with Alphonse Daudet's son Léon, who had written for *La Libre Parole*) a royalist reactionary journal called *L'Action Française*. Targeting Jews as well as Protestants, Freemasons and foreigners – the much-traduced *métèque* elements who were allegedly destroying France – it sought the restoration of the pre-Revolutionary order. During the inter-war period, during which he served for several years as a parliamentarian, Maurras grew shriller in his antisemitism. His antipathy towards Jews was exacerbated by the perceived threat of Bolshevism, by a sense of France's weakness in the face of external aggression, and by an influx of Jews from Germany and eastern Europe. It was especially apparent during the premiership of the Jewish socialist Léon Blum, who from 1936 to 1937 headed a Popular Front government consisting of his own party and other leftist and moderate groups. Such prejudices, held by nationalistic reactionaries who supported *L'Action Française*, helped to prepare the way for the anti-Jewish measures taken by Marshal Pétain's Vichy government formed after France's military collapse early in the Second World War and partial occupation by the Germans. The Vichy regime (1940–44) wasted no time in removing Jews from important posts in the military and the civil service, and followed this by imposing crippling quotas on the number of Jews to be employed in the professions and in educational institutions. It passed a law authorising government confiscation of Jewish property, and collaborated with the Nazis in the deportation of 100,000 Jews within its jurisdiction to their deaths.

During the inter-war period, European Jews also suffered from other negative pressures. The newly-independent states of central and eastern Europe, especially Poland, were trying to establish their own national identities, and saw little place for their Jews. Most such states believed that there were simply too many Jews in Europe, and that it would be best if most emigrated. As many Jews were living in poverty and oppression, a large number would have liked to emigrate, but it was at this time that the states of the 'New Diaspora' largely closed their doors to most new immigrants (non-Jews as well as Jews), especially the United States with its quota systems of 1921 and 1924. While some measure of prosperity and stability was restored to Europe in the mid- to late 1920s, the coming of the Great Depression in 1929, with the mass unemployment this engendered, made a difficult situation immeasurably worse, and was directly responsible for the rise of virulently antisemitic fascist and pro-Nazi parties and movements in the 1930s.

While the English-speaking democracies were largely immune to the worst of the trends, there also seems little doubt that the amount of antisemitism increased even there in the inter-war years. The equation of Jews with Bolshevism was also made in the English-speaking world. Even *The Times* described the non-Jewish Lenin and his motley crew of associates as 'adventurers of Russian–Jewish blood'. The period 1917–22 saw the propagation of conspiracy theory antisemitism there, the stock-in-trade of Henry Hamilton Beamish, founder of an extreme right-wing organisation known as The Britons; of Arnold S. Leese, head of the Imperial Fascist League; and of Nesta M. Webster, author of *World Revolution* (1920). Right-wing antisemitism was to become associated with Oswald Mosley and his British Union of Fascists during the 1930s. Not all of it, however, was confined to the lunatic fringes of public life. For example, Viscount Sydenham, a respected former colonial governor, was convinced that Jews were plotting the disintegration of the British Empire. While not antisemitic, in a reflection of public panic over the Bolshevik menace, both *The Times* and *The Morning Post*, a respectable Tory newspaper of long standing, published *The Protocols of the [Learned] Elders of Zion* and discussed whether they might in fact be genuine: *The Times* concluded, in a definitive statement issued in 1921, that they were not.

The United States witnessed the rise of movements like the second Ku Klux Klan, which was outspokenly antisemitic (as well as virulently anti-Catholic and anti-black; the first Ku Klux Klan, which existed after the American Civil War of 1861–65, was not antisemitic). Antisemitic public figures such as Father Charles Coughlin, the 'radio priest' whose broadcasts consisted of anti-Jewish invective, also flourished. Social and economic antisemitism was also widespread, with, for instance, most of America's elite private universities – such as Harvard, Princeton, and Yale – limiting the number of Jews in each entering class of freshmen to 10 per cent, and Jews were discriminated against by many employers, landlords, and country clubs. Of course, these trends should not be exaggerated: there was less antisemitic discrimination of this kind in Britain and in Commonwealth countries such as Australia, while America's national politicians and public institutions were never antisemitic. Indeed, President Franklin D. Roosevelt was virtually worshipped by American Jews and did everything possible to fight fascism.

The deterioration in the position of Jews in much of the Western world after 1918 set the scene for the rise of German National Socialism, the most virulently and destructively antisemitic movement in history. The Nazi Holocaust is, of course, covered in another chapter of this work, and only certain very fundamental questions concerning Nazi antisemitism can be addressed here. All such questions are very controversial, and only rarely does a consensus exist as to their answer. It seems inarguable that Hitler's antisemitism was more extreme than any previous version of Jew-hatred in history, for never before had all Jews been killed without exception, and without any chance of saving their lives through conversion or assimilation. Hitler's biological-type antisemitism manifestly went far beyond anything ever known previously, however much the 'Final Solution' might have been hinted at by previous theorists of antisemitism. Moreover, his antisemitism also differed from previous variants in another crucial respect: during the Second World War he was able to apply his genocidal policies not merely in Germany, but from the Pyrenees to the gates of Moscow. All other previous antisemites excoriated the Jewish presence in their own country, but seldom or never went beyond this to embrace all of Europe.

It also seems unarguable that Hitler consistently altered his Jewish policies, always in the direction of making them more extreme. Until 1940, or even later, the central policy of the Nazis towards the Jews consisted of expelling them to beyond the German sphere of influence. Only in mid-1941 (at the earliest) did this policy change to one of extermination, for reasons which are much debated, just as the precise timing of the decision to turn to genocide is endlessly debated by historians. While Hitler was the most extreme of all antisemites, putting a crude version of his theory of the malign influence of the Jews in German history and on modern German culture in *Mein Kampf* (1924), the Nazi movement also produced a number of other notable 'theorists' and propagandists of antisemitism. Alfred Rosenberg (1893–1946) wrote the closest approach to a considered Nazi view of racial factors in history in *The Myth of the Twentieth Century* (1925), in which he denounced the Jews directly and also attacked such institutions as the Catholic Church and Freemasonry, which were heavily influenced by Judaism. Julius Streicher (1885–1946) was known as the foremost 'Jew-baiter' of the 1930s through his newspaper *Der Stürmer* (The Stormer), an illustrated publication full of vile antisemitic images bordering on pornography, showing, for example, grossly caricatured Jewish men as sexual predators on blonde Aryan women, and as ritual murderers gleefully setting about their task. Both Rosenberg and Streicher were hanged in 1946, having been found guilty at Nuremberg of 'crimes against humanity'. Nazism also produced numerous other influential German racial nationalist 'theorists' who included virulent antisemitism in their writings, such as the social anthropologist Hans Günther (1891–1968) and propagandist Johann von Leers (1902–65).

Another question which has been much debated by recent historians is whether Germany was uniquely antisemitic and, specifically, whether the 'exterminationist' ideology of the Nazis was uniquely German and founded in German traditions and precedents. As noted in Chapter 9, this question has become widely discussed due chiefly (though not wholly) to the publication of Daniel Goldhagen's *Hitler's Willing Executioners* in 1996, which argues, among other things, that the genocide of the Jews was unique to Germany and founded in German traditions. Most historians and commentators have, probably justifiably, disagreed with Goldhagen. However, there seems little doubt that Germany's defeat in the First World War, with the loss of the traditional ruling class, traditional symbols, and economic prosperity, greatly radicalised the extremism of Germany's antisemites, making them more receptive to Hitler's message when it was voiced. The 1918 defeat, occurring almost simultaneously with the Bolshevik Revolution in Russia, certainly altered and radicalised German antisemitism as, however, these events did elsewhere in Europe.

During that conflict 80,000 German Jews served the Fatherland under arms, out of a total German Jewish population of just over 500,000; moreover, 12,000 died for their country and tens of thousands were decorated for bravery. Yet a perception that Jews, at the head of a traitorous combination of profiteers, leftists and pacifists, had administered a 'stab in the back' that led to Germany's military defeat culminated in Hitler's rise to power. 'It took four and a half years to poison our people to the point that it defeated itself,' he proclaimed in the 1920s. 'How could a people that waged such heroic battles lose its national spirit all at once? Through moral contamination by the Jews.' The widespread view of Jews as internationalists, bound to one another by ties of 'race' across national boundaries and thus untrustworthy, unpatriotic citizens, bolstered belief in this claim. Jews were also blamed for the harsh and humiliating Versailles peace treaty, which completely demilitarised Germany, removed 13 per cent of its territory (including Alsace and Lorraine, restored to France), and stationed black French colonial troops in the Rhineland. An antisemitic newspaper called it a 'syphilitic peace' which no 'true German' would have accepted, while Hitler viewed the treaty as a declaration of war by Jews ('the foul enemy of mankind') against Aryans, who must accordingly fight against them.

It seems unquestionable that Nazi antisemitism represented the climax of the 'new' radical antisemitism and had little direct relationship with the 'old' religious antisemitism. The Nazis did not conceive of the Jews as a religious group but as a racial group whose religion emphasised and enforced endogamy (marriages only among Jews). Many Nazis, however, did accept all the defamations of traditional religious antisemitism such as the 'blood libel' and the notion that the Talmud enjoins hatred of gentiles. Hitler, on the other hand, appears to have hated Jews only because they represented a racial 'threat' to 'Aryan' Europe, and disliked religious Jews only because they were likely to have a high birth rate. It should not be overlooked that Hitler and the other leading Nazis were not practising

Christians and also detested the Christian message of brotherhood and forgiveness.

With the liberation of the concentration camps in 1945 and the revelation of the horrors of the Holocaust at Nuremberg and other post-war crimes trials, it might be supposed that antisemitism would virtually disappear as a widely-enunciated belief, and that prejudice against Jews would have quickly ended. In the western world, by and large, this has happened, although the diminution in antisemitism has not been a straightforward process. For instance, a component of the fierce opposition by Britain in the period 1945–48 to the creation of the State of Israel was certainly antisemitic (although there were various other causes). In the United States, many overt forms of antisemitism, for instance in the unofficial quotas on Jewish entrants to elite universities, were indeed greatly liberalised at this time, although other forms persisted until the 1960s or even later. By and large, however, it is probably fair to say that overt expressions of antisemitism increasingly became 'beyond the pale' after 1945, largely in response to a realisation of the horrors of the Holocaust. Additionally, the creation of the State of Israel, whose image was of the 'new fighting Jew', a David against the Arab Goliath, also fundamentally altered the perception of Jews, just as the early theorists of Zionism claimed that the creation of a 'normal' Jewish society would do.

Antisemitism since the Second World War

Antisemitism has, however, certainly not vanished entirely since 1945. The Soviet Union and its satellites, until their collapse in the late 1980s, remained vituperatively and indeed increasingly hostile to Jews and to the State of Israel, for a variety of reasons, discussed in Chapter 13. In the Arab world, lurid and vicious antisemitism has been (and still is) widely disseminated by extremist Arab nationalist sources, usually in opposition to the State of Israel or to Western Jewish supporters of Israel. Antisemitic tracts, including *The Protocols of the [Learned] Elders of Zion*, are widely available in Arab countries, while nationalist Arab newspapers have produced an unending stream of antisemitic and extreme anti-Zionist propaganda. Arab regimes have also overtly or covertly collaborated with acts of terrorist violence directed against Israelites or Jews. Antisemitism of this type also exists in Muslim countries where there are no Jews (such as Malaysia and Indonesia) and also in a number of countries, such as Japan, which have never had a local Jewish population at all.

Within the Western world, both extreme right-wing and left-wing antisemitism have continued to exist. Extreme right-wing groups still propagate many of the old claims of traditional antisemites. Since the Second World War, perhaps the most dramatic and offensive new charge made by right-wing antisemites is that the Holocaust did not occur but was a 'Zionist hoax' invented by Jews after the war. This nonsensical claim has obviously been invented to whitewash Hitler and the Nazis. In the United States and other Western countries, an antisemitic underground of shadowy neo-Nazi and Aryan supremacist groups certainly continues to exist. During the period between 1967 and the mid-1990s much of the extreme left in the Western world, especially small Trotskyite and Marxist groups, turned against Israel and Zionism with a virulence reminiscent of extreme right-wing antisemitism, often disseminating the absurd claim that Zionists collaborated with Nazis to carry out the Holocaust. In 1975, the irresistible Arab–Third World–Soviet bloc majority at the United Nations General Assembly steamrollered through a resolution which declared Zionism to be a form of racism, an edict which was regarded by most Jews as antisemitic. This was not repealed until 1991, after the dissolution of the Soviet Union and of Communism in Europe.

Nevertheless, despite all this it seems unarguable that the amount of anti-semitism, in the Western world at any rate, has diminished so greatly that it is probably fair to say that it is virtually absent from the mainstream. It would be extraordinary, for instance, for any public figure in the Western world to utter an antisemitic remark, and anyone who did would probably commit instantaneous political suicide. As well, strong laws exist today throughout the Western world which criminalise racialist incitement, laws which generally did not exist before the 1960s. While the terrible experience of the Holocaust has probably been primarily responsible for this, the situation today builds upon a surprisingly strong tradition of philosemitism (support and admiration for Jews by non-Jews), especially in the English-speaking world, which has always existed.

Among the numerous household names in Britain who supported the Jewish cause were Charles Darwin, Lewis Carroll, and Arthur Conan Doyle. There were also members of the royal family, whose staunch philosemitism is well-documented: these included two of King George III's sons, the Dukes of Sussex and Cambridge, King William IV's wife, Queen Adelaide, as well as Queen Victoria and her son, King Edward VII. Victoria's favourite prime minister, after all, was Benjamin Disraeli. She honoured Sir Moses Montefiore expressly for his efforts on behalf of oppressed communities overseas, and both she and Edward VII remonstrated with the Russian tsars over their treatment of Jews.

These supporters of the Jews made their views known not as a token gesture, but out of earnest and genuine conviction that their combined protests might actually shame persecutory rulers into ceasing to oppress their Jewish subjects. Philosemites also opened relief funds on behalf of Jewish victims of violence and persecution overseas, as well as during famine and distress in Eretz Israel. Invariably donations poured in generously: from town and country, from high and low, from clergymen and lay persons alike. The most noteworthy features of the many great rallies that were held in Britain to protest the ill-treatment of overseas Jewry were the ecumenical and bipartisan nature of the gatherings and the illustrious public figures from all fields who spoke or sat in the audience. The lie is thereby surely given to the popular assumption that the British upper classes have been inherently anti-semitic. For example, the great rally in London in 1890 called to protest tsarist persecution was requisitioned by 85 distinguished non-Jews, including peers, senior clergymen, distinguished naval and military figures and 24 parliamentarians of various political allegiances, as well as by eminent writers, artists and intellectuals. Rallies of that kind, usually chaired by London's lord mayor, were held down to the Nazi period, and were replicated in other English-speaking countries.

During the Dreyfus Affair it was widely stated that 95 per cent of all intellectuals and public figures in Britain supported Dreyfus and regarded the charges brought against him as calumnies. Newspaper articles, letters, pamphlets and petitions also appeared condemning the persecution of Jews. The British petition condemning the infamous ritual murder accusation in Russia in 1911 involving Mendel Beilis was signed by 240 influential persons from politics, the military, academia, journalism, and the arts, a veritable 'Who's Who' of British society.

Four main types of champions of the Jewish cause can be identified, all of them evident at the time of the British and American rallies called to protest the 1840 Damascus blood libel and subsequently. First, liberal philosemites considered all human beings as deserving of fair treatment. Many philosemites of this sort had no special love for Jews, but supported them because of their common humanity, and also championed the cause of downtrodden peoples everywhere. Nevertheless, scores of liberal philosemites did have a particular interest in Jews and Judaism, visiting synagogues, for instance, or learning Hebrew. Second, philosemites who were practising Christians supported Jews either because they felt morally obliged to do so, or, more positively, because they felt a bond based upon a shared scriptural tradition. There was in particular a powerful tradition of Protestant philosemitism. While some philosemites of that sort befriended Jews in the hope of converting them to Christianity, others had no ulterior motives. 'To the foreigner the word Jew is a hissing in the street; to us the word suggests Solomon and Moses and a thousand cradle stories,' wrote Colonel Josiah Wedgwood, a prominent and sincere twentieth-century philosemite of Nonconformist background. A member of the famous pottery family, he hoped that a future Jewish State would become part of the British Commonwealth. From as early as 1840 there were Christian philosemites who, far from viewing Judaism as a flawed and superseded tra-dition, esteemed it as an alternative path to redemption. Third, Zionist philosemites advocated the Jews' right to Eretz Israel, either on the basis of scripture (some were millenarians who believed that the return of Jews to their ancient homeland and their subsequent conversion to Christianity was necessary to bring about the Second Coming of Jesus) or on the more secular grounds that they deserved a secure refuge from persecution. This latter kind of Zionist philosemite was especially prevalent during the Nazi period, but was available much earlier. Fourth, conservative/elitist philosemites admired Jews because they regarded them as an economic and intellectual elite, and as one of the oldest continuing peoples in the world, traits which accorded with traditional values. Particular individuals often displayed more than one strain of philosemitism; there was in practice considerable overlap.

Since the mid-nineteenth century, the Jewish communities of the West have responded to antisemitism by forming self-defence organisations to monitor and combat outbursts of hostility to Jews. Probably the best-known such organisation in the English-speaking world is the Anti-Defamation League (ADL) of B'nai Brith. Founded in the United States in 1913, it has kept detailed records of antisemitic activities, and other forms of hostility to minority groups, and has vigorously defended Jews and other minorities from bigotry and discrimination. Most Jewish communal representative bodies around the world (such as the Board of Deputies of British Jews) also have anti-defamation or defence committees to counter antisemitism. Such organisations are, of course, only as successful as the political culture of democracy and tolerance in which they operate, and would be virtually useless in totalitarian societies such as Nazi Germany and the Soviet Union: indeed in those they would be ruthlessly persecuted.

In the contemporary world, Jews are also well aware that they must seek out allies among non-Jews. Since the Holocaust, this has become much more common than before. Among such ventures are the various Councils of Christians and Jews which have been established in most English-speaking countries. The British Council of Christians and Jews was established early in 1942, just as news of the Holocaust began to filter back to the West. Embracing most Protestant churches and mainstream Jewish synagogues (the Catholics have always been more reluctant to join) it has served to enhance interfaith understanding, especially sympathy for the Jews. Similar bodies have been established in the United States and the Commonwealth. Arguably the most important single change in Jewish–Christian relations in modern times, however, has been the almost total reversal of the attitude of the Roman Catholic church towards the Jews. In 1965 the Catholic church formally removed its age-old accusation of 'deicide' against the Jewish people, the root cause of so much anti-semitism, and relations between the two faiths have improved steadily, especially under the papacy from 1978 of the Polish-born Pope John Paul II, who as a youth had many Jewish friends in pre-war Poland.

As the twenty-first century began, it seemed unarguable that the amount of antisemitism in the world had greatly diminished in the decades since 1945, and is today confined to a limited number of right-wing extremist groups around the world, and to Muslim anti-Zionist groups in Arab countries and elsewhere. In most Western countries the enunciation of an antisemitic opinion by a public figure was enough to destroy his or her career. The main reason for this change has, of course, been the Holocaust, which by the 1980s was almost universally internalised throughout the Western world as the archetypal symbol of evil. Hitler discredited anti-semitism, probably forever, to such an extent that virtually no one wished to be associated with anything smacking of it, however remotely. The legacy of Adolf Hitler and the Nazis to the Jewish people has, paradoxically, been a reborn State of Israel and a world with less antisemitism than ever before in history.

Further reading

Norman Cohn, *Warrant for Genocide: The Myth of the Jewish World Conspiracy and the Protocols of the Elders of Zion* (London, 1967)

Sander L. Gilman and Steven T. Katz, eds, *Anti-Semitism in Times of Crisis* (New York, 1991)

Richard S. Levy, *Antisemitism in the Modern World: An Anthology of Texts* (Lexington, Mass., 1991)

Albert S. Lindemann, *The Jew Accused: Three Anti-Semitic Affairs (Dreyfus, Beilis, Frank), 1894–1915* (Cambridge, 1991)

Albert S. Lindemann, *Esau's Tears: Modern Antisemitism and the Rise of the Jews* (Cambridge, 1997)

Paul Mendes-Flohr and Jehuda Reinharz, comps and eds, *The Jew in the Modern World: A Documentary History*, 2nd edn (Oxford, 1995), Part VII

Leon Poliakov, *The History of Anti-Semitism*, 3 vols (New York, 1965–76)

Dennis Prager and Joseph Telushkin, *Why The Jews? The Reasons for Antisemitism* (New York, 1983)

Peter G.J. Pulzer, *The Rise of Political Anti-Semitism in Germany and Austria* (Cambridge, Mass., 1988)

Jehuda Reinharz, ed., *Living with Antisemitism: Modern Jewish Responses* (Hanover, N.H., 1987)

Rosemary Reuther, *Faith and Fratricide: The Theological Roots of Antisemitism* (New York, 1974)

William D. Rubinstein and Hilary L. Rubinstein, *Philosemitism: Admiration and Support in the English-Speaking World for Jews, 1840–1939* (London, 1999)

Fritz Stern, *The Politics of Cultural Despair* (New York, 1965)

Joshua Trachtenberg, *The Devil and the Jews: The Medieval Conception of the Jew and its Relation to Modern Antisemitism* (New Haven, 1943)

Meyer Weinberg, *Because They Were Jews: A History of Antisemitism* (New York, 1986)

Robert S. Wistrich, *Anti-Semitism: The Longest Hatred* (London, 1991)

|7|

The 'zone of antisemitism': eastern Europe from 1918

The collapse of the old regimes throughout central and eastern Europe in 1917–18 as a result of the First World War produced a fundamental redrawing of the boundaries of old Europe and the rise of many new states. For the Jews, this was initially a time of hope, marked by the end of the Pale of Settlement and the enactment of democracy and minority rights in the new states. These hopes were, however, increasingly dashed, and, in most countries of eastern and central Europe, the Jews had to endure a vicious circle of ever-increasing oppression and poverty. The rise of Nazi Germany, with racialist antisemitism at its very core, greatly augmented this process, and the outbreak of war in 1939 brought unspeakable catastrophe for the Jews. The small remnants of survivors had then to endure two generations of often antisemitic Communist oppression; only with the fall of Communism in the late 1980s could the tiny remaining Jewish communities lead a life of freedom.

The Russian, Austria-Hungarian, and German empires fell as a result of the First World War. In their place emerged new states, most of which had significant Jewish minorities. The largest Jewish community, numbering 2.9 million in 1921 and probably about 3.3 million at the outbreak of the Second World War, existed in Poland. The new Polish republic, created out of 'Congress Poland' of tsarist Russia, Galicia from Austria, and parts of Lithuania and Belorussia, had a population of 27 million in 1922 and 31 million by the 1930s. Jews thus numbered ten per cent of Poland's population, and as much as one-third of the population of its largest cities – such as Warsaw and Lodz. Poland's Jewish community was the second largest in the world, exceeded only by that of the United States. The collapse of tsarism also brought independence to the three Baltic republics of Lithuania, Latvia, and Estonia. Lithuania had a Jewish population of about 158,000 in 1923, just over 7 per cent of the total population. In Latvia, just over 5 per cent of the total population of 1.8 million were Jews. Estonia had a tiny Jewish population of just 4500 in a country numbering 1.1 million.

Before 1918, Hungary existed as a large kingdom, ruled by the

Hapsburgs, in Austro-Hungary. By the Treaty of Trianon (1920), Hungary lost nearly all of the former kingdom where other nationalities (Romanians, Serbs, Slovakians, etc.) were in a majority, and was much reduced in size. In the mid-1920s Hungary had a population of about 8.5 million, of whom 473,000 (5.9 per cent of the population) were Jews. The new state of Czechoslovakia was created out of several different regions formerly part of Austria-Hungary. Bohemia and Moravia in the west were relatively advanced, inhabited by Czech-speaking Slavs and a substantial German minority in Sudetenland. Slovakia and the Subcarpathian Rus, in the east, were more backward. In 1930, there were 357,000 Jews in Czechoslovakia, about 2.4 per cent of its population of 14.7 million.

By siding with the Allies in the First World War, Romania greatly increased its size, adding Transylvania and other former Hungarian areas and Bessarabia (today Moldavia) from Russia. It had a large Jewish population of about 757,000 in 1930, about 4.2 per cent of its total population of 18 million. In addition, there were smaller Jewish populations in Bulgaria (43,000 in 1923, within a total population of 5 million) and Yugoslavia (64,000 in a population numbering 12 million). Also in central and eastern Europe were Germany, Austria, and the Soviet Union, whose histories in this period are considered in other chapters.

Status of central and eastern European Jewry

Owing to boundary changes and the very uneven pace of social development among the Jewish populations of these areas, Jewry in eastern and central Europe differed radically in their stage of socio-economic evolution in the inter-war years. The Israeli historian Ezra Mendelsohn has drawn a useful distinction between what he terms the 'West European type' and 'East European type' of Jewish community throughout this region at this time. The 'West European type', marked by high acculturation, the abandonment of Yiddish and Strict Orthodoxy, and high rates of urbanisation, was found among the countries we are studying here, in Bohemia–Moravia, in Hungary, in most of Latvia, and in parts of 'Old' Romania. The 'East European type', marked by low acculturation, the use of Yiddish and the continuing popularity of Strict Orthodoxy, and a village or (if urbanised) lower middle-class or working-class socio-economic structure, was found in most of Poland, Lithuania, Bukovina, the Subcarpathian Rus, and in Transylvania. These great differences in Jewish communal development often made unity of purpose between the Jewish communities of central and eastern Europe very difficult. They were also one of the main reasons for the development of so many different and rival ideologies among the Jews, although most of these had emerged before 1914. By and large, too, eastern European Jewry was increasingly urbanised in the inter-war period, with the old-fashioned *shtetl* the place of residence of a minority.

The treaties of 1918–22 which granted independence to the new states of eastern Europe (or, in the case of pre-existing states, brought an official end to war with the Allies) all obliged their governments to secure and protect the rights of minorities living within their boundaries, including the Jews. Jewish interests were represented at the post-war peace conferences by influential western Jews, for example Lucien Wolf (1857–1930), an Anglo-Jewish journalist and writer who was close to many influential British leaders. Wolf and other Jewish representatives at the peace conferences tended to be anti-Zionist and aimed at creating a viable Jewish life in eastern Europe. The new states were willing to give certain guarantees to protect the rights of many nationalities within their boundaries, but were unwilling to grant anything like full internal autonomy to the Jews or other minority groups. In Poland, the new government was very cool on allowing publicly-funded Jewish schools to teach in Yiddish, fearing the creation of a 'nation within a nation'. Some Jews at the post-war conference, such as Zionist Menahem Mendel Ussishkin (1863–1941), wanted legal recognition of an international Jewish entity, with Jews everywhere recognised as a nationality with special rights. While, on paper, Jews secured some protection in these treaties, there was no way, in practice, to enforce these rights, and extreme nationalists and xenophobes throughout eastern Europe were soon able to turn the region into what has been described as a 'zone of antisemitism', where ever-increasing hostility to Jews became one of the major features of the inter-war years (Czechoslovakia being the major exception to this trend). In particular, the refusal of the United States to join the League of Nations made the international enforcement of the protection of Jews and other minorities impossible, while the rise of Nazism in Germany, a movement which had rabid antisemitism at its core, acted as both a role model and an instigator of more extreme governmental steps against the Jews throughout eastern Europe. Nevertheless, as historians we must at all times resist the temptation to look at eastern European Jewry between 1918 and 1939 with hindsight as inevitably doomed to genocide: 'on the edge of destruction', as one history of Polish Jewry in this period is titled. But for the onset of the Great Depression in 1929 and the coming to power of Hitler four years later, eastern European Jewry would have survived and might well have found growing acceptability had the world economy been more prosperous and the international situation more peaceful and co-operative. In addition, eastern European Jewry produced a rich and diverse culture during this period, under conditions of great and ever-growing adversity, as well as a wide range of political and religious stances.

Poland

By far the largest Jewish community of eastern Europe was in Poland, which became independent in 1918. Poland was a republic, headed by a strong president, with most parliamentary power centred in the lower house, known as the Sejm. The majority of Catholics in Poland were peasants, although there was a growing industrial proletariat in the mines and factories. Poland had a large traditional aristocracy but only a small Catholic entrepreneurial class. The Catholic Church was probably the most important institution in the country. Poland had a strong grouping of left-wing socialist parties, especially the Polish Socialist Party, which at least tolerated Jews in the new state and was not overtly antisemitic. On the right, however, the largest party in inter-war Poland was the virulently antisemitic National Democratic Party, known as Endek, which had attempted to organise a boycott of Jewish shops as early as 1912, well before independence. In the centre was the largest peasant party, the Piast, and several groups affiliated with the Catholic Church. At the end of the First World War several major leaders of the new state emerged, especially General Josef Pilsudski, who had led the Polish legions in the war, and was a liberal in the context of Polish society, and Roman Dmowski, the leader of Endek, an extreme nationalist and an antisemite who believed that Jews were a harmful element in Polish society and unassimilable.

It is usual to divide the history of inter-war Poland into three phases. The first, – from its foundation in 1918 (and especially from the adoption of the Polish Constitution in 1921) until 1926 – saw the electoral triumph of right-wing parties. It became increasingly clear that the Jewish minority would not achieve their goal of internal autonomy, despite the promises of Versailles. In May 1926 Pilsudski staged a military coup and became the effective ruler of the country until his death in May 1935. Although he was relatively friendly to the Jews, and was certainly not an overt antisemite, the dictatorial nature of his government and the economic depression which began in 1929 led to conditions for the Jews being no better than before. A new constitution, adopted just before Pilsudski's death, effectively turned Poland into a quasi-fascist corporate state. The last period of Polish independence, from 1935 until the German invasion in September 1939, saw a right-wing military dictatorship under General Edward Smigly-Rydz, with a concomitant deterioration in the status of Jews and a sharp rise in violent right-wing antisemitism. Only in the immediate prelude to the outbreak of the Second World War, when the near-certainty of German aggression against Poland became the central concern of the Polish government, were attempts made to woo Polish Jewry as, by definition, the most anti-Nazi element in the Polish population. By then, however, it was too late to prevent the disaster which overtook Poland, or the genocidal catastrophe of Polish Jewry.

While no political grouping in Polish society genuinely welcomed the presence of the large Jewish minority, there were varying degrees of coolness. The Polish Socialist Party (PSP) was not antisemitic and continued to maintain distant but not unfriendly relations with Jewish socialists and the Jewish community. It favoured a long-term policy of assimilation of the

Jewish minority similar to that which occurred in western Europe and else-where in the Diaspora, where Jews spoke the language of the host nation, dressed in similar ways, attended mainstream schools, and so forth. This would inevitably occur, it argued, under socialism and as Poland modernised. It thus rejected the demands for a Yiddish-based Jewish autonomous culture in Poland favoured by the Bund and most (though not all) Jewish socialists.

It is not unfair to say that the whole of the Polish right was endemically antisemitic and basically hostile to the Jewish presence in Poland *per se*, certainly in the vast numbers which existed in the new state. Ideologues of the Polish right based their hostility to Jews in the usual charges and claims made by right-wing nationalist antisemites everywhere in Europe after 1870. According to Poland's antisemites, Jews were an unassimilable, alien minority whose interests were diametrically opposed to those of the Polish nation. They allegedly dominated Poland's urban economy and engendered Bolshevism and cultural modernism, which directly threatened Poland's conservative Catholic heritage. While small numbers of Jews might just be tolerated, especially apolitical Strictly Orthodox Jews, Poland simply had too many Jews and the only long-term solution to Poland's Jewish problem, according to both right-wing ideologues and most mainstream Poles, was mass emigration elsewhere. For this reason many Polish antisemites were supportive of Zionism, especially of the radical 'Revisionist' Zionist pro-gramme of Vladimir Jabotinsky, who (unlike most mainstream Zionists) advocated the mass migration of Jews to Palestine, with up to one million Jews leaving in ten years. During the 1930s the Polish government bizarrely attempted to secure foreign colonies from the League of Nations in order to send its excess Jews overseas. It even attempted to gain control of Madagascar, then a French colony, which would have become a homeland for the Jews. (The Nazis later also flirted with this idea, prior to embarking on genocide.) Virtually everyone in the gentile Polish mainstream believed that Poland simply had too many Jews, and that mass emigration was the only long-term solution.

No fewer than 25 extreme right-wing and antisemitic parties and move-ments existed in inter-war Poland. Although some extreme Polish anti-semites were overt racists, who feared the 'pollution' of Polish blood by Jewish admixtures, most opposed Jews because they were an alien element with a different 'psyche' who were inherently hostile to Polish interests and the Polish heritage. Polish right-wingers also opposed the rights of the other ethnic minorities in Poland: the Belorussians, Ukrainians, and Germans.

While some Polish antisemites would doubtless have wished to support the Nazis after the German invasion of 1939, paradoxically, this proved impossible: according to Nazi ideology, the Poles were ethnically little better than the Jews, to be treated by the Germans as a helot people. It is generally estimated that three million Catholic Poles died during the Second World War, including at least 100,000 Poles killed at Auschwitz. Just as many Poles disliked the Jews, so they found themselves victims of racial hatred.

Polish antisemitism intensified during the inter-war period, especially after the Depression began in 1929. Poland, with its peasant majority and relative lack of modern industries, was one of the most backward countries in Europe, with chronic poverty even during the relatively prosperous 1920s. With the onset of the Depression, scapegoating the 'rich Jews' became an ever more popular activity of the Polish right wing. Demands to limit the number of Jews at Polish universities to under 13 per cent (the Jewish total in the population) became increasingly common. Extreme right-wing student groups demanded the creation of so-called 'ghetto benches' in university classrooms, where Jewish students would be compelled to sit. Severe outbreaks of anti-Jewish violence occurred throughout Poland in 1930–31, 1934, and, especially, in 1935–37. During this last phase of antisemitic rioting, about 2000 Polish Jews were injured and between 20 and 30 were killed. Violence against Jews ranged from the beating up of Jewish students and Jews in their homes to the petrol-bombing of Jewish institutions. Even before the radicalisation of Polish antisemitism, the Polish government appeared actively to discriminate against the employment of Jews, with Jews constituting only 1.3 per cent of all government employees in 1933, and less than 3 per cent of school teachers in state schools. The percentage of Jews attending a Polish university fell from 25 per cent in 1921–22 to only 8 per cent in 1938–39, while Jewish doctors were virtually debarred from working in state hospitals. The Polish army was virtually without Jewish officers. These manifestations of blatant anti-semitic discrimination – and there were many others – were carried out by the mainstream (and in some respects liberal) Polish government, not by antisemitic extremists. Nevertheless, it is also important to note that, unlike other eastern European states, Poland never enacted any specifically anti-semitic legislation. Despite the strength of the extreme right in Poland, no important Polish fascist movement ever emerged, and the Polish government remained in the hands of the centre-right.

Probably the most important single institution in inter-war Poland was the Catholic Church. In general, the Catholic press was almost always at least moderately antisemitic. In particular, it maintained that Polish Jews had too much power, especially in the economy and the cultural sphere, and were inherently disloyal to the Polish state. More extreme Catholic publications, especially in the mid-1930s, openly advocated a boycott of Jewish businesses whose prosperity, it was claimed, came at the expense of Catholic businesses. Nearly all Catholic organs of opinion thought that there were simply too many Jews in Poland, and advocated mass emigration. Some very extreme Catholic sources advocated stripping Polish Jews of their citizenship. Catholic sources also consistently linked the Jews with 'international Freemasonry', a traditional object of much Catholic hostility. On the other hand, all Catholic sources were unanimous in decrying violence against the Jews, which was consistently denounced as 'unChristian'. Polish Catholicism also opposed the Nazi government of Germany, viewing it as neo-pagan in its orientation and hostile to the Catholic Church. Almost alone among eastern European nations Poland lacked a significant local fascist movement of the kind found almost everywhere, and in some respects Poland had a highly developed and sophisticated party system and political culture.

Because Polish Jewry was so large and because the Polish majority always resisted very extreme forms of antisemitism, Polish Jews were able, to a certain extent, to protect themselves against the worst manifestations of antisemitism. In 1925 the Polish prime minister, Wladyslaw Grabski, enacted a tough budget which many Jewish businessmen felt was aimed primarily at them. Following fierce protests, the government was forced to modify its taxation measures. In 1936, a serious attempt to outlaw *shechita* (ritual slaughtering, according to the laws of *kashrut*) was masterminded by right-wingers in the Polish parliament. The Polish government was again forced to back down after Jewish protests. The slide by Poland into overt antisemitism in the late 1930s was also halted by growing hostility to Nazi Germany, which after 1938 came to be seen as Poland's greatest enemy.

One factor which enhanced Polish antisemitism was the Jewish socio-economic structure, which was virtually the mirror-image of Catholic Poland. As almost everywhere, Jews were heavily engaged in commerce and trading, especially in small workshops, and were largely absent from agriculture. Virtually debarred from the state sector, Jews also formed a disproportionate share of the free professions, comprising no less than 56 per cent of all doctors in private practice in Poland, 34 per cent of lawyers, 43 per cent of private teachers (i.e., those not employed in state schools), and 22 per cent of journalists. In contrast, the majority of the Catholic Polish population consisted of peasants, with a growing proportion of working-class Poles in heavy industry and mining. Although one might expect the Catholic and Jewish socio-economic structures to complement one another, in reality many Catholic Poles, as we have seen, bitterly resented the alleged Jewish 'domination' of the urban economic elite and the free professions, areas which they thought rightfully belonged to Poles. While their critique was obviously exaggerated (and ignored the depths of Jewish poverty in Poland), it is a fact that Catholic Poland had notably failed to produce an urban business class which might have held more liberal attitudes towards Jewish commerce and to the Jewish presence in Poland. Poland's backward and unfortunate economic structure was at the heart of much of its endemic antisemitism. Had consistent economic growth and development produced a prosperous Catholic population, it is likely that the more extreme forms of Polish antisemitism would have been muted. Regrettably, Poland's economic performance in the inter-war period was generally dismal, especially after the start of the Depression in 1929.

Paradoxically, too, while Polish antisemites regarded the Jews as an economic elite, most Jews in inter-war Poland were grindingly poor, even in the context of the backwardness of the Polish economy. In 1931, 62 per cent of all urban homes in Warsaw had no electricity, 84 per cent no running water, and 66 per cent no indoor toilet. Nearly 30 per cent of Warsaw's Jews lived in one-room dwellings. Conditions in the remaining *shtetlekh* (small towns) were even worse, with Jews often living in shacks. There was an emerging Jewish middle class, but it was relatively small. It was also evident to most observers that Polish Jewry contained a large number of unemployed to semi-unemployed adults, often *luftmenshen*, petty traders earning a catchpenny, hand-to-mouth existence, always one step away from dire poverty. Many Orthodox Jewish men refused in any circumstances to let their wives and daughters find employment outside the home. The socio-economic picture among Polish Catholics was equally desperate, with a great mass of over 19 million peasants and farmers in a population of non-Jewish Poles of 31.9 million, and another three million manual workers in factories and public utilities. As bleak as was the Jewish economic scene in inter-war Poland, the situation among Polish gentiles was probably worse, with endemic Polish poverty heightening the appeal of extremist and anti-semitic movements.

A number of other broad demographic trends among inter war Polish Jewry should be highlighted. Increasing numbers of Jews lived in large cities, constituting 30–35 per cent of the population of Warsaw, Lublin, Lodz, and Lvov. In Warsaw, Poland's capital, Jews numbered 353,000 in 1931, 30 per cent of the city's population. Jews were thus a highly visible portion of Poland's urban population. The *shtetlekh* continued to decline, except in the remoter areas of eastern Poland and Galicia. Still, in 1931, nearly 24 per cent of Poland's Jews lived in villages, nearly 700,000 people. Only 6 per cent of Polish Jews were involved in agriculture, compared with 1.1 million (in 1921) employed in commercial pursuits, and 940,000 in industry. The urban profile of Poland's Jews was, again, largely the reverse of Poland's Catholics and led, not to perceptions of complementarity, but to deep hostility and mistrust towards the Jews by the Catholic majority, who often saw the Jews as a sinister urban mass.

Throughout the inter-war years, Yiddish continued to be the predominant language among Poland's Jews. In the 1931 Census, 80 per cent declared themselves to speak Yiddish as their native language. Another 7–8 per cent stated that Hebrew was their native language. (This is almost certainly false. There were no native speakers of Hebrew in Poland. In reality, the Zionist movement had asked its supporters to state that Hebrew, rather than Yiddish, was their native language. Almost certainly, nearly all of this group spoke Yiddish.) The remainder of the Jewish population spoke Polish. In some cities the percentage of Jews who spoke Polish was far higher – 35 per cent of the Lvov district, and 19 per cent of the Jews of Cracow, for instance. Because the Polish government insisted that instruction in state high schools must be exclusively in Polish, this percentage was probably rising, and there was, in the 1930s, a significant Jewish newspaper press in Polish rather than Yiddish. Although Yiddish would have survived (especially among Strictly Orthodox Jews) had the Holocaust not occurred, it is likely that, within a generation or two, many, possibly most, Polish Jews would have spoken Polish, just as in the Soviet Union most, in the post-1945 era, spoke Russian.

It has often been observed that the Jews of inter-war Poland were the most highly politicised in the world. Most Jews supported one or another of the many Jewish political parties. Notoriously, Jewish political and ideological conflict was both fragmented and bitter. New parties and factions appeared with alarming frequency, while relations among the Jewish political parties and factions was often more bitter and venomous than relations with the Poles. Jewish political parties in inter-war Poland existed not merely to contest elections to the *kehillot* (Jewish community councils), the Sejm (the Polish parliament), or local government councils, but as ongoing, multifaceted institutions with important functions apart from party politics.

A number of reasons may be offered for this state of affairs. Poland's Jewish population was the largest in Europe, and therefore had the greatest potential to produce rival movements. In Poland, there was genuinely no Jewish consensus on the most basic questions of Jewish identity or of the correct Jewish responses to the challenges of antisemitism, minority status, chronic poverty, and modernity. There could be no possible compromise between, say, the Strictly Orthodox and the Marxist or quasi-Marxist responses to these issues. Nor was there a common, universally-recognised representative body among the Jews of Poland similar to the Board of Deputies of British Jews, which could act as the community's mouthpiece. Nor did a single charismatic or universally-recognised figure ever come to dominate Polish Jewry's leadership structure, or act as its recognised spokesman. Secondly, Jewish political parties in Poland normally acted as what political sociologists have termed 'way of life' parties. These parties published daily and weekly newspapers, held social gatherings, formed youth groups, and even offered help to its members looking for employment. Each party had an infrastructure of officials who became prominent leaders in the Jewish community. Zionist parties largely had control of admission certificates to Palestine. Jewish youth in Poland joined one or another party in considerable numbers, often because their own futures looked bleak. Thirdly, in the absence of the normal institutions of self-government and in a society with endemic antisemitism, Jewish parties offered some measure of protection to their adherents in dealings with the Polish government, and some form of collective bargaining power. It has also been suggested by political sociologists that the bitter hostility which marked relations between the Jewish political parties constituted the internalised response to the weakness of Polish Jewry and their minority status with the anger and frustration which nearly all Polish Jews must have felt turned against each other rather than against their common oppressor. Finally, the inter-war period in

Europe generally was a time of the most bitter ideological hostility and of deep political fragmentation. Catholic Poland also produced a plethora of rival parties and movements. Nevertheless, the fragmentation and deep ideological tensions among Polish Jewry certainly exceeded those found anywhere else in the Jewish world at this time.

Throughout the inter-war years, three main political movements predominated in the Polish Jewish scene: the social democratic Bund, Agudas Israel, the focus of many Strictly Orthodox Jews (fragmented as it was into many factions), and the Zionist movement. Besides these, there were also a number of other significant minor Jewish political movements.

As we saw in Chapter 4 above, the Bund had been founded by Jewish workers in tsarist Russia in 1897. In Russia it stood for the creation of a socialist society, and was often close to the Menshevik party of revolutionary socialists. As such, it was long distrusted by the rival Bolshevik party, especially by Lenin, and was persecuted in the Soviet Union. In Poland, the Bund stood for a socialist future but always affirmed the right of the Jewish community of that country to full internal autonomy. It championed a progressive, secular Yiddish-based culture. Throughout its history the Bund claimed to be a party of 'revolutionary socialism' but also strongly opposed orthodox Communism. In the context of inter-war Poland, it continuously tried to forge an alliance with the Polish socialists. Although it met with some success, the depths of Polish antisemitism meant that a working alliance proved very difficult.

The Bund was adamant in rejecting Zionism as a solution to the Jewish dilemma in Poland, terming it 'reactionary' and a product of 'petty-bourgeois nationalism'. What most clearly distinguished the Bund from the Zionists was the former's emphasis on what was widely termed 'hereness', i.e. that the battle against antisemitism and poverty must be fought here in Poland, and that the migration of significant numbers of Jews to a desert wilderness was romantic folly. (It thus, paradoxically, shared opposition to Zionism with the Strictly Orthodox Agudas Israel party.) It strongly emphasised the authenticity and legitimacy of the Yiddish language and Yiddish secular culture, and always argued that antisemitism would disappear under socialism. As noted, it always sought to co-operate with Polish socialists, and believed that sooner or later the forces of socialism would triumph over reaction.

It is easy now to dismiss the Bund as hopelessly and tragically blind and naive, and even to view its opposition to Jewish emigration to Palestine while there was still time as virtually criminal. With the Holocaust and the creation of the State of Israel, the Bund and its ideology has nearly vanished (although offshoots of the Bund still survive in Canada and Australia); it was certainly one of the great and most tragic losers of modern Jewish history. Yet it is also important to realise that the Bund was not, in inter-war Poland, regarded as quixotic or marginal. On the contrary, in the 1930s it was certainly the largest Jewish party in Poland, with a strong base of support in Jewish trade unions and a real hold over many poor urban Jews. The Bund's policy of 'hereness', and on fighting antisemitism directly in Poland, its emphasis on Yiddish, and its rejection of the central Zionist plank that the culture of the Jews in the Diaspora was inauthentic and unworthy, all found considerable popular appeal. In 1936–38 the Bund won a series of notable victories in the Jewish *kehilla* (community council) and other local elections, chiefly at the expense of Agudas Israel. When Polish independence came to an end in 1939, there was no reason to suppose that the Bund was less popular than at any previous time in the inter-war years.

Like all other Polish Jews, the leaders and followers of the Bund were decimated by the Holocaust. Unlike their rivals, however, it was impossible for the Bund to re-emerge after the war, with the Jewish 'masses' virtually wiped out and nearly all survivors wishing to emigrate as soon as possible, chiefly to Israel. The Bund was also heavily persecuted by Soviet Communism, particularly when the Soviet Union occupied the eastern half of Poland in 1939–41. Two of the most important leaders of the Bund, Victor Alter (1890–1941) and Henryk Erlich (1882–1941), were murdered by Stalin during the war, and hundreds of the Bund's supporters were shot or imprisoned.

The second broadly popular political movement among the Jews of inter-war Poland was Agudas Israel ('Union of Israel', sometimes transliterated Agudas Yisroel), the party of Strictly Orthodox Jews. Founded as recently as 1912, it was strong in central Poland and had links to the Gerer *rebbe*, the head of the Hasidic dynasty with the largest following. It consistently claimed to receive more than 20 per cent of the vote at *kehillah* and other elections; its numbers remained high despite the probable numerical decline of the Strictly Orthodox community and the bitter rivalries between different Hasidic groupings. Agudas Israel was, in particular, fiercely opposed to the Bund and to all socialistic, secular movements within Polish Jewry. For most of the inter-war years it also strongly opposed Zionism, believing that the Jews would be restored to Palestine by the Messiah, not by a secular political movement. By the late 1930s, however, many leaders of Agudas Israel came to favour a Jewish state in Poland and were moving closer to the Zionist movement. On the other hand, Agudas always favoured Yiddish as the Jewish vernacular and opposed the popular usage of Hebrew.

Agudas had a relatively modest political agenda, and wished to use its political influence to obtain state aid for its religious schools and a recognition of the exclusively religious nature of Judaism. It was resolutely anti-socialist and anti-secular and consistently hostile to all manifestations of Jewish radicalism. It supported its own newspaper *Der Tog* (*The Day*). In so far as the Polish authorities favoured any Jewish political party, they were often seen as favouring Agudas, whose conservative, religious values they largely shared. On the other hand, the anti-Zionist sentiments of Agudas prior to the late 1930s, with its corollary that Jews should remain in

Poland, could not have been welcomed. While most supporters of Agudas dressed and engaged in the lifestyle of the traditional Strictly Orthodox, many of its leaders, especially in the cities, were engaged in business and the professions and had been secularly educated.

The third of the great political movements was Zionism. Collectively, all of the strands within the Zionist matrix probably constituted the largest political movement among Polish Jewry, although it should also be kept in mind that (certainly until the late 1930s), a majority of Polish Jews were non-Zionist in orientation and rejected its goals. Perhaps 15–20 per cent of Polish Jews were 'shekel-holders' (financial members of the Zionist movement), a high figure by international standards. Zionism in Poland was particularly strong in Galicia and in the eastern areas of Poland (the so-called *Kresy*). Among other segments of Polish Jewry, Zionism always had a large following. It differed from other Jewish political movements in that the goal of establishing a Jewish state or homeland in Palestine could be combined with virtually any ideological position, and Zionism was notable in fragmenting into a number of factions or sub-movements which differed markedly in their outlook and social bases. On balance, this probably helped the growth of the Zionist movement in Poland, by enabling Jews representing a wide variety of outlooks to join, but it also definitely enhanced the mutual distrust and even hostility of those Zionist factions. As well, the Polish Zionist federation in post-1918 was divided territorially into three separate groups, representing central and eastern Poland, Galicia, and western Galicia and Silesia, which never agreed to merge.

The largest ideological faction within Polish Zionism was the General Zionists, who, broadly, supported the World Zionist Organization but also played a considerable role within Polish Jewish politics. The dominant leader among the General Zionists, Yitzhak Grunbaum (1879–1970), was often recognised as the most important political figure in Polish Jewry, and he attempted to forge an alliance with other minorities in Poland, the Ukrainians and Germans. Zionists split into two factions in the early 1920s, with a more moderate grouping representing middle-class Zionists. To the left of the General Zionists were the Left-Zionists, heirs to the tradition of working-class Zionism. The best-known Left-Zionist group was the Poalei Zion ('workers of Zion') which, again, split into several rival groups. The Poalei Zion was also strong in Palestine, where it dominated the Histadrut (the Jewish trades unions) and included David Ben-Gurion and other notables of the Yishuv. One of the main aims of Poalei Zion was to prepare Zionist youth for emigration to Palestine. To the left of the orthodox Poalei Zion was the Poalei Zion-Left, a breakaway, pro-Communist group which rejoined the World Zionist Organization in 1937.

While most Orthodox Jews opposed Zionism as sacrilegious, increasing numbers not merely became reconciled to the Zionist movement, but actively supported it. Religious Zionism was represented in the Zionist matrix by Mizrachi (literally 'eastwards'), formed in 1902 but since 1917 a separate party within the Zionist matrix. Mizrachi was very large and in 1929 was the largest single Zionist party in Poland. It consistently opposed the radicalism of the secular Zionist left. Most Strictly Orthodox Jews, especially those connected with the Hasidic dynasties, mistrusted Mizrachi, which they believed was not only too Zionist but not sufficiently Orthodox.

The strongly nationalistic right wing of the Zionist movement in Poland was represented by the Union of Zionists-Revisionists, formed in 1925 by the remarkable Zionist leader Vladimir Jabotinsky (1880–1940). The Revisionist movement stood for the mass emigration of hundreds of thousands of Jews to Palestine as quickly as possible, with unrestricted emigration to both sides of the River Jordan (the east bank of the Jordan had been closed to further Jewish emigration by the British in 1922). It was militant and, many leftist Jews believed, very close to a kind of Jewish fascism, with the charismatic Jabotinsky seen as a possible Jewish dictator. In economic policy the Revisionists were anti-socialist, and Jabotinsky's romantic Jewish integral nationalism was always anti-Marxist. (Jabotinsky, an intellectual, writer, linguist, and life-long anglophile, was certainly a more substantial and intelligent figure than his opponents believed.) While the Revisionist movement was purely secular, it moved increasingly close to Mizrachi and had a following among conservative religious Jews.

The Revisionist movement had a stormy relationship with more mainstream Zionist groups. The Revisionists formally seceded from the World Zionist Organization in 1935 and Jabotinsky founded a rival body, the New Zionist Organization, which advocated the speedier formation of an independent Jewish state in Palestine than did rival Zionist groups. Jabotinsky and his followers were stridently attacked by other Zionists, especially for his willingness to work openly with Polish antisemites in order to expedite Jewish emigration to Palestine. Estimating the strength of the Revisionists is difficult. Jabotinsky claimed to have 700,000 supporters in Poland, but more objective historians suggest that about 5 per cent of Polish Jews, about 150,000 persons, supported the Revisionists in the late 1930s. After Jabotinsky's sudden death in New York in 1940, his younger followers carried on, forming the Herut party in Israel. In 1977 Menahem Begin, whom Jabotinsky apparently saw in the late 1930s as eventually likely to head his movement, became the first Revisionist prime minister of Israel.

Apart from these three major political movements, there were a number of significant smaller parties and groupings among Polish Jewry. The Folkists (the Jewish Democratic Peoples' party) were formed during the First World War. They were a kind of middle-class Bundist party, standing for the maintenance of an autonomous Yiddish-based secular culture, but with none of the Bundists' support for socialism and the trade unions. Almost forgotten today, during the early years of the Polish republic they were quite significant, winning more than 10 per cent of the total Jewish vote. On the extreme left were small groups of Polish Jewish Communists. The pro-Soviet and pro-Stalinist Communist Party of Poland was, of course, not a Jewish party as such, but it included a significant Jewish minority of members, estimated at up to half of the party's total membership. The Communist party was both banned and ferociously persecuted by the Polish government. Its aims always included adamant hostility to Orthodox Jews, Zionists, and the Bund. Jewish Communists were, moreover, mistrusted by Stalin, and large numbers were purged or even killed on his orders from the late 1930s. Those who managed to survive all this and the Holocaust briefly found themselves, for a few years after 1945, holding a disproportionate number of senior posts in the new Communist regime in Poland. Finally, in the early years of the Polish republic there was an active movement of assimilationists, known as the Union of Poles of Mosaic Religion of All Polish Lands. Pervasive antisemitism by Polish Catholics made their position an impossible one, although smaller groups of Jewish war veterans, with somewhat similar aims, continued to exist. Paradoxically, the number of Polish Jews who spoke Polish and conformed to Polish ways continued to grow.

These sharp divisions were indicative of the air of mutual hostility and mistrust which prevailed among the many Jewish political parties and groupings which existed in inter-war Poland. Sometimes the disputes between the parties had a rational basis. For instance, the Zionist groupings were each allotted a certain number of emigration certificates to Palestine by the British authorities, and they often fiercely contended over the size of the allocations. Disputes were often very bitter indeed, with violence erupting among Polish Jewish groups a number of times, for instance following the assassination of Haim Arlosoroff (1899–1933), a prominent Labour Zionist leader, on Tel Aviv beach in 1933. A Revisionist was arrested for the deed and convicted (his conviction was overturned on appeal). When Jabotinsky, the Revisionist leader, toured Poland at that time, he was given a bodyguard by the antisemitic Polish government to protect him from violence at the hands of other Zionists, a real possibility. Endemic hostility and vituperative denunciations of competing Zionist parties and movements were a chronic feature of Polish Zionist life. Strictly Orthodox rabbis and leaders issued anathemas against secular Jews, while Bundists and Marxist Jews regarded conservative elements in the Polish Jewish population as 'social fascists'. With all this, it is difficult to point to an ideological core among inter-war Polish Jewry, only to the most bitter and seemingly irreconcilable of hostile disputes. The pervasive antisemitism of inter-war Poland unified the Jews, yet served to produce deep divisions over the best strategy to adopt to deal with the animosity of the gentile majority. These divisions often persisted literally up to the moment of annihilation at the hands of the Nazis, with resistance groups in the Warsaw ghetto and elsewhere typically being organised along party-ideological lines.

Jewish cultural life in inter-war Poland was rich and diverse, but perhaps not as rich and diverse as one might have hoped. A number of younger Yiddish writers of great eminence arose, especially Isaac Bashevis Singer (1904–91), who emigrated to America in the late 1930s, was awarded the

Nobel Prize in Literature in 1977, and became world famous, as well as a number of other very notable authors, such as the poet Peretz Markish (1895–1952), Melech Ravitch (1893–1976), Y.Y. Trunk (1887–1961), and Singer's brother Israel Joshua Singer (1893–1944). Yiddish writing in Poland at that period tended to be less conventional and more experimental than before the First World War. Many authors of potential greatness died in the Holocaust, were persecuted by Stalin, or survived the war but were compelled to emigrate abroad. In other spheres, Jewish cultural and intellectual life in inter-war Poland probably did not flourish as it might have done, owing to the grinding poverty of so many Jews, antisemitism, and the lack of university positions for Jews in Poland. There were, however, two mass-circulation daily Yiddish newspapers in Warsaw, *Haynt* (*Today*) and *Der Moment*, and dozens of other Jewish publications in Yiddish, Hebrew, Polish, and even German. Finally, it should not be overlooked that a great many Jews engaged in intellectual work were Orthodox Jews who worked in the context of the *yeshivot* and the communal schools. Most of these perished in the Holocaust, but a minority were fortunate enough to survive, re-establishing Talmudic academies in Israel, the United States, and elsewhere.

While most Jews were deeply pessimistic about the situation facing them in the 1930s, it is fair to say that no one, anywhere, foresaw the scale or horror of the catastrophe which was about to unfold. To most Polish Jews, antisemitism meant hostility and persecution by the Polish authorities and right-wing groups. While Hitler was feared and hated, few foresaw his invasion and conquest of Poland or that he would turn to genocide. It was the deeply divided and persecuted Polish Jewish community which was, between 1939 and 1945, to be virtually destroyed, so that the re-establishment of a viable Polish Jewish community after the Second World War proved impossible.

The Baltic republics

The situation in the three newly-independent Baltic republics, Lithuania, Latvia, and Estonia, paralleled to a large extent the history of the Jews in inter-war Poland. The largest of the three Jewish communities was that in Lithuania, a nation immediately to the north of Poland which achieved independence in 1918. Historically, Lithuanian Jewry also constituted part of the Pale of Settlement and consisted of Yiddish-speaking, chiefly Orthodox Jews who differed little sociologically, if at all, from the Jews of Poland, and, indeed, had at one time been part of the Polish Commonwealth. When Lithuanian independence came, the territory of the new republic excluded the largest Lithuanian-speaking city, Vilna (which was, of course, also a great centre of Jewry). Vilna was instead forcibly incorporated into Poland, and Kaunas (known in Russian as 'Kovno') became Lithuania's capital. There were 157,527 Jews in Lithuania in 1923, just over 7 per cent of the population. Kaunas contained 25,000 Jews, and many lived in small towns. Despite the absence of Vilna, a number of notable *yeshivot* existed in Lithuania.

Initially, relations between Lithuanians and Jews were surprisingly good. Jews were granted full equality, and the right to establish totally autonomous communal institutions. The Lithuanian government looked to the Jews as a well-educated urban element with important links to the outside world; in general, it mistrusted Russia, Germany, and Poland, its large and powerful neighbours, more than its Jewish minority. Down to 1939, there were no pogroms in Lithuania, and much less overt antisemitism than in many comparable countries.

Nevertheless, the situation of Lithuanian Jewry deteriorated steadily during the inter-war period, especially after an authoritarian, nationalist government seized power in 1926. Strong efforts were made to create a Lithuanian bourgeoisie (almost non-existent before the First World War), and to 'Lithuanise' the local economy and culture. Jews were largely excluded from government employment, and the Jewish percentage of university students declined from 32 per cent in 1922 to 16 per cent by the mid-1930s. Unemployment was high and there was widespread pessimism about the future. These trends were aggravated by the Great Depression, and by the rise of Nazism in Germany, and by perceptions of Jews as disproportionately involved in the Communist party.

The Jewish economic structure in Lithuania was more 'backward' even than in its Polish counterpart, with few large-scale industries of any kind. As a result, the Bund and Jewish socialist movements were weaker than in Poland, and Zionism stronger. Lithuania had one of the highest percentage of shekel-holders (financial members of the Zionist movement) than virtually any country, with nearly half of Lithuania's adult Jewish population purchasing 'shekels' in the mid-1930s, an incredibly high proportion. More than 9,000 Lithuanian Jews emigrated to Palestine in the inter-war years, also a high percentage. Agudas Israel and the Folkists were also strong.

A considerable number of young Lithuanian Jews did join the local Communist party, chiefly out of despair over their future prospects. When the Soviet Union invaded and forcibly incorporated Lithuania in 1940, it persecuted many mainstream, religious, and Zionist Jewish groups, but also used Jewish Communists in the new government and the state bureaucracy. The perception of Jews as lackeys of the Soviet Union unquestionably made many Lithuanians only too ready to accept the enormities of the Nazis when Germany invaded Lithuania in mid-1941.

As elsewhere in eastern Europe, while most Lithuanian Jews spoke Yiddish, increasing numbers spoke Lithuanian. By 1936 one-fifth of Jewish elementary students were being educated in Lithuanian-language schools. Lithuanian Jewry thus entered the Second World War in economic and cultural depression, even despair, and was moving along the road to rapid assimilation.

The other Baltic republics, Latvia and Estonia, contained smaller Jewish communities than did Lithuania. Latvia contained 96,765 Jews in 1925, 5.2 per cent of the total population, and Estonia 4,566 in 1922, only 0.4 per cent of the population. The two countries differed in many other respects from Lithuania. The majority of the Lithuanian population was Catholic, but most inhabitants of the other two Baltic states were Lutherans. Both countries had a more advanced middle class, with many Germans playing a leading role in the economy. While most Jews were small-scale tradesmen and minor producers of goods, in Riga (the Latvian capital) Jews were prominent in banking and in the professions. Much of Latvia and all of Estonia had been outside of the Pale of Settlement in tsarist times, and the small number of Jews who had settled there had often been 'privileged' in some way; many were veterans of the tsarist army (who were able to settle outside the Pale). Neither Latvia nor Estonia had much of a tradition of antisemitism. Nevertheless, the history of the two countries in the inter-war period was fairly similar to that of Lithuania. In both, early hopes for pluralistic democracy, with full autonomy for the Jews, failed. In Latvia, a right-wing authoritarian government seized power in 1934, and Jews were gradually squeezed out of the local economy, although not to the same extent as in Lithuania. Zionism was very strong, with Revisionist Zionism in particular gaining a significant following. Many young Jews favoured Communism and, by a familiar pattern, became prominent in the Soviet 'republics' established in Latvia and Estonia in 1940. This led many Latvians and Estonians (who were 'racially' acceptable to the Nazis) to favour the Nazi-style treatment of the Jews when the Germans invaded in mid-1941. 'Latvianisation' of the Jews, however, had proceeded less far than the equivalent process in Lithuania when the end came.

Hungary

The history of Hungary in the inter-war years differed considerably from that in other eastern European countries. While most other central and eastern European states had not existed at all prior to 1918, or were much smaller in size, Hungary, in contrast, had been much larger and lost much of its territory as a result of the war. In 1910, the population of Hungary, an autonomous kingdom within the Austro-Hungarian Empire, with the Hapsburg emperor as its monarch, was 18.3 million. Magyars numbered about 9.0 million of this total; about 3.5 million were Romanians, while Slovaks and Ruthenians numbered about 2.5 million. The Jewish total in Hungary in 1910 was 911,227, about 5 per cent of the total population. By the Treaty of Trianon (1920), which officially ended the First World War for Hungary and defined its post-war boundaries, Hungary lost approximately 60 per cent of its pre-war territory, while its population decreased to 8,454,000 (in 1924). Trianon Hungary (as the post-1919 state is known) was, however, ethnically much more homogeneous, with 90 per cent of the population being Magyars (ethnic Hungarians). Through boundary changes, the Jewish population was reduced to 473,355 in 1920, about 5.9 per cent of the population (and actually a slightly higher percentage of Hungary's total population than before 1914). The Jewish population, as measured by religious observance, declined still further during the inter-war years, to about 445,000 in 1930.

There is also very general agreement that the position of the Jews changed markedly before the days of the Hapsburgs and the Trianon regime. Uniquely, prior to 1914 the Magyar majority appeared not merely to tolerate its Jewish minority but in some respects to have been allied to it, perhaps closely allied. Magyars are not Slavs, but speak a language unique in central Europe, distantly related to Turkish and Finnish. Magyars saw themselves as a non-Slavic nation in a sea of largely hostile Slavs, and looked to two non-Slavic groups as natural allies, Germans and Jews. For their part, Jews often prospered exceedingly in pre-1914 Hungary, comprising an unusually large proportion of the economic elite, especially in Budapest, as well as contributing a growing number of professionals, approaching a majority in some fields. Most of the Magyar elite consisted of great landowners with little economic prowess (although a Magyar industrial elite had emerged by 1914), and Jews enjoyed an unusual symbiosis with the Magyar leadership class. Jews often Magyarised their names and, in Budapest, almost always spoke Hungarian (or German) rather than Yiddish. A good many had converted to Christianity. The situation in pre-war Hungary resembled that in Imperial Germany, although, if anything, the situation in Hungary appeared to be more favourable to the Jews. As well, the Austro-Hungarian Empire was a 'multi-national' one, whose Hapsburg rulers actively discouraged extreme manifestations of nationalism which might disturb the tranquillity of the regime.

Needless to say, not all Jews in pre-1914 Hungary shared in this beneficent picture. Outside Budapest there was a mass of poor Jews in small towns, especially in the Transylvania region (which was ceded to Romania in 1918) and in Slovakia (which became part of Czechoslovakia). Religiously, pre-1914 Hungarian Jewry was divided into three sects, the Orthodox, Neologs (Reform), and a smaller group between the two known as the 'Status Quo' group. The Orthodox were strongest in the remote parts of Hungary, and were often Hasidic and very traditional in orientation and dress. In contrast, most Budapest Jews, especially those in the middle classes, belonged to the Neolog (Reform) movement, which formally split off from Orthodoxy in 1868. Neologs increasingly conducted their sermons and affairs in Hungarian, and were generally patriotic supporters of the Hapsburgs. Hungarian Jewry also failed to develop the plethora of political parties and movements so common in Poland. Although Theodor Herzl was born in Budapest, paradoxically Zionism failed to gain more than a minor foothold among Hungary's Jews. Jews were mainly divided between a vaguely liberal-conservative majority of assimilated, pro-Hapsburg moderates, and a smaller group of highly secularised, often very ideologically left-wing people, especially among the scions of Budapest's middle classes.

There is universal agreement among historians that the First World War and its attendant consequences were an unmitigated disaster for Hungarian Jewry, probably worse than in most other eastern European societies. There, typically, the situation for Jews prior to 1914 had been very bad, and the post-war situation represented no manifest deterioration until the Nazi catastrophe. In Hungary, by way of contrast, there was a marked decline in the status of the Jews *vis-à-vis* the Magyar majority, and an ominous increase in antisemitism.

There were several main reasons for the deterioration in the condition of Hungary's Jews. Hungary lost the war, sustaining, along with the rest of the Central Powers, a deep sense of the sacrifice of a generation which was utterly in vain. It also suffered, in common with the rest of the world, from a prolonged economic recession and from the Great Depression which began in 1929. Specific to itself, the Trianon settlement not merely greatly decreased the size of the Hapsburg kingdom of Hungary, but also placed millions of ethnic Hungarians beyond the country's new boundaries; in particular, as many as three million Hungarians found themselves in the enlarged boundaries of Romania. During the inter-war years, the Hungarian ruling elite thus felt a pervasive sense of national relative deprivation and a chronic feeling that it had been treated unfairly and shabbily by the post-war settlements of 1918–20.

Probably the most important single specific reason for heightened antisemitism in inter-war Hungary was the country's experience of the Marxist regime, headed by Béla Kun, which held power between March and August 1919. Kun (1886–1939), a Hungarian Jew from Transylvania, had spent the war years as a prisoner of war in Russia, where in early 1918 he joined the Bolshevik party. Returning to Hungary in late 1918, he founded a Communist newspaper and joined the inner circle of the revolutionary movement in Hungary which grew in the chaos following the end of the war. By early 1919 he was the virtual dictator of a short-lived Bolshevik republic which had seized power from moderate liberals. A true fanatic, Kun pursued a rigid and doctrinaire programme of extreme socialism and nationalisation while launching a reign of terror against all 'internal enemies'. Like so many 'non-Jewish Jews' of the far left, Kun did not regard himself as a Jew in any more than an accidental sense and he persecuted Orthodox Jews and Jewish capitalists. Nevertheless, his government was perceived by virtually all conservatives as 'Jewish'. It did, indeed, contain an extraordinary number of Jewish revolutionaries, who, everywhere in Europe, had a penchant for seizing power in the midst of the breakdown of settled society following the end of the war. By one estimate, of 45 'commissars' in the Kun regime, 32 were of Jewish origin. Coming alongside the Bolshevik Revolution in Russia, with its prominent Jewish leaders like

Trotsky and Sverdlov, as well as other Marxist uprisings in Bavaria and elsewhere in Europe with an equally disproportionate Jewish leadership, it seemed to many right-wingers that there was, indeed, an 'international Jewish conspiracy' to undermine Christian, conservative society. For most Jews of Europe and America, themselves very much in the mainstream, the heavily visible Jewish leadership of these movements was deeply vexatious and embarrassing.

By late 1919, Kun and his regime had been ousted by an anti-Communist alliance of Hungarian conservatives and similar forces from elsewhere in Europe, especially Romania, with Allied backing. (Kun made his way to Russia and served as a high official of the Communist International. His impeccable revolutionary credentials were not, however, sufficient to save him from being executed by Stalin in 1939 as a 'Trotskyite'.) For the next 25 years, Hungary was ruled by the conservative Magyar nobility and gentry. Its head of state during this long period was Admiral Miklos Horthy (1868–1957). The crushing of Béla Kun was the signal for the Hungarian right and the old social order to engage in violence on a scale which dwarfed that of the short-lived Marxist regime. In the 'White Terror', as it was known, an estimated 6000 persons were killed, ten times the numbers who perished at the hands of Kun's 'Red Terror'. Many were Jews, who became the victims of antisemitic pogroms for the first time in modern Hungarian history. The allegedly close association of Hungarian Jews with the far left was to remain as part of the outlook of Hungary's right wing throughout the inter-war period, and obviously assisted both the Nazis and the Hungarian fascists in their murderous activities during the Second World War.

Until the late 1930s, however, the situation in Hungary settled down to something like normality. Horthy was declared to be 'regent' of Hungary, that is, to exercise all the powers of the former Hapsburg kings of Hungary in their absence. Paradoxically, the pretender to the throne was never allowed to return, and Horthy was thus named 'regent' of a country without a king, just as he was the admiral of a country without a seacoast. Power in inter-war Hungary remained in the hands of the landed nobility, with an unusual number of prominent Hungarian politicians being counts and barons. Secret societies also grew up at this time, often founded by former army officers, which were rabidly antisemitic. Once normality had been restored, life for the Jews, to a certain extent, returned to normal as well. Jews continued to sit in both houses of the Hungarian parliament, with the chief rabbi of the Neolog and Orthodox communities being *ex officio* members of the Hungarian upper house, which was modelled on the British House of Lords. Nevertheless, a degree of antisemitism largely unimaginable before 1914 became regarded as natural and acceptable. In 1920, the Hungarian parliament, dominated by extreme right-wingers, and in a vengeful mood after the overthrow of Béla Kun, restricted Jewish admission to institutions of higher learning to 6 per cent. Although later modified, this set the tone for much subsequent legislation in the 1930s.

In general, the Magyar elite almost always drew a sharp distinction between the 'Magyarised' Jews of Budapest and recent immigrants from Galicia and Poland. The Magyarised Jews were tolerable, so long as they were patriotic and anti-socialist. Indeed, many Magyars, even outspoken antisemites, had numerous Jewish friends from among the acceptable Magyarised component of Hungarian Jewry. (Horthy used to play cards several times a week with Jewish cronies.) The Magyar elite, however, hated and feared the unassimilated immigrant Jews, especially, for some reason, those from Galicia. They thus drew a very familiar distinction between 'good' and 'bad' Jews which reoccurred among some European antisemites down to the Nazis. As well, and in common with most antisemites in inter-war central Europe, Magyar antisemites felt strongly that there were simply too many Jews in Hungary, especially Budapest, and that they were disproportionately wealthy and dominant in the Hungarian economy, a position they had achieved through 'usury'. The traditional position of Jews in the Hungarian economy was thus in direct conflict with the implicit aim of Hungarian conservatives to 'Magyarise' the economy.

During the 1920s, after the relatively brief 'White Terror' and its antisemitism, tranquillity returned to Hungary during the premiership (1921–32) of Count Istvan Bethlen. Bethlen's main aim was to secure the ascendancy of Hungary's landed elite and also, like nearly all Hungarian politicians, to press wherever possible for the restoration to Trianon Hungary of the largely Magyar areas, especially Transylvania in Romania, which had been taken from it in 1918. Known as the 'Compromise Era', the time of Bethlen's leadership was marked by a considerable diminution in overt antisemitism, although 'alien Jews' who had 'infiltrated' Hungarian life in the previous generation continued to be freely attacked. As elsewhere in central Europe, this relatively placid era ended with the coming of the Depression and the threat which Hungary's conservative forces perceived as once again emerging from the extreme left.

In 1932 Gyula Gömbös became Hungarian premier. In the early 1920s he had been a ferocious antisemite, who wished (as he put it) to limit the number of Jews 'allowed to succeed in any field beyond the level of their ratio in the population', and supported Zionism in order to expedite 'the resettlement of the surplus of several hundred thousand Jews of Hungarian citizenship'. His policies had an appeal to the lower middle classes and to poorer peasants. Kept out of power during the 1920s, with the onset of the Depression Gömbös was increasingly seen as the leader Hungary needed, and he was given power in October 1932. By then he was no longer an extreme antisemite and actually promised Horthy that he would not introduce antisemitic legislation. In office, Gömbös made considerable efforts to appease the Hungarian Jewish community, whose leaders were at pains to proclaim their complete loyalty to the regime. Nevertheless, he decisively altered Hungary's international course by moving it ever-closer to Nazi Germany. He was the first head of government to visit Hitler as German leader, in June 1933. Gömbös (and many other Hungarians) viewed the Nazi aim of ending the 'injustices' of the Versailles settlement with approval. He increasingly linked Hungary's economy with that of Germany, and actively sought investment by German businessmen. He promoted Hungarians of German descent and permitted the widespread establishment of pro-Nazi organisations and newspapers. These churned out a steady stream of virulent antisemitic propaganda, and weakened the position of Jews in Hungary during the 1930s. Moreover, initially small Hungarian pro-Nazi groups were founded at that time, most notably the Arrow Cross (*Nyilaskereszt*), who wore green shirts and whose emblem consisted of stylised crossed arrows. This party eventually came to power in 1944, working closely with Adolf Eichmann and the genocidal Nazi SS, and unleashing a reign of terror against the Jews. The best-known leader of the extreme right was Ferenc Szalasi (1897–1946), who advocated a Hungarian fascism with himself as dictator. (Like so many ultra-nationalists, Szalasi was rather marginal to the country he championed, having been born in what is now Slovakia to parents of mixed Hungarian, Armenian, and Slovak backgrounds.) Szalasi briefly became virtual dictator of Hungary, under Nazi auspices, in 1944–45.

The end of the 1930s saw a decisive intensification of Hungarian antisemitism, especially under the premiership (1936–38) of Kálmán Darányi, Gömbös's successor. The turning-point came in the so-called Györ Programme (from the town in which it was announced) of March 1938. In this Darányi announced that Hungary intended to diminish the 'disproportionately large role' of the Jews in Hungary's economic and cultural life. (He also announced a military build-up and increased measures against 'Bolsheviks'.) He then introduced a parliamentary measure, Government Bill No. 616, designed to diminish Jewish influence in Hungary's life. Its aim was to reduce to 20 per cent the proportion of Jews in most areas of Hungary's business, professional, and cultural life. As many as 50,000 Jews in excess of this 20 per cent figure were expected to lose their jobs as a result of this law. (The law specifically exempted many First World War veterans and Jews who had converted to Christianity before 1919.) The Bill had the support of most Christian leaders and virtually all conservatives. It was also supported by some Jews, who argued that it would end demands for more extreme antisemitic measures. It was opposed by many Magyar intellectuals (including the great composers Béla Bartók and Zoltán Kodály) and many social democrats, but by few others.

Horthy and the other aristocrats continued to mistrust Darányi, whom they regarded as too extreme, and forced his resignation in May 1938. His replacement was Béla Imrédy, a leading banker who was initially regarded as a moderate, and who tried to crush the more extreme pro-Nazi elements in the country. In November 1938, as a result of the Munich accords, Hungary acquired a portion of eastern Czechoslovakia. By aligning itself with Germany, it appeared that Hungary would be able to regain many of the territories it had lost in 1918 and, indeed, over the next few years expanded very considerably, acquiring the Subcarpathia (the easternmost portion of Czechoslovakia) in 1939, taking northern Transylvania from Romania in mid-1940, and portions of northern Yugoslavia in 1941. About 324,000 inhabitants of these areas were Jews, which, added to the 401,000 Jews in Trianon Hungary, brought Hungary's total Jewish population up to about 725,000 when the SS entered the country in 1944.

Despite his reputation for moderation, Imrédy, like his predecessor, moved increasingly close to Hitler (whom he visited in September 1938) and became more and more antisemitic. Although initially advocating no further antisemitic measures, in December 1938 Imrédy announced new measures against the Jews. In February 1939, however, he suddenly announced his resignation. One major issue which forced that action was the discovery that he had a Jewish great-grandparent. Horthy used this as an excuse to appoint a new premier, Count Pál Teleki, another extreme right-winger and an avowed antisemite. He proceeded with an even more drastic measure, the Second Anti-Jewish Law, which was enacted in May 1939. While continuing to exempt certain privileged categories of Jews and all converts to Christianity, it banned Jews from holding any government position, and aimed to reduce the Jewish percentage in business and commerce to between 6 and 12 per cent. As a result (and although frequently circumvented), tens of thousands of Jews lost their jobs and were impoverished. In another law passed in March 1939, Jews and other 'undesirables' were liable to be drafted into a military-related labour system. Teleki strengthened ties with Nazi Germany and allowed Nazi propaganda free rein in the country. He also joined the 'Anti-Comintern Pact', officially allying Hungary with Nazi Germany, Italy, and Japan. In April 1941 Britain declared war on Hungary in retaliation for its invasion of Yugoslavia. Like that of his predecessor, Teleki's reign was a short one: he committed suicide shortly before the invasion of Yugoslavia.

His successor was Lázló Bárdossy, another antisemitic extreme right-winger. Bárdossy went even further than his predecessors, enacting a Third Anti-Jewish Law in August 1941. This prohibited marriage between Jews and non-Jews and defined Jews in a racial rather than religious sense. Unlike the other acts it was strongly opposed by Hungary's religious leaders, who managed to get it watered down. Hungary also took part in the German invasion of the Soviet Union in June 1941. (Amazingly, tens of thousands of Hungarian Jews were conscripted to fight alongside the German armies in the Ukraine.) 'Alien' Jews were rounded up and deported in large numbers, and several antisemitic massacres, of 'alien' Jews deported to Galicia, took place in late 1941 and early 1942, in which about 25,000 Jews perished. The Hungarian ruling elite, frightened of the government falling into the hands of radical pro-Nazis, forced the replacement of Bárdossy with yet another premier, Miklós Kállay, in March 1942. Kállay came from the old landed gentry and was not pro-German. While expounding the Horthy regime's pronouncement about restricting Jews in the economic sphere, he was, by previous standards, a moderate, and Hungary's Jews managed to be the largest Jewry in Nazi-controlled Europe to survive intact.

In March 1944, however, the SS invaded the country, and herded them into a number of ghettos around the country. From 15 May until 8 July 1944 about 300,000 Hungarian Jews, almost all from country areas, were deported to Auschwitz, where most perished. These deportations (which included most Jews in Transylvania and other areas acquired by Hungary after 1938) were organised by Adolf Eichmann, who was tried and, in 1962, hanged by the Israelis chiefly as punishment for his role in the deportation of Hungarian Jewry. Owing to Horthy's intervention in early July 1944, the deportations were stopped before they affected most of the Jews in Budapest. Up to 150,000 Budapest Jews managed to survive the war, in part because of the assistance provided by a number of foreign diplomats like Raoul Wallenberg.

Many aspects of the Holocaust in Hungary remain particularly controversial, such as the notorious offer allegedly made by Heinrich Himmler and Eichmann to trade one million Jews for 10,000 trucks and other war supplies. The Arrow Cross, headed by Ferenc Szalasi, was in power in Hungary between October 1944 and early 1945. The conquest of Hungary by the Soviet Union in early 1945 brought about the total end of the old aristocratic regime. Horthy fled the country, living out his years in Portugal. Many Hungarian Nazis and pro-fascists, including Szalasi, were hanged after the war. To this day, Budapest contains the largest Jewish community of any city in central or eastern Europe outside the former Soviet Union.

Romania

In many respects, the political situation of Romania in the inter-war years was the opposite of that which characterised Hungary. An ally of France and Britain during the First World War, Romania greatly expanded in area as a result of the post-war settlements, obtaining Transylvania from Hungary, Bukovina from Austria, a region called southern Dobrogea from Bulgaria, and Bessarabia (now the Republic of Moldavia) from Russia. The Romanian monarchy remained in place without the fundamental loss of symbols as in Hungary. Similarly, the Romanian social structure was intact, and Romania never experienced anything like the Bolshevist regime of Béla Kun, although there was considerable land reform between 1917 and 1924. Victorious, enlarged, and stable, it seemed that an upward path lay ahead for Romania. Although before 1914 Romania was notorious for its antisemitism, it also seemed at first as if its Jews might share in the national ascent. In 1919, indeed, Jews were officially given full equal rights for the first time. (Prior to the First World War, 98 per cent of the Jews of Romania were classified as 'foreigners' who were not entitled to full citizenship rights, and were also handicapped by a wide variety of other restrictions.) Nevertheless, after the relatively calm (by later standards) 1920s, the situation of the Jews of Romania deteriorated sharply, to the extent that Romanian antisemitism in the 1930s was certainly as virulent, if not more so, as anywhere else in eastern Europe. Yet, most paradoxically, after an initial wave of mass murders and pogroms in northern Romania in 1940–41, the Jews of Old Romania (the heartland of the country within its boundaries prior to 1918) survived the Nazi era intact. There were no deportations of Jews from Romania to death camps, and in 1945 there were still 430,000 Jews there, the largest surviving number of Jews in any central or eastern European country apart from the Soviet Union.

Romania was part of the Ottoman realms in south-eastern Europe until 1878, when it was given independence in a truncated form at the Congress of Berlin. A minor Hohenzollern prince was proclaimed King Carol I in 1881; he ruled until 1914. Although originally allied closely to Germany and Austria, the complicated politics of the Balkans meant that Romania remained neutral in the First World War until 1916, when it declared war on Austria, Hungary and Germany. Despite severe losses to the Central Powers (who, in late 1917, occupied the Romanian capital, Bucharest), Romania was rewarded in 1918 by a doubling in size, adding, in particular, the Transylvanian region of Hungary. During the inter-war years Romania continued to be headed by relatives of the former monarch – by Ferdinand I (1914–27), Michael I (1927–30 and 1940-47) and Carol II (1930–40), who provided continuity and the ascendancy of the old social forces. Romania remained a backward peasant society, lacking much of a native entrepreneurial class. The Orthodox Church also played an important role in Romanian society.

Romanian antisemitism strongly resembled other forms of antisemitism which arose in eastern Europe after 1918, viewing Jews as alien exploiters, as threats to the integrity of traditional Romanian culture, and as agents of Bolshevism, hated by virtually everyone on the Romanian political spectrum except for the far left. As elsewhere, there were also other forms of ethnic hostility, especially that aimed, in Transylvania, at Hungarians. As well, many Romanians drew a familiar distinction between 'good' and 'bad' Jews, with the familiar Jews of Old Romania being regarded as tolerable (so long, of course, as they were patriotic and useful), while newly-arrived Jews and those in remote areas, especially the Strictly Orthodox, were regarded with much more hostility. As almost everywhere, too, a native Romanian fascist movement, virulently antisemitic, arose during these years, especially after 1930, which was in many respects viewed by the traditional Romanian 'establishment' as threatening and disruptive.

The Jewish community of Romania also exhibited many similar characteristics to other eastern European Jewries. Jews in 'Old Romania', especially Bucharest, were relatively modernised, while Jews in remoter areas often lived Strictly Orthodox lives in *shtetlekh*. In socio-economic terms,

Jews were overwhelmingly engaged in commerce and industry (often as petty traders, even virtual beggars) with scarcely any (4.1 per cent in 1930) in agriculture, the exact opposite of the socio-economic situation among non-Jewish Romanians, who were overwhelmingly engaged in agriculture, as farmers and peasants. In 1930, out of 756,930 Romanian Jews, a total of 516,938, or 68.3 per cent, spoke Yiddish. By then, many urban Jews spoke Romanian, while those in Transylvania, which formerly belonged to Hungary, often spoke Hungarian. There was little in the way of a flourishing Jewish culture, although Zionism was relatively strong, especially in Bessarabia. As in Poland, the Jewish community was fragmented into innumerable political and ideological movements, ranging from Strict Orthodoxy to Marxism, and it was difficult to speak of a Jewish 'core' ideology. In 1931, however, a Jewish Party emerged in Romania, intending to give the Jews a single voice. In 1932 it received 67,582 votes in the Romanian parliamentary election, from perhaps 15 per cent of all adult Jews. Relations between Jewish political movements and the Romanian political parties were initially fairly good, although they rapidly deteriorated after the 1920s.

In Romania, and elsewhere in eastern Europe, the 1930s saw a marked increase in the importance of pro-fascist and antisemitic movements. In Romania the local extreme right-wing parent movement was known as the Iron Guard, headed by Corneliu Codreanu. He had been prominent in extreme right-wing politics since 1919, building a power base among students and peasants. His ideology was the usual one of extreme Romanian ultra-nationalism, hatred of the cities, urban elites, and the corrupt Romanian political system, virulent anti-Bolshevism, and the idealisation of the peasantry and the Romanian Orthodox church. It was, of course, extremely antisemitic, arguing that Jews ran Romania and exploited ordinary Romanians. 'The Jews are our greatest problem ... We shall destroy the Jews before they can destroy us' Codreanu told a visiting journalist in 1937. The Iron Guard also wanted to link Romania with Nazi Germany. As elsewhere, the Iron Guard remained a minority within the Romanian political spectrum for most of the 1930s, and was feared and even hated by the Romanian political elite. Nevertheless, nearly everyone in the political mainstream was to a greater or lesser extent influenced by the Iron Guard's antisemitism. Virtually everyone felt that there were simply too many Jews in Romania, who were too powerful, although, as elsewhere, they were almost always willing to draw a distinction between 'good' and 'bad' Jews. Most favoured Zionism as the long-term solution to the 'Jewish problem'.

In December 1937 an overt antisemite, Octavian Goga, briefly became prime minister. His National Christian party was in some respects at least as virulently hostile to Jews as were the Nazis in Germany. He embarked on what has been described as 'an orgy of antisemitic legislation', which forbade Jews to own land, deprived all Jews who were naturalised after

1920 of their citizenship, and barred Jews from the professions. Jewish newspapers and libraries were shut down. Goga's extremism led to an immediate international outcry from Britain, France, and other western countries, which was seen as potentially threatening to Romania. King Carol, a relative 'moderate' (although sharing many of the presuppositions of Romanian antisemitism) also feared an Iron Guard takeover which might weaken the monarchy, and dismissed Goga early in 1938. (King Carol had a Jewish mistress and many Jewish friends.) Although the new Romanian Cabinet, headed by an Orthodox patriarch, Miron Cristea, was seemingly less hostile to Jews, the next prime minister, Armand Calinescu, appointed after Cristea's death in March 1939, was almost as bad as Goga, especially after Romania was forced to cede Bessarabia to the Soviet Union in 1939 and much of Transylvania to Hungary in 1940. Another sweeping set of antisemitic laws were passed in 1940, defining Jews in racial terms and greatly limiting their rights, although certain groups of Jews who had been citizens for many years were exempted from the worst of these laws.

In 1940 the situation deteriorated even further. In September General Ion Antonescu, a very extreme antisemite and pro-fascist, assumed dictatorial power. King Carol fled abroad and was replaced by his son, Michael V. German forces entered Romania in considerable numbers in October 1940, while a month later Romania officially became an ally of Nazi Germany. Antonescu began a purge of moderates. Jewish property was confiscated. The Iron Guard briefly became powerful (although Codreanu and other former leaders had been executed in 1938), organising pogroms. Fearing the Iron Guard, Antonescu then crushed this organisation so as to rule dictatorially.

The war saw the mass murder of Jews in Bessarabia and in Jassy in Moldavia, chiefly by pogroms and executions. The Jews of Transylvania and other areas annexed by Hungary were mainly deported to Auschwitz in 1944, where most perished. Nevertheless, nearly all of the Jews of 'Old Romania' survived the war, with Antonescu explicitly forbidding their deportation to death camps. Antonescu retained some scruples against mass murder and also feared retribution from the Allies, especially the Soviet Union, if he was too closely identified with Nazi policies. More puzzling, and still unanswered, is why Hitler and the SS allowed him successfully to forbid the deportation of so many Jews. In all likelihood, Romania was simply too far away for them to exercise direct influence, although, obviously, had Nazi Germany been more powerful, or had it won the war, the Jews of 'Old Romania' would have shared the same fate as all others caught in the Nazi death machine. From mid-1943 Antonescu tried to disengage Romania from its alliance with Germany and in 1944 changed sides and joined the Allies. In August 1944 the Soviet army entered the country and the surviving Jews of Romania were saved from mass murder.

Bulgaria

In some respects the history of Bulgaria in the inter-war period, with its small Jewish community, resembled that of its neighbour Romania, but in some dramatic respects it differed. Formerly part of the Ottoman Empire, Bulgaria had been recognised as semi-independent since 1878, headed by a monarch chosen from the Saxe-Coburg dynasty, and was fully independent from 1908. Despite the many affinities between Bulgaria and Russia, the very complicated Balkan situation during the early years of the century, and Bulgarian perceptions that she would achieve more from a German than an Allied victory, led her to declare war in 1915 on the side of the Central Powers. Near-chaotic conditions reigned in Bulgaria in the years just after the war, although the monarchy and traditional power structure remained intact. Despite being ruled by a variety of right-wing military dictatorships, there was little sympathy for Nazi Germany, and racist antisemitism, although not entirely absent, made surprisingly little headway. The Jewish community of Bulgaria also differed considerably in its socio-economic structure from other eastern European Jewries in containing almost nothing in the way of a financial elite or a visible commercial or professional presence. Many, moreover, were Sephardi Jews of long presence in the country, and there were few recent immigrants or refugees.

For these reasons and others, extreme antisemitism was genuinely unpopular among most of Bulgaria's elites, and Bulgaria's King, Boris III, although allied with Germany, refused to allow the Nazi SS to deport the nation's 50,000 Jews. Himmler and the SS evidently found Bulgaria too remote and marginal to invade and take over, with the result that 50,000 Jews survived the war. All of Bulgaria's Jews were spared, with the exception of about 7,000 in regions formerly owned by Bulgaria which had been ceded to Greece. In 1945, Bulgaria was the only country under Nazi influence whose Jewish population was larger at the end of the war than in the 1930s. In the late 1940s, most of Bulgaria's Jews, whose community had been strongly Zionist, migrated to Israel, where they and their descendants live today.

Yugoslavia

Yugoslavia was formed in 1922 as an amalgam of several pre-existing states such as Serbia and Montenegro, and from areas previously in the Austro-Hungarian Empire. It was an uneasy coalition of several rival ethnic groups, especially Serbs and Croats, a situation which gave rise to constant ethnic rivalry and bitterness. Most power was in the hands of the Serb majority, and the Yugoslav monarch was a member of the Serbian royal house of Karageorgevic, not a foreign import. The country numbered about 15.5

million in the late 1930s, of whom 43 per cent were Serbs and 34 per cent
Croats; the remainder were Slovenes, Macedonians, and other minority
groups. There were about 80,000 Jews in the country in 1941, about 0.5 per
cent of the population. Although they demonstrated the usual socio-
economic profile, with an urban and commercial/financial predominance,
there was little or no antisemitism until it grew as a direct result of Nazi
influence in the late 1930s. Owing to Nazi pressure, the Yugoslav government introduced some antisemitic legislation in 1940, including a *numerus
clausus* in schools and universities.

In mid-1941, just before the invasion of the Soviet Union, the Germans
thrust their way into Yugoslavia and brutally suppressed an anti-Nazi Serb
revolt. They then divided Yugoslavia into a German-administered Serb state
and an independent pro-Nazi Croatia, with parts of the former Yugoslavia
also being taken over by Bulgaria, Hungary, and Italy. The Nazi death
machine then rolled into action in a particularly efficient way: it is commonly estimated that perhaps 80 per cent of Yugoslavian Jewry perished in
the Holocaust. (Some estimates are substantially lower, but still in the range
of 60 per cent.) Croatia, under its pro-Nazi fascist dictator Ante Pavelic,
was especially brutal, with Pavelic murdering hundreds of thousands of
Serbs as well as thousands of Jews, gypsies, and left-wingers.

Czechoslovakia

The history of Czechoslovakia differed significantly from nearly all the other
states of eastern Europe in that it was a successful, indeed model, democracy
for most of the inter-war period, with liberal values and an efficient
economy. Additionally, Czechoslovakia had never existed in the past, but
was an amalgam of Bohemia, Moravia, and Silesia in the west, which before
1918 had belonged to the Austrian portion of Austria-Hungary, and in the
east of Slovakia and a remote province, Subcarpathian Rus (Ruthenia),
which had belonged to Hungary. Bohemia, Moravia, and Silesia, the Czech
lands, were among the most advanced parts of central Europe, with a strong
Hussite Protestant tradition (although most of the inhabitants were
Catholic) and a large middle class, largely Czech and German. Slovakia and
Ruthenia were much more backward and almost wholly Catholic. The new
state, which declared its independence in October 1918, also contained very
substantial minorities of Germans, Hungarians, Poles and others. In
particular, several million Germans lived in the Sudetenland, the mountainous region bordering Germany. Nevertheless, the new state worked surprisingly well, headed throughout most of this period by Thomas Masaryk
(1850–1937), its president from 1918 until December 1934, and Edward
Benes (1884–1948), formerly foreign minister, his successor as president
until his resignation in October 1938 following the Munich Pact. Both were
liberals, with Masaryk, in particular, being internationally renowned for his

staunch defence of democratic values. Masaryk's outlook reflected the older type of liberal nationalistic tradition, represented by Garibaldi and Kossuth, which was wholly or almost wholly free of any form of antisemitism or post-1870 racist xenophobia. Indeed, Masaryk was a considerable philosemite and pro-Zionist who was highly regarded by Jews around the world. Until the rise of Nazi influence in the late 1930s, his country was almost entirely free of antisemitic parties or propaganda in a way which, again, was nearly unique in central or eastern Europe. Considerable populist antisemitism did exist, however, in Slovakia, whose nationalists, closely allied with the most reactionary elements of the Catholic Church, claimed that Jews 'dominated' the economy and the professions.

The Jewish community was widely dispersed throughout the whole country. Numbering 356,830 in 1930, they comprised only 2.4 per cent of the total Czechoslovak population of 14.6 million, one of the lowest proportions in the area. A total of 117,551 Jews lived in the Czech areas, 136,737 in Slovakia, and 102,542 in Ruthenia. Jews comprised only about 1 per cent of the population of the Czech areas, and only about 4 per cent of the population of the two largest cities in this area, Prague and Brno. Jews comprised about 4 per cent of the population of Slovakia and 12 per cent of its largest city, Bratislava. In contrast, Jews numbered over 14 per cent of Ruthenia, and no less than 43 per cent of its largest city Mukacevo (Munkacs). The very low Jewish proportion of the population in the Czech lands, combined with the existence of a relatively large Czech and German bourgeoisie, unquestionably diminished Czech antisemitism. Czechoslovak Jewry also varied between a highly westernised, often secularised, community in Bohemia and Moravia (writer Franz Kafka, 1883–1924, posthumously becoming its most celebrated member), a community of petty tradesmen and professionals such as lawyers in Slovakia, and a heavily Strictly Orthodox community of the old Polish type in Ruthenia. Zionism was not strong in Czechoslovakia until the rise of Nazism, nor was any other Jewish ideology or party apart from the fiercely anti-Zionist and anti-modernist Agudas Israel in Ruthenia.

This relatively fortunate state of affairs for the Jews of Czechoslovakia was, as elsewhere, dealt a blow by the Depression, and was then destroyed by the brutal force of Nazi aggression. As a result of Munich and later accords, the Sudetenland was ceded to Germany and a German protectorate was established in Bohemia and Moravia (which, in March 1939, lost all of its remaining independence). Slovakia became semi-independent (and in 1939, fully independent) as a fascist state under the so-called Hlinka Guard. Monsignor Joseph Tiso, an arch-reactionary, became Slovak head of state, unleashing a regime of antisemitism. Other parts of the former state were taken over by Hungary and, initially, by Poland. Many Czechoslovak Jews emigrated, although this was particularly difficult in view of the fact that so many German and Austrian Jews were also seeking asylum elsewhere. Upon taking over the Sudetenland in 1938, the Germans expelled all of that region's Jews to Bohemia-Moravia, and severe antisemitic legislation was instituted there and in Slovakia. About 315,000 Jews lived in the former boundaries of Czechoslovakia when war broke out in September 1939. Although the Czech figures are open to dispute, probably between 233,000 and 243,000 perished in the Holocaust, constituting about 75 per cent of the Jewish population that remained in the former Czechoslovakia at the outbreak of the war, and about 65 per cent of the total number of Czech Jews in 1930.

Inter-war central and eastern Europe, 1945–68

The Jews of central and eastern Europe suffered severely from antisemitism in the two decades of the inter-war period. They were all but decimated by Nazi genocide, with the exception of the Jews of Romania, Bulgaria, and Budapest, who had escaped deportation to Auschwitz. It is important, however, to distinguish between the types of antisemitism which prevailed in those regimes, and the chronology of its imposition. Although conditions for Jews were never at any time ideal, during the relatively prosperous 1920s some degree of normality could be found in Jewish life in eastern and central Europe. The Depression and, still more, the rise of Nazism resulted, almost everywhere, in a sharp rise in virulent antisemitism and in the popularity of fascist and antisemitic parties, movements, and regimes. Nevertheless, the destruction of most Jewish life in central and eastern Europe was accomplished by Nazi Germany and not by the local pre-war right-wing regimes. Without the Nazi death machine, while life for the Jews of those areas would have been hard, there would not have been a deliberate policy of genocide.

It goes without saying that the catastrophe which overtook European Jewry between 1939 and 1945 affected the Jewish communities of eastern and central Europe more comprehensively than virtually anywhere else. Hundreds of smaller Jewish communities disappeared, their inhabitants annihilated, and the few survivors were often like ghosts from beyond the grave. Nevertheless, the Nazi death machine was not entirely comprehensive, and much-reduced Jewish communities remained, after liberation in 1944–45, in every country. Estimating their size is rather difficult. Considerable numbers of Jews managed to flee to safety after the late 1930s; several hundred thousand may still have been alive as slave labour or in German concentration camps; several hundred thousand Polish and other Jews were alive in the Soviet Union. Nevertheless, some estimate may be given for the number of Jewish survivors. It is probably most difficult to estimate the number of Jews surviving in Poland, an endeavour made more difficult by boundary changes: post-1945 Poland 'moved west', ceding very considerable portions of the pre-1939 state to the Soviet Union but incorporating large areas of eastern Germany. In April 1946 it was estimated that there were 240,000 Jews living in Poland, in addition to 110,000 former Polish Jews living in other European states apart from the Soviet Union. In addition, several hundred thousand former Polish Jews were alive in the Soviet Union, perhaps more, although their precise number is unknown. It is equally difficult to estimate the number of survivors in the Baltic countries, but apparently about 30,000 Jews returned to Latvia or remained alive in hiding, 25,000 in Lithuania, and 5,000 in Estonia. The three Baltic states were reincorporated into the Soviet Union in 1944–45, and the history of their remaining Jews then formed a part of the history of Soviet Jewry until the breakup of the USSR in 1989–91. Approximately 180–200,000 Jews survived in Hungary, chiefly in Budapest, within the Trianon boundaries of the state. About 80–85,000 Jews remained alive in Czechoslovakia, along with another 40,000 or so who had managed to emigrate in 1938–39. It would appear that 15–20,000 Jews survived in Yugoslavia. The survival rate in Romania and Bulgaria was much greater. Probably 450–480,000 Jews remained alive in Romania and 50,000 in Bulgaria. Thus, between 1,185,000 and 1,245,000 Jews probably remained alive in these eastern and central European states in 1945–46, in addition to several hundred thousand others who had fled elsewhere, chiefly to the Soviet Union. This compares with perhaps 4.8 to 5 million, and possibly more, alive in these countries at the outbreak of the war.

Thus, there were still substantial, albeit catastrophically reduced, Jewish communities in eastern and central Europe at the end of the war. Poland still had more Jews than France and Romania had perhaps 100,000 more than did Great Britain. It was thus just possible that some kind of settled Jewish life might have been re-established in eastern Europe. In reality, only rarely did this prove possible. A number of crucial reasons may be offered as to why normality seldom returned to eastern European Jewish life. First and foremost, surviving Jews naturally felt that they were living in the cemeteries of their families and their civilisation, and many wished to leave as quickly as possible. Although this factor may seem crucial it is also important to realise that Jews in Western Europe, even those like the Netherlands where the local community was decimated, nevertheless picked up the threads of Jewish life and, to this day, remain where they were. Therefore, other factors were also vital to the future viability of these communities. The degree of antisemitism – which had, alas, not vanished even with Hitler's death – was extremely important. Furthermore, the tyranny of the newly-installed Communist regimes was vital; given the choice, few Jews wished to remain in a Soviet satellite, particularly once these regimes themselves became openly antisemitic. In addition, the creation of the State of Israel gave the survivors of eastern and central Europe a state of their own, while Jews in Displaced Persons camps and elsewhere were also often able to emigrate in considerable numbers to the United States and to other Western democracies. Finally, as the number of eastern European Jews continued to shrink, a vicious cycle set in by which communities ceased to be viable, especially as the religious and cultural basis of Jewish life was made almost impossibly difficult by the Communist regimes. As a result of all this, Jewish life in central and eastern Europe between 1945 and the fall of Communism largely became a story of persecution and tragedy.

These processes are well illustrated by the history of the surviving Jews of Poland. For the first few years after liberation, survivors made their way back to Poland from all over Europe, so that several Polish cities briefly had visible Jewish communities (of course greatly reduced in size) once again, especially in Warsaw and Lodz. Hopes that Jewish life in Poland might revive, however tenuously, were dashed by Polish antisemitism, especially by the notorious pogrom in Kielce, in southern Poland, on 4 July 1946. This massacre, in which 43 Jews died, was the culmination of innumerable anti-semitic incidents which occurred in Poland in 1945–46, in which 108 Jews had been killed. This antisemitic violence was apparently stirred up by extreme right-wing elements which perceived Jews as agents of the newly-installed Communist government, although another school of thought holds that the Soviet secret police instigated these activities, in order to distract attention from the tyranny of the new regime. Polish Jews had also to con-tend with the increasingly harsh and regimentary nature of the Communist system, which forbade most private enterprise and cracked down on any deviant political views. As a result, a very large portion of Polish Jewry emi-grated to Israel as soon as the new state was established – 32,245 in 1948, 47,343 in 1949, 10,054 in the first six months of 1950, in addition to 'illegal' immigration that occurred before independence. Many thousands of others migrated elsewhere, to the United States, Canada, South Africa, or Australia. (There is a famous anecdote of three Polish Jews in a Displaced Persons' camp who are discussing where they are going next. 'To New York,' says one. 'To Israel,' says the second. 'To Melbourne, Australia,' says the third. 'Why so far?' the first two ask. 'Far?' comes the reply. 'Far from where?')

Although a notable percentage of the pro-Communist leadership which had been installed by the Soviet army in Poland in 1945 was Jewish, includ-ing the prominent economics minister Hilary Minc (a relative moderate in the context of the new regime), the Polish Communist government, taking its orders from Moscow, was deeply hostile to Zionism and to any sign of an independent Jewish life. The very reduced Jewish population of Poland, estimated at 65,000 in 1951, found itself the subject of renewed antisemitic hostility, in which the Communist regime exploited traditional Polish anti-semitism to deflect popular opinion away from its own repressive failings. Overt antisemitic feelings were expressed by anti-Communist activists in the movement against the regime in 1956, and more openly during the unrest of 1968. Most of the remaining Jews in Poland emigrated, leaving a commu-nity with as few as 10–15,000 members by the 1980s. In 1967, at Moscow's behest, the Polish government broke off diplomatic relations with Israel. The achievement of a democratic government in the late 1980s did, however, mark a new beginning, with the restoration of diplomatic relations with Israel and a renewed interest by Poles and Jews from around the world, in Poland's Jewish heritage. Auschwitz became a recognised place of international pilgrimage, although one marred as a symbol by pervasive quarrels between Jews and Catholics over such matters as the placing of a Catholic convent and Catholic religious imagery on the site. Nevertheless, at the end of the twentieth century a paradoxical situation emerged, as it did elsewhere in eastern Europe, namely, that there was both more understanding and freedom for Jews at the same time as the Jewish population had declined to negligible levels. The change in Polish Catholic perceptions of Jews was most visibly illustrated by the pronouncements of Pope John Paul II, who in 1978 became the first Polish pontiff. In pre-1939 Poland he had had many Jewish friends, and deeply and personally felt the tragedy of the Holocaust, an event to which he referred in official pronouncements on many occasions. Such outspoken sympathy for Poland's Jews by the most prominent of Polish Catholics would have been very difficult to conceive at any time before the late twentieth century.

The pattern found in post-1945 Poland was repeated in fairly similar ways throughout eastern Europe. In Czechoslovakia, about 80,000 Jews remained alive at the end of the war, with, as in Poland, a disproportionate number in the ascendant Communist Party. After a particularly unpleasant Stalinist regime seized power in 1948, overt antisemitism increased markedly, culminating in the Slansky trial of 1952–53. In late 1952 a prominent Jew, Rudolf Slansky, until 1950 the general secretary of the Czech Communist Party and until 1951 vice-premier of Czechoslovakia, was arrested along with 13 of his associates (most of whom, but not all, were Jewish) and charged with 'Trotskyite–Titoist–Zionist activities in the service of American imperialism' (*sic*). A year later, Slansky and ten others (of whom seven were Jews) were found guilty and executed. Previously, in 1950, the American Joint Distribution Committee, a long-established, highly-esteemed Jewish welfare society, was banned by the Communist government, as, in 1957, was the local Zionist organisation. About 24,000 Czech Jews emigrated to Israel in 1948–53, while others emigrated subsequently, leaving a tiny residual community estimated at 12,000 in the early 1990s. The short-lived Dubcek regime of 1968 liberalised conditions for Jewish life, but freedom did not return until the end of Communism in 1989.

Conditions in Hungary, with a relatively large surviving community of 180–200,000, chiefly in Budapest, were somewhat better, with Jews enjoying relatively more freedom. The Hungarian capital was also the home of the Budapest Rabbinical Seminary, unique in Communist Europe. Thousands of Jews left Hungary in the wake of the briefly-successful 1956 Revolution (whose nationalistic elements included a considerable antisemitic component), but a community of over 120,000 Jews remained, of whom, in 1990, over 80,000 lived in Budapest. With the coming of democracy in the 1990s, Hungarian Jewry remained the largest and best-organised in eastern Europe.

In 1995 Romania contained the largest surviving Jewish population in eastern Europe outside the Soviet Union, with over 450,000 still alive. Here, the familiar pattern occurred once again. A Communist regime took power, which included a number of prominent Jews, especially Ana Pauker (1890–1960), a rabbi's daughter who served as Romanian foreign minister from 1947–52, but was then purged by Stalin. From 1948 until 1952 no fewer than 122,000 Romanian Jews emigrated to Israel, mainly in 1950–51, when 87,000 Romanian Jews left for the Jewish state. Many others left Romania in the latter 1950s and 1960s. Romania pursued an independent line towards the Middle East in the wake of the Six Day War of 1964, being the only Soviet satellite to retain diplomatic links with Israel. Romanian chief rabbi Moses Rosen emerged as the best-known Jewish leader in eastern Europe, and was controversially close to the regime of dictator Nicolae Ceausescu, which was overthrown in 1989. Only about 20,000 Jews remained in Romania in the early 1990s. In Bulgaria, whose Jewish community survived the war, and where the Zionist movement had always been strong, almost the whole Jewish population emigrated to Israel in the few years after 1948. Nearly 45,000 Bulgarian Jews went to Israel, leaving only a residual community of 5,000 or so. Only about 10,500 Jews remained in Yugoslavia in 1946, a number which had declined to about 6,000 in the early 1990s, and which was, in many parts of the former nation, threatened by the ethnic violence which gripped the successor states to Yugoslavia after the break-up of the country in the early 1990s.

Further reading

Michael Bar-Zohar, *Beyond Hitler's Grasp: The Heroic Rescue of Bulgaria's Jews* (Holbrook, Mass., 1998)

Randolph L. Braham, *The Politics of Genocide: the Holocaust in Hungary* (2 vols, New York, 1990)

Randolph L. Braham, ed., *The Tragedy of Romanian Jewry* (New York, 1994)

Yisrael Gutman *et al.*, eds, *The Jews of Poland between Two World Wars* (Hanover, N.H., 1989)

Celia Heller, *On the Edge of Destruction: Jews of Poland between the Two World Wars* (New York, 1977)

Andrew C. Janos, *The Politics of Backwardness in Hungary, 1825–1945* (Princeton, 1982)

The Jews of Czechoslovakia: Historical Studies and Surveys 1968–84, 3 vols (New York and Philadelphia, 1968)

Kenneth Jowitt, ed., *Social Change in Romania, 1860–1940* (Berkeley, Cal., 1978)

Paul Lendvai, *Anti-Semitism in Eastern Europe* (London, 1972)

Joseph Marcus, *Social and Political History of the Jews in Poland, 1919–1939* (Berlin and New York, 1983)

William McCagg, *Jewish Nobles and Geniuses in Modern Hungary* (New York, 1972)

Ezra Mendelsohn, *The Jews of East Central Europe between the World Wars* (Bloomington, Ind., 1983)

Peter Meyer *et al.*, *The Jews in the Soviet Satellites* (Syracuse, N.Y., 1953)

Bela Vago, *The Shadow of the Swastika: The Rise of Fascism and Anti-Semitism in the Danube Basin, 1936–1939* (London, 1975)

B. J. Vlavianos and F. Gross, eds, *Struggle for Tomorrow: Modern Political Ideologies of the Jewish People* (New York, 1954)

(Note: The works listed above concerned with the Holocaust contain extensive material on the pre-1939 situation.)

Polin, an annual volume of essays on Polish-Jewish history, has been published by Oxford University Press since 1986. *East European Jewish Affairs* (formerly known as *Soviet Jewish Affairs*), published in London, also contains articles on eastern European Jewish history.

|8|

The Soviet Union from 1917

On 12 March 1917 (27 February, according to the Russian calendar), after nearly four years of disastrous war in which millions had been killed, tsarist Russia collapsed following a liberal revolution. The new government, headed first by Prince George Lvov and then by the lawyer Alexander Kerensky, abolished all legal discrimination against the Jews of Russia and ended the Pale of Settlement, allowing Jews to move freely throughout Russia for the first time. For most Russian Jews, it seemed as if they were to enter the Promised Land, moving into a new era of democracy and equality. Eight months later, on 7 November 1917 (25 October, according to the Russian calendar), unable to extricate Russia from the disastrous war, the Kerensky regime fell, and a Bolshevik government of uncompromising, dictatorial socialism, headed by Vladimir Lenin, took its place. For Jews, this began a period of nearly 75 years which, despite some real gains within the context of a totalitarian system, might be described as an unending nightmare for Jewish identity and freedom, a nightmare in many ways far worse than that experienced under tsarism. The history of the Jews in the Soviet Union was one of the darkest in modern history, but also provides evidence of how Jewish identity can survive in even the most difficult of circumstances.

It is important to understand that the Soviet state which emerged from the First World War was, until 1939, substantially smaller than the old Russian Empire and contained many fewer Jews. As a result of the 1918–19 settlement of the war, Poland emerged an independent republic, as did the three Baltic states (Estonia, Latvia, Lithuania). Moldavia (Bessarabia) became part of Romania, and Finland became independent. Especially as the bulk of the former Pale of Settlement was now in Poland, these changes meant that the Jewish population of the Soviet Union was much less than half of what it had been under the tsarist regime. It appears that the Jewish population of the Russian state declined from about 6.9 million in 1914 to about 2.4 million in 1923. Of this later figure, about 1.5 million lived in the

Ukraine, containing such Jewish centres as Kiev, with a Jewish population of 129,000 in 1923, and Odessa, with 130,000 Jews in the same year. Only 525,000 Jews lived in the Soviet Republic itself in the early 1920s, with only 86,000 in Moscow and only 52,000 in Leningrad (Petrograd). Although the Jewish populations of these great cities were to increase significantly, in the early days of the Soviet regime they still bore the impress of the tsarist regime's virtual ban on Jewish settlement outside of the Pale. In 1923, another 423,000 Jews lived in Belorussia, with Minsk as its capital, and perhaps 100,000 other Jews (not included in the 1920 population figures) in the remoter areas of the interior of Russia not yet wholly subject to Soviet control. In 1926, at the time of the first official Soviet census, the Jewish population of the Soviet Union stood at 2,680,000. Although sharply reduced from the pre-war figure, this was still the third highest Jewish population in the world, behind only the United States, with perhaps 3.7 million Jews, and Poland with 2.9 million. The percentage of Jews in the total population of the Russian state also declined sharply, from about 4.0 per cent on the eve of the First World War to about 2.2 per cent in the early 1920s. Because most of the Jews of the Pale were situated, after 1918, in the new state of Poland, Jews were probably less visible and less over-concentrated in a few areas in the new Soviet Union than in tsarist Russia, although paradoxically they were invariably perceived by antisemites as far more numerous and significant than they actually were.

Bolshevik aims and their repercussions

The victory of the Bolshevik regime in 1917 was soon followed by a civil war of great violence between the 'Whites' (anti-Bolsheviks, often ultra-nationalists) and the Bolshevik 'Reds'. The course of this civil war, which continued until the early 1920s, was marked by extraordinarily brutal pogroms against the Jews between 1918 and 1920, especially in the Ukraine, where they were perpetrated by followers of the nationalist leader Simon Petlyura. The Germans had occupied western Russia in the later stages of the First World War, and after their exit at the end of the war a period of anarchy ensued in much of this region. These pogroms were generally led by anarchist ultra-nationalist bands who combined traditional antisemitism with a fierce hatred of Bolshevism, which they viewed as dominated by Jews. Petlyura did little to curb the antisemitic rampages of his followers; he eventually settled in Paris, where in 1926 a Bessarabian-born Jew whose relatives had been among those killed assassinated him. The Jewish death toll during 1918–20 has been estimated at as high a figure as 200,000 (with a lower figure given by other historians of 60,000 Jewish dead). It has been estimated that about 10 per cent of Ukrainian Jewry perished. These figures, if accurate, dwarfed anything seen in the pogroms under the tsars and were almost certainly the most appalling slaughter of

Jews killed in modern times prior to the Holocaust. Atrocities were committed by both sides in the Russian civil war, with Jews often being killed by marauding Bolshevik bands, and with the Red army killing vast numbers of their enemies.

The triumph of the Bolshevik regime produced an entirely novel political, economic, and social regime in the areas which came under its control. From the first, a totalitarian regime was established in which virtually no dissent was permitted, no non-Bolshevik political organisations could be established, and the press was entirely muzzled. The aim of Bolshevism was to produce a wholly socialist society, and the regime declared war on all 'reactionary' elements in society. Organised religion (of any variety) was at the top of their list of 'primitive' social forces to be eliminated. By definition, capitalism was to be replaced by socialism, with the state owning all of the means of production, distribution and exchange, although until the mid-1920s some remnants of the market economy were allowed to remain and even to flourish. Nationalist movements which did not slavishly obey the Soviet model were also deemed 'reactionary'. Each of these aims, pursued ruthlessly by the Soviet state, was to be particularly deleterious to Jewish life in the Soviet Union, and it is no exaggeration to say that the survival of a self-conscious Jewish community in the Soviet Union for the 74-year history of the regime was nearly miraculous. There was, however, another side of the coin which made the history of the Jews in the Soviet Union rather paradoxical: that antisemitism was officially outlawed and severely punished. Especially in the earlier decades of Soviet rule, Russia's Jews found themselves living in a society where most areas of economic, professional, and social life were now opened to them for the first time in Russian history, at least in the context of the Soviet Union's Communist system and ideology. Thus the truly paradoxical situation arose that while almost all forms of Jewish consciousness and communal organisation were being systematically destroyed by the Soviet regime, with a thoroughness which most would term antisemitic, Jews were consistently overrepresented in the higher professional and economic structure of the Soviet Union, and entered fields such as the higher reaches of the military, the universities, and the diplomatic corps, which had been entirely closed to them in tsarist times. In a sense, the type of persecution experienced by the Jews in the Soviet Union was the opposite of that which they knew under the tsarist regime. In those times the Jewish religion, education, and most aspects of Jewish culture were largely left intact. On the other hand, practising Jews were virtually debarred from any public position or post in the administration. In Soviet Russia, at least officially, all the barriers to full Jewish participation in the Soviet system came down and antisemitism was made a crime, however nominal this ban was in practice. On the other hand, the Soviet state ruthlessly and relentlessly waged destructive war on the traditional bases of the Jewish community, especially Jewish religious practice, Jewish education, and most aspects of Jewish culture and cultural identity. It is a real contest as to which was worst for the Jews of Russia, although the Soviet attempt to wipe out Jewish religious and cultural identity probably had the more deleterious effects.

Bolshevik attitudes to Jews

For better or worse, the Bolshevik regime was firmly in power in the Soviet Union by the early 1920s, and Russia's Jews found themselves having to deal with the new regime. The attitude of the Bolshevik party, headed by Lenin, towards the Jews and the 'Jewish question' was conditioned by two basic factors: specific Bolshevik theory about the Jews enunciated by the leaders and theorists of the party, and the relationship between Bolsheviks and other socialist parties in pre-revolutionary Russia, especially the Social Democratic Bund, the Jewish socialist party. The main Bolshevik theories on the Jews were enunciated by Lenin, in a number of pre-1917 essays, and, in particular, by Stalin in his 1913 essay *Marxism and the National Question*. Both agreed that the Jews were *not* a nation in the true sense, and could not be treated as a fully-fledged, separate national group. According to Stalin, 'a nation is a historically evolved, stable community of language, territory, economic life, and psychological make-up manifested in a community of culture'. By this definition, the Jews were lacking in a number of basic criteria to be regarded as a nation. Most obviously, they had no common territory or common language. To the Bolsheviks, what united the Jewish people were, essentially, a common religion or religious origin, and a shared pariah status as money-lenders and outcasts which had been imposed by both feudalism and capitalism but would vanish under socialism. Therefore, to Bolsheviks, it was inevitable that Jews would assimilate into the majority nationality among whom they found themselves, with, for example, Russian Jews becoming Russians within a few generations of the end of tsarism. Furthermore, the two factors which had unified the Jewish people, a common religion and pariah status, would both vanish after the triumph of socialism. Bolsheviks of course refused to regard a common religion as in any way legitimate or as a viable basis for recognition as a nation. To them, religion was a relic of medievalism and would soon disappear under socialism. It should be noted that in an odd way the views of Bolsheviks towards the Jews were echoed among many Jews of the time, especially liberal assimilationist Jews and many Strictly Orthodox Jews, to whom the Jews were also, ultimately, a religious group and not a separate nation. As a result, these groups also opposed Zionism as an ideology which regarded the Jews as a separate nation rather than, in the former case, equal citizens of the nation in which they found themselves and, in the latter case, a religion. Bolsheviks, however, increasingly used their denials of Jewish national status as a means of disadvantaging and persecuting Jews, which obviously no Jewish group would have done.

Bolshevik opinion on the Jews also emerged from the party's relationship, before 1917, with other socialist groups. Most Jewish socialists in tsarist Russia had been Bundists, who, as a rule, supported the more moderate and idealistic Menshevik faction. Bundists emphasised the specifically Jewish nature of their struggle, which fell short, according to Lenin, of 'proletarian internationalism'. The Bolshevik faction had included relatively few Jews, and those who did join were virtually oblivious to the particular oppression represented by antisemitism, and had no real links to or sympathy with Russia's Jewish community.

The outcome of the Revolution did compel the Bolsheviks to include many Jews in its leadership elite, most notably Leon Trotsky (1879-1940), who became the second most important man in the regime until his loss of power at the hands of Stalin and others in the late 1920s. Many other early leaders of the Soviet Union, such as Jacob Sverdlov, Grigori Zinoviev, Karl Radek, and Leo Kamenev were Jews (the last three of whom, together with many others, were murdered by Stalin.) Whatever its faults, the Soviet Union was absolutely opposed to pogroms or to the antisemitism of the tsarist regime. Initially, many Jews welcomed the opportunities presented by the new regime, while the Bolsheviks also welcomed the often well-educated, urbanised Jewish component of the population as reasonably loyal and capable of running the state apparatus.

Jewish Bolsheviks

For all these reasons, from its accession to power in 1917 and for many years thereafter, the Bolshevik regime was widely seen in the West, and by anti-Bolshevik forces in Russia, as heavily 'Jewish' and dominated by Jews. For many Conservatives and anti-Communists in the West, the assumption that the Bolshevik regime in Russia was 'Jewish' became a stock-in-trade for decades to come, and was perhaps absolutely crucial in influencing Hitler's murderous antisemitism. The paradoxical element in this perception was, of course, that the pre-1917 Bolshevik party contained relatively few Jews and was insensitive, and extremely hostile to Jewish claims. Even more ironically, this allegedly 'Jewish' regime deliberately crushed organised Jewish life in the Soviet Union and, from the 1940s, can accurately be described as overtly antisemitic. Like all half-truths, however, there is an element of accuracy in the critique of the new regime as disproportionately Jewish. A very high percentage of the leaders of the new regime were Jews – not a majority, but a very significant minority, probably around one-third of the regime's most senior leadership. To be sure, Lenin was certainly not Jewish (he came of the minor Russian aristocracy, although he is sometimes alleged, without proof, to have had Jewish ancestors on his mother's side), nor was Nikolai Bukharin, the regime's most important Marxist theorist, Mikhail Kalinin, the Soviet Union's first 'president' (a ceremonial post),

Felix Dzerzhinsky, head of the dreaded 'Cheka', the anti-'White' secret police, nor, most significantly, in the long run, Joseph Stalin, the increasingly important secretary of the Soviet Communist Party and its all-powerful director between around 1929 and his death in 1953. Jews also comprised a disproportionate proportion of the members of the 'Cheka', the agents of the so-called 'Red terror' which ruthlessly eliminated opponents of the new regime (including socialists). In areas such as the Ukraine (where about 75 per cent of Cheka agents were believed to be Jewish), this led to the ready identification of the worst aspects of the new regime as 'Jewish' and to heightened antisemitism (which, of course, needed little to foment it). In the Western world outside Russia, the new regime was also widely perceived by conservatives and nationalists as 'Jewish', an impression which was augmented by the Jewish origins of many other Marxist revolutionary leaders who became prominent at this time, such as Béla Kun (1885–1937) in Hungary and Rosa Luxemburg in Germany. It was also greatly increased by the wide dissemination at this time of the *Protocols of the [Learned] Elders of Zion*, the notorious tsarist forgery. The allegedly 'Jewish' nature of the Bolshevik Revolution probably did more than any other single factor to spark the heightened antisemitism of the inter-war period on the political right.

Assault on Jewish communal life

That, despite this widespread belief, the Bolshevik regime was anything but 'Jewish' was quickly shown by its immensely hostile and destructive stance towards Jews and their institutions. In January 1918 the Soviet government withdrew legal status from all church organisations and prohibited all religious instruction in schools. While chiefly aimed at the Russian Orthodox Church, the effects of this decree upon Jewish religious life were hardly less deleterious, at a stroke ending all Jewish religious schools. In June 1919 the Soviet regime officially dissolved the *kahals* (quasi-governmental institutions of individual Jewish communities which carried on many social welfare and educational functions). The Soviet regime then carried out a far-reaching, relentless mission of destruction against the Jewish religion in the Soviet Union. To this end the regime established special Jewish branches of the Communist party, known as the *Yevsektsiya* ('Jewish Sections'), manned by particularly extreme Jewish Communists, whose function was to 'impose the proletarian dictatorship among the Jewish masses' and to 'enlighten the Jewish masses in the material world view'. It is not wholly inappropriate to compare the *Yevsektsiya*, which often employed terrorist methods, with the *Judenräte* ('Jewish Councils', established by the Nazis in Jewish ghettos prior to extermination), with the proviso that the members of the *Yevsektsiya*, unlike the *Judenräte*, were voluntary enthusiasts, and much more destructive to the bases of Jewish life. From 1918 until they were dissolved by Stalin in 1930, the *Yevsektsiya* carried on a diabolical series of measures and anti-religious propaganda designed to woo the 'Jewish masses' from their traditional religious loyalties. These included so-called public 'trials' of Jewish religious institutions such as the *hadarim* and *yeshivot*, use of the laws to secure the mass closure of synagogues and the confiscation of property, and the arrest and deportation of rabbis and other Jewish religious officials. The officially approved Yiddish press launched a tremendous anti-religious campaign, headed by 'Fighting Atheists', just before Jewish holidays. By the late 1920s, it was almost impossible for religious Jews to observe the Sabbath by refraining from work on Saturday, or to secure *matzah* (unleavened bread; plural *matzot*) for Passover.

Apart from this concerted attempt to destroy the Jewish religion, the regime also attempted to outlaw the Hebrew language. The Communists hated Hebrew because it was the language of the Jewish religion and also the language of the Zionist enterprise in Palestine, which they condemned as 'bourgeois nationalism'. Yiddish was allowed to continue as the language of the 'Jewish masses', although material was permitted to be published in Yiddish only so long as it strictly conformed to Marxist dogma.

The Bolshevik regime also nationalised the whole economy, although Lenin's 'New Economic Policy' (NEP) briefly (*c.*1921–27) allowed a class of independent merchants, shopkeepers, and craftsmen to continue, many of whom were Jewish. By nationalising virtually the entire economy and confiscating all holdings of private wealth, the Communist regime also eliminated a traditional means by which persecuted Jews could negotiate with an oppressive regime by bribery or the granting of economic favours to those in power. Whatever the grinding poverty of the Jews in tsarist Russia, a considerable number of Jews had succeeded in becoming capitalists, merchants, or petty traders. The percentage of Jews in commerce before 1917 was certainly far in excess of that among the whole population, and Jews paid a price for this, too, in the new regime. The Bolshevik regime created a class of 'deprived' persons (*lishentsy*), that is, of persons who were propertied or held office or official status under the tsarist regime. The 'deprived' class were denied political 'rights' under the new regime, such as the 'right' to vote (which were, in any case, quite meaningless, although *lishentsy* were not as a rule allowed to join the ruling Communist party). Because so many Jews had been merchants or tradesmen before 1917, no less than 35 per cent of Jews in the Soviet Union were declared to be *lishentsy*, compared with only 6 per cent of the total population of the Soviet Union.

Occupational opportunities

As black as this picture is, there was also another side of the coin of Jewish life in the Soviet Union which must be mentioned. For the first 20 years or more of the regime, many of its aspects appeared distinctly to benefit the

Jews. The propagation of 'antisemitic propaganda' was made a criminal offence in 1922. While the regime was wholeheartedly engaged in the destruction of traditional Jewish life in the Soviet Union, it should not be forgotten that its chief enemies were the 'reactionary' remnants of the former regime who were, as a rule, endemically antisemitic and responsible for pogroms and the massacre of Jews. These now ceased, at least in an overt form. All avenues of employment were now, at least theoretically, open to Soviet Jews, including those fields which no Jew could conceivably have entered prior to 1917. There were Jewish generals, including Y.E. Yakir, one of the two most famous generals of the earlier phase of the Soviet regime (brutally executed by Stalin in his purge of the Red Army in 1937), Jewish ambassadors, senior Jewish civil servants in all departments, and many Jewish university professors. Until the later 1930s, Jews were probably overrepresented among the senior leaders of the Soviet regime, although their numbers declined quickly after Stalin came to supreme power in 1929. Many of the most characteristic and best-known cultural figures of the Soviet regime (especially, again, before the 1940s) were Jews, such as David Oistrakh the violinist, and the famous writers Isaak Babel, Osip Mandelstam, and Boris Pasternak. (Babel was almost certainly murdered by Stalin in 1941; Mandelstam died, probably in a Siberian prison camp, a victim of Stalin's Purges, in 1938; Pasternak was forced by Khrushchev to decline the Nobel Prize for Literature in 1958.) Young Jews flocked into the university system in considerable numbers, comprising 9.4 per cent of all students in institutions of higher education in the Russian Republic in 1929 (10,852 of 102,438). As a literate, urbanised sector of the population, Jews comprised an important strand among what would be termed the 'white collar' and 'managerial' sectors of the employed population, in the context of Soviet society. In 1934, about 41 per cent of the economically active Jewish population was employed as civil servants, state employees, and in the liberal professions, a vastly higher percentage than among the Soviet population as a whole, with its vast numbers of agricultural workers and manual labourers. In 1939 – when Stalinist repression had already taken on an antisemitic tenor – Jews (about 2 per cent of the Soviet population) comprised 16 per cent of all physicians, 10 per cent of all so-called 'cultural workers' (journalists, librarians, and so on), and 9 per cent of university professors and scientific workers. As well, the Soviet Union claimed as part of its *raison d'être* to have ended unemployment. While this may not have been strictly true, it is probably accurate enough that the new regime provided jobs (however meagre and however a product of Communist ideology) for most who wanted them. In particular, the *lumpenproletariat* of so-called *luftmenshen* (men who lived 'on air', without permanent employment), so well-known a feature of ghetto life in the Pale, now disappeared. For many poor Jews, the Soviet system unquestionably provided greater economic security, and, within the context of the Communist regime, greater employment opportunities, than had existed previously. It seems safe to say that during the Great Depression which began in 1929, a considerably lower percentage of Soviet Jews were unemployed than in any Western country. For these reasons, Soviet Jews were, in the majority of cases, probably not as hostile to the Soviet regime in the pre-1939 period as one might expect.

Jewish culture and religion

There is also some evidence that – again, strictly within the context of the Soviet system – a Jewish culture was emerging in the 1920s and early 1930s. The number of students in Yiddish-language schools peaked in the early 1930s. A number of Jewish scholarly journals, which briefly in the 1920s allowed a surprising amount of free discussion within the context of the Communist system, existed at this time. A Yiddish press and literature, strictly reflecting Soviet values but also republishing old classics, grew in the 1920s. In particular, a very distinguished Yiddish theatre grew up in the same decade, continuing until the Purges of the late 1930s (and, in a skeletal form, until 1949). By the mid-1930s there were 20 professional Yiddish theatre groups in the Soviet Union. The best-known Yiddish actors, such as the great Shlomo, or Solomon, Mikhoels (1890–1948), murdered on Stalin's orders in a 'motoring accident' in 1948, were known throughout Jewish Russia.

Traditional Jewish life in the new Russia could only be kept alive with the greatest difficulty, and after the advent of Stalin, only behind the backs of the Soviet secret police. Of special note were the efforts during the 1920s of Rabbi Joseph Isaac Schneerson (1880–1950), the Lubavitcher *rebbe* (the father-in-law of the celebrated Lubavitcher *rebbe* of the post-1945 period) to organise a Committee of Rabbis in Soviet Russia which managed to keep alive some traditional religious education in Jewish homes, and even some *yeshivot* life. Schneerson viewed the Jewish *Yevsektsiya* as more anti-religious than the Soviet regime, and also hoped to keep alive Sabbath observance by the creation of self-employed Jewish craft co-operatives (which, until about 1929, enjoyed some autonomy). With the advent to power of Stalin that year, any open continuation of Jewish religious life in Soviet Russia became virtually impossible, and rabbis faced the real likelihood of execution. While the death of Stalin in 1953 removed the most barbaric features of this persecution, essentially traditional Jewish religious life in Russia only began again, except in underground fashion, in the 1980s. (Lubavitcher Jews did maintain important underground contacts with religious Jews in the Soviet Union from the 1950s onwards.) Schneerson enjoyed some financial support from the American Joint Distribution Committee and other Western Jewish bodies during the early and mid-1920s, and even some *de facto* support from some open-minded Soviet officials. A crackdown on religious life, begun in 1927, forced

Schneerson into exile. After the 1920s, more Jewish religious life managed to survive in the non-European republics of the Soviet Union than in Russia and the western Soviet Union. In 1939, no fewer than 60 synagogues managed to survive in Georgia (in the Caucasus), compared with only a handful in Moscow and Leningrad.

Stalin and the Jews

Joseph Stalin (*né* Iosif Djugashvili, 1879–1953), born into a Georgian Orthodox Christian peasant family, came to power in 1929. He was seemingly a mild-mannered, cautious, and reticent man (and initially preferred by many 'moderate' Bolsheviks to the fiery radical Trotsky for that reason). However, he proved to be one of modern history's greatest villains, one of the most ruthless and evil tyrants and mass murderers ever known, who relentlessly crushed all opposition and killed millions of innocent people. Indeed, only Hitler can compare with Stalin in murderous evil. Of the two, Stalin was the more cunning and possibly the greater psychopath, a paranoid megalomaniac who distrusted everyone, in particular his closest supporters. It has been noted by some historians that while about 90 per cent of Hitler's closest associates remained in power throughout the Nazi era, approximately the same percentage of senior Communists holding office when Stalin became Russia's supreme leader around 1929 had perished by the time of his death in 1953, usually murdered on his orders. The most obvious difference between Hitler and Stalin, however, is that while Hitler hated only some specific groups (with Jews being at the top of the list), Stalin hated and feared everyone impartially. To Stalin, the world was virtually composed of enemies and conspirators, who had to be crushed and annihilated.

Stalin's impact on the Jews was thus two-edged. Virtually everything about the Stalinist regime was, of course, bad for the Jews and this period was one of the blackest in the annals of Jewish repression. Yet Stalin did not, until his last years, single out the Jews for especially bad treatment and the Stalinist regime cannot, until the 1940s (and particularly the five years before Stalin's death), be described as antisemitic. While unquestionably tens of thousands of Jews perished in Stalin's Purges, so did millions of others: literally everyone was at risk. In the last five years of his life, Stalin clearly became much more blatantly antisemitic, and it is quite possible that hundreds of thousands of Jews in the western Soviet Union might have been deported to Siberia had Stalin lived longer.

Stalin's ascent to supreme power around 1929 marked an end to whatever signs of pluralism, even liberalism, had existed in the 1920s. A period of forced collectivisation of the economy began at this time, ending the quasi-capitalist New Economic Policy experiment. Increased repression began as soon as Stalin came to power. Internal passports (which recorded the nationality of each person) became mandatory in 1933 and no worker was allowed to leave his place of employment without permission. The powers of the secret police, already very great, were further increased. Forced collectivisation became the rule in the Soviet countryside, where millions of peasants died as a result (especially in the Ukraine) in 1932–33. In early 1930, the 'nationality' sections of the Soviet Communist party were dissolved, including the *Yevsektsiya*. However negative and perverse it had been, its dissolution marked the end of any toleration by the regime of any form of Jewish separatism, no matter how loyal to the regime. All autonomous literary and cultural groups were dissolved in 1932, and 'socialist realism' became the only permissible literary or cultural style, one which slavishly praised Stalin and the Soviet regime without cessation. Although many Jewish (and, of course, non-Jewish) writers did their best to adapt, many others could not, fearing that dissent would be the preamble to an automatic death sentence. 'We must cultivate a new genre – silence,' was Isaak Babel's celebrated commentary on the Stalin era.

Inter-war demographic and socio-economic change

For Soviet Jewry, the 1920s and 1930s also witnessed considerable demographic and socio-economic change. In particular, a movement from small towns to big cities took place, as well as a migration from the western Soviet Union – areas in the Ukraine and Belorussia formerly in the Pale of Settlement – to the Russian Republic, especially to Moscow and Leningrad. Moscow (virtually without Jews in 1914) was estimated to be the home to about 86,000 Jews in 1923, 131,000 in 1926, and to no fewer than about 400,000 in 1939, when it contained more Jews than any city in Europe with the possible exception of Warsaw. In the same period, Leningrad's Jewish population grew from 52,000 (1923) to 84,000 (1926) to 275,000 (1939). Whereas in the early 1920s only two Soviet cities (Odessa and Kiev) held more than 100,000 Jews, by 1939 there were six (the two just mentioned plus Moscow, Leningrad, Kharkov and Dnepropetrovsk). As well, there occurred what is sometimes known as the 'proletarianisation of the Jews' (side by side with their overrepresentation in the Soviet 'middle classes'). Particularly in the areas of the former Pale, the number of Jews in factory jobs or engaged in manual work increased substantially, with the percentage of Jews in the larger cities employed in factory jobs rising from 16 per cent in 1930 to 30 per cent in 1939. Normally, there were former artisans in small towns of the Pale. This trend, however, was balanced by the almost inevitable tendency of Jews to gravitate into the 'white collar' and professional sectors of the economy, as they did, by and large, almost everywhere else where educational opportunities engendering social mobility were open to them.

Despite the Stalin period's complete refusal to countenance any form of

Jewish self-identity, the Soviet regime did encourage some forms of peculiarly Jewish endeavour. There was a concerted attempt by both the Soviet state and the *Yevsektsiya* to create Jewish agricultural communities. This effort was seen as an attempt to make 'productive' workers out of the middlemen traders and the former *luftmenshen* of the Pale. A number of specific organisations were established to facilitate the creation of Jewish agricultural settlements, especially OZET ('Society for Settling Jewish Toilers in Agriculture'), founded in 1924. Land was set aside, especially in Belorussia, the Ukraine and the Crimea, and these schemes received financial support from Jewish bodies overseas. Initially, these schemes enjoyed considerable success, and five autonomous Jewish agricultural regions were established. The percentage of economically active Jews engaged in agriculture (only 3.5 per cent in 1897) rose to 8.3 per cent in 1926 and to 11.1 per cent in 1930. Some Jews viewed wholly Jewish agricultural settlements as likely *de facto* to retain local self-governance and a modicum of Jewish culture. Communists looked upon these agricultural settlements as an alternative to Zionism, especially to the *kibbutzim* of Palestine which had a somewhat similar aim of bringing about the 'productivisation' of the Jews.

An even more direct attempt to rival the popularity among Russian Jews of Zionism was the creation of a Jewish autonomous region at Birobidzhan. The leadership of the Soviet Union was also motivated by a desire to draw significant numbers of Jews into new areas of settlement (and away from areas of dense Jewish population, where antisemitism flourished), and by a desire, in the 1920s, to 'settle' the Jewish question in Soviet Russia. In 1928–31, plans were formulated to create a 'Jewish Federative National Unit' on the banks of the Amur River, just north of Manchuria on the Chinese border. It seems clear that Birobidzhan also came into existence when and where it did in order to deter Japanese aggression from Manchuria into Soviet Siberia. The Jewish Autonomous Region officially came into existence in May 1934. The Soviet leadership apparently held great hopes for Birobidzhan at this time, envisioning the migration of hundreds of thousands of Jews there and seeing it as a potential rival to Palestine. (In this, Birobidzhan can be seen as a facet of the long-standing 'Territorial Movement' aimed at finding a national home for the Jews outside Palestine.)

Birobidzhan was, of course, almost a complete failure. The Soviet regime was unable to persuade more than a handful of Jews to move to this remote, utterly unlikely region. In 1936 the Jewish population of Birobidzhan numbered only 18,000, out of a total population of 76,000. The Birobidzhan scheme did have a few minor triumphs. Yiddish was declared to be its official language (on the Manchurian border!), and two Yiddish newspapers were founded (one, *Birobidzhaner Shtern*, continuing as the Soviet Union's only Yiddish newspaper until the end of the Soviet regime). Yiddish schools, and even a well-known Yiddish theatre group, emerged. Nevertheless, any positive developments were soon wiped out entirely by the Great Purges, which began at this time. Although Birobidzhan continued until the end of the Soviet Union as a 'Jewish Autonomous Region', it was never predominantly Jewish and was never autonomous. It is possible that a genuinely autonomous Jewish Region founded by the Soviet government in, for example, the Crimea, might have been much more successful, but a totalitarian state never permitted this to occur.

The Great Purges

The year 1934 is usually seen as the beginning of Stalin's Great Purges, which eliminated whatever elements of pluralism remained in the Soviet Union and crushed any remaining hopes of a viable Jewish existence there. In December 1934 Sergei Kirov, the young Communist boss of Leningrad, and in the context of the regime a liberal, who was widely seen as a rival to Stalin, was murdered, certainly on Stalin's orders. This marked the beginning of a mass purge of any and every rival to Stalin for power within the Communist party. Nearly all of the 'Old Bolsheviks' were murdered, usually after show trials at which they 'confessed' to absurd crimes. Tens of thousands of ordinary members of the party were executed or sent to Siberia. The Purges spread to every institution of Soviet society, to the military, the intelligentsia, the factories and farms. By the most recent estimates of historians, probably 4–5 million people met their deaths in the four years between 1934 and 1938 (other historians put the figure vastly higher at up to 20 million). Literally everyone in the Soviet Union lived in perpetual fear of the 'knock on the door' after midnight, when the secret police would come to take away another 'spy and wrecker'. The Purges were organised by the three successive People's Commissars for Internal Affairs of this period: Genrik Yagoda (1934–36), Nikolai Yezhov (1936–38), and Lavrenti Beria (1938–46). In their inhumanity and mindless dedication to Stalin's every whim, they are strongly reminiscent of Heinrich Himmler and the Nazi SS, their only superior in mass murder and organised terror. (Yagoda, it might be noted, was of Jewish descent.)

The Great Purges could not but affect Soviet Jewry adversely. Hundreds of thousands of Jews were arrested, and tens of thousands (at the very least) were executed. Virtually all of the Jews, leaders of the former *Yevsektsiya*, and of all other Yiddish and Jewish publications and groups in the Soviet Union, were shot. Jews were probably more likely than the average Soviet citizen to be under governmental suspicion, since any past association with a foreign or dissenting body of any kind was evidence, to Stalin and his henchmen, of subversion and disloyalty. Zionists, former Bundists, religious Jews, and Jews with a connection with Western Jewry, were under particular suspicion. The fact that so many of the 'Old Bolsheviks' who were particularly detested by Stalin were of Jewish origin, above all his arch-enemy Leon Trotsky (murdered on Stalin's orders in Mexico City in 1940), added to the suspicion felt by the regime towards all Jews who were not blindly obedient. On the other hand, the Great Purges were not antisemitic as such. Millions of people of every background were persecuted: Ukrainian and Armenian nationalists, adherents of Russian Orthodoxy, non-Jewish composers and artists like Shostakovitch and Prokofiev, and Russian members of the former capitalist class, were persecuted with as great a vigour as were Jews.

One area in which there was a definite and clear decline in the position of Jews was in their prominence in the Communist party, especially in senior posts. In 1921 five of 25 members of the Central Committee of the Communist party (20 per cent) were Jews. By 1929, after a decade of Stalinism, this figure declined to 12 per cent (11 of 95). Jews in particular were, with the rarest exceptions, no longer included in Stalin's innermost circles. Only Lazar Kaganovitch (1893–1991), a particularly ruthless stooge of Stalin, remained in the Politbureau, the Communist Party's 'Cabinet', after about 1930. Jews were better represented among senior ministers, with Maxim Litvinov (1876–1951), a relative 'liberal', serving as Soviet foreign minister from 1930 until 1939. At lower levels of the Communist party and administration, however, the Jewish percentage diminished steadily during the 1930s. There were several reasons for this: overt antisemitism, now given freer rein; the fact that the Soviet government had trained a new generation of leaders from all nationalities; the lack of a Jewish 'republic' (apart from Birobidzhan) with its own ethnic infrastructure. By the outbreak of the Second World War, while Jews were probably still somewhat overrepresented in the Soviet Union's governing infrastructure, it was certainly absurd to view that country as 'Jewish' or governed by Jews. Jews, were, in fact, being steadily squeezed out of the positions of influence they had previously held.

The Nazi–Soviet pact

The year 1938 is generally seen as marking the end of the most nightmarish phases of the Great Purges, with the Soviet Union reverting to 'merely' being an appalling totalitarian society. By the outbreak of the Second World War Stalin was all-powerful, his image omnipresent. It was considered daring to omit his name from a single paragraph of *Pravda* (the Soviet Union's best-known newspaper), and the 'cult of Stalin' strongly resembled a primitive religion. By 1939, however, a new and most formidable potential challenge to the continuing existence of the Soviet Union had emerged from Nazi Germany, whose own murderous, all-powerful dictator, Adolf Hitler, was a sworn enemy of Communism and of the Jews and Slavs of the Russian state. Step by step, war drew closer, with Hitler taking over the Rhineland, Austria, and Czechoslovakia and meeting no resistance from the democracies. It seemed clear to many that sooner or later Hitler was likely to attempt a war of conquest against the Soviet Union. The granaries, mineral resources, and *lebensraum* ('living space') of western Russia had traditionally been envied by aggressive German ideologues and militarists, while Hitler regarded the 'Judeo-Bolshevism' of the Soviet Union as the root of all evil. In order to deter German aggression, during the 1930s half-hearted attempts were made to reach some kind of alliance between the two key European democracies, Britain and France, and the Soviet Union. These attempts had always foundered on the deep mistrust and mutual hostility of the democracies and the Soviet Union as well as on the internal turmoil caused in Russia by Stalin's Purges. After the Anglo-French collapse at Munich in September 1938, when Germany was allowed to seize the Sudetenland, Stalin attempted to buy time for what he viewed as an inevitable 'showdown' with Hitler by becoming increasingly friendly to Nazi Germany. In May 1939 Maxim Litvinov, who, as mentioned, was Jewish, was suddenly replaced as Soviet foreign minister by V.M. Molotov, by origin a middle-class Russian. This was widely interpreted as a sign that Stalin wished to have closer dealings with Nazi Germany: Hitler would almost certainly not have negotiated with, or even met with, a Soviet foreign minister who was Jewish. On 23 August 1939 the two dictatorships stunned the whole world by entering into a non-aggression pact, effectively removing the prospect of war between the Soviet Union and Germany in the near future. Once Hitler was assured that he would not have to fight against the Soviet Union, he invaded Poland only a week later, sparking the outbreak of the Second World War. By a secret protocol of the Nazi–Soviet pact, Germany and Russia divided eastern Europe into spheres of influence, with Russia being given hegemony in eastern Poland, Estonia, Latvia, and Bessarabia (part of Romania). Lithuania, the third Baltic republic, was also later added to the Soviet sphere of eastern Europe.

While this amazing pact between two ideologies which supposedly stood at opposite ends of the political spectrum startled the whole world, it was particularly shocking to Jews, and well-nigh incomprehensible. During the 1930s, many Jews in the Western world looked admiringly at the Soviet Union as a land without antisemitism and without unemployment. Ignoring the enormities and crimes of the Stalinist regime, they joined the Communist parties of the Western world in disproportionate numbers (although they were, of course, far from being the only group to join). To them, the Soviet Union alone appeared to have stood up to Hitler. The Nazi–Soviet pact came as a shattering blow to many Jews in the West who were sympathetic to the Soviet Union (and to many non-Jews). Many left the party. The Communist party explained the Pact as, essentially, removing the Soviet Union from an 'imperialist war'. Britain and France, at war with Nazi Germany, ironically now became the chief ideological enemies of the Soviet Union. This was to change categorically less than two years later, when Germany invaded the Soviet Union, and Stalin was forced into an alliance with Britain's Churchill. For the Soviet Union, the major consequence of the

Nazi–Soviet pact was the takeover of very significant areas of eastern Europe, and their incorporation into the Soviet Union in 1939–40. All of these areas had very large Jewish populations. The areas comprised the eastern half of the Polish republic, including such Jewish population centres as Bialystok, Lvov, and Pinsk; the three independent Baltic republics of Estonia, Latvia, and Lithuania, and Bessarabia and Northern Bukovina, formerly in Romania. The incorporation of these areas brought an additional 1,775,000 Jews into the Soviet Union, of whom 1,300,000 were in eastern Poland.

The Jewish population of the Soviet Union in mid-1939, just before the Nazi–Soviet pact, was, according to the 1939 Soviet Census, 3,020,000; thus, the Jewish population of that country grew to about 4.8 million, giving it the second largest Jewish population in the world after the United States. The Soviet Union would rule over these areas for less than two years before Nazi Germany launched its invasion on 22 June 1941, but even in that short period of time vast changes were made in the social structure of the Jewish people in these areas. The way of life in the *shtetlekh* was destroyed, religious life brought to an end, pupils receiving Jewish education transferred to Communist schools, and private property was confiscated. Tens of thousands of Jews (estimates of 250,000 are common) were arrested and deported to the interior of the Soviet Union, including many Jewish community leaders. Most apparently perished in Siberia (little of a precise nature is known of their fate) but some may, ironically, have survived the Holocaust by being beyond the Nazi line of military advance, while those who remained behind largely perished. As well, a large and steady stream of Jewish refugees from Nazi-occupied Poland entered the new areas of Soviet administration. As bad as the situation was in the Soviet Union, in Nazi-occupied Poland, with its forced ghettoisations preceding genocide, life for Jews was, even before the 'Final Solution' was instituted, vastly worse. It is generally estimated that about 300,000 Jews from western Poland entered the new areas of the Soviet Union in these two years (many were subsequently deported by the Soviet Union back to German-occupied areas).

Despite the complete hostility of the Soviet administration to traditional Jewish culture and religion, the situation for these Jews was not all bad. Antisemitism, an endemic feature of Polish, Romanian, and Lithuanian societies, was ended at least in its overt forms. As elsewhere in the Soviet Union, Jews could enter the universities and all professions freely, without the *numerus clausus* and legal and extra-legal prejudice of the previous regime. Although the standard of living for most Jews (meagre as it had been) declined under Soviet rule, many poor Jews found themselves better off. A kind of secular Communist Jewish culture, albeit greatly attenuated by Stalin, replaced traditional Jewish culture. The lifestyle of these Jews, in other words, quickly became similar to that of all other Jews of the Soviet Union.

Soviet Jewry during the Holocaust

How the history of Soviet Jewry might have evolved from this point is unknowable, for on 22 June 1941, the Soviet Union was suddenly invaded by Nazi Germany. By October, Germany was in possession of most of the western portion of the country, although it was unable to take either Moscow or Leningrad. It was in Russia, following the invasion of 22 June, that Hitler and the Nazis first began their policy of the genocide of the Jews, launching a campaign for the deliberate mass murder of Jews without parallel in history. This was in full swing by September or October 1941. In the western Soviet Union, genocide was chiefly carried out by the Einsatzgruppen of the Nazi SS, who murdered thousands of Jews by machine-gunning them in clearings at the edge of Jewish towns and settlements. The most notorious single such killing place was Babi Yar, a ravine near Kiev, where on 29–31 September 1941 at least 33,000 Jews were killed. When Nazi Germany was at last defeated on 8 May 1945, the face of Jewish Russia had changed comprehensively.

Ascertaining how many Soviet Jews died in the Holocaust is among the most difficult demographic issues of the Second World War, and no consensus exists as to the actual number who perished. Boundary changes, the problems in separating murders committed by the Nazis from battle and other deaths, the vagaries of the Soviet census, and many other similar factors mean that no straightforward answer to this question is possible. Expert estimates of Jewish deaths at the hands of the Nazis in the Soviet Union during the Second World War range from 700,000 to 1.5 million. One recent, careful scholarly estimate placed the figure at 970,000. It should be noted that this figure (which may well be an overestimate) excludes a number of very important categories of Jewish deaths during the Second World War which considerably increases this statistic. At least 250,000 other Soviet Jews died as a result of other causes during the war, especially battle deaths, privations in the siege of Leningrad and persecution by Stalin. As appalling as they are, these figures *exclude* all deaths in areas added to the Soviet Union in 1939–40: the three Baltic Republics, eastern Poland, and Bessarabia. Including only those areas which were retained by the Soviet Union in 1945 (chiefly the Baltic republics, Bessarabia (Moldavia), and easternmost Poland) adds at least another 350,000 more victims to the death toll. The only firm guidelines to the effects of the war on the Jewish population of the Soviet Union are the censuses of 1939 and 1959, the first carried out after the war. In the 1939 Census, the Jewish population of the Soviet Union was 3,020,000 (a figure which was in all likelihood an exaggeration; the actual number was probably about 2.8 million), and in 1959 it was 2,268,000, a decline of 752,000. However, the vast areas added to the Soviet territory in 1939–40, which were retained in 1945, must be added to these figures. Overall, it seems likely that at least 1.6 million Soviet Jews failed to survive the war, about 40 per cent of the pre-war Jewish population, of whom probably 1.3 million or so perished directly at the hands of the Nazis and their genocidal policies.

In the early days of the war, a very large number of Jews from the western Soviet Union reached relative safety behind the front lines. It is difficult to give a more precise figure, but specialist historians believe that as many as 1.5 million Jews may have been evacuated, chiefly to the Urals and other new settlements in the interior of the Soviet Union, especially in central Asia. Although Jews in the West were under no illusion as to their treatment in Nazi-controlled areas, many Soviet Jews literally did not know that the Nazi regime hated Jews. During the two years in which the Nazi–Soviet pact was in force, there was a total ban in the Soviet media on reporting Nazi antisemitism. Had the treatment of Jews under Nazi rule been better reported, it is quite possible that more would have been able to flee in time to the interior of Russia.

The Nazi invasion of the Soviet Union meant that the Russian state was now engaged in a life-or-death struggle with Germany, in which its allies were Britain and (after the Japanese attack on Pearl Harbor) the United States. Although Russia's back was up against the wall in the early days of the war (with Stalin coming very close to surrender in October 1941), Nazi Germany was unable to deliver the quick *blitzkrieg* knockout blow it had hoped, and became bogged down in the terrible conditions of the Russian winter, for which its armies were completely unprepared. Gradually the tide turned, decisively after the celebrated Battle of Stalingrad in January 1943. Since they faced the fiercest, most murderous antisemite in history as their common enemy, Russia's Jews naturally gave their most wholehearted support to the Soviet Union and its allies, as tyrannical as the Stalinist regime was and as destructive to Jewish institutions and culture as Soviet rule had been. There were high hopes – shared by all 'ordinary' Russians – that victory in the war would see some liberalisation of the most totalitarian features of Soviet society. There were, indeed, some grounds for specifically Jewish hopes. A so-called Jewish Anti-Fascist Committee was formed in April 1943, the first explicitly Jewish organisation founded in the Soviet Union in many years. Headed by Shlomo Mikhoels, the great Yiddish actor, and Itzik Feffer, a colonel in the Red Army and orthodoxly Stalinist poet, its aim was, apparently, to heighten pro-Soviet feeling among Jews in the West. Nevertheless, it was also a body whose members were conscious of their Jewishness, openly voicing opinions not permitted in the Soviet Union since the beginning of the Purges. Feffer's wartime poem 'I am a Jew' seemed to summarise the newly-permitted freedom of expression. In 1943 Mikhoels and Feffer embarked on a tour of America and Britain where, amazingly, they praised Zionism and sent birthday greetings to Chaim Weizmann, head of the World Zionist Organization, previously reviled by Moscow as a 'reactionary nationalist'. The Soviet Union did seem to be moving at this stage to some kind of endorsement of the Zionist movement, probably in order to enhance Russia's influence in the Middle East at the expense of Britain, but also perhaps because of some feeling of sympathy for Jewish wartime suffering. During the war (especially in 1943–44) there were also more Yiddish publications, and many well-placed Soviet Jews held apparently realistic hopes for genuine liberalisation after the war, with plans openly made for an unprecedented wave of Jewish publications and cultural activities, even in the religious sphere.

None of these were to be, and, within a few years of the end of the war, the Jewish community of the Soviet Union was to enter into the darkest period it had known since tsarist times. Nevertheless, it cannot be emphasised too strongly that it was the Soviet army which, in the well-known phrase, 'tore the guts out of Nazi Germany', and saved whatever remnants of eastern European Jewry had managed to remain alive in the face of the relentless Nazi death machine. Probably 3.5 million Jews (and possibly more) survived the war in Eastern Europe and the Soviet Union, virtually all of whom would have perished had the Red Army not been victorious. It was the Soviet army which liberated Auschwitz in January 1945 and saved Budapest's 120,000 Jews a month later.

Soviet Jews, too, played a very notable role in the war effort. They were the only, or virtually the only, ethnic group in the Soviet population whose anti-Nazi proclivities were total and absolute and who could never, under any circumstances, desert the Allied side to fight for the Nazis. On the contrary, every blow given by Soviet Jews against the Nazi scourge was literally one of life or death. About 500,000 Jews served in the Soviet armies during the war. The number of Jews who died as military casualties of the war (as opposed to those who were killed by the Nazis) is unknown, but the usual estimate is in the range or 160,000–200,000. No fewer than 200 Soviet Jews rose to the rank of general, with Lieutenant-General I.D. Cherniakhovsky commanding the 3rd Belorussian Front which conquered East Prussia (where he was killed). At 38 years of age Cherniakhovsky was the youngest man to command a front, the equivalent, in Western terms, of an army. (In 1944, there were ten fronts in combat against the Germans.) A total of 60,000 Soviet Jewish soldiers were decorated during the war, with the highest Soviet award, 'Hero of the Soviet Union', given to 145 Jews. Jews also played an extremely important role in the Partisan forces which fought the Nazis in the occupied areas of the western Soviet Union. Probably 20,000 or more Jewish Partisans fought in the Western Soviet Union, despite the fact that virtually all of the Jews in this area had been killed. One 70-man Partisan detachment, commanded by Vladimir Epstein, a Jew who had escaped from Auschwitz, killed 120 men of the SS; thousands of Nazis and their collaborators were killed by the Partisans, or their war material destroyed.

Post-war Stalinism and the State of Israel

Despite all the losses suffered by Soviet Jewry in the war, in 1945 they probably still numbered over 2.5 million (including an estimated 200,000

Polish Jews who survived the war in Russia and were later repatriated). Soviet Jewry was still the second largest Jewish community in the world, behind merely the United States (with an estimated 5 million Jews) in size. In 1945 only about 600,000 Jews lived in Palestine, and Israel's Jewish population would not overtake that of the Soviet Union's for at least 20 years. Soviet Jewry was the largest surviving Jewish community in Europe by many orders of magnitude, dwarfing the remaining communities in Romania (500,000) and Britain (350,000). However, denied the leadership role it should have fulfilled, it was quickly forced into silence and invisibility by Stalinist repression until Jewish consciousness miraculously reawakened in Russia a quarter-century later.

The first few years after the war did not produce the overt antisemitism which became so prominent a feature of Stalin's last years, but it did see some ominous signs. There was certainly no 'thaw' towards liberalism, and no renaissance of Jewish publishing or culture. More worryingly, there was virtually no specific mention of Jews either as victims of the Nazis or as heroes of the liberation. Jewish victims of Nazism were almost always termed 'Russians' or 'Ukrainians' and Hitler's 'war against the Jews', arguably his ultimate *raison d'être*, was totally obliterated in Soviet histories and propaganda, with the mass murders attributed to fascism's hatred of socialism and the Soviet Union. No official Soviet publication between 1945 and 1963 so much as mentioned the Jews as victims of the Nazi invaders. Monument after monument erected after the war where the Germans carried out their massacres failed to mention that the overwhelming majority of the victims were Jews, only specifying 'Russians', 'Ukrainians', or other nationalities. Similarly, the specific and honourable role of Jews in the Soviet army and as Partisans was seldom or never mentioned; indeed, scholars have demonstrated a clear pattern of editing out the names of military heroes and commanders when these were obviously Jewish.

Nevertheless, at first some continuation of the hopeful wartime spirit continued. There was as yet no crackdown on the Jews. Six Yiddish theatres were still active in the period immediately after the war. While the storm against the Jews began to break no later than 1947, there was one crucial area which seemed to present a startling contradiction in the position of the Jews which was beginning to occur in the Soviet Union itself. This was the surprisingly friendly attitude taken in 1947–48 by the Soviet Union towards the establishment of the State of Israel. The Soviet Union's official policy towards Zionism had always been highly negative. In May 1947 Andrei Gromyko, the Soviet deputy foreign minister, made an astonishing speech at the United Nations which recounted the 'indescribable' nature of the 'sorrow and suffering' undergone by the Jewish people in Europe. 'A large number' of the survivors, Gromyko stated, 'are in camps . . . and are continuing to undergo great privations.'

> The fact that no Western European state has been able to ensure the defence of the elementary rights of the Jewish people . . . explains the

aspirations of the Jews to establish their own State. It would be unjust not to take this into consideration and to deny this right of the Jewish people ...

While the Soviet Union still preferred an independent bi-national Palestine, it was willing to consider partition of the mandate into Jewish and Arab states. The Soviet Union voted for the partition resolution at the United Nations in November 1947 and allowed Czechoslovak arms to be sent freely to the new State of Israel during the War of Independence, arms crucial to the state's survival. In 1948 Radio Moscow compared the Israeli struggle to that of the Republicans in the Spanish Civil War. The Soviet Union granted *de jure* recognition to the State of Israel on 18 May 1948, only a few days after its establishment, and long before most other countries had done so. This mood continued for at least a few months after the establishment of the new state. In September 1948 Golda Meir (known at the time as Meyerson, and later of course Israeli prime minister) arrived in Moscow as the first ambassador from the State of Israel. At *Rosh Hashanah* (16 October) 1948 there occurred the celebrated incident when 50,000 or more Jews crowded the streets in front of the main Moscow synagogue to greet Mrs Meyerson and the Israeli delegation who had come to pray. 'Thank you for remaining Jews,' she said to the crowd in Yiddish. This was arguably the largest group of people to congregate in Moscow for a common purpose not organised by the Communist authorities since 1917, and it apparently created deep disquiet, even fear, among the Kremlin's leaders.

Commentators and historians have attributed this short-lived honeymoon period between the Soviet Union and the new Jewish state simply to international power politics, in particular to the desire by Russia to hasten Britain's departure from the Middle East. The Kremlin apparently thought that the Israeli government, with its socialist traditions and the Russian–Polish origins of most of its leaders, would be friendly to Moscow, especially given the hostility of Zionists to Britain, the former Mandatory power. There was also a desire to curry favour with the Western left-liberal intelligentsia, which was at the time certainly pro-Zionist. Finally, it is entirely possible that among a certain stratum of the Soviet leadership there was a sincere feeling of sympathy for the Jews, whose unparalleled suffering was known to all from the Nuremberg Trials and from the evidence of mass murder found by the Red Army.

The 'Black Years' under Stalin

This mood of sympathy, however, proved extremely short-lived. From 1948 until 1953 the Soviet Union experienced what is often known as the 'Black Years' of the Jews in Russia, a period of persecution and danger, rarely equalled even in tsarist times. A number of reasons may be adduced why the situation for the Jews in Russia deteriorated so markedly. In the first place, Stalin, a paranoid megalomaniac before the war, now deteriorated still further. By the late 1940s it seems clear that he was clinically insane, deeply and murderously suspicious of everyone and everything that appeared not to treat him with abject abasement and cult-like worship. His tantrums were apparently characteristic of cerebral arteriosclerosis compounded by alcoholism (Stalin was a heavy drinker). The links of Soviet Jewry to Israel and, possibly, to Western Jewry, were tailor-made to arouse his venomous ire. Stalin's faithful henchman in enforcing absolute conformity in the cultural sphere, A.A. Zhdanov, a particularly virulent opponent of 'cosmopolitanism' (as any expression of Jewish identity came to be known), initiated the crackdown on intellectuals in the late 1940s. Secondly, as the Cold War began in earnest after 1947–48, any individual or group that seemed to have international links, especially to the West, came increasingly under suspicion as traitors and conspirators. Second-level Communist officials, often crudely educated and always keen to curry favour with the Kremlin, bent over backwards to root out any signs of dissent. Thirdly, overt antisemitism now made a considerable comeback throughout eastern Europe, fanned by the deprivations of the war, by the Great Russian chauvinism increasingly espoused by Stalin after 1945, and by the weakened position of Soviet Jewry, decimated in many places by the Holocaust. Stalin's latent antisemitism, possibly the product of his background in a seminary, and never far from the surface, now became full-blown, although it once again must be emphasised that literally no group in Soviet society was immune from persecution by Stalin and his minions.

The anti-Jewish campaign which took place in the Soviet Union between about 1948 and Stalin's death in March 1953 had a number of distinct components. The most important was the virtual liquidation of Yiddish culture in any form. This took place in 1948 and 1949 with the arrest and frequent execution of most of Russia's leading Jewish writers and theatre workers. The most important single blow suffered by Soviet Jewry during this period was the murder of Shlomo Mikhoels by the secret police in Minsk (the Soviet authorities claimed that Mikhoels had died in an 'automobile accident'). Mikhoels was, unofficially, the head of the Soviet Union's Jewish community and probably its best known spokesman at home and abroad. Mikhoel's death had something in common with the murder by Stalin seven years before of Henryk Erlich and Victor Alter, two very prominent leaders of the Bund in Poland, who fled to the Soviet Union to escape the Nazis. In the Soviet Union the two experienced both imprisonment and then, after the outbreak of the war, some esteem. Asked by Lavrenti Beria (head of the internal security forces) to write directly to Stalin to suggest creating a Jewish World Committee which would appeal to Western Jews, they had an unexpected response: Stalin had them shot, in December 1941. It is believed that Stalin remembered them as former Menshevik leaders who had opposed the October 1917 Revolution and, for whatever reason, decided they were traitors.

Mikhoels was, strangely, given a state funeral, probably indicating that some kind of power struggle was going on in the Kremlin. Worse, however, was to follow. At the end of 1948, the Jewish Anti-Fascist Committee, formed during the war, was dissolved, its journal *Einikayt* (Jewish for 'Unity') ended, and its publishing house closed down. So, too, was the Yiddish magazine *Heymland*. Leading members of the Moscow Yiddish Theatre were arrested. The Jewish section of the Writers' Union was abolished. Most of Russia's leading Jewish writers and intellectuals were also arrested, at least 430 in the winter of 1948–49. The two remaining Yiddish schools in Vilnius (Vilna) and Kaunas (Kovno) were closed down. Bookshops were purged of all Yiddish books. 'Yiddish was denied even the right to continue praising Stalin,' one wit commented.

In 1949 there followed the campaign against 'cosmopolitans', which had a heavily antisemitic bent to it. Cartoons appeared in Soviet newspapers depicting hook-nosed 'cosmopolites without a fatherland', Nazi-style. Newspapers denounced 'rootless cosmopolitan intellectuals'. This campaign did not aim only at Jews, and, indeed, Stalin's henchman Andrei Zhdanov concentrated the greatest public ire at several non-Jewish writers, especially Anna Akhmatova, widely regarded as Russia's greatest living poet. Nevertheless, it was reliably estimated that at least 60 per cent (some studies say 90 per cent) of intellectuals denounced were Jews. One notable feature of the Soviet press at this time was the so-called 'disclosure of pseudonyms', wherein the original Jewish name of a 'cosmopolitan' writer was suddenly revealed. 'Thus,' as the historian Benjamin Pinkus has noted, 'the public suddenly discovered that Yakovlev was none other than Khotsman; Melnikov turned out to be Melman; Kholodov was Meerovich; and Burlochenko, Berdichevsky.'

There was some moderation in this campaign at the end of 1949, possibly on the direct orders of Stalin, who, in one of his inexplicable changes of mood, at this stage still opposed overt antisemitism. In the early 1950s, however, the campaign began again with a vengeance. In August 1952 24 leading Yiddish writers, held in prison for several years, were executed. In November 1952 came the Slansky Trial in Prague, in which Rudolf Slansky (1901–52), the Jewish secretary of the Czechoslovak Communist party and 13 other leading Czech officials (11 of whom were Jews) were tried and executed for engaging in 'Zionist espionage' and for alleged links to the CIA. The Slansky trial was carried out on the express orders of Moscow, and was accompanied by openly antisemitic and anti-Zionist tirades in the Czech press. In the Soviet Union, Jews were dismissed *en masse* from most academic and official posts in a manner strongly reminiscent of Nazi Germany in the 1930s. Although Jewish officers were very prominent in the Soviet military until 1945, between 1948 and 1953 virtually every high-ranking Jewish military officer was dismissed, among them 63 generals and 111 colonels. The new editor of the 24-volume *Great Soviet Encyclopedia* published in 1953 gave precisely four columns to the subject of Jews, a fraction of the material in previous editions. The climax of the 'Black Years' came in January 1953, with the so-called 'Doctors' Plot'. Nine prominent doctors, six of whom were Jewish, were arrested in Moscow for having murdered Zhdanov (who died in 1948) and plotting to kill Stalin. Fear approaching total panic gripped Soviet Jewry. One Western historian was told by a Moscow Jew many years later that 'when the news of the arrests of the Jewish doctors came over the radio we felt as if Hitler's armies were once again at the gates of the city'. Soviet newspapers outdid themselves to denounce 'Zionist agents of the American Secret Service'. *Pravda* claimed that the 'exposure of the band of prisoner-doctors is a blow at the international Jewish Zionist organization.' Many rumours circulated that Stalin was about to deport the Jews of Moscow, Leningrad, and other large cities to central Asia and Siberia. Others believed that mass pogroms were about to begin, as in tsarist times. Many explanations have been offered for the madness of 1952–53: Stalin was now insane, or a power struggle of some kind was going on behind the scenes, with Malenkov (briefly Stalin's successor) or Beria actually responsible for the wave of anti-semitism. It was claimed in later years that some high-ranking Soviet officials, including Nikita Khrushchev, opposed the more extreme manifestations of this antisemitic wave.

On 5 March 1953 Stalin suddenly died. Many rumours about his death were heard: that he was murdered, that he had had a vehement argument with his underlings about moving the Jews to Siberia and suffered a stroke. With the sudden death of the tyrant, the very worst excesses of his last years ended. On 4 April 1953, amazingly, all charges against the seven surviving doctors of the 'Plot' (two had died from torture) were dropped. Crude anti-semitism (although not anti-Zionism) suddenly disappeared from the Soviet press. Malenkov and Beria, who may have been the instigators of the near-pogrom atmosphere, were purged by Khrushchev and Bulganin, who emerged as the victors in the post-Stalin Kremlin power struggle. Beria was arrested in June 1953 and shot in December as an 'enemy of the people.' (It was following Beria's death that the famous incident occurred in which subscribers to the *Great Soviet Encyclopedia* were told to remove the article on his life with a razor, and replace it with an extension of the entry on the Bering Sea!) The 'Black Years' were now over.

The Khrushchev regime

The Soviet Jewish community naturally had high hopes that the death of Stalin, and the ending of the grosser forms of antisemitism, would lead to a new dawn in Soviet Jewish affairs. They were to be cruelly disappointed. Shortly after the death of Stalin, it was increasingly clear that Nikita

Khrushchev (1894–1970), the grandson of a Ukrainian serf, would be victorious in the power struggle to succeed him. Khrushchev was the chief ruler of the Soviet Union from about 1954 until he was replaced by other Soviet officials in 1964. A voluble, emotional fat man who loved to mix with people, he appeared to be the exact opposite of Stalin in everything except his commitment to Marxist ideology. Khrushchev was not an anti-semite as such (he had a Jewish daughter-in-law, just as Stalin had a Jewish son-in-law) and lacked Stalin's criminal paranoia. Nevertheless, while on the one hand he was in many respects a breath of fresh air, who denounced Stalin's worst excesses in a celebrated secret speech to Communist officials in 1956, he did nothing to ameliorate the condition of Soviet Jewry and stubbornly refused to recognise any specifically Jewish suffering under Stalin. Khrushchev was torn, in his personal attitude to the Jews, between a certain liberalism and hostility to the grosser forms of antisemitism on the one hand, and a peasant mistrust of Jews on the other, combined with a narrow Communist interpretation of the position of Jews as not really a national group in the same sense as other nationalities. Under Khrushchev, the worst persecution of the 'Black Years' certainly ended, and many imprisoned Jews were released or (if dead) 'rehabilitated'. Certainly the imminent sense of deadly danger experienced by most Soviet Jews during Stalin's last years vanished. Khrushchev also began a policy of *détente* with the West, and briefly allowed a certain amount of free expression and the publication of dissenting opinions which, under Stalin, would have won for their authors an automatic death sentence. Nevertheless, in many ways the position of Jews in the Soviet Union probably deteriorated still further under Khrushchev. Certainly there was no dramatic improvement, and no Jewish renaissance even in the context of the Soviet system. The period of Khrushchev's rule was also deeply confused in its attitude towards Jews, with both (some) positive and (many) negative signs and signals at the same time.

This may be illustrated by considering the Soviet attitude towards the Jewish religion: a chief rabbi of Moscow was again recognised (in the person of Solomon Shlieffer) and, amazingly, early in 1957, a *yeshivah* attached to the Great Synagogue was permitted to be established, the first Jewish theological institution of any kind established in the Soviet Union since 1917. A Jewish prayer book, reprinted from the engravings of old prayer books, appeared in 1956, although a new prayer book, announced the following year, never appeared. The chief rabbi of Moscow was also permitted some contact with Western and Israeli Jewish figures. On the other hand, in 1953–54 and then, much more stridently, after 1958, there occurred a renewed 'anti-religious campaign' launched by the Soviet author-ities. While all religions were attacked, Judaism was attacked particularly often and with great vehemence. One historian has estimated that up to 20 per cent of all anti-religious attacks in the period 1959–64 were against Judaism, although Jews made up only 1 per cent of the Soviet population.

Worse still, numerous synagogues were closed by the Communist authorities, often for no reason and while still functioning and well attended. One estimate is that the number of functioning synagogues in the Soviet Union declined from about 1100 in 1926 to about 500 in 1945 and to 100–150 by the late 1950s. By the time of Khrushchev's fall, their number had declined to between 60 and 70. Most of these were in remote Central Asian areas and the Caucasus, where Judaism had been allowed much greater freedom than in the larger population centres, but even here numerous synagogue closures occurred. By 1964, there were only 17 functioning synagogues in the Russian Republic, and only three in Belorussia. Orthodox Jewish religious refinements, such as the baking of *matzot*, were maintained only with the greatest difficulty and only after Western protests. Because attendance at the few public synagogues in the big cities was often fraught with danger for anyone brave enough to try it, a movement for Jewish worship in the home grew up in Moscow and Leningrad. This movement was instrumental in sparking the revival of Zionist consciousness from the late 1960s. In 1961, it was estimated that 50,000 Moscow Jews held services on *Simchat Torah* ('Rejoicing in the Law', a Jewish festival held after the High Holy Days) in their homes. Western *Habad* rabbis were also allowed openly to begin some contacts in the Soviet Union from the mid-1950s.

Soviet relations with Israel also deteriorated in this period. After the reception given to the Israeli ambassador, Mrs Meyerson, by Moscow's Jews, the Kremlin had become deeply suspicious of Israel's effects upon Soviet Jewry. Russia was also deeply disappointed by Israel's foreign policy, which moved ever-closer to the United States and to American Jewry. Israel's Communist party and other leftist elements were increasingly excluded from that country's governmental structure. Moscow increasingly backed a pro-Arab, anti-'imperialist' foreign policy in the Middle East, although it also maintained a neutral and diplomatically 'correct' attitude towards Israel. In 1952–53, however, relations between the two states began to worsen rapidly, having fallen victim to the intensified Cold War and to the anti-Jewish paranoia engendered in Russia by the Kremlin. In February 1953, just before Stalin died, the Kremlin had broken off diplomatic relations with Israel. Stalin's fortuitous death a month later allowed diplomatic relations to be restored and, initially, something like harmony was briefly achieved, with even some very minor Jewish emigration to Israel permitted. Under Khrushchev, however, the Soviet Union adopted an increasingly militant pro-Arab stance, especially after the Suez war of 1956. This was accompanied by an especially virulent campaign of anti-Zionist propaganda in the Soviet press and media. Many Zionist activists were harassed, arrested, and even sent to Siberian camps, especially after an overly-enthusiastic display of support by Moscow Jews for a 200-strong Israeli delegation to a Moscow youth festival in 1957. Soviet export of oil to Israel was also stopped in 1957. By the time of Khrushchev's fall in 1964, Soviet–Israeli relations, while they continued to exist in the sense that embassies were open, were close to freezing point. Under Khrushchev, too, something like overt antisemitism reappeared in the Soviet Union. Jews were openly branded as 'economic criminals' and as villains (often, pro-Nazis) in Soviet novels. In 1963 there appeared Trofim Kichko's *Judaism Without Embellishment*, published by the Ukrainian Academy of Sciences. Attacking Jews and Judaism in terms strongly reminiscent of Nazi propaganda, and illustrated with repellent antisemitic cartoons, its publication caused a wave of protest from around the world, including many European Communist parties. The Soviet press was forced to repudiate the work, which was withdrawn from sale. The Ukraine in particular became known as a place which *de facto* encouraged venomous antisemitic propaganda, although virtually the entirety of the Soviet press and media was engaged in some form of antisemitic and anti-Zionist diatribe.

Not everything was black under Khrushchev. Jews were still overrepresented in the professional and managerial infrastructure. In 1964, 16 per cent of newly elected members of the Russian Academy were Jews, and Jews continued to be prominent as celebrities in a wide variety of high-profile Soviet activities, from classical music to chess (a prestigious field in which Soviet Jews have always been very prominent and successful). Many of the trends deleterious to Soviet Jews also affected other nationalities. For example, there were no Ukrainian-language schools for the three million Ukrainians living in the Russian Republic, while Armenian, Ukrainian and Baltic nationalists, and dissidents of all backgrounds, were severely repressed and punished. For a number of reasons, however, Jews were especially liable for harsh treatment: the fact that (apart from Birobidzhan) Soviet Jews had no distinct territory with some self-governing powers; the close association of Jews in Soviet eyes with Western, especially American, 'imperialism'; the deterioration of Soviet–Israeli relations; above all, the deep pre-existing traditions of antisemitism which were never eradicated and increasingly took hold again after the 1930s.

Between Khrushchev and Gorbachev

Khrushchev's fall in 1964 was followed by the rule of Leonid Brezhnev (1964–82), and then by the brief periods of leadership of Yuri Andropov (1982–84) and Konstantin Chernenko (1984–85). The era of Soviet rule from about 1970 until the coming to power of Mikhail Gorbachev in 1985 is widely known as the 'period of stagnation', marked by an increasingly gerontocratic and conservative party leadership in an unsuccessful economy with mounting problems at home and abroad. Indeed, the apparent ossification of Soviet society between the 1950s and the 1980s was remarkable. Russia exploded its first atomic bomb in 1949, only four years after the United States, and set off its first hydrogen bomb only a few months after its American rival, in 1953. In 1957 the Soviet Union electrified the world by sending the first artificial satellite, Sputnik I, into orbit, several months before the launch of the United States' first satellite, and in 1961 it sent the first man into space, Yuri Gagarin, again ahead of America's first astronaut. Until the mid-1960s the Soviet Union seemed to dominate the space race, and Russia seemed to be at the forefront of many scientific fields. Its educational system was widely praised in the West, and widely contrasted with capitalist school systems, which seemed to produce only juvenile delinquents and semi-literates. Rates of economic growth in the Soviet Union exceeded those in many Western countries until about 1970. By the 1970s, however, it was clear that the Soviet Union had ceased to advance and was caught in a straightjacket of fossilisation and inertia, while both the West (especially western Europe) and newer economies of capitalist east Asia were forging ahead. This straightjacket of inertia continued until the ascendancy to power of the arch-reformer Mikhail Gorbachev in 1985. Nevertheless, the Soviet Union was still a military superpower, crushing revolts in East Germany (1953), Hungary (1956), and Czechoslovakia (1968), and continuing to be highly influential in the world's geo-politics from the Middle East to Vietnam to Latin America.

The position of the Jews in the Soviet Union between 1964 and 1985 was one of continuing deterioration, with the trends towards open antisemitism, virulent anti-Zionism, and marginalisation of the Jewish community continuing as under Khrushchev. In 1967, the Soviet Union severed diplomatic relations with Israel in the wake of Israel's remarkable victories over the Arabs in the Six Day War. The Soviet Union also forced all of its satellites in Eastern Europe (except Romania) to follow suit. At the United Nations and other international bodies, the Soviet Union and its satellites headed a hysterical anti-Israeli coalition with the Arab states and much of the Third World which, year after year, steamrollered through one-sided and absurd anti-Israeli resolutions, including the notorious 1975 resolution officially declaring Zionism to be a form of racism. The Soviet Union also consistently supported, and armed, many Arab regimes and terrorist movements, and, at home, issued an unceasing stream of anti-Zionist propaganda and disinformation.

Overt antisemitism also became an ever more widely experienced part of the lives of Soviet Jews. Most Soviet universities now openly imposed quotas restricting the number of Jewish entrants. As a result of this (and also of the shrinkage of the total number of Jews in the Soviet Union), the number of Jewish university students steadily declined in this period, for the first time in Soviet history, from about 112,000 in 1968–69 to only 67,000 in 1975–76. In 1977–78 not a single Jewish student was admitted to the University of Moscow. At the same time the Soviet press continued to serve up a diet of explicitly antisemitic canards and stereotypes, and to ignore or marginalise Jews as a distinctive ethnic and religious group.

Within the Soviet Union itself, unquestionably the most important movement among Soviet Jewry was the birth of a new movement of nationalist-minded Jews who demanded the right to emigrate from Russia to Israel or the West. Chiefly Zionist in orientation, its members were also motivated by Hasidic religious fervour and occasionally by Yiddishist-based nationalism. The contemporary Jewish nationalist movement in the Soviet Union originated in the mid-1950s, and won a major place in the international political agenda in the 1970s, especially as part of the super-power deals between America and Russia. The years 1968–69, just after the break between Russia and Israel, were a turning point, when thou-sands of Soviet Jews discovered their Jewish heritage and demanded the right to emigrate to Israel. Many were tried and punished under the Soviet Criminal Code which made 'slandering' the Soviet system (as a demand to emigrate or to teach Hebrew in Russia was considered) a criminal offence. As well, even demanding the right to emigrate often caused a Jew to lose his job and his economic rights in the Soviet Union. Others were sent to Siberia, to prison, or to a mental institution. Jewish men and women who were 'refused' the right to emigrate became known as 'refuseniks' and received wide attention in the Western media. Many became world famous, such as Alexander Lerner, Anatoly Scharansky, Vladimir and Maria Slepak, Silva Zalmanson, and Ida Nudel. The 'refuseniks' arose at the same time as a new generation of non-Jews within Russia, who, from a variety of perspectives, were openly questioning the Soviet system, such as Andrei Sakharov, Alexander Solzhenitsyn, and Yevgeny Yevtushenko, often in *samizdat* sources (underground, illegal periodicals which circu-lated from hand to hand). This was also a time of heightened nationalist feelings among other Soviet minorities, and of increased religiosity. (Throughout Eastern Europe the local national churches often acted as a central force in opposition to the Communist regime.)

The Jewish nationalists attracted very wide support in the West, and the United States increasingly made it clear that the fate of Jews and dissidents in the Soviet Union was crucially linked to better relations between the two superpowers in other spheres. In particular, the central demand made by the Jewish nationalists, the right to emigrate to Israel and elsewhere, became paramount on the international agenda. Neither Jews nor anyone else in the Soviet Union had the right to emigrate freely, and Jews wishing to emigrate were literally 'prisoners of Zion', as they became widely known. The first major break in the prison walls occurred in 1971–74 when, largely as a result of pressures from the American government during the Nixon-Kissinger era, about 90,000 Soviet Jews were allowed to emigrate, over 90 per cent of whom went to Israel. Thereafter, for the remainder of the 1970s and early 1980s, emigration declined, with only 13–14,000 allowed to leave in the mid-1970s and only tiny numbers in the 1980s. (The year 1979 was an exception, when, possibly as a result of Moscow's wish not to arouse international hostility prior to the 1980 Moscow Olympics, nearly 52,000 Jews were allowed to leave.) In all, between 1971 and 1981 a total of 256,446 Jews emigrated from the Soviet Union, probably 15 per cent of the total Jewish population of the country. Of this total, nearly 62 per cent

(158,051) migrated to Israel. The 1970s and 1980s saw the zenith of the international campaign for Soviet Jewry, an effort which galvanised Jewish activists around the world, and which, while it existed, acted as one of the central unifying forces in the contemporary Jewish world. Countless demonstrations, resolutions, petitions, and acts of solidarity, some involving considerable personal risk and danger, were organised around the Jewish world from Britain to Australia, from California to Israel. For the most part, they seemed to little avail, and at the time that Gorbachev came to power in 1985, freedom for Soviet Jewry seemed as remote as at any time in the post-war era.

Events since *perestroika*

Between 1985 and 1991, in one of the most unexpected developments in modern history, the Soviet Union collapsed, peacefully democratised itself, and decomposed into independent republics. No one predicted this extraordinary change, which was accomplished with minimal violence. The policies which led to the break-up of the Soviet Union were pioneered by Mikhail Gorbachev (b.1931), a dedicated reformer who became general secretary of the Soviet Communist Party in 1995. Gorbachev instituted a policy of reform (*perestroika* in Russian), which initially entailed the beginnings of a market economy in place of a centrally-directed 'command' economy which was no longer working. By 1988 the Kremlin officially gave up trying to control the whole economy. More unexpectedly, the direct election of a democratic parliament followed in 1989. Nationalist movements in the Baltic republics and in Georgia declared independence. The situation was rapidly getting out of hand, with an Army or CIA coup widely feared. When it finally came, in 1991, it failed. The Union of Soviet Socialist Republics collapsed. The 15 republics of the former Soviet Union declared their independence (though they remained very loosely federated as the 'Commonwealth of Independent States'). Amazingly, the Communist Party of the Soviet Union was outlawed after the 1991 coup. At the same time Boris Yeltsin (b.1931), originally a protégé of Gorbachev but subsequently his bitter enemy and rival, became the first democratically-elected president of Russia (not, of course, of the Soviet Union, which no longer existed) in 1991. Despite unpopularity and poor health, he was re-elected in 1996.

These cataclysmic changes affected Soviet Jewry in the most fundamental way. From about 1987, emigration to Israel and elsewhere became automatic. By mid-1996, no fewer than 630,000 ex-Soviet Jews had emigrated to Israel, increasing that country's total Jewish population by nearly 15 per cent. As well, perhaps 300,000 went to other parts of the world, having a perceptible effect on the demography of many Jewish communities. In Germany (of all places), the total Jewish population rose from perhaps

30,000 up to 100,000, chiefly as a result of emigration from Russia. Many a 'Little Odessa' (as the Russian Jewish neighbourhood in Brighton Beach, Brooklyn, became known) sprang up around the world.

The remaining Jewish community of the former Soviet Union was much smaller than in the past. The 1959 Census placed the number of Jews at 2,267,814. The next Soviet Census, in 1970, saw a decline to 2,151,000, through a combination of intermarriage and assimilation, low birth rates among European Jews, and some emigration. By the time of the 1979 Soviet Census, the number of Jews declined again to 1,811,000. By the mid-1990s, the Jewish population of the former Soviet Union was estimated at only 660,000, with 360,000 in Russia, 180,000 in the Ukraine, 28,000 in Belarus (Belorussia), 14,200 in Latvia, and 59,100 in the central Asian republics. Each year sees a further diminution of this number, as more Jews emigrate.

For those who remained, Jewish life was freer than at any time in Russian history. From about 1987, religious freedom was greatly extended. In 1989 the Solomon Mikhoels Jewish Cultural Centre was opened in Moscow, the first truly independent Jewish association in Russia since the 1920s. By the mid-1990s a network of Jewish religious, cultural, and educational institutions had opened for the remaining Jews of the former Soviet Union. In 1995, about 140 synagogues existed in the country. Each year 25 tons of *matzah* are baked locally for Passover. Judaism was officially recognised as an historical Russian religion, and was actually better treated by the Russian government than were many evangelising Protestant sects, whose presence was opposed by the predominant Russian Orthodox church. Several Jewish universities have opened in Russia, as well as 226 Jewish day schools, enrolling an estimated 22,000 children in 1995. There was also a rebirth of interest in Jewish history and culture by non-Jews. Jews were also very prominent in the reformist wing of the Yeltsin government, with two recent Russian prime ministers said to be of Jewish descent, and as successful businessmen in the new capitalist Russia.

There was another, darker side of the coin: the re-emergence of open antisemitism associated with extreme right-wing ultra-nationalist, and neo-Nazi movements, as well as with the 'conservative' wing of the reborn Communist Party. In particular, the emergence of ultra-nationalist leader Vladimir Zhirinovsky (said to be of Jewish descent), a demagogic extremist, in 1994, saw as well the growth of anti-Jewish sentiments. By the late 1990s, in the wake of Russia's notably poor economic performance under capitalism and in part also through the loss of its former superpower status, violent antisemitic incidents became commonplace. At the end of the twentieth century, Russian Jewry presented the paradoxical position that it was freer than ever before in its history, but possibly just as insecure as it had always been in the past. Only the reality of a truly prosperous and democratic Russia, committed to pluralism and tolerance, is ever likely to remove this sense of insecurity, or to give the much-reduced Jewish community hope for the future.

Further reading

Lucjan Dobroszycki and Jeffrey S. Gurock, eds, *The Holocaust in the Soviet Union* (Armonk, N.Y., 1993)

Lionel Kochan, ed., *The Jews in Soviet Russia since 1917*, 3rd edn (Oxford, 1978).

Joel Lang, *The Silent Millions: A History of the Jews in the Soviet Union* (New York, 1970)

Nora Levin, *The Jews in the Soviet Union since 1917: The Paradox of Survival*, 2 vols (London, 1990)

Ben-Zion Pinchuk, *Shtetl Jews under Soviet Rule: Eastern Poland on the Eve of the Holocaust* (Oxford, 1990)

Benjamin Pinkus, *The Jews of the Soviet Union: The History of a National Minority* (Cambridge, 1988)

Benjamin Pinkus, *The Soviet Government and the Jews, 1948–1967* (Cambridge, 1984)

Yaakov Roi, ed., *Jews and Jewish Life in Russia and the Soviet Union* (London, 1995)

Solomon M. Schwarz, *The Jews in the Soviet Union* (Syracuse, 1951)

|9|

The Holocaust

The Holocaust was the darkest event in Jewish history, perhaps in all of modern history, and the degree of evil it entailed remains incomprehensible and perhaps inexplicable. Today, 70 years after Hitler came to power, interest in the Holocaust remains greater than ever, with every year seeing book after book devoted to the Nazi attempt to exterminate the Jews, events commemorated in museums and memorials throughout the world.

Nazi attitudes towards the Jews had their origins in traditional German (and European) antisemitism but were, to an even greater extent, the product of the world-view held by Adolf Hitler. During the nineteenth and early twentieth centuries, Germany saw the growth of a virulent tradition of radical nationalism which was often linked with antisemitism. Such figures as Richard Wagner, Wilhelm Marr (who coined the term 'antisemitism') and Heinrich von Treitschke – the influence of whom is discussed in Chapter 6 above – became highly influential in right-wing German circles and, perhaps still more so, in Austria, the German-speaking portion of the multi-national Austro-Hungarian Empire. Anyone looking for the intellectual origins of Nazi antisemitism can certainly find much of it in Germany's previous history, especially in the German radical right-wing tradition which emphasised hostility to modernism and liberalism in a society which was renowned for its commitment to militarism, conformity, and unquestioning obedience to authority. Yet it would probably be a mistake to link the Holocaust directly to Germany's historical traditions. The nineteenth century saw the steady growth of toleration and acceptability for Germany's Jews, a trend which increased in the liberal Weimar Republic that replaced the German Empire in 1918. As late as 1928, the Nazi party secured only 2.6 per cent of the total vote in the German parliamentary election of that year, and Nazism had virtually no salience for the average German prior to the Great Depression, which saw a 40 per cent unemployment rate and the failure of the existing parties to provide a solution to Germany's economic and political problems. Nor should it be forgotten that at this time most continental European countries produced their own traditions of radical nationalism and antisemitism. Indeed, German antisemitism appeared mild, and the situation of German Jews fortunate, compared with the murderous antisemitism of the tsarist Russian pogroms and the Pale of Settlement. While the Dreyfus Affair split France politically in the 1890s, the treatment of Jews remained almost peripheral to the German political mainstream. Most German Jews were intensely loyal to Germany, and it is a cliché that very many were so assimilated that they almost literally did not realise they were Jews until Hitler made it a requirement for all Germans to search their family trees for 'Aryan' and Jewish ancestors. It should also be clearly noted that Jews were a tiny minority in Germany when Hitler came to power, constituting only 1 per cent of the population.

Recent historians have, however, pointed to a number of special circumstances relating to German antisemitism which, it is sometimes argued, set it apart from that found in other European nations. Many historians have claimed that Germany pursued a 'special path' (*Sonderweg*) to modernisation which differed from that in other major states. While France and America experienced revolutions which ushered in democracy, and Britain gradually evolved into a liberal, democratic state without revolution, Germany took a different route. In Germany, the old ruling elites maintained their grip on power down to 1918 or even beyond, while the German nation experienced unusually strong industrial and economic growth between 1870 and 1914. Thus, Germany's old aristocracy and the traditional German values of obedience, authority, and militarism remained in place, at the head of what by 1914 had become the most advanced economy in Europe. Attempts to re-establish Germany as a liberal state along British lines were crushed, especially with the failure of the 1848 revolution. As well, it is argued, Germany felt an enormous sense of 'relative deprivation', an inferiority complex, compared with other states such as Britain and France, especially in the fact that only the 'crumbs' of the Third World's colonies were left to it during the era of imperial expansion in the late nineteenth century. The defeat of Germany in the First World War, it is argued, left a vacuum at the head of the German state which the emperors and strong leaders like Bismarck had formerly filled. Hitler was able to exploit and fill this deep-seated German desire for a strong, authoritarian leader. While there is a good deal of plausibility in this interpretation of German history, it does not adequately account for Hitler's pervasive antisemitism, nor for the considerable success enjoyed by the liberal Weimar republic during the 1920s.

In 1996 a young American scholar, Daniel J. Goldhagen, published a work entitled *Hitler's Willing Executioners,* which achieved world-wide publicity. Goldhagen studied the activities of the Order Police in the Soviet Union, who carried out brutal massacres of Jews in 1941–42. Most of these were ordinary Germans, many aged well over thirty (and thus socialised into the pre-Hitler German value system), yet they engaged in mass murder,

CONCENTRATION CAMPS

Chelmno Death camp
■ Concentration camp

according to Goldhagen, with gusto and certainly with virtually no moral qualms whatever. Goldhagen argued that this was because, uniquely, 'eliminationist' antisemitism (his term) was deeply ingrained in the German consciousness well before Hitler came to power. Goldhagen's book led to an international debate, and placed the question of German guilt for the Holocaust in the spotlight of discussion. Goldhagen also argued that up to 100,000 'ordinary' Germans, rather than a much smaller number, took part in the killings of Jews, thus suggesting that the willingness to commit genocide was widespread in Germany.

While Goldhagen's work has found some adherents, it is probably fair to state that the great majority of historians have, for many reasons, rejected his findings. Goldhagen's claims that, pre-Hitler, an ideology of 'eliminationist' antisemitism existed in Germany, is based on little or no evidence. As noted, no German Jew perceived Germany in this light. The post-1945 Germany of the Federal Republic demonstrated little or no overt antisemitism, a fact that Goldhagen attributes, implausibly, to 'denazification' programmes imposed by the Occupying powers. Other historians who have studied the Order Police, especially Christopher Browning, have reached very different conclusions about that body's eagerness to engage in mass murder. Goldhagen presents no comparative evidence whatever about antisemitic ideologies in other countries. In summary, most historians doubt that Goldhagen has made the case that Germany was uniquely favourable to the murderous antisemitism of the Holocaust.

There may, however, be a certain element of truth in some of Goldhagen's arguments. It was probably the case that Germany's defeat in 1918 made that country more susceptible to far right-wing extremism than was the case in many other lands, and considerably increased the amount and virulence of German antisemitism. Recent research on the ex-Kaiser, Wilhelm II, who lived in the Netherlands following the Allies' victory, has noted a major heightening of his antisemitic rhetoric during his exile, and many other Germans, it seems, were only too ready to blame the Jews (and 'Judeo-Bolshevism') for Germany's defeat. It is, however, important not to push this argument too far, since no one or virtually no one in Germany prior to Hitler openly advocated the physical annihilation of the Jews.

The central role of Adolf Hitler

All attempts to link the Holocaust with deep-seated factors in Germany's historical evolution or national 'psyche' founder upon the fact that the genocide of the Jews was the work of one man, Adolf Hitler (1889–1945), who was Germany's dictator between 1933 and 1945. 'No Hitler, no Holocaust', is the way some historians have, correctly, summarised the situation. Many dozens of books and articles have been written which attempt to explain the origins of Hitler's monomaniacal and obsessive hatred of the Jews, and yet we really cannot fully account for his antisemitic attitudes and policies, which often appear to defy explanation. According to Hans Frank, a senior Nazi leader who was hanged in 1946 following the Nuremberg trials, in 1930 Hitler asked him to investigate claims that he (Hitler) had a Jewish grandfather, a man named Frankenheimer in Graz, Austria, in whose home Hitler's grandmother, Maria Schicklgruber was a cook. According to this story, Maria became pregnant by Frankenheimer and was paid money to support the baby. While it is just possible that Hitler had some Jewish ancestors, all attempts to identify a Jewish family in Graz named Frankenheimer have failed. Hitler, however, may well have believed this story, although whether this led to his fanatical antisemitism is very arguable. Other attempts to discover the origins of Hitler's hatred of the Jews focus on the fact that a Jewish doctor in Linz, Austria, Eduard Bloch, was the physician who treated Hitler's mother Klara for cancer, which killed her at the age of 47 in 1907. The problem here is that recent research has revealed that, far from hating Dr Bloch, Hitler continued to admire him. Bloch was one of the very few Jews who received favourable treatment from the arch antisemite, who personally allowed him to take all of his property with him to America in 1938, a privilege granted to virtually no other Austrian Jew.

Perhaps two other experiences of Hitler's life were more important in explaining his antisemitism. Between 1908 and 1913 the young Hitler lived in Vienna as a student, artist, and semi-tramp. Vienna was the capital of the polyglot Hapsburg Empire. There, Hitler discovered that he was a fanatical German nationalist and an equally extreme antisemite and anti-Slav. A voracious reader and autodidact, Hitler absorbed the pan-Germanic and antisemitic propaganda of the local right-wing, and saw, for the first time, Orthodox Jews in their strange traditional clothing, a sight which repelled him and which he never forgot. Recent research has shown that (after failing to gain admission to art school) Hitler earned a small income as a commercial artist of local tourist sights. Amazingly he had several Jewish business partners in these ventures. It is possible that he long harboured a sense of grievance that he, a great man (in his own eyes) should have been reduced to carving out a meagre, degraded living with the assistance of Jews. In Vienna, Hitler's position as a marginal German, a German from the edge of German-speaking Europe, came to the fore. He was, of course, not a German but a German-speaking Austrian. Like many men who are highly marginal to a national group, he became a fanatical super-patriot of that group, possibly in order to disguise the self-doubts which arose from his marginality.

The second key experience which probably engendered Hitler's antisemitism was his service in the German army during the First World War (Hitler was actually a member of the Bavarian Infantry, a semi-independent military force under German command). He served on the Western Front during virtually the whole of the war, and was awarded two decorations for bravery, although he was never promoted beyond the rank of corporal. In November 1918 Germany and the Central Powers were defeated by the Western Allies – Britain, France, the United States, and Italy. The defeat appeared to many Germans to come virtually out of the blue: as recently as August 1918 it appeared that Germany (which had just knocked Russia out the war) might actually defeat the Allies. Hitler suffered an apparent nervous breakdown as a result of the sudden defeat, and blamed Germany's defeat on a 'stab in the back' by Jews and socialists in Berlin, rather than on superior Allied military force.

After demobilisation Hitler joined a small extreme right-wing party, the German Workers' Party, and quickly became one of its chief leaders, changing its name to the *Nationalsozialistische Deutsche Arbeitpartei* (the National Socialist German Workers' Party), which quickly became abbreviated to the 'Nazis', the name by which it is universally known. In 1923 Hitler participated with General Ludendorff in the so-called Munich 'Beer-Hall *Putsch*', intended to foment a German revolution. As a result, he spent nine months in Landsberg Prison, where he dictated his autobiography *Mein Kampf* ('My Struggle') to Rudolf Hess, his associate and later the number two man in the Nazi regime. *Mein Kampf* was a turgid, crude, poorly organised but not unintelligent work which proclaimed Hitler's hatred of Jews and Slavs, his German ultra-nationalism and belief in German and 'Aryan' superiority, his desire for revenge for defeat in 1918, for *Lebensraum* ('living space') in eastern Europe and his utter contempt for democracy and socialism. The Nazi movement at this time also acquired its memorably frightening swastika symbol and flag, its brown-shirted uniforms, marching songs, annual Nuremberg rallies, and leadership structure. In the middle and late 1920s, a time of prosperity and international stability, it appeared that the Nazi party was doomed to perpetual fringe status. The coming of the Great Depression, mass unemployment, and the failure of the mainstream Weimar parties to ameliorate conditions led to a series of striking Nazi electoral gains between 1930 and 1933. In January 1933 President Paul von Hindenburg was forced to appoint Hitler as chancellor (prime minister) of Germany, but at the head of a coalition government which included non-Nazis such as former diplomat Franz von Papen. Hitler quickly disposed of any and all challengers to his supreme rule, both from outside and inside the Nazi party. In August 1934 von Hindenburg (still, technically, Germany's president) died at the age of 86, and Hitler combined the offices of president and chancellor into the post of *Der Führer* ('The Leader'), and from that point until the assassination attempt on his life in July 1944, virtually nothing was done to challenge his all-powerful rule.

As in fascist Italy, Stalin's Russia and more recent totalitarian states, Hitler's rule was absolute and enforced by every conceivable method of terror and propaganda. In particular he created private armies and secret police to enforce Nazi policy and destroy all opposition. When he came to power in 1933 he already had at his disposal a private army numbering over

400,000 men, the SA (*Sturmabtellung*, or Storm Troopers), which had been formed largely from ultra-nationalistic First World War veterans in 1921. (The SA's troops were known as 'brown shirts' from the colour of their uniform.) When it appeared that the SA under their leader Ernst Rohm (1887–1934) might challenge Hitler's authority, the *Führer* had Rohm killed in his bed in the so-called 'Blood Purge' or 'Night of the Long Knives' of 30 June 1934. The SA is sometimes confused with two other sinister Nazi bodies, the Gestapo and the SS. The Gestapo (from the initials of *Geheime Staatspolizei* or 'Secret State Police') crushed all opposition to Hitler in the Nazi state, and was responsible for sending any malcontents to concentration camps. The Gestapo was linked to, although semi-independent from, the SS (for *Schützstaffel* or 'Elite Guard'), the blackshirted army, originally Hitler's private guard but subsequently greatly expanded, under Heinrich Himmler (1900–45), who was officially known as the *Reichsführer SS* (National Leader of the SS). The SS was an elite force organised along the lines of an army, designed to destroy all opposition to Nazi rule and served as a parallel force to the regular army. During the Second World War the SS became infamous as the chief organisation which carried out the Holocaust. Yet another Nazi terror organisation was the SD (*Sicherheitsdienst*, or 'Security Service'), the intelligence branch of the SS, headed by Reinhard Heydrich (1904–42), a fanatical sadist even by Nazi standards. The SD was the SS's own secret police force and was responsible for many mass murders during the Holocaust and for innumerable atrocities against non-Jewish groups and 'undesirables'.

The Nazi regime

From the start Nazi Germany was notorious for its 'concentration camps' to which enemies of the regime were sent. The term 'concentration camp' is employed ambiguously, and one must be very careful about its use. Between 1933 and 1945, the Nazis established concentration camps throughout Germany, the most infamous being, perhaps, Bergen-Belsen, Buchenwald, Dachau, and Sachsenhausen. These were *not* extermination camps like Auschwitz, where hundreds of thousands were gassed, but brutal prison camps where enemies of the regime of all types were sent – an estimated 200,000 persons between 1934 and 1939. Although Jews were often despatched to these camps, especially after *Kristallnacht* in 1938, most people imprisoned there were not Jews, but Communists, socialists, Jehovah's Witnesses, pacifists, trade union leaders, and anyone else the Nazi regime found intolerable. During the Second World War many appalling atrocities were carried out in these places, and the photographs and newsreels of piles of corpses and living skeletons found in places like Belsen and Dachau when they were liberated by the Allies early in 1945 had an immediate and traumatic effect around the world. Nevertheless, these pre-1939 concentration camps must be distinguished from the extermination camps where many of the victims of the Holocaust perished. The six extermination camps, Treblinka, Chelmno, Sobibor, Maidanek, Belzec, and, most infamously, Auschwitz-Birkenau, were all situated in Poland, which was, of course, not in German hands until the outbreak of the war.

The Nazi regime instituted a reign of absolute totalitarian rule in many other ways. The press, radio, and publishing were, needless to say, totally under Nazi rule, as were all professional groups, most religious bodies, the entire educational system, the legal system, and all other facets of German society. Spies and informers were encouraged to report on their neighbours and, of course, any and all opposition was ruthlessly crushed, among 'Aryan' Germans no less than among Jews. For this reason, no serious opposition to Nazi rule emerged until nearly the end of the war. For instance, although the German Socialist and Communist parties were among the largest in the Weimar Republic, virtually no challenge to Nazi rule could be mounted from the German left. It is difficult for persons in a democratic society today to imagine what life was like in a totalitarian regime at that time, whether Nazi Germany or Stalinist Russia, or to imagine the futility of contemplating a successful revolt against the regime. It must also be said, in frankness, that the Nazi regime was certainly very popular among most Germans until the war started to go badly for their side around 1942. The Nazi regime ended unemployment and appeared to reverse the 'crime' of Versailles, with its severe treatment of Germany by the victorious Allies. Hitler was widely regarded as one of the greatest leaders Germany ever produced, especially when compared to either the leaders of the Wilhelmine Empire, which lost the First World War, or to the narrow, incompetent mediocrities of the Weimar Republic's political elite. Many 'Aryan' Germans unquestionably closed their eyes to the Nazi regime's horrors and enormities because of their perception of its positive achievements. Some historians and sociologists have also seen in Hitler's success the fulfilment of a deep-seated need in the German psyche for authority and for a strong leader, a need which dated from before Frederick the Great, which none of the leaders of the Weimar Republic could fulfil.

Nazi policy towards the Jews

The antisemitic ideology of the Nazi movement was an integral part of the party's doctrines from their inception. Among the 25 original points of the *Deutsche Arbeiterpartei*, issued in February 1920, were those stating that 'no Jew . . . may be a member of the [German] nation' and that a non-citizen could live in Germany only as a 'guest'. The party 'combats the Jewish-materialist spirit within us and without us'. *Mein Kampf* made clear the centrality of the Jews to Hitler's world-view. Yet there was also what one historian has termed a 'twisted road to Auschwitz', and there is no compelling evidence that the

Holocaust was already foreseen by Hitler (or anyone else) before it actually occurred. During the period 1933–39 Nazi policy was clearly to eliminate Jews from German life and to expel them from Germany. Jews were not systematically killed until the invasion of the Soviet Union in mid-1941, over eight years after Hitler came to power. The Nazi regime had no means of harming any Jews beyond Germany's borders until the war began.

Nevertheless, during the whole of the Nazi regime there appeared to be a consistent, continuing radicalisation of Nazi policy towards the Jews. Just as one might assume that the limits of Nazi intolerance had been reached, Hitler moved them in a still more extreme direction. The steps of this radicalisation were unpredictable, often occurring with no prior warning and for no obvious reason. From the first, the Hitler government enjoyed extraordinary powers, as a result of the so-called Enabling Act, which allowed it to pass laws without the consent of the German parliament. Moves against the Jews swiftly ensued. A one-day boycott against Jewish-owned businesses and shops was proclaimed by the Nazis on 1 April 1933, and there were spontaneous acts of violence against Jews in various cities, which Hitler, fearing that such behaviour might get out of hand, quickly stopped. On 7 April 1933 all Jewish civil servants (including judges) were removed from office, an ordinance which was extended to university lecturers the following month. Severe restrictions on Jewish lawyers and doctors were also instituted at this time. Originally, at the behest of President von Hindenburg, there were many exemptions, including all former Jewish front-line soldiers and any Jew holding government office when war was declared in 1914. Restrictions were also placed upon Jews in schools and universities, with a limit of 5 per cent placed on the number of Jews in any one school and a limit of 1.5 per cent on the total number of Jews in all schools and universities. Later in 1933 came the beginnings of the exclusion of Jews from journalism, and a ban on Jews owning farms. *Shechita* (the ritual slaughtering of animals for consumption by Orthodox Jews) was banned in April 1933, and in July the citizenship of all persons (including non-Jews) naturalised after 1918 was revoked. These legislative acts were accompanied by many other signs of barbarism, such as the book burnings of May 1933, when works by Jewish, Marxist, socialist, pacifist, and 'anti-patriotic' writers were collected by students and publicly consigned to flames. While books by Jewish authors such as Marx and Freud were among the main targets, the works of 'Aryan' writers regarded as hostile to the Nazi regime, like Thomas Mann, were also burned. Erich Maria Remarque's famous anti-war classic *All Quiet on the Western Front* was a particular target of Nazi venom, although Remarque was an 'Aryan' German.

Throughout the democratic world, newsreels quickly focused, unforgettably, on the sinister aspect of the Nazi regime, the book burnings, Hitler's ranting, maniacal speeches, the goose-stepping German troops, the other worldly Nuremberg rallies. Although some in the democratic world were fascinated by Hitler, especially right-wingers who applauded his all-out hostility to Communism, most normal people in the West were repelled by the new regime, regarding Hitler as an obvious madman. Because from the first the Nazis purged the universities of their Jewish and 'undesirable' professors and persecuted all dissident intellectuals, a steady stream of eminent academic and intellectual refugees from Nazi Germany came to the West, headed by Albert Einstein.[1] Einstein was already renowned as 'the cleverest man in the world' and the greatest scientist of the century, and the Nazi persecution of him and other celebrated intellectuals made an indelible impression on the conscience of the Western democracies. It seemed scarcely believable that the Nazi regime would expel many of its greatest minds and most valuable scientists instead of trying to use them. The United States, Britain, and other Western nations benefited immeasurably by offering shelter and employment to so many intellectual refugees from Nazism. Britain, for example, gained seven future winners of the Nobel Prize among the Jewish refugees from Nazism. It must also be stressed that many world-famous non-Jewish opponents of Nazism and other fascist regimes in Central Europe, such as Thomas Mann, Bertold Brecht, Arturo Toscanini, Enrico Fermi, and Béla Bartok, also fled to the democracies at this time.

The year 1934 was a relatively quiescent one for Jews in Nazi Germany, with many assuming that the worst was perhaps over. About 38,000 German Jews had fled the country in 1933 but only 22,000 in 1934 and 21,000 in 1935. Incredible as this may seem, about 10,000 Jews who had fled in 1933 actually returned in 1934, since economic conditions were improving in Germany. The next turning point came in September 1935 with the promulgation of the 'Law for the Protection of German Blood and German Honour', the Reich and Citizenship Law, and several supplementary decrees promulgated later in the same year, which are known as the 'Nuremberg Laws' from the town in Bavaria where the Nazis held their annual rallies and where Hitler and other Nazi leaders discussed further restrictions on the Jews. The Nuremberg Laws forbade marriage or sexual relations between Jews and Germans, declared that no Jew could be a German citizen (although they remained German subjects), and forbade the employment of 'Aryan' female servants in Jewish homes. A Supplementary Decree of November 1935 defined a 'Jew' as a person with at least three Jewish grandparents by 'race' or two Jewish grandparents by 'race' if he or she belonged to the Jewish religious community. 'Part-Jews' (*Mischlinge*) were divided into those 'of the first degree' with two Jewish grandparents and those 'of the second degree' with one Jewish grandparent. The *Mischlinge* retained certain rights and were not killed during the war. There were, as well, some curious provisions to the Nuremberg Laws. Jews were forbidden to display Germany's swastika flag, but were explicitly permitted

---

1 Strictly speaking, German-born Einstein was not a refugee. He was a Swiss citizen who held a chair at the University of Berlin. He was already in America when Hitler came to power, holding a visiting position in California, and never returned to Germany.

to 'display the Jewish colours' – that is, the Zionists' Star of David flag which is now the flag of the State of Israel. This was, in all likelihood, explicitly permitted because the Zionist movement wished Germany's Jews to emigrate to Palestine, a goal welcomed by many Nazis. The Nuremberg Laws also explicitly exempted Jewish (and other) religious organisations and Jewish schools from its requirements, and guaranteed that Jews formerly employed in the civil service who were war veterans could continue to receive their salaries. The Nuremberg Laws did not directly affect Jewish-owned businesses or Jewish communal or religious organisations, and it must be emphasised that Germany's synagogues remained open and largely unaffected until *Kristallnacht* in 1938.

While there were no further antisemitic measures until late 1937, Germany's Jews were subjected, at all times, to a stream of virulent anti-semitic propaganda from every institution of the Reich. Schools denounced the Jews as the root of all evil. Most Protestant churches – with honourable exceptions – accepted the Nazi line. Germany's Jews wrestled with their unprecedented troubles as best they could. The representative body of the Jewish community in Germany, the *Reichsvertretung Der Deutschen Juden* (Reich Representation of German Jews), under the leadership of the famous Reform rabbi Leo Baeck and of Otto Hirsch, co-ordinated a wide range of educational, retraining for emigration, and welfare measures on behalf of the Jews of Germany. Constantly watched by the Gestapo and SD, they helped, in particular, to train Germany's Jews (especially youth) for *aliyah* to Palestine. Forbidden to participate in 'Aryan' cultural activities, they organised Jewish cultural activities; consequently many Jews rediscovered their Jewish identities and heritage. This period of relative calm (by later standards) continued during the time of the Berlin Olympic games in 1936 and into 1937. In the meantime, however, Hitler decided, as part of a so-called Four Year Plan to expand the German economy, to drive the Jews out of the economic realm by the 'Aryanisation' of virtually all Jewish businesses (which had largely remained untouched by previous Nazi measures). As well, Hitler decided on a policy of military expansionism in central Europe with the aim of incorporating most German-speaking areas into the Reich. In March 1938 he annexed Austria (since 1918 an independent republic, and, of course, Hitler's own birthplace). This unleashed a wave of virulent antisemitism against Austria's Jews, with Austrians, if anything, even more barbaric than Germans in their hostility to Jews, especially to the cosmopolitan Jews of Vienna. In the middle of 1938 the Sudeten crisis erupted, resulting in Nazi Germany's annexation of the Sudetenland (the German-speaking areas of the western border of Czechoslovakia), owing partly to the inability of Britain and France to resist German aggression. At the same time, the world's fascist forces appeared to be in the ascendant almost everywhere, with Franco gaining the upper hand in Spain, Mussolini seizing Abyssinia, and Japan conquering much of China.

The year 1938 is usually seen as the decisive turning point in the history of Germany's Jews under Nazi rule. Probably the most important single event for the Jews in Nazi Germany was *Kristallnacht* ('Crystal Night') the night of 9–10 November 1938, also known as 'the Night of the Broken Glass' from the windows of Jewish properties vandalised by Nazis and their sympathisers. Two days earlier Ernst von Rath, third secretary at the German embassy in Paris, had been shot by a penniless Polish Jew aged 17 living in France, Herschel Grynszpan. Grynszpan's parents, Polish Jews resident in Hanover, had been deported to Poland by the Nazis under brutal circumstances as part of a campaign to expel all non-German Jews. Obsessed with the need to avenge their sufferings he assassinated the German official. Von Rath died on 9 November and within a few hours terrorist attacks on the Jews began in Germany. His assassination unleashed the full force of Nazi venom. On the night of 9–10 November 1938, hundreds of synagogues and thousands of Jewish businesses were vandalised and burned. Jewish cemeteries were desecrated and individual Jews attacked by SA-led mobs. About 30,000 Jews were arrested and sent to concentration camps (most were released soon afterwards), and over 90 Jews were killed. *Kristallnacht* was apparently orchestrated by Joseph Goebbels (1897–1945), a close confidant of Hitler who was boss of the Nazi propaganda machine and a major power in Berlin's local government. Goebbels was a fierce antisemite, but it is thought that he might have led the *Kristallnacht* campaign in order to curry favour with Hitler at the expense of his rivals, for instance Hermann Goering. It also appears that an attack on the Jews had long been planned.

In the wake of *Kristallnacht* the Nazis imposed a 'collective fine' of one billion marks (about $200 million or £40 million) on the whole Jewish community, and speeded up the process of 'Aryanising' Jewish businesses, that is, of their forced sale to 'Aryan' owners, usually at absurdly low prices. Between April 1938 and April 1939 the number of Jewish businesses in Germany declined in number from nearly 40,000 to 15,000, with most of the remainder under severe threat. By the outbreak of the Second World War, the Nazis had also instigated a wide variety of other anti-Jewish measures designed to make life intolerable and compel Jews to emigrate as quickly as possible. (For instance, by the outbreak of the war Jews were forbidden to drive cars, under the pretext that in a motor accident they might be responsible for shedding 'Aryan' blood.)

Exodus from the Reich

The German Jewish community now realised that the continued existence of a viable Jewish community in Germany was impossible and began emigrating to the four corners of the globe as quickly as possible. While 21,000 German Jews had emigrated in 1935, 24,500 in 1936, and 23,500 in 1937, in 1938 40,000 left the country and another 78,000 in 1939. By early 1942, when voluntary emigration became impossible and the remaining German

Jews began being deported to ghettos and extermination camps, no more than 140–160,000 Jews remained of the 500,000 living there in 1933 when Hitler came to power. Of the Jewish emigrants from Nazi Germany, about 55,000 migrated to Britain, 53,000 to Palestine, perhaps 80,000 to the United States, 50,000 to Latin America, 25,000 to France, and tens of thousands elsewhere – for instance, 10,000 went to Shanghai, the great seaport in China which did not require a visa for entry, and 9,000 to Australia. It appears that about 72 per cent of Germany's Jewish population managed to emigrate, by hook or by crook, including 83 per cent of German Jewish children. They were also soon joined by many thousands of Austrian and Czech Jews. As in all substantial waves of migration, the émigrés established distinctive residential neighbourhoods, such as Washington Heights in New York, where German Jewish culture was kept alive after a fashion. The *Anschluss* in March 1938 led to a mass flight of Austrian Jews which was, paradoxically, organised in a particularly efficient fashion by Adolf Eichmann (1906–62), head of the Reich Central Office of Jewish Emigration in Vienna. Eichmann was later infamous for his role in the Holocaust, and was hanged in Israel in 1962 after a trial which attracted world-wide publicity. About two-thirds of Austria's Jewish population of 250,000 managed to emigrate before the Nazis bolted the doors. Sigmund Freud (1856–1939), the founder of psychoanalysis, who settled in London, was probably the most famous of the emigrants from Nazi-occupied Austria.

Why was Jewish emigration from Germany so long delayed? One might point to a host of reasons and factors. Immigration, especially in the 1930s with massive rates of unemployment everywhere, was seldom easy, and many democratic countries already had particularly high immigration barriers in place. Many democracies regarded German Jews as undesirable immigrants, and there is evidence of explicit antisemitism in the reluctance of many countries to admit more Jews although, especially after *Kristallnacht*, this was often mitigated by compassion for Hitler's victims. In addition, many German Jews refused, until the last possible moment, to emigrate. Most thought that Hitler's brutalities would subside once the regime became institutionalised, and most German Jews regarded themselves as fully German, in spite of Hitler. Elderly German Jews were simply too old to adjust to life elsewhere, so that most who remained behind tended to be past middle age. Certainly until *Kristallnacht* surprisingly few German Jews made serious plans to emigrate. That event, however, unleashed a wave of emigration, such that Germany's Jewish population would probably have virtually disappeared through emigration by 1942–43, had the war not broken out.

Terror in eastern Europe

The outbreak of the Second World War in September 1939 now began a new and terrible phase of Hitler's terror, leading, after June 1941, to the greatest catastrophe in Jewish history. Between September 1939 and the invasion of the Soviet Union in June 1941 Nazi Germany greatly expanded its domain through foreign conquest, invading and taking over western Poland in 1939, Denmark, Norway, Belgium, the Netherlands, Luxembourg, and most of France in 1940, and Yugoslavia and Greece in early 1941. Probably two million additional Jews came under direct Nazi rule as a result of these conquests, with perhaps 1.5 million others living in such states as Hungary, Slovakia (independent after the conquest of Bohemia and Moravia in 1939), Romania, and Croatia, all closely allied to Nazi Germany. (However, in 1939–40 the Soviet Union also took over perhaps two million additional Jews in eastern Poland, the Baltic States, Moldavia, and elsewhere, as a direct result of the Nazi–Soviet pact.) The number of Jews in the Nazi realm was thus vastly enlarged. These eastern European Jews were, moreover, regarded by Nazi ideologues as especially odious, being seen as either traditionally Orthodox or pro-Marxist, and representing much of the former Pale of Settlement. Nazi treatment of the Jews in these areas became even worse than anything seen before. First, the Nazis ordered most of these Jews confined to ghettos, that is, to walled areas of large cities from which no Jew could enter or leave, day or night. Nothing so draconian had been seen in Europe even in the most barbaric period of the Middle Ages, and not even the Nazis had created ghettos in Germany. The first Jewish ghetto was created in the town of Piotrkow Trybunalski in central Poland in October 1939, followed in February 1940 by the creation of a ghetto in Lodz, a Polish city with one of the largest concentrations of Jews. In October 1940 a ghetto was created in central Warsaw, the largest of all Jewish population centres in Europe. In 1941–42, tens of thousands of Jews were deported from smaller Jewish cities in Poland and Germany to the Warsaw ghetto, which held over 400,000 Jews by mid-1941. Other ghettos in Poland were established in Cracow and Tarnow, and ghettos were created elsewhere in occupied eastern Europe during the Nazis' reign of terror. Conditions in the ghettos were indescribably awful. The Warsaw ghetto consisted of about 1,000 acres in the middle of the city, 2.4 per cent of Warsaw's total area. Jews were ostensibly employed, often by mainstream German firms (at subsistence wages, bordering on slavery), to supply goods for the German army. Disease, malnutrition, and hopelessness were rampant. In the year 1941 over 43,000 Jews died in the Warsaw ghetto, more than 10 per cent of the population. Although some Jews managed secretly to move in and out of the ghetto, movement was forbidden. Jewish councils (*Judenräte*) had been established by the Nazis in November 1939, whose leaders were required to carry out Nazi orders to the letter or be executed. Our knowledge of the ghastly conditions in the ghettos comes largely from Jewish historians and others who attempted to set down what they knew was something unique in the annals of inhumanity. The best-known of these recorders of events in the Warsaw ghetto was Emanuel Ringelblum (1900–44), whose archives, recovered in part after the war, have become widely known.

Secondly, the conquest of much of eastern Europe signalled a basic change in Nazi policy towards the Jews and, indeed, more generally. Previously, the Nazis' objective appeared to be the creation of a purely 'Aryan' German-speaking area in central Europe from which all Jews were to be expelled. With the takeover of eastern Europe, the Nazis no longer sought to limit their conquests to German-speaking areas alone, but to establish hegemony throughout the whole continent. They also now looked for a much broader 'solution' to the 'Jewish question'. The most immediate sign of this occurred in November 1940, when Jews in the General-Government of Poland (central Poland) were forbidden to emigrate. Thereafter, Jews throughout Nazi-occupied Europe were forbidden to do so. By 1942, no Jews could legally leave any part of Nazi-occupied Europe. Simultaneously, the Nazis initiated far-reaching plans concerning the Jews, aiming at a total 'solution'. Initially these consisted of proposals for the forced removal of all of Europe's Jews: in the first such plan, to a Jewish 'reservation' in central Poland, and then in plans drawn up in July 1940, to the island of Madagascar in the Indian Ocean, where a semi-self-governing Jewish entity was to be established under the administration of a German police governor. It appears that Hitler originally approved these schemes, and certainly some senior Nazis such as Hans Frank thought the 'Madagascar Plan' was a likely prospect at this time.

The 'Final Solution'

The issues of why and when Hitler decided on the genocide of European Jewry constitutes the most vexed of all queries surrounding the Holocaust. Jews were not deliberately and systematically killed by the Nazis prior to the invasion of the Soviet Union in June 1941. Jewish women and children were apparently not killed by the German invaders of the Soviet Union until several months later, while plans to kill all of Europe's Jews were not decided upon until this time or subsequently. No specific written orders from Hitler to embark on genocide exist. Hitler's orders to carry out genocide were given verbally to Heinrich Himmler, the leader of the SS. Since both Hitler and Himmler committed suicide at the end of the war, and no definitive documentation exists, the precise sequence of events remains unclear. According to Adolf Eichmann, when on trial for his part in the Holocaust, 'two' or 'three months' after the beginning of the invasion of the Soviet Union, he was told by Reinhard Heydrich, head of the SD and one of Himmler's most senior colleagues, that Hitler 'has ordered the physical destruction of the Jews'. This probably occurred in October or November 1941, although some historians put the date at September 1941.

The 'Final Solution' to the Jewish question began soon after the invasion of the Soviet Union in June 1941. At the time that country had a Jewish population of over five million and was regarded by Nazi ideologues as the

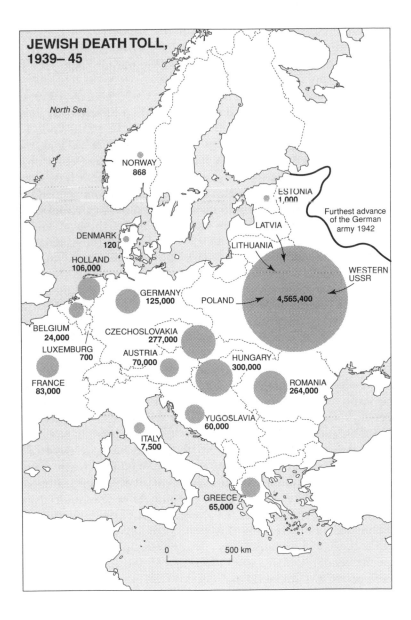

**JEWISH DEATH TOLL,
1939–45**

North Sea

NORWAY
868

ESTONIA
1,000

Furthest advance
of the German
army 1942

LATVIA

LITHUANIA

DENMARK
120

HOLLAND
106,000

GERMANY
125,000

POLAND

4,565,400

WESTERN
USSR

BELGIUM
24,000

CZECHOSLOVAKIA
277,000

LUXEMBURG
700

AUSTRIA
70,000

HUNGARY
300,000

FRANCE
83,000

ROMANIA
264,000

YUGOSLAVIA
60,000

ITALY
7,500

GREECE
65,000

0   500 km

very centre of the 'Judeo-Bolshevik' evil that they existed to oppose. Hitler may well have begun to think in terms of genocide in mid-1940, with planning for the invasion of the Soviet Union the following year. Hitler invariably thought in Social Darwinistic and demographic terms, and may well have reasoned that with the conquest of the Soviet Union perhaps nine million Jews would be under the rule of the Nazis or their allies, and that he could finish them off, as it were, in one fell swoop, thus ending the Jewish 'threat' to Germany for an indefinite period.

Hitler's well-known speech to the Reichstag on 30 January 1939 is often cited as evidence of planning for the Holocaust. In it he stated 'Today I will be a prophet: if the international Jewish financiers in and outside Europe should succeed in plunging the nations once more into a world war, then the result will not be the Bolshevising of Europe, and thus the victory of Jewry, but the annihilation of the Jewish race in Europe!' Nevertheless, in a little-known passage in the same speech Hitler definitely recommended emigration as the 'solution' to the 'Jewish question', and did not actually embark on genocide until nearly two years after the start of the war. Hitler also believed – actually believed – that the Jews 'controlled' the Allied powers – Britain, the United States, and the Soviet Union – and that killing the Jews would constitute 'revenge' for the deaths of hundreds of thousands of German troops and civilians. (He gave this as his motive for killing the Jews in his 'Political Testament' written a few hours before he committed suicide on 29 April 1945.) The precise reason or reasons for his decision remains unclear, and perhaps it is pointless to look for reason or logic in a psychopath.

Historians have also engaged in a lively debate over whether Hitler always intended to kill the Jews or whether his decision somehow emerged, possibly owing to pressure from below, from even more extreme Nazis wielding authority in eastern Europe. Those who hold the former view are known as 'intentionalists' and the latter as 'functionalists'. In reality, such a dichotomy does not do full justice to the reality of how the Holocaust emerged. At all times Hitler intended to do the maximum harm possible to the Jews under his authority, but the extent of this harm altered (and increased) as his empire expanded and the number of Jews under Nazi rule grew. What seems incontestable, however, is that Hitler, and Hitler alone, was responsible for ordering the Holocaust (although many other Nazis and Nazi allies bear full responsibility for carrying it out). Hitler was the absolute master of Nazi-occupied Europe and opposition to the Jews, whom he described as 'the universal poisoners of all peoples', was his central driving force. It is inconceivable that the Holocaust, in many ways unprecedented in modern history and entailing the diversion of very considerable resources in wartime, could have been carried out without Hitler's direct orders and continuing approval.

The invasion of the Soviet Union saw the beginnings of the mass murder of the Jews. These were carried out by the SS Einsatzgruppen

(SS task forces), special mobile formations attached to the RSHA (Reich Central Security Office). Four Einsatzgruppen were established for operation in Russia, containing about 3,000 men in all. Originally, the Einsatzgruppen (who advanced into Russia with the German army) had explicit instructions to execute all 'Jews in the service of the [Communist] Party or the [Soviet] State' (as well as all Communist party officials), but quickly widened their activities to include the mass murder of all Jews in the German-occupied areas of Russia. Most victims were machine-gunned to death in pits and fields at the edge of large towns. The most infamous of these places of wholesale slaughter was probably Babi Yar, a ravine on the outskirts of Kiev in the Ukraine. In September 1941 approximately 34,000 Jews were killed there by the Einsatzgruppen, as well as thousands of Russians, Ukrainians, and gypsies. Decades later, the Babi Yar massacre became the subject of a celebrated poem by the Russian poet Yevgeny Yevtushenko. The Einsatzgruppen may well have killed as many as one million Soviet Jews (although this number includes hundreds of thousands in eastern Poland and the Baltic areas, annexed by the Soviet Union in 1939–40).

The Wannsee Conference and its aftermath

The Hitler regime now decided to kill all the Jews in Nazi-occupied Europe. Traditionally, the Wannsee Conference, held in the Berlin suburb of Grossen-Wannsee on 20 January 1942, is seen as the defining moment when the Nazi regime turned to Europe-wide genocide. Chaired by Reinhard Heydrich, it was attended by 15 people including Adolf Eichmann. The Conference noted that Hitler had given his sanction to the 'evacuation to the east' of all Jews, who would be worked to death, with the few survivors killed. Europe was to be 'combed from West to East' for Jews. A lengthy country-by-country list of the eleven million Jews of Europe was drawn up. The precise relationship of the Wannsee Conference to the extermination of Europe's Jews has, however, been debated by recent historians. The genocide of the Jews was not as systematic as the conference protocol indicated, and was headed by Himmler, who was not present. It appears that Wannsee was chiefly intended to begin the discussion, among senior SS men, of a genocide decided upon by Hitler before then. Why Hitler turned to genocide has been endlessly debated. The question has never been satisfactorily answered, but has been linked by some historians to Hitler's euphoria at his successful invasion of the western Soviet Union and by others to the opposite motivating factor, Hitler's dread that he would certainly lose the war, and his desire to kill as many Jews as possible before the end came. These historians note that Wannsee was originally scheduled for 8 December 1941, the day after the Japanese attack on Pearl Harbor which brought the United States into the war, thus ensuring Germany's certain eventual defeat.

In the absence of further archival discoveries of fundamental importance, there the matter rests.

The Nazis also decided at this time to carry out the genocide of the Jews not by mass machine-gunning, which was regarded as psychologically difficult for the SS to carry out, but by mass gassings in purpose-built gas chambers. To this end the Nazis established six major extermination camps, all in Poland: at Treblinka and Chelmno in central Poland, Sobibor, Maidanek, and Belzec in the east of the country, and Auschwitz in the south. The Nazis had already experimented with poison gas in killing Russian prisoners of war, and had engaged in a euthanasia programme for the incurably ill in Germany from 1939–41. As is now universally known, Jews (and others) were deported to these extermination camps from all over Europe. It is believed that nearly three million Jews died in the extermination camps, 800,000 at Treblinka and between 950,000 and one million at Auschwitz. Additionally, hundreds of thousands of non-Jews were put to death in such places, including 100,000 Poles in Auschwitz alone. Auschwitz became certainly the most notorious of the camps, and is today universally synonymous with evil in its most diabolical form. There are several reasons for this, apart from the fact that more people were killed there than anywhere else. Auschwitz was the last of the camps to be closed down, in January 1945, whereas the other camps were closed or liberated earlier. Moreover, Auschwitz also contained a large Nazi synthetic rubber factory and other industrial works, thus offering a minority the chance for survival. As a result of both of these factors, it is believed that as many as 200,000 persons managed to survive deportation to Auschwitz, whereas only tiny numbers stayed alive in the other camps. The Nazis systematically destroyed the Jews of Poland first, mainly in 1942–43 (although the Cracow ghetto remained until mid-1944) before turning to the rest of Europe. Hungarian Jewry was the last to perish, between 15 May and 8 July 1944, when 440,000 Hungarian Jews were deported to Auschwitz, under the auspices of Adolf Eichmann.

Although the killing of the Jews by the Nazis was systematic enough, its comprehensiveness varied from country to country, with Polish and Soviet Jewry suffering the worst, and French, Belgian, Romanian, and Bulgarian Jewry showing the smallest percentage of victims. Historians have pointed to several factors for these differences. The Nazis did not establish puppet governments in Poland or Russia, nor did they work through an already-established right-wing regime (as in Hungary and Romania). The Nazis regarded the Poles and Russians as helot races, only slightly better than the Jews, and fit only for slavery. As a result, Jews had no intervening government in these areas which could offer some measure of protection, as they could elsewhere, but had to face the SS murder machine directly. Elsewhere, however, local right-wing regimes, even those which were already venomously antisemitic as in Vichy France or Romania, often drew the line at genocide, and were sometimes able to resist Nazi pressures for the deportation of the Jews. Thus, no Jews at all were deported from central Romania or Bulgaria, where semi-independent regimes continued to exist. Survival was, however, most often a matter of sheer luck, with no logical rhyme or reason.

Historians generally estimate that about 5.7 million European Jews died at the hands of the Nazis during the Second World War, a figure which includes death from all causes, such as starvation in ghettos, as well as direct mass murder. (Some well-known historians, such as Gerald Reitlinger and Raul Hilberg, put the death toll considerably lower, at 4.2–5.1 million.) In an era of world-wide conflicts, diabolical mass murders, and human catastrophes, this still stands out as probably the moral nadir of humanity in modern times. The Nazis and their allies also killed a vast number of non-Jews, possibly exceeding the number of Jews killed, including three million Russian prisoners of war and hundreds of thousands of Russian civilians, three million non-Jewish Poles, one million Serbs, and 500,000 gypsies. Had the Nazis won the war, the genocide of the Jews would probably have been only the first step towards the demographic transformation of Europe. Himmler apparently had active plans to deport virtually all Poles to Siberia, and millions of other people would also have been affected by the Nazis' diabolical schemes. It should, however, also be appreciated that the Nazis could not have carried out the 'Final Solution' without the active assistance of others. In the extermination camps and mobile death squads, Ukrainians, Balts, and other non-German Eastern Europeans were often prominent. (Others, of course, were active anti-Nazis.) Fascists and antisemites throughout Europe, from France to Croatia, participated in carrying out atrocities against Jews, sometimes exceeding the Germans themselves in zeal. Only in a number of countries such as Denmark, Italy and Bulgaria were the Nazis' antisemitic policies genuinely unpopular.

The Nazis persisted in attempting to kill all the Jews in Europe until literally the last minute. In 1944, perceiving that the Allies would win the war, Himmler allowed very small groups of Jews to escape to the West, in order, it would appear, to curry favour with the Allies as a post-Hitler ruler of Germany. Few historians, however, believe that Himmler was serious in offering to trade one million Hungarian Jews for 10,000 trucks and other war supplies, as he reportedly offered to do in mid-1944. After the extermination camps were closed down (chiefly to avoid discovery by the Allies) the SS under Himmler forced the surviving prisoners to undergo 'death marches' for hundreds of miles throughout eastern Europe. About 15,000 of 60,000 surviving Auschwitz prisoners forced on 'death marches' died along the way. Tens of thousands of prisoners also died in concentration camps in Germany itself such as Dachau and Buchenwald, some being killed in hideous medical experiments. In these camps, however, thousands managed to survive as 'living skeletons' as seen in newsreels and photographs shown around the world with the liberation of the camps by American and British troops in early 1945. Hitler committed suicide on 29 April 1945 with his former mistress and newly-married wife Eva Braun, as the Soviet armies were about to conquer Berlin. In his 'Political Testament', the last document he dictated, he enjoined Germans to continue their 'hatred against those finally responsible whom we have to thank for everything, International Jewry and its helpers.'

Consequences of the Holocaust

Retribution came to the majority, but not all, of those most closely involved in the Holocaust. Himmler and Goebbels committed suicide at the end of the war, while such notorious Nazis as Hans Frank, the governor-general of central Poland, and Artur Seyss-Inquart, the Reich commissioner for the Netherlands (where 80 per cent of Dutch Jewry perished, the highest percentage in Western Europe), were hanged in 1946 following the Nuremberg Trials. Rudolf Hoess, the commandant of Auschwitz, was hanged (appropriately, at Auschwitz) in 1947. Many others responsible for carrying out the mass murders of Jews and others were executed at that time. Some, however, escaped justice, often by fleeing abroad, especially to Latin America, which became a notorious haven for former Nazis. In 1960 Adolf Eichmann, who was chiefly responsible for organising the deportation of Jews to Auschwitz, was kidnapped in Argentina (where he had been living since the late 1940s), taken to Israel, tried and hanged in May 1962, the only person ever executed in the history of Israel. The Eichmann trial is often seen as a turning-point in the world's perception of the Holocaust, the beginnings of the avalanche of research and publicity on the Nazis' crimes which has continued ever since. Nevertheless, only in the 1980s did near-universal internalisation of the Holocaust as the most evil event in modern history lead to calls for identifying and trying suspected former Nazis at lower levels in the hierarchy who were responsible for the actual killing of Jews, especially in the Soviet Union. Previously, there was a feeling that once the senior Nazis were punished, there was no point in apprehending the minor functionaries of the Nazi death machine. As a result of this change of mood, many countries, including the United States and Britain, made great efforts to identify former Nazis who had emigrated to their shores after the war. Most of those tried were, ironically, not Germans but members of eastern European nationalities, especially Balts and Ukrainians, who killed Jews under the aegis of the Nazis. Aspects of these trials carried out so long after the Holocaust were often controversial and contested, and mistakes were sometimes made in the identification process, for instance in the trial of Ivan Demjanjuk, allegedly a notorious extermination camp guard known as 'Ivan the Terrible', who was convicted of genocide by an Israeli court but acquitted on appeal by the Israeli Supreme Court in the 1990s owing to doubts over his identity. Trials of former Nazi war criminals have continued into the twenty-first century, 60 years after the start of the Holocaust.

The Holocaust has had innumerable long-term consequences. First and foremost, it decimated Jewish numbers on the European continent, especially in central and eastern Europe. In Poland, where this process was most comprehensive, between 2.3 and 2.9 million Jews perished. Estimates for the Soviet Union (including the Baltic states) vary from 700,000 to 1.2 million, and for Romania from 200,000 to 420,000. In Hungary in its pre-1939 boundaries, between 180,000 and 200,000 perished. Estimates for other countries are as follows: Czechoslovakia, 200–300,000; Germany, 130–200,000; the Netherlands, 105,000; France, 80,000; Yugoslavia, 65–75,000; Greece, 60,000; Austria, 40,000; Belgium, 35-40,000; and very small numbers in Luxembourg, Norway, and Bulgaria. Although there were at the end of the war perhaps 1.2 million surviving Jews in these countries (apart from the Soviet Union, where there were probably 2.2 million), the re-establishment of viable communities in eastern and central Europe proved impossible. Most Jews fled once the hostility towards them of the new Communist governments of these countries became clear, and once Israel and the democracies opened their doors to Jewish immigration. As a result, the age-old Jewish culture of central and eastern Europe became virtually extinct, at least for the next half century. (There are now signs that it is reviving.) The Yiddish language was decimated by the Holocaust, with its main population centres destroyed and the survivors moving to countries (including Israel) where other languages are spoken. As a result, Yiddish survives today chiefly in Russia, and among some Strictly Orthodox communities elsewhere. Strictly Orthodox Jews perished in catastrophic numbers in the Holocaust (although since the 1950s they have revived in almost miraculous fashion in Israel and other Diaspora communities). Characteristic Jewish ideologies such as Bund Socialism came to a virtual end, as did most of the Jewish contributions to the culture of Central and Eastern Europe, so important in places like Berlin and Vienna.

To the surviving Jews of the world, the Holocaust has marked an obvious watershed of the most fundamental kind, surely the most significant event in modern Jewish history. The most immediate beneficiary of the effects which the Holocaust had upon Jewish consciousness was the Zionist movement. At the end of the war, Zionism became the secular ideology of probably the majority of the world's Jews, who saw in the creation of a Jewish state some compensation for the catastrophe in Europe. The Holocaust appeared to bear out the underlying presuppositions of Zionism in the starkest possible way, especially the message taught by Herzl and his followers that anti-semitism was virtually ubiquitous and that it could best be fought by the creation of a 'normal' Jewish society which would, among other things, enhance Jewish power. American Jewry, in particular, moved fairly decisively in the Zionist direction during the Second World War. In May 1942 the so-called 'Biltmore Declaration' (named for the Biltmore Hotel in New York, where the Zionist movement was meeting) stated – for the very first time – that its goal was henceforth the creation of an independent 'Jewish Commonwealth' in Palestine. With revelations of the Holocaust in

1945, American Jewish pressure and lobbying was decisive in moving the American government to advocate the creation of a Jewish state in Palestine, which became a reality in 1947–48, only a brief time after the end of the war. The State of Israel is, in a real sense, a phoenix which has arisen out of the ashes of the Holocaust.

Furthermore, the Holocaust decisively altered the balance of power within the Jewish world, giving English-speaking Jewry, especially American Jewry, a centrality it did not possess before 1939. Increasingly, the world's Jewish scene was bifurcated after 1948 between American Jewry and Israeli Jewry, with other Jewish communities playing a minor role. There is general agreement that American Jewry did not yet really possess the sophistication adequately to take on its new role at the head of world Jewry, a role which was thrust upon it by the events in Europe.

The Holocaust also did much to discredit both antisemitism and racism in the Western world. It is probably no exaggeration to say that frank and overt antisemitism of the kind so common in Europe before 1945 became virtually impossible to imagine as soon as the crimes of the Nazis became known. Within a few decades even a hint of antisemitism became almost unimaginable in the Western mainstream, and little or nothing remained of the social and economic antisemitism found in America before the Second World War. Right-wing nationalist ideologies which emphasised anti-semitism simply disappeared after 1945, except on the lunatic fringe.

The long-term effects of the Holocaust have also been profound in a number of other significant areas. In international law, the Nuremberg trial of major Nazi war criminals of 1945–46 established the principle that 'crimes against humanity' were punishable – indeed, punishable by the death penalty – by an international judicial tribunal acting *ex post facto* (that is, acting although it had not been established when the crimes them-selves occurred) and consisting of non-nationals of the country whose citizens carried out these crimes. Twelve of the Nuremberg defendants were sentenced to death and three to life imprisonment. (The last of these to die, Hitler's deputy Rudolf Hess (1894–1987) spent 41 years in prison following his conviction.) In the 1990s, when the end of the Cold War made their establishment possible, international tribunals to try those accused of 'crimes against humanity' began to flourish under United Nations' sanctions to deal with atrocities carried out in Yugoslavia, Rwanda, and other scenes of mass murder and carnage.

The Holocaust took some time to become central to the Western world's cultural life. It seems that something of a taboo on discussing the Holocaust existed prior to the Eichmann trial of the early 1960s (although the *Diary of Anne Frank* became world-famous from its publication in 1952). Since the 1960s, however, writers and artists using the Holocaust as the basis of their work have proliferated, with some like Primo Levi (1919–87) and Elie Wiesel (b.1928) becoming world-famous. Holocaust-inspired films, most famously *Schindler's List* (1993), have proliferated. Whether the Holocaust can be adequately depicted in any medium has been furiously debated by artists and scholars, with the consensus that its horrors cannot be adequately portrayed or understood by normal human beings. There has also been a consensus that the limits of the human condition altered in the Holocaust, the sheer evil of which had been previously unknown. One commentator acutely noted that, before the Holocaust, the human imagination had outdistanced reality, but the Holocaust showed that reality could exceed anything imaginable by the human imagination in its most diabolical mood.

Relations between Jews and Christians altered significantly as a result of the Holocaust, although, as with other aspects of its influence, this took some time. In particular, from the early 1960s onwards, the Roman Catholic church retracted all of the anti-Jewish statements and teachings which had been prominent in its liturgy, especially those proclaiming the guilt of today's Jews for the crucifixion of Jesus. Relations between Jews and Catholics became even warmer under Pope John Paul II (elected in 1978), who, as a young man in Poland, had had many Jewish friends and was an anti-Nazi during the war. Nevertheless, a host of areas of disagreement remained, especially over such matters as the placing of a convent at the site of Auschwitz, and over the Catholic Church's lukewarm policies towards Israel. The Holocaust also sensitised most Protestants to the effects of anti-semitism. Interfaith organisations such as the various Councils of Christians and Jews which were established from the 1940s onwards, can be viewed as a direct legacy of the Holocaust.

Jewish resistance in the Holocaust

Although the events of the Holocaust are incontestable, a great many historiographical debates and controversies have emerged from the Nazis' attempt at genocide, possibly more than have been produced by any similar occurrence in modern times. A few of the more prominent such debates ought to be highlighted here. From the end of the war, the degree to which Jews resisted the Nazi death machine has been a matter of controversy. During the war, the ghetto fighter Abba Kovner (1918–87) asked his fellow Jews whether they should go to their deaths 'like sheep to the slaughter' and whether Jews did indeed die like sheep, without effective resistance, has been a matter of fierce controversy. The contention that Jews offered insufficient resistance was made most commonly in Israel in the 1950s and around the time of the Eichmann trial in the early 1960s, when, in particular, the famous Jewish writer Hannah Arendt (1906–75), a refugee from Germany, contended in her book *Eichmann in Jerusalem* (1963) that the Jewish Councils established in Jewish communities and ghettos actually facilitated the Nazis' work for them. Arendt also questioned the role of the Zionist movement during the Holocaust, claiming that it did little or nothing to assist Jews and that, in Hungary in 1944, it may have, in a sense,

co-operated with the Nazis. (Obviously, her claims aroused fierce controversy.) Many others have asked how the Nazis could organise such an
efficient death machine without greater resistance on the part of the victims.

The tenor of virtually all historiographical analysis of this question since
the 1960s, however, has been to emphasise both the extent of Jewish resistance and the enormous obstacles to any successful resistance. Historians
have documented hundreds of examples of Jewish resistance to the Nazis in
the ghettos, as Partisan resistance fighters, and in the concentration camps,
throughout Nazi-occupied Europe. The most famous example of Jewish
resistance was the Warsaw ghetto uprising, which lasted from 19 April to
16 May 1943. Only 50–60,000 Jews remained in the Warsaw ghetto at this
stage, chiefly young people. With only minimal weapons and a fighting force
of no more than about 750 men and women, the Jews managed to hold off
the Nazi death machine for nearly a month before being crushed; individual
leaders of the uprising such as Mordecai Anielewicz (1919–43) became
heroes of the Jewish people. Major uprisings also occurred in the Bialystok
and Vilna ghettos, and even in the extermination camps.

More basically, ill-considered criticism of alleged Jewish supineness during the war ignores the extraordinary difficulties which faced any attempt at
resistance. The Jews had no armies or military leaders, no satisfactory way
of communicating with other Jewish communities, few weapons or supplies.
They were utterly terrorised and demoralised, as well as starving. While
regular armies consist overwhelmingly of young men aged 18 to 30, a
majority of Jewish ghettos and other population centres consisted of
women, children and the elderly, whose lives were under constant threat in
any case, and particularly so if Jewish resistance fighters appeared to be
active. Jews lived among host populations who were themselves often antisemitic (if not murderous) and could not rely on them for help. Until mid-
1944 the Western Allies and the Soviet forces were hundreds of miles away.
Nazi Germany was initially militarily hegemonic throughout Europe.
France, with an army of 1.5 million, had collapsed within a few weeks in
1940. In view of all this, it is absurd to criticise the Jews for not offering
greater resistance. Similarly, the Zionist movement was realistically unable
to help. The sole aim of Jews under Nazi rule was to survive one day longer,
not to engage in Hollywood-style heroics. Although mistakes may well have
been made in the conduct of Jewish leadership and other aspects of resistance, it is inappropriate for those of us who were not directly presented
with the imminent prospect of genocide to criticise those who were, under
conditions unique and unprecedented in modern history.

The role of the democracies

Another vexed question in the historiography of the Holocaust concerns
the attitude of the Western democracies: could more have been done to

save the Jews of Europe? Prior to the early 1970s few Jews and few historians voiced any direct criticism of the allies, and still less of the great wartime leaders Winston Churchill and Franklin D. Roosevelt. Most Jewish refugees and survivors were happy to be alive, and viewed any criticism of those who saved their lives as monumental ingratitude. Since the 1970s, however, book after book has appeared which has criticised the behaviour of the Allies. In the United States, probably the best-known of these works is David S. Wyman's *The Abandonment of the Jews: America and the Holocaust, 1941–1945* (1984), which has been extremely influential in depicting American policy as highly unsympathetic to Jewish refugee immigration. Since then, something of a backlash has occurred, with the position held by Wyman and others being attacked by one of the authors of this textbook, William D. Rubinstein, in *The Myth of Rescue: Why the Democracies Could Not Have Saved More Jews from the Nazis* (1997).

There is a good deal which might be said in support of the view that the democracies did too little to rescue the Jews of Europe. Nowhere during the 1930s was immigration unrestricted, and barriers, often severe, existed in the United States, Britain, Canada, Australia, and other Western nations. The United States imposed an annual quota of about 26,000 Germans (of any religious background) able to migrate to America, a limit which was never varied. While Britain did not set an annual quota, permission to settle in that country was not automatic and depended upon the good will of the British Home Office. Immigration to Canada, South Africa, and other countries was limited by restrictions, often rooted in antisemitic prejudice. While considerable German Jewish migration to Palestine occurred in the mid-1930s, this was severely limited by the notorious MacDonald White Paper of May 1939. During the war, little or nothing of a deliberate nature was done to rescue Jews, although the West certainly knew of Nazi plans to exterminate Europe's Jews by the end of 1942. Only in January 1944 did the United States establish a specific government body (the War Refugee Board), which attempted to rescue Jews. Auschwitz was never bombed, although this had been requested from May 1944 onwards. The rescue of Jews was, in fact, never an Allied priority.

While superficially plausible, these arguments are almost certainly very misleading and rooted in a hindsighted analysis of events. The Western democracies had no way of knowing, prior to the war, what the fate of Jews in Germany who were unable to emigrate would be. Despite this, over 70 per cent of Germany's Jews managed to leave the country. Indeed, the West's treatment of Jewish émigrés from Germany was unusually generous, by the standards of the time. Hitler did not conquer the millions of Jews outside Germany until the war began: before the war they were not refugees. Once the war started, they were unable to emigrate, not because the Allies refused to admit them, but because, from 1940, Jews were not allowed by the Nazis to leave the countries the latter occupied. Those Jews were, in effect, prisoners.

The Allies' failure to bomb Auschwitz is more complex. No one, anywhere, proposed the bombing of that camp before May 1944. When it was proposed it was rejected by many Jewish groups on the grounds that Jewish lives were likely to be lost in such air raids. Certainly no one at the time perceived the proposal as a panacea. It is difficult to see why the democracies and their leaders should be blamed, even indirectly, for the crimes of the Nazis and, as noted, most criticisms of the Allies are made with hindsight, lacking any real notion of the realities of the war raging at the time. Roosevelt and Churchill led a great international coalition which wiped Nazism off the face of the earth, and are surely owed a supreme debt of gratitude by today's Jews.

Other aspects of the behaviour of the so-called 'bystanders' during the Holocaust have come under continuing scrutiny. Perhaps the best known is that of the Vatican and, in particular, Pope Pius XII, the leader of the Catholic Church at the time. Pius's 'silence' during the Holocaust has been endlessly debated since his death in 1958. It is a fact that Pius appeared to be far more concerned with the evils of Communism than of Nazism. More questionable, however, is whether loud statements by him attacking Nazi genocide could have saved more Jews, or whether the quiet, often secretive, efforts by the Church in saving Jews were not the most efficacious which could be taken at the time. Other institutions have also come under the spotlight, especially the International Red Cross and its failure to condemn Nazi genocide. Curiously, the role of the Soviet Union and left-wing groups in saving Jews during the war has not come in for similar scrutiny and criticism, although most Jews were killed in the Soviet Union or in areas which fell under their control in 1944–45.

The role of 'bystanders' to the Holocaust also raises the question of so-called 'righteous gentiles', non-Jews who risked their lives to save Jews during the Holocaust. The term derives from the Hebrew *hasidei umot haolam* ('the righteous among the nations of the world have a place in the world to come'). Since 1953, Yad Vashem, the Israeli Holocaust memorial, has officially commemorated 'righteous gentiles' and since the early 1960s has recognised such individuals by name, with the award of a medal, and the planting of a tree at Yad Vashem. Over 8,000 such persons have been recognised. Some, like the Swedish diplomat Raoul Wallenberg (1912–1945) and Oskar Schindler, are world famous, but most remain virtually unknown. Moreover, their motives often still remain obscure. Few were previously known as humanitarians or anti-Nazis, and some, like Schindler, appeared, if anything, to favour Germany. Yet all considered the genocide of the Jews a diabolical evil, and risked their lives to save the lives of imperilled Jews. Much more research needs to be done before fruitful generalisations can be drawn.

The uniqueness of the Holocaust

One historiographical question which has aroused tremendous debate is that of the uniqueness of the Holocaust. Most scholars of the Holocaust regard it as unique in many salient respects, especially in the combination of the Nazis' intention to kill every Jew in Europe without exception, and, perhaps especially, in the efficiency of the conveyor-belt death machine operated by the SS. Some scholars of the Holocaust have gone so far as to suggest that any questioning of the uniqueness of the Holocaust is itself antisemitic. Most scholars are, however, confident that no seemingly comparable event in modern history, perhaps in recorded history, was truly like the Holocaust.

As with so many other aspects of the Holocaust, this view has itself come under heavy, indeed furious, criticism in recent years. Critics of the uniqueness of the Holocaust have claimed that an even higher percentage of American Indians (95 per cent) and Australian Aboriginals (90 per cent) died following the coming of Europeans than the percentage of European Jews killed by the Nazis, that Stalin certainly murdered more people than Hitler, and that there were precedents to the Jewish Holocaust in the Armenian genocide of 1915 and parallels in more recent mass murders in Cambodia and Rwanda. Some extreme critics also claim that the notion that the Holocaust is unique is promulgated by Jewish groups for political ends, especially to gain sympathy for Israel. Plainly, these views, often put intemperately, have been bitterly rejected by those who view the Holocaust as unique. The latter point out, for instance, that the American Indians and Australian Aboriginals who died mainly succumbed to disease (although many were certainly killed as a matter of deliberate policy), and that there was no general deliberate policy of genocide, as there was in Europe under Nazi rule. Historians have also asked whether the genocide of gypsies (Roma and Sinta) by the Nazis was comparable, and if Nazi Germany had plans to deal with other peoples, for instance the Poles, in like manner to the Jews if they had won the war.

There are no ready or obvious answers to the most basic questions of all about the Holocaust, namely, why did it occur and what was its meaning? The Holocaust showed the potentiality for evil in humankind when unrestrained by ordinary morality, and the evils of totalitarianism compared to democracy. The rise of Nazism may also be linked with the rise of Soviet Communism in showing the malign results of the breakdown of the old institutions and elite structure of central and eastern Europe as a result of the First World War. Given that democracy was triumphant over Nazi tyranny, at least in western Europe and eventually everywhere, the Holocaust also provided a powerful vindication of pluralism and democracy over totalitarianism. In a sense, too, the existence today of the State of Israel and of strong Diaspora Jewish communities shows that Hitler failed. The deepest questions of all, the theological issues raised by the Holocaust, are unanswerable by the historian.

Further reading

There are literally thousands of books on the Holocaust, and only a small number can be cited here. Dozens of important books and articles on the subject appear every year. The American journal *Holocaust and Genocide Studies* contains recent research and reviews, as do the *Leo Baeck Institute Yearbook* (published in London) and *Yad Vashem Studies* (published in Jerusalem), which appear annually.

References and documents

Yitzhak Arad, Israel Gutman, and Abraham Margaliot, eds, *Documents on the Holocaust* (Lincoln, Nebraska, 1999)

Abraham I. Edelheit and Hershel Edelheit, *History of the Holocaust: A Handbook and Dictionary* (Boulder, Col., 1994)

Martin Gilbert, *The Dent Atlas of the Holocaust* (London, 1993)

Israel Gutman, ed., *Encyclopedia of the Holocaust*, 4 vols (New York, 1990)

Yechiam Halevy, *Historical Atlas of the Holocaust* (New York, 1996)

J. Noakes and G. Pridham, eds, *Nazism 1919–1945: A Documentary Reader*, 4 vols (Exeter, 1988); Volume 3: *Foreign Policy, War and Racial Extermination*, is particularly relevant.

Louis L. Snyder, *Encyclopedia of the Third Reich* (New York, 1976)

Robert S. Wistrich, *Who's Who in Nazi Germany* (London, 1995)

General histories

Yehuda Bauer, *A History of the Holocaust* (New York, 1982)

Dan Cohn-Sherbok, *Understanding the Holocaust: An Introduction* (London, 1999)

Lucy S. Dawidowicz, *The War Against the Jews, 1933–1945* (New York, 1976)

Saul Friedlander, *Nazi Germany and the Jews: The Years of Persecution, 1933–39* (London, 1997)

Raul Hilberg, *The Destruction of the European Jews*, 3 vols (New York, 1985)

Michael R. Marrus, *The Holocaust in History* (London, 1989)

Gerald Reitlinger, *The Final Solution: The Attempt to Exterminate the Jews of Europe 1939–1945* (London, 1953)

Karl A. Schleunes, *The Twisted Road to Auschwitz: The Nazi Policy Towards German Jews, 1933–1939* (Urbana, Ill., 1970)

Leni Yahil, *The Holocaust: The Fate of European Jewry* (Oxford, 1984)

Works on specific topics

Yitzhak Arad, *Belzec, Sobibor, Treblinka: The Operation Reinhard Death Camps* (Bloomington, Ind., 1999)

John Bierman, *Righteous Gentile: The Story of Raoul Wallenberg, Missing Hero of the Holocaust* (London, 1995)

Rudolph L. Braham, *The Politics of Genocide*, 2 vols (New York, 1994)

Christopher R. Browning, *The Path to Genocide* (Cambridge, 1992)

Philippe Burrin, *Hitler and the Jews: The Genesis of the Holocaust* (London, 1994)

David Cesarani, ed., *The Final Solution: Origins and Interpretation* (London, 1994)

Gerald Fleming, *Hitler and the Final Solution* (Berkeley, Ca., 1984)

Martin Gilbert, *Auschwitz and the Allies* (London, 1991)

Daniel J. Goldhagen, *Hitler's Willing Executioners* (New York, 1996)

Yisrael Gutman, *The Jews of Warsaw, 1939–1993: Ghetto, Underground, Revolt* (Bloomington, Ind., 1982)

Yisrael Gutman and Michael Berenbaum, eds, *Anatomy of the Auschwitz Death Camp* (Washington, D.C., 1998)

Jochen von Lang, ed., *Eichmann Interrogated: Transcripts from the Archives of the Israel Police* (New York, 1983)

Alan S. Rosenbaum, ed., *Is the Holocaust Unique? Perspectives on Comparative Genocide* (Boulder, Col., 1996)

William D. Rubinstein, *The Myth of Rescue: Why the Democracies Could Not Have Saved More Jews from the Nazis* (London, 1997)

Robert R. Shandley, ed., *Unwilling Germans? The Goldhagen Debate* (Minneapolis, 1998)

Robert G.L. Waite, *The Psychopathic God: Adolf Hitler* (New York, 1993)

Robert S. Wistrich, *Hitler's Apocalypse: Jews and the Nazi Legacy* (London, 1985)

David S. Wyman, *The Abandonment of the Jews: America and the Holocaust, 1941–1945* (New York, 1984)

|10|

Jews in Britain and the United States

At the present time, about half of the world's Jews live in the English-speaking world: Britain and the 'Old Commonwealth' (Canada, Australia, South Africa, New Zealand), the United States, and a number of other very small communities such as Ireland. (Canada, Australia, South Africa, and other Commonwealth Jewish communities are considered in Chapter 11.) Although these societies differ in many respects, they also have a good deal in common, which set them apart from the Jewish communities of Europe and elsewhere. There was no Jewish presence in Britain during the crucial period between 1290 and 1656 when Britain became a Protestant, capitalist society and when many political liberties were achieved. In a real sense, post-1656 Jewish life in the English-speaking world was 'born free', lacking most of the medieval antisemitic elements found on the European continent. For the most part, the English-speaking world has seen only minimal levels of antisemitism, which never became a political force, and Jewish life has almost always been a success story. Although Jews often had to fight to secure their rights, they did this in societies where the concept of the freedom of the individual always enjoyed the support of the majority and the denial of equal rights to one particular group was, in the long run, always seen as anomalous.

The history of the Jews until the early nineteenth century

While the history of the Jews in Britain since the seventeenth century has almost always been a success story, this was far from true during the earlier period of Anglo-Jewish settlement. From the time of the Norman Conquest until they were expelled in 1290, there was a substantial Jewish community in medieval Britain whose history is an object-lesson in what might have been had Britain not experienced the great changes in its society which occurred in the early modern period. The Jews who migrated to medieval England were, legally, the chattels of the English kings, who were the absolute owners of the Jews' persons and property. The Jews were there as royal tax collectors and money-lenders, living in separate quarters in cities and towns throughout the country ('Old Jewry', a street in the City of London, is the most famous reminder of the medieval Jewish presence). Tax collectors and money-lenders are seldom admired in the best of circumstances, but in medieval England the Jews became increasingly reviled. The first recorded ritual murder charge since ancient times, made at Norwich in 1144, the 'blood libel' at Lincoln in 1255 leading to the cult of 'Little Saint Hugh of Lincoln', allegedly murdered by the Jews, and the mass murder of Jews at York in 1190, are among the most infamous events in medieval Jewish history. In 1290, the Jews were expelled from England by Edward I, the first time that Jews had been driven out en masse from any country in Europe.

For the next 366 years, England officially was without Jews, and was certainly without an organised Jewish community. Some Jews did live there, most famously Queen Elizabeth I's physician Dr Roderigo Lopez (1525–94), who was hanged for allegedly conspiring to poison her at the behest of the King of Spain. Lopez is often said to have been the model for Shakespeare's Shylock in *The Merchant of Venice*. Critics have long debated whether this work is essentially antisemitic, reflecting still-current stereotypes of the Jews, or more deeply humanistic. A small Marrano community existed in London in the Elizabethan and Jacobean period, and Shakespeare is believed by some to have had Jewish acquaintances.

Jews were formally readmitted to Britain in 1656 by Oliver Cromwell, the Lord Protector of England following the execution of King Charles I in 1649. As a Puritan, Cromwell was particularly sympathetic to the Hebrews of the Old Testament, and believed that the Second Coming of Jesus would occur only when Jews were permitted to settle everywhere on earth, including Britain. He was also influenced by an appeal by the Amsterdam-based Rabbi Menasseh ben Israel (1604–57), who argued that a Jewish presence would be advantageous to English commerce. As a result, Jews were formally allowed to settle in Britain again in 1656. In 1660 the British monarchy was restored and Charles II (son of the executed former monarch) became king. Arguably the attitude of the king and Parliament towards the Jews in the years after 1660 was as important as the actions of Cromwell. Charles II, who had been impressed by Jews during his exile in Europe, confirmed Cromwell's decision to readmit the Jews. Over the next few decades, attempts were made to levy a special tax on Jewish merchants in England, as was commonly done throughout the Continent. These were always defeated, and by the end of the seventeenth century it became universally accepted that no special measures of discrimination could be aimed specifically at Jews. As early as 1667 Jews were permitted to be sworn on the Old

THE JEWS OF THE UNITED STATES, 1860–1960

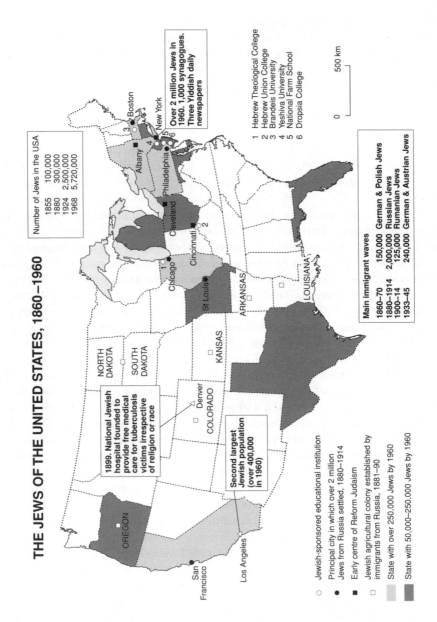

Number of Jews in the USA	
1855	100,000
1880	300,000
1924	2,500,000
1968	5,720,000

Over 2 million Jews in 1960. 1,000 synagogues. Three Yiddish daily newspapers

1 Hebrew Theological College
2 Hebrew Union College
3 Brandeis University
4 Yeshiva University
5 National Farm School
6 Dropsia College

0   500 km

Boston
New York
Albany
Philadelphia
Cleveland
Cincinnati
Chicago
St Louis
ARKANSAS
LOUISIANA
KANSAS
COLORADO
Denver
NORTH DAKOTA
SOUTH DAKOTA
OREGON
San Francisco
Los Angeles

1899. National Jewish hospital founded to provide free medical care for tuberculosis victims irrespective of religion or race

Second largest Jewish population (over 400,000 in 1960)

Main immigrant waves

1860–70	150,000	German & Polish Jews
1880–1914	2,000,000	Russian Jews
1900–14	125,000	Rumanian Jews
1933–45	240,000	German & Austrian Jews

○ Jewish-sponsored educational institution

● Principal city in which over 2 million Jews from Russia settled, 1880–1914

■ Early centre of Reform Judaism

□ Jewish agricultural colony established by immigrants from Russia, 1881–90

State with over 250,000 Jews by 1960

State with 50,000–250,000 Jews by 1960

Testament when testifying before a law court. Some extreme voices actually called for the creation of Jewish ghettos in England, but were ignored. Jews were thus never singled out for special opprobrium, as they were throughout Europe.

There were several important historical reasons for this state of affairs, most of which had their origins in the long period, from 1290 until 1656, when there was no Jewish communities in Britain. During the sixteenth century England and Scotland became Protestant by religion. The symbols and much of the liturgy and usages of Catholicism were swept away, among them most of the imagery which had encouraged antisemitism, especially the emphasis on the Crucifixion. British Protestantism was heavily Scripture-oriented, with the smaller sects that emerged during the sixteenth and seventeenth centuries – such as the Baptists, Independents, and Quakers – being highly sympathetic to the ancient Hebrews, and preferring the Old Testament to the New. Moreover, the British Reformation saw the end of Catholic hostility to 'usury' (money lending) and to capitalism in general. Britain now emerged as one of the world's leading commercial nations, with its own growing, highly successful class of rich merchants. The British aristocracy had little or no prejudice against capitalism or money-making, and Britain did not have feudalism, serfs, or peasants, as on the European continent. Thus there was absolutely nothing specifically 'Jewish' about capitalism as it emerged in Britain. Britain's successful class of wealthy businessmen were all Protestant gentiles, including its bankers and moneylenders. Jews were not reviled as moneyed exploiters, as on much of the Continent. Thirdly, the political struggles which occurred in Britain at this time led to the triumph of representative government, the rule of law and the notion of inalienable human rights, which became institutionalised in the Bill of Rights and the 'Glorious Revolution' of 1689. The Bill of Rights applied to everyone in Britain, including Jews.

The Reformation in Britain had, indeed, created a category of detested and often persecuted religious believers, namely Catholics. In Britain, Catholics were often depicted in the same negative imagery as were Jews in Europe. Catholics in Britain were both hated and feared, and many British people regarded the Pope as the 'Anti-Christ'. These attitudes persisted into the twentieth century, and may still exist in Northern Ireland. Certainly, Jews did not have the same rights as Anglicans (adherents of the established Church of England), and there was to be a protracted struggle, lasting until the late nineteenth century, to secure fully equal rights. Yet British laws never singled out Jews for forms of discrimination experienced by no one else, as was common in Europe. When it existed, the exclusion of Jews from certain rights and privileges was almost always precisely that suffered by other non-Anglican groups. Normally, this discrimination existed because persons had to take an Anglican-based oath to be admitted as a member of Parliament or holder of a public office, a requirement which applied equally to Protestant dissenters (i.e. Protestant non-Anglicans such as Baptists and

Quakers), Catholics, Jews, and agnostics. The struggle for the 'emancipation of the Jews' in Britain normally took the form of widening such oaths
to be conscientiously acceptable to Jews, not to the removal of discriminatory measures aimed specifically at Jews. Jews were increasingly seen as a
small, low-profile minority little different from any other Englishmen. They
were often widely respected, and were rarely, or never, seen as demon-
figures as was so common in Europe. Neither were they seen as 'controlling'
the British state or economy, or as being part of an international conspiracy
of evil. Few in Britain termed them 'Christ-killers', and extremist sentiment
of this kind was aimed far more often at Catholics than at Jews. An extraordinary example of British liberalism towards the Jews occurred in 1732
when an English newspaper publisher printed a variation on the 'ritual
murder' theme, accusing a London Sephardi of killing a Jewish woman
recently settled in Britain and her infant child because the infant had been
fathered by a Christian. The judge in this, the 'Osborne Case', described the
report as 'likely to raise tumults and disorder among the people and inflame
them with a spirit of universal barbarity against a whole group of men, as if
guilty of crimes scarce practicable and totally incredible.' Remarkably,
therefore, group defamation involving Jews was held to be illegal by an
English judge in the eighteenth century. Other tokens of tolerance occurred
at this time as well, for instance the Marriage Act of 1753, which gave Jews
(and Quakers, who were also seen as virtually non-Christian) a privilege
withheld from other non-Anglicans in recognising the legality of marriages
contracted according to their rites.

Not everything was rosy, however. In 1753, the same year as the Marriage
Act, the Whig government (which had links to wealthy members of the Jewish
community) decided to alter the rules of naturalisation to allow Jews to
become British subjects without (as was required) taking the Anglican sacra-
ments. This legislation, known as the 'Jew Bill', passed Parliament but caused
a fury of anti-Jewish agitation led by the opposition Tory party, anxious to
harm the government, in alliance with conservative Anglican clerics and some
jealous commercial interests in the City of London. Widespread agitation led
to the repeal of the 'Jew Bill' the following year. That some degree of antisemitic hostility to the Jews existed in England at this time is evidenced by
the writings of William Cobbett (1762–1835), an enormously popular radical opponent of the aristocracy who detested Jews, Quakers, and Scotsmen
as urban capitalists. Poorer Jews also acquired a reputation for urban crime,
especially dealing in stolen goods (as the famous character of Fagin in
Dickens' *Oliver Twist* illustrates). On the other hand, a good deal of
philosemitism also existed in Britain. Jews were welcomed into Masonic
lodges, and many notable British writers were extremely friendly to Jews, for
instance Sir Walter Scott and George Eliot.

The Jewish 'struggle for emancipation' in Britain aimed at putting British
Jews on a precisely equal footing before the law, and in particular at allowing practising Jews to sit in the British House of Commons. Before 1828,

only Anglicans (or Presbyterians in Scotland) could be elected to the House of Commons, for all MPs, upon their election, had to swear their allegiance to the Thirty-Nine Articles of the Anglican faith. In 1828, Protestant Nonconformists were allowed to be elected to the Commons, and in 1829, Roman Catholics. At first, it was assumed that Jews would also be allowed to take their seats with an oath tolerable to Jews, but Parliament, and particularly the House of Lords, insisted on maintaining that newly-elected MPs would have to take an oath which included the words 'on the true faith of a Christian'. Although not antisemitic, many Tories argued that Britain was, by its Constitution, a Christian state, and that it was not inappropriate to allow only Christians to become legislators. Some traditional Jews actually supported the status quo, arguing that the participation of Jews in national politics would lead to their secularisation and apostasy. Nearly all liberals, and some conservatives, were of course fully in favour of allowing Jews into the House of Commons, and the famous attack on the legal disabilities of the Jews by the great historian Thomas Babington Macaulay (1800–59) in 1839 remain among the most cogent arguments for Jewish emancipation. Baron Lionel de Rothschild (1808–79), head of the British branch of the celebrated banking dynasty, was elected to Parliament in 1847. He entered the chamber of the House, hoping to be permitted to swear the oath using the words 'So help me God' instead of 'On the true faith of a Christian'. This was, however, not allowed, and an enormous campaign grew up throughout Britain to allow him to take his seat, with hundreds of thousands of persons signing petitions on his behalf. Rothschild was repeatedly re-elected, and the House of Commons was always ready to seat him, but the Tory-dominated House of Lords always refused to allow the oath to be altered. Finally, in 1858, the Lords agreed to allow each House to decide its own oath, and Rothschild took his seat in July 1858. In 1885 another Rothschild became the first practising Jew to be given a peerage; he took his seat in the House of Lords without incident.

Other barriers to Jewish participation in British society also fell during the nineteenth century. Jews began to hold local office, as sheriffs (an important municipal position) and councillors from the 1830s. In 1855 Sir David Salomons (1797–1873) became the first Jewish Lord Mayor of London and the first Jewish member of the Privy Council. Jewish barristers and solicitors began to appear. A significant Jewish presence in the cultural life of Britain was hampered by the fact that Oxford and Cambridge universities (until the nineteenth century the only universities in England) required that all students swear adherence to the Thirty-Nine Articles of Anglicanism, Oxford on matriculation, Cambridge on graduation. This requirement excluded Protestant Nonconformists, Catholics, and Jews from university education in England. As a result, non-Anglicans, including the wealthy Jewish financier Sir Isaac Lyon Goldsmid (1778–1859), helped to found University College, London (the nucleus of London University), a non-sectarian institution, which was incorporated in 1837. In 1871, Parliament passed the

University Tests Act which abolished the Anglican oaths at Oxford and Cambridge, opening the old universities to all. This was done, in part, because of the experience of a gifted Jewish student at Cambridge who was permitted, through a special 'act of grace' by the university's senate, to be admitted to his degree without subscribing to the Thirty-Nine Articles. Nevertheless, he was still barred from a College Fellowship which he would have been offered if he had taken the Anglican oath. The opening of the old universities to Jews (and, it should be remembered, all other non-Anglicans) is often seen as completing in full the process of 'Jewish emancipation'.

Something must be said here about the crucial and unique position of Benjamin Disraeli (1804–81; created Earl of Beaconsfield in 1876). Born to a Sephardi family in London and boasting an extravagantly Jewish name, Disraeli was baptised as an Anglican at 13, following a feud between his father and his synagogue. Disraeli's spectacular career unquestionably represented the greatest political achievement of anyone born a Jew in the nineteenth century. Despite much antisemitic prejudice and many other obstacles, Disraeli became Britain's Prime Minister in 1868 and 1874–80. He did this, most remarkably, at the head of the right-wing Conservative party, which consisted at the time chiefly of hereditary landowners. Disraeli's 'one nation Toryism' put its stamp on the Conservative party's philosophy for over a century. He was hero-worshipped by the Conservative rank-and-file, and his career unquestionably did much to diminish levels of antisemitism in Britain. Disraeli was also one of the most distinguished novelists and writers of his time. No one like Disraeli appeared anywhere else in the nineteenth-century Western world.

The forging of Anglo-Jewry

The Jewish community which grew up in England following readmission was very small, numbering only about 8000 in the mid-eighteenth century. It mainly consisted of Sephardim, with some German-origin Ashkenazim, and was centred in London and seaports such as Portsmouth. None of the traditional institutions of eastern European Jewry, such as the *yeshivot*, were established by the new community, although synagogues quickly emerged. The eighteenth century saw the establishment of the two leading Jewish institutions which came to characterise Anglo-Jewry, the Board of Deputies of British Jews and the post of chief rabbi. The Board of Deputies, established in 1760 as the London Committee of Deputies of British Jews to parallel a similar body which emerged among Protestant Nonconformists, became a kind of parliament of the Anglo-Jewish community, a role it still maintains. It consists of delegates ('deputies') from synagogues (and, since the early twentieth century, other bodies such as Zionist groups) who meet to discuss common concerns. The community as a whole does not elect independent deputies. It is not a *kehillah* in the eastern European sense, since it cannot tax individual Jews and directly maintains few if any institutions, much less an educational or welfare network. The Board of Deputies was, however, given official recognition by the British Parliament when, in 1837, it was legally empowered to approve Jewish marriage celebrants in connection with the new Marriage and Registration Act. For most of the nineteenth century the leading figure of Anglo-Jewry was Sir Moses Montefiore (1784–1885), a wealthy Italian-born Jew, closely connected with the Rothschilds, who served as the Board's President from 1834 to 1874. Montefiore was especially concerned with the plight of persecuted Jewish communities in other countries, making many foreign journeys to intercede on their behalf. Drawing on the example of the Court Jews, he was primarily responsible for instituting the pattern whereby wealthy and influential Jews in the democracies work to alleviate the plight of oppressed Jewries overseas. Montefiore was also a notable proto-Zionist and, in Britain, a determined opponent of any official recognition of non-Orthodox forms of Judaism. He remained the dominant figure in Anglo-Jewry until his death at the age of 101.

The institution of chief rabbi grew up informally in the late eighteenth century. The chief rabbi was the rabbi of the Great Synagogue in London; his recognition as official religious head of Ashkenazi Orthodoxy throughout England came during the early nineteenth century, with Solomon Hirschell (1762–1842) being the first officially-recognised chief rabbi. His successors – such as Nathan Marcus Adler (1803–90) – strengthened the position. In 1870 most of the mainstream Ashkenazi synagogues in England joined together to form the United Synagogue, the most important Jewish religious grouping in Britain, whose head and spokesman is the Chief Rabbi. (The Sephardi community in Britain has a separate religious head, the Haham.) By the late nineteenth century the United Synagogue had evolved a distinctive ambience, somewhat like German neo-Orthodoxy, which emphasised decorum, British patriotism, and respectability, and was sometimes derided as an attempt to mimic Anglicanism. It always retained middle-of-the-road Orthodoxy as its religious position, eschewing both traditional Strict Orthodoxy and non-Orthodox forms of Judaism. To this day, the chief rabbi remains the foremost religious spokesman for Anglo-Jewry, and recent incumbents, such as Immanuel Jakobovits (1921–99) and Jonathan Sachs (b.1948), have been well-known public figures. The Anglo-Jewish community also evolved a network of other characteristic institutions, such as the weekly *Jewish Chronicle* newspaper, founded in 1841. By the year 1880 or so, Anglo-Jewry was in a fortunate position. The battle for emancipation had been won; many members of the community were prosperous and respected; there was little overt antisemitism.

This fortunate situation changed somewhat with the arrival of thousands of eastern European Jews in the decades following the Russian pogroms of 1881. Between 100,000 and 150,000 Jews settled in Britain in the period 1881–1914, increasing the total Jewish population of the United Kingdom to about 250,000 by the outbreak of the First World War, approximately two-thirds of whom lived in London. Most eastern European Jews settled in or near Whitechapel in the East End of London, transforming parts of it into something like a Jewish ghetto. Many more Jews – hundreds of thousands, perhaps – went from London to America. Cities such as Manchester, Leeds, and Glasgow also developed substantial Jewish populations. Until 1905 Britain allowed unrestricted immigration: there were no barriers to anyone settling in the country. In that year, Britain passed the Aliens Act, which attempted to limit the volume of immigration from Europe. (In British law, an 'alien' is a person who is not a citizen of Britain or – in the past – of the Empire; it has no pejorative connotation.) The enactment of this legislation occurred in large measure because of local opposition, in the East End, to further Jewish immigration. It is generally believed that the level of Jewish immigration to Britain declined by about one-third as a result of the Aliens Act (which also affected Italian and German migration). Only after 1918, however, was virtually all foreign immigration to Britain halted. Many of the Jewish newcomers were Orthodox Jews. Nearly all spoke Yiddish. Many were socialists or involved in the working-class movement. Many, paradoxically, were small businessmen, especially in the clothing trade, whose aim was to move up the economic ladder as quickly as possible. Relations between Jews and their gentile neighbours could be warm, and there were no violent outbreaks against the Jews anywhere in Britain at this time, the anti-Jewish rioting in South Wales in 1911 being perhaps an exception.

The established Jewish community of Britain aimed to assist and, where possible, acculturate the newcomers as soon as possible. Leaders of the established community helped to establish such institutions as the Federation of Synagogues (a Strictly Orthodox network of synagogues, chiefly in the East End of London, loosely connected with the United Synagogue) and the Jews' Free School. Most newcomers quickly learned English and many had begun to make an impact, even before the First World War. The famous retail chain of Marks and Spencer was established by two Jewish immigrants in Leeds, while Burton, the men's tailoring chain, was established by a Lithuanian Jew. At the top of the social scale, practising Jews now entered the British Cabinet for the first time, the earliest being Herbert Samuel (1870–1963) in 1909.

The First World War, in which nearly 42,000 British Jews fought, further encouraged acculturation. The Star of David was officially recognised by the War Office as a symbol, and appears on many war graves. Following the Armistice memorials to the war were deliberately designed in a non-sectarian manner rather than as Anglican icons, most notably the Cenotaph in Whitehall. General Sir John Monash (1865–1931), a distinguished Australian Jew, rose to become one of the most senior commanders on the Allied side. In November 1917, the British Cabinet remarkably promulgated the Balfour Declaration, promising Palestine (which British troops conquered from Turkey) as a 'national home' for the 'Jewish people'. It is difficult to believe that any other European power would have made such an offer.

Anglo-Jewry from 1918 to 1945

The first few years after 1918 unquestionably saw a rise in the levels of anti-semitism in Britain, fanned in part by perceptions of 'Jewish Bolshevism' in the Russian revolution. Yet, compared with other European countries, this mood soon faded and there was remarkably little mainstream antisemitism, as the failure of Sir Oswald Mosley's British Union of Fascists shows. Unlike Germany and most of central and eastern Europe, Britain's institutions were intact and its Empire was larger than ever. The British middle classes were not impoverished by the war. British politics continued to be dominated by moderate parties, and the British electorate notably failed to support extremists.

The rise of Hitler in 1933 presented Anglo-Jewry with a great challenge. The bulk of British public opinion was deeply antipathetic to early Nazi antisemitism. In 1933 the British Board of Deputies gave an undertaking that it would pay for all Jewish refugees allowed to migrate to Britain, and by 1939 raised £2 million for this purpose. Non-Jewish charities, especially the Lord Baldwin Fund (founded by former Prime Minister Stanley Baldwin in 1937) also raised very considerable finances. From *Kristallnacht* in November 1938, British refugee policy became increasingly more liberal. Between 55,000 and 75,000 German Jews migrated to Britain in the period 1933–40, with probably another 53,000-60,000 to Palestine, and 30,000 to other parts of the Commonwealth. Mosley's British Union of Fascists received virtually no electoral support and remained on the political fringes. After the outbreak of the Second World War in September 1939, Britain was unable to assist the Jews of Nazi-occupied Europe directly, but fought Germany alone between the fall of France in June 1940 and the German invasion of the Soviet Union a year later, and was a major part of the Allied coalition which vanquished Nazi Germany. A number of aspects of wartime British policy towards the Jews have come under severe criticism. In 1940, faced with invasion, Britain arrested and interned many German-born Jews (and non-Jews) as security risks, sending thousands to Australia and Canada. In 1942 the *Struma*, a Romanian vessel carrying fleeing Jews intending to enter Palestine, was detained at Istanbul following British political pressure, and was sunk in the Black Sea, probably by a Soviet submarine. The fate of the *Struma* was indicative of Britain's failure to allow more Jews into Palestine. In June 1944, Britain did not bomb the Auschwitz concentration camp, despite requests to do so, citing the difficulty of carrying out such a raid. More centrally, Britain never made the rescue of Jews an explicit wartime priority. While historians have debated the validity of these claims, it is very difficult to see what more Britain could realistically have done to rescue Europe's Jews, given the absolute determination of the Nazis to exterminate them, and Britain's military weakness.

Britain governed Palestine between 1917 and 1948, and its policies deserve examination. The 1920s saw a period of relatively peaceful growth of the *yishuv* in Palestine, backed by and large by the support of Britain's Jews, who were sympathetic to 'practical Zionism'. British policy changed perceptibly after the 'Wailing Wall' incident in 1929, and especially after the beginnings of the 'Arab revolt' in 1936, when the appeasement of the Arabs became increasingly marked. This affected, in particular, heightened barriers placed on Jewish immigration, most notably the 'MacDonald White Paper' of May 1939 (named after Malcolm MacDonald, the Colonial Secretary), which placed a limit of 75,000 on the number of Jews allowed to enter Palestine. This caused fierce resentment within the Zionist movement, and was probably the central factor in increasing support for Zionism among Diaspora Jewry. It also helped to fan the wave of anti-British terrorism in Palestine which led to Britain's withdrawal from the country in 1947–58 and the establishment of the State of Israel.

British Jewry in the post-1945 period

British Jewry emerged from the Second World War as one of the largest remaining Jewish communities in Europe. Estimating its size is difficult, but it probably reached a peak size of 380,000 in the mid-1950s. (Higher estimates, especially the much-cited figure of 450,000, are probably exaggerations.) From the 1960s the Jewish population of Britain began to decline, through the combination of a low birth-rate, emigration overseas, and intermarriage, although the extent of shrinkage is also probably exaggerated. By the early twenty-first century there were probably about 300,000 Jews in Britain. They were heavily centred in and around London (about 205,000), with sizeable concentrations in Manchester (26,000) and Leeds (10,000). Many smaller provincial communities declined sharply or virtually disappeared altogether. Nevertheless, London contained several visible and distinctive Jewish communities, especially those centring around Golders Green and, slightly to the east, the Strictly Orthodox community around Stamford Hill. Most Jews lived in the middle-class areas of London. The Jewish East End, heavily bombed during the Second World War, had virtually disappeared by the 1960s.

The first few years after the Second World War were surprisingly troubled ones for Anglo-Jewry. These difficulties stemmed from the Palestine question. The refusal of the British government to increase the number of Holocaust survivors and others allowed to enter Palestine led to a Zionist revolt against the British Mandate in 1945–48. That a Labour government, with Ernest Bevin as foreign secretary, enforced these restrictions, made them particularly galling. Two incidents, in particular, had repercussions in Britain: the blowing up of the King David Hotel in Jerusalem by extreme Zionists in July 1946 and the kidnapping and hanging of two young British sergeants by extreme Zionists in Palestine in July 1947. The latter incident, in particular, caused widespread antisemitic rioting throughout Britain, probably without real parallel. Although this mood quickly passed, it left a legacy of bitterness.

Since the 1960s, a period of general tranquillity and prosperity for the Anglo-Jewish community has ensued. The arrival of so many eminent Jewish intellectuals as refugees from central Europe brought a level of cultural distinction to British Jewry which had been largely lacking before. Intellectuals and writers such as Ludwig Wittgenstein, Sir Karl Popper, Sir Lewis Namier, Sir Ernst Gombrich, Arthur Koestler, Karl Mannheim, and Melanie Klein were among the most influential of their time. While relations between Britain and Israel were initially cool, they warmed considerably during the ill-fated Suez campaign of 1956. Anglo-Jewry supported Israel almost unanimously during the 1967 Six Day War, since which Britain has experienced the same rise of left-wing anti-Zionism as in most Western countries. Unlike the American Jewish community, the Anglo-Jewish community moved steadily to the political right, with a majority of the community voting Conservative at most recent general elections and many Jews receiving high-profile appointments, especially under Margaret Thatcher's government. Religiously, the dominance of the United Synagogue and its moderate Orthodoxy has been challenged from both the right and left, with both Strictly Orthodox congregations and Reform and Liberal Jewry growing in size. These tensions have occurred under all recent chief rabbis, but became especially pronounced under Dr Jonathan Sachs. The refusal, in 1996, of Dr Sachs to attend the funeral of prominent Reform Rabbi Hugo Gryn, and other high-profile incidents of this kind, left the Anglo-Jewish religious situation in some turmoil. Most concern within the community has been voiced over its apparent demographic decline, although even here there are some signs of renewal, for instance the dramatic rise in the number of children attending a Jewish day school. As elsewhere, there has been an escalation of interest in Jewish history and affairs, with the Holocaust taught in all British secondary schools.

The United States: the genesis of Jewish settlement

During the centuries between the 1650s and the 1920s, three waves of Jewish immigrants came to the United States (which achieved independence from Britain in 1775–83), each putting their stamp upon the nature of American Jewry. Most Jewish migrants during the seventeenth and eighteenth centuries were Sephardim. During the nineteenth century down to 1880 most migrants were Ashkenazim from Germany and elsewhere in central Europe. During the great wave of migration between 1881 and 1824, millions of Russian Jews and others from eastern Europe came to the United States.

The first Jews to come to what became the United States were a shipload of about 23 Dutch citizens, mostly Sephardim, who reached the Dutch trading centre of New Amsterdam (on Manhattan island) in 1654. Previously merchants and planters in Brazil, they were resented by New Amsterdam's celebrated Dutch governor Peter Stuyvesant, who inveighed against the 'deceitful race' of 'hateful enemies and blasphemers of the name of Christ' and wanted them gone. However, the Jews brought pressure to bear from their co-religionists in Amsterdam, and Stuyvesant was obliged by his government to agree to let them stay. In 1657 they were granted burgher rights, becoming more or less equal citizens. Dutch New Amsterdam was taken by the British in 1664 and renamed New York. Freedom of religion was guaranteed to everyone. The Jewish community remained surprisingly small, numbering only about 200 in 1730 when the first synagogue in New York was dedicated. With British colonisation of North America, however, a Sephardi community gradually emerged, with synagogues established from Newport, Rhode Island, to Savannah, Georgia. Most Sephardim were heavily involved in commerce. It has been estimated that by the mid-eighteenth century 15 per cent of the import–export trade was conducted by Jews, who dealt in a variety of goods from textiles to sugar to lumber. Although there were certainly Jewish slave-dealers and slave-owners, the overwhelming majority were gentiles, and the contention sometimes advanced today by antisemites that Jews were disproportionately involved in the slave trade is simply untrue. Some colonial American Jews amassed considerable fortunes, such as the New York-based fur dealer Hayman Levy (d.1763) and the Rhode Island merchant Aaron Lopez (1731–83). Nevertheless, most, as elsewhere, were petty dealers and many were poor.

The American Revolution and the American Constitution which followed enacted a form of government which was without precedent and of the greatest benefit to Jews. By law, there was no king or aristocracy. Crucially, under the First Amendment to the Constitution, enacted in 1790, the separation of church and state, and freedom of religion for all, were guaranteed. Other provisions of the Constitution guaranteed a range of liberal human rights, including freedom of speech and the press, and jury trial. The deliberately divided nature of the American system of government, with power split between the President, the Congress, and the courts, made it almost impossible for a dictator to arise, while each of the many American states enjoyed considerable authority in their own right. The principles of democracy and legal equality were universally respected, even by America's elites, with black slaves and American Indians being the chief ethnic groups initially outside the consensus on equality. Furthermore, America's national ethos centred on upward social mobility in the capitalist system. Virtually everyone in America believed in this central ethos in one form or another.

Washington Irving, the famous nineteenth-century writer, coined the phrase 'The Almighty Dollar' to describe 'the one universal item of veneration in the United States'. *The Federalist Papers*, the influential essays supporting the enactment of the American Constitution in 1788, argued perceptively that no human political system would ever curtail human greed or self-interest, and that the object of the wise constitution was to create conflicting interest groups which would set examples of greed against one another, thus checking the potential power of each. Thus, from the first, self-interest and material gain were recognised as inseparable from the spirit of America. Clearly, the encouragement of capitalism as perfectly legitimate, and of rapid social mobility as admirable, were beneficial to groups such as the Jews, whose commercial involvement stemmed from their pariah status. The combination of these two factors – complete legal equality for all citizens and the extolling of capitalist entrepreneurship – would make the United States seem a kind of earthly paradise for groups which had been ostracised from the European mainstream owing to their religious nonconformity and commercial pursuits. Additionally, America had a long tradition of offering refuge to the victims of religious oppression, a tradition which began with the Pilgrim Fathers in 1620. America was, moreover, a frontier society and Jews have traditionally done well in frontier societies, achieving greater acceptance in milieus with fluid social structures.

It would seem that most of the 4000 Jews in the American colonies in the late eighteenth century were supporters of independence. Polish-born Hyam Salomon (1740–85) of Philadelphia, sometimes known as 'the financier of the American Revolution', lent huge sums to fight the War of Independence and apparently engaged in anti-British espionage. America's earliest Jewish legislator, English immigrant Francis Salvador (1747–76) – who was killed and scalped by Indians – was a member of the revolutionary provincial congress of South Carolina. In 1787 the local Jewish spiritual leader joined Christian clergymen in a grand procession held in Philadelphia to celebrate ratification of the Federal Constitution, and at the banquet held on that occasion there was a table of kosher food. America's first president, George Washington, movingly summed up the significance of American democracy for Jews when he observed to Jewish leaders in 1790 who had sent him their congratulations that the United States provided the rest of the world with 'an enlarged and liberal policy worthy of imitation', in which all citizens enjoyed equal rights and liberties. 'It is now no more that toleration is spoken of as if it were by the indulgence of one class of people that another enjoyed the exercise of their inherent natural rights. For happily the Government of the United States which gives to bigotry no sanction, to persecution no assistance, requires only that they who live under its protection shall demean themselves as good citizens in giving it on all occasions their effectual support.' Washington also paraphrased the Bible with supreme eloquence: 'May the children of the stock of Abraham who dwell in this land continue to merit and enjoy the good will of the other inhabitants, while every one shall sit in safety under his own vine and fig tree, and there shall be none to make him afraid.' It is inconceivable that any other national leader would, at that time, have written to the local Jewish community in this manner, or expressed such views.

A number of Jews, chiefly Sephardim, rose to prominence in American life in the decades after the establishment of the United States. Uriah Phillips Levy (1792–1862), from a Sephardi family in Philadelphia, became the country's first Jewish naval commander, rising despite antisemitic prejudice from rival officers. He was instrumental in ending corporal punishment in the United States Navy. Mordecai Manuel Noah (1785–1851), another Sephardi Jew from Philadelphia, was a pioneering Zionist. A journalist and editor associated with New York publications, and briefly an early Jewish diplomat, he expressed hope, in a much-publicised speech in 1818, for the Jews' restoration to Palestine, but added that in the meantime 'the United States is their chosen country'. John Adams, America's second President, welcomed Noah's speech, stating that 'I wish your nation may be admitted to all the privileges of citizens in every country of the world'. The most remarkable early American Jewish career was probably that of Judah Philip Benjamin (1811–84). Born to a Sephardi family in the British West Indies, he became a successful lawyer in New Orleans and then senator for Louisiana. During the American Civil War he sided with the Confederacy, and was appointed by its president, Jefferson Davis, as its attorney-general and then, from 1862–65, its secretary of state, the most senior political position held by a Jew in American life before the twentieth century. After the Civil War he went to England, and became a successful barrister in London. David Levy Yulee (1810–86) was a representative and senator for Florida. It is notable that these early American Jewish figures came from the South, a region later associated, for many decades, with antisemitism. Sephardim gradually became a less important and visible component of American Jewry. Benjamin Cardozo (1870–1938) was a distinguished justice of the American Supreme Court, succeeding the celebrated jurist Oliver Wendell Holmes in 1932.

German Jewish immigrants to the United States

Most early Jewish immigrants to the United States were Sephardim. Ashkenazi Jews began to arrive in numbers in the mid-nineteenth century, especially from Germany and adjacent Hapsburg territories such as Bohemia and Slovakia, in the wake of the 1848 revolution. When this revolution, with its promise of liberal reform, failed almost everywhere, America seemed especially welcoming. As well as the motive of freedom, there was also the motive of escape from poverty, with many Jews from villages and small towns, petty dealers, tradesmen and craftsmen, being prominent among the wave of 1848 migrants. What has been termed 'emigration fever' gripped a component of German Jewry, particularly among its poorest elements. As a result, the Jewish population of the United States rose from 50,000 in 1848 to about 240,000 by 1880 (still a tiny percentage of the total population of the United States, which numbered 23.2 million in 1850 and 50.2 million in 1880). The newcomers strengthened (and, in some cases, almost created) the Jewish presence in large East Coast cities such as New York, Philadelphia, and Baltimore, and founded new Jewish communities elsewhere, especially in cities in the mid-west and west like Cincinnati, Chicago, and San Francisco. Some made fortunes, founding businesses which became household names. Among these were Leib (or Levi) Strauss (1829–1902), who in 1850 conceived the idea of making strong trousers for the miners on the Californian goldfields: thus Levi's denim jeans were launched, one of the best-known products in the world. During the same period Macy's department store in New York (known as 'The World's Largest Store') was founded by German Jewish immigrants named Straus. One of its members, Oscar S. Straus (1850–1926), became the first Jew to serve a federal government Cabinet, becoming secretary of commerce and labor from 1906 to 1909 under President Theodore Roosevelt. A remarkable number of renowned American retail shops were founded by German Jewish immigrants of this time, including Saks Fifth Avenue, Bloomingdales, and Gimbels. Many of their founders were former peddlers. German Jews also founded, for the first time, a visible network of banking and financial dynasties, among them such renowned families as the Belmonts, Guggenheims, Lehmans, Loebs, Seligmans, and Warburgs. Many members of these families became renowned philanthropists.

The range of notable and important Americans produced by this wave of immigrants and their offspring was truly remarkable. Louis D. Brandeis (1856–1941) became, in 1916, the first Jew to serve on the American Supreme Court. In 1948 America's best-known university founded by the Jewish community, Brandeis University in Waltham, Massachusetts, was named in his honour. In 1896 Adolph S. Ochs (1858–1935) bought the ailing *New York Times* newspaper and transformed it into the best-known newspaper in the United States. Since that time, the *New York Times* has been owned by the interrelated Ochs and Sulzberger families. Henry Morgenthau (1891–1967), a close friend of President Franklin Roosevelt, served as secretary of the treasury from 1934 to 1935. Albert A. Michelson (1852–1931) conducted the famous Morley-Michelson experiments which established that there was no 'ether' in outer space; this led directly to Einstein's Theory of Relativity. In 1907 Michelson became the first American to win the Nobel Prize in Physics. Walter Lippmann (1889–1974) became America's foremost political commentator. Few German Jewish immigrants were Orthodox in the eastern European sense, and, in America, became the most prominent founders of Reform and Conservative Judaism. Such famous Reform synagogues as Temple Emanu-El in New York were founded by German immigrants.

Probably the best-known institution founded by German Jewish migrants, however, was the B'nai B'rith ('Sons of the Covenant'), founded in New York in 1843 by a group of young men from Germany as a specifically Jewish fraternal society. It offered its members sickness and funeral benefits, and sponsored cultural events. A network of B'nai B'rith lodges spread across the United States and in 1909 women's chapters were introduced. In 1913 it established the Anti-Defamation League to monitor American antisemitism, which still continues as probably the best-known such body in the world. (It is no longer a component of the B'nai B'rith.) In 1882, in what was at the time a unique example of a Jewish institution being exported from the New World to the Old, it opened its first European lodge in Berlin, and has spread to other countries.

The wave of German Jewish immigrants also encountered some of the most notable examples of early American antisemitism. In 1862, Jewish traders and peddlers were specifically targeted by an extraordinary order issued by General Ulysses S. Grant, who, alleging that 'Jews, as a class, are violating every regulation of trade established by the Treasury Department', ordered their expulsion from the military district under his command. (His order was quickly rescinded by President Lincoln, and Grant demonstrated no antisemitism in his later career.) After the Civil War, a strong tradition emerged of excluding Jews from many resorts, hotels, and country clubs. Typically, this was aimed by Anglo-Saxon Protestants at newly-rich German Jews. One of the most notorious examples of such discrimination involved the wealthy German-born merchant banker Joseph Seligman (1819–80). In 1877 Seligman arrived in a popular upper-class resort, Saratoga Springs in upstate New York, intending to stay at the Grand Hotel. But the hotel's management refused to admit him, explaining that Jews were considered 'obnoxious to the majority of guests'. This was the beginning of a wave of social antisemitism which remained common in the United States until the Second World War, excluding Jews from purchasing upper-class real estate and imposing unofficial quotas on the admission of Jews to elite universities such as Harvard and Yale.

The great migration from eastern Europe

The 45-year period from 1881 was that of large-scale migration from eastern Europe, primarily the tsarist Empire. During the 1870s over 65,000 left Russia, many settling in the United States, and by 1880 perhaps 50,000 of the 250,000 Jews living in the latter country originated in eastern Europe. Between 1881 and 1924 about 2.5 million Russian Jews, plus many thousands from Romania, poured into the United States. 'The gates of the land are open wide to any healthy person who loves work and hates the bread of laziness' ran one of the many relevant articles in Yiddish newspapers in eastern Europe which, along with enthusiastic letters from those who had already reached the United States, praised opportunities in the *goldene medina* ('golden country') and stimulated the influx. These new-comers were very noticeable owing to their distinctive clothing, their over-whelming tendency to settle in enclaves in their ports of disembarkation on the eastern seaboard, pre-eminently New York, and in other big cities of the north-east such as Chicago. Their large and clustering Yiddish-speaking presence made members of the old-established Jewish community nervous, for the latter feared that popular resentment at this flood of immigrants would heighten antisemitism. Their arrival coincided with a surge of American nativism, and there were loud and persistent grumblings from nativist ranks about the number of non-Anglo-Saxon Protestants – not only Jews – who were flocking into the country at that time, particularly from eastern and southern Europe. Huge crowds of them could be seen at Ellis Island, the immigrant reception centre in New York Harbour, and similar arrival points, wearing clothes which were quaint and exotic to American eyes, speaking in a score of languages, and having to pass a health exami-nation, including testing for the dreaded eye disease trachoma, before being allowed to disembark.

Old-stock Americans worried that the Anglo-Saxon Protestant cultural and ethnic foundations of the country would be destroyed by this unprece-dented influx of people who originated outside the British Isles. These anxieties found expression in such works as Madison Grant's *The Passing of the Great Race* (1916), and a nativist poem which warned:

Wide open and unguarded stand our gates
And through them press a wild, a motley throng –
. . .
Flying the Old World's poverty and scorn;
These bringing with them unknown gods and rites,
. . .
In street and alley what strange tongues are these,
Accents of menace alien to our air,
. . . For so of old
The thronging Goth and Vandal trampled Rome,
And where the temples of the Caesars stood
The lean wolf unmolested made her lair.

American Jewish leaders, people of Sephardi, German and central European background, were certainly not unmoved by the woes facing their co-religionists in eastern Europe. In 1906, at the time of pogroms in Russia, a number of them, including Louis Marshall, Jacob H. Schiff, Cyrus Adler, Oscar S. Straus, and Judge Mayer Sulzberger, formed the American Jewish Committee in order to liaise with the federal government on matters of Jewish concern. Primarily the brainchild of Marshall, the Committee aimed 'to prevent the infraction of the civil and religious rights of Jews in any part of the world', and 'to secure for Jews equality of economic, social, and educational opportunity'. Earlier, at the outbreak of the Russo-Japanese War, Schiff, at financial risk to himself, arranged a massive loan to Japan prompted by his loathing of the antisemitic tsarist regime. In 1911 the Committee spearheaded a campaign to abrogate the Russian–American Commercial Treaty of 1832 owing to tsarist discrimination even against Jews holding United States passports travelling within Russia. In 1919 Henry M. Morgenthau headed a commission to investigate the plight of pogrom-stricken Polish Jewry.

In their concern to dissipate the antisemitism engendered by mass immigration, American Jewish leaders tried to encourage the newcomers to discard their distinctive clothing and, as soon as they had acquired a workable smattering, to speak English in public rather than Yiddish, which drew attention to their substantial presence. Coincidentally, at the time that this influx was occurring the notorious Frank Affair took place, probably the only example in American history during this period of the murder of a Jew for antisemitic reasons. Leo Frank (1884–1915), a Texan-born Jew of German parentage who had been educated at Cornell University, managed his uncle's pencil factory in Atlanta. He was arrested in 1913 and charged with murdering a 14 year-old girl who worked at the factory and whose body had been found there. Suspicion fell on Frank because the factory was closed at the time of her death, a weekend, and she had made a special trip there to collect her wages from him. He was found guilty on very questionable testimony, and condemned to death. Widely supported demands for a retrial were rejected. But at length Georgia's governor, satisfied that there had been a mishandling of the prosecution's case, commuted the sentence. With that, an angry mob from the girl's home town broke into Frank's cell and hanged him from a tree. The episode undoubtedly shook American Jewry and, despite the groundswell of support for Frank, who was almost certainly innocent, increased their feelings of vulnerability.

American Jewish leaders attempted, with initiatives such as the Industrial Removal Office (IRO), which existed from 1901 to 1917, to encourage eastern European Jews to leave their crowded, ghetto-like enclaves in the big cities of the north-east for locations elsewhere. The IRO, which was dedicated to securing employment for Jewish immigrants who were prepared to relocate, placed about 75,000, who went largely to the mid-west. Partially financed by Jacob H. Schiff, the Galveston Plan (1907–14) was a Jewish agricultural project in Texas, which had the co-operation of the London-headquartered Jewish Territorial Organization and the Berlin-based Hilfsverein (founded in 1901 to assist underprivileged Jews). It attracted about 10,000 settlers. These experiments laid the foundations of Jewish communal life in many fairly remote parts of the United States, but they failed in their essential purpose, for the eastern Europeans remained overwhelmingly in the urban centres of the north-east.

The immigrants perceived the established community as, at worst, antagonistic and, at best, patronising, towards them; they referred to the old-established Jews, whom they considered snobs, as *yahudim*, in contrast to themselves, characterised as *yidn* ('yiddishers'). Yet the advice of the American Jewish leaders was basically well-meant, if high-handed, and many of them worked hard on behalf of the newcomers. This is especially true of Louis Marshall, who learned Yiddish in order to communicate with them and who in 1902 established a newspaper for them. As time passed, the two groups of Jews laid aside their mutual misgivings and co-operated with each other, realising that they must make common cause on various issues, including proposals to curb immigration.

The highest annual total for Jewish emigration out of Russia occurred in 1907, immediately following the pogroms of 1905–06, when 200,000 left, 154,000 of them arriving in the United States, its democratic freedoms symbolised by the towering Statue of Liberty in New York harbour and the evocative lines by Emma Lazarus (see Chapter 16) inscribed on its base. The First World War temporarily halted this flow, but immediately afterwards it recommenced. In 1921, and again in 1924, against a background of increasing public concern about the scale and effects of the mass immigration of people from non-northern European societies, quota acts were passed restricting the influx. As in the case of an earlier enforcement of a neglected law against pauperism, which targeted indigents of all origins, these acts were not aimed specifically at Jews: there was in particular a great deal of unease about the immigration of southern Europeans, especially Italians from backward and Mafia-ridden Sicily. The legislation of 1921 limited the annual maximum number of immigrants permitted to enter the United States from each country to 3 per cent of the number of foreign-born persons of such nationality present according to the federal census of 1910. The 1924 legislation went further, limiting the annual quota to 2 per cent, based on the federal census of 1890. It further stipulated that from 1927 (subsequently altered to 1929) annual immigration should be restricted to a total of 150,000 persons, drawn from various countries in proportion to the relative strength of the natives of those countries in the federal census of 1920.

Impact of the great migration

The mass migration of some 2.5 million eastern European Jews to the United States between 1881 and 1924 transformed the centre of gravity of the Jewish world – that is, even before the Holocaust – from Poland to the United States. It also ended the communal dominance of American Jews of chiefly German background.

It seems that the typical Jewish immigrant from eastern Europe was young, in their twenties or thirties, and, overall, less religious than those remaining in Russia. There were many young single women among them. Over 65 per cent of these immigrants were skilled workers, of whom the number with experience in the clothing trade – as tailors, dressmakers or seamstresses – was especially high. Although Jews comprised only 10.3 per cent of the total immigrant population of the United States between 1900 and 1924 they made up 25 per cent of the skilled industrial workers of the country.

About 70 per cent of the eastern European Jewish immigrants remained in New York. They were originally concentrated in the so-called Lower East Side of Manhattan, an insalubrious district which they turned into a replica of an old-world *shtetl*, consisting of synagogues, prayer groups, market stalls and pushcarts. Something of its ambience is captured in the movie *Hester Street* (1975). The district consisted of tall, run-down tenement buildings which were badly ventilated and lacked proper sanitation. Entire families lived in single rooms in such buildings, that cramped space typically serving as their living quarters and their workplace, for thousands of Jews were occupied in contract sewing for the clothing trade; this was known as 'sweating' and the tenements were consequently dubbed 'sweatshops'. The appalling conditions in them were graphically depicted in such works as *Children of the Tenements* (1903) by the crusading Danish-born (non-Jewish) New York journalist Jacob Riis. By 1897 three-quarters of workers in Manhattan's garment industry were Jews, and Jews dominated related fields such as the fur trade. They established trade unions (called labor unions in the United States), including the famous International Ladies' Garment Workers' Union.

By the 1920s Jews comprised 25 per cent of the population of New York City. Their number peaked in the 1940s when it reached 2.5 million, out of a total metropolitan population of 8 million inhabitants. It was the greatest concentration of Jewish residents in one small area in history. To put this figure into perspective: during the 1930s Warsaw had 500,000 Jews and Berlin 200,000, while London Jewry numbered 250,000 during the 1940s and 1950s, and until the 1970s there were more Jews in New York than in Israel. By the end of the Second World War most Jewish families had moved out of the Lower East Side and into Brooklyn and the Bronx. The Brooklyn neighbourhoods of Brownsville and Flatbush were particularly heavy areas of Jewish settlement, and in time, with increased prosperity, many Jews moved on again, to adjoining neighbourhoods such as Crown Heights and Carnarsie, as well as to parts of New Jersey. Since New York City was the largest Jewish metropolis in the world, it became indelibly associated with Jewish culture.

On the eve of the First World War there were over 320 Orthodox Jewish congregations on the Lower East Side. But New York Jewry, in common with the rest of American Jewry, failed to develop a Jewish day school system. Instead, Jewish children learned Hebrew and the fundamentals of Judaism in classes held after school until *Bar Mitzvah* age; state school education was free, secular and compulsory. Orthodox Jews in the United States did not develop a body analogous to the United Synagogue organisation in Britain.

Most Jews were nominally or unobservantly Orthodox, never setting foot inside a synagogue except on the High Holy Days.

A flourishing Yiddish culture was established by the immigrants. By 1917 there were seven Yiddish theatres in New York, while other cities accounted for five more. In 1922 there were over 20 Yiddish newspapers in the United States with a combined readership of over 400,000, a remarkable figure. Established in 1897, the most important of these, the New York-based *Jewish Daily Forward*, boasted 175,000 readers by 1918.

The marked sympathy among the eastern European newcomers for radical political parties and trade unions was reflected by the wide-circulating *Jewish Daily Forward*, and in electoral statistics in areas with high Jewish populations. In 1914 a Jewish attorney specialising in labour law was elected as a socialist member of the United States Congress from a Lower East Side seat. In 1917 ten socialists, mainly from seats in the same neighbourhood, were elected to the New York Assembly. This clear preference for the political left continued into the second generation. As in many other Diaspora communities during the 'devil's decade' of the 1930s many secularised Jews turned to Marxism as a kind of substitute for religion and as a panacea for the world's ills. New York's radical young students and intellectuals were sharply divided between Stalinists and Trotskyites. By that time there were thousands of Jewish students enrolled at the City College of New York, the well-known free university, and they were caught up in this divisiveness. It was the era of radical intellectual periodicals such as *Partisan Review* and *New Masses*, of left-wing theatre groups and writers' groups, and the like. Many young Jews were ignorant of, or chose to ignore, the excesses of Stalinism, including its antisemitism (which became truly apparent in the 1950s). They were preoccupied with fighting Nazism and fascism, and in coping with the discrimination that they encountered in American society, including the quotas that prevailed at many prestigious educational institutions. Moreover, the antisemitism of motor car manufacturer Henry Ford's newspaper *The Dearborn Independent*, which in the 1920s had raised the spectre of the sinister, all-powerful 'International Jew', had been succeeded by the anti-Jewish diatribes of Father Charles Coughlin, 'the radio priest'. On the other hand, there was much philosemitic activity from clergymen and other Christian and liberal elements regarding prejudice against Jews and their persecution in Europe.

One field in which Jews attained remarkable success was the entertainment industry. Hollywood in its classic period, from its foundation in about 1920 through the rise of the great studios in the early 1930s until the demise of the studio system in the early 1950s, was very disproportionately Jewish. Virtually every major studio had a Jewish head, and a majority of Hollywood producers were Jewish. Daryl Zanuck was a rare non-Jewish exception among such moguls as Harry Cohn, Samuel Goldwyn, Louis B. Mayer, David O. Selznick, and the Warner Brothers. It has been argued that these Jews, selfmade men, usually with little formal education, compensated for their exclusion from mainstream high society by creating in Hollywood 'an empire of their own', as one recent historian has put it. This empire, however, drew no attention to the Jewish plight. It is now notorious, for instance, that possibly not a single Hollywood movie before the late 1940s dealt with antisemitism, and not a single Hollywood movie ever attacked Hitler or the Nazis until the non-Jewish British radical comedian Charlie Chaplin made *The Great Dictator* in the late 1930s.

The renowned Yiddish humorist and novelist Sholem Aleichem (pseudonym of Shalom Rabinovich, 1859–1916), who had established his reputation in his native Russia, lived in New York for a few years before his death. The Nobel Prize-winning Yiddish novelist Isaac Bashevis Singer (1908–91), who emigrated from Poland in 1935, also settled in New York. Eventually the rich Yiddish-based cultural world to be found in New York and other American cities with large eastern European immigrant populations declined, as few of the second and third generations spoke or read that language. They identified Yiddish with the impoverished and foreign world of the immigrants, with elderly men and women who failed to understand the modern world and were often regarded by younger generations as an embarrassment. In addition, Zionists looked to Hebrew, rather than to Yiddish, as the Jewish language of the future. By the 1950s Yiddish newspapers collapsed one after another, and subsequently Yiddish was spoken only by a small minority who, ironically, were mostly Strictly Orthodox Jews, rather than by secular, socialist-oriented people, which is what so many of the immigrants were.

Jews were also highly visible on Broadway, and the Jewish joke – half Yiddish, half American, based on the Shakespearean premise that brevity is the soul of wit – began to dominate Jewish humour. Typically the Jewish joke is short and snappy, and often involves self-denigration; self-analysis or psychology is often involved too. Notable exponents of Jewish humour, who began their careers between the wars, were Jack Benny and George Burns. Samuel Goldwyn (*né* Goldfish, 1882–1973), the famous Hollywood producer, was celebrated for such pronouncements as, 'If you see a psychiatrist, you should have your head examined', and 'Why did you name your son John? Every Tom, Dick, and Harry is named John.' (Goldwyn claimed that he never said any of the 'Goldwynisms' attributed to him.) Similarly, Aaron Copland (1900–90) became perhaps the archetypal composer of American classical music, virtually defining 'American'-sounding music in such works as *Appalachian Spring* and *Billy the Kid*, although he was born to Russian Jewish parents in Brooklyn, New York. Moreover, during the 'golden age' of popular song from about 1920 to 1955 most standard songs were written by Jews. Popular composers such as Harold Arlen, Irving Berlin, George Gershwin, Jerome Kern, Richard Rodgers and many others were representative of the secularised second generation of immigrant Jews in New York. Among that milieu there was a genuine love of the United States, seen in their drive towards swift 'Americanisation' without fully relinquishing their

Jewish roots. Two of the most popular songs of the era were Irving Berlin's 'God Bless America' (which has become an unofficial national anthem) and his 'I'm Dreaming of a White Christmas' (a most unlikely song from the pen of a Russian Jew, but one readily appreciated by the many Jews in America who never saw the inside of a synagogue except on the High Holy Days and who each year had a Christmas tree in their homes). The attempt by American Jews to redefine an American identity led to the hero-worshipping of Hank Greenberg (1911–86), the greatest Jewish baseball player, and to evolving a distinctive niche in the world of jazz, with such notable Jewish performers as Benny Goodman (1909–86) and Artie Shaw (b.1910).

As noted, American Jews did, however, encounter considerable discrimination in many areas of life. This appeared to increase in the interwar years. The country's prestigious private universities, like Harvard, Princeton, and Yale, routinely imposed a 10 per cent quota on the number of Jews permitted to enter any class, forcing many highly promising prospective students to attend less prestigious universities. This situation continued until after the Second World War. Economic discrimination preventing the appointment of Jews in many businesses and professions (such as many law firms) was rampant, as were so-called 'gentlemen's agreements' in the sale of prestigious housing, restricting purchases to 'Protestant Caucasians'. Such discrimination also existed against other American groups, especially Italian Catholics, and, of course, was virtually ubiquitous against blacks. This situation also changed for the better only after the Second World War.

During the 1940s a Jewish Congressman observed that 'the Jews have three *velten* [worlds]: *die velt* [this world], *yene velt* [the next world], and Roosevelt'. American Jews, especially in New York, gave Democrat President Franklin D. Roosevelt, with his New Deal, overwhelming support. Although many first generation Jewish immigrants were nominally socialists and would have preferred more overtly socialistic policies than his, virtually every part of the American Jewish community rallied behind him. This enhanced the political power and centrality of the Jewish community, especially via the electoral college system under which presidents of the United States are voted into office, a system whereby all of New York's very large electoral college vote goes to the winning party. Roosevelt became increasingly dependent upon the Jewish vote and was often perceived by antisemites as being a tool or puppet of the Jews. After the Second World War a strong and effective 'Jewish lobby' did emerge, based in New York, over the key issues of support for Israel and for Soviet Jewry. But it is doubtful whether before the Second World War the Jewish community had any real political power at all. Rather, Roosevelt seems to have taken the Jewish vote while giving little in return. In particular, his administration failed to liberalise the country's immigration quotas during the Nazi period, and failed to put pressure on Britain to admit more Jews to Palestine or create a Jewish state there. As with the British case, however, it is too easy to be wise after the event, and to blame Roosevelt and the American government for events beyond their control. The United

States admitted 161,000 Jews as immigrants between 1933 and 1942, with 80,000 arriving in the two years 1938–40 alone. This total was higher than the number admitted to any other country, and included thousands of cultural luminaries (for instance, Albert Einstein) who helped to reshape America's intellectual scene. It is a sad fact that once the Second World War began, the United States had no realistic means of saving the lives of many, or perhaps any, of the Jews of Nazi-occupied Europe without defeating Nazi Germany. At the time, Roosevelt and the American government were almost universally viewed by America's Jews as the 'arsenal of democracy' and as their greatest and most powerful defenders. Posterity should respect the verdict of most men and women of the time, who actually lived through those dark days, unlike today's critics. About 500,000 Jews fought in the American armed forces during the Second World War, and few B-grade Hollywood movies were made about army life which failed to include a recognisably Jewish soldier 'from Brooklyn' along with other American stereotyped characters such as the Southerner, the Westerner, the upper-class recruit, and so on, in a typical army platoon.

Some aspects of Jewish life as it evolved in the United States after 1880 do require some comment. While the Roman Catholic community in the United States established a vast system of Catholic parochial schools and universities, American Jewry made no attempt to found or organise a system of Jewish day schools, and virtually all the children of the immigrant Jews were educated at local public (i.e. state) schools. Only a handful of Jewish universities (like Yeshivah University) were established by America's Jews. (The best-known Jewish-foundation university in America, Brandeis, was founded in 1948, just after the Second World War.) One might suggest that the entire ambience of American Jewry would have been quite different had such a Jewish day school and university system emerged, with the community likely to have comprised many more Orthodox Jews. Another puzzle is the failure of American Jewry to evolve a single recognised leadership body similar to the Board of Deputies of British Jews. Of course, in such a vast community, spread out across a nation larger than Europe, the emergence of such a body was arguably impossible. Nevertheless, the absence of a unified American Jewish representative body probably handicapped and weakened the community, leading to the rise of recognised but unelected leaders such as Rabbi Stephen Wise (1874–1949). Wise, America's best-known Reform rabbi and a leading Zionist, acted as the generally-accepted leader of American Jewry during the Roosevelt era, although he lacked the legitimacy which election by a constituency of millions might have provided.

American Jewry since the Second World War

Owing to the Holocaust and other fundamental demographic factors, American Jewry emerged from the Second World War as immeasurably the largest and most powerful Jewish community in the world. The Jewish population of the United States in 1945 probably numbered about 4.5 million (no precise figures exist). The next largest, Soviet Jewry, probably numbered about 2.0–2.2 million at the end of the war (the Soviet Jewish population at the time of the first post-war Soviet census in 1959 was about 2.2 million). Most of eastern European Jewry had been decimated in the Holocaust and, in Europe, only Romania (430,000) and Britain (350,000) had as many as 300,000 Jews. The Yishuv in Palestine contained about 550,000 Jews but was, of course, as yet without national rights. Almost uniquely, America was physically unscathed by the war, and its Jewish community was relatively prosperous, although it still contained a surprisingly large working-class component. Within American Jewry, New York was by far the largest community and, indeed, constituted probably the largest Jewish population centre in one city in history. In the mid-1940s New York City was home to about two million Jews (among its 7.5 million inhabitants), of whom about 950,000 lived in the Borough of Brooklyn alone. Another 200,000 or more Jews lived in the suburbs of New York. Other very large American Jewish communities existed at that time in Philadelphia (245,000), Chicago (300,000), Los Angeles (225,000), and Boston (140,000), Detroit (90,000), Cleveland (80,000), Baltimore (75,000), and San Francisco (60,000). Outside New York most cities had recognisably Jewish neighbourhoods, ambiences, and histories. For instance, Chicago Jewry (the third largest community in the United States), had existed since before the Civil War, and grew rapidly with the large-scale immigration of Russian Jews after 1880. In the mid-twentieth century it was heavily centred in the (geographically discrete) Lawndale, Hyde Park, South Shore, and Humboldt Park areas. Chicago Jewry managed to produce a surprising variety of notable and varied figures in American life, including Supreme Court Justice Arthur Goldberg, boxer Barney Ross, singer Mel Tormé, jazz clarinetist Benny Goodman, Admiral Hyman Rickover, labor leader Sidney Hillman, actor Paul Muni, cartoonist Herbert Bloch ('Herblock'), media baron William S. Paley, authors Meyer Levin, Leo Rosten, and David Mamet, as well as Edna Ferber (1887–1968), who was the first Jewish writer to win a Pulitzer Prize, Academy Award-winning scriptwriter Ben Hecht (1893–1964), and Nobel Prize-winning novelist Saul Bellow (b.1915), to name only a few of the most eminent; certainly by any standards a remarkable list.

The largest Jewish community in America was in New York, which was in every respect the centre of Jewish life in the United States. Among America's major Jewish organisations only one or two had their headquarters in another city (generally Washington DC), and virtually all religious, charitable, cultural, and Zionist bodies were located in New York. Most Jews there lived in the two 'dormitory' boroughs of Brooklyn and the Bronx, with the very rich and (in the Lower East Side) very poor Jews remaining in Manhattan. Jewish life in New York appeared settled and permanent. While further movement to the suburbs and other parts of the

United States had already begun, it was not yet more than a trickle. Hundreds of thousands of Jewish schoolchildren were being educated in New York's state schools, institutions that were intensely secular and 'American', with Jewish education reserved for after-hours and weekend schools, generally ceasing at thirteen. Most New York Jews were still probably nominally Orthodox, although the Reform and Conservative movements were very large. Strict Orthodoxy had hardly made more than a minor impact, although the arrival of Orthodox Holocaust survivors marked the beginning of an enlarged Strictly Orthodox presence.

At the end of the war, many Jews feared that a recrudescence of antisemitism was likely to occur, perhaps in the midst of renewed economic depression and American isolationism. In fact, antisemitism not only did not emerge in force after the war, but greatly diminished, a trend which has continued to the present day. Antisemitism was notably absent from the Cold War hysteria associated with the name of Senator Joe McCarthy which gripped America from about 1946 until 1955. The absence of antisemitism from McCarthyite anti-Communism was in marked contrast to the anti-Bolshevist 'Red Scare' which the United States experienced just after the First World War, which included a notable component of nativist antisemitism and anti-foreigner feeling. McCarthy's chief targets appeared to be rich old stock WASP (white Anglo-Saxon Protestant) alleged 'subversives' like Alger Hiss rather than Jews; indeed, McCarthy's main aide, Roy Cohn, was Jewish. Jews did, however, suffer disproportionately in the 'blacklisting' of notable Broadway and Hollywood figures who had been involved, during the Depression or Second World War, in alleged pro-Communist activities, chiefly because, in the age of fascism and Depression, Jews had of necessity often been heavily associated with the political left. The famous playwright Lillian Hellman (1906–84) revealed in her autobiography *Scoundrel Time* that after being blacklisted for left-wing activities her yearly income fell from $140,000 to only $10,000 and she was forced to take a part-time job in a department store to make ends meet. The actor Howard da Silva (1909–86, *né* Howard Silverblatt) was blacklisted on the flimsiest grounds and could not obtain work on Broadway or Hollywood during the 1950s; eventually, after the McCarthy era had ended, he landed a part in a Broadway musical playing the American patriot Benjamin Franklin. Perhaps the most controversial and disturbing single Jewish aspect of the McCarthy era was the trial of Julius (1918–53) and Ethel (1920–53) Rosenberg on charges of passing American atomic secrets to the Soviet Union after the war. The couple, born in the Lower East Side, had joined the Communist party in the 1930s. It would appear that Julius did pass atomic secrets to the Soviet Union but that his wife was innocent. Their highly controversial trial, on a charge of conspiracy to commit espionage rather than treason, resulted in the death sentence being imposed on both, despite world-wide protests. The judge who imposed the death penalty and most of the other participants in the Rosenberg trial were also Jewish.

Despite all this, between the start of the Cold War around 1946 and the end of McCarthyism a decade later, by any reasonable criteria, antisemitism in the United States certainly diminished rather than increased. Quota systems imposed against Jews at universities and other forms of social and economic discrimination largely vanished. Antisemitic violence and vandalism was all but unknown, overt antisemites largely disappeared from the American scene, and the extreme anti-Communist political right generally took pains to dissociate itself from antisemitism. Increasingly Judaism was viewed as one of the legitimate co-equal 'three faiths' of the United States, along with Protestantism and Catholicism, and rabbis and other religious leaders enjoyed enhanced visibility and prestige. The title of the well-known study by Will Herberg (1901–77), *Protestant, Catholic, Jew* (1960), seemed to summarise the apparent, and widely-accepted, parity of America's major religions, despite the fact that only 3 per cent of the American population was Jewish.

One important, possibly seminal, factor in this transformation was the creation of the State of Israel. The role of the American government was crucial to the creation of the Jewish state and from the first the United States was probably Israel's foremost backer. Relations between America and Israel apparently cooled somewhat around the time of the Sinai War of 1956 (and, more generally, during the Eisenhower presidency, from 1953 till 1961), but they always remained good. Jewish support for Israel was one of the most important factors in crystallising the so-called 'Jewish lobby' in the United States. A 'Jewish lobby' had, in some sense, long existed in the United States, with Jewish leaders pressuring presidents and congressmen over matters of concern, especially foreign outbursts of antisemitism. In the 1950s, however, a professional, well-funded 'Jewish lobby' arose which attempted to influence the American government over Israel and, as well, over antisemitism, human rights issues, and the plight of Soviet Jewry. For many American Jews, Israel was increasingly central to their religious, ethnic, and, indeed, human identity. The 'new fighting Jew' of Zionism was a potent antidote to the negative stereotype of Jews as cowards and cringers. Israel represented a kind of compensation for the Holocaust, and, under Ben-Gurion and his successors, seemed to typify a social democratic ideal as the Middle East's only democracy. By the 1960s many American Jews saw their identity as Jews in significant part through the achievements and success of the State of Israel. This was, paradoxically, not inconsistent with the fact that only a minute percentage of American Jews seriously contemplated moving to Israel, while hardly more even visited that country. Israel gradually became a classical 'homeland of the mind' for hundreds of thousands of American Jews.

Organisationally, the American Jewish community which existed after the Second World War bore the stamp of its peculiar evolution and uniquely large size. As noted, no equivalent to the British Board of Deputies came into existence in the United States, and all attempts to form an American

Jewish *kehillah* (Jewish council) failed. Although American Jewry was distinguished by its plethora of disunified and single-purpose Jewish bodies, often fiercely resistant to any attempts to control them from above, a number of recognised national bodies stood out in twentieth-century America, and were regarded as representative institutions of major sections of the community. These included the American Jewish Congress (a branch of the World Jewish Congress, founded 1917) and the American Jewish Committee (founded 1906); the American Joint Distribution Committee, commonly known as the 'Joint', founded in 1914 to give relief to persecuted and impoverished Jews; the B'nai B'rith and its Anti-Defamation League, probably the primary and best-organised Jewish body fighting antisemitism. The United Jewish Appeal, established in 1939, became the most important Jewish fund-raising body in the United States, raising hundreds of millions of dollars annually, especially for the United Israel Appeal. Jewish religious life also remained deeply fragmented, but a number of widely-recognised representative bodies also arose in the American Jewish religious sphere, such as the Union of American Hebrew Congregations, the nation-wide body of the Reform movement, founded in 1873, and the Union of Orthodox Jewish Congregations of America, a leading Orthodox body founded in 1898. At the local level, most communities maintained a federation, a single fund-raising body which raised revenues, by voluntary donations, for most Jewish bodies in that area. Inevitably, a Council of Jewish Federations (CJF), founded in 1932, with over 200 local federation members, arose. The federation model was not found in precisely the same form in many other Diaspora communities, few of which maintained so sophisticated a range of local bodies and which were, in some cases, beset by religious conflict. (In America, the non-Orthodox synagogues greatly outnumbered the Orthodox, which were often reluctant to co-operate with non-Orthodox bodies.)

As bewildering as this array of institutions seems, it only scratches the surface of the vast number of Jewish groups in post-war America. While no formal overarching leadership structure exists among American Jewry, the leaders and spokesmen of these major bodies generally became recognised as the leaders of the Jewish community in the United States. They maintained an elaborate, well-organised, and professional lobbying presence in Washington DC and New York, which in part accounted for the considerable success enjoyed by the post-war American Jewish community. Another factor in this success has been that American Jewry has been relatively united on a small range of (to it) extremely important issues, especially American support for Israel and for fighting antisemitism and defending civil liberties in the United States. Not all of American Jewry was necessarily a part of this mainstream. Probably the best-known American Jewish leader of any kind in the 15 years prior to his death was Rabbi Menahem Schneersohn (1902–94), the celebrated 'Lubavitcher *rebbe*' from Brooklyn. Like many other Strictly Orthodox leaders, Schneersohn in great measure dissented from much of the civil liberties emphasis of American Jewish lobbying, and the large and growing Strictly Orthodox component of the American Jewish community remained largely outside the mainstream leadership and lobbying structure.

The first 20 years after the end of the Second World War also witnessed a sustained ascent in the economic status and educational achievements of American Jewry, which underpinned the structure of voluntary donations to communal institutions. While American Jewry was always extraordinarily rapid in its rise from the immigrant slums, as recently as the early post-war period very substantial numbers of American Jews remained outside the middle class. One comprehensive national survey of the occupations of members of leading American religious groups in 1945–46 found that, among Jews, 14 per cent were professionals, 22 per cent businessmen, and 37 per cent in white collar occupations, but that 28 per cent still remained in the service trades or working-class occupations. (Among all respondents, from all religious backgrounds, the respective totals were 11, 9, 20, and 61 per cent.) American Jews were, thus, already heavily entrenched in the middle classes, but with a large 'tail' of the relatively disadvantaged. In some Jewish communities this 'tail' was much larger, especially in industrial towns. Hundreds of thousands of Jews continued to work in blue collar trades, especially in the garment trade in New York. During the post-war years, as discriminatory barriers fell and opportunities increased, university attendance, probably always higher than among most other ethnic groups, became virtually ubiquitous, leading to the famous joke (or cliché) that a 'Jewish dropout' was 'an MA'. Probably 80–90 per cent of American Jews attended a college or university, compared with 30–40 per cent of the entire American population. Building upon the success already achieved by many American Jews, this led to growing prosperity in many cases. By the 1960s Jews had the highest *per capita* household income of any religious group in the United States. In the 1970s Jews, who numbered about 2.5 per cent of the American population, comprised about 7 per cent of the country's middle and upper classes. Obviously this did not mean that poverty had vanished from American Jewry. During the 1960s poorer Jews who had been 'left behind' in decaying areas of New York formed the backbone of Meir Kahane's Jewish Defense League, and many observers discerned a basic division between affluent Jews, especially in Manhattan, who were often left-liberal on social issues, and poorer Jews in Brooklyn and Queens, whose social attitudes, especially towards blacks, were often right-wing. Most observers of the American Jewish scene have also highlighted the large number of elderly Jews, often living on or near the poverty line, who comprise a disproportionate percentage of the Jewish community.

American Jewry's typical political stance has often attracted wide comment. Since the New Deal of the 1930s, American Jews have overwhelmingly supported the Democratic Party, especially its liberal wing. Normally, about 80 per cent of American Jews vote for the Democratic presidential candidate, a percentage which has decreased only at a handful of recent elections (for instance in 1980, when Republican Ronald Reagan received nearly half of the Jewish vote). Most observers have been both struck and puzzled at the failure of the American Jewish vote to move to the right, in line with its high income and status attainments. Many theories have been offered to explain this paradox, for instance the Jewish emphasis on 'social justice', lingering memories of right-wing antisemitism and fascism, and mistrust of the heavily Anglo-Saxon Protestant Republican Party, especially a perception that it might be more pro-Arab than the Democratic Party. The American situation, however, appears to be unusual if not unique among notable Jewish communities. In Israel, the Likud, religious, and fringe right-wing parties have together won majorities at most elections since 1977, while survey research on the Jewish communities in Britain, Australia, and elsewhere suggests that most Jews support centre-right rather than centre-left parties. One factor at work here might well be the non-Orthodox majority among American Jews. There appears, throughout the Jewish world, to be a nexus between religious Orthodoxy and political conservatism and between non-Orthodoxy (or secularism) and left-liberalism. As well, some erosion of American Jewish left-liberalism has occurred in recent decades. American neo-conservatism has often stemmed from Jewish intellectual organs such as *Commentary* magazine. The deterioration of black–Jewish relations in the United States led to the growth of a 'backlash' among, especially, poorer Jews in the big cities against extreme demands for black rights. This tendency was manifested especially in the mid-1960s in New York, and particularly in proposals which would apparently have advantaged blacks at the expense of Jews in matters like municipal employment. As well, the growth of strong left-wing hostility to Israel, and the reality of Soviet antisemitism, also alienated Jews from the political left. Nevertheless, the nature of the contemporary Democratic Party in the United States, a party of the upwardly mobile, often from previously excluded groups, which has never been anti-capitalist and has always been strongly pro-Israel, remains attractive for most Jewish voters.

The post-war phase of American Jewish life probably peaked around the time of the Six Day War in 1967, when American Jewry showed unprecedented support for Israel's struggle. In the decades since then, a number of important changes have overtaken American Jewry, not all of them positive. Demographically, perhaps the most striking alteration in the situation of American Jewry has been the shift of the Jewish population away from New York to the south and west, so that American Jewry was much more geographically variegated than at any previous time. In 1999, of a total American Jewish population estimated at 56.1 million, about 1.9 million lived in the New York City metropolitan area (with 1,450,000 in New York City), about 33 per cent of the total Jewish population. Greater Los Angeles, the second largest Jewish centre, had 590,000 Jews (more than any country in Europe with the possible exception of France and Russia). The third largest centre of American Jewry was now Miami–Fort Lauderdale, Florida, with 382,000 Jews, followed by the metropolitan areas of Philadelphia (280,000), Chicago (263,000), Boston (235,000), San Francisco (216,000), Washington DC (166,000), West Palm Beach–Boca Raton, Florida (151,000), and Baltimore (105,000). Four other cities (Cleveland, Detroit, St Louis, and San Diego) had at least 50,000 Jews in their metropolitan areas. In the previous half-century, many areas in the south and the west experienced phenomenal rises in their Jewish populations. Between 1950 and 1996 the Jewish population of Phoenix, Arizona, increased from 3500 to 50,000; of Denver, Colorado, from 16,000 to 46,000; of Atlanta, Georgia, from 10,200 to 77,300; of Albuquerque, New Mexico, and Los Vegas, Nevada, from zero to, respectively, 6000 and 20,000. These trends mirrored those of the American population as a whole, which also moved south and west in great numbers.

Conversely, the older centres of Jewish life drastically declined. Brooklyn, New York, the home *par excellence* of the 'typical' American Jew, saw its Jewish population drop from 950,000 to only 379,000, and the Bronx from around 400,000 to only 84,000. In the period from around 1955 to about 1980 many old-established Jewish neighbourhoods were literally deserted by their inhabitants – for instance the Flatbush and East New York areas of Brooklyn – generally as a consequence of 'white flight', the mass movement of whites from encroaching black and Hispanic neighbourhoods, with their extraordinarily high rates of violent crime and drug abuse. Many New York Jews relocated to more suburban and family-oriented areas of Metropolitan New York such as Queens and Long Island. In Chicago, similarly, Jews abandoned their old neighbourhoods and relocated the centre of Jewish life to the Albany Park–North Park area, in the north of the city, and to the West Rogers Park district, as well as to Chicago's suburbs like Skokie and Highland Park. The very affluent moved to the ritzier parts of Manhattan when they had 'made it'; retirees went to Florida; thousands of others moved west, south, or abroad, or made *aliyah* to Israel. Within the older areas of New York, the nature of the remaining Jewish community also changed significantly in the four final decades of the twentieth century. By the early twenty-first century, Brooklyn Jewry was disproportionately composed of Strictly Orthodox Jews in Borough Park, Crown Heights, and other Orthodox enclaves, and of recent Russian immigrants in Coney Island. They had often replaced the second-generation Americanised Jews whose families had come to the United States between 1881 and 1924, and had largely moved on.

The relocation of American Jewry to the south, west, and the suburbs necessitated the creation of a network of new Jewish institutions and an altered framework of relationships. Families no longer lived in the same neighbourhood, but were strewn across a continent. The frequency of marriage breakdowns produced non-traditional families and relationships, as did the rise of a visible fringe of Jewish homosexuals and those living a singles life-style. *Yiddishkayt* in its old neo-European sense largely became a matter of nostalgia, with the Yiddish language determinedly being championed by young activists who had to learn Yiddish from scratch. To most observers, probably the most alarming aspect of Jewish life in America in recent decades was the great increase in intermarriage among younger age-cohorts, which, according to some estimates had reached nearly 50 per cent by the 1990s. Only in a minority of cases, it would seem, were the children of such marriages raised as avowed Jews. Because of these trends, there emerged a surprisingly vast penumbra group in the American Jewish community, estimated at nearly three million persons in the 1990s, consisting of persons of Jewish descent but practising other religions or non-Jewish members of a household with at least one Jew. Increasingly, too, Judaism in America was viewed as a religion of choice rather than of birth, with several hundred thousand conversions into Judaism by persons born to another religion, and Judaism often seen as simply another religious identity, like Lutheranism or Presbyterianism, into or out of which one might move as one wished. A situation such as this had not arisen in the history of the Jewish people since late Roman times, if there were any historical parallels at all, and, in terms of its identity and self-perception, American Jewry was increasingly operating in completely uncharted waters. The geographical mobility of so many American Jews, the lack of a core definition of Jewish identity universally shared, the sharp decline of antisemitism, and the virtually complete normalisation of Jewish life in America, all contributed to these trends.

From the early 1960s, the Holocaust became more and more central to the self-identity of American Jews as Jews, and, indeed, became almost universally internalised as the ultimate expression of evil in the modern world. As some commentators have noted, the Holocaust increasingly became 'Americanised' and was, as it were, adopted by millions of non-Jewish Americans as their own tragedy. Many historians have also observed that in the first 15–20 years after the war, something of a taboo on the widespread discussion of the Holocaust existed in the American Jewish community (despite the fact that many significant books on the Holocaust had already appeared). In 1957, for example, a 458-page collection of essays on the recent history of American Jewry, *Two Generations in Perspective: Notable Events and Trends*, edited by Harry Schneiderman, devoted just six pages to the Holocaust. In the early 1960s one academic looked through every college and university catalogue in the United States to discover courses on the Holocaust. He discovered precisely one – at Brandeis, the Jewish university. By the end of the twentieth century, it had become inconceivable that American Jewry's response to the Holocaust, and the impact of the Holocaust upon American Jewry's self-identity, would not form a major theme of any historical account of the recent American Jewish community, while probably hundreds of college and university courses on the Holocaust existed throughout America, to say nothing of dozens of Holocaust museums, memorial institutes, archives, and the like. Historians believe that this transformation was chiefly engendered in the 1960s by the Eichmann trial of 1960–62 and the Six Day War of 1967. 'The Holocaust', a television mini-series of the late 1970s, informed millions about the Jewish tragedy.

From the mid-1960s onwards, a steady stream of works drawing attention to the alleged inactivity (or worse) of the United States during the Holocaust in rescuing Jews appeared, beginning, seemingly, with Arthur Morse's *While Six Million Died* (1968) and culminating in David Wyman's *The Abandonment of the Jews* (1984). The question of why the Auschwitz camp was not bombed became, in particular, a matter of wide controversy. In the late 1970s the Carter administration agreed to the public funding of a major museum on the Holocaust in Washington DC. After a great deal of controversy this opened in 1993 as the United States Holocaust Memorial Museum. Situated in central Washington near other national museums devoted to purely American subjects and memorials to American heroes, this museum is extraordinary in commemorating an event in which no Americans were involved (except as liberators) and which occurred 4000 miles from the United States. Critics (including many Jews) of this project were concerned that the erection of such a museum, while no display existed in Washington to memorialise black slavery, would be interpreted as ethnic favouritism and an example of 'Jewish power'. Others questioned how non-Jewish victims of the Holocaust should be treated, among them controversial groups such as Communists and homosexuals. Despite these pitfalls, the Museum proved an enormous success, attracting two million visitors annually and arousing little controversy once it opened. Other major museums and memorials to the Holocaust have been opened elsewhere, from New York to Los Angeles. While the Holocaust has often been depicted on film, from *The Diary of Anne Frank* (1959) onwards, mainstream Hollywood had never made a 'blockbuster' about these events until Steven Spielberg's *Schindler's List* (1993). Seen by hundreds of millions around the world, and awarded the Academy Award, this moving film brought the Jewish tragedy to the centre of consciousness as, arguably, no depiction had done before. By the end of the twentieth century, the Holocaust, its memorialisation and depiction, had become a veritable industry with literally hundreds of books and articles published each year, and discussion ubiquitous in every conceivable forum. While this phenomenon occurred throughout the Western world, it was probably most marked in the United States.

At the same time as the Holocaust moved into the centre of consciousness, antisemitism continued to decrease. A world-wide wave of synagogue vandalism in the early 1960s was never repeated, and antisemitic organisations like the Ku Klux Klan have undergone a steady decline in membership. All barriers to full Jewish participation in American society have vanished, and no one believes that they will ever return. In 2000, an Orthodox Jew, Senator Joseph Lieberman, was the Democratic party's candidate for vice-president, and two persons of Jewish descent – Henry Kissinger and

Madeleine Albright – have served as secretary of state in the years since 1970. Once limited by tacit restrictive quotas from entering America's most prestigious private universities in great numbers, by the year 2000 persons of Jewish background served as presidents of nearly half of the best-known private universities in the United States. Yet American Jews were not truly at peace, and many surveys have revealed that they were much more conscious of antisemitism, and concerned that it was likely to increase, than were American non-Jews. In recent decades, hostility to Jews can be found on three points of the spectrum: among the residual antisemites of the extreme right, among the anti-Zionist extreme left, and among some blacks. Neo-Nazi 'Aryan Power' groups, often violent and near-insurrectionary, have arisen during the past few decades, especially in the American West. Some are virulently antisemitic and attached to fringe Christian fundamentalist groups. Furthermore, a pseudo-intellectual infrastructure of 'Holocaust denial' authors and groups has arisen. Left-wing anti-Zionism became common among Marxist fringe groups in the period between roughly 1967 and 1990. Often venomous in their rhetoric and bordering on antisemitism, they exerted some influence on campus radical bodies and activities. Some among the growing number of Arabs and Muslims in the United States are also viciously hostile to Israel and, less commonly, to Jews. The relationship between Jews and blacks in the United States has long been ambiguous. Jewish liberals were disproportionately active in the struggle for black civil rights. Despite this, surveys have consistently highlighted higher levels of antisemitism among blacks than whites. Many theories have been offered to explain this, ranging from black religious fundamentalism to the exploitative nature (as perceived by many blacks) of Jewish ghetto businesses. In the 1980s, the Reverend Jesse Jackson offended Jews by referring to New York as 'Hymietown', and the Nation of Islam, a religious group founded by Rev. Louis Farrakhan, has been obsessively and vocally antisemitic. In 1991, rioting occurred in the Crown Heights district of Brooklyn between blacks and Orthodox Jews, which resulted in the murder of a Jewish university student. Some of this strife declined with full employment in the 1990s, but underlying tensions remain. Despite these remaining pockets of antisemitism, by the beginning of the twenty-first century antisemitism could truly be described as a fringe phenomenon, and most unlikely ever to enter the mainstream as a significant force.

By the opening of the twenty-first century, American Jewry had produced a significant contribution to American civilisation, contributing disproportionately in virtually every conceivable intellectual and cultural field. The Jewish contribution to American culture was arguably nearly as great as that of Jewry in central Europe between 1850 and 1939, although in the context of a society which largely welcomed and nurtured Jewish (and non-Jewish) intellectual achievement. Yet American Jewry itself was deeply and increasingly divided. While survey research indicated that (by 1990) most American Jews defined themselves as religiously Conservative (40 per cent) or Reform (39 per cent) rather than Orthodox (only 6 per cent), Orthodox Judaism became the fastest-growing and in many respects most visible and dynamic religious component of the community. Its birth-rate, barriers to assimilation, and 'outreach' programmes to non-Orthodox Jews meant that it would become more significant as time passed. American Jewry's love-affair with Israel peaked in 1967 but diminished, at least somewhat, with Israel's controversial West Bank policies and the ascendancy of Israel's right-wing parties. Much of American Jewry had been active, in the 20 years or so before 1990, in the struggle to support Soviet Jewry, but this effort ended with the collapse of the Soviet Union. It may well be that the price of success for American Jewry will be heightened disunity and a steady loss of influence.

Further reading

Great Britain
Geoffrey Alderman, *Modern British Jewry* (Oxford, 1992)
Eugene C. Black, *The Social Politics of Anglo-Jewry, 1880-1920* (London, 1988)
Chaim Bermant, *The Cousinhood: The Anglo-Jewish Gentry* (London, 1971)
David Cesarani, ed., *The Making of Modern Anglo-Jewry* (Oxford, 1990)
Todd M. Endelman, *The Jews of Georgian England, 1718–1830* (Philadelphia, 1979; rev. ed. 1999)
Todd M. Endelman, ed., *Radical Assimilation in English Jewish History, 1656–1945* (Bloomington, Ind., 1990)
David Feldman, *Englishmen and Jews: Social Relations and Political Culture, 1840–1914* (New Haven, Conn., 1994)
Niall Ferguson, *The World's Bankers* (London, 1998)
Lloyd Gartner, *The Jewish Immigrant in England, 1870–1914* (London, 1960)
Colin Holmes, *Anti-Semitism in British Society, 1876–1939* (London, 1979)
David S. Katz, *The Jews in the History of England, 1485–1850* (Oxford, 1994)
Tony Kushner, *The Persistence of Prejudice: Antisemitism in British Society during the Second World War* (Manchester, 1989)
V.D. Lipman, *Social History of the Jews in England, 1850–1950* (London, 1954)
Cecil Roth, *A History of the Jews in England* (Oxford, 1964)
W.D. Rubinstein, A *History of the Jews in the English-Speaking World: Great Britain* (London, 1996)
M.C.M. Salbstein, *The Emancipation of the Jews in Britain: The Question of the Admission of Jews to Parliament, 1828–1960* (Rutherford, N.J., 1982)

Bernard Wasserstein, *Britain and the Jews of Europe, 1939–1945* (London, 1979)

United States
There is by now an enormous literature about Jews in the United States, only a small portion of which can be mentioned here. The journal *American Jewish History* presents reviews of most recent works, while the distinguished annual publication *The American Jewish Year Book* contains comprehensive information on American (and world) Jewry. The following is a representative sample of significant works.

General histories
Arthur Hertzberg, *The Jews in America: Four Centuries of an Uneasy Encounter – A History* (New York, 1989)

Henry L. Feingold, general editor, *The Jewish People in America*, 5 vols (Baltimore, 1992). The most comprehensive general history.

Jacob Rader Marcus, ed., *The Jew in the American World: A Source Book* (Detroit, 1996)

Howard M. Sachar, *A History of the Jews in America* (New York, 1992)

Jonathan D. Sarno, ed., *The American Jewish Experience* (New York, 1986)

Gerald Sorin, *Tradition Transformed: The Jewish Experience in America* (Baltimore, 1997)

Aspects of American Jewish history
Yehuda Bauer, *American Jewry and the Holocaust: The American Jewish Joint Distribution Committee, 1939–1945* (Detroit, 1981)

Stephen Birmingham, *'Our Crowd': The Great Jewish Families of New York* (New York, 1968)

Stephen Birmingham, *'The Rest of Us': The Rise of America's Eastern European Jews* (New York, 1984)

Lenni Bremner, *Jews in America Today* (London, 1986)

Naomi W. Cohen, *Jews in Christian America: The Pursuit of Religious Equality* (Oxford, 1992)

Irving Cutler, *The Jews of Chicago: from Shtetl to Suburb* (Urbana, Ill., 1996)

Leonard Dinnerstein, *The Leo Frank Case* (New York, 1968)

Leonard Dinnerstein, *Anti-Semitism in America* (New York, 1994)

Eli Faber, *Jews, Slaves, and the Slave Trade: Setting the Record Straight* (New York, 1998)

Roberto Rosenberg Farber and Chaim I. Waxman, eds, *Jews in America: A Contemporary Reader* (Hanover, N.H., 1999)

Leonard Fein, *Where Are We? The Inner Life of American Jews* (New York, 1988)

Henry L. Feingold, *Bearing Witness: How America and its Jews Responded to the Holocaust* (Syracuse, N.Y., 1995)

Myrna Katz Frommer and Harvey Frommer, *Growing Up Jewish in America: An Oral History* (New York, 1995)

Sidney Goldstein and Alice Goldstein, *Jews on the Move: Implications for Jewish Identity* (Albany, N.Y., 1996)

Leon Harris, *Merchant Princes: An Intimate History of Jewish Families who Built Great Department Stores* (New York, 1979)

Samuel Halperin, *The Political World of American Zionism* (Silver Springs, Md., 1985)

Ben Halpern, *A Clash of Heroes: Brandeis, Weizmann and American Zionism* (New York, 1987)

Irving Howe, *World of Our Fathers* (New York, 1976)

Frederic Cople Jaher, *A Scapegoat in the New Wilderness: The Origins and Rise of Anti-Semitism in America* (Cambridge, Mass., 1994)

Jenna Weissman Joselit, *The Wonders of America: Reinventing Jewish Culture, 1880–1950* (New York, 1994)

Abraham J. Karp, *Jewish Continuity in America: Creative Survival in a Free Society* (Tuscaloosa, Ala., 1998)

Thomas Kessner, *The Golden Door: Italian and Jewish Immigrant Mobility in New York City 1880-1915* (New York, 1977)

Bertram W. Korn, *American Jewry and the Civil War* (New York, 1961)

George Kranzler, *Hasidic Williamsburg: A Contemporary American Hasidic Community* (Northvale, N.J., 1995)

Seymour Martin Lipset and Earl Raab, *Jews and the New American Scene* (Cambridge, Mass., 1995)

Louise A. Mayo, *The Ambivalent Image: Nineteenth-century America's Reception of the Jew* (Cranbury, N.J., 1988)

Deborah Dash Moore, *To the Golden Cities: Pursuing the American Jewish Dream in Miami and Los Angeles* (Cambridge, Mass., 1994)

Ewa Morawska, *Insecure Prosperity: Small-Town Jews in Industrial America, 1890–1940* (Princeton, N.J., 1996)

Peter Novick, *The Holocaust in American Life* (Boston, Mass., 2000)

Dan A. Oren, *Joining the Club: A History of Jews and Yale* (New Haven, 1985)

Stuart E. Rosenberg, *The New Jewish Identity in America* (New York, 1985)

Stanley Rothman and S. Robert Lichter, *Roots of Radicalism: Jews, Christians, and the Left* (New Brunswick, N.J., 1996)

David Schoenbaum, *The United States and the State of Israel* (Oxford, 1993)

Robert M. Seltzer and Norman J. Cohen, eds, *The Americanization of the Jews* (New York, 1995)

Charles E. Silberman, *A Certain People: American Jews and Their Lives Today* (New York, 1985)

Marshall Sklare, ed., *The Jews: Social Patterns of an American Group* (Glencoe, Ill., 1958)

Melvin I. Urofksy, *American Zionism from Herzl to the Holocaust* (Lincoln, Neb., 1975)

Beth S. Wenger, *New York Jews and the Great Depression: Uncertain Promise* (New Haven, Conn., 1996)

Jack Wertheimer, ed., *The American Synagogue: A Sanctuary Transformed* (Hanover, N.H., 1995)

|11|

The world-wide Diaspora

Throughout modern history, Jewish communities have existed in many countries of the world. The history of the Jews in America, Britain, Russia, Eastern Europe, the Afro-Asian world, and Israel is considered in other chapters of this book. Here, we examine the evolution of modern Jewish history in the Commonwealth, Western Europe, and Latin America, significant areas of Jewish settlement in the contemporary world.

The Commonwealth

The British Commonwealth comprise a number of countries with substantial and interesting Jewish communities. Although relatively small, they have become of increasing importance on the world Jewish scene. While they have much in common, to a surprising extent they are marked by differing patterns of development and different communal profiles.

Australia and New Zealand

The European presence in Australia began on 26 January 1788 with the arrival, in what is today Sydney, New South Wales, of the 'First Fleet', consisting largely of 1500 convicts from London's prisons. Among them were a number, estimated at between six and 14, who were Jewish. Jews were thus present in Australia literally from the first day of European settlement. This fact gave Jews a kind of historical legitimacy seldom enjoyed elsewhere. Jews consistently comprised about 0.5 to 1 per cent of convicts deported from Britain to Australia (normally for petty robbery and property crimes) between 1788 and the 1830s. The first free Jewish settlers arrived in Australia in 1809. Organised communal life began with the formation of the first synagogue (in Sydney) in 1828–30. By 1841 there were 1183 Jews in Australia, comprising 0.57 per cent of the total population. By the late Victorian period synagogues had been established in the large cities (Sydney, Melbourne, Adelaide, Brisbane, Perth, Hobart) and in many smaller towns and country settlements where Jews played a prominent role as traders and merchants, especially after the start of the Victorian gold rush in 1851.

Most of the early settlers were English-speaking Jews from Britain, who assimilated into the wider society very quickly. Intermarriages and conversions were high. By 1901 there were 15,239 Jews in Australia (the Australian census has always included an optional religious question), comprising 0.40 per cent of the population. The two largest communities were in Sydney and Melbourne, which have long been the main bases of Australian Jewry. Synagogues, all Anglo-Orthodox, comprised the centres of Jewish life. There were neither Jewish schools nor *yeshivot*.

In Australian society down to the Second World War, Jews played a remarkably prominent role in public life, a role so extraordinary that it was arguably not paralleled anywhere else at the time. The most prominent Australian Jew of this period was probably Sir John Monash (1865–1931), Australia's senior commander in the First World War, one of Australia's greatest heroes. At Monash's state funeral in Melbourne in 1931, one-third of the city lined the route, 'as if the king had died'. Monash's contemporary, Sir Isaac Isaacs (1855–1948), served as chief justice of Australia and its first native-born governor-general (head of state) in 1931–35. Jews served in many other senior public offices, including Speaker of the House of Representatives, state governors, and Cabinet ministers. There appears to have been remarkably little serious antisemitism in Australia until the 1930s, although Jews (and other groups) were depicted in negative stereotypes in some press cartoons. In 1938 Australia agreed to take 15,000 refugees from the Reich, and actually admitted about 9000 by the outbreak of the Second World War.

In the post-war world, Australian Jewry was marked by heavy immigration, in particular of Holocaust survivors, and, after 1970, of Soviet Jews, as well as a continuing stream of migrants from Britain and other democracies. About 35,000 Holocaust survivors settled in Australia (especially Melbourne) after the war. This immigration was instrumental in bringing about a substantial increase in Australia's Jewish population, from 23,553 in 1933 to about 52,000 in the early 1950s and to perhaps 105,000 at the opening of the twenty-first century. Melbourne (with about 50,000 Jews) and Sydney (with about 40,000) are the two chief centres of Jewish life, often rivals. Perhaps the most notable feature of post-war Australian Jewish life has been the establishment of nearly 20 full-time Jewish day schools (nine of which are in Melbourne and six in Sydney), founded by various denominations and movements within the Jewish community. Mount Scopus College in Melbourne, with over 2000 students, was believed to be the largest Jewish day school in the Diaspora. In 1995 there were 81 synagogues in Australia, of which 14 were Liberal and nearly all the others Orthodox. In a reversal of the pre-1939 pattern, very few Jews have entered public life in post-war Australia, although Sir Zelman Cowen (b.1919) was Australia's governor-general in 1977–82. Jews are, however, prominent in business and professional life. In many respects post-war Australia stands in marked contrast to most other Diaspora communities, with a vigorous, committed Jewish community which is continuing to grow in size. Indeed, some demographers regard Melbourne's Jewish community as virtually the only one in the Diaspora whose fertility rate is above the replacement level. Relations with non-Jews are unusually good, barring the usual right-wing antisemites and left-wing and Arab anti-Zionists. *Schindler's Ark*, a novel by the non-Jewish Australian writer Thomas Kenneally, served as the basis of Steven Spielberg's celebrated Holocaust film *Schindler's List*. The Executive Council of Australian Jewry (ECAJ), founded in 1944, is the national representative body of the Australian Jewish community. Australia and Israel have enjoyed highly favourable relations, with Australian foreign minister Dr H.V. Evatt being among those responsible for the UN's adoption of the Palestine Partition plan in 1947–48.

The pattern of successful development found in the Australian Jewish community was not really replicated in the much smaller Jewish community of New Zealand. Both countries have a similar origin, New Zealand being settled by English Jews in the 1830s. New Zealand Jewry consisted of free settlers, mainly merchants and storekeepers (no convicts were sent to New Zealand), which also grew after a minor gold rush in the 1860s. But New Zealand's community was always only a fraction of Australia's, numbering about 1300 in the early 1860s, 2380 in 1921, 4006 in 1961, and (after some Soviet Jewish and other migration) 4812 persons in the 1996 census. (Since the religious question in the New Zealand census is optional, as it is in Australia, the actual number is probably higher.)

The early period of New Zealand Jewish history is also similar to Australia's in the unusually high number of Jews who rose to high places in this 'frontier' society where social class boundaries were fluid. Sir Julius Vogel (1835–99) served as New Zealand's prime minister in 1873–75 and 1876, Sir Michael Myers (1873–1950) was New Zealand's chief justice from 1929 to 1946, and four Jews served as mayors of Auckland between 1869 and 1941. Thereafter, the paths of the community diverged sharply, with New Zealand admitting only about 900 Holocaust refugees and survivors, compared with 45,000 who came to Australia. New Zealand's Anglo-Jewish community, without fresh blood, largely atrophied in the post-1945 era. Since the 1970s, the community has been reinvigorated by some Soviet Jewish immigrants and by the establishment of Jewish day schools in Auckland and Wellington and other communal institutions. Nevertheless, in contrast to Australia, the long-term prognosis for such a remote community, divided among regional centres, must remain problematical.

Canada

The history of the Jewish community of Canada has naturally been lived in the shadow of the United States' much larger Jewish presence. Nevertheless, the Jewish population of Canada is very considerable, numbering 360,000 in the 1990s, making it one of the six or seven largest Jewish communities in the world. Canada belonged to France until it was conquered by Britain in 1759 (Quebec is, for this reason, French-speaking). Jews and Huguenots were forbidden to settle in French Canada; a permanent Jewish presence dates only from after the British conquest. Jews became prominent as merchants, especially in Montreal; the first synagogue dates from 1768. Some Jews, especially the Hart, de Sola, and Franks families, became prominent, with Ezekiel Hart being elected to the legislature of Lower Canada in 1807 but unable to take his seat because of its Christian oath. Full Jewish civil rights came to Lower Canada (Quebec and the east) in 1832, a quarter-century before the right of Jews to sit in the British Parliament was enacted. A Jewish presence in Upper Canada (Ontario and the west) dates from the 1840s. Until the 1880s the Jewish population of Canada remained microscopic, with only 1115 Jews in the entire country in 1871, of whom 549 lived in Quebec and 518 in Ontario. Significant migration – although by the standards of the United States, very small – began with the 1881 pogroms, which saw the Jewish population rise to 6414 in 1891, 16,493 in 1901, and then to no less than 125,000 by 1920, of whom 85,000 were migrants who came between 1901 and 1921. It is difficult to account for a rise of this magnitude; in particular it is difficult to see why they did not settle in the United States, as so many hundreds of thousands did. It is possible that the Aliens Act, passed by Britain in 1905, made Canada a more popular destination for those who wished to settle in the British Empire but who were unable to come to Britain. By the time the Depression began, about 58,000 Jews lived in Montreal, 46,000 in Toronto, and 17,000 in Winnipeg, the next largest Jewish community.

As almost everywhere else, in Canada the First World War ended the age of the relatively liberal migration policy and greatly enhanced nativist and, often, explicitly antisemitic rhetoric and political action. Jews, especially those from eastern Europe, were increasingly seen as an unassimilable mass of urban dwellers, engaged in dubious financial practices and often the bearers of the viruses of Bolshevism and destructive modernist tendencies. In Canada it is arguable that hostility to Jews in the inter-war years went further than anywhere else in the English-speaking world. In particular, the fact that only a tiny percentage of Jews settled in rural areas or engaged in agricultural pursuits enhanced antisemitic hostility. As in many other countries, the onslaughts of the war, continuing economic recession, and the perceived threat of Communism and modernist values and moral standards, made many democratic Canadians fear any substantial increase in Jewish numbers. Among Canada's rural communities, and in particular among the devoutly Catholic French Canadians, hostility to Jews and other southern and eastern European migrants – but especially to Jews – increased enormously after 1918. Between 1919 and 1923 a series of immigration measures made it virtually impossible for Jews to migrate to Canada, the only exceptions being Jews from Britain or the United States, or close relatives of Jewish Canadians. Italians, Greeks, Turks, and Levantese suffered from similar restrictions. A few exceptions apart, Jews, however, were restricted virtually regardless of where they were born or their economic status. Canada did, anomalously, admit some Russian Jewish refugees stranded in Romania in 1923, but thereafter virtually closed the doors. One well-known account of Canada's Jewish refugee policy during the Nazi period (by Irving Abella and Harold Troper) is called *None is Too Many*, a reference to the alleged response of one Canadian official who asked how many refugee Jews Canada would like to take. This description of Canadian policy may be somewhat overdrawn, since 11,000 Jewish immigrants did enter Canada between 1930 and 1940, but it seems consistent with what is known of Canadian society at the time. Despite Canada's image as a 'clean, outdoors' society of Royal Mounted Police, and despite its unquestioned commitment to democracy, Canada was in many respects a country gripped by irrational fears and hostilities. Jews, for instance were often accused of holding undue economic power, but one careful study of Canadian company directors in 1937 found that only 44 out of 4670 directors (0.94 per cent) were Jewish, less than their total portion in the Canadian population.

Although a good deal of antisemitism existed everywhere in Canada in the inter-war years, it was worst in Quebec, French-speaking Canada, where hostility to Jews was truly virulent, probably the worst of any area in the British Commonwealth. In 1934 a Jewish medical student was offered an internship at a hospital in Montreal. All 14 of his fellow-interns walked out, stating that Catholic patients would find it 'repugnant' to be treated by Jews. Numerous instances of antisemitic violence were recorded. Campaigns against Jewish businesses were organised. One rabbi stated that 'In Quebec antisemitism is a way of life.' French Canadians, whose culture was deeply traditional and whose conservative Catholicism was radically anti-modernist, feared all outsiders, Jews in particular. In Western Canada, the Social Credit movement of Major Douglas, which was opposed to banks and financiers, gained considerable influence; many of its members were also antisemites. Unlike Britain, Australia, and other Commonwealth countries, in Canada virtually no Jews held high political office before the Second World War.

For reasons which are not entirely clear, the picture has changed almost entirely since 1945. The Canadian government allowed very considerable refugee immigration, permitting 40,000 Jews to migrate to Canada between 1945 and 1960. As a result, the Jewish population of Canada rose enormously, growing to 255,000 in 1961 and to 356,000 in 1991. The contemporary Canadian Jewish community is unusually well-organised, with many day schools and a plethora of communal institutions. Most Jews continue to live in Toronto, with a Jewish population of 142,000 in 1990, or in Montreal, with 96,000 Jews. Vancouver (18,000), Winnipeg (16,000), and Ottawa (9000) are the next largest communities. In general, contemporary Canada has seen little antisemitism, although right-wing 'Holocaust deniers' and French Canadian xenophobes have caused alarm. Canada's voting record on Israel in the UN has been good, but left-wing critics of Israel and a growing Muslim population exist. In contrast to the pre-war situation, the number of Jewish elected office-holders has risen significantly. The Bronfman family of Seagram's whisky are among the best-known of contemporary Jewish leaders, with Edgar Bronfman (b.1929) serving as President of the World Jewish Congress from 1981. A number of Canadian Jewish writers have become internationally known, including A.M. Klein (1909–72) and Mordecai Richler (b.1931). The Canadian Jewish Congress, founded in 1919, is the national representative body of the Jewish community in Canada.

South Africa

During the twentieth century South Africa contained one of the larger and more important Jewish communities in the Commonwealth, one which differed from the others in marked respects. South Africa consisted of four provinces – the Cape of Good Hope, Natal, the Orange Free State, and the Transvaal – which were merged into the Union of South Africa in 1910. The Orange Free State and the Transvaal were founded and chiefly populated (among the white population) by fiercely Calvinistic Afrikaans-speaking Boers of Dutch origin. The other two provinces were chiefly British. Above and beyond everything else in South African history is the fact that whites have always comprised a small minority of the population: 1.3 million out of 6.0 million in 1911, and only 3.7 million of 21.4 million in 1970. This fact led to the institution of *Apartheid* by the South African Nationalist government in 1948, to the struggle to end the South African regime, and to its collapse and replacement by a black-led government in 1994. Jews, as whites, were always considered part of the political nation by both the British and the Afrikaaners, but met very considerable pressures and some hostility. The institution of a black-led government has, if anything, in many respects made their position more precarious than before.

Although Jews (and Christians of Jewish descent) were probably living in South Africa from the seventeenth century, a significant community of merchants, traders, and storekeepers emerged in the early nineteenth century. The discovery of diamonds in the Kimberley (in the Orange Free State) in 1869 and gold in the mines of Witwatersrand (near Johannesburg) altered the economic nature of South Africa and sparked significant Jewish migration. The Jewish population of South Africa stood at about 4000 in 1880 and grew to about 38,000 by 1904. Many came from Britain, but the majority migrated from eastern Europe, especially Lithuania. (South African Jewry has long been known as a 'Litvak', that is Lithuanian, community.) The Jewish population of South Africa grew to nearly 59,000 in 1918 and to 90,645 in 1936, comprising 4.52 per cent of the white population. This was a significantly higher Jewish percentage of the population than virtually anywhere else in the world outside eastern Europe (although if blacks, denied political rights, are included the Jewish population was of course markedly lower).

South African Jews became renowned in the late nineteenth century for their important role as 'Rand lords', exploiters of the fabulous gold and diamond mines of South Africa, and in associated financial trades. Such multi-millionaires as Barney Barnato (*né* Barnett Isaacs, 1852–97, originally from the East End of London), Sir Alfred Beit (1853–1906), and the Joel and Oppenheimer families became world-famous, especially for their connections with De Beers Consolidated, the diamond syndicate. As such, they were frequently depicted in antisemitic stereotypes, especially during the Boer War period, which many radicals in Britain opposed, seeing it as an imperialist struggle against the independent Boer republics by 'finance capital'. Many of the famous 'Rand lords', for instance the celebrated Cecil Rhodes, were not Jews, but Jews often became depicted as 'behind' the Boer War and Britain's imperial expansion.

Jews generally encountered little overt antisemitism in South Africa itself, and some strongly Calvinistic Boers were philosemites, seeing in Jews the 'people of the Bible'. Nevertheless, Jews did not win full civil rights throughout South Africa until British annexation in 1902. The Transvaal Republic, founded by Boers, had restricted office-holding to Protestants, debarring both Catholics and Jews. The Jewish community became organised in the late nineteenth century, with dozens of synagogues (mainly Orthodox) established by the First World War, and a South African Jewish Board of Deputies formed in 1912. Perhaps the most distinctive feature of the South African Jewish community has been the central influence of the Zionist movement, which probably became more integral to the community's identity and structure than in any Jewish community outside some parts of eastern Europe. This has been linked by some historians to the origin of much of the community in Lithuania, once one of the bastions of the Zionist movement in eastern Europe. The first all-South African Zionist conference was held in 1905. By 1922 no fewer than 177 bodies of various kinds (including synagogues) had affiliated to the South African Zionist Federation, a figure that rose to 347 by 1948. The Zionist Federation thus became the community's *de facto* all-embracing representative body, in a way to which few other Zionist Federations could aspire. Elsewhere, Zionism had considerable ideological opposition *per se*, or remained on the fringes of the community, with synagogues or non-Zionist secular bodies holding centre-stage. Elsewhere in the Commonwealth, the central bodies of the community had been founded by wealthy old families who were often lukewarm to Zionist claims, and were joined by a variety of anti-Zionist strands among Jewry, from Strict Orthodoxy to Marxism. In South Africa, Zionism became a consensual communal ideology and mass movement.

The tensions inherent within South African society between the English, Boers, and the black majority could not have failed to have impacted upon the Jewish community. While some Boers regarded Jews as outside agitators or financial exploiters, many originally gave them, and especially the Zionist movement, their strong support. Probably the most important example of this was Jan Christian Smuts (1870–1950), originally a Boer senior officer and Cabinet minister who then supported the British after the formation of the Union of South Africa in 1910 and became a member of the British Cabinet during the First World War. Smuts was one of the most fervent 'gentile Zionists' of modern times, a consistent friend of the Jews who helped to steer the Balfour Declaration through the Cabinet. A relative liberal in South African terms, in 1945 Smuts was the author of the United Nations Charter. During the inter-war years, however, relations between Jews and Boers deteriorated markedly. A pro-Nazi and antisemitic element emerged among the Afrikaaner community, especially in the extreme National Party, which became strong among the Afrikaaner population in the 1930s. A variety of 'shirt' movements (the Greyshirts, Blackshirts, and so on) emerged in imitation of the Nazi Stormtroopers and Italian fascists. The chief aim of these movements was to prohibit further Jewish immigration and to limit Jewish participation in South African economic life in the interests of 'poor white' Afrikaaners. Jewish immigration to South Africa had already been severely limited by the Quota Act of 1930, which affected immigration from outside the Commonwealth and Western Europe. In 1937, however, immigration was liberalised somewhat, although refugee immigration from Germany remained insignificant, with fewer than 3000 Jews entering the country between February 1937 and March 1940. It should be stressed that South Africa's government in this period was in the hands of the United Party, led by moderates like Smuts and strong among the English community, and not led by extreme Afrikaaner nationalists.

During the Second World War South Africa formally declared war on Germany. In 1948 the Jewish community was considerably disturbed when the National Party, which had supported the antisemitic restrictions of the 1930s, came to power. To its surprise, the party's leaders went out of their way to emphasise that it was no longer antisemitic, welcomed Jews as members, and supported the creation of a Jewish state. Over the next 45 years, until the collapse of *Apartheid*, the Jewish community became increasingly integrated into the governing elite of South Africa. In many respects, the Jews of South Africa were as well off as they were anywhere in the world. A wealth of Jewish institutions flourished, especially a successful day school movement. The Jewish population of South Africa continued to grow, to 115,000 in 1961 and to around 120,000 at its peak in the 1980s.

In the 1960s about 65,000 Jews lived in and around Johannesburg and 23,000 in Cape Town, with smaller numbers in other centres. South Africa was an early supporter of Israeli independence and of Israel's admission to the United Nations. Officially, Israel deplored *Apartheid* (although it maintained normal relations with South Africa), leading, especially in the early 1960s, to a strained relationship between the two. Unofficially, however, the two 'pariah' governments co-operated clandestinely on military projects, including, it was widely rumoured, Israel's test of atomic bombs off the coast of South Africa.

The central, unavoidable political question in South Africa was the fate of its black majority. Here, the Jewish community was deeply divided. It is probably fair to say that most mainstream Jews were perfectly happy with *Apartheid*, especially if its worst features could be ameliorated. Many were uncomfortable with the prospect of a Marxist-dominated black government whose international stance might well be oriented in a sharply pro-Arab, anti-Israel direction. On the other hand, individual Jews were extremely prominent in the anti-*Apartheid* struggle. Helen Suzman, a Progressive Party MP, gained world-wide publicity for her attacks on *Apartheid*, while Joe Slovo, a Jewish Communist, was one of the few senior members of the African National Congress.

The ending of *Apartheid* in 1994 has seen a deterioration in the circumstances of the Jewish community of South Africa. While Nelson Mandela and other black leaders were sympathetic to Jews and (after a fashion) to Israel, the astronomical increase in the crime rate in urban areas and the inevitable pressures to 'Africanise' the South African economy have inevitably disturbed the Jewish community. Its numbers declined from 120,000 to about 50,000 in less than twenty years, with heavy emigration to Australia, Israel and elsewhere. Whether a stable relationship will be reached by the Jewish community with the new South Africa remains to be seen. It is possible that, with further economic and social deterioration, the community will virtually disappear, although this is an extreme prognosis. The Jewish community of Southern Rhodesia (now Zimbabwe), which numbered 7000 in the 1960s and was prominent in the economic life of the country, declined to around 1000 by the 1990s, under the particularly extreme rule of Robert Mugabe.

South African Jewry produced a number of very notable writers, including Nadine Gordimer (b.1923), recipient of the 1991 Nobel Prize in Literature, and the well-known novelist Dan Jacobson (b.1929).

Ireland

The history of the Jews in Ireland presents some interesting features. Ireland was, of course, part of the United Kingdom until 1922 (largely Protestant, Northern Ireland still is) and its history was mostly shaped by this fact. On the other hand, Southern Ireland was overwhelmingly Roman Catholic, a mainly illiterate peasant society and an economic backwater in stark contrast to the dynamism of England and Scotland. The Catholic Irish population had a history which revolved (for most) around a shared history of oppression by Britain, the catastrophe of the Potato Famine of the 1840s (in which over one million Irishmen died), the spread of the world-wide Irish Diaspora, and the struggle for independence from British rule. Since gaining independence in 1922 Ireland has shaped its own society in which the very conservative Irish Catholic church was *de facto* the legally established religion and in which traditional Gaelic culture was central to Irish identity, a situation which prevailed until more liberalising trends set in after the 1970s. The very small Irish Jewish community was thus an outsider minority in a society where neither the Catholic church nor Irish nationalism would necessarily be sympathetic to it.

Only a handful of Jews lived in Ireland before the early nineteenth century, with the size of the community even then rising to only 450 in 1881 and to 3796 in 1901, the majority living in Dublin. The community was too small to attract much hostility, although anti-Jewish rioting occurred in Limerick in 1884, and in Cork in 1894. In 1904 Father John Creagh led an overtly antisemitic campaign against the Jewish community in Cork which led to a two-year economic boycott of the local Jewish community, resulting in a sharp decline in its size. After Irish independence, the Jewish community suffered from little or no direct antisemitism. Eamon De Valera, Ireland's leader for most of the half-century after 1920, was friendly to Jews, and Judaism was officially recognised in the 1937 Irish Constitution as a minority faith. Nevertheless, the post-1922 atmosphere of conservative Catholic triumphalism inevitably made Jewish (and Protestant) life more uncertain. A certain undertone of Catholic antisemitism is readily discernible. Ireland took in virtually no refugees, and Charles Bewley, Ireland's envoy in Berlin, was a notorious pro-Nazi and antisemite. In April 1945 De Valera committed one of the most incredible acts of his career when he, as Irish Prime Minister, visited the German legation in Dublin to express his condolences at the death of Hitler! (Ireland, which was neutral during the war, still maintained diplomatic relations with Nazi Germany.) The small local Jewish community voiced no protest at this inexplicable act.

In the post-1945 world relations between the Irish government and the local Jewish community have been good, with much less in the way of overt hostility. De Valera was close to Ireland's chief rabbi, Isaac Herzog (1888–1959, the father of Chaim Herzog, who later became president of Israel), and despite his 1945 lapse, was widely admired by the Irish Jewish community. He had visited Israel as early as 1950. Ireland extended *de facto* recognition to Israel in 1949 and *de jure* recognition in 1963. For most of its history, the Irish Jewish community has kept a low profile. It produced few figures of note, although Robert Briscoe (1894–1969), who was active in the

Irish Republican movement, was a long-serving member of the Irish parliament and achieved international visibility as Mayor of Dublin in 1956–57 and 1961–62. Throughout the post-war period, however, there has been a sharp decline in the number of Irish Jews, from 3907 in 1946 to only 1581 in 1991. Another 1000 Jews live in Northern Ireland, chiefly in Belfast. Possibly the most renowned Irish Jew was a fictional character, Leopold Bloom in James Joyce's 1922 novel *Ulysses*. In surveying Irish Jewish history, one has the feeling that if a larger and economically more important community had existed, it would probably have provoked very considerable hostility from the Catholic majority. In reality, however, it was too small, insignificant, and assimilated to be noticed, while Ireland's national hostilities were always directed against Britain.

Western Europe

Western Europe, like eastern Europe, experienced the full force of the Holocaust; unlike eastern Europe, however, it contained relatively few Jews prior to the mid-nineteenth century. Unlike eastern Europe, too, democracy came to western Europe after 1945, allowing these communities to re-establish themselves, often in much-reduced numbers. Nevertheless, today France has one of the largest Jewish communities in the world, while the reborn German Jewish community has been growing rapidly through immigration.

France

In many respects, France, rather than Germany or Britain, was the society in which the 'normal' evolution of a European nation was best exemplified. The French Revolution of 1789 has been interpreted by many historians as the overthrow of feudalism by democracy and capitalism and of the aristocracy by the middle classes. For millions of people it heralded the coming of the modern age. France prided itself on being the nation of 'liberty, equality, and fraternity', yet was split down the middle, from 1789 until after the Second World War, between those who accepted the implications of the 1789 Revolution and those who rejected them. France's Jewish population could not fail to have been affected by these trends. Although small and in many respects very marginal to the political development of France, the French Jewish community often found itself in the very middle of French political debate, while French antisemitism was an important force for a century after the mid-nineteenth century.

The struggle for Jewish emancipation, and the relationship of French Jewry to Napoleon and other French governments down to the 1830s, has been discussed in Chapter 2 above. By 1846, the removal of the 'Jewish oath', regarded by most Jews as humiliating, completed the process of emancipation. In 1834 Achille Fould (1800–67), a prominent banker, became the first Jew to sit in the French parliament, the Chamber of Deputies, and became Minister of Finance under Napoleon III in 1849 and 1861–67. Adolphe Crémieux (1796–1880), regarded as the leader of the Jewish community in France, was also elected, in 1842, to the Chamber of Deputies. The period from the revolution of 1830 (which brought Louis-Philippe to the throne as king) until the abdication of Napoleon III in 1870 was something of a golden age for French Jewry, which made great strides in all spheres of public life. French Jews entered the civil service and became prominent in the arts – for instance, the composer Jacques Offenbach (1819–80) and the famous actress 'Rachel' (Elisa Rachel Felix, 1821–58) became famous at this time – scientific life and, above all, in business life. As elsewhere, the Rothschild family became enormously influential. The head of the French branch of the renowned banking family, James de Rothschild (1792–1868) was certainly the richest man in France and possibly in Europe. The Péreire brothers, Emile (1800–75) and Isaac (1806–80) were almost as celebrated as bankers. They founded the Crédit Mobilier, the great banking cartel, and financed much of France's railway building. In general relations between French Jewry and the rest of French society at this time was extremely good.

The Franco-Prussian war of 1870 marked something of a turning-point. France lost Alsace-Lorraine to Germany, an area with a substantial Jewish population which regarded itself as French, but whose Jews appeared to many right-wing Frenchmen as pro-German. The establishment of the Third French Republic in 1871 split French society, creating a deeply alienated body of conservatives and ultra-conservatives. Mainly Catholic and rural, and influential among the old aristocracy, conservative France rejected the republic, the French Revolution of 1789, secularism, and modern life. It developed, surprisingly quickly, an overt antisemitic edge, seeing in Jews the personification of urban, modernist materialists and viewing them, of course, as deeply hostile to Catholic France. (France's conservatives were also anti-Protestant, anti-Freemason, and anti-leftist: Jews were not necessarily singled out.) The failure of the Union Générale, a major Catholic bank, in 1882 was widely attributed to the unfair competition of Jewish banks. Antisemitic newspapers appeared, closely associated with royalist and conservative Catholic sources. The first of these, *La Croix* ('The Cross'), began in 1883. Its central theme was that the French Revolution of 1789 and its consequences had been fomented by Jews and Freemasons. (Jews had, in fact, played virtually no role whatever in the revolution.) The most important work of French antisemitism, Edouard Drumont's *La France Juive*, was published in 1886 and became enormously popular. A near-hysterical work of 1200 pages, it attributed most of the ills of modern France to the Jews, especially in the economic sphere. In 1892 Drumont founded a daily newspaper, *La Libre Parole* ('Free Speech') which accused Jews of financial scandal and intrigue. A National Anti-Semitic League had also been founded in France in 1889. One should not exaggerate the strength of these movements: this type of antisemitism remained on the political fringes, and was closely associated with the most reactionary elements in the Catholic church.

Antisemitism was, however, integral to the celebrated Dreyfus Affair which took centre-stage in French politics in the 1890s. Briefly, Alfred Dreyfus (1859–1935), a captain on the French general staff, was accused of having sold secrets to the Germans. He was convicted in 1894 and sent to Devil's Island, France's infamous prison off French Guiana, for life. It soon became clear to many that he was innocent, the victim of a far-reaching conspiracy based on forged documents. It was also clear that he was victimised, at least in part (there were also other factors), because he was Jewish: a Jew from the 'German' Alsace. The Dreyfus Affair split France, with liberals and socialists supporting the move, spearheaded by Emile Zola, Bernard Lazare (1865–1903, a great leader of French Jewry), and others, to secure him a pardon, and with many Catholics and conservatives convinced that he was guilty. By 1906 Dreyfus had been pardoned and the forces of liberalism had won a resounding political victory which resulted in the separation of church and state in France, in 1905. By 1914, much of the previous mood of antisemitism had vanished, and Jews fully participated in the First World War as French soldiers. From a French Jewish population of about 120,000 in 1914, 46,000 served in the army and 6500 were killed. There was almost certainly less antisemitism in France in 1930 than there had been 40 years previously.

Nevertheless, factors existed which would see an upsurge in hostility to Jews. There was (for France) a massive influx of eastern and central European Jews, with between 150,000 and 200,000 foreign Jews entering the country between 1906 and 1939. About 110,000 foreign Jews settled in France between 1880 and 1939. Most of these newcomers were Yiddish-speaking, foreign-looking, and poor, and attracted some hostility, despite the basic mood of French tolerance. They also aroused very mixed feelings from the longer-established French Jewish community, concerned that the arrival of so many visibly alien Jews would undermine their own position. The 1920s, however, are generally seen as a time of communal good will and prosperity in France. Three Jews served in the Cabinet of Georges Clemenceau just after the First World War, while Jewish intellectuals, such as Henri Bergson (1859–1941), the philosopher, were among the most distinguished in France. Relations between the Catholic Church and the Jews notably improved at this time, presaging in some respects the situation after the Second World War.

As almost everywhere in Europe, the Depression and, above all, the rise of the venomously antisemitic Nazi party to power in Germany in 1933, resulted in a serious deterioration of the position of the Jews in France. Antisemitic movements, especially *Action Française*, again flourished. An unpleasant scandal revolving around a Jewish swindler named Alexander

Stavisky led to rioting and mass demonstrations in 1934. France, next door to Germany, became the home to more than 30,000 Jewish refugees from the Nazi regime, leading to anti-foreign agitation at a time of mass unemployment. In 1938 and 1939 the French government greatly tightened the admission of immigrants to the country.

In September 1939 France declared war on Germany when the Nazi regime invaded Poland; nine months later France capitulated before a *blitzkrieg* campaign launched by the German army. Within France, the Third Republic, in existence since 1871, was dissolved, and Marshal Philippe Pétain, a hero of the First World War, established a quasi-fascist French government, under Germany's central authority, at Vichy in southern France. (A Free French government-in-exile was established in London by Charles de Gaulle.) From June 1940 until liberation after D-Day in June 1944 France was ruled by the Vichy regime, with France divided into 'occupied' and 'unoccupied' sectors, the former being effectively ruled by the Nazis. Antisemitic legislation was immediately introduced, with Jews forced to wear the yellow star. Between 1941 and August 1944 about 77,000 French Jews were deported to Auschwitz or other concentration camps and perished there, or were shot by the Nazis. Drancy, a housing estate on the outskirts of Paris, served as the place where Jews were imprisoned before being deported. Nevertheless, and rather amazingly, about 253,000 French Jews (including those who fled abroad) managed to survive the war, over three-quarters of the French Jewish population. Nearly 90 per cent of French-born Jews survived the war, with recent immigrants being the most likely to be deported to their deaths. Although the Vichy regime contained its full share of murderous and sadistic antisemites, most in Vichy had little stomach to assist the Nazis in mass murder. Jewish communal organisations and non-Jewish 'Righteous Gentiles' also helped many to survive, often by placing Jewish children with non-Jewish hosts. Thousands of Jews also managed to flee to neutral countries like Spain and Switzerland. The survival rate among French Jewry was among the highest in Europe.

In general, the post-war years have been a benign era for France's Jews. The French Jewish population, in the region of 250,000 in 1950, grew by about 100,000 during the 1950s, through heavy immigration of north African Jews. In 1962, 110,000 Algerian Jews moved to France, following Algerian independence. Another 16,000 north African Jews arrived in 1967–68. By 1970 more than half of the French Jewish population was Sephardi. By the beginning of the twenty-first century, at least 525,000 Jews lived in France (many estimates place the actual figure even higher, at up to 700,000). France's Jewish community is actually the largest in Europe, larger than the remaining Jewish population of Russia, or that of Britain. About 60 per cent of France's Jewish community live in Paris which, with 3–400,000 Jews, is the largest Jewish city in contemporary Europe. French-speaking Jewry is the largest linguistic component among the contemporary Jewish people after those who speak English and Hebrew. Significant Jewish communities also exist in Marseilles (70,000), Lyons (25,000), Toulouse (20,000), Nice (16,000), and Strasbourg (12,000). The Marais area of central Paris is recognisably Jewish, with a plethora of Jewish restaurants and shops.

In the post-war period levels of antisemitism have greatly diminished, and the traditional Catholic reactionary locus of antisemitism has virtually disappeared. President Charles de Gaulle, who had many Jewish confidants, caused concern in November 1967 when he referred to Jews at a press conference as an 'elite' and 'domineering' people, apparently in an effort to win support from the Arabs, and in attacking Israeli policy. Since then, 'Holocaust denial' propaganda (although outlawed by French law) has spread. On the other hand, most hostility by the extreme right in the recent past has been generated against recent Arab and African immigrants. On the extreme left, France has been the home of a virulently anti-Zionist faction, and a favourite target of pro-Arab terrorists. The worst of such attacks against Jewish targets occurred in an explosion in the Rue Coupernic liberal synagogue in October 1980, in which four persons were killed, and another at Goldenberg's restaurant in the Marais, in August 1982, in which six people were killed and 20 injured.

Jews have played an extremely prominent role in many aspects of post-war French politics and culture, with men and women of distinction ranging from Marc Chagall and Claude Lévi-Strauss to Simone Weil. Most post-war French governments have included a number of Jewish ministers, and, starting with Léon Blum in the 1930s, there have been Jewish prime ministers of France. Most French Jews are Orthodox, and, as elsewhere, the community has a representative body to coordinate its activities and relations with the wider French community, the *Conseil Représentatif des Juifs de France* (CRIF), founded in 1944.

The Netherlands

The Dutch Republic of the seventeenth century was renowned for its toleration towards Jews (and others), probably unique anywhere at that time. Originally chiefly Sephardi, and finding itself in a nation which had won its political and religious freedom from Spain, the local Jewish community gradually gained more and more rights. By the early eighteenth century it appears that Dutch Jews had achieved most rights, and the formal emancipation of Dutch Jewry came with the French invasion of 1795. By the late eighteenth century most of the community was Ashkenazi – there were about 50,000 Ashkenazim and 5000 Sephardim in 1810 – and included a small number of wealthy merchants, although most Jews were extremely poor. The late nineteenth century saw the major development of the diamond-cutting industry in Amsterdam, which employed many Jews and, indeed, was widely seen as an archetypal Jewish industry. In the early twentieth century the number of Dutch Jews declined, chiefly because of widespread intermarriage, and the community was on something of a downhill path, possibly because Dutch society was so tolerant.

Despite its previously harmonious history, Dutch Jewry suffered more heavily from the Holocaust than any other western European Jewish community, with an estimated 102,000 out of 140,000 Jews perishing, chiefly through deportations between 1942 and 1944. Some Jews managed to survive by hiding – Anne Frank and her family are the most celebrated example of a Dutch Jewish family attempting to survive in this respect – while Jews in mixed marriages were left alone. In 1946 about 30,000 Jews lived in the Netherlands. Despite its liberalism and tolerance, surprisingly little was done by the Dutch government to help them adjust. Despite some *aliyah* and other forms of emigration, between 25,000 and 30,000 Jews lived in the Netherlands at the end of the twentieth century, two-thirds in Amsterdam. Dutch Jewry has also seen the arrival of some Sephardi and ex-Soviet Jews in recent years. The Holocaust effectively ended, for the most part, the highly visible presence of Jews in distinctively Jewish neighbourhoods, although a much-reduced community remains. Relations between the Netherlands and Israel have consistently been very good.

Belgium

The history of the Jews in Belgium presents something of a paradox, especially as compared with the Netherlands. Belgium is overwhelmingly Catholic, and the local Jewish community was much smaller, and much more heavily persecuted than its counterpart in the Netherlands. The French Revolution gave the very small (800 persons) Jewish community its rights, and full emancipation was granted in 1831. Nineteenth-century Belgium saw two centres of Jewish life: Brussels, where a more assimilated community emerged, and Antwerp, whose community was largely Yiddish-speaking and Orthodox. The 1930s saw a rise in pro-Nazi antisemitism and a local fascist movement. At the outbreak of the Second World War, between 90,000 and 110,000 Jews lived in the country, 55,000 in Antwerp and 35,000 in Brussels. Only a small minority were Belgian citizens. With the German invasion of May 1940, it is believed that about one-third of Belgian Jewry fled the country, chiefly to France, leaving about 70,000 Jews in place to face the Nazi death machine. The usual measures of identification and persecution were introduced by the Nazis. When liberation came in 1944, about 24,000 Belgian Jews had been deported to their deaths. Nevertheless, the majority of Belgian Jews managed to survive the war, in contrast to their neighbours in the Netherlands. The reasons for this are complex, but it appears that the Catholic Church effectively intervened to save Jews and even organised resistance. At the end of the war about 45,000 Jews remained in Belgium, with about 40,000 today. The two largest communities remain

Brussels (18,000) and Antwerp (12,000). Antwerp, which is now the centre of the European diamond trade, is virtually unique in continental western Europe in possessing a pre-war 'ghetto'-like Jewish quarter, with many distinctive Orthodox Jews. As with the Netherlands, Belgium has been notably pro-Israel since its foundation.

Germany

It is often said by historians that the Jews first encountered modernity in Germany and that the German-Jewish experience has been central to understanding the evolution of the Jewish people in modern times. However, only to a certain extent can this generalisation be viewed as accurate. Germany was never the demographic centre of Jewish life; the German Jewish community exhibited some characteristics found nowhere else; the catastrophe which overtook German Jewry in 1933–45 was only loosely paralleled elsewhere (although the effects of Nazism were felt throughout Europe). Additionally, many historians have argued that Germany itself experienced a 'special path' to modernity which, until 1945, set that country apart from most other western societies.

Germany itself was a disunified group of states until 1871, with two competing centres of power and authority, Protestant Prussia, whose capital was Berlin, and Catholic Austria, whose capital was Vienna. Until the late eighteenth century Austria was regarded as the most important part of German-speaking Europe, and Austria's Hapsburg kings automatically became rulers of the 'Holy Roman Empire', the loose amalgam of German-speaking states, until it was abolished in 1806. From the time of Frederick the Great (Frederick II, king of Prussia 1740–86), Prussia gradually became dominant in Germany, absorbing much of the Rhineland and Poland during the Napoleonic period. Between 1864 and 1871 the great Prussian statesman Prince Otto von Bismarck (1815–98) cleverly and ruthlessly engineered Prussia's dominance in Germany. In 1871 Wilhelm I of Prussia was proclaimed Emperor of Germany. As previously mentioned, Prussia and Germany, it is often said, experienced a 'special path' to modernisation, characterised by the continued existence of a powerful, reactionary elite of 'Junkers' (Prussian aristocrats), an obsession with military greatness and authority, and an extremely rapid and decisive period of industrial growth between about 1860 and 1914. Unlike France or Britain, it is argued, Germany's middle classes never achieved real power (although a German parliament existed), being happy to leave the governance of Germany in the hands of the old Junker/military elite. Indeed, Germany's businessmen, especially its industrialists, themselves abandoned liberalism and fully accepted the rule of the old governing classes. Post-1871 Germany also felt an overriding sense of 'relative deprivation' compared with Britain or France, having conquered only the 'crumbs' of colonial rule in the Third

World. These elements in the German spirit, it is often argued, came together during the reign of Kaiser (Emperor) Wilhelm II (1888–1918), and inevitably led to the First World War. It was unquestionably true that ideologies centring around German racialism and expansionism, which rejected liberalism and modernism, were increasing in centrality and importance in Germany after 1870.

Germany's Jewish community experienced all the pressures engendered by Germany's path to modernity. In the late eighteenth and early nineteenth century German Jewry was chiefly responsible for the *Haskalah*, and produced most of its foremost leaders, such as Moses Mendelssohn. Non-Orthodox forms of Judaism originated in Germany, as did neo-Orthodoxy. The Jews of Germany were gradually emancipated, a process completed by 1869–71. Nevertheless, some formal or informal barriers to full Jewish participation in the period 1871–1914 remained. Jews could not be appointed to officer rank above lieutenant unless they converted. They could not (and certainly did not) serve in the governance of the country as Cabinet ministers, although they could and did gain election to the *Reichstag* (Germany's parliament). Few Jews became university professors or senior diplomats. Nevertheless, Jews did participate fully in the commercial, professional, and intellectual life of imperial Germany. In business life, Jews were disproportionately important in banking, retailing, and in newspapers and publishing, although they played a less important role in heavy industry. Jews formed a large and growing portion of the German 'free professions', especially law and medicine, and the stereotyped image of the 'German scientist' of this period was shaped in part by Jews. Significant (although not overwhelmingly large) Jewish communities existed throughout pre-1914 Germany, especially in Berlin (54,000 Jews in 1880, 144,000 in 1910), Frankfurt (10,000 in 1871, 26,000 in 1910), Hamburg (14,000 in 1871, 19,000 in 1910), Cologne (4500 in 1880, 13,000 in 1910), Breslau (14,000 in 1871, 20,000 in 1910), and many other cities, as well as small towns and some rural areas. By and large, most German Jews were loyal Germans and wished for nothing more than to be accepted as fully German by their fellow-citizens. Both Reform Judaism and neo-Orthodoxy in Germany made efforts to adapt to the religious norms and styles of their fellow Germans. Many German Jews feared an influx of large numbers of exotic-looking Yiddish-speaking eastern Jews, whose numbers and appearance threatened to undermine the position of Germany's established Jewish population, and made efforts to help them emigrate to newer areas of settlement overseas.

Virtually everything about pre-1914 German antisemitism is necessarily coloured by what occurred after 1933, and a sensible and balanced account of this subject is therefore difficult. Antisemitism existed in force in Germany during the period between 1850 and 1914. Most historians believe that the financial depression of 1873, which was especially severe in Germany, greatly increased the strength of ideological antisemitism.

Extreme nationalist antisemitic candidates and parties emerged in late nineteenth-century Germany, electing 16 deputies to the *Reichstag* in 1893, while a variety of ultra-nationalist, racialist, and Christian anti-semitic movements flourished. Nevertheless, all of this should be seen in context. Political antisemitism and parties devoted to antisemitism were actually in decline after 1900. The major political issues in imperial Germany had little to do with Jews. The *Kulturkampf* between Protestants and Catholics, Germany's drive for imperial expansion, and even the battle to suppress the ever-growing socialist movement had little to do with Jews. When Germany entered the First World War, the Kaiser stated that 'I recognise only Germans' rather than members of political parties or of different religions. Germany's Jews were emphatically included in the Kaiser's description. Whatever hostility remained, most German Jews believed that they had become fully integrated into German society. It is also important to emphasise that none of the notorious incidents of European antisemitism in this period, from the Russian pogroms to the Dreyfus Affair, occurred in Germany. It is therefore very difficult to accept the proposition put forward by Daniel J. Goldhagen that Germany was uniquely antisemitic or had uniquely evolved a tradition of what he terms 'eliminationist' antisemitism.

Over 100,000 German Jews served during the First World War (nearly one-fifth of Germany's Jews) and 12,000 were killed. Jews reached high places in the wartime administration, for instance Albert Ballin (1857–1918), who was one of the major directors of Germany's economic life. With the German defeat and the end of the Empire, Germany's Jews appeared to have become fully emancipated. The Weimar Constitution of 1918–19 (which was drafted by a Jew, Hugo Preuss) removed all remaining barriers to Jewish participation in any sphere of German life. As well, two trends emerged at the end of the war with very great long-term consequences. In the wake of the Bolshevik Revolution of 1917 and the collapse of the German empire, short-lived reactionary socialist regimes were established in a number of places, including Hungary and the German state of Bavaria. The extreme left-wing Bavarian government of 1918–19, modelled on the Soviet Union, contained a disproportionate number of Jewish leaders, including its head, Kurt Eisner (1867–1919), who was assassinated early in 1919 after five months in power. Moreover, on the extreme right ultra-nationalist parties and movements were founded at the end of the war, which were fiercely anti-Bolshevik and often had virulent antisemitism at their core. One such party, founded in 1918, was joined the following year by a former corporal who had been gassed at the front and suffered a nervous breakdown when he heard that Germany had been defeated; he quickly became head of the party. That party was the German National Socialist Workers' Party (or Nazis), and its leader was Adolf Hitler. Imbued with ferocious antisemitism before the war in his native Vienna, Hitler emerged in 1918–19 as a demagogue of undoubted genius and probably the most extreme antisemite in history, who believed that he had been given a divine mission to rid the world of Jews.

Nevertheless, it is also important not to exaggerate the dangers in which Germany's Jews had been placed. In many ways the Weimar period constituted a golden age of Jewish participation in German intellectual and economic life, with hundreds of renowned Jewish intellectuals such as Einstein prominent in German life. Jewish religious life was invigorated by the writings of such men as Franz Rosenzweig (1886–1929) and Martin Buber (1878–1965). Particularly during the mid-period of the Weimar Republic, roughly 1923–29, Jewish life in Germany appeared highly successful and likely to continue indefinitely. Germany's Jews possessed an impressive representative body, the *Centralverein Deutscher Staatsbürger Jüdischen Glaubens* ('Central Union of German Citizens of the Jewish Faith'), or *Centralverein*, to which about half the community belonged, which existed from 1893 until 1938. A wide range of Jewish institutions existed in Weimar Germany, concerned with welfare, education, youth, religious, and Zionist matters, and many Jewish schools existed. There were, of course, many straws in the wind, for instance the assassination by right-wing extremists of Walter Rathenau (1867–1922), Germany's Jewish foreign minister. Yet until the Depression set in with full force around 1930, no one would have believed that German Jewry was doomed, and only with hindsight does it seem as if it was.

The Nazi period (1933–45) and its consequences are covered in the chapter on the Holocaust, above. There were about 500,000 Jews in Germany in 1933 but only about 28,000 living there when Germany surrendered in May 1945. Probably about 360,000 German Jews had emigrated and a number estimated at between 120,000 and 180,000 had been deported to the east and murdered in extermination camps or perished in other ways. The 28,000 remaining Jews included about 5000 who had survived in hiding or through sheer good fortune, about 15,000 Jews who were married to non-Jews and hence 'protected' (these Jews were left alone), and about 8000 German Jews who had returned from concentration camps. Soon, however, they were joined by very significant numbers of 'Displaced Persons' (or DPs), Holocaust survivors from eastern Europe, fleeing from their former homelands, who briefly came to the refugee camps established by the Allies in occupied Germany. By late 1946 there were 160,000 DPs in Germany, chiefly in the American zone. Most regarded their stay there as temporary, waiting only until they could re-emigrate to America, Israel, or some other democratic country. Only about 12,000 Jewish DPs settled permanently in Germany. Nevertheless, a Jewish community was re-established after the war, with a new representative body the *Zentralrat der Juden in Deutschland* ('Central Council of Jews in Germany') founded in 1950. Nearly all of Germany's Jews lived in the Federal Republic or in West Berlin. Considerable help and financial assistance was given by the West German government, which took enormous pains to distance itself from the

Nazi past. While antisemitism has continued to exist, its public expression is illegal and now considered beyond the pale. The Communist regime in East Germany, which existed from 1949 until 1989, did little or nothing to help its small remaining Jewish community.

There were about 35,000 Jews in Germany in 1970. Many of these were elderly persons who had known Germany before 1931 and continued to regard themselves as Germans. Since few were young, the future of the German Jewish community was extremely precarious. Owing to the fact that Jewish emigration from the Soviet Union has been allowed, from the late 1980s onwards, Germany's Jewish community has grown very considerably, and probably now numbers 80–100,000. At the end of the twentieth century about 11,000 Jews lived in Berlin, 6000 in Frankfurt, and 5000 in Munich. Because so many of today's German Jews are former Russians, the community is still largely a migrant one, and one which has virtually no historical continuity with pre-1939 German Jewry. As elsewhere, the Lubavitcher movement has led to a significant number returning to Orthodoxy, and a variety of communal institutions exist. Whether a truly viable, dynamic, and permanent Jewish community can emerge on the ashes of the Nazi period remains to be seen, but the possibility is more hopeful than during any time since the 1930s. Germany's relations with Israel are generally very good, and, since 1952, the Federal Republic has paid billions of dollars to Israel in restitution for the crimes of the Nazis.

Austria

Austrian Jewish history in modern times is sharply bifurcated by the end of the Hapsburg Empire in 1918. In the century or so before the break-up of the Austro-Hungarian monarchy, Austrian Jewry flourished as the community *par excellence* of a modern intelligentsia and bourgeoisie in the midst of an often backward and hostile majority. After 1918, when Austria became a tiny republic, the situation of its Jews deteriorated and virtually ended when the country was absorbed by Nazi Germany in early 1938.

Prior to 1918, 'Austria' was a vast area which comprised Galicia (southern Poland), Czechoslovakia, and northern Yugoslavia (Slovenia, Croatia, and so on) besides the post-1918 state of Austria wedged between Germany, Italy and Hungary. Jews (except those in Austria's Turkish realms) were technically debarred from living in Austria during the eighteenth century, and only 450 Jews lived in Vienna in 1752. In the late eighteenth century Austria acquired Galicia, with a substantial Jewish population, while both Maria Theresa (queen in 1740–80) and Joseph II (1780–90) officially 'tolerated' wealthy Jews as useful to the community, with Joseph II's *Toleranzpatent* of 1782 giving Jews basic rights in some cases in an attempt to normalise their position in Austria.

In the early nineteenth century, although they did not receive full civil rights, Jews were very active in the Austrian economy and, increasingly, in the free professions such as law and journalism. By the time of the revolution of 1848 Jews already comprised a disproportionate share of the Viennese middle classes. Religious discrimination persisted until the Austro-Hungarian constitution of 1867, when all legal discrimination against Jews was abolished. As a result, the size of the Austrian (in its post-1918 sense) community grew rapidly, with Vienna's Jewish population increasing from only 6300 in 1860 to 120,000 by 1890 and to 175,000 in 1910. (Remarkably, the earliest synagogue in Vienna was opened only in 1826.) The 50 years or so before the First World War is celebrated as a golden age of Jewish achievement, with Sigmund Freud, Gustav Mahler, Arnold Schönberg, Stefan Zweig, Max Reinhardt, Ludwig Wittgenstein, and innumerable other eminent Jewish cultural achievers appearing in the Austrian Jewish community. Jews owned many of Vienna's newspapers, and were extremely prominent in business and professional life. Although there was a relatively friendly symbiosis with the cosmopolitan Hapsburg monarchy and the old nobility, *fin-de-siècle* Vienna is also notorious for the range and virulence of its antisemites, such as Vienna's mayor Karl Lueger and the pan-Germanic nationalist Georg von Schönerer. The young Adolf Hitler lived in Vienna from about 1907 until 1914, and is widely believed to have absorbed much of his virulent, murderous antisemitism from Viennese sources and in reaction to the Jews he met there (although he did probably not become a vocal and obsessive antisemite until 1918–19). Austria as a whole was largely Catholic, rural, and very conservative, and many Austrian right-wingers detested Jews as a dangerous and destructive element, although one should be careful not, with hindsight, to exaggerate the importance of this factor. As in Germany, political antisemitism appears to have been in decline in the decade or so before the First World War. *Fin-de-siècle* Austrian Jewry is also notorious for its 'degenerate' air, with the frequently-cited example of Otto Weininger (1880–1903), a misogynistic, self-hating Jewish intellectual who committed suicide at the age of 23 after publishing the antisemitic tract *Sex and Character*. This element, too, with hindsight, appears more important than it was. Theodor Herzl, the founder of Zionism, although born in Budapest, lived most of his life in Vienna and was buried there in 1904. (He was later reinterred in Jerusalem.)

The First World War proved, at least in the long run, to be a catastrophe for Austria's Jews, just as it was for Jews throughout most of Europe. The new republic of Austria, founded in 1918, was only a fraction of the size of the previous Austrian monarchy. It lost many of the economies of scale and transport links which grew out of the large size of the empire, and was, as a rule, a sad relic of former glory. Post-1918 Austrian politics were headed by two major parties, the Social Democratic and the conservative, largely Catholic, Christian Social party. Most Jews supported the Social Democrats, whose party included some Jewish leaders such as Otto Bauer. The Catholic and rural Christian Social party was not antisemitic, but was uneasy with 'Jewish' Vienna and urban modernity generally. In 1934, as the Depression struck hard in Austria, Engelbert Dollfuss, leader of the Christian Socialists, became, in effect, dictator of Austria, suppressing the Social Democrats. An attempted coup in July 1934 by Nazis (who assassinated Dollfuss) was put down with the co-operation of Italy and Yugoslavia, Germany not yet being strong enough to gain the upper hand in Austria. From 1934 until March 1938 Austria was ruled by Dr Kurt Schuschnigg, a collaborator of Dolfuss and an extreme conservative. A Hapsburg restoration seemed likely. From 1937, however, as Hitler's position became ever stronger, Austria was gripped by a rise in Nazi strength and an increasing inability to stem a takeover of Austria by Germany. In March 1938 Schuschnigg was forced to resign and Artur Seyss-Inquart, the leader of the Austrian Nazis, became Chancellor (Prime Minister). A few days later he proclaimed the *Anschluss* ('annexation') of Austria by Germany, which was approved by a 99.75 per cent yes vote in a plebiscite. Hitler toured Vienna in triumph. In contrast even to the Munich crisis over Czechoslovakia a few months later, Britain and France did nothing to protest.

Although the economic situation of Austria's Jews had greatly deteriorated in the early 1920s and then after the start of the Depression in 1929, there was no formal discrimination against Jews in Austria until the *Anschluss*. At that time, in March 1938, there were about 190,000 Jews in Austria, of whom 176,000 lived in Vienna. The new regime lost no time in launching a reign of terror against the Jews. All of the denial of civil rights and discrimination known in Nazi Germany were immediately enacted in Austria, and violent pogroms, with Jews beaten up and terrorised, occurred at once. Jewish property and businesses were confiscated. Despair set in among Austria's Jews, and many suicides occurred. In August 1938 Adolf Eichmann was made head of the Central Bureau for Jewish Emigration, which was given the task of forcing Austria's Jews to emigrate as quickly as possible and looting their property. Mass pogroms occurred during *Kristallnacht*, when 42 synagogues were burned in Vienna alone. Eichmann and the Nazis were nothing if not efficient, and by the outbreak of the Second World War, only 18 months after the *Anschluss*, 110,000 Austrian Jews had emigrated. Another 11,000 Jews also managed to emigrate during the first few months of the war, leaving only 60,000 Jews in the country when emigration became virtually impossible, of whom 53,400 lived in Vienna. Most deportations to death camps occurred in 1941–42. Owing to population movements, it is difficult to estimate the number of Austrian Jewish survivors, but probably about 8–15,000 were alive in May 1945, mainly Jews married to non-Jews. A disproportionate number of leading Nazis, including many of the most extreme antisemites (such as Hitler himself) were Austrians.

Following liberation, Austria temporarily became home to a significant number of survivors from slave labour camps and Displaced Persons, with about 42,500 Jews in Austria (chiefly in the American zone of occupation) in late 1946. After heavy emigration, a permanent community of 10–12,000 came into existence, of whom about 11,000 lived in Vienna. It resembled the post-war German community in being mainly composed of elderly Jews, with few younger members. Several waves of immigrants, from Hungary in 1956–57, and a larger wave from the Soviet Union in the 1970–90 period, used Vienna as a major transit point. From 1970–84 Austria's Chancellor (Prime Minister) was Bruno Kreisky (1911–90), a Jew who spent the war in Sweden. A highly controversial figure, he was regarded with mistrust by Israel, which he frequently criticised, and by much of the Jewish world. In the 1980s Kurt Waldheim, the Austrian secretary-general of the United Nations (and later president of Austria), became a figure of international controversy when it was revealed that he had concealed his role as a Nazi SS officer during the war. In general, most Jews believe that Austria has not gone far enough to admit its Nazi past, and there remains a certain mistrust of Austria's extreme right wing, for instance of the People's Party leader Jörg Haider, who is viewed by Austrian Jews as xenophobic and even pro-Nazi. Haider briefly became Austrian chancellor in 2000. Although the Austrian Jewish community will presumably never again attain the eminence it enjoyed before 1938, it seems that a small but vigorous community will continue to exist.

Switzerland

The history of the Jewish people in Switzerland is a curious and often unsatisfactory one. A medieval Jewish community in the area of what is now Switzerland disappeared through expulsion in the later Middle Ages, and only very small groups of Jews existed on the outbreak of the French Revolution. Despite the fact that the French armies established a 'Helvetian Republic' in 1798, Switzerland was among the very slowest countries in Western Europe to grant emancipation and equal rights to its Jews. When Jews were granted freedom of residency (this was often decided at the local level of the Swiss cantons), full citizenship rights were often denied them. Full equality for Swiss Jews did not come until the 1870s. There remained a fear of Jews in much of rural Switzerland until recent times. In 1893 *she-chita* (the Jewish ritual slaughtering of animals) was banned by the Swiss constitution on the highly questionable grounds that it was a cruel practice.

Despite these barriers, a small Jewish community numbering about 1400 in 1900 and 18,000 by 1930 had established itself. The very mixed attitude still held by the Swiss government towards the Jews became evident during the Nazi period. Switzerland did admit about 14,000 German and Austrian refugee Jews between 1933 and 1939, while an estimated 25,000 foreign Jews were resident in Switzerland in 1945. On the other hand, the Swiss severely discriminated against many would-be Jewish refugees, and, fearing a mass influx of Jews, failed to admit thousands who could have been saved. During the war, Switzerland was surrounded on all sides by Nazi Germany and Nazi-allied states, and feared a German invasion. In 1938 the Swiss government prohibited the incitement of racial or religious hatred, and things were generally quiet for Swiss Jews during this troubled period. Switzerland was also the home of the Red Cross and many other international bodies. The role of the Red Cross during the Holocaust has become hotly debated, with many seeing its failure to expose and condemn the concentration camps and its apparent acquiescence in the Nazi view of the Theresienstadt camp (visited by the Red Cross) as a 'model' institution as despicable. Switzerland's banks, in which some Jews who perished in the Holocaust deposited their money, have also been widely criticised in the recent past for foot-dragging over the location of heirs. In the last year of the war, Switzerland admitted 1700 Jews from Hungary and 1200 from the Thereseinstadt camp as part of deals between Jewish groups and Himmler and Eichmann.

Most Jewish refugees from Nazi Germany left Switzerland after the war, but a community of about 15,000 remained in 1960, mainly in Zurich (6100) and Geneva (3300). The community has continued to grow, and numbered about 19,000 in 1990. Relations between Israel and Switzerland have been good.

Sweden

The Jewish community in Sweden was always very small, and Jewish emancipation came to that Protestant country surprisingly late, with full emancipation not being granted to the local Jewish community until the decade of the 1860s. Only about 3000 Jews lived in Sweden in 1880, and only about 7000 in 1930, of whom 4000 lived in Stockholm.

Sweden remained neutral during the Second World War, and was not invaded by the Nazis. Prior to the war, a considerable part of the Swedish population was pro-German and, during the late 1930s, much pro-Nazi antisemitism had developed. Sweden took in only about 4000 Jewish refugees, and erected high barriers to immigration. During the war, however, as the horrors of the Holocaust became known, opinion in Sweden turned decisively in favour of the Jews and, from 1942, Sweden did more than most countries to assist the Jews of Nazi-occupied Europe when it could. In 1942–43 nearly 1000 Norwegian Jews managed to escape to Sweden. In October 1943 virtually the entire Jewish population of Denmark, nearly 8000 persons, were secretly spirited to Sweden in one of the great acts of rescue during the war. In 1944 Sweden was at the centre of diplomatic attempts to rescue the Jews of Hungary, with Raoul Wallenberg, a Swedish diplomat, generally credited with saving many of Budapest's Jews before his mysterious disappearance. Another Swedish diplomat, Count

Folke Bernadotte, also managed to rescue an estimated 3500 Jews from the Nazis in the closing stages of the war.

As a result of these efforts (and some subsequent migration) the Jewish population of Sweden significantly increased in the post-war years, reaching 13–14,000 by the 1960s and 15,000 today. About 7500 Jews live in Stockholm. As a general rule the post-war history of Swedish Jewry has been unremarkable, with a well-organised community life.

Latin America

Jews had very little to do with Latin America before the nineteenth century. Practising Jews were prohibited from settling in Spanish America during the colonial period. Nevertheless, a few 'New Christians' (Spanish Jews who converted to Catholicism but regarded themselves in some sense as Jews) were believed to be resident in Mexico, Peru, and elsewhere. Several alleged 'New Christians' were burned at the stake in the sixteenth and seventeenth centuries in these places. More happily placed was the Jewish community in the British West Indies, part of a world-wide trading and mercantile network, who were among the earliest to gain full civil rights, in the course of the eighteenth century. In Brazil, owned by Portugal, conditions were also somewhat better, with a large percentage of its estimated European population of 50,000 in the seventeenth century consisting of 'New Christians'. From the early seventeenth century, too, the Dutch gained a foothold in the north of the country, and a Jewish mercantile presence was felt there.

Independence came to most of Latin America between about 1811 and 1830. The new nations abolished the Inquisition and declared religious equality on the French and American models. Nevertheless, Jewish settlement in Latin America was initially very small, and in many countries only Catholics could hold high office. Large-scale Jewish settlement in Latin America essentially began with the Russian pogroms of 1881, increasing the total Jewish population throughout Latin America from a few thousand in 1880 to about 150,000 by 1920. The largest Jewish community appeared in Argentina, where the first *minyan* was formed in 1891. Between 1881 and 1900 about 26,000 Jews arrived in Argentina. Many were attracted there by the Jewish Colonization Association (ICA) founded by Baron Maurice de Hirsch in 1891. Hirsch (1831–96), a Paris banker and railway magnate who was one of the richest men in Europe, established the Association with funding of £2 million in large part to establish agricultural colonies of persecuted Russian and Romanian Jews in Argentina; slightly later, the ICA established similar schemes in Brazil, Canada, and tsarist Russia. (Hirsch was originally very cool towards Zionism, but later became more favourable.) The ICA succeeded in attracting relatively few Jews to Argentinian agricultural settlements, although it did attract some. To this day there are colonies of Jewish *gauchos* (cowboys) in Argentina. The growth of Buenos Aires as a world-class city in a temperate society was the main instigator in attracting Jewish migrants. Antisemitism was rare in Argentina until the 1930s. Heavy Jewish immigration continued until the Depression, with 79,000 Jews arriving in the decade 1920–29.

The 1930s saw an increase in Argentinian antisemitism. This was part of a world-wide trend, linked in the Argentinian case by the substantial German presence in the country and also by the increase in importance of the Argentinian military in politics. Nevertheless, 20–30,000 Jewish refugees entered Argentina between 1933 and 1943. In 1946 Juan Perón came to power as president. A right-wing populist and nationalist with fascist tendencies, he became virtual dictator of Argentina in 1949. As well, many former Nazis and Nazi war criminals (including, most notoriously, Adolf Eichmann) found refuge in Argentina, which became celebrated as a haven for former Nazis. These two factors were in part responsible for something of an increase in antisemitism in the post-war years. Nevertheless, there was no general trend to antisemitism in post-war Argentina. Indeed, Jewish life flourished and relations between Argentina and Israel were warm, despite the kidnapping of Eichmann. The Jewish population of Argentina reached 250,000 by 1947 (some estimates placed the number at 275,000), 310,000 in 1960, and 265,000 in 1975, although other estimates are far higher. The Jewish population of that country has declined in recent decades, owing to heavy *aliyah* and emigration elsewhere, and to assimilation. It was estimated at 228,000 in 1990 and 206,000 (possibly an underestimate) in 1995. Most Jews (about 180,000 in 1990) lived in Buenos Aires, with smaller communities in Rosario (15,000) and Cordova (10,000). The Buenos Aires community is well organised, with many Jewish day schools and synagogues. About 80 per cent of the community is estimated to be of Ashkenazi descent. As in many other places, the long-term viability of the community, while not in question, gives no grounds for complacency. Nevertheless, the community survived the troubled period of military rule in the 1960s fairly well.

The next largest Jewish community in Latin America is in Brazil. Settlement began somewhat earlier than in Argentina, with communities established in Rio de Janeiro, the capital, and in other cities like Sao Paulo, Belem, and Bahia by the late nineteenth century. From 1902, attempts were also made by the ICA to establish Jewish agricultural colonies in Brazil, with little success. As a general rule, Brazil's tropical climate has made it less attractive as a place of Jewish settlement than Argentina, with only about 7000 Jews resident in the country by 1914. The closing of immigration opportunities elsewhere did make for more Jewish settlement in the 1920s, when over 28,000 Jews arrived, mainly from eastern Europe. Despite the erection of new barriers in the 1930s, about 20,000 refugees from the Nazis arrived, bringing the official Jewish population of the country to 56,000 in 1940 and to 70,000 by 1950 (many experts place the actual figure at those dates far higher). By 1990, demographers estimated

Brazil's Jewish population at either 100,000 or 150,000, with (on the higher figure) about 75,000 in Sao Paolo, 55,000 in Rio de Janeiro, and 15,000 in Porto Alegre. There has been little antisemitism in Brazil, and a Jewish public figure, Horacio Lafer (1893–1965), served as the country's finance minister from 1951–59 and foreign minister from 1959–61.

Four other Latin American countries have Jewish populations of 20,000 or more: Mexico (41,000), Uruguay (24,000), Chile (21,000), and Venezuela (20,000). These figures are regarded as underestimates by some experts. All four communities appear to be relatively well-organised and have suffered from little antisemitism, even (as in Chile during the 1970s) during times of general repression and turmoil. Largely Catholic Latin America has provided if not a haven for Jewish life, at least one which has been less troubled than almost anywhere else. As in most places in the contemporary Diaspora, the primary challenge facing Latin American Jewry is how to continue as viable, Jewish-conscious communities in a place where there is little intolerance and the pressures to assimilation or emigration are great. Smaller Jewish communities exist throughout Latin America: for instance, Peru has 2900 Jews, Costa Rica 2500, and Ecuador 900. In 1995 an estimated 435,000 Jews lived in Latin America, although some demographers would place the number considerably higher, at perhaps 600,000 or more.

Apart from the communities mentioned here, a number of other countries with Jewish populations greater than 15,000 exist at the present time. Italy's age-old community, the last to be released from the medieval ghetto system, today numbers about 34,000. About 8000 Italian Jews are believed to have perished in the Holocaust with deportations commencing with the German *coup d'état* of 1943. The majority of the Italian Jewish community managed to survive. Turkey's Jewish community was much diminished in size with the emigration of about 37,000 Jews to Israel after 1948. Previously, in 1919, Constantinople (Istanbul) had a Jewish population of about 90,000, many of whom emigrated. Remote Uzbekhistan, in central Asia, still contains a Jewish community of about 19,000, much reduced through recent emigration to Israel. In many countries, the Jewish community today is considerably smaller than it was 70 years ago. The Holocaust and the subsequent emigration of so many Jews to the State of Israel, as well as other waves of migration, have substantially reduced the Jewish populations of many countries. World Jewry is today concentrated in fewer places than at any time since the emancipation process began.

Further reading

The Commonwealth
Irving Abella and Harold Troper, *None is Too Many* (Toronto, 1982)
Paul R. Bartrop, *Australia and the Holocaust* (Melbourne, 1994)

Lisa-Rose Betcherman, *The Swastika and the Maple Leaf: Fascist Movements in Canada in the Thirties* (Toronto, 1975)

Robert J. Brym, William Shaffir, and Morton Weinfeld, eds, *The Jews in Canada* (Toronto, 1993)

Daniel J. Elazar and Peter Medding, *Jewish Communities in Frontier Societies: Argentina, Australia, and South Africa* (New York, 1983)

Dermot Keogh, *Jews in Twentieth-Century Ireland* (Cork, 1998)

Stephen Levine, *The New Zealand Jewish Community* (Lanham, Md., 1999)

Moses Rischin, ed., *The Jews of North America* (Detroit, 1967)

Moses Rosenberg, *Canadian Jews: A Social and Economic Study of Jews in Canada in the 1930s* (1939; republished Montreal, 1993)

Hilary L. Rubinstein and W.D. Rubinstein, *The Jews in Australia: A Thematic History* (2 vols, Melbourne, 1991)

W.D. Rubinstein, ed., *Jews in the Sixth Continent* (Sydney, 1986)

Suzanne D. Rutland, *Edge of the Diaspora* (Sydney, 1988; revised edition 1998)

Gustav Saron and Louis Hotz, eds., *The Jews in South Africa* (Cape Town, 1956)

Milton Shain, *The Roots of Antisemitism in South Africa* (Charlottesville, Va., 1994)

Gideon Shimoni, *Jews and Zionism: The South African Experience (1910–1967)* (Oxford, 1980)

Europe and general

Steven Beller, *Vienna and the Jews, 1867–1938: A Cultural History* (Cambridge, 1988)

Evan Burr Bukey, *Hitler's Austria: Popular Sentiment in the Nazi Era, 1938–1948* (Chapel Hill, N.C., 2000)

Jean-Claude Favez, *The Red Cross and the Holocaust* (Cambridge, 1999)

Ruth Gay, *The Jews of Germany: A Historical Portrait* (New Haven, 1992)

Brigitte Hamann, *Hitler's Vienna: A Dictator's Apprenticeship* (Oxford, 1999)

Alfred Haesler, *The Lifeboat is Full: Switzerland and the Refugees* (New York, 1969)

Michael Pollack and Gerhard Botz, eds., *Jews, Antisemitism, and Culture in Vienna* (London, 1987)

Jehuda Reinharz and Walter Schatzberg, eds., *The Jewish Response to German Culture: From the Enlightenment to the Second World War* (Hanover, N.H., 1985)

Marsha L. Rozenblit, *The Jews of Vienna, 1867–1914: Assimilation and Identity* (New York, 1985)

Howard M. Sachar, *Diaspora: An Inquiry into the Contemporary Jewish World* (N.Y., 1985)

Jonathan Webber, ed., *Jewish Identities in the New Europe* (London, 1994)

Robert S. Wistrich, *Socialism and the Jews: The Dilemmas of Assimilation in Germany and Austria-Hungary* (London, 1982)

David Vital, *A People Apart: The Jews in Europe 1789–1939* (Oxford, 1999)

Latin America

Judith Laikin Elkin and Gilbert W. Merkx, eds, *The Jewish Presence in Latin America* (Winchester, Mass., 1987)

|12|

The development of modern Zionism

Proto-Zionism

Throughout their centuries of exile, Jews everywhere kept alive the dream that they would eventually be restored to Palestine as the rightful rulers of the 'Promised Land'. For most Jews during these centuries of exile, this dream was purely religious in nature, centring around profound hopes that a Messiah would eventually restore the Jews to the Land of Israel and to Jerusalem. With the exception of so-called pseudo-Messiahs like Shabbetai Zevi in the seventeenth century, however, Jews did not actively embark on any proto-nationalistic crusade to restore Jews to the Holy Land, and most religious Jews would have rejected any such efforts as sacrilegious. Although only a small percentage of the world's Jews lived in Palestine, during these centuries there was always a Jewish presence there, especially in the so-called holy cities of Jerusalem, Hebron, Tiberias, and Safed. With the coming of modernity and the rise of modern nationalism and modern antisemitism, it was probably inevitable that many secular Jewish thinkers would turn their minds to the re-establishment of a Jewish state in Palestine, or at least to the movement of significant numbers of Jews to Palestine as a permanent and growing settlement. Before the rise of the modern Zionist movement in the late nineteenth century a number of significant proto-Zionist theorists emerged, secular thinkers who turned to such a project as a solution to the difficulties of Jewish existence in the Diaspora. Paradoxically, in view of America's commitment to religious equality, perhaps the very earliest such thinker arose in the United States. He was an American, Mordecai Manuel Noah (1785–1831), a Jewish diplomat, author, and newspaper owner. Noah was conscious that antisemitism existed even in democratic America and, in 1818, proposed that the world's seven million Jews should 'march in triumphant numbers, and possess themselves once more of Syria, and take their ranks among the governments of Earth.' (By 'Syria' Noah meant Palestine and the Fertile Crescent area.)

Noah also proposed that a Jewish army of 100,000 men should conquer their ancient homeland. Later, in 1844, he also suggested that a Jewish national territory be created in northern New York state near the Canadian border, thus presaging the so-called 'Territorialist' movement, which aimed at creating a Jewish homeland in any available region of the world rather than in Palestine – even in areas to which the Jews had no historical claim – in order to solve the problems of Jewish homelessness and persecution.

In 1843, a Jerusalem-born Serbian rabbi, Yehuda Alkalai (1798–1878), proposed the restoration of a Jewish national state in his book *Minhat Yehuda*. Alkalai was one of the first Orthodox figures to discuss directly the crucial point that the Return to Palestine would be brought about by divine intervention, not by human beings. Alkalai postulated that humans must begin this process, with only the final stages likely to witness divine intervention. Alkalai rejected the concept of a Jewish army, postulating instead that Jewish notables should create an agency to purchase land for resettlement from the Ottoman authorities. He also suggested that Jews should readopt Hebrew as their vernacular language. His programme was, in many respects, amazingly prophetic, foreshadowing the main method by which the Jewish world would indeed obtain land in Palestine and the re-emergence of Hebrew as a vernacular language. Nevertheless, it had little immediate impact upon wider Jewish opinion.

Another important proto-Zionist was Zvi Hirsch Kalischer (1795–1874), who in 1862 published *Derishat Zion* ('Seeking Zion'). Kalischer was an Orthodox rabbi in Thorn, Prussia, who was concerned at the rising tide of Reform Judaism and assimilation. Unlike most Orthodox thinkers, he rejected the possibility of turning inward, in order to insulate the observant community from these trends. Instead, he believed that the most positive response was a return to Palestine, where assimilationist tendencies would be considerably reduced. Kalischer argued that full Jewish participation in the political and social life of the nations of the West – an increasingly realistic prospect in his time – would inevitably increase assimilationist pressures and weaken traditional Orthodoxy (as, indeed, has almost always proved to be the case). No mere theorist, Kalischer established several bodies for Jewish agricultural settlement in Palestine, especially the Central Committee for Palestine Colonization, which he founded in Berlin in 1864. Kalischer also realised that nationalism represented perhaps the most important political force of his time, and saw it as a key factor to energise the Jewish world.

Probably the most important of the early Zionists was Moses Hess (1812–75). Born in Germany and raised as an Orthodox Jew, Hess moved sharply to the left as a young man, and was briefly an associate of Karl Marx on a left-wing newspaper. Gradually he returned to his Jewish roots, and in 1862 produced his seminal work *Rom und Jerusalem* ('Rome and Jerusalem'). In this he set out his views that the Jews were a nationality, like any other, but denied that emancipation represented the end of Jewish exile.

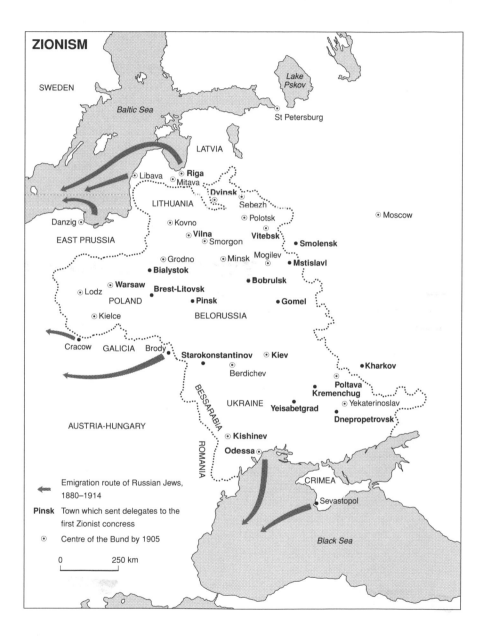

ZIONISM

SWEDEN

Baltic Sea

SWEDEN

Lake Pskov

St Petersburg

LATVIA

Libava · **Riga**
Mitava

Dvinsk

Danzig

LITHUANIA

Sebezh

Polotsk

Moscow

EAST PRUSSIA

Kovno

Vilna
Smorgon

Vitebsk

Smolensk

Grodno

Minsk

Mogilev

Mstislavl

Bialystok

Lodz · **Warsaw**

Brest-Litovsk

Bobrulsk

POLAND

Pinsk

Gomel

Kielce

BELORUSSIA

Cracow GALICIA Brody

Starokonstantinov

Berdichev

Kiev

Kharkov

AUSTRIA-HUNGARY

BESSARABIA

UKRAINE

Yeisabetgrad

Poltava
Kremenchug

Yekaterinoslav

Dnepropetrovsk

ROMANIA

Kishinev

Odessa

CRIMEA

Sevastopol

Black Sea

Emigration route of Russian Jews,
1880–1914

Pinsk Town which sent delegates to the
first Zionist concress

⊙ Centre of the Bund by 1905

0   250 km

He accepted the notion that there was a Jewish mission based in the creation of an equitable society, but asserted that this mission would only be fulfilled in a Jewish state.

As conditions for Jews in the Russian Pale of Settlement continued to deteriorate after the 1860s, it became apparent that the only realistic defence which Jews could offer to their plight was mass migration elsewhere. In the period from 1881 to 1914, nearly three million Jews left the Russian Empire for newer societies, chiefly the United States. The majority remained behind, however, and no obvious solution presented itself for their situation. Although many eastern European Jews lived a traditional lifestyle, this no longer offered meaningful answers to the problems of the day. Accordingly, a new definition of Judaism was needed; in this milieu Jewish intellectuals began to discuss some form of Jewish self-emancipation through a return to Jewish nationalism.

The murderous tsarist pogroms of 1881 sparked the creation, in 1882, of the first explicit Zionist organisation, known as *Hibbat Zion* ('Love of Zion' in Hebrew). *Hibbat Zion*'s ideological father was Dr Leon Pinsker (1821–91), a physician who had earlier advocated assimilation as the answer to the problems of Jewry. Pinsker was disturbed by the pogroms and, more significantly, by the positive attitude of some Russian intellectuals to their perpetrators. As a result, in 1882 he wrote *Auto-Emancipation*, a pamphlet with very important repercussions among Russian Jewry.

Pinsker argued that the pogroms of 1881 were not really a new phenomenon in Jewish history, but had repeatedly occurred, and would occur again, because the Jew 'is everywhere a guest, and nowhere *at home*'. Antisemitism was eternal and arose from the ambiguous and anomalous status of the Jews everywhere: 'for the natives, an alien and a vagrant; for property holders, a beggar; for the poor, an exploiter and a millionaire; for patriots, a man without a country'. Apart from the sweeping nature of his diagnosis, Pinsker differed from previous proto-Zionists in the success he enjoyed among the Jewish masses of eastern Europe. In November 1884 he organised the Kattowitz Conference, at a small town in Poland, where the *Hibbat Zion* movement was organised. By 1890 *Hibbat Zion* had 138 local chapters with perhaps 14,000 members. It aimed to establish agricultural colonies in Palestine and to build factories there, manned by Jewish labourers. A few years earlier, in 1882, a movement known as *Bilu* had come into being, with similar aims. *Bilu* (the initials, in Hebrew, of the Biblical passage 'O house of Jacob, come ye and let us go') was founded by Jewish students at Kharkov whose aim was emigration to Palestine. It was probably the first secular Zionist body to lead the return to Palestine by personal example. By the time of the Kattowitz conference, *Bilu* had established two colonies, at Rishon-le-Zion and Gedara. At the same time, other groups of Russian and Romanian Jews had established colonies in Palestine. This wave of Jews migrating to Palestine is known as the First

Aliyah, and is usually dated from 1882–1903. By 1903, almost 25,000 *olim* ('ascenders' in Hebrew) had settled in Palestine, or Eretz Israel ('the Land of Israel'), as it is often known. By 1903, Jews held a total of 400,000 dunams of land in Eretz Israel, about 1.5 per cent of the total area, had established settlements in the port city of Jaffa as well as the traditional areas of Jewish settlement, and had established 700 independent farms.

These early settlers (often known as *halutzim*, Hebrew for 'pioneers') encountered innumerable difficulties, especially the backwardness of the land, the lack of a modern infrastructure, depredations by Bedouin raiders, and hostility from the Turks. The *Bilu* movement did benefit, however, by extensive financial assistance from Baron Edmond de Rothschild (1845–1934), of the French branch of the banking family. Rothschild's somewhat heavy-handed patronage was often resented, and in 1899 a Palestine Jewish Colonization Association was established. Despite the gains made, however, the impetus behind the First Aliyah had considerably weakened by the end of the nineteenth century, lacking a leader of stature in the years after Pinsker's death in 1891. The Turks temporarily banned *aliyah* (migration to Palestine) in 1891. The great majority of émigrés from the Russian Empire continued to settle in the countries of the 'New Diaspora', especially the United States.

Another strand in late nineteenth-century Zionism was that of 'Spiritual Zionism', associated with Asher Ginsburg (1856–1927), better known by his pseudonym of Ahad Ha-am ('One of the People' in Hebrew). Born in the Ukraine to a wealthy Hasidic merchant's family, he attended several central European universities and became a Zionist, although he was a persistent critic of the Zionist organisations of his day. While Ahad Ha-am accepted the basic proposition advanced by Zionism, that the Jews were a separate nation, he believed that the decline of Judaism as a unifying factor in Jewish identity was the central element imperilling the Jewish collective determination to survive. Jewish nationalism had to address this problem by focusing on what he termed *Tehiat ha-Ruah*, or the revival of the spirit. He thus identified two separate crises in Jewry: those of the political fate of the Jews and of Judaism as a religion. To him, the latter was the more pressing of the two problems.

Ahad Ha-am also concluded that the creation of a new Jewish national home would never offer a complete answer to the difficulties faced by the Jewish people: Palestine was simply too infertile and backward ever realistically to attract more than a restricted minority of Jews. Instead, he argued that Eretz Israel should become a spiritual centre for the world's Jews, populated by an elite portion of Jewish youth, somewhat in the manner of ancient Israel during the Greco-Roman period. Ahad Ha-am laid great stress on the cultural and spiritual roles of Zionism; success in reviving the Jewish spirit could be accomplished only if a small number of Jews were relocated to Eretz Israel. In the years since he wrote, Ahad Ha-am's position has remained very controversial, being seen by some Zionists as impractical and even as slowing Zionist development. His attempt was to steer a middle way between maximalist Zionists and non-Zionists.

Theodor Herzl: the man and his mission

The event which brought Zionism to the forefront of Jewish and world affairs occurred in France in 1893–94, in the shape of the Dreyfus Affair. Captain Alfred Dreyfus, a Jewish member of the French general staff, was falsely accused of having sold military secrets to Germany, France's arch-enemy, and was sentenced to life imprisonment on Devil's Island. The Dreyfus Affair split France politically over the next decade, and led to an upsurge in antisemitism, in which all Jews were regarded as evil-doers by France's anti-Dreyfusards. Dreyfus's trial and sentence were reported for the liberal Viennese newspaper *Das Neue Freie Presse* by a young Austrian journalist, Theodor Herzl (1860–1904). Herzl was to write later that the taunts of witnesses to Dreyfus's public degradation, calling for death to the Jews, contributed greatly to his decision to write *Der Judenstaat* (*The Jewish State*), the book destined to become the Zionist classic par excellence.

Herzl's family came from Semlin, Serbia, the city where the major proto-Zionist Rabbi Yehuda Alkalai had lived; Herzl's grandfather was one of Alkalai's followers. While this may well have affected Herzl's own attitude, his upbringing, especially after his *bar mitzvah*, was only slightly more than marginally Jewish, and in many respects Herzl was an archetype of the highly assimilated, cosmopolitan middle-class intellectual Jew who emerged in central and western Europe during the nineteenth century. Nevertheless, he had long been obsessed with the problems faced by European Jewry, and the seeming intractability of antisemitism. Although some recent historians have questioned whether the Dreyfus Affair was as crucial to the evolution of Herzl's thought as was previously believed, as late as 1892 he had explic-itly rejected a proto-Zionist scheme of Palestinian settlement. The Dreyfus Affair both crystallised and fundamentally altered his views on a viable solution to the endemic problems of European Jewry. Shortly after the Dreyfus trial, Herzl wrote a play, *Das Neue Geto* (*The New Ghetto*), and then, in March 1896, his most important work, *Der Judenstaat*. Like Pinsker and the other proto-Zionists, Herzl held that the Jews were a nation, that a 'Jewish question' continued to exist, but that the emancipa-tion process had failed to solve the fundamental plight of the Jews. For Herzl, the solution to the 'Jewish question' lay in the Jewish people obtain-ing sovereignty 'over a portion of the earth's surface that is sufficient for our rightful national requirements'. To accomplish this goal, he proposed the creation of two bodies: a society of Jews to deal with all the technical issues related to the creation of a Jewish national home, and a Jewish company to undertake the financial arrangements to ensure success. Rather surprisingly to us, Herzl was initially not certain where the Jewish state should be, and considered both Argentina and Eretz Israel. (At the time, large-scale Jewish settlement on the Argentinian pampas was being organised by the Parisian banker Baron Maurice de Hirsch, one of the richest men in Europe.) Initially, Herzl had no firm views on the matter, and even later, in 1903, he accepted the British offer of East Africa as a place of settlement. More and more, however, Herzl came to see Eretz Israel as the only viable location for a Jewish national home, the only place which would arouse the enthusiasm of the Jewish masses and to which the Jewish people had a valid historical claim. The rest of *Der Judenstaat* was taken up with the technicalities of the Jewish state, which Herzl wished to have organised as a modern democratic society (and not as a theocracy).

Der Judenstaat proved an instant sensation, and almost overnight Herzl became internationally known. He was, apparently, almost totally ignorant of the writings of proto-Zionist thinkers like Moses Hess, and did not even realise that a movement of Zionist resettlement already existed. Nor did he reckon on the hostility his proposals would arouse among Jews. Orthodox rabbis and leaders repeatedly denounced his proposals as false messianism and heresy; assimilated Western Jews argued that demands for a Jewish state or homeland would increase antisemitism and undermine their status in the West; some Jewish (and other) socialists attacked the 'reactionary' nationalism of Herzl's theories. Nevertheless, Herzl found an enormous groundswell of support for his proposals, and was inundated with calls that he assume the role of a new Moses. At this crucial juncture, Herzl's abilities as an organiser and leader also became apparent, a role which was fundamental in laying the groundwork for the creation of the State of Israel half a century later. To realise his dreams, he created a tentative organisation and summoned its inaugural conference, soon dubbed the First Zionist Congress, which met in Basle, Switzerland, in August 1897.

Herzlian diplomacy

Herzl's seminal role in Zionism lay, as much as anything else, in his abilities as a diplomat who understood the realities of European politics. He also recognised the need for a clear indication of support from within the Jewish community which would be dramatic and highly visible. He brought visibility to his movement with the formation of the World Zionist Organization (WZO), and with other actions, such as the foundation in 1897 of a Zionist newspaper, *Die Welt*. At the First Zionist Congress, attended by 204 delegates, the WZO was officially constituted. Herzl was elected president, and the well-known writer Max Nordau (1849–1923) vice-president. The Congress adopted the so-called Basle Programme, which became Zionism's official platform. It declared that the 'aim of Zionism' was 'to create for the Jewish people a home in Palestine secured by public law', vowed to promote 'the colonisation of Palestine by Jewish agricultural and industrial workers', to create appropriate Zionist bodies, and to strengthen and foster 'Jewish national sentiments and consciousness'. This agenda left much unstated: there was nothing about creating an independent Jewish state, which would obviously have turned the Ottoman rulers of Palestine against the scheme, nor anything on how Europe's oppressed Jews were to be lured to Palestine rather than the 'New Diaspora'. There was nothing on the role of the Jewish religion in the Zionist venture, nor on the language to be spoken. To allay Turkish fears, nothing was said about the restoration of Jews to Palestine by historical right. Nevertheless, it should be noted that Palestine – rather than a Jewish homeland somewhere else – was explicitly mentioned in the programme and that it passed unanimously. After the Congress, Herzl penned an eerily prophetic passage in his diary: 'At Basle I founded the Jewish state. If I said this out loud today, I would be answered by universal laughter. Perhaps in five years, certainly in fifty, everyone will know it.' Herzl was out by just eight months, the State of Israel being founded in May 1948, slightly more than fifty years later.

In addition, Herzl had begun an international approach to world leaders to further his aims, an effort which had few positive results. He met the Turkish grand vizier (prime minister) but not the sultan. Three times in 1898 he met the German Kaiser, Wilhelm II, who was polite but non-committal. Rather surprisingly, Tsar Nicholas II declined to support Zionism – rather surprisingly since one might suppose that a movement whose aim was to rid Russia of its Jews would have his full support. The stumbling block diplomatically lay chiefly in the intrusions which Zionism would make into Ottoman sovereignty; moreover, the new movement had yet to prove itself. The Second Zionist Congress, of 1898, also held in Basle, did see notable gains in the movement, with a larger attendance that included delegates from Britain and the United States, some Orthodox rabbis, and the leading French pro-Dreyfusard Jewish author Bernard Lazare (1865–1903).

Zionist aims and methods, 1898–1903

The sudden growth of a viable Zionist movement, but one lacking immediate success, highlighted the great differences about what the aims of Zionism should be. Herzl himself was clearly a 'Political Zionist' (as those of his viewpoint came to be known), advocating immediate mass immigration to Palestine and a political and legal change in the status of Eretz Israel, based in the securing of a charter from the Ottomans which would guarantee the Zionist future. In contrast, there also soon emerged 'Practical Zionists', who believed in the slow but steady growth of Jewish settlement in Palestine. Many argued that mass *aliyah* was impossible (America and other Western countries still permitted unrestricted Jewish immigration) and that emphasis should be on 'infiltration' of Jews into Palestine to build up a small but viable centre of Jewish life, somewhat along the lines of Ahad Ha-am's 'spiritual Zionism'. Herzl's position was also weakened by the fact that the Ottoman authorities had virtually banned mass *aliyah*. In 1903 a branch of the Jewish Colonial Trust, the Anglo-Palestine Company, was established in Jaffa to facilitate limited immigration.

Frustrated in his continuing efforts to achieve some measure of success in his dealings with Turkey, Herzl next turned to Britain, the imperial power in Egypt and a likely beneficiary if the Ottoman Empire disintegrated. In October 1902 he secured some success in getting the British tentatively to accept the establishment of an autonomous Jewish colony at El Arish in northern Sinai. Although this plan eventually failed, it did show that the British government was at least sympathetic to Herzl. In 1902–03 a new series of murderous pogroms broke out in Russia, making the task of Zionism more urgent. At all times Herzl believed that the immediate aim of the Zionist movement was the seeking of asylum, even on a temporary basis, for oppressed Jewry, eventually leading to settlement in Eretz Israel. When the El Arish proposal collapsed, Britain's colonial secretary Joseph Chamberlain made an extraordinary parallel offer: to permit the creation of an autonomous Jewish colony in East Africa (commonly, if incorrectly, identified with Uganda) and generally known as the 'Uganda Scheme'. Initially Herzl rejected this proposal. But in May 1903 he accepted it, possibly, it would seem, so that any commission which examined the practicalities of the plan would conclude that Uganda was unfit for European habitation and return to a serious discussion of Palestine. Nevertheless, Herzl offered the 'Uganda Scheme' to the Zionist movement as a serious proposition. While he admitted that Uganda 'is not and can never be Zion', it represented 'an emergency measure designed to allay the present helplessness . . . of our people.' He also famously referred to Uganda as a 'night shelter' for a time of emergency.

The 'Uganda Scheme' was debated acrimoniously at the Zionist congresses of 1903 and (after Herzl's death) 1905 and bitterly split the Zionist movement. Herzl found himself opposed by the young Chaim Weizmann (1874–1952), Russian Zionist leader Menahem Mendel Ussishkin (1863–1941), and many others. By a narrow majority, the 1903 Congress allowed Herzl to continue negotiating with the British on the 'Uganda Scheme'. As a result, the young Zionist movement was gravely split. The acrimony surrounding the 'Uganda Scheme' apparently destroyed Herzl's health. He died at the age of only 44 in July 1904, arguably the most important Jewish political leader in modern history who, tragically, did not live to see the fruits of his endeavours.

Although the 'Uganda Scheme' was swiftly dissolved – the British investigating team rejected it as impractical – the Zionist movement remained internally fragmented, divided into a number of political parties and factions whose adherents all regarded themselves as Zionists. An Orthodox strand emerged within the movement, the Mizrachi Party ('Mizrachi' is the

Hebrew abbreviation of *merkaz ruhani*, spiritual centre; *mizrach* also means 'east', the direction of Jerusalem, in Hebrew), founded in 1902, under the slogan 'The Land of Israel for the People of Israel according to the Torah of Israel'. Mizrachi was highly significant for removing the hostility of many Orthodox Jews to Zionism, and for formulating a religious alternative to the secular nationalism (and secular socialism) of most Zionists. Another major strand formulated at this time was Socialist Zionism, which opposed Herzl's idea of deferring social and economic reforms within the Jewish community until the Jewish state actually came into existence. Socialist Zionism most directly confronted the growing force of Bund Socialism among Russia's Jews, who were adamantly anti-Zionist. Socialist Zionists often advocated immediate settlement in Palestine, and were among the most visible immigrants of the Second Aliyah (1904–14) and originated many of the characteristic institutions of the Yishuv (the Jewish community in pre-independence Palestine) and of the State of Israel. A third strand, the so-called Democratic Faction, was vaguer in its orientation, having some things in common with the theories of Ahad Ha-am. Its members opposed the 'cult of personality' which emerged around Herzl and favoured 'work in the here and now' to ameliorate the plight of Russian Jewry as well as continuing settlement in Palestine. Chaim Weizmann was perhaps the best-known of the younger leaders of this more moderate faction.

It should also be noted that the impetus behind the 'Uganda Scheme' – the securing of a temporary 'night shelter' somewhere in the world and not necessarily in Palestine for Jews in immediate peril – was not dead. Efforts to find any suitable homeland for the Jews somewhere on the globe became formalised through the foundation of the Jewish Territorial Organization (known as ITO, from its Yiddish initials) in 1905, organised by 40 dissident members of the Zionist Congress of 1905, and led by Israel Zangwill (1864–1926), the famous English author (who coined the phrase 'the melting pot'). The ITO lost most of its impetus following the Balfour Declaration, and was formally dissolved in 1925. During the Nazi period 'territorialist' proposals were again revived; there was, for instance, a serious effort, in the late 1930s, to found a settlement for Jewish refugees from Nazism in a remote part of north-west Australia. In the late 1920s Stalin actually formed a territory for Soviet Jews as a kind of pseudo-rival to Zionism, the Birobidzhan Autonomous Region in eastern Siberia. All such proposals finally withered with the establishment of the State of Israel in 1948; all such schemes lacked the popular support and moral impetus of Zionism and Eretz Israel.

The Zionist movement, 1904–14

The Zionist movement was in crisis following Herzl's sudden death, and many feared that it might disappear without his charismatic leadership. In fact, the movement he had founded took on a life of its own under his pre-Balfour Declaration successor David Wolffsohn (1856–1914) and of Wolffsohn's replacement, Otto Warburg (1859–1938). Under the presidency (1905–11) of Wolffsohn, efforts (often known as 'Synthetic Zionism') were made to produce an amalgam of 'Political' and 'Practical' Zionists within the WZO. Active membership of the latter continued to rise, reaching 127,000 dues-paying members in 1914. Within the Zionist movement, three broad political 'parties' became crystallised in this period. Two of these, the Socialist Zionists and Mizrachi, are noted above. The third, the General Zionists, aimed at a broad mainstream approach. The movement also produced a number of significant theorists, especially among the Socialist Zionist strand. Russian-born Nahman Syrkin (1868–1924) viewed the Zionist enterprise as making possible the creation of a classless Jewish society, although one funded by middle-class Jews in the Diaspora; his views were in some respects a socialist parallel to Ahad Ha-am's view of Eretz Israel as a 'spiritual centre' of the Jewish people.

Another prominent Socialist Zionist theorist was the Ukrainian-born Dov Ber Borochov (1881–1917), founder of the Poalei Zion ('Workers of Zion' in Hebrew) party which played a leading role during the Mandate period. Borochov, who left Russia in 1907, was more radical than Syrkin. He was an avowed Marxist, whereas Syrkin favoured class co-operation. Borochov argued that the abnormal socio-economic structure of European Jewry in the context of rising antisemitism would inevitably lead to massive Jewish emigration overseas, but that the exploitation of Jewish workers would cease only in a socialist Jewish homeland, which could only realistically exist in Eretz Israel. (For a discussion of the special features of Jewish participation in the European economy see Chapter 17). Borochov died at the age of only 36 in Russia, to which he returned during the brief Kerensky regime.

Mizrachi, the Orthodox Jewish movement, also struggled to develop a characteristic attitude towards the Zionist movement. Rejecting secular and 'cultural' interpretations of Zionism, Mizrachi's leaders – such as the Lithuanian rabbi Yitzhak Yaakov Reines (1839–1915) – supported Zionism essentially as an effort to find a safe haven for the Jewish people. Ironically, for this reason many welcomed the 'Uganda Scheme', despite their attachment to Eretz Israel. Mizrachi was also plagued by being opposed not merely by secular Zionists but by the majority of Strictly Orthodox rabbis and Jews, for whom secular attempts to re-establish a Jewish state remained sacrilegious. Some *Haredi* (Hebrew for 'God-fearing'; the term was adopted by non-Zionist Strictly Orthodox Jews to define themselves and is today often used by Strictly Orthodox communities in Israel and elsewhere) regarded Orthodox Zionists as a greater threat to Judaism even than secular Zionists.

By the eve of the First World War, the Zionist movement had thus already developed a surprisingly wide range of factions and internal ideo-logical strands under its umbrella. This diversity was to continue through-out the pre-state history of Israel and beyond. That so many antipathetic strands could coexist within the Zionist movement was a sign of strength, not weakness.

The decade between the death of Herzl and the outbreak of the First World War was one of growth of the Zionist movement without, of course, achieving either real success in Palestine nor, it should be noted, hegemony rather than merely wide support among the Jewish people. One survey of the attitudes of 520 Jewish university students in Kiev in 1909 found that, of 277 who claimed to be active members of a political party, 66 (24 per cent) described themselves as Zionists, compared with 44 (15 per cent) who viewed themselves as Bundists (Jewish socialists who were anti-Zionist). Nearly half of these students did not regard themselves as members of any political party. If anything, these figures may exaggerate the popularity of Zionism among Jewish youth, since proletarian Jewish youth, likely to be socialists, were underrepresented among university students. These figures would suggest that the Zionist movement had made major headway among eastern European Jewry in a short time, but it certainly did not represent a majority viewpoint.

In the more prosperous Diaspora, the Zionist movement had also made major headway. Many prominent American Jews became active supporters of the Zionist movement, including such influential members of the American Jewish community as Louis D. Brandeis (1856–1941), the first Jewish Supreme Court justice, Judge Julian W. Mack (1866–1943), Solomon Schechter (1847–1915), the founder of Conservative Judaism, and Cyrus L. Sulzberger (1858–1932), whose family owned the *New York Times*. In Britain the movement also had many influential supporters, and an important centre of Zionist strength emerged in Manchester, which was the home of Chaim Weizmann and of the Sieff and Marks families, owners of the retail chain Marks and Spencer, who were strong Zionist supporters.

The Second Aliyah, 1903–14

Growth also continued during this period in the Yishuv, sparked by such developments as the Jaffa branch of the Anglo-Palestine Bank (in 1903), and the WZO's Palestine Office (in 1908). In 1903, a short-lived representative body among Jewish settlers in Palestine was created, the first expression of Jewish self-government in Eretz Israel in modern times.

The so-called Second Aliyah of 1903–14 also increased Jewish settlement in Palestine. Begun as a result of the pogroms in Russia in 1903, it centred on the development of agricultural settlement in Eretz Israel. Members of the Second Aliyah had to fight against the tendency by members of *moshavim* (agricultural settlements) to hire Arab labour, and therefore emphasised *Avodah Ivrit* ('Hebrew labour'), entailing the desire that all substantial labour in the Yishuv should be performed by Jews. The centrality of Jewish labour in the ideology of the Second Aliyah is particularly associated with the Russian-born Zionist theorist Aaron David Gordon (1856–1922). Gordon argued that restoration of a Jewish national home perforce required the regeneration of individual Jews by creating a bond with nature through agricultural work; his ideology is sometimes termed a 'religion of labour' (*Dat ha-Avodah*). In this period, too, the first co-operative Jewish agricultural settlements, working as a collective unit, were founded. Known individually as *kevutzah* (Hebrew for 'group') they were the forerunners of the better-known *kibbutzim* founded after the First World War. The first continuing *kevutzah*, Deganyah in the Galilee, was established in 1909. More followed; they emphasised cooperative life, in terms of obligations, rights, property, and communal child-care, all well-known features of the *kibbutzim* to this day.

Other important achievements can be credited to the Second Aliyah. In 1909 Tel Aviv, the first modern all-Jewish city, was founded on the Mediterranean coast near Jaffa, with 60 housing units by Jewish settlers who found Jaffa overcrowded and squalid. Tel Aviv, meaning 'Hill of Spring' in Hebrew, became a separate city from Jaffa in 1934, and grew to become Israel's largest city and economic and social centre. By the year 2001 over two million people lived in the Tel Aviv metropolitan area. In Eretz Israel, Jewish settlers took the first steps towards a systematic development of Jewish self-defence. Self-defence became an issue among Diaspora Jewry in the wake of the appalling Kishinev pogrom of 1903, and the notion that Jews, traditionally without a defence force of their own, ought to protect themselves from physical attacks by their enemies, took root at that time. In Eretz Israel marauding Bedouins and Arab thieves regularly threatened the new community. In 1907 a group of ten young Jews formed the *Ha-Shomer* ('The Watchman' in Hebrew) society, offering themselves as guards to Jewish farmers. By 1911, *Ha-Shomer* was responsible for security in all Jewish settlements in the Galilee. As yet, *Ha-Shomer* did not have to protect Jews from militant Arab nationalists, and, indeed, sought good relations with the Arab communities.

By 1914, 85,000 Jews had settled in Eretz Israel, forming a visible community in the Lower Galilee and around Tel Aviv. They had developed some highly characteristic and unique institutions, especially the precursors of the *kibbutzim*, an ideology based upon the redemption of the land by Jewish labour, and considerable international support. While America and the 'New Diaspora' remained by far the most popular destination of Jews leaving eastern Europe, the Yishuv had been placed on a secure foundation. Within the next few years the Zionist movement was to secure a diplomatic breakthrough of profound significance.

Further reading

Alex Bein, *Theodor Herzl: A Biography of the Founder of Modern Zionism* (New York, 1970)

Alex Bein, *Toldot ha-Hityashvut ha-Zionit me-Tekufat Herzl ve-Ad Yamenu* (History of the Zionist Settlement from Herzl's Time to Today), 4th edn (Ramat Gan, Israel, 1970)

Isaiah Friedman, ed., *Herzl's Political Activity, 1897–1904* (New York, 1987)

Peter Grose, *Israel in the Mind of America* (New York, 1983)

Arthur Hertzberg, ed., *The Zionist Idea: A Historical Analysis and Reader* (New York, 1976)

Theodor Herzl, *The Jewish State* (New York, 1946)

Theodor Herzl, *The Complete Dairies of Theodor Herzl*, edited by Raphael Patai, 5 vols (New York, 1960)

Herzl Year Book

Moses Hess, *Rome and Jerusalem*, edited by Meyer Waxman (New York, 1943)

Herbert Samuel, *Memoirs* (London, 1945)

Gideon Shimoni, *The Zionist Ideology* (Hanover, N.H., 1995)

Leonard Stein, *The Balfour Declaration* (London, 1961)

David Vital, *The Origins of Zionism* (Oxford, 1975)

David Vital, *Zionism: The Formative Years* (New York, 1982)

|13|

Zionism, 1914–47: from settlement to state

The First World War and the Balfour Declaration

The position of the Zionist movement towards the rivalry between the Great Powers in the years before 1914 was one of strict neutrality. Many Zionists saw that the Jewish inhabitants of the Yishuv would be in potentially grave peril from the Ottoman sovereigns, and were determined to do nothing to upset the Turks. As the First World War became more deadly, however, the Zionist movement realised that it was in a potentially strong position to be courted by both sides. As Germany made major gains in eastern Europe, conquering much of the tsarist Pale of Settlement, the Zionist movement expected some kind of declaration of support for the movement by imperial Germany. None was forthcoming until after the issuance of the Balfour Declaration by the British in October 1917, chiefly for fear of alienating Germany's Turkish allies. It should be realised, however, that both sides in the war were seen as at least potential supporters of the Zionist movement, a striking indication of the growth of Zionist strength and perceptions of its importance to millions of Jews. As well, to a later generation it is striking that during the First World War Germany was not explicitly antisemitic and was seen by the Zionist movement as its potential supporter; indeed, Germany's armies were seen as liberators by many Jews suffering under the tsarist regime.

It was, however, not Germany but Britain which was to take the momentous step of conquering Palestine and promising that it would become a Jewish national home. Several pathways converged to produce this end. Britain and France had been at war with the Ottoman Empire, a German ally, since November 1914. An Allied victory would therefore see a basic redrawing of the boundaries of the Middle East, with, in all likelihood, a reduction of its boundaries to purely Turkish areas. Furthermore, Britain had become the home of considerable Zionist strength. Herbert Samuel (later Viscount Samuel, 1870–1963), of a wealthy Anglo-Jewish family, had sat in the British Cabinet since 1909 and was widely respected. In January 1915 he composed a memorandum to the Cabinet advocating that the British occupy Palestine and the Trans-Jordan, with Jewish restoration to the Holy Land as official British policy. Chaim Weizmann, a powerful figure in the international Zionist movement, lived in Manchester and was an effective lobbyist on behalf of the Zionist cause. The British Cabinet contained a number of leading figures, especially David Lloyd George (1863–1945), prime minister after December 1916, and Arthur Balfour (1848–1930), who were convinced Zionists. Lloyd George, a Welsh Baptist, had grown up knowing the Old Testament chronicles virtually by heart, and had a deep affinity for the Jews as a small persecuted people. Britain was also well aware of the importance of winning over Jewish support for the Allies against Germany, especially in America. From 1915 on, the British gradually permitted the creation of a Jewish fighting force to help liberate Palestine from the Turks. The idea for a 'Jewish Legion' came from a number of sources, especially Vladimir Jabotinsky (1880–1940), later the leader of Revisionist Zionism, and Joseph Trumpeldor (1880–1920). Trumpeldor, who had lost an arm fighting for Russia in the Russo-Japanese war of 1904–05, had settled in Palestine in 1912 and (since Russia was at war with Turkey) became an exile in Egypt during the First World War. In 1920 he was killed by Arabs in defence of Jewish settlements in the Upper Galilee and became a great posthumous hero of the Yishuv. Initially, in 1915, the British permitted the creation of the Zion Mule Corps, a company of Jewish mule-drivers who acted as ammunition carriers at the Battle of Gallipoli. In 1917, the British permitted the creation of the 'Jewish Legion', consisting initially of the 38th battalion of the Royal Fusiliers. Lead by a non-Jewish British colonel, it participated in the British conquest of Palestine. Composed of Jews from many countries, especially Palestine, it numbered 5000 men. David Ben-Gurion and Yitzhak Ben-Zvi, later Israeli statesmen, enlisted in it, as did Jabotinsky.

In the middle of 1917, the British Cabinet decided to place on record its commitment to the establishment of a Jewish national home of some kind in Palestine. Apart from the pro-Zionist leanings of many influential members of the Cabinet, Britain was also keen to lure the Jewish masses of Russia, following the overthrow of the tsar in February 1917, to continued support of the Allied cause. As well, Britain saw the establishment of a Jewish homeland under British sovereignty in Palestine as a strategic asset, especially in safeguarding the Suez Canal. Opposition to any move to creating a Jewish national home in Palestine came not at this stage from Arab sources – Arab nationalism as yet hardly existed and could be disregarded – but chiefly from non-Zionists within the Jewish community itself, such as Edwin Montagu (1879–1924), a prominent Jewish Cabinet minister, and David C. Alexander, president of the Board of Deputies of British Jews. On the other hand, it seems clear that most influential British Jews strongly supported the move to the creation of a British-backed Jewish national state, among them

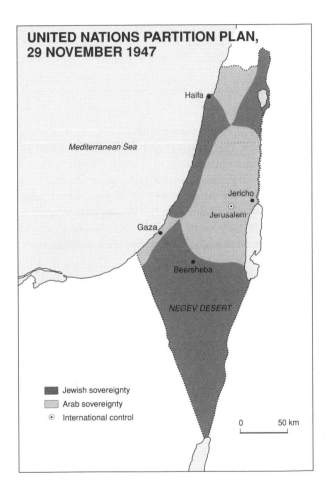

UNITED NATIONS PARTITION PLAN,
29 NOVEMBER 1947

Mediterranean Sea

Haifa

Jericho

Jerusalem

Gaza

Beersheba

NEGEV DESERT

Jewish sovereignty
Arab sovereignty
International control

0   50 km

Lord Rothschild (the unofficial head of Anglo-Jewry), the chief rabbi, Joseph H. Hertz, and the leader of the Sephardi community, Haham Moses Gaster. In the summer and autumn of 1917 a series of proposals indicating Britain's support for a Jewish national homeland were debated by the Cabinet. Finally, on 2 November 1917, the British Cabinet issued the celebrated Balfour Declaration, a letter from the foreign secretary, Arthur Balfour, to Lord Rothschild, which stated that

> His Majesty's Government views with favour the establishment in Palestine of a national home for the Jewish people and will use their best endeavours to facilitate the achievement of this object, it being clearly understood that nothing shall be done which may prejudice the civil and religious rights of existing non-Jewish communities in Palestine, or the rights and political status enjoyed by Jews in any country.

While the meaning of the Balfour Declaration in practice was highly ambiguous, its seminal importance cannot be overstated. It was the long-sought-for charter of the Zionist movement, the guarantee by a Great Power of Zionist legitimacy. Not since Cyrus of Persia had declared that Jews could return to Judaea in 517 BCE had anything comparable, or as momentous, occurred in the Jewish world. Now Zionism's task would change from attaining a Jewish national home to turning idea into reality.

Formalising the Jewish national home

The Balfour Declaration would have been meaningless without the occupation of Palestine by Britain in place of Turkey. This occurred at about the same time as the issuance of the Balfour Declaration, although in reality Britain did not fully occupy Palestine until after its promulgation. Moving in from Egypt, in October 1917, General Edmund Allenby successfully attacked the Turks in the Gaza-Beersheba area and on 9 December 1917 entered Jerusalem. The decisive Battle of Megiddo (19 September 1918) swept the Turks from Syria. At the same time as the British formally endorsed Zionism, it also supported Arab national aspirations. Many 'Establishment' Englishmen viewed the Arabs as a romantic people who fought with honour and deserved respect, for instance Colonel T.E. Lawrence ('Lawrence of Arabia', 1888–1935) the celebrated British leader of the 'Arab Revolt'. Some in the British 'Establishment' were hostile to Jews and to Zionism. For the next thirty years the two competing forces, the pro- and anti-Zionists, remained in conflict over determining British policy in Palestine.

In 1918–19 the nature of the Jewish 'national home' in Palestine began to take shape. Initially, the leaders of the Arabs were willing to make major concessions to Zionism, and in January 1919 Weizmann and Faisal ibn

Hussein of Transjordan reached agreement in which the Arabs recognised the legitimacy of the Balfour Declaration. Although this agreement collapsed within a year, initially the Balfour Declaration was not opposed by key Arab leaders.

At the Paris Peace Conference, the Zionists proposed a national home (not, as yet, an independent state) in Palestine with a large territory stretching from the Litani River (now in Lebanon) to areas in what is now Jordan and the Sinai. Initially, British and international support for Zionism was considerable. In 1919 the League of Nations, the newly-formed international body, tentatively assigned Palestine to the British, and, in September 1922, officially made Palestine into a British mandate, a new form of territorial rule which was like that of a colony, but with at least theoretical oversight by the League of Nations in its international capacity. In practice, from 1918 until Israeli independence in 1948, Palestine was a British colony, its jurisdiction determined by the British Colonial Office and the British colonial secretary. (The era of British rule in Palestine, 1918–48, is always known as the 'mandate' period.) Initially, many of the expansive territorial dreams of the Zionist movement were granted, although no part of the Sinai (a component of Egypt) was included in the mandate. At first, however, the whole of what is today the kingdom of Jordan was included in the Palestine mandate, although in 1922–23 Jordan (then known as 'Transjordan') was separated off from Palestine and declared to be an autonomous state, ruled over by Abdullah ibn Hussein, son of the Sharif (ruler) of Mecca (and grandfather of King Hussein of Jordan). The provisions of the Balfour Declaration were also officially applied to the mandate of Palestine.

In 1920, Sir Herbert Samuel, one of the leading Anglo-Jewish Zionists and a former Cabinet minister, was appointed high commissioner for Palestine, the first Jewish governor of the Holy Land since Roman times. About 35,000 Jewish immigrants migrated to Eretz Israel in the first few years of the mandate (1919–23), known as the Third Aliyah. Mainly socialists, they chiefly became engaged in Jewish agriculture in the *kibbutzim* and *moshavot*. Nevertheless, at this time the Zionist movement made a conscious decision not to endorse mass Jewish migration to Palestine, and rejected the proposals by Max Nordau, the venerable Zionist leader, for the *aliyah* of 600,000 Jews in two or three years. Instead, they decided to endorse such *aliyah* as would be realistically consistent with Palestine's absorptive capacity. Until 1948, the mainstream Zionist movement never favoured mass Jewish migration, but only the careful, limited immigration of an elite of mainly young and committed Zionist enthusiasts. This attitude (which, during the 1930s, was fiercely contested by Jabotinsky and his 'Revisionist' Zionists) must strike us today as extremely puzzling, in view of the crying need of so many Jews for a place of a refuge, and was entirely reversed by the newly-independent State of Israel in 1948.

In 1922, when the League of Nations formally recognised the principles of the Balfour Declaration, it stipulated that the World Zionist

Organization 'shall be recognised' as the 'Jewish agency' for Palestine, thus officially incorporating the Zionist movement in the development of Eretz Israel. In 1929, the Jewish Agency for Palestine, the body established to channel funding and other assistance to the Yishuv, was broadened to include friendly non-Zionist Jewish leaders from around the world. During these years economic development did occur in Jewish Palestine in virtually every sphere. In 1900 Jews had cultivated approximately 119,000 dunams of land; by 1927 the figure had reached 463,570 dunams, with another million owned by overseas Zionist bodies. During the early-mid 1920s the *kibbutzim* took shape in their present form, having chiefly originated during the Third Aliyah of 1919–23, based upon the pre-existing *kevutzah* format. The first true *kibbutz*, Ein Harod, was established in 1921. Industry and wage labour was added to the original purely agricultural models. Much growth occurred in the infrastructure of Eretz Israel, with the creation of an electricity grid, a railway system, irrigation, and the growth of Tel Aviv and other Jewish or largely Jewish cities in place of what had been almost entirely a primitive desert. The year 1925 saw the opening, to international acclaim, of the Hebrew University of Jerusalem, the first Jewish university in the Holy Land, while the King David Hotel, the first luxury hotel in Eretz Israel, opened in 1930. The growth of Hebrew as the vernacular language of Jewish Palestine also now became an established fact. That Eretz Israel would be Hebrew-speaking was not preordained: most immigrants of course spoke Yiddish, while many would have preferred a Western language, such as German. The rise of vernacular Hebrew was chiefly due to the efforts of Eliezer Ben-Yehudah (*né* Perelmann, 1858–1922), a Lithuanian-born journalist who had settled in Palestine in 1881 and edited Hebrew-language journals. His personal example, of speaking only Hebrew, had a profound effect, as did his efforts to produce a comprehensive Hebrew dictionary. From the 1880s, too, a distinguished authorship in modern Hebrew began to emerge both in Palestine and in the Diaspora, most notably Haim Nahman Bialik (1873–1934), the Russian-born poet whose most famous work, *Be-Ir ha-Hareghah* ('In the City of Slaughter'), to commemorate the Kishinev pogrom of 1903, became celebrated. Living in Tel Aviv from 1924, he became the centre of a revival of modern Hebrew literature. In Eretz Israel, the first daily newspaper in Hebrew began in 1886, while from 1913 the Jewish community in Palestine enforced the exclusive use of Hebrew in its schools. It was officially recognised as one of the official languages of the Palestine mandate (with English and Arabic) in 1921. The Yishuv's insistence on the use of Hebrew as a vernacular marked a striking, and deliberate, break with Diaspora life, since few if any Diaspora Jews spoke Hebrew as a vernacular. It also placed the Zionist movement at loggerheads with some Strictly Orthodox Jews, for whom the use of Hebrew in everyday speech was anathema.

By the end of the 1920s, the Jewish community in Palestine numbered an estimated 154,300 – tiny by comparison with the Diaspora communities but much more substantial than it had been only a generation earlier. As a percentage of the total population of Palestine, the Jews had increased from 13 per cent in 1922 to 19 per cent in 1929.[1] Yet despite its achievement, all was not well with the Zionist project. Immigration by Jews to Palestine remained surprisingly small throughout the 1920s, despite the closing of the United States to heavy Jewish immigration in 1924. While severe limitations on Jewish settlement in Palestine were set in place by the British in most years of the 1920s, immigration to Palestine was much lower than it could have been, even among the impoverished communities of eastern Europe. In some years, indeed, more Jews left Palestine than emigrated there. The Zionist movement, too, remained deeply divided by ideology and in its aims. Three major blocks which had developed within the WZO – the General Zionists, the Socialist Zionists, and the Religious Zionists – continued, with further internal divisions emerging within these groupings. The Socialist Zionists had fragmented into a social democratic and a Marxist wing, reflecting the world-wide divisions in the socialist camp. A fourth major strand also emerged within Zionism at this time, Revisionist Zionism. Revisionist Zionism embodied a right-wing nationalistic vision of Eretz Israel. Founded and led by Ze'ev Jabotinsky, it advocated rapid mass migration to the Yishuv, in contrast to the gradual approach supported by the mainstream. It despaired of any realistic possibility of peaceful accommodation with the Arabs, at least in the short-term. It tended to be opposed to socialism in the economic sphere, but advocated such concepts as *hadar* ('self-respect') for the new Jews of Palestine, a disciplined, unified Zionist movement, and the eventual goal of an independent Jewish state. Revisionism also contained a number of militaristic elements, including uniforms and paramilitary drills among its youth group Betar, which were widely condemned by Jabotinsky's enemies as redolent of fascism. (Jabotinsky denied this, believing that these innovations were made to instil dignity and discipline into Jewish youth.) During the 1930s, relations between Revisionist Zionism and the mainstream deteriorated further. Although Jabotinsky remained a liberal anglophile, some of his more extreme followers developed ideas and doctrines friendly to fascism and to the use of terrorism against the British and Arabs.

Probably the main reason why the Zionist movement encountered apparently insurmountable obstacles to its goals was the growth of Arab nationalism and of militant, often violent, opposition to the Zionist enterprise by the local Arabs and their leaders. The growth of Arab (and, particularly, Palestinian) nationalism during this period was itself slowed by the backward and illiterate nature of Arab society, where local chieftains, clan leaders, imams and other religious leaders, commanded followers in competing fiefdoms. Western-style nationalism was itself confined to a small minority among the

---

1 About 62,000 immigrants, mainly from Poland, had settled in Palestine in 1924–29, known as the 'Fourth Aliyah'.

well-educated urban elite. Many of these urban elites themselves welcomed the modernising trends introduced by the Zionists and the British, and the Palestinian Arabs were themselves deeply divided. Leadership of the Palestinians became centred in the person of Haj Mohammed Amin El-Husseini (1893–1974), appointed mufti of Jerusalem and head of the Supreme Muslim Council by the British in 1921. El-Husseini was a ruthless, uncompromising opponent of both the Zionists and the British, and was especially keen to portray Zionist domination of the Muslim Holy Places in Jerusalem as a threat to all Arabs. While violent disturbances against the Jews and the British had broken out in 1920–21, the extremely bloody disturbances of August 1929 marked a turning-point in the history of the mandate. Arab massacres of Jews occurred on an unprecedented scale in Hebron (where 700 Jews lived) while a fierce and violent confrontation at the Western Wall in Jerusalem (the 'Wailing Wall' incident) inflamed relations between the two communities. A total 133 Jews were murdered by the Arabs, while thousands of others became homeless, and old-established Jewish communities temporarily ceased to exist. The British authorities responded with a series of investigations which, irrationally, rejected further large-scale Jewish migration to Palestine unless large-scale development plans were implemented. In October 1930 the minority British Labour government accepted the thrust of these reports in the so-called Passfield White Paper (named for Sidney Webb, Lord Passfield, the famous socialist theorist who was colonial secretary). Although the British Labour party might be seen as more sympathetic to Zionism than the British Conservatives, the earliest change in British policy in a pro-Arab direction came from a Labour government. Henceforth, British policy would become ever more mindful of Arab anti-Zionism. The British Empire comprised tens of millions of Muslims, while Britain also had vast economic interests throughout the Middle East. Under pressure in India and elsewhere, Britain was increasingly keen to deter or prevent an anti-British Arab nationalist uprising which would threaten its imperial role. Establishment antisemitism in Britain might have influenced this shift in British policy, but this was less significant than Britain's need to appease Arab and Muslim opinion. For its part, the mainstream Zionist movement was keen to reach some workable compromise with the Arabs which would allow the growth, and eventual independence, of a state with a Jewish majority, and repeatedly sought agreement with Arab leaders aimed at achieving a *modus vivendi*. These efforts were always uncompromisingly rejected by the Arabs, who made an accommodation with the Jews of Palestine impossible.

There the matter stood until 1933, when an event of the most profound and tragic significance affected Eretz Israel, as it did the whole of the Jewish people: the rise to power of Adolf Hitler in Germany. Hitler's uncompromising antisemitism triggered an outflow of German Jews seeking refuge wherever they could. Many went to Eretz Israel: some because they were Zionists, some because emigrating there was relatively less painful than elsewhere. Initially, Nazi ideology favoured Zionism as a 'solution' to

Germany's Jewish 'problem', and allowed more favourable terms of emigration to German Jews who settled in Palestine. This was formalised by the so-called Haavara Transfer Agreement of November 1933, which remained in force until about 1937, when Nazi Germany turned against Zionism. (German and Austrian Jews continued, however, to emigrate to Palestine until 1940–41). Between 1933 and 1941, 55,000 German and 9500 Austrian Jews emigrated to Palestine. Immigration, however, also continued from other parts of the Jewish world, especially Poland. This wave of immigration, known as the Fifth Aliyah, brought about 230,000 Jews to Palestine from abroad, three-quarters of whom came from other sources than Germany, Poland in particular. Immigration to Palestine was never unrestricted but was based upon Eretz Israel's alleged ability to absorb different categories of persons (such as workers, capitalists, students, etc.) and was the subject of fierce rivalry and struggle between various Zionist groupings and the British. As the Jewish situation in Europe continuously darkened, more Jews sought to enter Palestine. This demand rose as, from 1936, Britain began to tighten immigration controls to appease the Arabs. As a result, 'illegal' immigration (popularly known as *Aliyah Bet*) developed. Between 1933 and 1939, at least 25,000 *ma'apilim* ('defiers' in Hebrew; i.e. illegal immigrants) are thought to have entered Eretz Israel, in addition to perhaps 12,000 during the Second World War.

As Jewish immigration to Palestine rose during the 1930s, it again touched off a wave of Arab anti-Zionism and nationalism. This wave coincided with outbursts of anti-colonial feeling in other parts of the Arab world and in India. The Arabs were actively encouraged by Nazi Germany and fascist Italy. In April 1936 the mufti of Jerusalem headed a general strike, aimed at both the Jews and the British, which touched off what has become known as the 'Arab Revolt'. Rioting and terrorism continued for six months; ninety-one Jews were killed. In response, Jews organised self-defence forces which, in the summer of 1936, began to attack Arab terrorist targets. A system of stockades and watchtowers was organised throughout Jewish settlements. Tel Aviv was developed as a purely Jewish port, to replace Jaffa harbour, dominated by Arabs.

The British responded harshly to the 'Arab Revolt', disbanding the Arab Higher Council. It also established the so-called Peel Commission to decide on the future of Palestine. Named for Earl Peel, a British politician, its members toured Palestine late in 1936 and held separate meetings with Arab and Zionist leaders in London in 1937. The Peel Commission concluded that the Palestine mandate should be divided into a Jewish state, a Palestinian Arab state, and a British mandatory zone. The small Jewish state was, under the Commission's proposals, to include the coastal region from Jaffa northwards and the whole of the Galilee, areas where most of the Jews in Eretz Israel lived. The British were to retain Jerusalem, Bethlehem, and a strip of land to the coast; the Arabs were to have the rest, including all of the Negev, Gaza, and what is today the West Bank.

The Peel Commission thus proposed, for the first time in modern history as a serious proposition, the creation of an independent Jewish state, albeit a very small one, and one which excluded Jerusalem. With the menace of Nazism constantly rising, and the need for refuge becoming ever clearer, it may seem as if the Jewish world would enthusiastically embrace this proposal, whatever its obvious deficiencies. In fact, the Peel Commission's proposals bitterly split the Jewish world. Although Weizmann, David Ben-Gurion and other Zionist luminaries supported the plan (along with a majority of the WZO), it was also bitterly opposed by many other Zionists, including Jabotinsky. The Arabs adamantly opposed any partition proposal and flatly refused to consider the establishment of a Jewish state in any form. Although Britain initially accepted the Peel report, it quickly came to reject it. Arab terrorism continued throughout 1938 (nearly 250 Jews were murdered in this year), and Britain was keener than ever not to alienate Arab opinion. A further British inquiry into Palestine in 1938, the Woodhead Commission, modified the Peel proposals to decrease the territory allocated to the Jews and increasing that which remained in British hands. With the approach of the war, partition became a dead issue for the time being.

As if the rejection of the Peel proposals was not enough, in 1939 the British government delivered what seemed to be a hammer blow aimed at the entire Zionist movement, the so-called MacDonald White Paper of May 1939. (A 'White Paper' is an officially published statement by the British government; this White Paper was named for Malcolm MacDonald, Britain's Colonial Secretary.) In it, Britain set extremely severe restrictions on the number of Jews allowed in future to enter Palestine, limiting the total to only 75,000 over the next five years. The White Paper also foresaw the creation of an independent Arab-dominated Palestine within ten years, and virtually revoked the principles of the Balfour Declaration. Britain made no bones about the fact that it issued the White Paper purely in order to appease the Arabs: with the outbreak of war a virtual certainty, the support of Jews against the Nazi peril would be automatic, but the Arabs had, at all costs, to have no grievances against Britain which Germany could exploit. While Britain liberalised its own immigration policies towards Jewish refugees at this time, the whole Jewish world reacted with fury to the MacDonald White Paper, engendering a legacy of ill-will which negated the effects of Britain's heroic stand against the Nazis.

During the later 1930s, there was a demonstrable increase in the strength of the Zionist movement around the world, with the number of 'shekel-holders' (dues-paying members of the WZO, who paid a small sum of money, called a 'shekel', to join the Zionist organisation) rising significantly, from 425,987 in 1931 to 978,033 in 1935 and 1,042,054 in 1939.[2]

---

2 Including Jabotinsky's New Zionist Movement would probably add about 150,000 to the 1939 figure.

Nevertheless, despite the Nazi threat, Zionism remained a minority movement within the Jewish world, with important ideological strands, such as Bund socialism in Poland, remaining fiercely opposed to Zionism. In the West, many Jews also remained lukewarm to 'political Zionism', still fearing that the creation of a Jewish state would threaten their civil status. Few if any foresaw the extent of the catastrophe which was about to occur throughout Europe, or the urgent necessity for a place of refuge not just for Germany's Jews but for all those on the Continent.

The inter-war years also saw many political developments within the Yishuv. A party infrastructure continued to emerge, with, in particular, important developments on the social democratic left. In 1930 Mapai (the acronym of *Mifleget Po'alei Eretz Israel*, Hebrew for the 'Party of Workers of Eretz Israel') was formed from pre-existing labour parties. Mapai was a pragmatic party of the left which contained many of the Yishuv's important political figures. It was keen to establish a good working relationship with non-socialist and Jewish religious parties, and was also virtually coterminous with the Histadrut. The Histadrut (officially 'The General Federation of Workers in Eretz Israel') was the overarching trade union body of Israel, the equivalent of the AFL-CIO in the United States and of the TUC in Britain, but relatively much more important than either, since it was also a mutual aid society, a centre of cultural activity, and an employer of labour. Between 1921 and 1935 its secretary-general was David Ben-Gurion (1886–1973), also the leading figure in Mapai. Ben-Gurion was the dominant political figure in Eretz Israel during much of the mandate period, and became the country's first prime minister after independence in 1948. A Polish-born socialist Zionist, lawyer, and newspaper editor, he was an early advocate of an independent Jewish state but also a pragmatist who abhorred both Marxism and extreme Jewish nationalism. Other major Mapai leaders of the time included Berl Katznelson (1887–1944), editor of Histadrut's newspaper *Davar*, and Yitzhak Ben-Zvi (1884–1963), Ben-Gurion's close associate and, from 1952–63, Israel's second president.

On the right of the Zionist political spectrum, this period also saw the continued growth of Jabotinsky's Revisionist movement. Appalled by what he saw as the failure of mainstream Zionism to achieve either independence or large-scale *aliyah*, in 1935 Jabotinsky and his followers founded the New Zionist Organization (NZO), which aimed at the immigration, by whatever means required, of 1.5 million eastern European Jews to Palestine over ten years and the rapid creation of a Jewish state. The NZO established a rival body to the WZO which remained estranged from mainstream Zionism until Jabotinsky's death in 1940 and, indeed, perhaps until the creation of the State of Israel or afterwards. Relations between Jabotinsky and his followers and mainstream Zionism were almost always bad during this period. In 1933 Haim Arlosoroff (1899–1933) a rising young Labour Zionist figure, was assassinated on Tel Aviv beach. A Revisionist follower of Jabotinsky's, Avraham Stavsky, was arrested for his murder, convicted, and sentenced to death (his conviction was later overturned by a British appeals court). As a result, relations between Revisionists and Labour Zionists deteriorated still further, and actual violence erupted between their followers throughout the Jewish world. Relations between Ben-Gurion and Jabotinsky, probably the two outstanding Zionist leaders, remained frigid during this crucial period.

The coming of the Second World War in September 1939 found the Yishuv in grave peril and deeply divided, a situation which intensified with the seemingly inevitable German conquest of all Europe apart from Britain. The restrictions on *aliyah* imposed by the British had crucially alienated Zionist support, but the Jews of Palestine knew that a German victory would be infinitely worse than a continuation of British rule. As a result, the vast majority of Zionists emphasised the need for a truce with Britain for the duration of the war. The Yishuv, however, remained in an almost constant state of conflict, with Jews largely confined to the limited territory they already held and even heavier restrictions placed on *aliyah* (although, it should be emphasised, it was the Nazis who forbade Jewish emigration from Europe). With the German and Italian victories in north Africa, a Nazi conquest of Palestine became an ever more realistic possibility. Had Germany's Erwin Rommel defeated Britain's Bernard Montgomery at El Alamein in Egypt (rather than the other way round) in November 1942, there is no reason to suppose that the Jews of the Yishuv would have survived: Hitler specifically promised the mufti of Jerusalem at their notorious meeting in Berlin in 1941 that he would 'exterminate' the Jews of Palestine once he conquered the country. Although the area was not directly a battlefield, war came to the Yishuv when Italian aircraft bombed Tel Aviv and other places in Palestine in late 1940, killing over one hundred. There were advanced plans for Jews to retreat to the mountainous areas of the Galilee and establish a centre of resistance, if German armies invaded Palestine. The British did not permit the formation of a specifically Jewish combat corps in its army until late in 1944 (previously, Jews from Eretz Israel were accepted into British or Commonwealth armies, but not in separate units). The Jewish Brigade Group, as it was known, consisted of about 5000 Jewish soldiers who were permitted to fly the Zionist flag.

On the other hand, a Yishuv self-defence force, the Palmach (from the abbreviation of 'shock companies' in Hebrew) was established in May 1941 to defend the country in the event of a German invasion. It was a branch of the Haganah (Hebrew for 'defence'), organised in the interwar period to protect Jewish lives; it later became the backbone of the Israel Defence Force. Once the German danger diminished, Palmach (and the Haganah) became strike forces against the British mandatory authorities and, during the War of Independence, against the Arabs. At the fringes of the Yishuv's political spectrum, two independent military groups also emerged, the *Irgun Zva'i Le'umi* (IZL – 'National Military Organization' in Hebrew) and the Lehi (the acronym of *Lohamei Herut Yisrael*, 'Fighters for the Freedom of

Israel'). The Irgun, founded in 1931, was closely associated with Jabotinsky's Revisionists. With the 1939 White Paper, it began attacking British targets, a policy it discarded with the outbreak of the war. In February 1944 it began a 'revolt' against British occupation of Palestine, led by its youthful commander Menahem Begin (1913–92), later prime minister of Israel. The Lehi, or 'Stern Gang' as it was often known after its founder Abraham Stern, adopted a policy of anti-British terrorism throughout the war, and helped to assassinate Lord Moyne, the British minister of state in Cairo, in November 1944. Stern (1907–42) had himself been shot dead by British policemen in February 1942. Very extreme members of Lehi, not realising the extent of the Holocaust, actively sought an alliance with Nazi Germany against the British. During the war, most Jews of the Yishuv found the anti-British activities of these organisations odious, and they were marginalised by the Zionist mainstream, although they became central to winning independence after 1945.

News of the Holocaust began to trickle out of Europe from late 1941, although the full extent and horror of the catastrophe unfolding in Europe did not become known for several years and, perhaps, not until after the war. The Yishuv was virtually helpless to assist European Jewry, who were under the total domination of the Nazi monsters and their diabolical policy of genocide. In addition, the lack of a specific fighting force established from Palestine Jewry conceivably deterred any rescue efforts. In mid-1944, a group of Yishuv volunteers was parachuted into Nazi-occupied Hungary; the most famous was Hannah Szenes, a celebrated poet. Most (including Senesh) were murdered by the Nazis. Other Yishuv volunteers were also parachuted into Nazi-occupied Europe, but could accomplish virtually nothing. In the post-war years, some historians have criticised the alleged 'inertia' of Ben-Gurion and other Yishuv leaders during the Holocaust, but it is very difficult to see how they could have assisted Europe's Jews, who were prisoners of Hitler.

During the war, there was a significant, perhaps decisive, shift of opinion among Diaspora Jewry in the direction of supporting Zionism which was instrumental in creating the State of Israel a few years later. Diaspora support for Zionism had been rising before the war. During the early stages of the war, the Zionist movement made a fundamental shift in its policy, explicitly calling for the first time for the creation of an independent Jewish state. This was accomplished in the so-called Biltmore Declaration of May 1942, named for the Biltmore Hotel in New York, the scene of an 'Extraordinary Zionist Conference' attended by more than 600 delegates, mainly American, and some notable international Zionist leaders including Weizmann and Ben-Gurion. The Biltmore Declaration also called for large-scale Jewish settlement of Palestine, thus overturning mainstream Zionism's traditional stance of advocating limited 'elitist' immigration. American Jewry now became the main driving force behind the quest for an independent Jewish state. The number of 'shekel-holders' among American Jewry rose enormously, from 134,497 in 1934–35 to 954,886 in 1946–47, just after the war. While the Biltmore Declaration was passed before the full horror of the Holocaust became known, the decisive shift in Diaspora opinion was largely the product of international Jewish frustration at its inability to rescue European Jewry. Increasingly, Diaspora Jewry saw the creation of a Jewish state as a kind of 'compensation' for the Holocaust, and a phoenix which would rise from the grave of European Jewry. This shift was also the product, in part, of British foolishness in its Palestine policy, most notably over such incidents as the *Struma* episode of 1941–42. The *Struma*, an illegal Romanian immigrant vessel with 770 Jews bound for Palestine, was prevented by British pressure from leaving Istanbul. Eventually towed out to sea by the Turks, it was torpedoed (probably by a Soviet submarine) in February 1942, with the loss of nearly all passengers. Britain appeared in the worst possible light, and (although it had nothing to do with the ship's sinking) as inhumane. While Britain liberalised some of its Palestine immigration policies as a result, the *Struma*, and other similar incidents, heightened hostility to its rule in Palestine.

The end of the Second World War in May 1945 presented a paradoxical picture in Eretz Israel. The Yishuv had survived the war and numbered 554,329 in 1945, a sharp increase from its size in 1935 (335,147) or even in 1939 (445,457). It now numbered 31 per cent of the total population of mandate Palestine, and had evolved a sophisticated political system, press, and culture, many distinctive institutions, and its own language. Because of the Holocaust, it had become one of the largest surviving Jewish communities in the world. But also because of the Holocaust, it surveyed a Jewish world which had just been visited by a catastrophe unprecedented in modern history, one which had affected, in particular, the Jewish 'masses' of eastern Europe whose plight Zionism had come into existence to ameliorate. Nor was it necessarily any closer to achieving either independence from Britain nor peace with the Arabs.

The election of a British Labour government with a large majority in July 1945 naturally raised Zionist hopes. Labour was viewed as sympathetic to Zionism, especially to the socialist Zionist tradition of Ben-Gurion and his colleagues, and as highly sensitive to the plight of the Jewish survivors of Nazism. It soon became clear, however, that the Labour government was almost wholly unsympathetic to Zionist claims and that it was, in practice, if anything worse than previous Tory governments. The foreign secretary, Ernest Bevin (in charge of Palestine policy), a rough-hewn, powerful trade union leader, was viewed, in particular, as bitterly hostile to Zionist goals. The three years between the end of the war and the achievement of Israeli independence in May 1948 were among the bloodiest ever experienced in the history of the Yishuv.

Britain not only refused to grant independence to Eretz Israel, but continued to place strict limits on the number of Jews allowed to enter Palestine. It forbade the hundreds of thousands of Holocaust survivors in

Displaced Persons camps in Germany and elsewhere to enter Eretz Israel, and cracked down even harder on attempts to bring 'illegal' immigrants into Palestine. American President Harry S. Truman (who had succeeded Franklin Roosevelt in April 1945), soon demanded that Britain permit 100,000 Jewish survivors to enter Palestine. Ernest Bevin refused, reaffirming, in November 1945, that only 1500 per month would be permitted to enter. Bevin also established an Anglo-American Commission of Enquiry into the Palestine question. It reported in May 1945, recommending that 100,000 Jewish refugees be permitted to enter Eretz Israel and the 1939 White Paper be abrogated, and that the mandate become a single independent state, divided into Jewish, Arab, and British provinces. This proposal (the Morrison–Grady Plan) pleased no one, and Britain reluctantly promised to implement the Plan only if all private armies in Palestine disbanded.

Palestine now descended, for the final two years of the mandate period, into virtual anarchy and civil war. A Hebrew Resistance Movement, established in late 1945 and including elements of the Haganah, IZL and Lehi, aimed at bringing in 'illegal' immigrants, freeing those captured and imprisoned by the British, and attacking British military targets. After mid-1946, co-operation between the groups deteriorated, with IZL and Lehi engaged in overt terrorism. The most famous examples of violent action by extremist factions in this period included the blowing up of the King David Hotel in Jerusalem in July 1946, in which 91 persons were killed, and the hanging of two British sergeants in July 1947 by Etzel terrorists, in retaliation for the hanging of three Etzel fighters by the British. Both of these became internationally notorious, leading to antisemitic outbreaks in Britain, and were denounced by mainstream Zionist leaders. In contrast, the Zionist movement received much positive publicity for Britain's short-sighted and hamfisted actions in preventing ships carrying illegal immigrants from reaching Eretz Israel. The most famous of these was the *Exodus* episode of July 1947. The *Exodus*, carrying 4515 Holocaust survivors from France to Palestine, was boarded by British sailors and taken back to France. Its passengers refused to disembark and were forcibly taken back to Hamburg and to Displaced Persons Camps in Germany, amidst world-wide negative publicity and ill-will for the British, especially in the United States.

By mid-1947 Palestine had become virtually ungovernable, for the Arabs also began a violent renewal of their 'revolt' against the British and Zionists at the same time. Arab terrorism against the Yishuv escalated dramatically, with dozens of Jewish civilians murdered by the Arabs. The cost, in money, manpower, and negative publicity, to war-exhausted and virtually bankrupt Britain, of remaining in Palestine now became so high that the Labour government decided, in the spring of 1947, to wash its hands of Palestine and to turn the entire problem over to the United Nations, founded two years before (and, as the legal successor to the old League of Nations, technically the sovereign of the mandate). Turning the problem over to the UN meant that the United States and the Soviet Union would now have a greater say in the future of Palestine. America, with its enormous Jewish population, had moved to become strong a supporter of Zionism, while the Soviet Union was also going through one of its infrequent periods of at least lukewarm support for Zionism (probably to hasten the exit of Britain from the Middle East).

In the spring of 1947, a special session of the UN General Assembly was convened to consider the future of Palestine. In August 1947, its investigative committee, composed of members representing eleven countries, unanimously recommended that the mandate be ended immediately. A majority of seven counties also recommended that the mandate be partitioned into a Jewish and an Arab state, with Jerusalem to be internationalised. The Jewish state was to include most of the areas which actually comprised the State of Israel after the 1948–49 war, but with the Arabs holding areas in the upper and western Galilee and Negev that were taken by Israel. A minority of three countries submitted a separate report recommending the establishment in Palestine of a binational federal state in the whole of the mandate. On 29 November 1947 the UN General Assembly approved the majority report by a vote of 33 to 13 (with ten abstentions), meaning that, after nearly 2000 years, an independent Jewish state was likely to come into existence, with widespread international support. Nevertheless, support for an independent Jewish state was far from unanimous. The Arabs continued to oppose it tooth-and-nail, and there was never any chance of the Arab or Muslim block of countries acquiescing in the creation of such a state. While the Soviet Union and its satellites at this stage endorsed Israeli independence, this was soon to change. Newly-independent India was notable for endorsing the minority report, recommending the creation of a binational state, and within a decade or two much of the Third World would become hostile to post-independence Israel.

Further reading

Shlomo Avineri, *Arlosoroff (1899–1933)* (New York, 1989)

Abraham J. Edelheit, *The Yishuv in the Shadow of the Holocaust: Zionist Politics and Rescue Aliya, 1933–1939* (Boulder, Co., 1996)

Isaiah Friedman, ed., *Tension in Palestine: Peacemaking in Paris, 1919,* Rise of Israel series, Vol.10 (New York, 1987)

Martin Gilbert, *Israel: A History* (New York, 1998)

Chaim Herzog, *The Arab–Israeli Wars* (New York, 1982)

Efraim Karsh, ed., *Israel: The First Hundred Years.* Volume 1: *Israel's Transition from Community to State* (London, 2000)

Aaron S. Klieman, ed., *The Intensification of Violence,* Rise of Israel Series, Vol. 20 (New York, 1987)

Walter Laqueur, ed., *The Israel–Arab Reader,* 2nd edn (New York, 1971)

Joseph B. Schechtman, *The Life and Times of Vladimir Jabotinsky* (New York, 1961)

Zc'cv Schiff, *A History of the Israeli Army, 1870–1974* (San Francisco, 1974)

Tom Segev, *One Palestine Complete: Jews and Arabs under the British Mandate* (London, 2000)

Shabatai Teveth, *Ben-Gurion: The Burning Ground, 1886–1948* (Boston, 1987)

Ronald W. Zweig, ed., *David Ben-Gurion: Politics and Leadership in Israel* (London, 1991)

Dina Porat, *The Blue and Yellow Stars of David* (London, 1992)

Yonathan Shapiro, *The Formative Years of the Israeli Labor Party: the Organization of Power* (London, 1976)

Abba Hillel Silver, *Vision and Victory* (New York, 1949)

Bernard Wasserstein, *Britain and the Jews of Europe, 1939–1945* (Oxford, 1979)

|14|

Israel from Independence to the Six Day War, 1948–67

Although an independent State of Israel now became, for the first time, a strong possibility, it was by no means a certainty, and the form the new state would take was far from clear. The fateful two years or so between the passage of the UN's partition resolution in July 1947, and the conclusion of the War of Independence in mid-1949, determined the nature of the State of Israel. A consideration of the fateful events of 1948–49 ought to be divided into a number of separate subjects: the decision to declare the independence of the State of Israel; the state of the military forces of the Yishuv; the stages of the War of Independence; the exodus of the Palestinians; and the creation of the apparatus of a sovereign state with international legitimacy. The leaders of the Yishuv were surprisingly reluctant to declare Israeli independence, fearing that a premature declaration of self-government would lose the crucial support of the United States. As violence in Palestine increased, the United States' government actually began to qualify its support for partition, and was heavily pressured to do so by American oil companies, whose interests in the Arab world were already enormous. Various senior officials of the State Department, including the secretary of state, George Marshall, and the American UN Security Council representative, Warren Austin, were extremely cool to Zionist claims, fearing loss of American influence in the Middle East and a blood bath. In the meantime, the initial stages of the warfare between the Jews and Arabs was going very badly for the outnumbered Zionists. On top of everything else, Britain was doing everything possible to delay or prevent the creation of a Jewish state in Palestine, chiefly under the belief that an Arab-dominated Palestine would give it the best chance of retaining its old imperial interests in the area. It was at this stage, in April–May 1948, that Ben-Gurion decided to force the issue, especially when confronted with the final withdrawal of Britain's troops in Palestine on 1 April, and the final end of the British mandate on 15 May 1948. At the same time, the tide of war began to turn in favour of the Zionists. In early May 1948 Ben-Gurion and most, but not all, of his colleagues decided to declare Israeli independence, come what may, despite continuing American State Department pressure to delay or modify any such declaration. The decisive vote in the Provisional State Council (shortly to become the Israeli Cabinet) to declare independence, taken on 12 May 1948, only three days before the end of the mandate, was only 6:4 in favour of an immediate declaration of Israeli independence.

On 14 May 1948 at 4 pm, in the hall of the Tel Aviv Museum, David Ben-Gurion read out the Israeli Declaration of Independence to the thirty-two delegates who were present, each of whom then signed it. The first act of the new government was to rescind the British White Paper of 1939 and its restrictions on Jewish immigration. A few hours after Israeli independence was declared, President Harry Truman, acting on his own and without the advice of the State Department, extended *de facto* recognition to the State of Israel (the name the new state had chosen to call itself). Truman, a philosemite who had once had a Jewish pro-Zionist business partner, had become friendly with Chaim Weizmann, who crucially influenced him in support of Zionism. That a presidential election was less than six months away was not lost on cynics. Within a few days several other nations, including, extraordinarily, the Soviet Union, recognised Israel's existence, although Britain did not extend even *de facto* recognition to the new state until 30 January 1949, following a period of very bad relations indeed.

All of this took place against the background of a destructive war which Israel nearly lost. Analysts often divide this war into a number of separate phases. The first, usually seen as lasting from the partition vote in November 1947 until the end of March 1948, witnessed Arab violence directed at Jewish targets, frequently with British connivance. Late in 1947 the Arabs attempted to capture outlying Jewish settlements but were repulsed. Early in 1948 an Arab volunteer army under Fawzi al-Qawudji entered Palestine and took control of the Arab north, while other Arab forces entered from the south. These achieved some success in isolating the outlying settlements and Jerusalem from the main areas of Jewish settlement. The Yishuv, of course, had no formal army of its own (while the independent Arab states like Egypt had large armies) and had to form one from whatever existed. It used the remnants of the existing self-defence force, the Haganah, and, in addition, two unofficial forces of extreme Zionist groups outside the mainstream's formal structure, the Irgun or IZL and Lehi. Both bodies were renowned for their ruthless attacks on the British and the Arabs. Although they co-operated, these various forces were not centrally led and lacked modern weaponry.

Between early April and 14 May 1948 the Haganah recaptured much of the ground it had lost, taking Tiberias and Haifa. It was also at this time that Lehi and the Irgun captured the Arab village of Deir Yassin. A terrible massacre occurred – of up to 250 Arab civilians – which was condemned by the Zionist mainstream. The brutal treatment accorded to these Arabs probably spurred the Arab exodus from Jewish areas. The Arabs engaged in

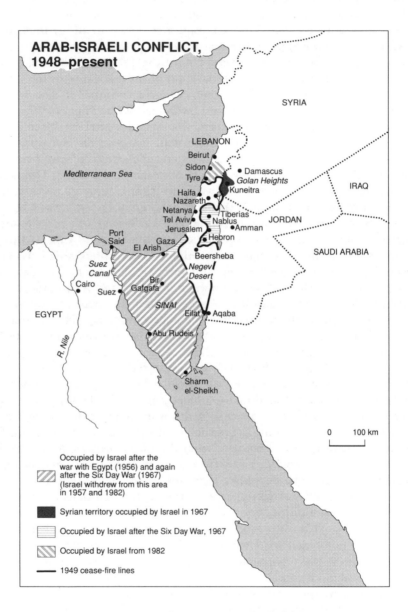

ARAB-ISRAELI CONFLICT, 1948–present

SYRIA

LEBANON

Beirut

Sidon
• Damascus
Tyre
Golan Heights

IRAQ

Haifa
Kuneitra
Nazareth

Netanya
Tiberias

Tel Aviv
Nablus

JORDAN

Jerusalem
Amman

Port
Hebron
Said
Gaza
El Arish
Beersheba

SAUDI ARABIA

Mediterranean Sea

*Suez
Canal*
Bir
*Negev
Desert*
Cairo
Gafgafa
Suez

SINAI

EGYPT
Eilat • Aqaba

•Abu Rudeis

R. Nile

Sharm
el-Sheikh

0   100 km

Occupied by Israel after the
war with Egypt (1956) and again
after the Six Day War (1967)
(Israel withdrew from this area
in 1957 and 1982)

Syrian territory occupied by Israel in 1967

Occupied by Israel after the Six Day War, 1967

Occupied by Israel from 1982

—— 1949 cease-fire lines

massacres of their own: for instance, a particularly infamous slaughter of 77 Jewish doctors, nurses and patients on the road to Hadassah Hospital on Mount Scopus, in Jerusalem, on 15 April 1949, a week after Deir Yassin.

Israeli independence on 15 May 1948 changed the character of the war. In place of volunteers, five Arab armies, led by Egypt's King Farouk, now invaded Palestine with the aim of destroying the Jewish state. This invasion was obviously in violation of every canon of international law, and was apparently prompted in part by Farouk's wish to foil Transjordan's King Abdullah, who supposedly had plans to annex Arab Palestine. Syria, Lebanon, and Iraq also entered the war, although the campaign of the Arab Legion, as it became known, was never co-ordinated. Nevertheless, it initially met with considerable success, with Egyptian forces moving to within 25 miles of Tel Aviv, the Jordanians capturing the Old City, the Jewish quarter of Jerusalem, and Syria moving into Galilee. The Arab high-point came around June 1948.

Thereafter, the tide turned strongly in Israel's favour. Aircraft and weaponry from Czechoslovakia, France, and (illicitly) the United States began pouring in; Ben-Gurion unified the Haganah, Lehi, and the Irgun into a single body, the Israel Defence Forces (IDF), on 31 May 1948, and a UN-imposed ceasefire took effect on 10 June 1948, relieving the tired and beleaguered Israeli forces. The resumption of the war on 10 July 1948 saw swift gains by the Israelis, which continued after another ceasefire in late July. By October 1948 the Israelis had captured most of Galilee and the Negev and had even penetrated into the Sinai. The only unsuccessful phase of the war was Israel's failure to recapture Jerusalem, which, despite desperate attempts, remained in Arab hands until 1967. The area of the new Jewish state was thus considerably larger than that envisioned by the UN Partition Plan, with the Jews having gained the whole of Galilee, the southern coast to Ashkelon, and the northern Negev, including Beersheva, all areas which were to have been included in the proposed Palestinian state. The almost miraculous Israeli victories had been achieved despite the expectations of virtually every 'expert' that the pacific Jews would surely be annihilated by the large, professional armies of the Arab states.

Early in January 1949 Egypt, with its back now to the wall, agreed to a ceasefire, and negotiations between Egypt and Israel took place on the island of Rhodes the same month, chaired by the celebrated black American diplomat Ralph Bunche. A formal armistice, setting the boundary between Israel and Egypt, was signed on 24 February 1949, and other armistices quickly followed with Transjordan, Lebanon, and, on 20 July 1949, with Syria. Expectations that these would lead to normal diplomatic relations between Israel and its Arab neighbours were high, but no Arab state made a formal peace treaty with Israel until the Camp David accords between Israel and Egypt of September 1978, almost 30 years later. Even in the early twenty-first century Israel had formal diplomatic relations with only six of the 20 or more Arab states. A considerable measure of international legitimacy for

Israel came with its admission to the United Nations as a member state in May 1949.

Although Israel did indeed win the War of Independence, the costs to it were very great indeed. In November 1948 the first census of the new state was conducted, which found a total population of 713,000 Jews and 69,000 Arabs. In the War of Independence, Israel lost about 6000 dead (4000 of whom were soldiers), just under 1 per cent of its total Jewish population. To put this in perspective, during the Second World War Great Britain, with a population of 45 million, lost almost precisely the same proportion of its population, 463,000 persons (398,000 military dead and 65,000 civilian). But these British deaths occurred over six years of fighting, in campaigns which extended from Normandy to El Alamein to Burma, and through German bombings of British cities, in a war which was fought (from 1941) in alliance with the Soviet Union and the United States. In contrast, Israel's losses were recorded between November 1947 and January 1949, in an area the size of Wales, and in a war fought without allies against five murderous if not genocidal hostile armies. Tens of thousands of Jews, a people lacking a military tradition or infrastructure for 2000 years, became successful soldiers, knowing that the penalty for military failure was literally destruction.

The victorious War of Independence utterly changed the demography of Palestine. Whereas the area set aside by the UN for a Jewish state had contained 528,000 Jews and 397,000 Arabs, while the proposed Arab state held 804,000 Arabs and 10,000 Jews, in December 1949, after the ending of the War of Independence and high levels of *aliyah*, the Jewish population of the new state, in its post-armistice boundaries, was 1,014,000 and the Arab population only 174,000. The Jews thus accounted for 85 per cent of the total population, a vastly higher percentage than ever before in the history of the Yishuv, and enough to make the new state overwhelmingly and assuredly Jewish.

Part of the reason for this Jewish population ascendancy lay in heavy immigration, but the decline in the Arab population was caused by the flight of hundreds of thousands of Palestinian Arabs to other parts of the mandate and to neighbouring Arab states, where they festered as impoverished and resentful refugees. The emigration of so many Palestinian Arabs – the most generally accepted figure is that about 600,000 Palestinians fled from their homes, although other estimates range from 500,000 to 750,000 – is unquestionably the most controversial aspect of the circumstances surrounding the creation of Israel. The lengthy controversy surrounding their flight cannot possibly be examined in full here, but some points appear clear. First, repeated Israeli claims that they fled in response to radio appeals by Arab leaders that they do so cannot be substantiated. On the other hand, it does appear that the typical social structure of the mandate Palestinians, with heavy reliance by the masses on clan and village leaders and chieftains, greatly spurred the general exodus: when the Palestinian leadership emigrated (as they did from Haifa and elsewhere), the masses followed. Most

Palestinians left hurriedly, packing few belongings, believing their leave-taking to be temporary and that they would return once the Arab Legion had annihilated the Zionists. One important point worth making, but which is noted too seldom, is that most of the Arabs fled to areas set aside by the UN for an independent Palestinian state. This state (unlike Israel) did not come into existence in 1948, in large part because the Arab states would not allow it, but also because the Palestinians refused to recognise the legitimacy of the partition plan. *Had* an Arab Palestinian state come into existence in 1948, as was planned, in a larger area (and possibly including Jerusalem) than that seriously discussed half a century later, the whole history of the Arab–Israeli conflict could have been entirely different and immeasurably more peaceful.

The effects of the 'catastrophe' (as the Palestinians term it) on the Palestinian psyche and culture were, of course, profound. Israel's attitude was that the Arabs refused to accept Israel's independence and launched a war of annihilation to destroy it, and the exodus of the Palestinians was therefore permanent, to be resolved by the Arab states or, perhaps, in a general and final settlement of the conflict. Originally, Israel offered to take back 100,000 fleeing Palestinians but withdrew this offer in 1950 after continuing Arab intransigence. About 174,000 Palestinians remained in Israel, and Israel absorbed, over the next few decades, up to one million Jews expelled from the Arab world: so why, it asked, could the Arab states not absorb the Palestinians? Most remained, and in part remain, in wretched refugee camps, their situation still unresolved more than a century later.

Many decades after the events of 1947–49, a group of so-called 'New Historians' in Israel questioned many of the long-held assumptions pertaining to the state's foundation, arguing, for instance, that the Israelis had always intended to expel the Palestinians and that they won the War of Independence by collusion with Jordan's King Abdullah, who acquiesced in their victory in exchange for the West Bank (which was, in fact, absorbed by Transjordan in 1949–50). Many other historians dispute these interpretations, which assume that Israel's leadership could somehow have known in advance how the Middle East would evolve in the 1940s and which understate the sheer desperation of the Zionist struggle against the odds in 1947–49. The 'New Historians' also rely on full access to Israeli and Western archival documentation, but cannot see or consider confidential Arab sources. Nevertheless, their work is evidence that these events remain as controversial as ever and that the last word has obviously not been said on the foundations of Israel.

Ben-Gurion and his colleagues founded a functioning state in May 1948, and had to decide on everything related to the nature of that state. The first task was to decide what to call it, for it had no commonly-accepted name until immediately before independence, and the founders of the nation were torn between 'Israel', 'Judea', and 'The Jewish State' (as in Herzl's book) before choosing the first. The flag, coat of arms, and symbolism of the state were taken from that of the Zionist movement, and, invariably and without exception, emphasised the unbroken continuity of the State of Israel with the Biblical kingdom of Israel, with the 1800 years between them being regarded as an unfortunate interregnum. The entirety of Jewish history in the Diaspora – *galut* ('exile') as it is known in Zionist circles – was omitted from the symbolism of the new state.

The nature of the political institutions of the State of Israel will be considered below, but a number of other matters should be noted here. The first law passed by the new government was to abolish the restrictions on Jewish immigration to Palestine contained in the MacDonald White Paper (see Chapter 13), and the Israeli Declaration of Independence promised that the state 'will be open to the immigration of Jews from all countries of their dispersion.' Hundreds of thousands of Jewish immigrants immediately flocked in. This itself represented a reversal of mainstream Zionist thinking, which looked to immigration based upon a selective, committed elite, and represented the triumph of the views of Jabotinsky, who called for mass immigration. This new situation was given official status by the famous Law of Return, passed by Israel's parliament, the Knesset, in July 1950, which gives every Jew in the world the automatic right to emigrate to Israel. Soon after the War of Independence, the nature of the Israeli military was also settled. The Israeli Defence Forces (IDF) were organised into a regular army and a reserve (together with an Air Force and Navy). All Israeli men normally must serve for three years, and all women for two years, although *yeshivah* students are exempt. Moreover, all men must serve an additional 30–45 days per year in reserve duty until they are 55, the aim being to place a substantial, well-prepared army in the field instantaneously during an emergency. Arabs in Israel are exempt from conscription, although since 1955 the Druze (a separate religious-ethnic group which broke away from Islam in the eleventh century, and who number about 70,000 in Israel) have been eligible for conscription. The IDF is, of course, subject to civilian authority, specifically to the Ministry of Defence, but throughout Israeli history it has acquired more of a life of its own than its counterparts in most other Western countries. The leading generals, especially the chiefs of staff, are national (indeed international) figures who have frequently entered politics, sometimes rising to the highest places. For most of its history the IDF has been one of the most prestigious institutions in Israel, and military life and its consequences have permeated every aspect of Israeli society.

While Israel's Declaration of Independence guaranteed 'freedom of religion' to everyone, Judaism plays a far more central role in Israeli society than religion does in other Western states. There is, for instance, no civil marriage or divorce in Israel, and all marriages have to be conducted by Jewish, Muslim, Christian, or other recognised clergymen. Most of Israel comes to a halt on Saturday, the Jewish Sabbath. A separate Orthodox school system exists side-by-side with the state school system. Only Orthodox Judaism is officially recognised, and efforts to establish a large Reform or Conservative Jewish presence have met great opposition. Most

Jewish religious matters, including such things as *kashrut* (dietary regulations) and burial, are decided by the two chief rabbis and their councils, those of the Ashkenazi and Sephardi communities. From the foundation of the state, Orthodox political parties became deeply involved in politics, being included in nearly all governments and Cabinets, with the aim of securing state aid for their members and halting secularist tendencies in Israel.

Key personalities in the early history of Israel

From before its foundation the State of Israel's political scene was dominated by a number of key personalities who set their stamp on the Jewish state, and whose careers and viewpoints must be examined in any account of Israeli history. The most important figure in the early history of the State of Israel was, of course, David Ben-Gurion (1886–1973), who was born in Plonsk, Russia, under the name of David Gruen ('Ben-Gurion', adopted by him in 1910 after making *aliyah*, means 'Son of a Lion' in Hebrew; it had been the name of one of the last defenders of Jerusalem against the Roman occupation).[1] As noted above, Ben-Gurion built up a strong power base in the Histradut and in the Mapai party of mainstream socialist Zionists. From 1935 he was also chairman of the Zionist Executive and the Jewish Agency, in effect the formal government of the Jewish community in Palestine. By the outbreak of the Second World War, Ben-Gurion was thus effectively the recognised leader of the Yishuv and its prime minister-in-waiting. As a general rule, he worked effectively with Chaim Weizmann (1874–1952), the suave leader of the World Zionist Organization, who lived in Manchester. In general, Weizmann was better able to deal with Britain's governing elites than was the rough-hewn Ben-Gurion, and was much better known to the general public until Israel's independence. Ben-Gurion's leadership of the Yishuv was contested from a number of sources, especially by the right-wing Revisionist Zionists led by Jabotinsky. Until the Second World War, Ben-Gurion favoured the step-by-step approach to Jewish immigration to Palestine found among most mainstream Zionist leaders. In 1937 he supported the Peel Commission's proposal (which came to nothing) for the creation of a small Jewish state in Palestine. Despite Ben-Gurion's hostility to the MacDonald White Paper of May 1939, which severely limited Jewish immigration to Palestine, he supported Britain's war efforts against Nazi Germany, famously saying that the Jews would 'fight the war as if there were no White Paper and the White Paper as if there were no war'. In reality, he could do neither well, but certainly did not hinder Britain's war

---

1 Most early leaders of the Yishuv and the State of Israel were born in eastern Europe under a typical Ashkenazi surname. In Palestine most changed their original surname to a more Hebrew-sounding one, by which they are known to history.

efforts (as some extreme Zionists wished), recognising Nazi Germany as plainly the supreme evil, and did his best to crack down against extremist anti-British terrorist groups.

The war radicalised Ben-Gurion's stance in a number of ways. In May 1942 he became the driving force behind the so-called 'Biltmore Declaration', named after the place where it was formulated, which, as described in Chapter 13, defined the Zionist movement's goal, officially for the first time, as that of the creation of an independent Jewish state. Ben-Gurion's attitude to the Holocaust has given rise to endless debate, and remains puzzling: he, it seems, simply did not know what to make of the catastrophe unfolding in Europe and, it is sometimes argued, did much less to fight Nazism than he might have done.

By 1947, however, Ben-Gurion was ready to assume power as the head of an independent Jewish state. He lost no time in declaring Israeli independence in May 1948, becoming prime minister and minister of defence. He fought the War of Independence with ruthless efficiency, organising a unified army, the Israel Defence Forces, which triumphantly defeated the Arab attempt to annihilate the Jewish state, although it was unable to conquer the Jewish holy places in Jerusalem. The first years of Israeli independence were largely taken up with absorbing vast numbers of new immigrants, especially the total of 685,000 *olim* who arrived between May 1948 and 1951. Ben-Gurion oversaw the immigration of most Holocaust survivors and of most Jews in the surviving eastern European communities, especially Romania and Bulgaria. He also supervised the transfer of over 250,000 Sephardi Jews from the Afro-Asian world, sharply altering the demographic nature of the new state, whose population had previously been heavily Ashkenazi. Ben-Gurion put his stamp on the Israeli constitution through his adoption of the Basic Law of 1950, which has remained Israel's *de facto* constitution, the Law of Return of 1950, and many other measures. Although not politically associated with Orthodox Jewry, he granted *yeshivah* students exemption from military conscription in order to build up a significant centre of Orthodoxy in Israel to compensate for the destroyed world of the *yeshivot* in eastern Europe. He also initiated the settlement of the largely uninhabited Negev in the south of the country. Ben-Gurion's most controversial act was his establishment of diplomatic relations with West Germany, resulting in the Restitution Agreement of 1952, under which West Germany agreed to pay vast amounts in compensation to Israel for Nazi crimes against the Jews. The Restitution Agreement was vehemently opposed by many elements in Israeli society, especially by Menahem Begin's Herut Party, and violent demonstrations ensued, the worst in Israel's history.

While Ben-Gurion bestrode the Israeli political scene like a colossus, he was unpredictable and an enigma to even his closest colleagues. In 1953 he suddenly left the government to live on a *kibbutz* in the Negev, rejoining the government in 1955 after the Lavon Affair (see pp. 354–55). He entered into the bizarre agreement with Britain and France to invade the Sinai, leading to the Suez Crisis in 1956. All of his attempts to reach accommodation with the Arabs failed, chiefly because of the absence of moderate Arab leaders willing to engage openly in negotiations with Israel: these would have to await another generation. Perhaps stung by the Kasztner Affair of 1955–57, which reopened the question of alleged Zionist inactivity (some said collaboration) during the Holocaust, Ben-Gurion masterminded the kidnapping and trial of Adolf Eichmann in 1960–62. The Eichmann trial is often seen as a fundamental turning-point in the world's consciousness of the Holocaust, opening the floodgates of histories and memoirs which have continued until today. In all, Ben-Gurion was prime minister of Israel for nearly 14 years, from 1948 to 1954, and then from 1955 until 1963. In June 1963, at the age of 77, he resigned from his offices, although he remained a member of the Knesset, and an active participant on the political scene, until 1970. In his retirement he wrote widely on Biblical topics and archaeology.

David Ben-Gurion was the 'father of his country' in much the same way as were Nehru, Masaryk, de Valera, Nkrumah, and, indeed, George Washington. His political philosophy stressed the concept of what he termed *mamlakhtiyut* ('statism'), in which the Israeli state ran most of the country's institutions. He remained staunchly pro-Western, and his attractive brand of social democracy, together with the universal perception at the time of Israel being the 'David' to the Arabs' 'Goliath', gave him unmatched prestige in the West, especially among Americans. He favoured a relatively moderate course in dealing with the Arabs, recommending the return of most territories conquered in the Six Day War. Despite this, he opposed the creation of a Palestinian state or the resettlement of Palestinian refugees. Many Western observers of the Israeli political scene believe that the downhill slide in Israel's reputation began with Ben-Gurion's retirement. His colleague Golda Meir called him 'the greatest Jew in our generation', and there are few other claimants to this title who can match Ben-Gurion's extraordinary list of achievements.

Although Ben-Gurion dominated the Israeli political scene during his lifetime, there were many other leading politicians who should be mentioned in any account of the history of Israel between 1948 and 1973. Three other persons held the office of Israeli prime minister during these years: Moshe Sharett, Levi Eshkol, and Golda Meir. Moshe Sharett (1894–1965) was born in Russia and emigrated to Palestine at the age of 12, completing his education in Tel Aviv and serving in the Turkish army. He began to rise in Labour Zionist circles in the early 1930s, becoming head of the Jewish Agency's political department following the assassination of Haim Arlosoroff in 1933. More cautious and pro-British than Ben-Gurion, he helped to establish the Jewish Legion during the Second World War with British co-operation. He led the successful diplomatic efforts to secure the UN's partition of Palestine in 1947, and became Israel's first foreign minister in 1948, an office he held until 1956. Sharett unsuccessfully sought an accommodation with the Arabs. His two years as prime minister were very difficult, being marked by the 'Lavon Affair', increasing armed militancy against the Arabs, and a sense that he was merely keeping the seat warm until Ben-Gurion returned to power; this indeed came about in 1955. Sharett opposed the 1956 Sinai war. Although he served as chairman of the Jewish Agency Executive in the early 1960s, his softer line in international affairs gradually became less popular. Sharett was a distinguished writer and a linguist who knew seven languages.

Following Ben-Gurion's final retirement in 1963, Levi Eshkol (1895–1969) became Israel's third prime minister. His early years were like those of so many other early Israeli leaders; born in the Ukraine and educated in a traditional Orthodox fashion in Vilna, he became a keen Zionist as a teenager and emigrated to Palestine in 1914. Active in both the Yishuv's self-defence forces and Labour politics, he was head of the Tel Aviv Workers' Council, a powerful trade union body, from 1944 to 1948. In 1948 he became deputy defence minister and then a long-serving (1952–63) and successful minister of finance. He enjoyed a reputation as a mediator and conciliator, which, with his wide experience, led to his appointment as prime minister after Ben-Gurion relinquished that office. He drew closer to the United States and also to the European Community, but was attacked by Ben-Gurion and his followers as a maladroit leader. As the international situation deteriorated in 1967, Eshkol was forced to give up the Defence Ministry to Moshe Dayan, the famous general who was, politically, closely associated with Ben-Gurion's faction. Eshkol also broadened the Israeli Cabinet to become a Government of National Unity, even including Menahem Begin, leader of Herut and a virtual pariah during much of his career, as minister without portfolio. The triumphant Six Day War of 1967 (see below) witnessed one of the greatest feats of arms in modern history, yet few give much credit to Eshkol for the victory. Few, indeed, even remember that he was Israel's prime minister at the time. Eshkol continued as prime minister until his death in 1969. He was well-aware that Israel's sweeping victory was a very mixed blessing, with two million conquered Palestinians likely to be a source of endless trouble for the Jewish State, but, in view of Arab hostility to Israel, could see no alternative to holding on to the acquired territories pending a peace treaty. Eshkol's most important achievement may well be seen as the reorientation of Israel's foreign policy towards a staunchly pro-American position, which he pursued with high profile visits to President Lyndon Johnson and other leading American officials.

Israel's most unusual leader during these years, and certainly one of its most renowned, was Golda Meir (*née* Mabovitch, but generally known by her married name of Meyerson until the 1950s, when she changed this to 'Meir', 1898–1978). Like so many others born in tsarist Russia (where she survived a pogrom), she emigrated at the age of eight not to Palestine but to Milwaukee in the United States, where she trained as a schoolteacher. A keen Labour Zionist from an early age, she emigrated to Palestine in 1921 with her husband (from whom she separated) and rose within the Council of Working Women in the Histadrut. Gaining a reputation as a skilful and intelligent operator, she became head of the Political Department of the Jewish Agency in 1946 when Moshe Sharett was arrested by the British. In 1947–48 she held a number of important secret negotiations with Jordan's King Abdullah in an effort to achieve peace. In 1949 she was appointed Israel's initial Ambassador to the Soviet Union, her arrival in Moscow being greeted with unprecedented scenes of Jewish jubilation, despite Stalinist oppression. She served as Israel's minister of labour from 1949 to 1956 and then as foreign minister, 1956–66, when she built up Israeli links with Africa. When Eshkol died in 1969, she became prime minister, in part because of her skill as a negotiator among Labour's rival factions, and in part, perhaps, because of her American links and fame there. As one of the few women heads of state (and the only Israeli woman who had risen to such heights) she was naturally regarded as a pioneer and was certainly one of the most visible of world leaders. Her record as prime minister, however, was very mixed. A natural peace-maker, she was forced to contend both with adamant Arab hostility to negotiations with Israel and to a growing Israeli mood of invincibility and hubris. The Soviet Union and most of its satellites severed diplomatic links with Israel in 1967, and the Jewish state became the subject of innumerable hostile motions in the United Nations. It was also during the period 1969–73 that Palestinian terrorism became ubiquitous, culminating in such events as the massacre of Israeli athletes at the Munich Olympics of 1972. At home, a deep sense of resentment at the 'Ashkenazi Establishment' arose among many Sephardim. Although Golda Meir wished to retire in mid-1973, she stayed on, only to find that Israel had become the victim of a surprise attack by the Arabs in October 1973, the Yom Kippur War described in Chapter 15. She proved a successful war leader, and, 18 days after the conflict had begun on 6 October 1973, Israel found itself on the road to Cairo and in possession of the whole Golan Heights. Although Meir accepted the UN-imposed ceasefire, she felt deep remorse at the human cost of the war for which Israel had been unprepared, and finally resigned as prime minister in April 1974. She died four years later, opposed to the Camp David Accords.

Apart from its prime ministers, Israel had many other leading politicians of note in the period 1948–73. There were three holders of the largely ceremonial office of president: Chaim Weizmann, Yitzhak Ben-Zvi, and Zalman Shazar. Weizmann (1874–1952), the renowned president of the World Zionist Organization for most of the period from 1920 until the foundation of the state, was generally a moderate and, as such, was frequently opposed by extreme Zionists. Nevertheless, his great prestige was highly significant in securing Israeli independence, and Ben-Gurion insisted that Weizmann become, first, president of the Provisional Council of Israel and then the country's foundation president, a post he formally took up in February

1949. His powers were almost entirely ceremonial, while his poor health prevented him from playing much of an official role. When Weizmann died, Ben-Gurion offered the presidency to Albert Einstein, who declined (Einstein was a long-time, if unorthodox, Zionist; had he taken up the offer he would undoubtedly have brought enormous esteem and prestige to the new state). Instead, the post went to Ben-Gurion's lifelong friend and collaborator Yitzhak Ben-Zvi (1884–1963), who had known Ben-Gurion since 1907. Closely associated with the Histadrut, Ben-Zvi had served as chairman of the *Va'ad Le'umi* (the Jewish National Council, the community council of the Jews of Palestine established in 1920; it administered local government, education, and taxation among the Jews of the Yishuv). Ben-Zvi served as president for ten years, from 1953 until 1963, longer than anyone else. Israel's third president was Zalman Shazar (1889–1974). Like so many others Russian-born, he received an Orthodox education, became a Zionist, and migrated to Palestine in 1924. A leading Labour Zionist in the Ben-Gurion mould, he served as minister of education and culture and then as chairman of the Jewish Agency Executive. Holding the presidency from 1973 to 1978, he travelled widely and also welcomed Pope Paul VI to Israel in 1964. Like his predecessors, he was a scholar of substance.

Israel also produced other notable Cabinet ministers, only a few of whom can be mentioned here. Pinchas Sapir (1907–75), Polish-born, made *aliyah* in 1929 and served as Levi Eshkol's deputy before independence. He held a variety of important positions from 1953 through 1972, including minister of finance for most of the period between 1963 and 1972. Sapir was renowned as a power-broker and 'numbers man' in the Labour party, jotting down notes in a black book he carried around with him. In politics he was a moderate, opposing Israeli expansion, largely on economic grounds. Abba Eban (b.1915), the South African-born, Cambridge-educated diplomat, educator, and politician, became certainly one of the three or four most famous Israeli public figures in the 1960s and 1970s, especially during his term as foreign minister from 1966 to 1974. A renowned and eloquent orator, he frequently presented Israel's case at the United Nations, becoming widely known for his lucidity and cogency. He was also the narrator of the nine-part television series on Jewish history, *Heritage*, which was shown in many countries. Yosef Burg (b.1909), who was born in Germany and ordained as a rabbi, migrated to Palestine in 1939. After Israel's independence he was one of the founders of the National Religious Party (NRP), holding Cabinet office in virtually every government from the early 1950s until 1986. He was one of the first leaders of Orthodox Judaism to appreciate the electoral potential of the Orthodox bloc in the context of the Israeli political system. Burg was associated with Hamizrachi, a relatively moderate (by later standards) Orthodox grouping; he was regarded as relatively moderate for an Orthodox Jewish political leader.

The early years of the Jewish state also saw the emergence of many renowned military leaders, some of whom subsequently entered Israeli politics and became significant figures; some became famous for other reasons. Only a few of the most significant can be noted here. Yigal Yadin (1917–84), born in Jerusalem, was the second chief of staff of the Israel Defence Forces. Serving as active chief of staff during the War of Independence, he was frequently at odds with Ben-Gurion, and resigned his military posts in 1952. Yadin became world-famous as an archaeologist, especially in the excavation of Masada, and served as deputy prime minister in Menahem Begin's Cabinet from 1977 until 1980. Moshe Dayan (1915–81) was unquestionably Israel's most famous soldier; with his eye-patch he was instantly recognised around the world. Born on a farm in Palestine, Dayan was arrested by the British as a member of the Zionist underground in 1939 but later released and served in Lebanon, where a sniper shot out one of his eyes. He served with distinction in the War of Independence and was a protégé of Ben-Gurion, rising to Israeli Chief of Staff in 1953 at the age of only 38. Dayan led the Sinai campaign of 1956, and was appointed defence minister just before the outbreak of the 1964 war, in which he lead Israel to its remarkable victory. His reputation as one of the greatest soldiers in history was somewhat tarnished by his erratic performance in the opening stages of the 1973 war. Dayan served as a Cabinet minister under David Ben-Gurion, Levi Eshkol, Golda Meir, and, remarkably in view of his Labour affinities, from 1977 until 1979 as foreign minister under Menahem Begin, who was instrumental in forging the Camp David Accords with Egypt. Dayan was surely one of the most remarkable figures produced by the State of Israel in its early decades. Many other personalities who were highly important in Israel during the period 1948–73, including Menahem Begin and Yitzhak Rabin, are discussed in Chapter 15.

The government of Israel and its political history, 1948–56

The rather peculiar format of the government of the State of Israel chiefly emerged from the Jewish quasi-governmental institutions of the Yishuv. Early in 1948, before independence, a 37-member People's Council, headed by David Ben-Gurion, was constituted, proportionately representing each party in the main elected Jewish bodies of the Yishuv. This council in turn declared itself to be the provisional government of Israel and, on 15 May 1948, formally declared Israeli independence. The Israeli Declaration of Independence authorised the election of a Constituent Assembly or parliament no later than October 1948. Owing to the war of independence, its election was postponed until January 1949, when the first elections for Israel's parliament, the Knesset (Hebrew: 'assembly'), were held. The Constituent Assembly maintained essentially the same unusual electoral system which had existed for elections to the *Va'ad Le'umi* (which administered local government in the Yishuv) and the Jewish Agency before independence. Under this system, which has continued to exist throughout Israeli history, there are no constituencies in the sense known in most other parliaments: no one is, for instance, the member of the Knesset for Tel Aviv north-west. Instead, the entire Israeli Knesset of 120 members is regarded as a single constituency, with each political party nominating a list of potential members in descending order of preference, and the leader of the party placed first on the ballot. When the totality of votes in an Israeli election is counted, each party is allotted the number of Knesset members proportionate to its share of the vote, provided that it has obtained at least 2 per cent of the total vote. For instance, if Labour receives 30 per cent of all the votes cast in an election, it receives roughly 30 per cent – 40 seats – of the Knesset's 120 seats, the top 40 nominees (in descending order) being elected. Every Knesset member is thus elected for the entire country rather than a particular locality. Consequently, members are totally beholden to the party which has nominated them, and can only establish a separate power base by forming a separate party and successfully contesting an election.

The most important outcome of this procedure is that small parties, those representing particular (often extreme) political positions or special interests, are greatly advantaged and are assured of having seats in the Knesset provided that they can obtain a mere 2 per cent of the vote. This feature has prevented Israel from developing a two-party system, and has, in practice, greatly advantaged Orthodox religious parties, which have used their bloc votes to gain many concessions from the government. The method of election has also worked to prevent the growth of particular local loyalties or constituencies, and has thus arguably enhanced the Knesset's sense of working for the national interest. It has also greatly increased the power of the political parties as such, especially their permanent infrastructures, as pathways to successful patronage and public spending.

The Constituent Assembly also gave the vote to every 'inhabitant' of Israel, including all non-Jews. Israel was thus the first nation in the Middle East to give the vote to Arab women and, indeed, one of the very few Middle Eastern nations with electoral democracy in the Western sense. It also set the minimum voting age at 18. Most Western countries did not set the minimum age at 18 (rather than 21) until two decades later.

In the first election of the Constituent Assembly, Mapai, headed by Ben-Gurion, won 46 of the 120 seats. Although it was the largest single party, it was forced into coalition with most of the other significant parties in the Knesset, except those of the extreme left and right. In Ben-Gurion's famous phrase, he would govern in coalition with anyone but 'without Herut and Maki'. (Herut was the right-wing nationalist party founded by the followers of Vladimir Jabotinsky, while Maki was the Israel Communist Party.) Throughout its history Israel has usually been governed by a coalition of parties; until 1977 these coalitions were always based in the centre-left and headed by Ben-Gurion or one of his followers. Israeli political parties have come and gone in a remarkably bewildering fashion, often dividing into factions or suddenly growing from nothing. It might, therefore, be helpful to examine the more important parties during the first 25 years of Israeli history.

The largest single party for this period was Mapai, which existed from 1930 until 1968. It was a democratic Zionist socialist party, very pragmatic in dealing with other forces in Israeli society and generally very pro-Western in its foreign policy orientation. Mapai was dominated by Ben-Gurion until his retirement in 1963. In 1964 it joined with several other left-of-centre parties to form the Alignment, which, from 1968, has been known officially as the Israel Labour Party. To the left of Mapai was Mapam, a left-wing socialist party which was pro-Moscow in its foreign policy, yet never a Communist party in the strict sense. Although it was the second largest party in the first Knesset, electing 19 members, its numbers have declined since the mid-1950s. Mapam has, since 1967, been friendlier than many other Israeli parties to the West Bank Arabs. The third largest party in the first Knesset was the United Religious Front, which elected 16 members. It was a coalition of all Orthodox Jewish factions; in subsequent Israeli elections this unity broke down and the various Orthodox strands (which had very different constituencies and policies) contested elections separately. Among the most notable Orthodox Jewish parties which contested elections after 1948 were: Agudat Israel (which had been strongly opposed to the establishment of the State of Israel); Poalei Agudat Yisrael, a more moderate breakaway movement which supported Zionism; Hamizrachi, an emphatically pro-Zionist Orthodox group, and Hapoel Hamizrachi, a labour Orthodox party. In 1956 the pro-Zionist Orthodox parties united to form the National Religious Party (NRP), which has been a coalition party in many Israeli governments. All the Orthodox parties are united in opposing secular trends in Israeli society and in attempting to gain as many privileges as possible for the institutions of Orthodox Judaism in Israel, especially the *yeshivot*. They have also supported the long-standing exemption of *yeshivah* students from conscription and a change in the 'Law of Return' to delegitimise conversions to Judaism carried out by non-Orthodox rabbis. In the early days of Israel, their aims were acquiesced in or supported by many secular political leaders, including Ben-Gurion, in part owing to recognition of the catastrophic losses suffered by the Orthodox world in eastern Europe during the Holocaust (and under Soviet rule), and the historic necessity for Israel to emerge as a centre of Orthodox Jewish life. In recent decades, however, a major divide has opened between the secular and Orthodox communities of Israel, with many secular Jews believing that the Orthodox have become too powerful.

Another successful party in the early Knessets were the General Zionists. This grouping was originally formed at the 1929 Zionist Congress, and represented the non-socialist, non-religious strands within Zionism, chiefly based among the Zionist movement's middle-class supporters. In 1931 it split into two factions (formally known as Faction A and Faction B!), the former (headed by Chaim Weizmann) closer to Labour Zionism and the latter more right-wing. With the formation of the State of Israel, the two factions contested the Knesset elections under different names, respectively the Progressive Party and the General Zionists or Centre Party. The latter was the closest thing to a centre-right party that the new state possessed, although it was also very liberal (in the Western sense), calling for a secular, liberal constitution. It elected seven members to the first Knesset but no fewer than 20 to the second, elected in 1951, while the Progressive Party elected five and four members at these elections respectively. After the early 1960s the General Zionists moved closer to Herut, establishing first (1961) the Liberal Party and then, in 1965, Gahal (the acronym of *Gush Herut-Liberalim*), a formal coalition with Herut.

On the right of Israeli politics was Herut ('Freedom' in Hebrew), founded by supporters of Jabotinsky and former members of the Irgun. From the start it was headed by Menahem Begin, who was to become one of the most dominant and controversial figures in Israeli history between 1977 and 1983. Herut theoretically stood for Israeli dominion over the whole of mandate Palestine *and* Jordan and for private enterprise. Although secular, it was more sympathetic to Orthodox Jewry than was Labour. In the early days of Israel's history most of the Israeli political elite and intelligentsia regarded Herut as beyond the pale, a group of quasi-fascist fanatics leading an ignorant mass rabble. The party was indeed associated with mass protest (especially, in 1952, over the proposed Reparations Accord with West Germany) and attempted to win votes from the disaffected elements of Israeli society. Herut always did reasonably well in Israeli elections, winning 14 seats in the first Knesset and, generally, about 15 in most subsequent elections. From the mid-1960s Herut entered into a broader electoral coalition, first as Gahal, and, from 1973, as Likud (Hebrew for 'Union'), and finally formed a government under Begin in 1977.

Another grouping formed to contest the 1949 elections was the Sephardi List, which joined the General Zionists in the early 1950s. It represented the traditional Sephardi elites, and elected four members to the first Knesset.

On the extreme left of the political spectrum was Maki, the Israeli Communist Party. Despite being split into Arab and Jewish factions, it won four seats in the first Knesset and five or six in most others until the mid-1960s. Although a substantial Arab population remained in Israel, they did not establish significant parties of their own until much later.

In early 1949 the first government of Israel took shape. The Constituent Assembly was formally renamed the Knesset in February; a speaker was chosen; Weizmann was formally sworn in as Israel's first president; and, in March 1949, Ben-Gurion formally appointed a Cabinet of 12, consisting of the leaders of the Mapai and other ministers drawn from the United

Religious Front (which, rather remarkably, received four ministries), the Progressives, and the Sephardis. Ben-Gurion held both the prime minister-ship and the Defence Ministry. The pre-existing civil service and govern-mental infrastructure were reformulated in new Israeli state ministries, and the Israeli Defence Force took shape following the disbanding of the Palmach, the Irgun, and Lehi.

Few new nations in history faced the range of serious problems which Israel did in 1948–49. Apart from its very survival, by no means guaranteed even after the 1949 Armistice Agreement, Israel had to create a Constitution, oversee the settlement of hundreds of thousands of immi-grants, develop a viable economy from nothing, and create a single national entity from Jews of many diverse backgrounds. It had, as well, to deal suc-cessfully with all of the world's great powers at a time of rapidly deteriorat-ing relations between East and West, and establish a new and successful relationship with Diaspora Jewry, not all of whom had previously been Zionists. That it was reasonably successful at doing all of these is far more surprising than that it was not wholly successful.

The new government quickly passed a series of laws setting out the powers of the government, especially the Transition Law of 1949, which became known as the 'Little Constitution', and established the functions of the branches of the Israeli government. Much preparatory work went into drafting a formal Israeli Constitution. Nevertheless, no written Constitution for the State of Israel was enacted then (or since). Ben-Gurion and his advisers decided to postpone adopting an official Constitution, arguing that it was premature and that the Orthodox members of the Knesset (who were included in the ruling governmental coalition) would insist on making the state as religiously Orthodox as possible. For these reasons, no formal Israeli Constitution was drafted. Israel remains, with Great Britain, one of the few nations without a written Constitution.

The most important and pressing internal problem confronting the young state was the absorption of vast numbers of immigrants. Between May 1948 and December 1949 350,000 immigrants arrived, increasing Israel's population from 650,000 to one million, possibly the greatest rate of increase of any country in history. The two largest groups of arrivals were Holocaust survivors, frequently the only living members of their families or indeed of their communities, and Afro-Asian Jews, often from pre-modern societies. Probably the best-known such Afro-Asian migrants were the 50,000 Jews of Yemen and Aden who were airlifted to Israel in 1950. It has frequently been pointed out that most of these migrants had never been in a wheeled vehicle before flying to the Jewish state. Another 170,000 immigrants arrived in 1950 and 175,000 more in 1951. To deal with this enormous influx, from 1951 immigrant transit camps (*ma'abarot* in Hebrew) were established. By the end of 1951 no fewer than 139 such settlements had been built, holding, at the time, over 200,000 immigrants. *Ma'abarot* consisted of jerry-built huts and tents, and living conditions were harsh. Migrants from many cultures and speaking different languages were thrown in daily contact with one another. A change in immigrant absorption policy in 1954 led to the siting of immigrant communities in virtually uninhabited areas of the country, particularly in the Negev. Development of the (by Israeli standards) vast but primitive Negev region had long been a dream of Ben-Gurion's. The *ma'abarot* often lasted well into the 1950s, until a permanent housing infrastructure could be developed.

Israel's enormous defence burden, combined with the cost of receiving such a vast number of immigrants, led to an economy constantly on the brink of bankruptcy. Young Israel produced few manufactured goods and was known, in economic terms, only for its agricultural exports. Price controls and rationing were the order of the day, and a flourishing black market in goods for which there was a popular demand obviously led to mass dissatisfaction. This harsh policy, *tzenah* (austerity), continued until 1952, when the so-called 'New Economic Policy' was introduced. The new policy abolished price controls, devalued the Israeli pound (at the time the unit of currency), and offered export incentives. Attempts to increase investment in Israeli bonds among Diaspora Jewry were increased. American foreign aid to Israel began in 1952, the same year that the Restitution Agreement with West Germany initiated very substantial German payments to the Jewish state. From 1953 Israel began a long period of rapid economic growth, with an average annual rate of growth in gross national product of about 10 per cent per annum over the next twenty years.

The first eight years of Israeli history were not without their major political difficulties. Three events stand out in particular. The Holocaust, of course, loomed over everything else in recent Jewish history, despite the belief of many Zionists that this was a tragedy which happened to Jews in *galut* ('exile') and might well have been avoided had Israel existed earlier. In 1949 Konrad Adenauer, a conservative Catholic who had spent the Nazi years in retirement and obscurity, became the first chancellor of the newly-established Federal Republic of Germany (West Germany), consisting of the three zones of occupation in western Germany conquered by the Western powers in 1945. Adenauer understood the centrality of re-establishing relations with the Jewish people as a prerequisite for Germany's own re-emergence, and almost immediately spoke out in the German press in favour of both German recognition of the State of Israel and of German reparations to the Jewish state. Formal talks between Jewish and German leaders began in 1950. In September 1951 Adenauer addressed the West German parliament, formally stating Germany's obligation to support Israel morally and financially. As the possibility of substantial West German economic assistance for Israel became more realistic, an enormous storm of hostile opinion broke out in Israel. In many respects, public hostility to German reparations in the early 1950s dwarfed anything seen later in Israel's often turbulent domestic political scene.

Although opposition came from the left, centre, and right of the Israeli political spectrum, it was associated, in particular, with Menahem Begin and his Herut supporters, whose hostility to any agreement with West Germany appeared to cross the line from spirited dissent to something like insurrection. Begin, whose parents had perished in the Holocaust, denounced reparations as 'an abomination' and 'blood money'. In January 1952 Ben-Gurion summoned the Knesset to approve detailed negotiations with Germany. On the same morning Begin addressed a crowd of 15,000 of his supporters in Jerusalem saying 'Today I give the order – Yes! This will be a war of life or death.' A great mass of demonstrators marched on the Knesset building (then in central Jerusalem), setting fire to motor cars and attacking anything in its path. The windows of the Knesset were smashed and dozens of police were injured. Ben-Gurion denounced Begin as 'a fascist', called in the army, and broadcast to the Israeli nation, attacking 'the hand of evil ... the first step ... to destroy democracy in Israel'. Despite the emotive nature of the issue, Ben-Gurion won a vote of confidence in the Knesset by 61:50. Begin was expelled from parliament for fifteen months. This show of strength worked, and Herut never again threatened the legal order. After intensive negotiations, an agreement between Israel, Diaspora Jewish organisations, and West Germany was reached in September 1952 under which Germany agreed to pay about $750 million to Israel and $125 million to the Conference on Jewish Material Claims Against Germany (representing Diaspora bodies concerned with Holocaust victims and survivors) over the next 12 to 14 years. In 1956 West Germany also paid personal compensation to Holocaust survivors and the relatives of victims. Few continued to question the ethics of German reparations, which poured dollars into the Israeli economy and did show a sincere and practical attempt to atone for the unique crimes committed by Germany between 1933 and 1945.

Another major affair involving the Holocaust in a direct and painful manner also occurred during these years. In 1953 an elderly muck-raking Israeli journalist, Malkiel Grunwald (often spelled 'Greenwald') who had been born in Hungary and migrated to Palestine in 1938, launched an attack on Dr Rudolf Kastner (or Kasztner, 1906–57), another former Hungarian who was then employed as public relations director for the Israeli Ministry of Commerce and Industry. Grunwald accused Kastner of having directly collaborated with the Nazis during the Second World War when the extermination of Hungary's Jews occurred. Specifically, he accused Kastner, who in 1944 was chairman of the Jewish Rescue Committee in Budapest, of reaching a deal with Adolf Eichmann whereby 200 Jewish families were to be allowed to emigrate to Switzerland while Kastner's associate Josef Brand tried to negotiate the notorious 'blood for goods' proposal with the Allies. Kastner provided Eichmann with a list of 1700 Jews to be saved: many of them were his relatives or associates, or originated in the same village. Eichmann indeed allowed these Jews to emigrate; they survived the war while hundreds of thousands of Hungarian

Jews were deported to Auschwitz. Even more seriously, Kastner was also accused of keeping silent about the fate of Hungary's Jews just prior to their deportation, and of aiding Kurt Becher, an SS associate of Eichmann, after the war.

In Israel, Kastner was an important member of the ruling Mapai party, while Grunwald was known for his slanderous attacks on Mapai leaders. Mapai decided to make an example of Grunwald, and helped Kastner to bring a libel suit against him. In 1954, a lengthy and emotional trial was held in Jerusalem which gripped the nation and opened and reopened many questions which had lain dormant about the response of world Jewry to the Holocaust. Grunwald's lawyer, Shmuel Tamir (b.1923) was a fiery Herut supporter (and, much later, a minister in Begin's Cabinet), who was happy to embarrass Ben-Gurion and Mapai. In June 1955 a District Court judge found that Grunwald had indeed been defamed by Kastner who, in the judge's words, 'had sold his soul to the devil'. Mapai decided to appeal; this led to a successful no confidence vote in the Knesset by the Opposition parties which produced the resignation of prime minister Sharett. In particular, Herut supported extreme action against Kastner. In early 1957 Kastner was shot and killed outside his home by three men associated with the Israeli extreme right, the first political assassination in the country's history. Paradoxically, in 1958 the Israeli Supreme Court reversed the verdict of the lower court, and ruled that Kastner had not collaborated with the Nazis. It is sometimes said that one of the effects of the Kastner trial was to influence Ben-Gurion to take steps to bring Adolf Eichmann to justice, as a response to criticisms made of Mapai during the affair.

The third of the great political _causes célèbres_ in Israel at that time was the Lavon Affair. Polish-born Pinchas Lavon had been appointed defence minister in late 1953 when Ben-Gurion retired to a _kibbutz_. He quickly fell out with senior commanders such as Dayan, and was not, he later argued, fully informed of clandestine operations. In particular, he claimed not to have been informed of an elaborate security plot being undertaken by Jewish agents in Egypt to prevent a full British military evacuation from Egypt which, Israel feared, would remove a restraining influence on Egypt's dictator, Colonel Nasser. In 1954 Israel's agents planted bombs (injuring no one) in British and American buildings in Cairo and Alexandria. Unfortunately, for Israel, one such bomb accidentally went off in the pocket of an Israeli agent, leading to Egypt's seizure of the entire network. In January 1955, two of the Israeli spies were hanged in Cairo. Arab opinion was inflamed, and both Britain and the United States were temporarily alienated from Israel. Blame for the fiasco fell on Lavon, who angrily denied any knowledge of the plot. Lavon's claim was itself contradicted by the head of Israeli Intelligence and by Moshe Dayan. An investigative committee apparently agreed with Lavon, who nevertheless resigned in February 1955 when, chiefly as a result of this affair, Ben-Gurion re-entered politics, becoming defence minister and, shortly thereafter, prime minister again.

The Affair continued to rumble on until the mid-1960s. In 1961 another committee concluded that Lavon had not known of the plot. As late as 1965 the Affair temporarily split Mapai, and has never been fully clarified.

Despite these imbroglios, by 1956 Israel was a sovereign and developing society of growing importance and strength. Its existence had also brought about a fundamental reformulation of the Zionist dream among world Jewry. In the mid-1940s (to say nothing of an earlier period) there were still very considerable reservoirs of Jewish anti-Zionism hostile to the creation of a Jewish state in Palestine. These spanned the political spectrum. On the right, many highly assimilated Jews in the English-speaking world and elsewhere continued to regard Jewish identity as wholly religious and the creation of a Jewish state as threatening to Jewish equality in their own countries. On the left, a variety of groups continued to oppose Zionism, including surviving Bundist and many Yiddish groups and most Marxists. Similarly, many Strictly Orthodox Jews still regarded the Zionist goal as sacrilegious. By 1956, however, most of this opposition had vanished. In particular, there was no longer an outspoken group of right-wing opponents of Israel's existence. One could no longer plausibly argue that a Jewish state threatened the civil rights of Diaspora Jews. On the contrary, Israel's military prowess and national achievements enhanced the self-esteem of Jews everywhere. On the left, the fact that the Soviet Union and its allies were bitterly hostile to Israel led to a decline in Jewish Communism, although a very vocal anti-Zionist left grew up among fringe Trotskyites, many of Jewish origin. Most social democrats around the world were, at that time, strongly pro-Zionist. While some Strictly Orthodox groups, especially Neturei Karta ('Guardians of the City' in Aramaic), still refused to recognise Israel's existence, most had overtly or *de facto* made their peace with Israel. Growing numbers lived in Israel, especially in Jerusalem, and played the Israeli political game very successfully.

Most of this change came from the spontaneous realisation by Jews everywhere of the mighty achievement of Israel's existence, especially one so closely following the Holocaust, an epochal, even miraculous achievement, which perforce redefined Jewish identity everywhere. This was well-illustrated in remote Melbourne, Australia. There, the St Kilda Hebrew Congregation (St Kilda is a district of Melbourne) was long headed by Rabbi Jacob Danglow (1880–1962), known as 'Anglo Danglow' for his firm loyalty to Britain and its policies. In December 1947 its management adopted an unenthusiastic motion of support for the establishment of Israel which 'noted the establishment of the Jewish state and wished it every success'. Owing to members' dissatisfaction, this was altered to one praying that 'it will not only enhance and advance the Jewish name but will become a blessing in the midst of the earth'. Finally, again through congregational pressure, this became 'the St Kilda Hebrew Congregation records with profound gratitude to Almighty God this blessed event in our time'. From mid-1948 the Congregation ended its services not with *God Save the King* but with *Hatikvah* ('The Hope'), the Zionist song that had become the Israeli national anthem. 'When the choir sang *Hatikvah*, I knew the world had changed,' one congregant later recalled. In New York, on 14 May 1948, the day Israeli independence was proclaimed, tens of thousands of Jews crowded into Madison Square Garden for celebrations and another 75,000 who could not get in listened to proceedings in the streets via loud-speakers. Israel's military victory, it was widely claimed, enhanced Jewish self-esteem everywhere with vicarious 'macho' pride. Nevertheless, the precise nature of the relationship between Israel and Diaspora Jewry remained highly ambiguous. Calls by Ben-Gurion and other Zionist leaders for massive *aliyah* from the United States and other democracies fell on deaf ears, and have continued to remain unheeded ever since.

From the Sinai Campaign of 1956 until the Six Day War of 1967

Despite the gains made by Israel during its first eight years, relations with the Arabs were still at the zero point. While some of the reasons for this may well have been due to the failure of Israel to pursue every avenue towards conciliation with the Arabs, unquestionably the main reason for failure to achieve rapprochement came from the Arab side, with the adamant refusal of their leaders to recognise Israel's existence or make peace with the Jewish state. A number of important factors, indeed, seemed to indicate that, from the Israeli viewpoint, the situation *vis-à-vis* the Arab world was actually deteriorating. In July 1953 the playboy King Farouk of Egypt was overthrown by a junta of 'young officers' led by General Mohammed Naguib and Colonel Gamal Abdel Nasser. In April 1954 Nasser assumed full control in Egypt. Although there were some initial hopes that the modernising new regime might be more likely to arrive at a peace settlement with Israel than the reactionary Egyptian monarchy, in practice Nasser proved to be the first of a long stream of radical Arab dictators who used extreme anti-Zionist rhetoric as a means of retaining popularity among the Arab masses and Islamic fundamentalists. Nasser was also only too happy to exploit Palestinian discontent and to harass Israel through terrorist attacks, at minimal cost to Egypt. He also made clear that he believed another war was inevitable with what he termed 'the State of the Zionist gangs'. He also took steps which caused great alarm throughout the Western world. In September 1955 Egypt announced an enormous arms deal with Czechoslovakia, a satellite of the Soviet Union, whereby (according to Israeli intelligence) 300 tanks, 200 MIG-15 jet fighters, and 50 Ilyushin bombers were supplied to Egypt, obviously made available by the Soviet Union. In 1955 Britain announced the withdrawal of its remaining troops from the Canal Zone and, in July 1956, Nasser nationalised the Suez

Canal, in violation of international law. Egypt had previously repeatedly contravened international law by refusing (contrary to the 1949 Armistice Agreement between Egypt and Israel) to allow passage through the Suez Canal for Israeli ships. In 1953–55 Palestinian terrorists (known as *feda'iyin*, or 'suicide squads') launched many murderous attacks against Israelis, including civilians, from bases in the Gaza Strip, which was directly controlled by Egypt. (Similarly, Palestinian terrorist incidents also occurred along the Jordanian border.) In February 1955 Israel retaliated with a massive attack against an Egyptian army base in Gaza, in which 38 Egyptian solders were killed. By 1956 it appeared that some kind of war between Egypt and Israel was more than likely.

Despite the Czech arms shipments, Israel was already militarily stronger than Egypt, and Shimon Peres (then director general of Israel's Ministry of Defence, and later Israeli prime minister) estimated that it would take Israel only five to seven days to conquer the Sinai, an area – held by Egypt – larger than Israel itself. Nevertheless, in that period Israel was also lacking in powerful allies. The Soviet Union was, of course, increasingly an enemy. The United States' government, while supportive, was chiefly interested in promoting international peace and was not yet as close to Israel as it would subsequently become, while Britain was still heavily under pro-Arabist influences. This left France, to which Israel in this period drew closer. The leaders of the Fourth French Republic perceived Israel as fighting the same enemy that they were in Algeria, and began to sell considerable quantities of armaments to Israel. The Israeli government debated whether to attack Egypt in a pre-emptive strike, but decided against it. France and (more reluctantly) Britain under prime minister Sir Anthony Eden also decided to attack Egypt in order to regain the Suez Canal.

In October, a French general, Maurice Challe, proposed to Israel a truly astonishing course of events. Israel would attack Egypt, seizing the Sinai up to the Suez Canal. Britain and France would then intervene, ostensibly to keep the peace between Israel and Egypt, but in reality to retake the Suez Canal. Even by the historical standards of diplomacy, this marked a new departure in cynicism. After many negotiations (Ben-Gurion wanted a much more sweeping plan which would greatly increase Israel's territories), agreement between Britain, France, and Israel was reached. On 29–30 October 1956 Israeli parachute battalions seized the Mitla Pass, while three Israeli land columns marched into the Sinai. Within four days Egypt's armies in the Sinai had been routed. The Anglo-French invasion of Egypt began a few days later. At the UN, a rarely seen common front between America and Russia led to condemnation of Israel and calls for an immediate ceasefire. The UN also voted to create its own Emergency Force to replace the withdrawing troops. In the meantime, the Soviet Union (which had just suppressed the Hungarian Revolution) threatened a missile attack against Israel. The United States, which had opposed the Suez campaign, refused to support Israel or the Anglo-French venture. In Britain, the Suez campaign unleashed great opposition and hostility, and Sir Anthony Eden, an ill man, could not proceed to seize Suez as he had hoped. ('Suez 1956' is always seen as a major turning-point in Britain's role as a major power.) Under extraordinary pressure, Israel agreed to withdraw its troops from the Sinai, having gained, at most, only some concessions about the right of its shipping to sail in the Straits of Tiran near Sinai (which were maintained until shortly before the 1967 War). By March 1957 Israel had withdrawn all of its forces from the Sinai.

This curious and unattractive affair produced some lessons. The Israeli army showed itself to be far stronger and more successful than many imagined, and gained a brief experience of the kind of sweeping victory it would achieve in 1967. Accommodation between Israel and Egypt, never a very realistic prospect, now became almost impossible, and Nasser brooded over revenge. Nevertheless, ironically, the Egyptian–Israeli border became much quieter after 1956 than it had been. New radical Arab regimes arose in Iraq and Syria, and a drive towards a 'Pan-Arabism', headed by Nasser, took shape. The Soviet Union became an emphatic supporter of the Arab cause and a determined opponent of Israel, although diplomatic relations between the two countries continued until the Six Day War of 1967.

Somewhat surprisingly, the Sinai Campaign did little harm to Ben-Gurion or the Mapai-led coalition, which dominated Israeli politics for almost the whole of this period. Mapai won 46 seats at the first Knesset election, and then 45 at the second general election in 1951, 40 in 1955, 47 in 1959, and 42 in 1961, being by far the largest party at each election, although forced into coalition with other parties to form a government, generally those religious parties which were agreeable to working with Mapai. Ben-Gurion's stature ensured that the party he led would not be seriously challenged. There was, moreover, no credible opposition leader. Menahem Begin, who headed Herut, the nearest approach Israeli politics had to an opposition party, lost election after election. From 1955 he initiated talks with the General Zionists (B Faction), the middle-class mainstream Zionists, with the aim of forming a non-socialist electoral bloc, but no such coalition would come into being for a decade. The close interconnections between Mapai, the Histadrut, and the institutions of the Israeli state and economy, as well as the close linkages of all these with the Israel Defence Force and its leadership elite, also greatly assisted Mapai's electoral success. This would not be seriously challenged for many years.

In 1960 came one of the most famous and momentous events in Israeli history: the capture and trial of Adolf Eichmann (1906–62), the SS Chief of Operations during much of the Holocaust. Eichmann was chiefly responsible for organising the rounding up and deportation of many of Europe's Jews who perished in the extermination camps. He was especially visible, and infamous, during the deportation of Hungarian Jewry to Auschwitz in 1944. From 1945 until 1950 he lived under an assumed name in East Germany, Austria, and Italy. In 1950 he emigrated to Argentina, living there as 'Ricardo Klement'. Owing largely to renowned Nazi-hunter Simon Wiesenthal (b.1908), Israel's secret service was alerted to the fact that Eichmann was alive and well in Buenos Aires. In May 1960 Israeli agents kidnapped him from Argentina and took him to Israel to stand trial. Later that month Ben-Gurion made a dramatic announcement to the Knesset that 'the Israeli Security Services have captured one of the greatest Nazi criminals, Adolf Eichmann'.

Eichmann was allowed to choose his own counsel, and his trial, which lasted from April to August 1961, proceeded with the utmost fairness. Eichmann was seated in the prisoner's dock surrounded by bullet-proof glass. The prosecution was led by Israeli attorney-general Gideon Hausner (1915–90). The trial was certainly one of the most famous of the twentieth century, a turning-point in the history of Israel and in remembrance of the Holocaust. The overwhelming impression made by Eichmann was that, far from being a sadistic monster of evil, he was nondescript and bland, an archetypal civil servant. He admitted all the accusations against him, adding some important details to our knowledge of the Holocaust, but pleaded that he was just 'obeying orders' and was a 'cog in the machine'. In a sense he was right, for he was only a colonel in the SS who was delegated by his superior, Heinrich Himmler, to organise the killing of Jews, which he did in an efficient manner. (Before the war, he had organised the emigration of Austrian Jews, which he also did with great efficiency.) There is no evidence that Eichmann hated Jews in the visceral sense that Hitler did, and he would probably have acted in precisely the same way if he had been given the task of killing Bulgarians or Basques. Eichmann was, in the Nazi hierarchy, 'middle management'. He never met or spoke to Hitler, and apparently met Himmler fewer than half a dozen times. Hannah Arendt's celebrated *Eichmann in Jerusalem*, a study (in her words) of 'the banality of evil', summed up the man. Many have seen in Eichmann one of the most typical figures of the twentieth century. Almost alone of well-known Nazis, no biography of him has yet been written.

Hausner's remarkable opening speech, beginning 'As I stand before you, Judges of Israel, I do not stand alone. With me, at this place and hour, stand six million accusers,' set the tone of the trial, which lasted through 114 sessions and was publicised around the world. In December 1961 Eichmann was sentenced to death. There had been, and continued to be, much debate as to what to do with him, with such suggestions as making him live on a *kibbutz* being aired. Eichmann appealed to the Israeli Supreme Court, lost, and then appealed for clemency to the Israeli president, who turned down his request. He was hanged in the early hours of 1 June 1962. His body was cremated and his ashes taken aboard an Israeli police launch and thrown into the Mediterranean beyond the three-mile limit. The Eichmann trial was arguably the most important single catalyst for memorialisation of the Holocaust, removing something of a taboo about discussing it and opening a tidal wave of histories, survivors' accounts, and every other conceivable form of portrayal, which continues to the present. By the end of the twentieth century the Holocaust had been universally internalised around the world as the best-known evil event of modern history, indeed conceivably the most famous event of modern history.

Ben-Gurion finally retired as prime minister in June 1963 at the age of 77. The next few years, leading up to the 1967 Six Day War, probably saw Israel enjoying as close to a time of normality as it had ever experienced. In January 1964 Pope Paul VI arrived for a brief visit to Israel (the Old City of Jerusalem, with its Christian holy sites, was of course still in Jordanian hands). Although far from wonderful, Jewish–Catholic relations had improved categorically since the Vatican II Council of the early 1960s, with the attendant removal of overtly anti-Jewish statements from Catholic prayers. In March 1966 Israel received the dubious blessing of television, with the introduction of an educational television station. Internationally, old-fashioned antisemitism had declined markedly, and Israel enjoyed virtually universal support among the Western world's intelligentsia and, indeed, in popular opinion. There were, of course, many clouds as well. In 1966 a serious recession began in Israel. Terrorism by the Arabs continued, and relations with the Soviet Union continued to deteriorate. Above all, relations with the Arabs remained deeply hostile.

No one was, however, prepared for the momentous events of 1967. Relations between Israel and the Arab states continued to deteriorate throughout the 1960s. Nasser continued to make blood-curdling statements of his intentions, such as that made in a joint communiqué with the president of Iraq in 1963 that 'The aim of the Arabs is the destruction of Israel.' Nevertheless, few knowledgeable Israelis expected a major war to break out in 1967, when Nasser's best forces were committed to fighting in the civil war in Yemen. So long as Egypt was unprepared for war, most Israelis thought that no general conflict was likely. Nevertheless, tensions with (in particular) Syria had grown markedly, leading to a major clash in April 1967 in which Israeli planes struck at Syrian artillery positions. (Egypt failed to come to Syria's aid.) The major determining factor in the outbreak of the 1967 war appears to have been the provocative behaviour of the Soviet Union. Soviet leaders consistently misled Egypt regarding Israel's intentions, giving Egypt confidential 'information', in May 1967, that Israel was about to invade Syria. This led to a general mobilisation of the Egyptian military in the Sinai. The aim of the Soviet Union appears literally to have been that of trouble-making, creating another crisis spot for the United States and the West in the middle of the Vietnam war. The Soviet Union also apparently expected an Arab–Israeli war to provide a testing ground for the weapons it had given in large quantities to the Arabs.

As they do at the beginnings of most wars, events then spiralled out of control. On 16 May 1967 Egypt requested that the UN withdraw its emergency force from the Egypt–Israeli borders and from the Straits of Tiran and, two days later, from the whole of the Sinai. Several days later, Nasser reimposed a blockade of the Gulf of Arabia. Israel had previously announced that it would interpret any such act as a *causus belli*. Nasser, it seems, had gone well beyond what the Soviet Union was actually prepared to tolerate, and Egypt entered into a war-like situation without Soviet support. Egypt's actions also deeply alienated the Western powers. Preparation for a full-scale war now began, with Israel mobilising and Egypt making 'defence' pacts with Syria, Jordan, and Iraq. During this time the Israeli foreign minister, Abba Eban, made the rounds of the world's leaders, explaining the Israeli position and looking for support. The United Nations and other international bodies were powerless to stop the build-up to war.

In Israel and throughout the Jewish world, it appeared to many that a second Holocaust was at hand. In addition, Israel's government appeared to be literally at its wit's end, highlighted by the dismal performance by the prime minister, Levi Eshkol, in a national television broadcast. In view of the gravity of the situation, there were widespread demands for a Government of National Unity headed, if possible, by Ben-Gurion. This was formed on 1 June 1967, and marked a turning-point in Israeli political history. For the first time, Menahem Begin of Gahal (the bloc formed by Herut and the Liberals) joined a Cabinet, as did his colleague Yosef Sapir. So, too, did Moshe Dayan, out of office since 1964, who was looked upon as a potential national hero. Dayan was named minister of defence. Ben-Gurion, however, declined to join the new Cabinet.

On 5 June 1967 Israel launched a pre-emptive strike against the Sinai, with the Israeli Air Force destroying its Egyptian counterpart. Despite repeated warnings by Israel, Jordan then attacked Israeli territory south of Jerusalem. In retaliation, the Israeli Air Force destroyed that of Jordan and, on the same day, that of Syria as well. Within 16 hours of the start of hostilities over 400 Arab planes had been destroyed, with losses to Israel of just 19 aircraft.

Israel also launched a ground attack into Sinai. Despite Egyptian resistance around Abu Ageila, within two days the Egyptians were routed and the Sharm-el-Sheik (the southern tip of the Sinai) was taken. On 7 June 1967 occurred one of the most momentous events in recent Jewish history, the capture of the Old City of Jerusalem from Jordan, an area deliberately cut off by the Arabs even from visits by religious Jews. On the third day of the war (8 June), the UN demanded a ceasefire, which Israel accepted. Syria, however, refused to accept the ceasefire and continued to shell Israeli positions from the strategic Golan Heights, which, by 10 June, when the war ended, Israel had also captured.

At the cessation of the Six Day War, it dawned on all Israelis that their country had won what was arguably the greatest military victory in the history of the world, one equal to, if not surpassing, any triumph by the world's greatest military commanders from the time of Alexander the Great to Zhukov and Eisenhower. Israel found itself in control of an area three times its pre-war size, including the whole of the Sinai, the West Bank, and the Golan Heights. The Old City of Jerusalem was in Jewish hands for the fist time since the Roman era. The Israeli casualties were 700 dead and 2500 wounded. The Arab losses are not precisely known, but 1500 Egyptians were killed and 5600 taken prisoner. About 70 per cent of the heavy equipment of the three Arab armies was destroyed.

Around the world, there had been a spontaneous wave of support for Israel and, indeed, of philosemitism. Almost everywhere, thousands of non-Jews volunteered to fight or give blood for the Israeli cause. In the Jewish world, many thousands of Jews who had previously held no strong views on Israel suddenly realised that it was central to their identity as Jews.

In the long-run, however, victory in the Six Day War proved, arguably, a curse rather than a blessing. One million Palestinian Arabs of the West Bank were now under Israeli occupation. Many Israelis, especially on the political right but also on the left, increasingly refused to contemplate returning the territories of the West Bank, regarding them as 'liberated' rather than 'occupied'. Israel was now increasingly viewed as 'Goliath' rather than as 'David', and much of the support it had enjoyed in 1967 evaporated on the political left. The Arabs remained deeply embittered, and the Soviet Union proved even more hostile than in the past. As a result of the war, the Soviet Union and most of its satellites (Romania being the sole exception) broke off diplomatic relations with Israel, a state of affairs which persisted until 1989, well after the start of the *glasnost* era. Israeli society was increasingly polarised by the question of what to do with the West Bank. Palestinian nationalism and terrorism grew enormously over the ensuing few years.

Further reading

Ahron Bregman, *Israel's Wars, 1947–93* (London, 2000)

Martin Gilbert, *Israel: A History* (London, 1998)

Efraim Karsh, *Fabricating Israeli History: The 'New Historians'* (London, 1997)

Mordechai Naor, *The Twentieth Century in Eretz Israel* (Tel Aviv, 1996)

Susan Hattis Rolef, ed., *Political Dictionary of the State of Israel* (Jerusalem, 1993)

Howard M. Sachar, *A History of Israel: From the Rise of Zionism to Our Time* (New York, 1993)

Mark Tessler, *A History of the Israeli–Palestinian Conflict* (Bloomington, Ind., 1994)

S. Ilan Troen and Noah Lucas, eds, *Israel: The First Decade of Independence* (Albany, N.Y., 1995)

Ronald W. Zweig, ed., *David Ben-Gurion: Politics and Leadership in Israel* (London, 1991)

|15|

Israel since the Six Day War, 1967–2000

From the Six Day War (1967) to the Yom Kippur War (1973)

'The lightning pace of the [1967] war inevitably gave rise to myths,' noted Yitzhak Rabin, the IDF chief of staff in that war and subsequently Israel's prime minister shortly after the conflict. 'The myth-making ... simultaneously portrayed the Israel army as "invincible" and the Arab armies as a "pushover". Nothing could have been further from the truth.' Rabin also saw, with much wisdom, 'a strange phenomenon among our soldiers. Their joy is incomplete, and more than a small portion of sorrow and shock prevails in their festivities, and there are those who abstain from celebration. The warriors in the front lines saw with their own eyes not only the glory of victory but the price of victory ... It may be that the Jewish people has never learned or accustomed itself to feel the triumph of conquest and victory, and therefore we receive it with mixed feelings.'

Rabin's sage observations were not universally shared. It appeared to many as if the Israelis were invincible. Although this was indeed not so, it seemed true to many at the time. It has become common to look at the Six Day War as a turning-point in the history of Israel, when a righteous and liberal young republic was transformed into an aggressive expansionist super-state whose policies many critics have lambasted as unjust. Nevertheless, it is difficult to see how events could have unfolded very much differently.

After 1967, and in the wake of the war, Israel was faced with a number of daunting challenges which severely constrained the choice of policy her leaders could pursue. Probably the most important was the growth of Palestinian nationalism and terrorism. The elite which led that community during the Yishuv consisted of traditional Arab families and clans. After 1948 that leadership largely vanished, while both Jordan, which annexed the West Bank, and to a lesser extent Egypt, which controlled the Gaza, did their best to prevent the growth of a modern Palestinian nationalism. In the early 1960s, however, a new, more modern and extreme Palestinian nationalism arose, headed by westernised lawyers, intellectuals, and the like. In 1964 the Palestine Liberation Organization (PLO) was founded in Cairo. At the time it was headed by the lawyer Ahmed Shukeiri. It was this body which immediately drafted and adopted the notorious 'Palestine National Covenant', which explicitly called for abolishing the State of Israel and for expelling all Jews who entered Palestine after 'the beginning of the Zionist invasion'. It also committed the PLO to armed struggle by 'commando action'. In 1968 Yasser Arafat, head of the *Fatah* faction (from the initials, in Arabic, of the 'Palestinian Liberation Movement') became head of the PLO. In that year, in the wake of the 1967 War, an even more extreme version of the Palestine National Covenant was drafted. Whatever the political realities of the situation, this remained the PLO's official statement of principles until the mid-1990s. Israel was thus faced with dealing with a movement of Palestinian nationalism which was officially committed to destroying it, to expelling most of its population, and to using terrorism to achieve those aims. No country in the world would negotiate with a terrorist movement whose announced intention was to destroy it, and most nations would regard the existence of such a body as *ipso facto* an act of war.

The PLO also proceeded to make terrorism and the murder of Israeli civilians its stock-in-trade. To mention only a few examples: in March 1968 an Israeli school bus exploded a land mine planted near Eilat, and two school children were killed; in September that year explosives placed by PLO terrorists in the Tel Aviv bus station killed one person and wounded 70; and in November, a booby-trapped car exploded in a Jerusalem market, killing 12 and wounding another 70. Airline hijacking, virtually unknown before 1967, became a PLO device, beginning with the hijacking, in July 1968, of an El Al plane flying from Rome to Tel Aviv. It was forced to land in Algiers, and its last passengers were released only in mid-September, in exchange for the release of Palestinian terrorists. Thereafter, for years, hardly a month went by without some terrorist atrocity. Among the more infamous attacks carried out by Palestinian terrorists or their allies during these years were the blowing up in mid-air of a Swissair plane flying from Zurich to Tel Aviv (February 1970) with 47 dead; an attack on an Israeli school bus in the Upper Galilee in which nine children and three adults were killed (May 1970); indiscriminate machine-gunning at Tel Aviv's airport (May 1972) by Japanese terrorists connected with the PLO in which 25 persons were killed; the murder of 11 members of the Israeli Olympic team at Munich by the Palestinian 'Black September' movement (September 1972); the takeover of a school in Ma'alot by Palestinian terrorists resulting in the deaths of 21 pupils and three adults (May 1974); the explosion of a booby-trapped refrigerator placed by terrorists in the centre of Jerusalem in which 13 were killed (July 1975); and the hijacking of an Air France plane, en route from Tel Aviv to Paris, to Entebbe, Uganda, by German and Palestinian terrorists (June–July 1976). The last-mentioned led to 'Operation Yonatan', the world-famous 'Entebbe Raid' by the Israel Defence Force (IDF), in which nearly all of the passengers were released and flown to safety; however the leader of the expedition, Lieutenant-Colonel Yonatan Netanyahu, and three hostages were killed. (This raid caught the imagination of the world, engendering books and movies almost overnight.) Literally hundreds of other terrorist attacks were carried out during this period by the PLO and 'Terror International', in a way which spread to other, unrelated conflicts (for instance, the IRA's terror campaign in Northern Ireland began in 1969) and seemed at the time to threaten the very foundations of civilised society.

The attitude of the Arab states towards Israel ostensibly gave no further reason to expect that peace was near. Egypt had lost the whole of the Sinai and the Gaza, and Nasser was thirsting for revenge. In March 1969 he launched the so-called 'War of Attrition' with Israel, consisting of daily skirmishing on the border of the Suez Canal which almost always resulted in Israeli casualties. This 'war' lasted for 17 months, until August 1970, when its end was negotiated by the Americans. The first night after the ceasefire came into effect, the Egyptians violated it by moving anti-aircraft missile systems to the Suez Canal line. Nasser died unexpectedly in September 1970, and was succeeded by his deputy Anwar Sadat. Although Sadat was to prove a great and brave peacemaker, there was as yet, and for some years to come, little in his record to foreshadow any pacific intent. Lebanon and Jordan were also used as staging-camps for terrorist raids against Israel, resulting in Israeli retaliation. King Hussein of Jordan, who was very reluctant to become involved in the Palestinians' struggle (and who still, nominally, was regarded by some as legally sovereign over the West Bank), launched an all-out offensive against Palestinian terrorists in Jordan in 'Black September' of 1970. This effectively removed Jordan from the allies of the PLO; Arafat and the PLO were forced to move to Southern Lebanon.

Nevertheless, there were subtle (and not so subtle) changes in the rhetoric and strategy of the Arab states during this period. The primary goal of the Arabs became the regaining of the territories lost to Israel in 1967, not the liberation of the Palestinians. Since Israel was, in effect, a military superpower, this could be done only, however reluctantly, by trading land for peace. It was then, in 1967–69, that the goal of the United States and most Western diplomats came to be that of bringing a 'just and lasting peace' to the Middle East by persuading Israel to withdraw from the territories it had conquered in exchange for peace treaties and normal diplomatic relations with the Arab states. This goal was first enacted by the UN Security Council's famous Resolution 242, passed in November 1967, which called upon Israel to withdraw from the occupied territories in exchange for the 'acknowledgement of [its] sovereignty, territorial integrity, and political independence'. De facto, Nasser seemed to accept this potential outcome, as, more certainly, did Jordan. A gap, in fact, opened up between those states and more extreme regimes in Syria, Iraq, and elsewhere, which rejected any peace treaty. Many attempts at diplomatic negotiations were made in that period, for instance the UN's Jarring Mission of 1967–71 (named for Swedish diplomat Gunnar Jarring), but these accomplished little. For the Arabs, any peace treaty with Israel would leave the Palestinian question unresolved, while most Israelis rejected the notion of returning *all* occupied land to the Arabs, especially the Old City of Jerusalem and militarily strategic areas like the Golan Heights. In early 1971 a possible breakthrough came when President Sadat of Egypt hinted at the possible recognition of Israel in exchange for returning all of the conquered territories. Probably unwisely, the Israelis rejected this overture, although it is difficult to see how any Israeli government could have agreed to vacate all of the conquered territories.

It was during that period, too, that relations between Israel and the Soviet bloc became bitterly hostile. Except very briefly in the late 1940s relations between the two, fanned by Soviet antisemitism and strategic support for the Arabs, were never very good, but now they deteriorated to overt hostility. Before the Six Day War the Soviet Union had become the main supplier of arms to Egypt and Syria. The Soviet Union also greatly feared the encouragement which Israel was giving to Soviet Jews – and, by their example, to other dissidents who wished to exercise greater freedom or emigrate. The Soviet Union's satellites, especially East Germany and Czechoslovakia, also certainly became among the chief financiers of international terrorism. There were, however, limitations to Soviet hostility. Although removing its ambassador from Israel in 1967, the Soviet Union always continued to recognise Israel's right to exist in its pre-1967 boundaries, and to a certain extent restrained the more extreme Arab regimes (especially those which might have stirred up Muslim unrest within the Soviet Union). In 1970–72, also, as part of the international process of 'détente', it negotiated a deal with President Richard Nixon and Secretary of State Henry Kissinger of the United States, whereby up to 250,000 Jews were allowed to leave the Soviet Union for other countries, of whom 165,000 migrated to Israel. This unique emigration was the largest exodus from the Soviet soil between Stalin's rule and the collapse of the Soviet Union in the late 1980s.

At some stage between 1971 and 1973 President Sadat of Egypt decided on a limited war with Israel based on a surprise attack. His aims were to retake the Suez Canal and rupture the post-1967 stalemate with Israel. There is no evidence that Sadat wished to bring about the 'annihilation' of Israel, as Nasser might have done, and he involved himself in an alliance only with Syria, rather than with the whole of the Arab world (which showed no interest in actually fighting Israel). Syria was anxious to regain the Golan and to gain the upper hand in southern Lebanon. The Soviet Union was more than willing to provide Egypt and Syria with vast amounts of arms and satellite intelligence reports. Israel's response to this was curiously incompetent, based upon a stubborn refusal to believe the Arabs capable of a revenge attack or to take the uncharismatic Sadat seriously as a leader. Israeli Intelligence continued to view the Egyptian build-up across the Suez Canal as anything more serious than manoeuvres. In the early hours of *Yom Kippur* (6 October) 1973 – the Day of Atonement – it became manifestly obvious that Egypt and Syria were about to launch an attack. Nevertheless, the Israeli government turned down an urgent request by the IDF chief of staff for a pre-emptive air strike, deciding on a call-up of army reserves alone. This was certainly one of the worst military mistakes in Israeli history, for which the prime minister, Golda Meir, and the defence minister, Moshe Dayan, were chiefly to blame.

At 2 pm on 6 October 1973 the Egyptian and Syrian forces simultane- ously attacked Israel. Most Israelis were in synagogue on the holiest day of the Jewish year, and virtually all shops were shut and public transport was at a standstill. It has been pointed out that this timing was actually a mis- calculation by the Arabs: since most Israelis were not at work, mobilisation was actually easier than at other times. Nevertheless, the Israelis were unprepared. In the north, the war began fairly well for Syria, and, on the first day of the attack, its troops had penetrated 20 miles into the middle of the Israel-held Golan and 30 miles into the south, near the old boundary with Israel. Within two days, however, Israeli reinforcements had arrived. The tide now turned completely and Israel advanced still further into Syria, capturing the whole of the Golan. By 22 October, when a ceasefire began, the Syrian army had lost 1100 tanks and the Syrian Air Force had been destroyed.

Also on 6 October, five Egyptian infantry divisions (70,000 troops) crossed the Suez Canal, bypassing Israel's lightly-defended fortifications[1] and by 13 October had made substantial gains in the western Sinai, employ- ing anti-aircraft missiles to good effect against the Israeli Air Force. Then, having turned the tide in Syria, the Israelis counterattacked, fighting a great tank battle on 14 October. On 15–16 October General Ariel Sharon led a paratroop division across the Suez Canal, establishing the Israelis on the Egyptian side of the Canal. Additionally, the Israelis managed to push the Egyptians back to the Canal in the south (but not in the north) and crossed the Suez Canal with tanks and men in operation. By 22 October, when a general ceasefire was supposed to come into force (it was delayed for a few days), the Egyptian Third Army, with 20,000 troops, had been surrounded and was about to be captured. Had this occurred, the Israelis would literally have been on the high-road to Cairo. Like the Syrians, the Egyptians had lost heavily, with over 1000 tanks captured and 8000 soldiers taken prisoner.

---

1 These were known as the 'Bar-Lev Line' – from the name of Israeli chief of staff, Haim Bar- Lev (1924–94) – and consisted of thirty strongholds. Somewhat similar in concept to the Maginot Line in 1930s France, it proved just as useless to Israel in October 1973.

In the end, both the United States and the Soviet Union were only too happy to impose a cease-fire on the combatants via the United Nations; the United States feared that yet another Israeli rout of the Arabs would make a general settlement impossible while the Soviets dreaded another humiliation of their Arab allies. While both sides could claim some credit, de facto the war was an Arab victory, proving that the Israeli army was not invincible and that the Arab side was entitled to feel a measure of self-respect. This made moves to a compromise peace more likely than in the past, since it appeared that the two sides were negotiating as equals.

New leaders and new parties since 1967

While many of Israel's old leaders, of course, continued after 1967, and while many 'new' leaders had been prominent in Israeli politics much earlier, the retirement of Ben-Gurion in 1965 and the events surrounding 1967 do mark something of a turning-point in Israeli politics in terms of both leadership and parties. In both cases, one is immediately struck by the fact that the right-wing tradition in Zionist politics, founded by Jabotinsky, is much stronger than before, and the left-wing socialist Labour tradition much weaker, and certainly not completely dominant as in the past. During Israel's first 19 years of independence, all of that country's prime ministers belonged to Mapai, the main Labour party, or its allies. In the 34 years between 1967 and mid-2000, however, Labour prime ministers have held office for 17 years but prime ministers belonging to Likud, the right-wing coalition of parties, have held office for 14 years, nearly as long. Since the retirement of Golda Meir in 1974, Israel has had seven prime ministers: Yitzhak Rabin (1922–95), Menahem Begin (1913–92), Yitzhak Shamir (b.1915), Shimon Peres (b.1923), Binyamin Netanyahu (b.1949), Ehud Barak (b.1942) and Ariel Sharon (b.1928). Rabin, born in Jerusalem, was a professional military man for his entire career before entering politics. He was aged 26, already commander of the Hard Brigade on the Jerusalem front during the War of Independence, and rose to be a senior military commander during the 1960s and '70s. He was Israel's commander-in-chief during the victorious Six Day War. A political protégé of Ben-Gurion, he entered Golda Meir's Cabinet as minister of labour in 1973 after a stint as ambassador to the United States, and then became Israel's sixth prime minister in 1974. Although some moves towards peace were made during his first three years in that office, his term was marked by a deterioration in Israel's international standing, and a steady decline in Labour's political hegemony at home. A minor scandal involving Rabin's wife's illegal American bank account meant that Shimon Peres headed the Labour ticket at the 1977 general election (which Labour lost), although Rabin remained prime minister. He re-entered the Cabinet in 1984 as minister of defence in a National Unity government, and with an iron fist suppressed the *Intifada* which broke out in 1987. Rabin was also moving closer to making peace with the Palestinians, and, replacing Peres as Labour leader, he became prime minister again in 1992. As prime minister, he negotiated the momentous breakthrough to peace with the PLO which occurred in 1993. His handshake with Yasser Arafat on the White House lawn in September 1993 became one of the most widely-known events in modern diplomatic history, and, together with Peres and Arafat, he was awarded the Nobel Peace Prize for 1994. In the same year he signed an agreement making peace with Jordan. In Israel, a vociferous right wing opposed to further concessions became more visible. On 4 November 1995, after leaving a rally in Tel Aviv to support the peace process, Yitzhak Rabin was assassinated by Yigal Amir, a third-year law student at Bar-Ilan University, from a Yemenite immigrant background, who was linked to shadowy extreme right-wing groups. Millions around the world genuinely mourned Rabin as a man of peace, with President Bill Clinton's eulogy ending with the Hebrew words 'Shalom, chaver, shalom lekha yedidi' ('Goodbye, friend, goodbye to you my friend') becoming world famous.

The name of Menahem Begin has already been encountered; he lasted longer than virtually anyone else at the top of Israeli politics, serving in the Knesset from 1949 until he resigned in 1983; for all of that time he was the leader of Israel's largest right-wing party. Indeed, he lasted even longer than this, for he was already an important figure before the foundation of the State. Born in Brest-Litovsk, he joined Jabotinsky's Betar movement (the youth movement of the Revisionists) as a teenager, becoming a member of its national executive in Poland at the age of 19. In the late 1930s he clashed with Jabotinsky, demanding the 'conquest of the homeland' by force. In 1940 he escaped from Poland to Vilna, which was occupied by the Soviet Union, and was arrested and charged with espionage. Released into Polish General Ander's army in 1941, he made his way to Palestine and served as commander of the Irgun, barely escaping capture and possible hanging by the British. With Israeli independence he formed the Herut (Hebrew: 'freedom') party, leading the right-wing nationalist opposition to Ben-Gurion's hegemonic Mapai party for many years in a stormy manner. Realising that Herut was doomed to perpetual opposition, in 1955–65 he brought about the merger of it and the right-wing General Zionists into Gahal (an abbreviation for 'Herut-Liberal bloc'), which in 1973 became the more broadly-based Likud ('Unity'). Labour at this time was suffering from having been in power for too long, from internal divisions, from the deadlock with the Arabs, and from allegedly ignoring the poorer Sephardi immigrants. Likud capitalised on all of these, unexpectedly winning the 1977 Israeli general election. Begin appointed Moshe Dayan, previously a key Labour figure, as his foreign minister.

To universal amazement, in November 1977 came the historic visit of Egyptian President Anwar Sadat to Jerusalem and the signing, in September 1978, of the 'Camp David Accords', by which Israel agreed to evacuate the

Sinai in exchange for normalisation of relations between Egypt and Israel. In 1979, Begin and Sadat were awarded the Nobel Peace Prize for their historic efforts. Many observers noted that it was easier for an avowed right-winger to make peace with a former enemy (as Nixon had done with China) than a 'soft' liberal, and expected further momentum for peace on the West Bank. To Begin and Likud, however, the Sinai was Egyptian territory (and hence open to return to Egypt) while, for historic, religious, and strategic reasons the West Bank was not. Begin's strategy during the rest of his term as prime minister was far more militant than previously, with the bombing of the Iraqi nuclear reactor in June 1981, and the ill-fated Lebanon conflict of 1982. In poor health and dispirited after the death of his wife in 1982, Begin retired in 1983. To his supporters, he was nearly as great a national hero as Ben-Gurion; to his detractors, he was a mindless militant who, at Camp David, rose to the heights of statesmanship which his doctrinaire ideology otherwise prevented.

Begin was succeeded by Yitzhak Shamir, whose career before becoming prime minister was to some extent shrouded in mystery. Born in Poland and early joining the Zionist Revisionist youth group Betar, he went to Palestine in 1935 and, in 1940, joined the ultra-extreme Lehi. After independence, he was a businessman before becoming the head of Mossad, Israel's secret intelligence force, where his activities still remain obscure. Elected to the Knesset in 1974, he was, remarkably, elected speaker in 1977, only three years later. In 1980 he became foreign minister, and then became prime minister in 1983, stepping down in 1984 in favour of Shimon Peres in a National Unity government. Shamir became deputy prime minister and foreign minister. Two years later, by agreement, Peres and Shamir exchanged places, continuing to head a National Unity government until 1990. In June 1990 Shamir formed a Likud-based government which lasted until the 1992 election, won by Labour. Shamir's many positive achievements included the formation of a free trade agreement with the United States, the re-establishment of diplomatic links with most eastern European and many Third World states, enormous immigration from the Soviet Union, and a sharp drop in Israel's very high inflation rate, keeping Israel out of the Gulf War of 1991, and the repeal of the notorious 'Zionism is Racism' UN resolution of 1975. Shamir also agreed to the Madrid Peace Conference of 1991, the first at which the Arabs and Israel openly participated. Although flexible, Shamir had no truck with Palestinian claims to nationhood and refused to deal with the PLO. The violent Palestinian *Intifada*, which began in late 1987, occurred when he was prime minister.

Israel's ninth prime minister was Shimon Peres, who was born in Belorussia and emigrated to Palestine with his family in 1934. Closely associated with Ben-Gurion in his early career, he became deputy director-general of the Ministry of Defence in 1952 and director-general in 1953. In 1959 he was elected to the Knesset, again as a close associate of Ben-Gurion, entering the Cabinet in 1969. He was a successful minister of defence under

Rabin in 1974, and narrowly lost to him in a contest as leader of the Labour party in 1977. Peres finally became prime minister for two years under the National Unity government agreement of 1984. Although a long-serving and much-respected figure, he has been mistrusted by much of Israel's right wing and has often been surprisingly unsuccessful in Israeli politics. A dedicated social democrat of the old school, he often seemed wholly at odds with the nationalist forces in Israel which emerged strongly after 1967. He again became prime minister after Rabin's assassination in November 1995, but narrowly lost the national election for prime minister to Likud's Binyamin Netanyahu in June 1996. In mid-2000 Peres was also narrowly defeated for the Israeli presidency in the Knesset, although, shortly after, he again became foreign minister.

Peres's successor as prime minister was Binyamin Netanyahu, popularly known as 'Bibi', the first head of government born after Israel achieved independence and the first elected directly at a nation-wide poll rather than chosen by the Knesset. The brother of the hero Yonatan Netanyahu who led the Entebbe raid and was killed there, he lived in America during much of his youth, and became a captain in the IDF and then a businessman before attracting widespread attention as Israel's UN ambassador in the 1980s. Handsome and articulate, a master of the television 'sound bite', and very fluent in English, he became enormously popular in America. He was elected to the Knesset in 1988, holding a number of sub-Cabinet positions before becoming leader of Likud in 1993, and then, very narrowly, prime minister in May 1996. There is general agreement that his three years as prime minister were unsuccessful, marked by scandal and general drift. Following the Oslo Accords of 1993, by which the PLO was recognised, Likud lacked a real *raison d'être*, and Netanyahu could never quite make up his mind whether to wholeheartedly seek peace with the PLO or maintain a very guarded distance. His desire to privatise and modernise much of the Israeli economy was widely resisted by entrenched vested interests, although, for the first time in its history, Israel acquired an international reputation in the 'hi-tech' field. Netanyahu retired from politics, at least temporarily, after his resounding defeat at the 1999 general election.

He was succeeded by Ehud Barak, who was born on a *kibbutz*. A soldier from the age of 17, he became a major general in 1982, was deputy commander of the Israeli forces in the Lebanon incursion of 1982, and, in 1991, became chief of staff of the IDF, the highest rank in the Israeli military. Barak, who holds an advanced degree in engineering from Stanford University, California, entered the Knesset in 1995 and immediately became foreign minister. Chosen as leader of the Labour Party, he became prime minister in May 1999, winning the national poll against Binyamin Netanyahu by 56 per cent to 44 per cent. Barak withdrew Israel's forces from Lebanon but, commencing in September 2000, met an unexpected upsurge of violence on the West Bank which threatened to undermine the entire Arab–Israeli peace process. Only a few months earlier, an overall and possibly final peace settlement between Israel and the PLO seemed very close. Barak's government was also, politically, very fragile. Early in 2001, Barak was decisively defeated in a popular vote for prime minister by Ariel Sharon.

Sharon, one of the most controversial of all Israeli leaders, was a paratroop commander of great renown. Since his election to the Knesset in 1973, he has been associated with the right-wing of Likud, and with uncompromising attitude towards Jewish West Bank settlements. Most controversially, Sharon was virtually in charge of the Lebanon incursion of 1982, and was forced to resign as minister of defence after the Sabra and Chatilla massacres. In 1999, he became leader of Likud, and early in 2001 defeated Ehud Barak in the popular election for prime minister, forming a coalition government.

Recent Israeli politics has also produced many prominent Cabinet ministers below the prime ministerial level as well as other political and military figures who were well-known to the wider public, often internationally renowned. Only a few of the best-known can be mentioned here; this is necessary to illustrate the range of recent Israeli politics. Moshe Arens (b.1925) spent much of his youth in the United States before emigrating permanently to Israel in 1958, where he was a professor of aeronautical engineering. He became a Herut member of the Knesset, ambassador to the United States, and a prominent Likud minister in the 1980s. Geula Cohen (b.1925), of Sephardi background, has been one of the most prominent women politicians in Israel. A fervent, outspoken right-wing nationalist, she was responsible for the Basic Law declaring Jerusalem to be the undivided capital of Israel. Rafael Eitan (b.1929) was chief of staff of the IDF in 1978–83, and was officially criticised for failing to prevent the Sabra and Chatilla massacres of 1982. Mordecai Gur (b.1930) was also a prominent military leader, serving as chief of staff of the IDF in 1974–78. Meir Kahane (1932–90) was probably the most prominent and extreme ultra-nationalist in Israeli history. Kahane grew up in New York, where he founded the Jewish Defense League, devoted to protecting Jews from physical assaults and crime, and known for its violent methods. Around 1971 he migrated to Israel, where he founded Kach (derived from the motto on the emblem of the Irgun, a rifle on a map of Palestine, *Rak Kach*, meaning 'Only thus!'), an ultra-extreme party devoted to expelling virtually all Arabs from Israel and to the strict segregation of Jews and Arabs. From the mid-1980s Kach was, on the grounds of racism, banned by the Knesset from contesting elections. In November 1990 Kahane was assassinated in New York by an Egyptian. Teddy Kollek (1911–99), born in Austria, became internationally known as mayor of Jerusalem for nearly 30 years from 1966. He was chiefly responsible for governing and rebuilding the unified City of Jerusalem. Under his administration, Jerusalem enjoyed good relations between Jews and Arabs until the beginning of the *Intifada* in the late 1980s. Rabbi Moshe Levinger (b.1935) founded the Gush Emunim ('Block of the Faithful') movement, devoted to Jewish settlement on the West Bank and Gaza. Well before its foundation in 1974, Levinger was one of the first to initiate Jewish settlement in what he and his followers regarded as Judea and Samaria. David Levy (b.1937), born in Morocco, became a prominent and well-respected Likud minister under Begin and his successors, especially as foreign minister. Yuval Ne'eman (b.1925), a very prominent nuclear physicist and mathematician, was also a leading right-wing nationalist politician and a leading advocate of Jewish settlement on the West Bank. Mattitiyahu (or Matti) Peled (1923–95), a distinguished military leader, became politically prominent as an advocate of peace with the Palestinians. He was probably the first mainstream Israeli to meet Yasser Arafat, in the mid-1980s.

The years since 1967 have seen the consolidation of Israel's main political strands into two major party blocs: the Israel Labour Party and Likud. Israel was prevented, however, from developing into a true two-party system by the fact that a plethora of Orthodox religious, special interest, and *ad hoc* parties continued to exist and to win a considerable number of seats in the Knesset. In the recent past the system of popular election of the prime minister has further fragmented the Israeli party system. The Israel Labour Party was formed in 1968 as a coalition of Mapai, Ahdut Ha'avodah-Po'alei Zion, Rafi, and Mapam, all left-of-centre parties. A year later it formed with Mapam, a left-socialist party, a coalition known as the Alignment, but remained a separate though dominant grouping within that arrangement. The Alignment continued to dominate Israeli politics until the general election of May 1977, when it was seminally defeated, the number of its seats declining from 51 in 1973 to only 32. Many reasons have been offered for the collapse of Labour in this period, among them a reaction to the 1973 War, the disaffection of poorer Sephardi immigrants who constituted an ever-growing portion of the Israeli population; bickering and rivalry between Yitzhak Rabin, Shimon Peres, and other top leaders, and a number of well-publicised scandals. Additionally, the socialist Zionist impulse which animated Israel during its early years appeared to be wearing thin. Israel's international position was steadily deteriorating and constant terrorism was deeply frustrating. Likud took full advantage of this, winning the elections of 1977 and, narrowly, of 1981. In the elections of 1984 and 1988, there was a virtual dead heat between the two major parties, resulting in a National Unity government. In the 1990s Labour's fortunes improved, it having been the largest single party at the elections of 1992, 1996, and 2000, and forming the government much of the time. In recent decades Labour has discarded much of its socialist ideology (as have other Western social democratic parties) and has attempted to 'modernise'. At the 1999 general election it campaigned under the name 'One Israel'. Labour is much more flexible than Likud in its relations with the Arabs, although its mainstream has been far from advocating unilateral Israeli withdrawal from the West Bank. The historic breakthrough to recognition of the PLO in 1993 was taken by a Labour government, and could probably not have occurred under any Likud leader.

The fortunes of Likud, the right-wing opposition party, have mirrored those of Labour. Likud was formed in 1973 from a union of Gahal and several smaller centre-right and nationalist parties. Gahal was itself formed in 1965 by a previous right-wing merger. Likud is in some respects a typical right/centre-of-right party in the Israeli context, emphasising Israel's sovereignty and respect for tradition and the free market as opposed to socialism. It also stands for the economic betterment of Israel's disadvantaged. Menahem Begin was its leader for many years. Once Likud was launched it came to be viewed as a credible alternative party to Labour (which Herut alone had not been), and the 1973 general election saw its total number of seats in the Knesset rise to 39, from 26 for Gahal in 1969. In 1977 Likud won a watershed victory, chiefly by increasing its share of the vote among Sephardi immigrants. Likud has often been derided by left-liberal intellectuals for its populism and uncompromising stance towards the Arabs, although in practice it has shown considerable adaptability. From 1977 until 1992, Likud's electoral fortunes were the equal of Labour's. Since then, and notwithstanding Netanyahu's premiership, it has declined considerably, riven by internal rivalries (as Labour previously had been) and, in the wake of the Oslo Accords (see below), experiencing a considerable loss of its nationalistic *raison d'être*.

Israel has always had a plethora of smaller parties which have achieved significant Knesset representation. Many of these have been Orthodox religious parties, in particular Shas (the Hebrew acronym for *Shomrei Torah Sephardim*, 'Sephardi Torah Guardians'), a Sephardi Strictly Orthodox party headed by former Sephardi Chief Rabbi Ovadia Yosef and by Rabbi Yitzhak Peretz, and the older National Religious Party (NRP). Both are perceived as very right-wing, although they have worked with Labour when necessary. Left-wing, pro-peace parties have also gained Knesset representation, for instance Meretz, formed in 1992 among pro-peace elements. Meretz was headed by Shulamit Aloni (b.1929), a veteran fighter for civil liberties and women's rights. Many other ephemeral single-issue parties have also gained Knesset seats, as have several Israeli Arab parties. At the May 1999 general election the smaller parties gained seats at the expense of the larger ones, with One Israel (that is Labour) winning 26 seats, Likud 19, Shas a record 17, Meretz 20, and eleven other parties gaining 48 seats between them. This made stable government very difficult.

With its back to the wall? Israel 1978–90

In many respects the 17 years or so following the Yom Kippur War marked a time of trial and tribulation for the State of Israel, despite some solid achievements. While there were many reasons for this state of affairs, it was centrally due to Israel's failure to accomplish a lasting peace with the Arabs and, especially, to resolve the Palestinian question. This, in turn, led to a sharp deterioration of Israel's standing *vis-à-vis* the Soviet-Arab-Third World bloc which emerged strongly at the United Nations and other international bodies, and a loss of support among the Western world's leftist and left-liberal elements. In addition, Israeli society experienced internal divisions between Ashkenazim and Sephardim, considerable economic difficulties, significant emigration to Diaspora countries, and a continuing terrorist threat. Israeli society also saw the rise of a vocal ultra-nationalist element, especially among Jewish settlers on the West Bank, and the growth of a powerful Strictly Orthodox community, which appeared increasingly distinctive from, and hostile to, secular Jewish tendencies in the more liberal Diaspora. Throughout this period, Israel's 'special relationship' with the United States was sufficient to guarantee its survival and its strength, but only after the collapse of the Soviet Union at the end of the 1980s did its position improve significantly.

During the 1970s, Israel became increasingly the subject of grossly hostile and inflammatory condemnation at the United Nations and other international bodies. The most notorious manifestation was the resolution passed by the UN General Assembly on 10 November 1975 equating Zionism with racism, which was passed by a large majority after being steamrollered through by a bloc of Communist, Arab, and Third World states, holding between them an irresistible majority of the UN's votes. Countless other resolutions condemning Israel in one-sided and often absurd terms were passed, year after year, by the General Assembly and virtually all of the UN's affiliated bodies such as UNESCO. Owing to Arab and Muslim pressure, most African states broke off diplomatic relations with Israel after the Yom Kippur War. Throughout most of this period Israel had no diplomatic relations with any Communist state apart from Romania, with any Arab nation (except Egypt after Camp David), or with most Third World states where there was a significant Muslim element, or where Arab petro-dollars could influence diplomatic outcomes. The Arab states also instituted, wherever possible, an economic boycott of Israel. Moreover, much of the Western world's leftist and left-liberal intelligentsia (especially outside the United States) reversed their former strong support for Israel, and routinely attacked that country, often in extravagant terms. On the extreme Marxist left, Israel was regularly condemned in venomous language strongly reminiscent of right-wing antisemitism, and was often grouped with South Africa of the apartheid era, Taiwan, and a few other states as a right-wing pariah. Even in the political mainstream, newspaper editorials and television reportage in the West on the Arab–Israeli conflict almost always depicted the Israelis in a bad light, as the oppressors of the Palestinians. These trends, which had begun when Labour still ruled in Israel, were greatly accentuated after Likud's election to power in 1977, notwithstanding the gains for peace made by the Camp David accords.

Many liberal Diaspora Jews felt very uneasy with Likud's philosophy of nationalism and its opposition to negotiations with the PLO. The truculent rhetoric preferred by Menahem Begin, and his invoking of the Holocaust to justify any Israeli action, did little to win friends in the West.

Two events of this period also greatly added to Israel's unpopularity abroad, the Lebanon conflict of 1982, and the Palestinian *Intifada* which began in 1987. The former, in particular, probably marked the nadir of Israel's fortunes in the West, engendering hostility in the mainstream media so virulent that many Western Jews believed that it crossed the line to anti-semitism. The Lebanon conflict, officially known as 'Operation Peace for Galilee', began on 6 June 1982. For years the PLO had used its bases in southern Lebanon to launch rocket and terrorist attacks against settlements in Israel's north. The controversial Likud minister of defence, Ariel Sharon, had long favoured a full-scale military operation to clear the PLO out of southern Lebanon, in co-operation with the Phalangist (right-wing Christian) forces of Bashir Jemayel, Israel's chief Lebanese allies, who detested the PLO as well as Lebanon's Muslims. In early June 1982 the Israeli ambassador to Britain, Shlomo Argov, was shot and seriously wounded in London by a Palestinian terrorist. This was the signal for the unleashing of 'Operation Peace for Galilee', with Israeli forces advancing into Lebanon to destroy the PLO's forces there. This proved a complete success, with Israel destroying the PLO's terrorist bases, especially the Beaufort fortress, a major artillery stronghold, within a few days. By the fourth day of the operation, Israel had engaged in a full-scale air war with Syria (destroying most of its air force) and by 11 June, when a ceasefire came into operation, had marched to within a few miles of Beirut airport. At this point the war, already extremely contentious, became the most controversial in Israel's history. Linking up with their Phalangist allies, the Israelis besieged and, by early September, conquered Beirut, Lebanon's capital, forcing Arafat and the PLO to flee to Tunis. The conquest of Beirut was facilitated by a massive (11–12 August) aerial bombardment of Beirut. Western media and newspaper depictions, especially of the relentless and bloody march on Beirut, were almost universally hostile, and routinely contrasted with the defensive wars fought by Israel in the past. Arafat was widely seen as 'David', Israel as 'Goliath'. Many openly compared Israel's forces with those of Nazi Germany. Now things went even more badly wrong. On 14 September Bashir Jemayel, Lebanon's president-elect and Israel's ally, was assassinated. In retaliation, three days later Phalange forces entered two Palestinian refugee camps near Beirut, at Sabra and Chatilla, and cold-bloodedly massacred about 3000 Palestinian civilians.

These forces were technically under Israeli control, although the massacre was carried out without the knowledge or approval of Israel's forces, which, when alerted, did what they could to stop it. The international furore intensified, as did opposition to the war within Israel itself, on a scale unknown in the country's history. On 25 September 1982, a rally of

400,000 protesters, the largest in Israel's history, took place in Tel Aviv, which called for a commission of inquiry into the massacre. The Begin government agreed, in late September, to establish such a commission of inquiry. Chaired by Supreme Court Justice Yitzhak Kahan (and known as the Kahan Commission), it issued a report early in 1983. This heavily criticised defence minister Ariel Sharon for his actions during the massacre, and led to his resignation.

Israel withdrew from Beirut in mid-September, but remained in Lebanese territory as far as the Awali River until September 1983. In November, a suicide squad of Syrian-backed Shi'ites destroyed Israel's headquarters in Sidon, on the Lebanese coast, killing 36 people. In April 1985 Israel withdrew from Lebanon except for a narrow 'security zone' just north of the border. The IDF remained in this area, and under constant terrorist threat, until mid-2000. There is general agreement, at least on the left, that the Lebanon invasion was a terrible mistake, since it was not occasioned by the immediate need for self-defence, did not stop terrorism, destroy the PLO, or establish a pro-Israeli government in Beirut. Many questions have also been asked about the Begin government's exact knowledge of Sharon's intentions and actions. On the other hand, many on the Israeli right supported the war as a necessary step. The Knesset election held in July 1984 resulted in almost precisely the same results as the previous one, held in June 1981, with both Likud and the Alignment (Labour) suffering limited losses of seats. Many conservatives around the world strongly supported Israel's stance against terrorists, and American support for Israel remained firm, despite criticism. Possibly the most important long-term outcome of the conflict was the realisation that the PLO could not be destroyed by military action.

The failure of any real peace effort involving the Palestinians in the years following the Lebanon conflict led to an upsurge of unrest in the West Bank and Gaza. In December 1987 there began what is known as the *Intifada*, a popular uprising in the occupied territories in which Israeli soldiers and others were attacked by rioters and guerrillas. The initial phase of the *Intifada* lasted for two months and led to over 50 deaths. As with Lebanon, media depictions of armed Israeli soldiers dealing with rioters throwing stones and handmade weapons did considerable harm to Israel's image. Israel responded harshly to the uprising, restricting the movements of the Palestinians and making many arrests. The *Intifada* continued in diminished but chronic form in the early 1990s. By the end of 1992 over 1800 Palestinians had been killed (many were alleged 'collaborators' killed by other Palestinians). The initiation of a serious peace process between Israelis and Palestinians in 1992–93 saw a decline in instances of violence. Late in 2000 these resumed with a vengeance following the failure of Israel and the PLO to agree on terms for a final peace settlement.

Apart from the damage done to Israel by the Lebanon conflict and the *Intifada*, the period from 1973–91 saw many other serious and chronic problems for Israeli society itself. While these grew in part from the failure of the peace process and the continuing tensions between Israel and the Arabs, they were essentially unrelated to Israel's external policies; rather they were situated within Israeli society. Despite massive and continuing American foreign aid, Israel's economy for much of this period was in dire straits, experiencing massive inflation and a severe balance-of-payments problem almost continuously until the later 1980s. Each Israeli government offered a variety of nostrums to tackle this situation, but without much real relief. Raising already high taxation to lower demand and curb inflation inevitably diminished living standards, while any attempt to reorient the Israeli economy as a whole in a less interventionist direction (as Likud tried to do in the late 1970s) triggered inflation and outraged the vested interests which had been built up by Israel's highly centralised economy. In 1980 the Israeli currency was revamped, with the lira, in use since 1948, replaced by the shekel at a ratio of 10:1. The economic situation made it necessary for most Israelis to hold two jobs, or to engage in an orgy of speculation on the Stock Market, leading to the 'Bank Shares Crisis' of 1983. By 1984 inflation in Israel was running at 400 per cent, an incredible figure for a Western country. Israel's economic position was made worse by the Arabs' long-standing boycott of Israeli goods, which made it difficult for Israel to trade with its closest neighbours, and by the vast sums which had to be spent year after year on the military. Only in the late 1980s did inflation lessen, although at the cost of economic stagnation. Israel's economy did not begin to improve until the 1990s.

The economic difficulties of living in Israel were also in part behind the phenomenon of the *yordim* (literally 'those who go down', or 'drop outs'), Israelis who emigrated abroad in search of prosperity and a quieter life. By the 1980s communities of Hebrew-speaking Israelis were to be found in many Western cities, especially New York and Los Angeles. Estimates of their numbers (almost certainly exaggerated) ranged upward to 500,000. (Paradoxically, Israel's Jewish population continued to grow substantially, from 2,582,000 in 1970 to 3,283,000 in 1980 to 3,947,000 in 1990.) Only in the 1990s did this emigration appear to lessen.

Within Israeli society, there were also many sources of division and tension. The Sephardim from the Afro-Asian world, often immigrants from pre-modern societies, often found themselves at the bottom of the economic and political barrel. In the early 1970s a radical protest movement of second-generation Sephardim known as the 'Black Panthers', after the radical black movement in the United States, gained considerable attention.[2] Massive immigration from the Afro-Asian world (491,000 Jews migrated from North Africa, Iraq, Yemen, and other 'Oriental' nations between 1948 and 1960) altered the demographic balance of Israel; by the 1980s nearly

---

2 The deprived Sephardi communities from the Afro-Asian world are known as the *Edot Mizrach* ('Oriental communities'), and should be distinguished from the Sephardim of Europe. The *Edot Mizrach* typically spoke Arabic, Judeo-Arabic, or Judeo-Persian, rather than Ladino, and often resembled the Muslim host population in appearance.

half the Jewish population was of Sephardi origin. There is general agreement that their integration into Israeli society was not well-handled, and that too many remained at the fringes of society for too long. Herut and Likud successfully exploited their grievances against the Ashkenazi elite. Many Afro-Asian Jews, having experienced Muslim hegemony for centuries, were also less willing to make concessions to the Arabs than were Jews of Western backgrounds, with their expectations that the Arabs would produce a moderate, liberal element with whom Israel could negotiate. Only in the 1980s did the gap between the two communities appear to narrow, symbolised by the election in 2000 of Moshe Katzav, an Iranian-born Jew, as Israel's president.

Perhaps the deepest division to emerge within Israeli society at this time was over religion, between Orthodox and non-Orthodox or secular Jews. Throughout Israeli history there has been a steady rise in the Orthodox (known as *Haredi*, literally 'God-fearing') portion of the Jewish population. By the 1980s perhaps one-fifth of the population was Orthodox in a visible sense, with the Orthodox holding a majority in Jerusalem and elsewhere. While the Orthodox had always elected their own members to the Knesset, as the political monopoly enjoyed by Labour disintegrated they were able to exploit their balance of power position in the Knesset to extract concessions from the government of the day, always in the direction of making Israel more 'Jewish'. In 1981, for example, Begin's government was forced to agree to end flights by El Al, the national airline, on the Jewish Sabbath. Expenditure on Orthodox schools and institutions skyrocketed. Religious teachers were exempted from military conscription, a privilege previously unknown. Secular educational expenditure was cut. Religious violence aimed, for instance, at archaeological excavations at religious sites, intensified. The growth of political Orthodoxy in Israel has also resulted in a continuing clash over the so-called 'Who is a Jew?' question, which has long bedevilled Israeli politics. Under the Law of Return of 1950 all Jews have the automatic right to migrate to Israel. Naturally, therefore, the issue of Jewish identity must be legally clarified. Until 1970 Israel accepted that anyone would be considered a Jew who was born of a Jewish mother or who had converted to Judaism. This was set out in a law passed by the Knesset in 1970, which also established that someone born a Jew, but who was converted to another religion, is not to be considered a Jew. Since then, great controversy has raged over the meaning of 'conversion' to Judaism. Orthodox Jews have attempted many times to change the law to define as Jewish only those who have converted to Judaism according to the *Halakhah*, that is, according to Orthodox Jewish law and by an Orthodox rabbi. This proposed change has been fiercely and vociferously opposed by Reform and Liberal rabbis in the Diaspora, who see it as an attempt to delegitimise their movements. Many unsuccessful attempts have been made by Orthodox political parties and leaders to change the Law of Return, and such change remains an ever-present possibility. Furthermore, only

Orthodox Judaism is officially recognised by the Israeli state; non-Orthodox Jews cannot legally perform marriages or other ceremonials, and their institutions meet many official obstacles. Paradoxically, the Law of Return has always been interpreted liberally, allowing, for instance, thousands of Soviet Jews possessing the most tenuous association with Jewry (including the non-Jewish spouses of Jews) to migrate to Israel. Ironically, probably half or more of the Israeli population is wholly or largely secular in their lifestyle apart from observation of the basic rites of passage and festivals.

The period 1973–91 of course had its triumphs as well as its chronic problems and malaise. The day after Menahem Begin became prime minister in May 1977, he made a speech calling for peace with the Arabs and appointed the ex-Labour moderate Moshe Dayan as foreign minister. Secret talks were then held in Morocco between Dayan and Egypt's foreign minister. In November, the Egyptian president, Anwar Sadat, made the stunning announcement that he wished to visit Jerusalem, and Begin issued an official invitation. Most remarkably, on 19 November 1977 Sadat landed at Ben-Gurion airport for a three-day visit. Absolutely nothing like this had happened before in Israel's history. By October 1978, normalisation of relations between Israel and Egypt had become a reality, following the Camp David Accords (named for Camp David, in Maryland, where the negotiations were held). Israel also promised a 'framework of autonomy' on the West Bank. In exchange for normalisation, Israel agreed to hand the Sinai back to Egypt in stages, which it completed in April 1982.

Further progress towards peace with the Arabs did not eventuate, owing to the reluctance of the Israelis to withdraw from the West Bank or to negotiate with the PLO, and also owing to the continuing level of terrorist violence directed against Israel by the Palestinians and the radical Arab states. Most religious Jews and most of those in the Revisionist-Likud tradition believed that the West Bank and Gaza were legitimately a part of the Jewish state, belonging historically and religiously to Israel. Many secularists believed that Israel required all or much of the West Bank for strategic reasons, and that a tiny state like Israel could not return to its pre-1967 boundaries, which were termed by Abba Eban the 'boundaries of Auschwitz'. After 1967, many Israeli settlements were built on the West Bank and Gaza. Some were initiated by Orthodox Jews, but others, especially around Jerusalem, were simply 'dormitory suburbs' whose Jewish inhabitants often commuted to work elsewhere. The settlement issue became a burning one in Israeli politics, with most on the political and religious right strongly favouring Jewish settlements on the West Bank, especially Gush Emunim, the religious Zionist movement which strongly advocates Jewish settlement throughout the whole of the historic land of Israel. Most left-liberal Israelis believed that West Bank settlement was a tragic blunder, making overall peace with the Palestinians far more difficult. The settlement issue became a burning one in Israeli politics, with over 100,000 Israelis living on the West Bank by the year 2000.

Towards peace and prosperity? Israel since 1990

By the late 1980s, the profound changes in the world's geopolitics brought about by the collapse of the Soviet Union began to impact upon the Arab–Israeli conflict, making the period since about 1990 much more hopeful for Israel than the previous decades.

A distinct turning-point in the fortunes in the State of Israel came in the late 1980s with Mikhail Gorbachev's policy of *glasnost* and the subsequent collapse of the Soviet Union. Contacts between that country and Israel, unknown since 1967, were resumed in 1987, when several renowned 'prisoners of Zion' were allowed to emigrate. There was a steady, but slow, improvement of relations between the two countries, leading to massive Soviet Jewish emigration to Israel (and elsewhere, especially the United States) and to renewed diplomatic relations between the two, which were formally resumed early in 1991. (Israel also established or re-established diplomatic relations with dozens of other countries at this time.) Between the late 1980s and the end of the 1990s about 600,000 Soviet Jewish immigrants went to Israel, an extraordinary figure, including 200,000 in 1990 alone. They took with them a range of scientific skills, and considerably altered Israel's political balance. In addition, 50,000 Ethiopian Jews were airlifted to Israel in 1984–91 giving Israeli society a multi-racial aspect. Also in 1991, despite the severe provocation of Saddam Hussein's Scud missile attacks on its territory, Israel pointedly avoided becoming directly involved in the Gulf War waged by the American-led international coalition against Iraq. In January and February 1991 39 Iraqi Scud missiles hit Israeli targets, killing four persons (three died of heart attacks), wounding another 300, and damaging 9000 buildings, chiefly in Tel Aviv. Photographs of Israelis wearing gas masks (against assumed poison gas attacks) were published around the world. Although Israel could have launched deadly counter-measures against Iraq (and had every right to do so), strong American pressure, exercised for fear of alienating its Arab allies, meant that Israel did nothing. Its forbearance brought considerable international kudos, and an esteem unexperienced for some time. Coincidentally or not, in December 1991 the UN General Assembly voted by 111 to 25 to rescind the 1975 resolution equating Zionism with racism.

The American government now turned its attention to securing a far-reaching settlement in the Middle East. In October 1991 the Madrid Peace Conference opened, the first occasion since the foundation of the Jewish state at which Israelis and Arabs participated directly and officially in negotiations for peace. Yitzhak Shamir, Israel's prime minister, headed the Israeli delegation, while the Arabs were represented by the foreign ministers of Egypt, Jordan, Syria, Lebanon, and members of a joint Palestine–Jordan delegation. Israel's initially harder stance was softened when Rabin and Labour replaced Likud in 1992. Throughout, the Arabs adopted a hostile position, insisting on full Israeli withdrawal from all occupied territories.

Although few concrete results were achieved, in its way the conference marked a turning-point in the Arab–Israeli conflict.

In January 1993 American President Bill Clinton presided over one of the most dramatic turns in the history of Arab–Israeli relations. Beginning early in 1993, secret talks between Israeli and PLO negotiators took place in Oslo, Norway. Initially low-keyed and concerning chiefly economic co-operation, they became more serious when Shimon Peres, the new foreign minister, decided to upgrade them. This occurred against the background of a renewed *Intifada* and murders of Israelis by terrorists. By August, in strict secrecy, the Oslo Accords had been brokered. Their heart consisted of the mutual recognition of the PLO and Israel, leading to Palestinian autonomy. Announced on 20 August 1993, they caused universal surprise, exceeding even that produced by Anwar Sadat's visit to Jerusalem in 1977. A month later, on the White House lawn, occurred the celebrated handshakes between Yasser Arafat, Rabin, and Peres, as President Clinton looked on. Many diplomatic gains ensued over the next few years. In May 1994 the Gaza–Jericho agreement was signed, signalling the withdrawal from these areas by Israel. In October came a peace treaty between Israel and Jordan. Further agreements on the future of the West Bank followed in 1996. In contrast to the previous decades, strong economic growth occurred in Israel in the 1990s, and a 'hi-tech' sector of international note emerged. Relations with the Vatican markedly improved, as did Israel's linkages with the Third World.

Progress towards peace was most emphatically not straightforward. Most Israelis refused to contemplate a fully independent Palestinian state, in particular one with East Jerusalem as its capital. A significant radical right developed in Israel, vehemently opposed to any further concessions. In November 1995 a student extremist, Yigal Amir, assassinated prime minister Rabin. Protracted negotiations continued year after year. No agreement was reached with Syria, despite negotiations. In 2000 the entire peace process came to a virtual halt with the upsurge of anti-Israel *Intifada*-like violence on the West Bank following the failure, albeit narrowly, to reach a final settlement over Jerusalem and other remaining issues.

Despite all these failures, after half a century Israel had accomplished an enormous number of gains for the Jewish people. In the early twenty-first century nearly five million Jews (4,941,000 in mid-2000) lived there. The country seemed likely by 2010 to overtake the United States as having the largest Jewish community in the world. It was possibly the only Jewish community in the world, and clearly the largest, with a positive demographic balance, where the Jewish fertility rate was above the replacement level. Even after settling so many immigrants from the former Soviet Union, it continued to receive about 40,000 Jews each year. It was home to Orthodox Jewish life, which had recovered from the catastrophic losses of the Holocaust chiefly owing to Israel's existence. Israel was the Middle East's economic and military super-power, and the cause of enhanced self-esteem for Jews everywhere. The image of Israel probably did as much to reduce right-wing antisemitism in the West as any other factor, a feat for which the country is given too little credit. That full peace has not yet been achieved is primarily the result of Arab hostility and intransigence. In many respects Israel's achievements have occurred in contradistinction to trends elsewhere in the Western world, where liberalism, hedonism, and a lack of deeply-held principles have become the order of the day. Perhaps Israel's greatest contribution to the Jewish people has been to counteract the rampant assimilation which has occurred in the Diaspora.

Further reading

R.O. Freedman, ed., *Israel under Rabin* (New York, 1995)

Calvin Goldscheider, *Israel's Changing Society: Population, Ethnicity, and Development* (Boulder, Col., 1993)

Neill Lochery, *The Israeli Labour Party: In the Shadow of Likud* (Reading, Berks, 1997)

Ian S. Lustick, *For the Land and the Lord* (New York, 1988)

D. Makovsky, *Making Peace with the PLO: The Rabin Government's Road to the Oslo Accord* (Boulder, Col., 1996)

Howard M. Sachar, *A History of Israel, Volume II: From the Aftermath of the Yom Kippur War* (Oxford, 1987)

Ehud Sprinzak, *The Ascendancy of Israel's Radical Right* (Oxford, 1991)

Geoffrey Wheatcroft, *The Controversy of Zion: Jewish Nationalism, the Jewish State, and the Unresolved Jewish Dilemma* (Reading, Mass., 1996)

(Many of the works cited in the previous chapter's list of further reading are relevant here.)

16

Jewish women in modern times

In traditional Judaism men and women occupy different spheres, much as they do in virtually all other traditional religions and cultures. In traditional Judaism, women's maternal and domestic functions are central to their identity. They are exempt from most of the religious observances required of men, but are required to make a prescribed blessing over the Sabbath candles, cleanse themselves in a ritual bath (*mikveh*) before their wedding and following menstruation and childbirth, and keep a kosher kitchen. Traditionally, Jewish women are subordinate to their husbands. They are also regarded as sexually enticing to other men. Accordingly, men and women sit separately in synagogues, with, in many Orthodox synagogues, women seated in galleries above the men, often screened from view, so that the thoughts of male worshippers will not stray from prayer to lust. In traditional Judaism, women cannot become rabbis or scholars of Jewish law. While a wife cannot be divorced against her will, as in Islam, there have been instances of husbands refusing to grant their wives a writ of divorcement (*get*), thus trapping them in unhappy marriages, and of husbands deserting, thereby relegating them to the status of 'chained women' (*agunot*), unable to marry. Down the centuries, Orthodox Judaism has remained full of innumerable instances of apparent gender inequality.

All this should be seen in context, of course. Virtually every religion sanctions different roles for men and women, with the role of women invariably being more limited, if not overtly inferior. Women cannot become priests or bishops of the Catholic Church, and could not become priests of the Church of England until 1992. The inferior status of women in most fundamentalist Islamic countries is too self-evident to require much elaboration. If anything, the status of women in traditional Judaism was relatively higher than in other societies, with women, for instance, probably demonstrating higher levels of literacy than elsewhere in pre-modern times, and legally able to own and inherit property. The Torah and other holy books of Judaism reveres the Matriarchs (Sarah, Rebecca, Leah, and Rachel) as well as the Patriarchs (Abraham, Isaac, and Jacob) of the Jewish people, and highlights the achievements of other celebrated women, such as Deborah and Esther. Although women in traditional Judaism are viewed as having different roles from men, they are not regarded as inferior in any essential sense, but are seen as crucial to the maintenance of Judaism and the Jewish people across the generations: indeed, Jewish descent is matrilineal.

As in other religions and peoples, the traditional role of women has altered among the Jews in modern times, leading to conflicts between traditional and modern interpretations of Judaism. In particular, in the twentieth century the granting of political and economic rights to women throughout the western world, and the rise, after 1960, of 'Second Wave feminism' challenging gender stereotypes and inequalities, have had a profound impact upon Jewish women and among the strands of Judaism. Jewish women have suffered as women as well as Jews, for instance during the Holocaust. This chapter explains some of the ramifications of these events, especially of the changes in the role and status of women in recent times.

Traditional ways

During the eighteenth and nineteenth centuries the overwhelming majority of Jewish women lived as their female ancestors had done, presiding over the domestic sphere. In accordance with the modesty expected of them most wore long-sleeved high-necked gowns, and after marriage they took care that not a strand of their hair should be seen by any man other than their husbands. Thus in eighteenth-century central Europe married women wore variations of the headgear described by a Scotswoman visiting Holland in 1756. She described a cotton cap fitting snugly to the head, 'so that you see none of their hair, and some has a curl of wool round their faces, by way of a wig, some black and some white'. An Irishwoman visiting Poland a century later noted that Jewish married women shaved off their hair, 'substituting for it braids of black or brown satin, according to the original colour of the hair. On the old women these satin appendages are almost concealed by golden caps, which have a bordering of stiff ruching, while the young ones have theirs surmounted by richly trimmed headdresses, their foreheads, ears, and necks bedecked with pearls and diamonds, their garments, in many instances, being at the same time scarcely worth the acceptance of a beggar.' The wearing of wigs as substitutes for cloth head coverings began in the sixteenth century in imitation of gentile fashion and led to controversy. Some rabbis argued that their use contravened the spirit of the law since they looked like real hair, and that they should therefore be banned. Others, however, declared their use to be acceptable, a view heeded by countless women in eastern Europe, particularly those adhering to Hasidic and other strictly Orthodox sects.

In Islamic countries Jewish women's costume resembled that of Muslim women, and the decorative use of henna and kohl was widespread. An Englishman who in the 1760s visited the home of the British consul in the Dardanelles, a Turkish Jew, described the unmarried daughter as 'a girl in a long white vest, with a zone about her middle, her feet naked, her nails dyed red, her hair plaited and hanging down her back.' A traveller in Morocco described the Jewish women's attire as 'most fanciful and oriental', their eyes 'rendered more oriental by a dark powder'. Their clothes, especially those worn on Sabbaths and festivals, were 'remarkably rich', consisting of finely-woven scarlet or dark green robes, lavishly embroidered on the bodice and bound by a silk sash; on special occasions women of the wealthier classes sported 'splendid earrings, and a magnificent tiara of pearls, emeralds, and other precious stones, with numerous rings on their fingers of considerable value'. There were close versions of this costume throughout North Africa.

The status of Jewish women in Morocco at the turn of the twentieth century was described by westernised female teachers of eastern origin employed by the Alliance Israélite Universelle. The condition of women was one 'of complete servitude', reflecting the influence of the surrounding non-Jewish culture. 'From the moment of her birth, a woman feels the weight of her inferiority. Whereas there are cries of joy and endless celebration upon the birth of a son, it is cries of mourning which welcome into the world the young girl.' Daughters were married in childhood 'so that they may be all the sooner taken off the hands of the father'. Acquiring a second wife during the lifetime of the first was not uncommon, and wives owed 'passive obedience' to their husbands. There was segregation of the sexes at meal-times, with the husband, sons and male guests being given the best furniture and table linen, being served first, and having the pick of the food. Wives, daughters, and female servants usually ate together in the kitchen, not uncommonly making do with the leftovers of the all-male repast. (Similar accounts from other pens of the downtrodden condition of Jewish women in Morocco have survived.) In Turkey the stagnant conservatism which gripped rabbinic circles from the seventeenth to the nineteenth centuries had an adverse effect on the status of women within the family.

Before marriage Jewish girls in Islamic countries were secluded within their homes, venturing out in the evening, faces hidden, to visit close neighbours. After marriage many appear to have enjoyed greater freedom to come and go than did Muslim women, whose custom of wearing the veil was widely imitated by Jewish women in order to avoid the unwelcome attentions of Muslim men. The latter tended to regard them as fair game for sexual harassment if they left their faces bare. But ill-disposed regimes, such as Persia's, forbade Jewish women to cover their faces in a deliberate attempt to bring shame on them and their community, and very good-looking women were sometimes abducted and taken into the harems of rich men.

Beyond the domestic sphere

Despite the constraints of law and custom some women through force of personality or circumstance broke out of the purely domestic sphere in pre-modern times. The biblical archetype of the female achiever was Deborah the judge. One Talmudic sage went so far as to warn that 'Whoever teaches his daughter Torah teaches her *tiflut*' – generally translated as 'indecency' or 'frivolity'. That was, in fact, a minority opinion. There was, however, general consensus that such study was not incumbent upon women them-selves and that their chief responsibility in this area was to ensure that their sons were taught Torah and to encourage their husbands to continue to study it. Not all fathers were averse to teaching their daughters Torah. Beruriah, daughter of one rabbi and wife of another, was a celebrated second-century scholar of Jewish law, and over the ensuing centuries there was the occasional renowned and respected female religious authority. For example, the learned daughter of a prominent and important twelfth-century Baghdadi scholar sat at a window modestly concealed behind a lattice discoursing knowledgeably on Bible and Talmud to male pupils. There were female Jewish poets and intellectuals in early modern Italy, Holland, and England, notably the seventeenth-century Venetian poet Sara Copia Sullam, whose writings reveal a humanistic education. In anticipation of the salon hostesses of the *Haskalah* period her marital home served as a meeting place for Jewish and Christian scholars.

Jewish women engaged in commerce. Many helped their husbands with the family business, which was at least until the late nineteenth century typically situated in or adjacent to the family home, meaning that the wife was on the premises to divide her time between living-quarters and count-ing-house or shop-front. Wives of tradesmen often helped their husbands keep the accounts. Sometimes women found themselves in the role of principal breadwinner, either through desertion, divorce or widowhood, or because their husbands were lifelong, fulltime Talmudic scholars, a role regarded as desirable and honourable, especially in eastern Europe. It was common for wives, and in some cases daughters, of poor families to help supplement the household income. In North Africa married women in such families sewed and embroidered to earn extra household money, frequently squatting on the ground outside the *mellah* waiting for Arab women to bring them items to mend. Some very poverty-stricken women acted as water carriers in return for a meagre portion of food. Starting out at first light and continuing until nightfall, they trod a continuous path between the public fountain and the households that hired them, lugging the water in jars on their shoulders. Women in the Rome ghetto were so adroit at sewing, producing work of an exceptionally high standard, that they were in great demand from citizens to do fine needlework and invisible repairs. They were to be seen sitting at their windows from dawn to well after dusk busy with their thread. The close work involved, often performed of necessity in poor light, reputedly had deleterious effects upon their eyesight. A nineteenth-century account of Kazimierz, the Jewish quarter of Cracow, reported that Jewish women stood at the doors of their shops inviting 'every passer-by to become a purchaser', rapidly knitting all the while. The majority of garments thus created would become part of their stock.

In the *shtetlekh* of eastern Europe most of the inhabitants were poor, some even to the point of scraping to buy chicken or fish for the Sabbath meal, subsisting for the rest of the week on water, bread, and onions. It was not uncommon for wives to mind the family stores and stalls while their husbands were on business errands and for wives to fit in other types of work around their usually heavy domestic reponsibilities in order to help the household make ends meet. Stringing pearls, plucking and selling poultry, hawking dairy produce, bagels, potato pancakes and other foods, knitting and selling socks, gloves, and shawls, sewing garments and clothing accessories – these were among the ways in which married and unmarried women earned money. The Russian census of 1897 indicated that just over 21 per cent of the Jewish labour force in the Pale were women. This, it has been argued, was probably a significant underestimate since in concentrating upon workers engaged in industrial manufacturing it almost certainly excluded self-employed women in such categories as those listed above. Eastern European Jewish women who emigrated to Britain and the New World also contributed towards the family income, often working as machinists of clothing in 'sweatshops' and factories.

The celebrated memoirs of Hamburg-born Glückel of Hameln (1646–1724), written in Yiddish but since translated into English, provide a vivid insight into the conduct of a prosperous central European Jewish merchant's household. Her life in its basic respects typified the experiences of Jewish women not only in her own and previous generations but for several generations to come: she was betrothed to a man of her parents' choice at the age of 12, married at barely 14, had her first child a year later, and settled into a pattern of regular childbearing which made her the mother of a numerous brood. Widowed at the age of 44, she went on to prove that she possessed a shrewd head for business, enabling her to provide dowries for her unmarried daughters. However, ten years after her husband's death she married a wealthy financier of Metz, who went bankrupt, losing her money as well as his own in the process. Owing to the claims of creditors, at his death she 'received back very little of the money from my wedding-contract, not a third of what was due to me', and for the rest of her life she was dependent on the generosity of a son-in-law. Such a fate must have overtaken many women. A few Jewish women with commercial acumen actually managed to become Court Jews.

The Jewish hostesses and habituées of drawing-room salons operating in Berlin around the time that the *Haskalah* first began to make inroads into German Jewry were also among the earliest Jewish women to mix freely in general society. Sparkling conversationalists, and socially fashionable, they were able to mingle with upper-class and educated gentiles owing to the tolerant atmosphere engendered by the European Enlightenment and because of the interaction between their Jewish social milieu and aristocratic gentiles seeking financial loans. The salon women were the daughters and wives of very prosperous men, and had been educated at home by tutors who prepared them for a life of leisure and ornamentation. Their education in this respect differed little from that of non-Jewish girls of comparable socio-economic background. They could converse well in French, the preferred language of genteel German society at that time, and hold their own in polite company. They were fluent in German and largely ignorant of Yiddish. One of them recalled that at first they 'used their French to conduct elegant con-versations with army officers and court cavaliers who came to borrow money from their fathers.' Later, however, they utilised their knowledge of French for the more important purposes of familiarising themselves with French classics and modern writers. And thus a new world hove into view.

Henriette Herz, *née* De Lemos (1764–1847), author of the above quota-tion, and Rachel Varnhagen, née Levin (1771–1833) were the doyennes of the Jewish salon hostesses. An accomplished linguist, Henriette Herz was the daughter of a Portuguese physician who had settled at Hamburg, and the wife of a Berlin physician and *maskil*. She had belonged to a high-minded group of young people dedicated to ethical principles, among whom were several of the Jews and gentiles who would later grace her salon. They included Moses Mendelssohn's literary-minded daughter Dorothea von Schlegel (1763–1839), who was conspicuous in salon society. Rachel Varnhagen, daughter of a wealthy Berlin merchant, met her non-Jewish hus-band, a minor Prussian diplomat, at Henriette Herz's salon. Frequenting the salons of both women were leading *maskilim* and distinguished politicians, literary and cultural figures from home and abroad. The salon hostesses were in an influential position, facilitating the interchange between Jew and non-Jew, introducing acculturated Jews to liberals and intellectuals from the wider society and helping to break down barriers to Jewish acceptance. Two staunch Prussian warriors in the campaign for Jewish emancipation, brothers Alexander and Wilhelm von Humboldt, for example, were among the noted persons who frequented the salons of both Henriette Herz and Rachel Varnhagen.

Many of the 50 or so Jewish women of Berlin and Vienna who hosted or frequented salons lost their attachments to Judaism. A study of 20 Jewish salon women in Berlin shows that at least 17 became Christians, and ten married gentiles. The widowed Henriette Herz waited until the death of her mother before being baptised, influenced by a distinguished Protestant theologian whom she had long known. Dorothea Mendelssohn left her husband, a Jewish banker with whom she had sons, for a prominent non-Jewish philosopher and man of letters whom she eventually married, having converted to Protestantism along the way. She later embraced Catholicism and successfully prevailed upon her sons to become Catholics too.

Prominent salon hostesses Fanny von Arnstein (1757–1818) and Cecily
Eskeles (1759–1818) had their children baptised, and Fanny and her
husband eventually also converted. She did, however, retain lingering
feelings for her former faith and residual links of sentiment to her erstwhile
co-religionists. Rachel Varnhagen, who was raised in an observant Jewish
household, became a Lutheran upon marriage. She had always been deeply
troubled by her Jewishness: 'I can ascribe every evil, every misfortune, every
vexation that has befallen me to *that*,' she wrote privately when in her
twenties. Her attitude mellowed later in life. Many of these women seem to
have regarded Judaism as a fossilised relic in which they had a second-class
status, and as an encumbrance impeding their upward social progress.
Nevertheless, more men than women became Christians during the wave of
conversions of the late eighteenth and early nineteenth centuries, with more
women remaining in their traditional Jewish domestic and social roles.

The education of women

Glückel of Hameln's unedited manuscript was interspersed with Hebrew
words and phrases, excerpts from prayers, and aphorisms from the Bible
and Talmud. She wrote: 'My father gave his children, girls and boys, a
secular as well as a religious education.' This does not mean, however, that
she and her brothers learned their Judaism in the same way or to the same
depth. While a Talmud Torah for girls was established by the Rome community in 1745 this was unusual. And although there were certainly exceptions most women lacked competency in Hebrew. Glückel, like countless
other Jewish girls of her time, place, and class was almost certainly tutored
at home, and while she may well have been taught the rudiments of Hebrew
it was doubtless in Yiddish that the greater part of her instruction was
conducted, for it is evident that her knowledge of religion owed much to
Yiddish works which existed primarily for women. These included devo-
tional prayers (Yiddish *tkhinnes*; Hebrew *tekhinot*), published from the end
of the sixteenth century. Very many bore the names of female authors,
although these might in a number of cases – perhaps the majority – have
been pseudonyms of male scholars, including rabbinical students, reluctant
to be identified as writers of such simple homely prayers, with their special
relevance to the concerns and lifestyles of women. At least a few *tkhinnes*
were, however, certainly penned by women, one of whom was Leah
Horowitz (*c*.1720–*c*.1800), daughter of a Galician rabbi and apparently
well acquainted with the Talmud. Women also depended for instruction
upon ethical tracts and story books consisting of moralistic tales based on
the Bible, Talmud, and other sources. The classic text for the religious education of women (and men with inadequate command of Hebrew) was the
Zenah u-Reenah (literally 'Come and See,' from the *Song of Songs*, 3:11).
Compiled by a well-known Polish rabbi in the sixteenth century and

believed to have first appeared in the 1590s, it was written in a deliberately straightforward, engaging style. A miscellany of tales, homilies, and other instructive material composed around a Yiddish paraphrase of the Pentateuch, it became extremely popular with successive generations of Jewish women in eastern Europe. Books were available in Yiddish specifically on the dietary regulations and the laws governing family purity, those aspects of *Halakhah* of direct relevance to women. Because so few women had command of Hebrew, the custom emerged in eastern European synagogues of having prompters who helped female worshippers recite prayers and indicated appropriate behaviour at certain parts of the liturgy. There were, however, occasional eastern European Jewish women who became serious students of traditional Judaism. One such was Hannah Rachel Werbermacher (*c.*1815–1892), from Ludomir in the Ukraine, who gained a reputation as a *zaddik*, having both men and women followers. She eventually emigrated to Palestine.

As a result of the *Haskalah*, girls attended the newly-established modern Jewish elementary schools. A basic grounding in Hebrew and the tenets of Judaism was offered to all pupils regardless of gender, and the schools also prepared children for life in the wider society by introducing them to commercial subjects and trades. In the case of girls trades typically meant cookery and needlecraft, equipping them for positions as domestic servants in wealthy Jewish homes and for marriage. Commercial subjects proved useful for girls who went on to become the wives of tradesmen and merchants, because they could help their husbands with the bookkeeping. A similar purpose was served by the schools for girls established in North Africa and the Middle East by the Alliance Israélite Universelle. Their teachers, specially trained in Paris, were the first eastern Jewish females to receive a formal education, and they acted as role models when they returned to their native region. The Alliance schools sought to instil into the girls western standards of childcare, housewifery, and hygiene; they also sowed the seeds of confidence and a sense of self-worth in girls accustomed to feeling inferior to their brothers. Girls were taught sewing and dressmaking, and in due course secretarial and other office skills were added to the curriculum. At first, many of the girls sent to these schools were peremptorily removed by their fathers in order to be married at a very young age, but gradually more and more girls stayed on to complete their courses. Their schooling helped to raise their status within the family, and the provision of vocational education gave them the opportunity to earn an independent livelihood, at least until they wed. Sometimes, to the chagrin of older relatives, many also acquired western ways, abandoning their traditional attire for European clothes, hairstyles, and cosmetics, neglecting after marriage to adopt a subservient secluded lifestyle and thus playing their part in the transformation of eastern Jewry.

Among the traditional Jews of eastern Europe there could be found *hadarim* for girls, operated typically by rabbis' wives or widows. There the girls were taught prayers and the fundamentals of Judaism, how to read and write in Yiddish, and arithmetic. Sometimes a smattering of Russian or Polish was added. In other cases girls were sent to *hadarim* along with boys, but were removed once they had learned how to read; they did not stay on to study sacred texts as boys did. A survey in 1894 showed that there were just over 10,500 girls in these sorts of schools in the Russian Empire compared with nearly 191,000 boys. Girls whose parents could afford the services of a tutor, again typically a mature woman, received instruction at home in reading and writing and in the fundamentals of their religion for perhaps one hour a day. The Russian census of 1897 indicated that 30 per cent of Jewish females between the ages of ten and 19 could read and write in Russian compared with 41 per cent of Jewish males of the same age group. Those most likely to do so lived in the south-west provinces, where the *Haskalah* had penetrated. Most Jewish women received no formal education, yet the majority seem to have been able to read and write – usually exclusively in Yiddish. They had obviously picked up these skills informally at home, learning from relatives and friends, using the *Zenah u-Reenah* and related material as well as popular romances. For instance, a study in 1913 of Jewish working women in three cities showed that in Berdichev and Warsaw less than 7 per cent were illiterate while in Vilna over 99 per cent could read and write. These percentages were vastly higher than among non-Jewish Russians. A sample of 110 female Russian Jewish immigrants to the United States surveyed that same year showed that only 18 were totally illiterate.

In twentieth-century Poland an unmarried seamstress, Sarah Schenirer (1883–1935), founded the Beis Yaakov ('House of Jacob') school for girls from Orthodox homes which developed into an impressive network. In 1918 she opened a girls' school in Cracow, with an initial enrolment of 25 girls under the age of 17. Their number steadily increased to over 300 at the end of the first year. Before proceeding with the venture she had obtained the consent of the Belzer *rebbe*, the dynastic leader whom her family followed. She went on to receive the approval of no less an authority than the famed and respected Rabbi Israel Meir Kagan (known as the Hofetz Haim, meaning 'He who wants to live,' after a book of that title which he wrote). The Hofetz Haim, who was a leader of the strictly Orthodox Agudas Israel movement, pronounced that in view of the inroads into traditional Jewish family life that were taking place the old prejudice against educating girls must be jettisoned, for it was essential that girls – future mothers and exemplars to the next generation – be thoroughly instructed in the fundamentals of Judaism. In 1919 the Agudas Israel movement assumed responsibility for the Beis Yaakov school that Sarah had founded and in 1923 established an educational fund to pay for the establishment of more such schools. From Poland they spread into Lithuania, Latvia, Romania, Hungary, Czechoslovakia, and Austria. Teachers' training colleges were established and summer camps set up. By the outbreak of the Second World

War there were over 250 Beis Yaakov schools, with a total enrolment of almost 40,000. Feminism was constantly derided in school publications, because the Agudas Israel movement viewed it as yet another strand of secularism injurious to conventional Jewish life. Yet through these schools girls became familiar with Jewish religious texts once privy virtually exclusively to males, and they received vocational as well as domestic training, fitting them for work as teachers, secretaries, and bookkeepers as well as for the role of wife and mother. Although the movement was not a Zionist one, during the 1930s a training farm was set up for girls who wished to emigrate to Palestine.

Women in religious life

The Jewish girl attains her religious majority at the age of 12, but historically there has been no special ceremony to mark this rite of passage. It is no accident that, although Jewish identity descends in the maternal line, levitical and priestly status is taken from the father, for the activities associated with synagogue ritual have been traditionally an exclusively male concern. The conduct of services, the quorum (*minyan*) of ten adults – that is, of *Bar Mitzvah* age and above – necessary to hold public worship, the recitation of *Kaddish* at the funerals of parents and on each anniversary of their deaths, have been through the ages restricted to men. They alone have been called to the reading of the Torah in the synagogue on Sabbaths and festivals; they alone have occupied the chief space in the synagogue, for women have been traditionally segregated behind a partition, or in a separate room, or in a balcony, lest the sight of them should distract the minds of men engaged in prayer.

Only in the non-Orthodox streams of Judaism, those not bound by the letter of *Halakhah*, have women achieved some semblance of equality in the ritual and administration of the synagogue. The Reform Temple dedicated in 1818 in Hamburg in the wake of the *Haskalah* was set up partly in response to the wish of women for a service which they could understand, since their knowledge of Hebrew was scanty. Owing to its inclusion of a sermon and prayers in German, the new Temple attracted far more women to its services than did the city's traditional synagogues. However, unlike its Berlin contemporary, which had women seated opposite men, it retained the Orthodox practice of a balcony for women; pioneered by Rabbi Samuel Holdheim, mixed seating in German Reform congregations seems to have been generally introduced later than in their American counterparts.

Nineteenth-century German Reform rabbis fostered the then quite revolutionary notion of the equal treatment of women in the ritual of their synagogues, introducing a ceremony of confirmation for groups of girls who had attained their religious majority. Although falling far short of the *Bar Mitzvah* ceremony for boys, it at least recognised females as active participants in worship. Abraham Geiger and certain contemporary pioneers of Reform in the German states advocated the abolition of aspects of *Halakhah* disadvantageous or seemingly insulting to women. Geiger went so far as to include females in the *minyan*, the quorum of 10 adults necessary for holding public prayer, hitherto always confined to males. This sort of thing scandalised Orthodox rabbis, who stood by their conviction that since *Halakhah* was the word of God it was immutable. The foundation rabbi of Britain's earliest Reform congregation, established in 1840, wasted little time in arguing that women should participate 'in the full discharge of every moral and religious obligation', jettisoning 'eastern customs totally at variance with the habits and dispositions of enlightened people'.

There were many women among the founders of the Union Libérale Israélite in Paris, which held its first services, men and women sitting together, in 1907. Marguerite Brandon-Salvadore, compiler of an anthology of passages from the Bible, the Talmud, and other Judaic texts, was perhaps the most noteworthy. One of the most significant figures in the history of non-Orthodox Judaism, especially in Britain, was a Jewish peer's daughter, Lily Montagu (1873–1963). She co-founded the Jewish Religious Union, forerunner of the Liberal Jewish Synagogue in London. The Union held its initial service in 1902, and was to inspire an elderly Melbourne widow with firsthand experience of it to found Australia's earliest Liberal congregation in 1930. Lily Montagu was the chief organiser of a gathering in London in 1926 that established the World Union for Progressive Judaism. In 1928, when attending that body's inaugural conference in Berlin, she delivered the first sermon ever given by a woman in a German synagogue when she addressed the city's Reform congregation. She had delivered the occasional sermon at her synagogue in London since 1918, and read the service there for the first time in 1920.

During the Nazi era Regina Jonas (1902–44), became the world's first female rabbi. On graduating from Berlin's Academy for the Science of Judaism she began teaching. But, hankering after a rabbinic career, she returned to study, producing a thesis which, utilising the Bible and other sources of *Halakhah*, concluded that there was nothing in Jewish law to prevent women from becoming rabbis. The thesis failed to secure her the rabbinic ordination that she sought, for both the academy's principal and the spiritual leader of Reform Jewry, the renowned Rabbi Leo Baeck (1873–1956), declined to take so radical a step. They perhaps feared that to do so would alienate many within the Reform movement as well as outraging the Orthodox, and so unleash irreconcilable divisions in the ranks of the country's Jewish community at a time of horrendous persecution when it needed to stand united. However, one leading Reform rabbi was prepared to break ranks; he privately presented her with a rabbinical diploma in 1935. Thereafter she served in various chaplaincy and temporary rabbinic positions. Deported in 1942 to Theresienstadt (Terezin), where she applied her pastoral skills to maintaining morale, she perished at Auschwitz two years later.

From its origins in the nineteenth century American Reform Judaism avowed a fundamental commitment to women's equality reflected in mixed seating arrangements, the inclusion of female voices in Temple choirs, and in attitudes to marriage and divorce. In 1922 a daughter of the founder of the Reconstructionist movement, Rabbi Mordecai Kaplan, had the first known *Bat Mitzvah* ('Daughter of the Commandment') ceremony. Such ceremonies, rare at first, went on to become during the latter half of the twentieth century commonplace in synagogues in the United States and elsewhere affiliated to the World Union for Progressive Judaism. Women did not, however, play an equal part alongside men in the administration of Reform congregations, nor in Conservative ones, further to the right along the non-Orthodox spectrum. Their role was confined to so-called sisterhoods and analogous congregation-based organisations which confined themselves to suitably 'feminine' tasks, such as fundraising, arranging catering for functions, and helping out in the Sunday schools. Not until the final decades of the twentieth century were women found on boards of management in numbers, let alone in the position of synagogue president.

In the early 1920s two women studied at the Hebrew Union College in Cincinnati, the American Reform movement's rabbinical seminary, hoping to become rabbis. Another woman, with the same aim, studied during the 1930s at the Jewish Institute for Religion in New York (run by a very prominent Reform rabbi, Stephen S. Wise), which in 1950 amalgamated with the Hebrew Union College. All three aspirants were refused ordination. In the early 1950s the popular and capable widow of the rabbi of a Reform Temple in Mississippi served as her husband's replacement, despite her lack of formal qualifications, at the request of the congregation. During her two-year incumbency she encountered a surprising amount of goodwill and co-operation from ordained Reform colleagues. In 1956 the president of Hebrew Union College, Nelson Glueck, gave his official support to the American Reform rabbinate's recommendation that the ordination of women should proceed. Not until the feminist upsurge of the late 1960s were applications received from women; in 1972 Sally Priesand was ordained by the American Reform movement, becoming the first female rabbi since Regina Jonas. Many more have since followed. Women have also qualified as rabbis in the Reconstructionist movement, as well as at London's Leo Baeck College, the joint seminary of the Reform and Liberal movements in Britain. Some of these graduates have served in progressive congregations overseas. There are also female cantors.

Feminism made an impact, too, upon the Conservative movement in the United States, which in 1973 cautiously ruled that any of its congregations that wished to do so could count women in the *minyan* and call them to read from the Torah, both established practices of Reform Judaism. The question of admitting women to the Conservative rabbinate proved controversial; not until 1985 did the movement have its first female rabbi, Amy Eilberg. In response to her ordination at the Jewish Theological Seminary in New York the schismatic Union for Traditional Judaism was formed. But it failed to turn back the clock. From 1987 the seminary accepted women for training as cantors. The presence of non-Orthodox female spiritual leaders wearing prayer shawls and other ritual garments traditionally associated with men has inspired a growing number of non-Orthodox women worshippers, especially in the younger age brackets, to do likewise. To those girls who are presented with prayer shawls at their *Bat Mitzvah* ceremonies such conduct tends to come without self-consciousness.

Since the 1970s Orthodox women have been increasingly demanding, and in some cases obtaining, a decision-making role in the lay affairs of their synagogues, where in the past they have had no say or suffrage. Orthodox women have also sought, and found, ways to expand their participation in Jewish ceremonial without contravening *Halakhah*. Some have campaigned for a more flexible interpretation of Jewish law by rabbinical courts, in order to end the problem of *agunot*, and some would like the aspects of Judaism which they perceive to be archaic or degrading towards women quietly rendered obsolete. Among the pioneering advocates of an expanded role for Orthodox women within the bounds of *Halakhah* has been Blu Greenberg, wife of an Orthodox rabbi in the United States. She has written and lectured extensively on the subject. From the early 1970s innumerable women's prayer (*tefillah*) groups emerged in the United States, Canada, Britain, Australia, and Israel, and new ones are constantly being created. Their members are careful not to contravene the letter of *Halakhah*. They rely on sympathetic Orthodox rabbinical advisers who tell them what is and what is not permissible according to which authorities. Yet not everyone approves. Strictly Orthodox rabbis have dismissed the women's efforts as the work of troublemakers who are motivated by anti-Halakhic militancy rather than genuine feelings of piety, an accusation which has deeply hurt many women. Critics are unfazed by the knowledge that some women, frustrated at the limited opportunities for spiritual expression within existing congregations, have drifted away from Orthodoxy; some defectors have taken this step on being forbidden to recite *Kaddish*. Traditionalist rabbis have objected to women in the prayer groups touching the Torah scroll, on the old grounds that they could be, unwittingly, menstruating in which case their contact would pollute it. Instead, such rabbis reiterate women's conventional role and traditional obligations within Judaism, and regard with deep suspicion innovations introduced by Orthodox women's prayer groups such as specially crafted baby-naming ceremonies for infant girls and blessings pertinent to women's experience and life-cycles.

In contrast, by the dawn of the twenty-first century some Orthodox congregations allowed women to carry the (encased, covered) Scroll on the joyous festival of *Simchat Torah* ('Rejoicing in the Law'); a few allowed a Torah reading especially for women on this occasion, but they were exceptional. Some Orthodox congregations held *Bat Mitzvah* or *Bar Chayil* ('Daughter of Valour') ceremonies for girls. More commonly, girls were by then permitted to deliver a religious homily (*dvar Torah*) on Sabbath mornings, an honour tempered by the fact that this took place after the service when the Torah scroll had been returned to the Ark in the synagogue and many congregants tended to be non-attentive. Increasingly, Orthodox feminists were placing their faith in the efficacy of religious education in transforming women's status within the traditional congregations. They pointed to the increased opportunities for women to study sacred texts, and to attend all-female religious study sessions (*shiurim*) as well as to the example of two Orthodox synagogues in New York which had appointed women as rabbinic interns with responsibility for counselling, pastoral work, youth programmes, and adult education – functions which assistant rabbis habitually perform. And they took heart from the fact that the Jerusalem-based Women's Institute for Talmudic Law, headed by rabbi's wife Chana Henkin, had recently graduated six women as consultants on Jewish law.

Women in communal life

Since the Emancipation era Jewish women have risen to prominence in a variety of fields. There have been eminent Jewish actresses, writers, musicians, artists, politicians, lawyers, judges, intellectuals, academics, doctors, psychoanalysts, scientists, businesswomen, and sports champions. Between 1966 and 1986 four Jewish women received the Nobel Prize: the German-born Israeli poet Nelly Sachs (1891–1970) and the South African novelist and short story writer Nadine Gordimer (b.1923) for Literature and the American Rosalyn Sussman Yalow (b.1921) and the Italian Rita Levi-Montalcini (b.1909) for Medicine. More and more Jewish women are receiving professional qualifications and pursuing careers. But for all their visibility and participation in the wider world, they had not, by the dawn of the twenty-first century, won absolute equality within the organisational leadership of Jewish communities, whose male dominance, however, found itself increasingly under challenge. A noteworthy development was the election in 2000 of a woman as President of the British Board of Deputies.

The traditional exclusion of women from leadership positions in the synagogue and the Jewish community and their restriction to the private sphere is based on *Deuteronomy*, 17:15 ('Thou shalt set him king over thee ... one from among thy brethren'), and *Psalms*, 45:13 ('The King's daughter is all glorious within'), reinforced by the pronouncements of the medieval thinker Maimonides barring women from holding communal office. The traditional tasks of women in the *kehillot*, and after the Emancipation period in the less formalised community structure, consisted of welfare work of an appropriate 'feminine' nature. This entailed ministering to the sick and the needy, preparing female corpses for burial, comforting the bereaved, and similar good and charitable works. In the English-speaking world organisations sprang up in Jewish communities, often attached to specific congregations, with such titles as 'The Hebrew Ladies' Benevolent Society' and 'The Jewish Ladies' Guild'. Typically led by the wives of prominent members, these organisations were communally powerless. They collected alms for worthy causes, and met periodically for such purposes as sewing and knitting garments for distribution to the poor, decorating the synagogue hall with flowers and bunting on special occasions, and helping with the catering for communal events. Indeed, far into the twentieth century women did not as a rule belong to communal organisations apart from those they had set up themselves, even ones concerned with charity such as B'nai B'rith ('Sons of the Covenant'), the fraternal organisation founded in New York in 1843.

It seems that the first Jewish charitable organisation of the type described in the preceding paragraph was the Female Hebrew Benevolent Society set up in Philadelphia in 1819 by Rebecca Gratz (1781–1869), daughter of a prominent family of German origin. In founding the society, which distributed food and clothing to the poor, she was inspired by the work of a general charity for the relief of indigent women and children to which she belonged. In 1838 she and other Jewish women of Philadelphia established a free and independent Hebrew Sunday School open to all Jewish children in the city, the prototype for further such institutions in the United States. She served for the rest of her life as its president and superintendent. In 1855 she was instrumental in the establishment of the Jewish Foster Home and Orphan Asylum in Philadelphia. (Incidentally, she was the model for 'Rebecca,' the Jewish heroine in the novel *Ivanhoe* by Sir Walter Scott, who had been told about her by the American writer Washington Irvine.)

A notable milestone in the history of Jewish women's organisations in continental Europe was the foundation in 1904 in Germany of the Jüdischer Frauenbund ('Jewish Women's League') by an unmarried member of a prosperous family, Bertha Pappenheim (1859–1936), who was at that time housemother in an orphanage for Jewish girls. A feminist, albeit a conservative one in the mould of feminists of her day, she recognised that women's auxiliaries to the main (men-only) communal organisations were impotent, subservient institutions; for that reason she rejected a proposal by B'nai B'rith to set up a women's section. The Frauenbund originated as a federation of a number of Jewish women's charitable societies; by 1930 it had 50,000 members. It combined social welfare work with a feminist agenda, and in many respects mirrored the concerns of the general German feminist movement which emerged in the liberal climate of the 1848 revolution and peaked in 1919, when women were politically enfranchised. Most of its members were conventional middle-class women. They conducted classes in housewifery and mothercraft, set up childminding groups, and founded a children's home. But while Bertha Pappenheim believed that motherhood was a woman's highest calling and that every girl should learn home economics, she also championed the right of women who wished or needed to do so to pursue careers. She feared that economic hardship or idleness would force some girls and women into prostitution, and was aware that intermarriage and emigration on the part of men meant that some Jewish women would never find marriage partners, at least within the community, a problem exacerbated by battlefield casualties during the First World War: hence the need for employment. Additionally, she hoped that men, who tended to devalue the work of women based in the home, would come to esteem career women, thus helping to raise the general status of women within the Jewish community. Accordingly, the Frauenbund aimed to offer advice on job selection and vocational training to those who required it. Mindful that many eastern European Jewish migrant women had been tricked into prostitution by Yiddish-speaking pimps, it also campaigned for an end to the white slave trade. It did this despite strong communal pressure not to draw attention to Jewish criminals, and despite the uses to which antisemitic activists (later including Hitler) put reports of Jewish involvement in prostitution rackets.

The Frauenbund's campaign for female representation on Jewish communal organisations, which involved the right to vote and to stand for office, contravened tradition and custom and alienated Orthodox women as well as Orthodox men. All Jews living in a particular area were regarded as belonging to the local Jewish community run by elected officials, unless they had specifically opted out – a voluntary grouping unlike the *kehillah* of old – and were taxed according to income in order that each community (*Gemeinde*) could maintain synagogues, hospitals, libraries, newspapers, old people's homes, and cemeteries, and pay the salaries of rabbis and other communal employees. Many non-Orthodox men sympathised with the Frauenbund's demands for the enfranchisement of women and their access to communal leadership posts, yet acquiesced in the status quo because the Orthodox threatened to secede from the various communities if women were granted those things. In 1919, when German women won civil equality, the head of the Orthodox rabbinical seminary issued a formal statement, citing *Deuteronomy*, 17:15, reiterating that *Halakhah* forbade the election of women to communal office. At the same time, he declared that since God had commanded all Israelites to elect judges women had the right and the duty to vote for communal leaders. This announcement neither satisfied the Frauenbund nor won widespread support from the Orthodox rabbinate. Pressing on with demands for full equality, the Frauenbund drew encouragement from the statement of another Orthodox rabbi. He said that there was no objection in Jewish law to women either voting or standing for office. The Frauenbund treated his remarks as a propaganda victory, but by 1930 only 23 of the 1611 Jewish communities across Germany had changed their rules to allow women to vote and stand for communal office, while a mere eight had become liberal enough to permit women merely to vote. These were insignificant figures, and by the time the Frauenbund wound up its affairs in 1937 it had made little headway on the issue.

In 1902 the Union of Jewish Women was set up in Britain by a group of anglicised middle-class women involved in philanthropic work. London-based, and always at its most active in the capital, it established branches in Manchester and other centres. Dedicated to social welfare projects among disadvantaged Jews, including newcomers from abroad, it found jobs for young people of both sexes outside the overcrowded needle trades where prospects seemed limited. Although the clothing industry was to remain the principal employer of young Jewish women throughout the interwar period, numbers were steered by the Union into such fields as domestic work and, in the cases of the better-educated, into clerical work, nursing and teaching. The Union was not specifically concerned with combatting the risk of prostitution by poverty-stricken Jewish girls. That area was the especial concern of the Jewish Ladies' Society for Prevention and Rescue Work (later renamed the Jewish Association for the Protection of Girls, Women and Children) established in 1885, in response to the Great Migration from eastern Europe, by the Countess of Battersea, who was a member of the British Rothschild family. This society, which set up a 'Gentleman's Committee' to meet young immigrant women at docks and train stations to prevent them falling into the clutches of procurers, as well as to rescue 'fallen women' from their life of vice, rehabilitated former prostitutes and sponsored a home for unmarried mothers. The plight of *agunot* was tackled by the Council for the Amelioration of the Legal Position of the Jewess, founded in 1922, which drew attention to the difficulties facing women unable to remarry, in the vain hope that the Orthodox authorities would be willing and able to solve the problem.

An enduring and important organisation, the National Council of Jewish Women, was founded in 1893 by Hannah Greenberg Solomon (1858–1942), a middle-class Chicago woman of German background engaged in voluntary work. It too was a social service body with feminist, albeit conservative feminist, goals. Branches spread from Chicago to New York, Philadelphia and elsewhere, and in time the International Council of Jewish Women came into being, with members across over 20 countries. From the first the Council's members carried out voluntary welfare work among Jews in deprived areas, who comprised mainly new arrivals from eastern Europe, providing them with free baths, aid in finding lodgings, helpful practical advice, English language classes, vocational guidance and instruction. It set up Sunday schools for the religious education of Jewish children. Representatives in various centres offered assistance and shelter to young female immigrants in the fight against the white slave traffic. The Council lobbied for comprehensive American social welfare legislation, including slum clearance, public health schemes, the provision of mothers' pensions, and the regulation of child labour. During the Nazi era it embarked on a scheme which developed into the National Refugee Service; it and other Jewish welfare organisations helped in the placement of young refugee women as domestic workers in Jewish families (an occurrence not confined to the United States). Following the Second World War the Council implemented initiatives on behalf of Holocaust survivors, and established various educational and welfare projects in Israel. It has also been very active on behalf of women unable to remarry because their husbands refuse to grant them a divorce.

Excluded from mainstream Zionist organisations that sprang up in the wake of Herzl's *Der Judenstaat*, women established comparable bodies of their own. Here again the emphasis was on social welfare work and health issues, which seemed appropriately linked to what was taken for granted even by feminists to be women's innate maternal, nurturing nature and function. In 1912 New York-based Hungarian-born Henrietta Szold (1860–1945), an associate editor of the *American Jewish Year Book*, founded Hadassah, the Women's Zionist Organization of America. It grew to be the largest Zionist body in the world. (Hadassah, Hebrew for 'myrtle,' was the alternative name of the Biblical heroine, Queen Esther.) In her youth Henrietta Szold, daughter of a liberally-inclined Orthodox rabbi in Baltimore, had been involved in projects to ease the integration of Russian Jewish newcomers. As a prelude to collating and editing her late father's scholarly writings she had, somewhat extraordinarily, been permitted to sit in on classes at the Jewish Theological Seminary of America in New York (the training institution for Orthodox rabbis), in order to acquire helpful background knowledge. She founded Hadassah shortly after returning from a visit to Palestine, where the extent of disease and the scarcity of adequate medical facilities appalled her. Hadassah, known until 1914 as the Daughters of Zion, bases its work on the three central aims it has had since the outset: to raise the standard of health and healthcare in the Land of Israel, to promote Jewish institutions and enterprises there, and to foster Jewish ideals.

Another highly important women's organisation active in this field is the Women's International Zionist Organization, known as WIZO. It was established in London in 1920 at an international conference of female Zionists convened by the Federation of Women Zionists of the United Kingdom. Among its founders were Rebecca Sieff (1890–1966), daughter of one of the founders of Marks and Spencer, and Vera Weizmann (1882–1966), wife of Chaim Weizmann. It has about 250,000 members today.

One of the most visible Jewish organisations in Britain during the 1970s and 1980s was the Women's Campaign for Soviet Jewry, commonly known as 'The 35s' from the average age of its foundation membership. It tirelessly publicised the plight of the so-called *refuseniks* and strenuously campaigned for their right to leave the country which had become to them a virtual prison, and start new lives as they wished in Israel. It was a notable example of a high-profile communal initiative on the part of women, and more recently has supported needy Soviet immigrants in Israel.

During the closing years of the twentieth century Jewish women's organisations experienced ageing memberships and launched publicity drives to recruit younger members. Women's expectations and horizons had largely changed. As more and more Jewish women acquired higher education and professional qualifications and sought fulfilment outside the home there were correspondingly less potential full-time volunteers available to devote their time and energy to service organisations such as the National Council of Jewish Women as earlier generations of housewives had. Moreover, some younger and more radical feminists considered joining such old-style conservatively feminist organisations inappropriate, believing that instead of sidelining themselves in women-only bodies Jewish women aspiring to Jewish leadership positions should build up a power-base within the general organisational structure. Indeed, increasing numbers of women did achieve positions of influence on secular general communal institutions and umbrella organisations. On the other hand, the leadership of the average Jewish communal institution around the world was, at the close of the twentieth century, still predominantly male, and comparatively few communal forums featured women, except as occasional tokens. Those Jewish women for whom the pace of change was not proceeding quickly enough complained that, all too often, despite protestations to the contrary by male communal leaders, they felt patronised, trivialised, and marginalised.

Female radicals, philanthropists, and social reformers

As noted earlier in this work, Rosa Luxemburg and other women were active in the revolutionary socialist movement in eastern Europe. Often graduates of Russian high schools, sometimes also of universities at home or abroad, many grew alienated from society owing to disappointing career prospects. Additionally, although they were frequently distanced from their Jewish roots, they had in many cases imbued enough of Jewish teaching and tradition centring on the prophetic message to realise its inherent drive for social justice, and convinced themselves that a better world could and should be achieved through radical activism. While women shared these motivations with male radicals, the discrimination or outright exclusion faced by their sex in most areas of human endeavour was an additional cause for grievance and the consequent desire to overthrow the established order.

A number of women radicals, closer to the Jewish community, were involved in the Bund. From their ranks emerged the best-known female Jewish radical journalist in the Soviet Union, Malka Frumkin, *née* Lifshits (*c.*1880–*c.*1939), who used the pseudonym Esther. The daughter of an affluent Minsk *maskil*, she started teaching following graduation from the University of Berlin. After joining the Bund in 1901 she immersed herself into propagandising on its behalf, going on to become a well-respected Yiddish-language newspaper correspondent. Never forgiven by Bundists for ending up as a zealous apologist for Bolshevism, she fell foul of Stalin and became a victim of his purges. A very prominent female Jewish radical in eastern Europe was Ana Pauker (1890–1960), who strayed far from her origins as a Hebrew teacher from a religious family in Bucharest when she joined Romania's then illegal Communist party in 1920. From 1947 to 1952 she was her country's minister for foreign affairs. Having long since ceased to have formal links to the Jewish community, she was nevertheless expelled from the Communist Party in 1952 and put under house arrest, charged with having encouraged Romanian Jews to settle in the new State of Israel.

South African Jewish women were notable in the fight against apartheid. Helen Suzman (b.1917), an economics lecturer who was first elected to parliament in 1953, served until 1989. She was one of the founders of the Progressive party, and a persistent advocate of rights for non-whites. She was twice nominated for the Nobel Peace Prize.

Among the Russian Jews who settled in the United States in the 1880s was Lithuanian revolutionary Emma Goldman (1869–1940), who found work in clothing factories. Emerging as a leading anarchist and women's rights campaigner, she was suspected of complicity in the assassination of President McKinley in 1901. During the First World War she was sentenced to two years' imprisonment for opposing the draft, and upon her release in 1919, which coincided with the Red Scare in the United States that followed the Bolshevik Revolution, she was deported to Russia. Eastern European Jewish women played a significant part in the development of the American trade union movement. Most of the 20,000 shirtwaist makers who in 1909 staged the largest industrial strike by women held in the country up to that time were Jewish, and it was in the clothing industry that Jewish women made an impact as labour representatives and organisers.

Notable among American social workers was Lillian Wald (1867–1940), from a comfortable German-Jewish background. In 1895 she founded the Henry Street Settlement on New York's Lower East Side, a deprived area packed with immigrant families, in order to provide nursing care and other needed services, as well as to campaign for improved sanitation and disease control. Opposed to the United States' entry into the First World War, she became president of the American Union Against Militarism. Her work in the Lower East Side brought her into contact with her fellow Jews, but by orientation she was a universalist who did not identify specifically with her co-religionists. The poet Emma Lazarus (1849–87), who wrote often on Jewish themes, was very different in that respect. From a well-to-do family, she was deeply touched by the plight of Jewish refugees from Russia who were pouring into New York during the 1880s. Immersing herself in relief work on their behalf, and finding them accommodation, she used her own money to help them. 'Till this cloud pass,' she wrote, 'I have no thought, no passion, no desire, save for my own people.' She is best remembered for her deeply moving sonnet, 'The New Colossus', inscribed on the base of the

Statue of Liberty at the entrance to New York Harbour. It concludes with the celebrated words she imagines the Statue to be saying:

> ... Give me your tired, your poor,
> Your huddled masses yearning to breathe free.
> The wretched refuse of your teeming shore.
> Send these, the homeless, tempest-tost to me.
> I lift my lamp beside the Golden Door!

Jewish women were not, as a rule, particularly notable during the struggle for voting rights and civic equality in the English-speaking world and Europe during the period 1850–1920, although Ernestine Rose (1810–92) was a key participant in the inaugural National Rights Convention, held in 1850, which demanded equal rights for American women. Strikingly, however, American Jewish women have been in the forefront of the so-called Women's Liberation Movement that began in the late 1960s and grew into a powerful movement during the ensuing decade. It encouraged Jewish women to examine their role and status within Judaism and the Jewish community, and that self-awareness was given additional impetus by Israel's astounding victory in the Six Day War of 1967, which infused Jews with reinvigorated pride in their identity. The National Jewish Women's Conference held in New York in 1973 aired various issues of concern, and a feminist magazine defiantly titled *Lilith* (the name of the female demon of tradition) was launched around the same time. Israel's victory in 1967 had led to anti-Zionism and even antisemitism in radical and feminist circles. This became especially evident during the United Nations' Decade of Women (1975–85) which saw the UN Resolution equating Zionism with Racism (1975) and the unpopular Israeli invasion of Lebanon in 1982. The hostility towards Israel manifested at women's conferences caused Jewish delegates much unease.

Among the American Jewish feminists whose writings have brought them into prominence in the women's movement, and have attracted controversy both within and without feminist circles, are Betty Friedan, author of *The Feminine Mystique* (1963), a work generally credited with initiating the Women's Liberation Movement, as well as Susan Brownmiller, Andrea Dworkin, and Naomi Wolf, all authors of groundbreaking books. Since the 1970s a substantial number of books by Jewish feminists dealing with Jewish issues have appeared. These include: *On Women and Judaism: A View from Tradition* (1981), by Blu Greenberg; *On Being a Jewish Feminist* (1983), an anthology edited by Susannah Heschel; *Jewish and Female: Choices and Changes in Our Lives Today* (1985), by Susan Weidman Schneider; *The Tribe of Dinah: A Jewish Woman's Anthology* (1986), edited by Melanie Kaye-Katrowitz and Irena Klepfisz; *Standing Again at Sinai: Judaism from a Feminist Perspective* (1990), by Judith Plaskow; *Deborah, Golda, and Me: Being Female and Jewish in America* (1991), by Letty Cottin Pogrebin; *Daughters of the King: Women and the Synagogue*

(1992), by Susan Grossman and Rivka Haut; and *Voices of the Matriarchs* (1998) by Chava Weissler. There are many others. In addition, the outstanding American poet Adrienne Rich (b.1929), the acclaimed American novelists Erica Jong (b.1942) and Cynthia Ozick (b.1928), as well as many academics involved in Jewish studies, are all committed and outspoken feminists

The concern of some feminists who address specifically Jewish questions extends beyond demands for more meaningful participation in the ritual of the synagogue and the governing structure of Jewish congregations and institutions, and empowerment within the framework of *Halakhah*. For example, there have been criticisms of the male-centric nature of permanent exhibits at the United States Holocaust Museum in Washington DC, which fail adequately to depict the plight of women victims of Nazism, and there have been charges that the modern phenomenon of the 'JAP joke' is neither amusing nor harmless. Far from being jocular, many feminists insist that, describing well-dressed, seemingly affluent and upwardly mobile Jewish girls and women as JAPs ('Jewish American Princesses') is an iniquitous form of sexism: it heaps the old stereotype of Jews as ostentatious and avaricious squarely on the shoulders of the female, thus combining antisemitism with misogyny.

Women during the Holocaust

During the Holocaust women were subject to a number of gender-related perils and torments, including sexual exploitation and sexual sadism, rape, molestation, gynaecological experiments, the anguish of finding themselves pregnant at such a diabolical time, and the murder of their children, including babies torn from their arms and barbarically killed before their eyes. Hiding from the Nazis in forests, attics, out-buildings and so on was extremely difficult and hazardous for women encumbered by babies and small children. There were cases of fractious babies being deliberately smothered at the insistence of their mothers' companions in refuge, lest the infants' seemingly interminable crying should alert the enemy. Many women chose the heart-wrenching option of leaving their children with Christian friends and acquaintances, who agreed to pass them off as their own. It was not unknown for mothers on the insufferably close-packed cattle-cars bound for concentration camps, fearing what might lie in store, to toss their little ones from the vehicles at opportune points in the journey, begging strangers alongside the tracks to take care of them. While there were separate sections for women at Auschwitz and other camps, Ravensbrück was set up specially to house women. Forced labour, medical experiments, and executions by various methods took place there. For women, mingled with sheer terror was shame at being forced to undress by the Nazis and their collaborators prior to being put to death. Scenes of naked women on their way to the gas chambers and lining up at pits waiting to be killed were recorded in countless photographs by guards and soldiers. There is little doubt that many were put to pornographic purposes. It is believed that as a result of the Holocaust Jewish prayers and customs peculiar to women, orally transmitted over the generations, have been irretrievably lost to Judaic tradition because they were so seldom recorded on paper.

Through the efforts of feminist historians and other modern scholars, as well as via the written memoirs and oral testimonies of female survivors of the Holocaust, more has gradually become known of the specific ordeals endured by women during those terrible years, as well as of acts of bravery by women against overwhelming odds. Among the very earliest survivors' memoirs published, and among the most cogent and revealing, were those of a doctor's wife and surgical assistant from Transylvania, Olga Lengyel, who with her parents, husband and two young sons was sent to Auschwitz in 1944. Her account, *Five Chimneys: The Story of Auschwitz* (1947), provides a graphic and often chilling insight into life in the camp for those women who were not directed leftwards on arrival, to instant death. Deprived of their clothes, the new inmates were obliged to undergo a thorough and intimate physical examination, surrounded by soldiers 'chuckling obscenely'. The newcomers' hair was shorn – it was used in the German mattress and rope-manufacturing industries – and they were given ragged, ill-fitting, and frequently inadequately-fastened garments which had once belonged to other prisoners. The psychotic female commandant of the women's section mercilessly whipped those who incurred her wrath, and took sadistic pleasure in her powers of life and death. Sexual favours were expected of women by some of the male inmates of the camp, grown callous and cynical through their own despair and suffering, who came into contact with the female prisoners when on work assignments and in lunch breaks. Hunger induced many women, against their better nature, to surrender their bodies in exchange for an extra morsel of food or item of clothing.

Owing to her medical training Olga Lengyel was forced to act as a nursing assistant to the evil camp physician, Dr Josef Mengele, and in that capacity was confronted with harrowing scenes. These included horrific scientific experiments on living people, including many specifically concerned with the female genito-urinary system. Invariably, these practices resulted in unspeakable permanent injury to the victims or agonising death. As soon as a pregnant woman gave birth at the camp, both she and her baby were sent to the gas chamber. If the child was stillborn the mother's life was spared, and she was returned to slave labour. Eventually, Olga Lengyel and the other nurses decided to save the mothers' lives by suffocating the babies as they emerged from the womb and recording them as stillbirths: 'And so, the Germans succeeded in making murderers of even us.'

Despite the Nazi prohibition on sexual relations between Jews and gentiles, numerous Jewish women were held in brothels established for SS officers. Some exceptionally privileged male inmates of the concentration camps were also given access to them. Girls and women rounded up in actions were often raped before being killed. One notable act of martyrdom by Jewish women was that of 93 young teachers of the Beis Yaakov schools who committed mass suicide rather than be forced to become white slaves for the use of Nazi soldiers. Another well-known act of defiance was that of an attractive Jewish dancer who, on her way naked to the gas chamber, was ordered by a leering officer to dance for his amusement. She complied, moving ever nearer to him until she was able to grab the revolver from his holster and shoot him dead. She was immediately shot dead herself.

Such conduct is widely considered in the historiography of the Holocaust to fall within the category of resistance. There were innumerable Jewish women in the underground resistance movement, acting as messengers, carrying vital information, provisions, and ammunition, and fighting with partisan units and in the heroic but doomed Warsaw Ghetto uprising of 1943. Members of Jewish youth groups were conspicuous in activities of this kind, and there were numerous instances of outstanding courage. Representative of female participants in the Jewish resistance were Marianne Cohn (1924–44), who belonged to a Zionist youth group in France, and helped to smuggle Jewish children over the border into Switzerland until she was caught and axed to death; Gisi Fleischmann (1897–1944), a Zionist activist in Slovakia who was involved in ultimately abortive rescue initiatives and was immediately gassed on arrival at Auschwitz; Zivia Lubetkin (1914–76), one of the leaders of the Jewish underground in Poland who fought in and managed to survive the Warsaw Ghetto uprising and ended her days in Israel; and Roza Robota (1921–45), who while working in the ammunition factory at Auschwitz smuggled tiny amounts of explosives to underground organisers there, refused to reveal their names under torture, and was hanged together with three female accomplices. Haviva Reik (1914–44), born in Slovakia, and Hannah Szenes (1921–44), born in Budapest, were among groups of Jews from Palestine who parachuted into Nazi-occupied Europe to try to reach Jewish resistance leaders and gather information for the Allies; both were captured, tortured, and executed. It should not be forgotten that there were many women among the compassionate gentiles who gave shelter and other forms of aid to hunted Jews, often at mortal danger to themselves.

Two of the most posthumously famous victims of the Holocaust, who have, respectively, left behind a literary and a pictorial personal record of those dark years, happen to have been female. Anne Frank (1929–45), who died in Bergen-Belsen following her family's betrayal to the Nazis while concealed in a secret annex attached to her father's business premises in Amsterdam, was the author of a remarkable diary written during her two years in hiding. Recovered by one of the kind and brave Dutch friends who brought food and clothing to the family and to the four Jews who shared the annex with them, the diary was published after the war and has since been translated into numerous languages, while the building containing the annex has been turned into a museum commemorating those tragic events. Charlotte Salomon (1917–43) was a gifted artist from Berlin who in 1939 emigrated to France. There she married another Jewish refugee. In 1943 the newly-weds were seized by the Nazis and deported to Auschwitz, where they were gassed. Charlotte's paintings, which survived the war, were deposited in an Amsterdam museum. A sizeable proportion depict aspects of Nazi persecution, many as it affected Charlotte's own life, such as the poisoned atmosphere in her school, the destruction of her synagogue, and the deportation of her father, a doctor, to a concentration camp. Among the captions is one which reads: 'I cannot bear this life, I cannot bear these times.' These written and painted works by a girl and a woman whose young and promising lives were snuffed out so tragically have done much to bring home to countless readers and viewers the grim reality of Nazi persecution as it impacted on the lives of individuals. They help to illuminate the adage, coined by a male Holocaust survivor: 'Six million Jews were not murdered. One Jew was murdered, six million times over.'

Women in Israel

Although the imagery of the early Zionist movement frequently depicted biblical women as authoritative figures, it usually portrayed contemporary women in domestic and supportive roles. There were only a handful of women among the 250 delegates at the First Zionist Congress (1897) and they had no voting rights. Enfranchisement came with the Second Zionist Congress, held the following year. During the immediate prelude to the First World War the subordinate position of women in the Zionist Movement began to be challenged, for example in a forceful speech by a French feminist delegate at the Tenth Zionist Congress (1911). Women were among the idealistic pioneers who emigrated to the land of Israel during the Second and Third Aliyot (1904–14 and 1919–23), determined to create a Jewish national renaissance there. The mood was innovative, secular, and egalitarian, enabling women to enjoy an equal voice with men in the socialistic Ha-Shomer Ha-Tzair movement and in the running of *kibbutzim*. They worked in physically demanding outdoor capacities alongside men, preparing the soil, driving tractors, planting trees and crops, clearing swamps, and constructing homes and roads, as well as in more conventional occupations such as teaching and nursing. They shared with men the task of guarding *kibbutzim* and other settlements from attack. Through the Council of Working Women (Moetzet ha-Poalot), established in 1914 as the first women's organisation in the country – subsequently replaced by Na'amat, the women's sector of the Histradut – they made their views known on public issues. In the face of fierce objections based on religious precepts women were granted full civil, political and economic rights by the Jewish

National Assembly, the Yishuv's proto-Knesset, in 1925. Some were elected to that body. Women were active in the Habimah (the Jewish national theatre), the Bezalel School of Arts and Crafts, and other cultural ventures in the Yishuv. Several thousand Jewish women from Palestine volunteered for service with the British during the Second World War. Women served with the Haganah, and there were female members of the Irgun Zvai Leumi.

As a secular leftist, Israel's inaugural prime minister, David Ben-Gurion, was committed to egalitarian principles. Future prime minister Golda Meir (1898–1978) served as his minister of labour from 1949 to 1956, and as foreign minister from 1956 to 1966, having in 1948 been the new state's envoy to the Soviet Union. The Israeli Declaration of Independence, issued by Ben-Gurion in 1948, promised all the country's inhabitants regardless of religion, race, or gender 'complete equality of social and political rights'. Consequently women – including Muslims and Christians – were granted the vote, making Israel the first country in the Middle East to enfranchise women. In 1951 the Ben-Gurion government passed the Women's Equal Rights Law, which put women on an equal legal footing with men. Married women thereby obtained co-guardianship of their children with their husbands and the right to own and dispose of property. The status of Muslim women and of women from certain eastern Jewish communities was improved by the prohibiting of polygamy, and the law made divorce of the wife against her will, as practised in Islam, a criminal offence. Although the provisions of this legislation took precedence over Jewish, Muslim, and canon law, there was an escape clause allowing all freely willing parties aged 18 years of age and over to have their cases heard before religious courts. By the remarkably progressive Nationality Law of 1952 a child acquired Israeli nationality from either parent; non-Israeli women did not automatically acquire Israeli citizenship on marriage to an Israeli, and Israeli women did not lose it on marriage to a foreigner. The equally remarkable Women's Employment Law of 1954, applicable to both the public and private sectors, made it a criminal offence to dismiss female workers by reason of pregnancy, and guaranteed new mothers 12 weeks of paid maternity leave. Also binding on state and private employers alike was the Equal Pay for Equal Work Law of 1964. These laws can be attributed to the socialistic values prevalent in the country at the time, and on the developing economy's need for a large workforce.

Legislation of that sort, the drafting of young unmarried women for non-combat duty in the Israeli army (women from Israel's strictly religious community can and usually do claim exemption), and the *kibbutzim*, with their merging of male and female roles and their provision of childcare facilities, have led to the impression that Israeli women have long possessed a degree of liberation from 'biological destiny' and male supremacism unknown to most women in comparable advanced societies before the final three decades of the twentieth century. This impression is not entirely justified. In the years since statehood there has been what one writer has called a 'flight from feminism' among Israeli women. This can perhaps be partially explained by the willingness of many women themselves to put the country's early years of struggle behind them and turn to things 'feminine'. There seems to have been widespread apathy by women to achieving parity with men in the public domain, and the effects of the legal gains made before 1948 and in the Ben-Gurion years stalled, as women retreated into the spheres deemed appropriate for their gender: domesticity, motherhood, and voluntary work. The image of the fresh and natural 'girl fighter' and *kibbutz* worker was replaced by images of glamorous beauty contest queens, as Israel entered international pageants based on physical appearance such as the 'Miss World' competition, and by images of 'ideal' wives and mothers promoted by various contests that took hold based on their entrants' culinary and domestic skills, frequently with personal grooming and fashion sense added. Despite the egalitarianism offered in the *kibbutzim* regarding work roles, and the example of the early pioneers, women gravitated away from outdoor labour therein and into light industry or such tasks as minding and educating children, preparing communal meals, laundering, and tending poultry, vegetable gardens, orchards, and saplings. How much this polarisation within the *kibbutz* can be explained by physiological and psychological differences between the sexes must be a matter for conjecture.

Some feminist observers have argued that the relative absence of women from important decision-making posts in Israeli society is attributable to a chauvinistic, machismo attitude in Israeli men fostered partly by Zionist ideology and partly by war or the threat of war. This attitude, it is postulated, has its roots in the expectation of Zionism that in the Jewish homeland a new type of Jew – tough and combative – would develop in contrast to the passive, powerless Jew of the Diaspora, and has been reinforced by the need to protect Israel from the ever-present danger of annihilation. The retention of traditional sex roles by women from strictly religious and Afro-Asian Jewish families also helped to check the gender egalitarianism set in motion by the pioneers.

Aside from Golda Meir, two of the most prominent female politicians in Israel have been the left-wing Shulamit Aloni (b.1929) and the right-wing Geula Cohen (b.1925). Aloni has been a tireless champion of civil liberties and feminism; Cohen, a Zionist nationalist, has been an advocate of the annexation by Israel of the West Bank.

On the other hand, members of women's *tefillah* groups praying at the Western Wall in Jerusalem have been chased away by hostile male worshippers, some shouting abuse and even throwing missiles. A few years before her death in 1997 at the age of 92, Dr Nehama Leibowitz, a very eminent award-winning Israeli scholar and teacher of Jewish religious texts, was allowed by a strictly Orthodox religious ruling to lecture to a male audience on condition that she concealed herself behind a screen. This ruling, commensurate with the Talmudic precept that looking upon a woman would fill men with sexual desire, was greeted in many quarters with dismay and derision. There had been resistance to allowing Dr Leibowitz to lecture at all, on the grounds that a woman's voice is a seductive sexual instrument.

Israeli feminists have also drawn attention to the fact that, contrary to popular opinion, the problem of wife-battering exists in their country, and have been instrumental in opening refuges for its victims. They have also protested at the misogynistic nature of pornography available in Israel, and of offensive images of women in advertising. However, a feminist consciousness has apparently yet to pervade women in Israel as a whole. Nevertheless, during 2000 landmark legislation, sponsored by feminist politician Yael Dayan, was passed by the Knesset. Granting women equality in a wide range of spheres, it was supported by all political parties except those affiliated to the United Torah Bloc.

Further reading

(Books asterisked are especially useful anthologies.)

Judith R. Baskin, ed., *Jewish Women in Historical Perspective* (Detroit, 1991)*

Charlotte Baum *et al.*, *The Jewish Woman in America* (New York, 1976)

Michael Berkowitz, *Zionist Culture and West European Jewry before the First World War* (Cambridge, 1993)

Rachel Biale, *Women and Jewish Law* (New York, 1984)

Steven M. Cohen and Paula E. Hyman, eds, *The Jewish Family: Myths and Reality* (New York, 1986)

Rudolf Glanz, *The Jewish Woman in America: Two Generations*, 2 vols (New York, 1976)

S.D. Goitein, *A Mediterranean Society*, Volume 3: *The Family* (Berkeley, Ca., 1978)

Lesley Hazelton, *Israeli Women: The Reality Behind the Myth* (New York, 1977)

Leo Jung, ed., *The Jewish Library*, Volume 3: *Woman* (London, 1970)*

Marion A. Kaplan, *The Jewish Feminist Movement in Germany: the Campaigns of the Jüdischer Frauenbund, 1904–1938* (Westport, Ct., 1979)

Marion A. Kaplan, *The Making of the Jewish Middle Class: Women, Family and Identity in Imperial Germany* (Oxford, 1991)

Elizabeth Koltun, ed., *The Jewish Woman: New Perspectives* (New York, 1976)*

Steven M. Lowenstein, *The Berlin Jewish Community: Enlightenment, Family, and Crisis, 1770–1830* (Oxford, 1993)

Marvin Lowenthal, trans., *The Memoirs of Glückel of Hameln* (New York, 1977)

Ada Maimon, *Women Build a Land* (New York, 1962)

Jacob R. Marcus, *The American Jewish Woman: A Documentary History* (New York, 1981)

M. Maurel, *Ravensbrück* (London, 1958)

Ada Rapoport-Albert, 'On women in Hasidism: S.A. Horodecky and the Maid of Ludmir Tradition,' in *idem.* and Steven J. Zipperstein, eds, *Jewish History: Essays in Honour of Chimen Abramsky* (London, 1988)

Naomi Shepherd, *A Price below Rubies: Jewish Women as Rebels and Radicals* (London, 1993)

Shaul Stampfer, 'Gender differentiation and education of the Jewish woman in nineteenth-century Europe', in Antony Polonsky, ed., *From Shtetl to Socialism: Studies from Polin* (London, 1993)

Marie Syrkin, *Blessed is the Match* (Philadelphia, 1947)

Yonina Talmon, *Family and Community in the Kibbutz* (Cambridge, Mass., 1972)

Susan L. Tanenbaum, 'Jewish feminist organisations in Britain and Germany at the turn of the century', in Michael Brenner *et al.*, eds, *Two Nations: British and German Jews in Comparative Perspective* (London, 1999)

Sydney Stahl Weinberg, *The World of Our Mothers: The Lives of Jewish Immigrant Women* (Chapel Hill, N.J., 1988)

|17|

The demography and socio-economic status of the Jews; Jewish achievement

This chapter first explores a number of key facets of the evolution of the Jewish people in modern times, in particular changes in the Jewish population of the world, in their socio-economic status, and in Jewish languages. It then looks at the nature of Jewish achievement in modern times, in particular the Jews' contribution to the cultural development of the world. It also considers whether there is a 'Jewish mind' hallmarked by typical and distinctive modes of thought and attitudes.

Between the mid-eighteenth century and the beginning of the twentieth century the world's overall Jewish population grew enormously. Some levelling off occurred in the first decades of the twentieth century, followed (1939–45) by the unprecedented catastrophe of the Holocaust. Since the Second World War, the Jewish population of the State of Israel has grown immensely, but that of the Diaspora has stagnated.

Jewish population figures are notoriously difficult to compile in any more than an approximate way. There were no reliable censuses before modern times while in the contemporary world many nations (such as the United States) undertake no official censuses based upon religion or ethnicity. There is also the perennial question of 'who is a Jew?', and by what criteria Jewish identity should be assessed. Should persons of Jewish descent who are adherents of no religion, or another religion, ever be counted as Jews? Or persons of mixed Jewish and non-Jewish ancestry? There are no clear, or universally accepted, answers to those or other similar questions. For the most part, attempts to compile Jewish population statistics must be estimated, with a margin of error which may, in some cases, be very large.

Nevertheless, historians and demographers of the Jewish people have attempted to give answers to the question of Jewish numbers. It is estimated that in the time of the Emperor Caesar Augustus (14 CE) the Roman Empire had a population of 54 million, of whom 4.5 million (8.3 per cent) were Jews, a much higher proportion of the Western world's population than in modern times. It is also estimated that a further 20 million people lived in the environs of the Roman Empire, of whom perhaps 500,000 were Jews.

By the time of the late Roman Empire, Jews lived throughout the Western world, with the numbers living in Palestine certainly only a small minority of the total Jewish population after 135 CE. Since the world's Jewish population certainly diminished over the centuries – it is estimated that there were about 1.5 million Jews in the world before the expulsion of the Jews from Spain in 1492, divided almost equally between the Near East and Europe – very many Jews must have been absorbed through intermarriage, conversion, and assimilation into other national population groups. It is thus likely that there are today many hundreds of millions of people in the world with some remote Jewish ancestry, going back to Roman times. It would also appear that nearly all of today's Jews are related to one another (as DNA testing has recently shown), sharing a common gene-pool traceable to ancient Palestine.

It seems that Jewish numbers did not increase markedly until the late eighteenth century. It is believed that in the 1780s there were about 2.5 million Jews in the world of whom one million lived in the Near East, especially Turkey, and about 1.5 million lived in Europe, particularly Russia and Russian Poland (800,000), Austrian Galicia (300,000), Hungary (100,000), and Prussia (100,000). Very small numbers of Jews also lived elsewhere, especially in the western hemisphere. Over the next 120 years, however, vast changes occurred in the world's Jewish population. In particular, a Jewish population explosion occurred without historical precedent. The total population of the world's Jews probably rose to about 4,750,000 in 1850, to 7,750,000 in 1880, to 10,500,000 in 1900, and to 16,717,000 in 1938, just before the Holocaust. While the reasons for this enormous population increase are not entirely clear, a number of explanations can be offered. Much of the Western world experienced a sharp population increase in this period as well. For instance, the population of Great Britain rose from about 9 million in 1801 to 40 million in 1911, despite massive migration overseas and the chronic poverty of the Industrial Revolution. Like most other Western groups, Jews almost invariably married young and had, by later standards, enormously large families. Rates of infant mortality among Jews were probably lower than among other peoples; Jews were often spared the illnesses and accidents associated with heavy industry while, as a largely urban people, they had greater access to medical care than many other groups. Jews also moved in large numbers to newer areas of European settlement, especially to the United States, where living standards for all were higher than in most of Europe. Loss of numbers through conversion and intermarriage were relatively low, while Europe as a whole went for nearly a century (1815–1914) without a major war.

Prior to the First World War, the largest Jewish community in the world was to be found in tsarist Russia, which contained about seven million Jews on the eve of that conflict. By 1914, however, the United States, with about

2.5 million Jews, was already the second largest Jewish community in the world. In the late 1930s, after 150 years of Jewish population growth, about 9,924,000 Jews out of an estimated world-wide total of 16,717,000 (59.4 per cent) lived in Europe. The largest Jewish population centre was still to be found in Poland, which contained most of the old Pale of Settlement, where 3,325,000 Jews (19.9 per cent of the world-wide total) lived, generally in conditions of poverty and oppression. The European portion of the Soviet Union held about 3,000,000 Jews, while Jewish populations of 100,000 or more were to be found in nine European countries: Romania (758,000), Hungary (445,000), the United Kingdom (370,000), Germany (500,000 in 1933, a figure which constantly decreased after Hitler came to power, especially following *Kristallnacht* in 1938), Czechoslovakia (356,000), France (260,000), Austria (192,000), Lithuania (155,000), and the Netherlands (120,000). By the late 1930s about 5,300,000 Jews lived in the western hemisphere, and since 1918 the largest Jewish community in the world was, of course, in the United States, with about 4.7 million in 1938. At that time, two other countries in the western hemisphere had Jewish communities of 100,000 or more: Argentina (275,000) and Canada (175,000). Contemporaneously, five other countries also contained Jewish communities numbering 100,000 or more: Palestine (440,000), Morocco (200,000), Algeria (130,000), Iraq (100,000), and South Africa (100,000). At that time, too, about 665,000 Jews, or 4 per cent of the world's Jewish population, lived in countries which were predominantly Sephardi rather than Ashkenazi. There were Sephardi Jews living in other countries, but it seems unlikely that Sephardi Jews constituted more than 10 per cent of the world's Jewish population at that time. This indicated a sharp decline in the percentage of Sephardim among the world's Jews. As recently as 1800, about 40 per cent of the world's estimated 2.5 million Jews lived in the Near East, and perhaps half of the world's Jews were Sephardim.

The catastrophic and cataclysmic events of the period between 1933 and the early 1950s had, of course, the most far-reaching effects upon the world's Jewish population and its main centres. The Holocaust and other losses produced by the Second World War resulted in a decrease in the world's Jewish population of approximately one-third. In 1951, after some post-1945 growth in Jewish numbers, the most reliable estimate of the world's Jewish population was 11,533,000, or 5,184, 000 less than in 1938, thirteen years earlier. The bulk of this decline of course came in Europe, where Jewish numbers were estimated at 3,464,000, or 6,460,000 fewer than just before the Second World War. Most of this decline was, obviously, the result of losses in the Holocaust, but it also includes very considerable numbers of refugee and survivor emigration from Europe to Israel, America, and elsewhere. Whereas, in 1938, 59.4 per cent of the world's Jewish population lived in Europe, only thirteen years later the European percentage had declined to 30.0 per cent, just one-half of what it had been. In other parts of the world, however, Jewish numbers had grown. In 1951, according to this estimate, 5,828,000 Jews lived in the western hemisphere, with about five million in the United States and 201,000 in Canada. The number of Jews in Asia had also risen considerably, owing to heavy immigration to the newly-created State of Israel, whose population numbered 1,330,000 in mid-1951. 694,000 Jews continued to live in Africa, chiefly in the Arab lands of north Africa, and 56,000 in Australia and New Zealand. In 1951, fourteen countries were believed to have Jewish communities numbering 100,000 or more, compared with nineteen in 1938: the United States, the Soviet Union, Israel, Britain (450,000, almost certainly an overestimate), Argentina (360,000), Romania (280,000, the largest surviving Jewish community in a country of Nazi occupation), Morocco (260,000), France (235,000), Canada, Hungary (155,000), Algeria (140,000), Brazil (120,000), South Africa (110,000), and Tunisia (105,000). The effects of the Holocaust were evident in the Jewish populations of such countries as Poland, decimated from 3.3 million to only 45,000, Czechoslovakia (17,000), Germany (37,000), the Netherlands (27,000), and Yugoslavia (3500).

Similar estimates have been made for the very recent past. In 1995, the world's Jewish population was estimated at 13,059,000, an increase of 1,526,000 in the two generations since 1951. The trends apparent in the period 1938–51 had now heightened, with the Jews of the world increasingly bifurcated between Israel and the United States. In 1995, the American Jewish Committee estimated the 'core' Jewish population of the United States as 5,515,000, although, if persons of Jewish descent but not practice were included, American Jewish numbers were estimated at 6,840,000 persons. At the same time, the Jewish population of Israel was believed to be 4,550,000, an increase of no less than 3,220,000 since 1951, or 242 per cent. At the same time, the Jewish population of Europe had declined to only 1,741,000, half of what it had been in 1951, chiefly owing to mass emigration from the former Soviet Union. Only nine countries now contained Jewish populations of 100,000 or more: the United States, Israel, France (525,000), Canada (362,000), Russia (360,000), Britain (292,000), Argentina (206,000), the Ukraine (180,000), and Brazil (100,000). (The total Jewish population of the former Soviet Union, now composed of independent republics, was estimated at 660,000.) Some demographers would regard these figures as definite underestimates, consistently taking the lowest possible evaluation of Jewish numbers in most countries. For instance, Jewish numbers in France were estimated by other sources at 700,000 and in Britain at 370,000, while the Jewish population of Australia was believed by some to be 105,000 rather than the 92,000 given by those authorities. It is also difficult to account for the apparent decline in Jewish numbers in Argentina from 360,000 in 1951 to only 206,000 44 years later. While Jewish population figures are notoriously difficult to estimate, it is nevertheless also true that the broad trends shown by these figures are certainly correct, above all the key importance of the United States and Israel in the contemporary Jewish world. Together, these two countries held 10,065,000 Jews, 72 per cent of the world's total Jewish population.

The Jews: economics and education

In modern times, Jewish economic life has always been marked by a number of distinctive features. Since the Jews almost wholly lacked an agricultural class, nearly all European Jews were employed, during the Middle Ages, in the commercial trades as merchants, financiers, handicrafts workers, and the like. Their occupational pattern was almost precisely the reverse of that found throughout Christian Europe, where the great majority of the economically active population consisted of peasants, farmers, and other agricultural workers. Jews also obviously lacked a nobility or landed gentry, a military class or (before the nineteenth century) a professional category of lawyers or university teachers, while their religious class of rabbis and Talmudic scholars differed in many respects from the religious orders found among all Christian populations. Within the towns, Jews were automatically excluded from the guilds, and were seldom present in such trades as shipowning. The particular and peculiar economic structure of the Jews was often the very opposite of the host population's. In Poland in 1931, for instance, whereas only 4.4 per cent of Jews were employed in agriculture, no less than 67.5 per cent of Christians (mainly Catholics) worked in agriculture. On the other hand, whereas 78.6 per cent of Polish Jews were employed in industry and trade, the Christian percentage was only 19.7 per cent. Much of the difference can be accounted for by the far greater urbanisation of the Jews, but the figures are extraordinary. Within the industrial section there were very significant differences, too, with 78.6 per cent of Polish Jews in industry employed in small workshops and only 21.4 per cent in factories, while the Christian (mainly Catholic) figures were almost the precise reverse: 85.2 per cent in factories but only 14.8 per cent in small workshops.

Jews also had – and have – a reputation for often being very wealthy, and for 'dominating' much of a country's economy. This was, of course, one of the major items in the litany of European antisemitism. Plainly, the overwhelming majority of Jews were not wealthy; most, indeed, were extremely poor. Nevertheless, throughout continental Europe, especially in central and eastern Europe, Jews did comprise a disproportionate percentage of the economic elites of many countries. About 31 per cent of the richest families in Germany in the 1907–10 period were Jews or of Jewish origin, a fact known from comprehensive taxation records which historians have studied. Jews also comprised a very disproportionate percentage of the economic elite in countries such as Austria and Hungary, and even that of inter-war Poland. The Rothschilds, the legendary banking dynasty who originated in the Frankfurt ghetto in the late eighteenth century, were probably the richest family in nineteenth-century Europe. By the last third of the century their members had entered the aristocracies of most European countries and mixed freely with kings and princes. Antisemites often credited them with mysterious, even occult, powers of international influence and power. Elsewhere, however, Jews were not a very notable component of the economic elite, especially in the English-speaking world. Jews were almost entirely absent from the list of significant entrepreneurs of the British Industrial Revolution. Only a handful of the multi-millionaires of America's golden age of *laissez-faire* capitalism from 1865–1929 were Jews, most, such as Rockefeller, Ford, Carnegie, Astor, and the other famous American tycoons of the period, being Anglo-Saxon Protestants. Just as the apparent overrepresentation of Jews in the economic elites of central Europe did much to heighten antisemitism there, so their relative absence from the economic elites of the English-speaking world acted to dampen antisemitism in these countries.

Jews have also long had a reputation for engaging in newer trades or lines of business, presumably because they were often excluded from older established trades. In truth, however, only occasionally in the modern world does this image have much reality. Jews certainly were to be found in very large numbers in businesses which delivered American popular culture in the nineteenth century, especially in Hollywood and in radio and television. Jews also were to be found in significant numbers in newspapers and publishing and in the world of commerce, in the development of department stores and modern advertising. That, however, is about as far as this observation can be pushed. As noted, there was almost no Jewish presence in the factory industries and new technologies of the Industrial Revolution, just as today, with the possible exception of enterprises in Israel, there is no obvious Jewish presence in a highly visible way in 'hi-tech' computer and internet industries. Jews in fact were most often engaged in fairly traditional spheres of commercial capitalism and a number of other well-worn fields. For many years the 'rag trade', the clothing industry, was heavily Jewish in many Western urban centres. In the 1930–50 period possibly 500,000 Jews in New York were employed in the local garment industry. Jews have always been heavily involved in the diamond and jewellery trades and, down to the Second World War, in the tobacco industry.

Many Jews, especially Jewish intellectuals, were well-aware of the abnormal nature of the Jewish economic structure in many Western countries. The socialist Zionist Ber Borochov described the Jewish economic structure as an 'inverted pyramid', and also pointed out that Jews flourished in occupations which were 'furthest from nature', that is, from agriculture and mining. Many Jewish political activists of the 1880–1940 period deplored the economic structure of world Jewry, seeing in it a potent cause of antisemitism. They urged that Jews aim at producing a 'normal' economic structure like those found among most other peoples with, in particular, a greatly expanded 'productive' sector, especially in agriculture. This thinking was highly influential in the early Zionist movement, which specifically aimed at creating a 'normal' economic structure among the Jewish community in Palestine, and especially emphasised the 'reclaiming of the land' by Jewish agricultural work. Although the Jewish economic structure was indeed unusual, it should be noted that it was not unique. Other so-called 'middleman minorities', such as the Armenians and Greeks in the Levant and southeastern Europe, performed much the same commercial role as the Jews, as have groups such as East Asians in Africa and Chinese in south-east Asia. Nearly all such groups often encountered fierce hostility from the local population, with the Armenians in Turkey being the earliest victims of twentieth-century genocide.

While a minority of Jews were wealthy or at least successful in business life, it was also the case that the great majority in eastern Europe and initially among the waves of migrants to the 'New Diaspora' around the world were poor. In many countries, Jews were forbidden to enter a wide range of trades and professions while, in tsarist Russia, they were, with rare exceptions, legally confined to living in the Pale of Settlement. The great population explosion of European Jewry in the nineteenth century led to a chronic and grinding poverty among the majority of the Jewish population, poverty which was made worse by tsarist oppression. Many Jews with no capital or marketable skills, especially in the handicrafts trades, clothing, and food areas (bakers, butchers, etc.) were continuously on the verge of ruin. A significant portion of the population lived in chronic poverty bordering on permanent mediocrity. These *luftmenshen* ('air men', that is, men who lived on air) were a highly visible and typical part of Jewish life in the Pale. While there was, at first, some improvement in eastern Europe after the First World War, the coming of the Great Depression and greatly heightened antisemitic pressures produced a marked deterioration in Jewish living standards throughout eastern Europe during the 1930s. By the eve of the First World War, a major portion of Polish Jewry was saved from starvation only by substantial economic assistance from American Jews, and the situation in other eastern European countries was similar.

In western Europe and the 'New Diaspora' which grew up in the English-speaking world the situation was generally brighter. In countries such as Britain, Australia and, above all, the United States, Jewish immigrants made remarkable economic progress, at least until the beginning of the Great Depression. This progress was, however, very uneven, so that probably at least one-third of the Jews in New York and London in 1929 were still living in chronic poverty, especially those in London's East End and in New York's poor areas such as the Lower East Side and Brownsville in Brooklyn. This chronic poverty did not improve until after the Second World War. Today, while the majority of Jews in America are certainly well established in the middle class, there is still a surprisingly large Jewish component among lower middle-class trades, such as postal clerks and taxi drivers, as well as a large Jewish percentage among schoolteachers in many cities. As well, as among all other groups, poverty has often become age-specific, with elderly Jews, sometimes from immigrant backgrounds, often living in chronic poverty. It is often claimed that in Israel Sephardi Jews from Afro-Asian countries, generally poorly educated and from comparatively primitive Third World societies, comprise an economic and social underclass. During the 1960s and 1970s, the apparent gap in Israeli society between European and Afro-Asian Jews became a major political issue. Many Afro-Asian Jews, who felt excluded by the alleged domination of the Israeli Labour Party by Europeans, turned to Likud, the right-wing opposition party. It is often suggested that this shift to Likud by poorer Afro-Asian Jews gave it political power for the first time in 1977. In New York in the 1960s, a time of acute social change and racial conflict, it is also often suggested that poorer Jews in Brooklyn and Queens vehemently opposed 'reverse discrimination' measures designed to improve the educational and economic opportunities of blacks and Hispanics, while wealthier Jews in Manhattan supported them, the reverse of what one might have expected in advance. Nevertheless, it is unquestionably true that most Jews in America today, and in other Diaspora societies, are situated economically in the upper middle classes. In 1984, a study revealed that Jews have the highest average per capita income of any religious group in America, results which have been shown in many other surveys of American income patterns.

These patterns have been mirrored by the Jewish participation in the professions, such as law, medicine, and teaching, and in journalism and publishing. Throughout (in particular) central Europe down to the Holocaust, after the mid-nineteenth century Jews often comprised a grossly disproportionate percentage of the professional class; that is, in fields which they were permitted to enter freely. (Some areas, such as university teaching or the military, remained all but closed to Jews before the First World War or even afterwards.) Before emancipation, Jews were almost never found in the professions apart from medicine, but in the late nineteenth century became attracted increasingly to professional occupations. It is difficult to understand precisely why this was so, but clearly it can be linked to the far greater levels of urbanisation and literacy among Jews, and to the fact that the professions entail intellectual work, highly congenial to Jews. In Prussia in 1925 26.1 per cent of all lawyers, 15.5 per cent of physicians and surgeons, 15.0 per cent of dentists, and 8.7 per cent of journalists and writers were Jews, who made up perhaps 1.5 per cent of the total population. In Vienna in 1934 (four years before the Nazi takeover) Jews comprised 62.7 per cent of all dentists, 62.0 per cent of lawyers, 47.2 per cent of physicians and surgeons, and 28.6 per cent of university professors, compared with 9.3 per cent of the Viennese population. In Hungary the situation was similar: in 1920, Jews comprised 50.6 per cent of lawyers, 46.3 per cent of physicians, and even 39.1 per cent of engineers, compared with about 5 per cent of the population. As with the economic elite, the position of Jews in the English-speaking world was very different, with Jews possibly overrepresented in some professions such as the law after the late nineteenth century, but not

by much. On the European continent before 1939, Jews were highly prominent in some fields; by contrast, in the English-speaking world they were
certainly not notable at all. Even in 1991, for example, only 4 per cent of
physicians in Britain were Jewish. In the Edwardian period only one Harley
Street specialist was Jewish (Harley Street, in London, is where expensive
physicians and medical specialists in private practice have their offices). In
the United States, it would appear that about 10 per cent of all adult male
Jews were in the professional classes, a far higher percentage than for the
American population as a whole, but Jews certainly did not comprise a
visibly large portion of America's professional groups except perhaps in
New York. Since the Second World War the number of Jews in the professions has certainly risen, but again in the context of increases in professional
numbers among virtually all groups.

Underlying many of these patterns is the traditional Jewish emphasis on
education, a characteristic for which Jews have always been renowned.
Since emancipation, it has probably always been true, in every national
milieu in the Western world in which they have found themselves, that Jews
have attended secondary schools and tertiary institutions in greater numbers
than non-Jews. Prior to emancipation and down to the twentieth century
Jews almost invariably had higher levels of literacy (among both men and
women) than non-Jews. As with the economic and professional statistics,
the higher educational attainments of Jews were relatively greater in under-
developed countries in central and eastern Europe; elsewhere, in more
developed societies, such as in the United States, the differences between
Jews and other groups was also marked, but to a lesser and decreasing
extent. In Prussia in 1921, while only 9.7 per cent of Christian (Protestant
and Catholic) teenagers were attending a secondary school of any kind, no
fewer than 60.5 per cent of Jewish teenagers were attending a secondary
school. In Hungary in 1933–34, the ratios were, respectively, 10.6 and 41.4
per cent. Even in relatively advanced Czechoslovakia, the respective ratios
(in 1927–28) were 7.3 and 29.3 per cent. This same difference persisted at
the university level. In Germany in 1929–30, 3.4 per cent of all university
students were Jews, an overrepresentation compared with their numbers in
the German population of 3.7 times. In Czechoslovakia the Jewish overrepresentation in 1927–28 was 6.0 times, in Austria in 1936 4.3 times, and
in the Soviet Union in 1935 7.0 times. In the United States, for which precise
figures are lacking, one study found that, in 1937, despite the Depression
and despite well-documented antisemitic quota restrictions at many elite
private universities, about 9.1 per cent of all American college students were
Jews, an overrepresentation of 2.6 times. The degree of overrepresentation
in Great Britain at that time, based in incomplete statistics, appears to have
been very similar. Despite all the antisemitic and economic barriers which
existed to Jewish participation in higher education, until the Nazi period
there does not appear to have been any Western country with a substantial
Jewish population where Jews were not overrepresented among university

students. This trend has certainly continued (and, if anything, been enhanced) during the post-war period. One poll taken in 1947, just after the Second World War, found that more than two-thirds of all American Jewish high school seniors applied for admission to college or university, compared with only one-third of all Protestants and one-quarter of all Catholics. In 1976, one survey found that among Americans aged 30 to 49 (born, roughly 1927–46, and attending college or university between 1945 and 1968), no less than 75 per cent of Jews had graduated from college or university, compared with 54 per cent of Episcopalians, 41 per cent of Presbyterians, 26 per cent of all Protestants, and 24 per cent of Roman Catholics. American Jewish statistics for college or university enrolment were matched perhaps only by those of a number of small, 'elite' Protestant groups such as Quakers and Unitarians. Nevertheless, in the United States, where university education is a virtually universal expectation, differences between Jews and other groups were probably not as marked as in Europe, while the ratio between Jewish and non-Jewish rates of university attendance were in all likelihood converging.

This situation has been affected, too, by the growth of the Jewish day school movement and by the relative increase in the number of Strictly Orthodox Jews. Increasing numbers of Jewish students in the Western world, especially Orthodox students, attend full-time Jewish day schools. This represents a considerable difference from the past. Historically, in the United States, the great majority of Jewish children went to public (state) schools, obtaining a meagre Jewish education in afternoon and weekend religious schools to *Bar Mitzvah* age. In recent decades, however, the number of full-time Jewish day schools has increased markedly. Originally restricted to the Orthodox, these have increasingly been imitated by other strands in Judaism, concerned with rapidly increasing rates of assimilation and intermarriage. The failure of the American Jewish community to establish a full-time Jewish day school system (unlike the Catholics in America, who established a far-reaching 'parochial school' system) has put a distinctive and, arguably, unfortunate stamp on American Jewish life. In other Diaspora societies, much higher rates of education at full-time Jewish day schools have been achieved post-1945, particularly in South Africa, and, most remarkably, Australia, where more than 60 per cent of school-age Jews attend a full-time Jewish day school.

The Jews and urbanisation

One stereotype of Jewish identity is that they are overwhelmingly an urban people, a community of city-dwellers. For many antisemites, one of the worst facets of Jewish life was that, unlike other peoples, they had no farmers, peasantry, or agricultural sector: they were not 'rooted in the soil'. Like many stereotypes, there is a major element of truth in this depiction.

There is no doubt that Jews in modern times have for the most part possessed only a small rural component, and that, in many places, most Jews lived in urban areas. Yet there is also much about this notion which is false. Jewish agricultural settlements have existed in many places, and agriculture was one of the bases of the Zionist movement. Only in a few milieus did the majority of Jews actually live in very large urban centres. Since the Second World War, many Jews (like other middle-class groups) have left the inner cities for the suburbs.

There are rational reasons for explaining why Jews generally eschewed the countryside and rural life. First and foremost, Jews in Europe were almost always forbidden, prior to the nineteenth century, to own land. Secondly, Jews often felt extremely insecure wherever they lived, never knowing when they would be massacred or expelled. Most well-off Jews therefore preferred to keep their property in the form of 'portable' wealth, such as jewellery and cash, rather than invest it in land (which in any case they were not allowed to do) as most wealthy Christians did. Thirdly, Jews almost always preferred (and, to a certain extent, prefer) to live with their fellow Jews in recognisable Jewish communities. They have preferred to do this for self-protection, in order to live a Jewish life-style according to Jewish traditions, and because virtually all minorities prefer to live among their own people. Thus, most Jews lived in Jewish 'ghettos' even after the legal requirement for them to do so had disappeared. Finally, Jews functioned in the economies of most European nations in a number of clear-cut trades and professions, mainly in finance, retailing, mercantile activities, and (later) in the clothing industry. (They were often legally or semi-legally excluded from other trades.) These distinctively Jewish trades were mainly carried on in urban areas, whether in villages, small towns, or large cities.

In the early modern period, and throughout eastern Europe, most Jews lived in villages and small towns rather than very large cities. Many of these settlements were distinctively Jewish or with a large Jewish majority, and Jews often formed the commercial class of that area, sometimes together with other ethnic minorities like Armenians or Greeks. This pattern persisted down to the Second World War. In 1931, of a total Jewish population of 2.9 million, only 353,000 lived in Warsaw, Poland's capital, and 202,000 in Lodz, the next largest city, that is, less than one-fifth of the total Jewish population of Poland. No other Polish city had as many as 100,000 Jews (Lvov, in eastern Poland, had 99,595). Cracow had only 57,000 Jews, Vilna only 55,000, and Lublin only 39,000. Most Jews continued to live in smaller towns and villages, as their ancestors had done for centuries.

In the nineteenth century there was, however, a distinct tendency for Jews to move to larger cities in Europe, especially outside of the Pale of Settlement. Indeed, virtually all Jewish immigration and settlement outside of the Pale and its environs took place in large cities, which became the characteristic mode of habitation of Western Jewry. In particular, Jews tended to settle in the capital city, or the largest and most important commercial centre, of most nations. Thus, in twentieth-century Europe prior to the Second World War, the largest Jewish population centres outside Poland were in London (235,000 in 1937), Budapest (204,000 in 1930), Vienna (178,000 in 1934), Berlin (161,000 in 1933), and Moscow (200,000 by the mid-1930s). In parts of central and eastern Europe Jews constituted a major and very visible portion of the population of the largest city or cities. In 1930, for instance, Jews constituted 20.3 per cent of the total population of Budapest and 9.3 per cent of the total population of Vienna. The heavy Jewish presence in these places, and in such cities as Warsaw, where they comprised 30.1 per cent of the total population, unquestionably led to heightened prejudice, and the presence of so many Jews was seized upon by ultra nationalists to inflame antisemitism. In cities such as Berlin, Vienna and Budapest, Jews comprised a very disproportionate percentage of the middle classes, especially those in commerce and the professions, and were renowned as the driving force of the local intelligentsia, often possessing radical and modernist ideas at which conservatives and antisemites looked with fear and hostility.

The process of Jewish urbanisation was probably carried furthest in the United States (and above all in New York) which became the *goldene medina* ('golden land') to so many Jews, especially from eastern Europe, as well as to many other European minorities. New York's Jewish population had almost certainly passed one million by the early twentieth century, and it reached about two million by the 1930s. At the time, this amounted to just under 30 per cent of New York's vast population of seven million, and to around 40–45 per cent of America's total Jewish population. The borough of Brooklyn, in particular, became renowned as the residential centre of New York's Jewish community. In 1940 its Jewish population, estimated at 950,000, was greater than the entire Jewish population of western Europe. Other very substantial Jewish communities also grew up in Chicago, Philadelphia, Boston, and many other large American cities, numbering 200–350,000 at that time. Throughout the 'New Diaspora' large Jewish communities also emerged, from Buenos Aires to Montreal, almost always in the largest city, capital, or chief commercial centre. Within these cities there was often a distinctive pattern of internal residency, with Jews initially settling in an impoverished slum district, and then moving out to a more salubrious locale after two or three decades. In London, Russian Jews settled in large numbers in Whitechapel, the East End slum, from 1881. Just before the First World War, and more emphatically during the inter-war years, many of these Jews, or their children, moved to newer middle-class or lower middle-class suburbs in north and north-west London. In New York, the vast wave of post-1881 migrants initially settled in the Lower East Side of Manhattan, but, as in London, moved to the outer, more residential parts of New York City, especially Brooklyn and the Bronx, just after the First World War, when the subways expanded to these neighbourhoods. (This pattern was paralleled by many other immigrant groups.) Almost everywhere, too, well-to-do Jews disproportionately lived in a number of recognisable areas like Bayswater and, later, St Johns Wood and Golders Green in London, and the Upper East Side and Upper West Side of Manhattan in New York. Upper-class Jewish areas emerged in almost every city with a substantial Jewish population, even long after antisemitic barriers to Jewish residency had largely disappeared.

Despite the predominance of towns and cities in modern Jewish life, some Jews lived in rural areas throughout modern times. A number of deliberate attempts were made in the nineteenth and twentieth centuries to bring Jews back to the land, especially in Russia and the Soviet Union, and in remote parts of the Diaspora like Argentina. Agricultural settlement in Argentina began with the foundation of the Jewish Colonization Association in 1881 by Baron Maurice de Hirsch. Formed as a response to the pogroms of 1881, it purchased 1.5 million acres of land in Argentina, but could lure only minimal numbers of Jews from Europe. Agricultural settlement was also an integral part of the Zionist programme, with the *kibbutzim* being among the best-known features of Zionist life in Palestine. By 1939 there were about 240 Jewish agricultural settlements in Palestine, with a total population of about 100,000, more than one-fifth of the total Jewish population at the time. Since the Second World War, while the *kibbutzim* and other agricultural settlements of course remain, most Israelis live in cities or suburban areas.

Prior to the Second World War, there were also, surprisingly, Jewish agricultural settlements in Russia, numbering 200,000 persons in 1938, as well as in Jewish eastern Europe, and even in the United States, where it was estimated that there were 20,000 Jewish farming families (80,000 persons, or about 2 per cent of America's Jewish population), mainly in and around New York. Most of the efforts to settle Jews on the land received strong backing from representative Jewish groups, who saw in them a way to counteract the negative image of Jews as exclusively urban-dwellers. Unfortunately, only a very small proportion of the world's Jewish population chose the rural lifestyle, even when encouraged to do so.

In the post-1945 world, Jews have become largely an upper middle-class group, and, like most other such groups in Western countries, have significantly suburbanised away from the inner cities. This process had gone especially far in the United States, where 'white flight' from the older immigrant neighbourhoods became pronounced after the mid-1950s, as most inner cities became inhabited chiefly by black and Hispanic migrants and crime rates soared. Despite the political liberalism of most American Jews, they fled to the suburbs, or to the upper-class white enclaves within the cities, no less readily than other white groups. Today, there are an estimated 2.2 million Jews in metropolitan New York, of whom about 950,000 live in New York City and 1.25 million in the suburban areas of Long Island and New Jersey. Within the City itself, there are still huge Jewish enclaves, especially the Borough Park area of Brooklyn, often inhabited by poorer or

Orthodox Jews, but these people are now outnumbered by Jews in the suburbs. Many well-off Jews live in the luxury areas of Manhattan, reversing the pattern of suburbanisation. In other large cities, many traditional areas of Jewish settlement had almost vanished by the 1960s, for example the Lawndale and South Shore areas of Chicago, to be replaced by the growth of heavily Jewish districts in suburban areas. In all Diaspora countries with significant Jewish populations, there are recognisably Jewish areas in which most of the community's institutions and shops are located. This pattern has repeated itself virtually everywhere, from the Golders Green and Stamford Hill sections of London to the St Kilda–Caulfield neighbourhood of Melbourne, Australia. Often, a visible presence of Strictly Orthodox Jews proclaims such areas as obviously Jewish.

In the State of Israel most Jews have settled in the very largest urban areas, especially metropolitan Tel Aviv, Jerusalem, Haifa, and Beersheva. Tel Aviv, in particular, is now an enormous urban centre, probably today numbering two million or more including its many suburbs, which appears to stretch endlessly along the Mediterranean coast. Jerusalem has become the home of over 500,000 Jews, many Strictly Orthodox, who reject the hedonism and secularisation of the rest of Israeli society. While some immigrants, mainly poor Sephardi Jews from Afro-Asian countries, have settled in newer development towns, Israel has largely become a land of Jewish suburbs and urban areas, not unlike Jewish population centres elsewhere.

Jewish languages

Another field in which profound change has occurred over the past 200 years is in the vernacular languages spoken by the Jewish people. While Hebrew, the language of the Bible, has always been the language of Jewish religious discourse, no Jews spoke Hebrew as a vernacular from ancient times until Hebrew was deliberately revived in Palestine by the Zionist movement at the end of the nineteenth century. Instead, Jews employed a variety of languages. Some were spoken by no one else. Increasingly, however, Jews spoke the languages of the peoples among whom they lived. Indeed, the degree to which Jews normally spoke the language of the majority in the countries in which they lived was and is probably the most important single indication of Jewish assimilation and acculturation.

In the late eighteenth and early nineteenth centuries the great majority of Jews in Europe, especially those in the Pale of Settlement, spoke Yiddish, which remained the characteristic language of the Jews of eastern Europe prior to the Holocaust. Yiddish is a dialect of Medieval High German, and also includes words from Hebrew and other admixtures, especially from Slavic cultures as in Poland. It is believed that Yiddish was originally spoken by Jews in the Rhineland area of Germany, and retained when they began to migrate eastwards into Poland in the fourteenth century. Yiddish is, thus, an

Indo-European language, not a Semitic language like Hebrew. Yiddish is, in fact, as closely related to Hebrew as English is to Arabic. To those unfamiliar with Jewish languages it is, however, often confused with Hebrew because it is written in Hebrew characters. By the eighteenth century, Yiddish had developed a number of dialects in specific countries of Jewish residence, especially Poland and Lithuania. Outside the Pale, in south-eastern Europe and the Afro-Asian world, Jews spoke a variety of other languages, especially Arabic, Turkish, Ladino (sometimes known as Spaniole), a Jewish variant of Castilian, spoken by Jews exiled from Spain and Portugal, as well as a number of other Jewish admixture languages. In south-eastern Europe the characteristic language of Jews in countries such as Bulgaria and Greece was Ladino. Jews in the Afro-Asian world did not speak Yiddish. It should also be reiterated that no Jews at this time spoke Hebrew, although (theoretically) virtually all Jews could read it.

Until the Holocaust (and afterwards, in the Soviet Union) Yiddish remained the language of the great majority of Jews in the former Pale of Settlement. As late as 1897 no less than 98 per cent of the Jews living in the Pale of Settlement in Czarist Russia spoke Yiddish as their vernacular tongue, according to the Russian census of that year (the others spoke Russian, Polish, or German). However, after the First World War and, indeed, even before, Jews in eastern Europe began to speak the language of each country's majority population in ever-increasing numbers. In 1926, for instance, only 76.1 per cent of the Jews of Russia spoke Yiddish, the remainder speaking Russian, Ukrainian, or another non-Jewish language. Even in inter-war Poland, the percentage of Jews normally speaking Polish was steadily increasing, so that probably 15–20 per cent of Polish Jews spoke Polish as their vernacular on the eve of the Second World War.

In virtually all of the countries to which Jews emigrated in significant numbers in central and western Europe, as well as in other parts of the world, Jews quickly spoke the language of the majority and gave up any pretence of speaking a specifically Jewish tongue. In most countries of heavy Jewish immigration, such as the United States, all Jewish children rapidly mastered English, with Yiddish and other languages restricted increasingly to the original immigrants. Since all public discourse in the United States, as in Britain and the British Dominions, was in English, it was virtually inconceivable that any significant number of Jews would not speak English within a few decades of arrival, or would not wish to. The same process of linguistic assimilation was followed by all other non-English speaking immigrant groups which went to the United States, at least until very recently, when 'multi-culturalism' became legitimated, at least in some circles. Similarly, by the mid-nineteenth century, Jews in Germany invariably spoke and wrote in German, not Yiddish, and this was the case virtually everywhere else.

By the beginning of the twentieth century, then, very substantial numbers of Jews spoke the language of the majority in the countries in which they lived although a majority, in the Pale of Settlement and elsewhere in eastern Europe (and among recent immigrants elsewhere), still spoke Yiddish, with smaller groups also speaking Ladino or another Jewish language. In 1905, it was estimated that of 11,550,000 Jews in the world, 7 million (60.6 per cent) spoke Yiddish as their native tongue; 1,250,000 (10.0 per cent) spoke German (chiefly in Germany and Austria-Hungary); 1,100,000 (9.5 per cent) English; 600,000 (5.2 per cent) Magyar (Hungarian); 350,000 (3.0 per cent) Ladino. Only 20,000 Jews (0.2 per cent) spoke Hebrew, all in the small Jewish community in Palestine. This was changing rapidly on the eve of the First World War, as millions of Jews emigrated to the 'New Diaspora' and assimilation continued everywhere. In 1938, on the eve of the Holocaust, according to the same sources, the main languages spoken by the world's 16,717,000 Jews were believed to be as follows: Yiddish – 6,800,000 (40.7 per cent); English – 4,100,000 (25.1 per cent); Polish – 1,000,000 (almost certainly an overestimate; 6.0 per cent); Russian – 1,000,000 (6.0 per cent); German – 600,000 (3.6 per cent, and declining rapidly through Nazi-enforced emigration); Arabic and Turkish – 600,000 (3.6 per cent); Hebrew – 500,000 (3.0 per cent).

No similar estimates exist for the contemporary Jewish world, but it seems probable that, of the world's 13.1 million Jews at the beginning of the twenty-first century, about 6.5 million (49.6 per cent) speak English, and about 4 million Hebrew (30.5 per cent), with the Hebrew percentage constantly increasing. Thus, over 70 per cent of the world's Jews today speak one of two languages which fewer than 1 per cent of the world's Jews spoke 200 years ago, a change which may well be without parallel among any other ethnic group in modern times. The remaining languages spoken by Jews include Russian, French, Spanish, and Yiddish. Yiddish is still the vernacular language among some Strictly Orthodox Jews throughout the world, and among elderly Jews in Russia and elsewhere, but today it is spoken only by a small fraction of the number who spoke it 70 years earlier. This catastrophic decline was chiefly caused by the Holocaust and the migration of survivors elsewhere, but also by the adoption of Hebrew as the national language of the State of Israel. Hebrew is today spoken by over 200 times as many people as a century ago, an increase which, again, may be without any modern parallel. *Ivrit* (modern Hebrew), as adopted by the Yishuv and the State of Israel entailed the creation of innumerable new words and terms not found in Biblical Hebrew, and quickly came to produce a significant body of literature, such as the poetry of Haim Nahman Bialik (1873–1934), widely regarded as the father of modern Hebrew literature. Other languages spoken by Jews a century ago have also, like Yiddish, sharply declined in importance, ranging from German to Arabic, while Russian speakers are now rapidly diminishing. As with their residency patterns throughout the world, increasingly the Jewish people are bifurcated into two linguistic groups: those speaking English and those speaking Hebrew. There is no reason to suppose that this trend will not continue indefinitely.

Jewish achievement in the modern world

To write of Jewish achievement in the modern world is an impossible feat in a book that is not intended as a multi-volume encyclopedia. As a consequence, only a few of the most eminent and distinguished Jews in any field (let alone every field) can be mentioned in a work such as this. It is also not easy to define 'Jewish achievement'. Does high achievement in a specifically Jewish milieu, such as Talmudic scholarship by an eminent *yeshivah* rabbi or successful generalship in the Israeli army, count, or only activities conducted in a wider milieu, such as the work of an eminent scientist or composer? What kind of 'achievement' should be noted? Should great Jewish athletes and sportsmen be noted besides Nobel Prize-winning scientists? Although there are no easy answers to these questions, in general we are concerned here with Jewish achievement in a wider milieu, for instance of a scientist, cultural figure, or political leader. Not all fields can possibly be surveyed, although with greater space one would certainly wish to extend the number of areas discussed.

It is generally recognised that Jewish achievement since the eighteenth century has clustered particularly in certain fields – for whatever reasons, there were more famous Jewish physicists than Jewish engineers, for instance – and, more controversially, in certain distinctive modes of thought. Some scholars have claimed that there is a distinctive type of 'Jewish mind', characterised by originality, marginality, and criticism of the dominant group. According to this view, perhaps the archetypal examples of the 'Jewish mind' in modern times were the trio of Karl Marx (1818–83), Albert Einstein (1879–1955), and Sigmund Freud (1856–1939). All, it is claimed, put forward theories which were both revolutionary and deeply subversive of the established order, while their systems became dominant paradigms (in the case of Marx, enforced by totalitarian regimes). Marx, Einstein, and Freud, it is argued, were each in their way originally marginal intellectuals, all becoming objects of hatred to the extreme right. This thesis has its limits – Marx, for instance, was a Jew only in a biological sense; he was baptised as a Lutheran and became both an atheist and an antisemite – but many observers believe that it has considerable validity.

It is abundantly clear that, for whatever reason, Jews have, over the past 200 years, made a remarkable contribution to human achievement in virtually every field, and no account of modern Jewish history can fail to take note of some of the most important of these achievers.

Probably the most remarkable contributions of Jews to human knowledge have been in the sciences. Here, the overrepresentation of Jews, especially in the most important of scientific innovations, has been phenomenal. Between 1901 (when they were first given out) and 1995 Jews won 19.8 per cent of all Nobel Prizes awarded in Physics, 12.7 per cent of those in Chemistry, and 28.7 per cent awarded in Medicine, or 17.5 per cent of all the Nobel Prizes awarded in this period. Jews comprised no more than 1.2

per cent of the Western world's population, and often faced the handicaps of antisemitic discrimination and of poverty.

While providing a full list of the most notable Jews in any field is impossible here, a number were so distinguished that they cannot be omitted. Among scientists (in physics, chemistry, medicine, mathematics, and so on) no listing could omit Einstein, Niels Bohr (1885–1962) one of the founders of quantum physics along with Max Born (1882–1970); cosmologist Sir Hermann Bondi (b.1919); Sir Ernest Chain (1906–79), co-discoverer of penicillin; Ferdinand Cohn (1828–98), the 'father of modern bacteriology'; Paul Ehrlich (1854–1915), discoverer of the treatment for syphilis; atomic theorist Richard Feynman (1918–88); Rosalind Franklin (1920–58), co-discoverer of the structure of DNA, who died tragically young; Dennis Gabor (1900–79), who invented holography; particle physicist Murray Gell-Mann (b.1929); German chemist Fritz Haber (1868–1934); Soviet physicist Peter Kapitza (1894–1984); biochemist Sir Hans Krebs (1900–81); aviation engineer Theodore von Karman (1881–1963); Karl Landsteiner (1868–1943), discoverer of blood groups; genetics pioneer Joshua Lederberg (b.1925); investigator of nerve transmission Otto Loewi (1873–1961); Cesare Lombroso (1836–1909), founder of modern criminology; pioneer of fission Lise Meitner (1878–1968); biologist Elie Metchnikov (1845–1916); mathematician Hermann Minkowski (1864–1909), and 'games theory' pioneer John von Neumann (1903–57); nuclear physicist Isidor Rabi (1898–1988); conquerors of polio Albert Sabin (1906–93) and Jonas Salk (1914–95); astronomer Karl Schwarzchild (1873–1916); atomic researcher Leo Szilard (1898–1964); biochemist Selman Waksman (1888–1973); German cancer pioneer Otto Warburg (1883–1970) who was, amazingly, allowed to continue his research unmolested by the Nazis; pioneer of cybernetics (he coined the term) Norbert Wiener (1894–1964); and immunology researcher Rosalyn Yalow (b.1921). Innumerable other names could be added to this list; indeed a full account of notable Jewish scientists could fill a book many times this size.

Fewer Jews were to be found among the ranks of the world's great inventors or engineers, but there were some, for instance Emil Berliner (1851–1929), inventor of the phonograph which employs a wax disk (as all did, until replaced by CDs a century later); David Schwarz (1845–97), who built the first airship; Henry Dreyfus (1882–1944), discoverer of Celanese; Charles Proteus Steinmetz (1856–1923), the electrical pioneer; Mikhail Gurevich (1893–1976), who designed most of the Soviet's MIG planes; and Edwin Land (1909–91), developer of the Polaroid camera.

One scientific field in which Jews have made a particularly significant contribution is psychiatry. Apart from Freud himself, very important Jewish psychiatrists include Alfred Adler (1870–1937), who coined the term 'inferiority complex' and later broke with Freud; Hungarian Sandor Ferenczi (1873–1933) and German Karl Abrahams (1877–1925) among Freud's inner circle; and Austrians Otto Rank (1884–1939) and Theodore

Reik (1888–1969). Later Jewish psychiatrists of note include the controversial sexologist Wilhelm Reich (1897–1957), and child psychoanalysts Erik Erikson (1902–94) and Melanie Klein (1882–1960). Max Wertheimer (1880–1943) was the founder of 'Gestalt' psychology and Kurt Lewin (1880–1947) of 'group dynamics' psychology, while William Stern (1871–1938) invented the IQ test in its modern form. There would appear to be something in the 'Jewish mind', especially in central Europe and the United States, which is particularly attracted by psychology and psychoanalysis.

As in so many other areas, the number of renowned Jewish writers of literature are legion. From 1901–95, Jews were awarded 10.8 per cent of Nobel Prizes in Literature, a considerable overrepresentation, but not as great as in the sciences. One must, in considering this topic, also divide eminent Jewish writers into those who wrote primarily in Jewish languages, especially Yiddish and Hebrew, or other tongues, and, possibly as well, those whose work typically employs Jewish themes and those whose work does not do so, at least overtly. Probably the most distinguished and influential Jewish writers of the past 200 years have been Heinrich Heine (1797–1856), who wrote in German; Marcel Proust (1871–1922), the seminal French writer whose mother was Jewish and whose *A la Recherche du Temps Perdu* includes as a central character Swann, a Jew; the Czech Franz Kafka (1883–1924), whose works (written in German) were only known posthumously; and the Russian Boris Pasternak (1890–1960), author of *Dr Zhivago*. This illustrates something of the linguistic range among Jewish writers, who often have little in common apart from their origins. Eminent Jewish authors have written in most Western languages and cultural milieus. Those who wrote in English (from all over the world) include Saul Bellow (b.1915), Allen Ginsberg (1926–97), Nadine Gordimer (b.1923), Bernard Malamud (1914–86), Joseph Heller (1923–99), Norman Mailer (b.1923), Harold Pinter (b.1930), Henry Roth (1906–95), Philip Roth (b.1933), Mordecai Richler (b.1931), Neil Simon (b.1927), Muriel Spark (b.1918), Gertrude Stein (1874–1946), Elie Wiesel (b.1928), Leonard Woolf (1880–1969) and Herman Wouk (b.1915), among innumerable others. Writing in French were Paul Celan (1920–70), Eugene Ionesco (1912–94) and André Maurois (*né* Emile Herzog, 1885–1967); in German Elias Canetti (1905–97), Lion Feuchtwanger (1884–1958) and Stefan Zweig (1881–1942); in Russian Joseph Brodsky (1940–96), Isaac Babel (1894–1939), Osip Mandelstam (1891–1938) – both Babel and Mandelstam 'disappeared' in Stalin's Purges); in Italian Carlo Levi (1902–75), Primo Levi (1919–87), Alberto Moravia (1907–90) and Italo Svevo (*né* Ettore Schmitz, 1861–1928).

This is certainly an extremely distinguished list, yet it should not be forgotten that full lists of English-language, French or Russian writers of all backgrounds of the past two hundred years would be just as impressive. Jews have produced notable figures apart from serious literature, ranging from the enormously popular right-wing novelist Ayn Rand (1902–81), to the science fiction doyen Isaac Asimov (1920–92), to the detective fiction author and editor 'Ellery Queen' (the pseudonym of Frederick Dannay, 1905–82, and Manfred Lee, 1905–71), to cartoonists Al Capp (1909–79) of 'L'il Abner' fame, and Joe Schuster (1914–92) and Jerry Spiegel (1914–96), both of whom invented the comicbook hero Superman.

Only a minority of notable Jewish writers have produced their work in a Jewish language. The best-known writers in Yiddish, included Isaac Leib Peretz (1852–1915), Sholem Aleichem (*né* Shalom Rabinovitch, 1859–1916), Sholem Asch (1880–1957), and Isaac Bashevis Singer (1904–91). Yiddish literature was, of course, decimated by the Holocaust, but survives among Yiddish speakers in Israel, America, and elsewhere. Modern Hebrew literature is seen as having begun with the *Haskalah*, in the writings of such writers as Michal Lebensohn (1828–58) and Judah Leib Gordon (1830–92). From the 1880s a Hebrew literature associated with Zionism emerged, in the writings of such authors as Haim Nahman Bialik (1873–1934) and Shaul Tshernikovsky (1875–1943). Shmuel Agnon (1888–1970) became the first (and, so far, only) Hebrew writer awarded the Nobel Prize, while Amos Oz (b.1939) is probably Israel's best-known contemporary writer.

Jews have also been extremely notable in economics and the social sciences. The Nobel Prize in Economics (founded only since 1969), the only one in the social sciences, has, in the period 1969–95, been given to a Jewish recipient in a remarkable 37 per cent of all awards. Marx was the most influential of Jewish economists, but others have included the seminal English writer on economics David Ricardo (1772–1823); Richard Kahn, Lord Kahn (1905–89), who provided Keynes with much of the theoretical basis for his theories; Piero Sraffa (1898–1983); Simon Kuznets (1901–85); Paul Samuelson (b.1915); Peter Drucker (b.1909); and the renowned champion of free markets Milton Friedman (b.1912).

Among the most important Jewish social scientists and social thinkers were the sociologists Emil Durkheim (1858–1917); Karl Mannheim (1893–1947) and Raymond Aron (1905–83); anthropologists Franz Boaz (1858–1942) and Claude Lévi-Strauss (b.1908); controversial linguisticist and political commentator Noam Chomsky (b.1928); and such theorists of political ideas as Sir Karl Popper (1902–94) and Sir Isaiah Berlin (1909–97), and political commentators Hannah Arendt (1906–75), Isaac Deutscher (1907–67), and Walter Lippmann (1899–1974).

Jewish historians have been concerned with both Jewish and wider history. Among the former, Heinrich Graetz (1817–91), author of a remarkable eleven-volume history of the Jews, Simon Dubnow (1860–1941), a victim of the Holocaust, and Salo W. Baron (1895–1989) were of great importance, while Emanuel Ringelblum (1900–44) was the great recorder of events in the Warsaw ghetto, where he was captured and shot. Jewish historians concerned with wider events who have become well known to the general public include Sir Lewis Namier (1888–1960), Eric Hobsbawm (b.1917), Sir Martin Gilbert (b.1936), Marc Bloch (1886–1944), and Richard Hofstadter (1916–70). Sir Nicholas Pevsner (1902–83) became one of the best-known historians of architecture, as did Erwin Panofsky (1892–1968) and Ernst Gombrich (1909–2001) of art.

In philosophy, there is the same divide between Jewish philosophers concerned primarily with Jewish themes and those dealing with more general topics. Among the most eminent of the former were Franz Rosenzweig (1886–1929), Martin Buber (1878–1965), Abraham Joshua Heschel (1907–92), and Emil Fackenheim (b.1916). Well-known Jewish-born philosophers whose concerns are wider include Theodor Adorno (1903–69), Samuel Alexander (1859–1938), Walter Benjamin (1892–1940), Henri Bergson (1859–1941), Ernst Cassirer (1874–1945), Jacques Derrida (b.1930), Edmund Husserl (1859–1938), and Simone Weil (1909–43). After Baruch Spinoza (1632–77) in the seventeenth century, probably the philosopher of Jewish descent with the greatest influence on the mainstream of philosophical thought was Ludwig Wittgenstein (1889–1951).

Turning to music and the arts, the contribution of leading Jews is somewhat spotty: tremendous in some areas, less so in others. Only a handful of the great composers whose music forms the backbone of the Western canon of classical music were Jewish: Felix Mendelssohn-Bartholdy (1809–47), the grandson of the key figure in the *Haskalah* Moses Mendelssohn, and Gustav Mahler (1860–1911) were probably the most distinguished, with the Americans George Gershwin (1898–1937), and Aaron Copland (1900–90), the Austrian Arnold Schoenberg (1874–1951), the French composer Darius Milhaud (1892–1974), among the giants of twentieth-century music. Other very notable Jewish composers whose works are in the repertoire include Giacomo Meyerbeer (1791–1864), Jacques Offenbach (1819–80), Karl Goldmark (1830–1915), Paul Dukas (1865–1935), Reinhold Gliere (1875–1956), and Erich Korngold (1897–1957). The composer–conductor Leonard Bernstein (1918–90), and the American 'minimalists' Philip Glass (b.1937) and Steve Reich (b.1936) are enormously popular.

Famous Jewish classical musicians – conductors, pianists, violinists, and so on – have probably been far more numerous than great Jewish composers. Only a few can be listed here. Renowned Jewish conductors have included Daniel Barenboim (b.1942), Otto Klemperer (1885–1973), Serge Koussevitzky (1874–1951), Eugene Ormandy (1899–1985), and Bruno Walter (1876–1962). Among the great pianists are Vladimir Ashkenazy (b.1937), Dame Myra Hess (1890–1965), Vladimir Horowitz (1903–89), Artur Rubinstein (1887–1982), and Artur Schnabel (1882–1951). Violinists include Jascha Heifetz (1901–87), Joseph Joachim (1831–1907), Yehudi Menuhin (1916–99), David Oistrakh (1908–74), Isaac Stern (b.1920), and Joseph Szigeti (1892–1973), while Jacqueline Du Pré (1945–87) and Gregor Piatigorsky (1903–76) were virtuosi on other instruments.

One area in which Jews have truly excelled, perhaps dominated, is that of popular music, especially during the golden age of Broadway and Hollywood from 1920 through to about 1965. Apart from Gershwin and Bernstein, noted above, celebrated Jewish composers of 'standard' songs from musicals, movies, and radio include Irving Berlin (1888–1989), Richard Rodgers (1902–79), and both of his famous lyricists, Lorenz Hart (1895–1943) and Oscar Hammerstein II (1895–1960); Jerome Kern (1885–1945), Harold Arlen (1905–86), Frank Loesser (1910–69), Alan Jay Lerner (1918–86), Sammy Cahn (1919–93), Steven Sondheim (b.1930), London's Lionel Bart (1930–99), and many others; indeed, only a minority of America's famous popular composers of this period were (like Cole Porter) not Jewish. It is difficult to account for this remarkable record, which perhaps far exceeds the impact made by Jews as composers of classical music. This tradition has continued, albeit in a much-attenuated form, during the recent past, with such songwriters and performers as Jerry Leiber (b.1933) and Mike Stoller (b.1933), who wrote most of Elvis Presley's famous songs; Bert Bacharach (b.1929), Neil Sedaka (b.1939), Barry Manilow (b.1946), Carole King (b.1938), and Simon and Garfunkel (Paul Simon, b.1941, and Art Garfunkel, b.1942). Although jazz is a form of popular music which is closely associated with American blacks, Jews made a surprisingly important contribution to it, via such performers as Paul Whiteman (1890–1967), Benny Goodman (1908–86), Harry James (1916–83), Ziggy Elman (1914–68), and Artie Shaw (b.1910).

The contribution of Jews to painting and sculpture in modern times has also been significant, but, as with classical composition, certainly not genuinely remarkable. Prior to the nineteenth century, Orthodox Judaism forbade the painting of portraits. Much art (before the Renaissance, nearly all Western art) was church art, in which Jews, by definition, could not participate. Decoration within the nineteenth century synagogues tended to be less ornate and more ephemeral than that in churches. Much nineteenth-century art was patriotic or nationalistic; Jews, again, did not necessarily feel at home. From the mid-nineteenth century, however, Jews began to carve out a respectable record among notable artists. Some, like the renowned painter Marc Chagall (1887–1985), Moritz Oppenheim (1880–82), Arthur Szyk (1894–1951) and Maurycy Gottlieb (1856–79), whose death at the age of 23 cut short a career of immense promise, used Jewish themes, but most did not. Other famous Jewish artists include painters Max Ernst (1891–1976), Lucien Freud (b.1922), Isaac Levitan (1860–1900), Roy Lichtenstein (1923–97), Max Liebermann (1847–1935), Camille Pissarro (1830–1903), Sir William Rothenstein (1872–1945), Mark Rothko (1903–70), Chaim Sontine (1894–1943), and sculptors Sir Jacob Epstein (1880–1959) and Jacques Lipschitz (1891–1973).

Many Jews have been prominent as important and striking photographers, such as Dianne Arbus (1923–71), Robert Cápo (1913–54), Alfred Eisenstaedt (1898–1995), Alfred Steiglitz (1864–1946), and Roman

Vishniac (1897–1990). Important Jewish architects include Louis Kahn (1901–74) and Erich Mendelsohn (1887–1953).

Jews in Hollywood and the cinema have been too numerous and influential to mention, with Hollywood often said to be 'Jewish'. Adolph Zukor (1873–1976) was, indeed, the 'founder' of Hollywood, together with such other Jewish film magnates as the Warner Brothers, Sam Goldwyn (1897–1974), and Carl Lammerle (1867–1939). It is impossible here to name even the most prominent of Jewish producers, directors, and actors in Hollywood, a tradition which has continued through the present time with such personalities as Steven Spielberg (b.1947). Nevertheless, any discussion must surely include Al Jolson (1886–1950), the first man to talk on screen, the Marx Brothers ('Chico', 1886–1961, 'Harpo', 1888–1964, and 'Groucho', 1890–1972), Barbra Streisand (b.1942), and Woody Allen (b.1936). Jews have also been prominent in the cinema of other countries, as for instance with the celebrated Soviet film-maker Sergei Eisenstein (1898–1948). Jews also have a long tradition as leading theatrical actors and actresses, for instance the renowned French actresses Rachel (Elisa Rachel Felix, 1820–58) and Sarah Bernhardt (1844–1923), as well as the impresario David Belasco (1859–1931), Florence Ziegfeld (1869–1932) and Max Reinhardt (1873–1943).

In business life and entrepreneurship – a topic also discussed earlier in this chapter – again only a few names can be mentioned. The Rothschilds, the merchant banking dynasty, were of course the most famous of all Jewish business dynasties, but there were many others, including the Bronfmans, Canadian distillers; the Guggenheims, American mining tycoons and later philanthropists and art patrons; the Gunzbergs, bankers and railway builders in tsarist Russia; the Marks (Sieff) dynasty of British retailers (Marks and Spencer) and Zionist supporters; the Morgenthaus, American bankers and public figures; the Olivettis, Italian industrialists; the Oppenheimers, South African mining magnates; the Sassoons, Baghdadi/British merchants in the Orient; the Seligmans, American bankers; the Ullsteins, German publishers and newspaper magnates; and the Warburgs, German-American bankers. Among the notable individual Jewish businessmen who ought to be mentioned are Baron Maurice de Hirsch (1831–96), the immensely wealthy Munich-born railway magnate and philanthropist, the German shipping magnate and economic adviser to the Kaiser, Albert Ballin (1857–1918), and the German industrialist and politician Walther Rathenau (1867–1922). Among notable Anglo-Jewish businessmen were Sir Alfred Mond, Lord Melchett (1868–1930), founder of Imperial Chemical Industries; Sir Moses Montefiore (1784–1885), stockbroker and world-famous head of the Jewish community in Britain for over sixty years; Baron Paul Julius von Reuter (*né* Israel Beer Josaphat, 1861–99), founder of the renowned news agency; Sir Marcus Samuel, Viscount Bearsted (1853–1927), founder of the Shell Oil Company; and Sir Isaac Wolfson (1897–1991), retailer and philanthropist. Among the scores of notable American Jewish businessmen were Armand Hammer (1898–1990), petroleum tycoon and negotiator with the Soviet Union; Julius Rosenwald (1852–1932), head of Seers Roebuck, and philanthropist; Helena Rubinstein (1870–1965), cosmetics magnate and one of the earliest self-made women millionaires; David Sarnoff (1891–1971), radio pioneer and chairman of RCA; Jacob Henry Schiff (1847–1920), merchant banker and philanthropist; Levi Strauss (1829–1902), originator of blue jeans; and Adolph Ochs (1858–1935), who purchased the *New York Times* in 1896 and turned it into America's most prestigious newspaper. Motor car magnate André Citroen (1878–1935) became known as the 'French Henry Ford'.

Jews are not renowned as athletes and sporting champions, but have contributed their share: Daniel Mendoza (1764–1836) was the most famous boxer of his day, while Max Baer (1909–59) was heavyweight champion in 1934–35. The life of the sprinter Harold Abrahams (1899–1978) was immortalised in *Chariots of Fire*. Hank Greenberg (1911–85) and Sandy Koufax (b.1935) were among the greatest baseball stars, while Mark Spitz (b.1950) excelled in swimming. Irena Kirszenstein-Szewinska (b.1946), who won seven medals at Olympics between 1964 and 1976, has been described as 'the greatest women's track and field athlete of all time'. Jewish athletes have won more than three hundred medals at Olympic games.

Because practising Jews were excluded from the power structures of virtually all Western nations until the nineteenth century (or later), few Jews figured among the world's notable political leaders until modern times. In the nineteenth century, of course, Benjamin Disraeli (Earl of Beaconsfield, 1804–81) was among the greatest of British statesmen; as is well-known, he was baptised an Anglican as a 13-year-old and could thus take part in British political life. In Prussia, Frederick Julius Stahl (1802–61), like Disraeli both a convert to Protestantism and a political conservative, was an influential member of the Prussian Upper Chamber, while Ferdinand Lassalle (1825–64) was among the most important of German socialists. During the twentieth century, Jews played an increasingly visible role in governments. No Jew has yet become president of the United States, but two, Henry Kissinger (b.1923) and Madeleine Albright (b.1937), have served as secretary of state, and dozens of others have held senior positions. Bernard Baruch (1870–1965), became virtual dictator of the American economy during the First World War and was a renowned adviser to presidents. During the American Civil War Judah P. Benjamin (1811–84) was secretary of state of the Confederacy. In Britain, about fifteen Jews have sat in Cabinets, among them Herbert Samuel (1870–1963), home secretary and leader of the Liberal party, Rufus Isaacs, Marquess of Reading (1860–1935), foreign secretary and viceroy of India, and Nigel Lawson (b.1932), chancellor of the exchequer. Leon Blum (1872–1950), René Mayer (1895–1972), Pierre Mendes-France (1907–82), Michel Debré (1912–96), and Laurent Fabius (b.1946) were premiers of France (the latter two being of Jewish extraction), while Luigi Luzzatti (1841–1927) and Baron Sidney Sonnino (1847–1922) held the same position in Italy. Belgium's Paul Hymans (1865–1941) served as the first president of the League of Nations Assembly in 1920, and Simone Weil (b.1927), an Auschwitz survivor, was president of the European Parliament in 1979–82. Numerous Jews have served with great distinction as jurists, such as Americans Louis Brandeis (1856–1941), Benjamin Cardozo (1870–1938), and Felix Frankfurter (1882–1965).

When allowed to do so, Jews have distinguished themselves as military commanders, as the success of the Israeli Defence Force since 1948 shows. Despite all the obstacles in their way, Jews showed as much military prowess as any other group, as exampled by the careers of such men as Australia's remarkable commander in the First World War, Sir John Monash (1865–1931), the celebrated 'father of the nuclear submarine' Admiral Hyman Rickover (1900–86), and numerous Soviet generals such as Ivan Chernyakhovsky (1906–45), the youngest Army commander in the Soviet ranks during the Second World War. Israel's celebrated military leaders such as Moshe Dayan (1915–81) and Yigal Allon (1918–80), built on a surprisingly impressive tradition.

The Jews have also produced any number of achievers in unusual and eccentric fields. Nearly half of all chess world champions have been of Jewish descent, from Wilhelm Steinitz (1836–1900) to Gary Kasparov (b.1953). So, too, was the famous contract bridge champion Charles Goren (1901–91). Harry Houdini (*né* Erich Weiss, 1874–1926) was the most famous of magicians, and Uri Geller (b.1946) is the man today most renowned for 'telepathic' powers. Ludovic Zamenhof (1859–1917) invented Esperanto, the 'universal language'. Jews have even produced their share of explorers, such as Nathaniel Isaacs (1808–1860), explorer of Natal, Eduard Glaser (1855–1908), travelling in the interior of Arabia, and Sir Auriel Stein (1862–1943), explorer of central Asia.

Not every Jewish 'achiever' made his mark in a positive way, and, in fairness, one must also record the existence of Jewish gangsters like Meyer Lansky (1902–83) and Louis 'Lepke' Buchalter (1897–1944), the heads of 'Murder Incorporated' in the United States; Jewish spies such as George Blake (b.1922) and the Americans Julius (1918–53) and Ethel (1915–53) Rosenberg, whose executions for espionage aroused world-wide condemnation; and Jewish business frauds such as Robert Maxwell (1923–91).

What conclusions can be drawn from this extraordinarily impressive list of achievers? First, it seems clear that Jews made a remarkable contribution to virtually all spheres, even those, such as the military, from which they were often excluded. While Jewish achievement was found everywhere, it was probably most remarkable in two milieus: in central Europe from about 1850 to 1939, and in the United States since about 1920. Jewish contribution to some areas in particular, like theoretical physics and popular entertainment, is simply staggering. It must be emphasised that, in other areas, although the record of Jews is considerable, it has not been greater than that of many other groups.

Accounting for this record of over-achievement is extremely difficult, and no fully satisfactory explanation has ever been found. Clearly, the Jewish emphasis on education has been crucial. Some sociologists believe that the typical Jewish combination of high self-esteem and high marginality distinctly favours achievement, as it does in other groups – especially the smaller Protestant sects like Quakers and Unitarians – which demonstrate the same characteristics. The international nature and outlook of modern Jewry has also probably been a factor, together with their status as (until 1948) a perpetual Diaspora. Whether this record of achievement will continue during the twenty-first century, with a settled and 'normal' Jewish society existing in Israel and antisemitism markedly diminishing in the Diaspora, remains to be seen.

Further reading

Joan Comay, *Who's Who in Jewish History after the Period of the Old Testament*, 2nd, revised, edn (London, 1995)

Peter Y. Medding, ed., *Israel: State and Society, 1948–1988*. Volume 5 of *Studies in Contemporary Jewry* (Oxford, 1989).

Ezra Mendelssohn, ed., *Jews and Other Ethnic Groups in a Multi-Ethnic World*. Volume 3 of *Studies in Contemporary Jewry* (Oxford, 1987).

Geoffrey Wigoder, *Dictionary of Jewish Biography* (New York, 1991)

|18|

Conclusion: Jews in today's world

As the twenty-first century opens, the Jewish people find themselves in a position which is at the same time both enviable and fraught with danger. For the first time in modern history, no significant community of persecuted Jews exists anywhere, the only exceptions being the small communities of Iran and Syria. For the first time in modern history, no regime effectively imprisons Jews by forbidding them to leave. Almost everywhere Jews enjoy completely equal rights and can and do reach the highest places. Outside the Arab and Islamic world, there is no government anywhere on earth which would condone, or fail to condemn, antisemitism, while antisemitic statements and acts are confined to marginalised fringe groups. Jewish institutions of every kind abound; works of Jewish scholarship roll off the presses; while in the Western world the Holocaust has become one of the best-known and most universally-internalised events of modern times. For the most part Jews are prosperous and often successful.

Yet there is a far-reaching sense that all is not well. In a number of areas there is serious concern about where the Jewish people are heading. In the demographic sphere, it seems clear that the Jewish fertility rate throughout the Diaspora is seriously below the replacement level, and that, therefore, the total Jewish population of the Diaspora must inevitably decline, barring a totally unexpected increase in Jewish birth rates, or mass conversion to Judaism. The unfortunate condition of the Jewish Diaspora is, to a certain extent, being compensated for by the relatively rapid increase in Israel's population and by the high birth rates in Strictly Orthodox communities in the West, but overall the long-term situation is worrying to many. This particular problem is also being heightened by a number of related trends, including high rates of assimilation and, in particular, of intermarriage not followed by the conversion of the non-Jewish spouse to Judaism. Moreover, the Jewish people have an unusually large component of the elderly who, increasingly, require considerable financial support. In the Diaspora, especially in the United States, many programmes have been put in place to counteract the negative demographic threats of low birth-rates and inter-marriage, but it remains to be seen if they will have any real effect.

In addition, the Jewish world is deeply divided on a number of funda-mental issues, especially the relationship of Orthodox and non-Orthodox Judaism (and of Orthodox and non-Orthodox Jews). In the past half-century the Strictly Orthodox strand within the Jewish matrix has made great strides in numbers, virility, and influence, and is extremely important in the Israeli political process. At the other extreme, Reform Judaism has adopted a number of positions on the ordination of women rabbis, abortion, partilineal descent as a test of Jewish identity, and homosexuality, which are anathema to most Orthodox (and to some Conservative) Jews. The two extremes seem as far apart as they have ever been in modern times.

There are, in addition, other major points of division in the Jewish world, especially the relationship between Israel and the Diaspora, above all American Jewry. Israel's Jews are often fervent nationalists and reluctant to reach peace at any price with the Arabs. American and many other Diaspora Jewish communities are often, in contrast, keen to reach peace with the Arabs and, by and large, eschew extreme nationalistic positions unless Israel's security is threatened. There are many other cultural differences, too, between the two poles of Jewish life, English-speaking America and Hebrew-speaking Israel.

As discussed a number of times in this work, many of the sources of unity in the Jewish world since 1945 have increasingly disappeared. The 'prisoners of Zion' in the Soviet Union and its satellites have, since the fall of Communism, been free to leave, removing a potent source of unity and action throughout the Jewish world. Israel's existence is no longer in ques-tion, and the PLO is no longer considered anathema by virtually anyone in the Jewish world. In this climate, divisions between Jews about the future of Israel and, indeed, what role Israel occupies in the Jewish world, have surfaced and increasingly become more central. Only the memory of the Holocaust remains as a unifying force among all Jews, and, even here, there are many fierce debates, for instance on the uniqueness of the Nazi genocide of the Jews.

It is difficult, therefore, to know what the future holds for the Jewish people. As this book has shown, their response to modernity since the mid-eighteenth century has been extremely diverse, possibly more diverse than that of any other Western people. Since 1939, an unusual degree of unity has prevailed amongst them (except in the religious sphere), given the over-arching factors of the Holocaust and antisemitism on the one hand, and of the rebirth of Israel on the other. It is possible, even likely, that now much greater disunity will be evident amongst them – a product, ironically, not of the fact that Jews are persecuted, but of the fact that they are free.

Index